This page is intentionaly left blank.

Prof. Dr. 'Umar Sulaymān al-Ashqar

History of Islamic Fiqh

Published by: Mishkah University's Academic Committee

Translation by: Mishkah Translation Committee

Reviewed by: Mohammad Elshinawy

Editing of English Text by: Scott Jaspen

Supervised by: Dr. Hatem al-Haj

Cover Design by: Janis Mahnure

A CIP record for this book is acailable from the Library of Congress Cataloging-in-Publication Data

ISBN-13: 9798688801156

Prof. Dr. 'Umar Sulaymān al-Ashqar

HISTORY OF ISLAMIC FIQH

Mishkah University's Academic Committee

History of Islamic Fiqh

PROF. DR. ‘UMAR SULAYMĀN AL-ASHQAR

Contents

Unit 1
Introducing Fiqh and its Relationship to Sharia and Man-made Law

Contents of Unit 1

• Introducing *Fiqh*, its linguistic and technical definition
• The branches of Islamic *Fiqh*
• Islamic *Fiqh* encompasses all branches of man-made law
• The Islamic Sharia is broader than man-made law

Importance of this Unit

In the Arabic language, the term *fiqh* refers to knowledge and understanding. Among the early generations of Islam, the term was used in reference to the entire religion. Later, it became specific to the science of practical legal rulings that were derived from their detailed proofs. Fiqh includes both the definitive and speculative rulings in Sharia. These legal rulings are divided into two branches: acts of worship (*'ibādāt*) and transactions (*mu'āmalāt*). Between the two branches are a number of differences, but together they form a comprehensive and unparalleled system. The Islamic Sharia includes all branches of man-made law and more, for it tackles matters that man-made law has never addressed.

By studying this unit, we shall come to know – by Allah's bounty – these details and more. Let us begin.

Learning Objectives

At the end of this unit, readers are expected to be able to:

1) Define *fiqh* from both a linguistic and technical point of view
2) Refute the allegations and claims of those who accuse Islamic *Fiqh* of being incompatible and inadequate for addressing ever-changing developments.
3) Clarify that the Islamic Sharia covers all branch-

الوحدة الأولى: تعريف الفقه وعلاقته بالشريعة والقانون الوضعي

محتويات الوحدة الأولى

• تعريف الفقه في اللغة والاصطلاح.
• أقسام موضوعات الفقه الإسلامي.
• اشتمال موضوعات الفقه الإسلامي على فروع القوانين الوضعية.
• الشريعة الإسلامية أوسع من القانون.

أهمية دراسة الوحدة:

يطلق الفقه في لغة العرب على الفهم والعلم، وقد كان الفقه في اصطلاح أهل الصدر الأول شاملاً للدين كله، أما المتأخرون فقد خصوه بالعلم بالأحكام الشرعية العملية المكتسب من أدلتها التفصيلية، وهو- أي الفقه- شامل للأحكام الشرعية القطعية والظنية، والأحكام الشرعية تنقسم إلى قسمين: عبادات ومعاملات، وبينهما عدة فروق، والشريعة الإسلامية اشتملت على جميع أقسام القانون الوضعي وزيادة؛ ذلك أنها تعرضت لأمور لم تتعرض لها القوانين الوضعية.

وفي دراستنا لهذه الوحدة، نتعرف- بفضل الله سبحانه- على جميع هذه التفصيلات وزيادة، فهيا بنا لدراسة الوحدة.

الأهداف التعليمية:

يتوقع منك أيها الدارس الكريم بعد دراستك لهذه الوحدة أن تكون قادراً على أن:

١- تُعرف معنى الفقه في اللغة وفي اصطلاح الفقهاء.

٢- تُفند دعاوى ومزاعم الذين يتهمون الفقه الإسلامي بالقصور وعدم صلاحيته لمواكبة تغيرات الزمان.

es of man-made law more comprehensively

4) Compare and contrast the differences between acts of worship and transactions

5) Compare and contrast the differences between Sharia and *Fiqh*

Defining *Fiqh*: Linguistic Definition

In the Arabic language, *fiqh* refers to understanding or comprehension.

When Prophet Moses (ﷺ) was commissioned with the divine message at Mount at-Tūr in Sienai, he supplicated to his Lord and said, **"And loosen the knot from my tongue, that they may *yafqahu* (comprehend) my saying."**[1]

When Prophet Shu'ayb called his people to embrace what Allah had sent him with, his people said to him, **"O Shu'ayb, in no way do we *nafqahu* (comprehend) much of what you say."**[2]

As well, the Arabs say, "So and so was given *fiqh* (comprehension) of religion." Allah also said, **"...*liyatafaqqahu* (to gain comprehension for themselves) in the religion,"**[3] meaning to become knowledgeable in the religion.

Similarly, the Prophet (ﷺ) invoked Allah for Ibn 'Abbās and said, "O Allah, *faqqihhu* (grant him comprehension) in the religion, and teach him the interpretation (of religious texts)."[4] Allah accepted the invocation of the Prophet, and Ibn 'Abbās was the most knowledgeable of his era about the Book of Allah.

1 Sūrah Ṭa Ha – Verses 27-28
2 Sūrah Hūd – Verse 19
3 Sūrat at-Tawbah – Verse 122
4 This narration of the hadith was reported by the author of Lisān al-'Arab. Both al-Bukhāri and Muslim reported this hadith with a slight variation, wherein the Prophet (ﷺ) said, "O Allah, make him understand the religion." Imām al-Bukhāri mentions this hadith in *Ablution, the Chapter on Placing Water near the Water Closet* (See: *Fatḥ al-Bāri Sharḥ Ṣaḥīḥ al-Bukhāri* 1/244). Imām Muslim mentions this hadith in *The Merits of Ibn 'Abbās* (See: *Sahīh Muslim bi Sharḥ an-Nawawi*). In his commentary on *Mishkāt al-Maṣābīḥ*, Shaykh Nāṣir ad-Dīn al-Albāni denied that this hadith is in *Sahīh al-Bukhāri*.

٣- تُوضح اشتمال الفقه الإسلامي على جميع أقسام القانون الوضعي وزيادة.

٤- تُقارن بين العبادات والمعاملات.

٥- تُقارن بين الشريعة والفقه

تعريف الفقه في اللغة والاصطلاح

الفقه لغة:

مدار الفقه في لغة العرب على الفهم.

قال موسى في دعائه لربه عندما كلفه بالرسالة عند طور سيناء: ﴿**وَاحْلُلْ عُقْدَةً مِّن لِّسَانِي يَفْقَهُوا قَوْلِي**﴾(١)، أي يفهموه.

وعندما دعا رسول الله شعيب ﷺ قومه إلى ما بعثه الله به قال له قومه: ﴿**قَالُوا يَا شُعَيْبُ مَا نَفْقَهُ كَثِيراً مِّمَّا تَقُولُ**﴾(٢)، أي لا نفهمه.

وتقول العرب: «**أوتي فلان فقهاً في الدين**»؛ أي فهماً له، قال الله عز وجل: ﴿**لِيَتَفَقَّهُوا فِي الدِّينِ**﴾(٣)، أي ليكونوا علماء به.

ودعا النبي ﷺ لابن عباس، فقال: «**اللهم علمه الدين، وفقهه في التأويل**»(٤)؛ أي فَهِّمه تأويله ومعناه، فاستجاب الله دعاءه، وكان من أعلم الناس في زمانه بكتاب الله تعالى.

١ طه: ٢٧-٢٨.
٢ هود: ١٩.
٣ التوبة: ١٢٢.
٤ هكذا أورد صاحب لسان العرب هذا الحديث، وقد رواه البخاري ومسلم في صحيحهما بلفظ «اللهم فقهه في الدين»، والحديث في صحيح البخاري في كتاب الوضوء، باب وضع الماء عند الخلاء، انظر البخاري بشرحه فتح الباري: ١/ ٢٤٤، وهو في صحيح مسلم في كتاب فضائل ابن عباس، انظر مسلم بشرح النووي: وقد أنكر الشيخ ناصر الدين الألباني في تعليقه على مشكاة المصابيح أن يكون الحديث في صحيح البخاري.

The Arabs use *fiqh* to denote both knowledge and understanding. Al-Fayrūz Ābādi said, *"Fiqh* refers to knowing a matter as well as having an understanding of it."

Also, interpreting *fiqh* to mean comprehension teaches us that *fiqh* is associated with concepts, not individuals. Concepts are understood, whereas individuals are known.

The Arabs did not differentiate in their usage of the term *fiqh* between clear or ambiguous meanings. Abū Isḥāq al-Marwazi differed regarding this, and viewed that *fiqh* was the understanding of the subtle matters and not those that were clear and obvious.[1]

This latter opinion is refuted by the fact that the leading linguists reported that to the Arabs *fiqh* simply meant understanding and that [definition] covers both the subtle and obvious matters. This is further asserted by the fact that the Noble Qur'an used this word regarding mere comprehension. The Most High said about the disbelievers, **"What is it, then, with these people? They almost do not *yafqahūn* (comprehend) any discourse."**[2]

The Qur'an also described the people found by Dhul-Qarnayn as **"...a people who could hardly *yafqahūn* (comprehend) speech."**[3]

1 *Uṣūl al-Fiqh* by Abūn-Nūr Zuhayr, 1/6.
2 Sūrat an-Nisā' – Verse 78
3 Sūrat al-Kahf – Verse 93

وواضح من التعريف أن العرب تفسر الفقه بالعلم كما تفسره بالفهم، يقول الفيروز آبادي: «الفقه بالكسر: العلم بالشيء والفهم له»(١)

ولا فرق عند العرب في كون المعنى المراد فهمه واضحاً أو خفيّاً، فكله يدخل في دائرة الفقه، وقد خالف في هذا أبو إسحاق المروزي، فذهب إلى أن الفقه فهم الأمور الخفية دون الواضحة الجلية(٢).

ويرد عليه أن أئمة اللغة نقلوا عن العرب أن الفقه مطلق الفهم، فهو يتناول فهم الأمور الواضحة والخفية، ويؤكد هذا أن القرآن الكريم استعمل الكلمة في مجرد الفهم، قال تعالى في شأن الكفار: ﴿**فَمَا لِهَـؤُلاءِ الْقَوْمِ لاَ يَكَادُونَ يَفْقَهُونَ حَدِيثاً**﴾(٣)، ووصف القرآن القوم الذين وجدهم ذو القرنين بأنهم: ﴿**لاَّ يَكَادُونَ يَفْقَهُونَ قَوْلاً**﴾(٤).

١ بصائر ذوي التمييز للفيروزآبادي: ٤/ ٢١٠.
٢ أصول الفقه لأبي النور زهير: ١/ ٦.
٣ النساء: ٧٨.
٤ الكهف: ٩٣.

Fiqh from a Technical Point of View

According to the terminology of the early Muslims: We have previously established that the Arabs used the term *fiqh* in reference to understanding and knowledge, and did not differentiate in that between any particular speech and science. Whoever learned a science was a *faqīh* in that science, and someone who mastered many sciences is considered to be the scholar or *faqīh* of the Arabs in the absolute sense.

Following the advent of Islam, *fiqh* became used predominantly in reference to the science of religion because it is greater than and superior to all other sciences.[1]

Therefore, when the earlier Muslim scholars used the term *fiqh*, they meant the religious sciences. In this era, the religious sciences were solely referring to the Book of Allah and the Sunnah of the Prophet (ﷺ). In one hadith, the Prophet (ﷺ) said, "May Allah brighten [the face of] a man who hears a tradition from us, and memorizes it to convey it to others. Perhaps a bearer of *fiqh* [may convey] to one who is *afqah* (more comprehending) than him, and perhaps a bearer of *fiqh* may not himself be a *faqīh*."[2]

This hadith clearly indicates that the Messenger (ﷺ) was referring to his words that were carried as being *fiqh*.

الفقه في الاصطلاح:

(أ) اصطلاح أهل الصدر الأول:

بيَّنا فيما سبق أن الفقه عند العرب الفهم والعلم، لا يفرقون في هذا بين كلام وكلام وعلم وعلم، وكل من علم علماً فهو فقيه في ذلك العلم، والذي أحاط بعلوم كثيرة، فذلك هو فقيه العرب وعالمها.

وبعد مجيء الإسلام غلب اسم الفقه على «علم الدين لسيادته وشرفه وفضله على سائر أنواع العلم، كما غلب النجم على الثريا، والعود على المَنْدل»(١).

فإذا أطلق علماء الصدر الأول اسم «الفقه»، فإنه ينصرف في عرفهم إلى علم الدين دون غيره من العلوم، وكان علم الدين في ذلك الوقت يتمثل في كتاب الله وسنة رسول الله ﷺ، وفي الحديث يقول الرسول ﷺ: «**نضر الله**(٢) **امرأً سمع منا حديثاً فحفظه حتى يبلغه، فرب حامل فقه إلى من هو أفقه منه، ورب حامل فقه ليس بفقيه**»(٣)، وواضح من الحديث أن مراد الرسول ﷺ بالفقه المحمول هو كلامه صلوات الله وسلامه عليه.

---

1 *Lisān al-'Arab* 2/1119 and *Baṣā'ir Dhawit-Tamyīz* 4/210.

2 Reported by Abū Dāwud in his *Sunan* in *The Book of Knowledge, Chapter on the Virtue of Disseminating Knowledge* 3/438. The verifier of the book said, "It was also reported by at-Tirmidhi and an-Nasā'i, and at-Tirmidhi said that it is *ḥasan-ṣaḥīḥ*." It was also reported by Ibn Mājah in his *Sunan* on the authority of 'Abbād al-Anṣāri, who narrated it on the authority of Zayd ibn Thābit. It was also reported in *Mishkāt al-Maṣābīḥ* 1/78. Shaykh Nāṣir ad-Dīn al-Albāni, the verifier of *Mishkāt al-Maṣābīḥ*, said, "It was reported by ash-Shāfi'i with an authentic chain."

١ لسان العرب: ٢/ ١١١٩، بصائر ذوي التمييز: ٤/ ٢١٠.

٢ دعاء له بالنضارة، وهي النعمة والبهجة والحسن، فيكون تقديره: جَمَّله الله وزينه.

٣ رواه أبو داود في سننه، كتاب العلم، باب فضل نشر العلم: ٤٣٨/٣، وقال محقق الكتاب: وأخرجه الترمذي والنسائي، وقال الترمذي: «حسن صحيح»، وأخرجه ابن ماجه في سننه من حديث عباد الأنصاري عن زيد بن ثابت، وأورده صاحب مشكاة المصابيح: ٧٨/١، وقال محقق المشكاة الشيخ ناصر الدين الألباني: «رواه الشافعي بإسناد صحيح».

Reflecting on this hadith, it indicates that the *faqīh* is the one who has insight into his religion – the one that has grasped the meanings of the religious texts, and is capable of deducing the rulings, lessons, and wisdoms contained in these texts. This is indicated in the statement of the Prophet (ﷺ), "Perhaps a bearer of *fiqh* [may convey] to one who is *afqah* (more comprehending) than him, and perhaps a bearer of *fiqh* may not himself be a *faqīh*." The phrase "more comprehending than him" means more capable of knowing the intent of Allah, His rules, and His legislations. The phrase "...not a *faqīh*" means incapable of deducing the rulings and facts that the texts imply.

The *fuqahā'* (plural of *faqīh*) among the Companions and Successors were well known. In the hadith narrated by al-Bukhāri, on the authority of Anas ibn Mālik, regarding the spoils of war that Muslims obtained from the tribe of Hawāzin, the Messenger (ﷺ) had distributed them among some men from Quraysh. As a result, a number of men from the Anṣār expressed objection about that, and the words they said reached the Messenger (ﷺ), who summoned the Anṣār and said to them, "What are these words which have reached me about you?" The *fuqahā'* among them said, "O Messenger of Allah! As for the wise among us, they did not say anything."[1]

When 'Umar ibn al-Khaṭṭāb wanted to deliver a sermon regarding an important issue during the Hajj season, 'Abdur-Raḥmān ibn 'Awf said to him, "During Hajj, there are mobs of people, and I believe that you should delay this matter until you arrive in Madinah and are in the midst of the people of *fiqh*."[2]

1 Reported by al-Bukhāri in *The Book on the Obligatory Share of the One Fifth, Chapter on the Share Given by the Prophet* (ﷺ) *to the Recent Converts* no. 19. See *Fatḥ al-Bāri* 6/251.

2 Reported by al-Bukhāri in *The Book on the Merits of the Anṣār, Chapter on the Prophet's Arrival in Madinah*. See *Fatḥ al-Bāri* 7/264.

والتأمل في الحديث السابق يدلنا على أن الفقيه هو صاحب البصيرة في دينه، الذي خلص إلى معاني النصوص، واستطاع أن يخلص إلى الأحكام والعبر والفوائد التي تحويها النصوص، يدلنا على هذا قوله ﷺ: «**رب حامل فقه إلى من هو أفقه منه، ورب حامل فقه ليس بفقيه**». فمراده بقوله: «**أفقه منه**» أي أقدر منه على التعرف على مراد الله وأحكامه وتشريعاته، وقوله: «**ليس بفقيه**» أي ليس عنده القدرة على استخلاص الأحكام والعلم الذي تضمنته النصوص.

وقد كان الفقهاء من الصحابة والتابعين معروفين بارزين، ففي الحديث الذي يرويه البخاري عن أنس بن مالك في شأن الأموال التي غنمها المسلمون من قبيلة هوازن، وكان الرسول ﷺ قد وزعها على رجال من قريش، فعتب رجال من الأنصار على رسول الله ﷺ، وقالوا كلاماً بلغ الرسول ﷺ، فدعا الرسول الأنصار وقال لهم: «**ما كان حديث بلغني عنكم؟ قال له فقهاؤهم: أما ذوو آرائنا يا رسول الله فلم يقولوا شيئاً**»(١)

وأراد عمر بن الخطاب أن يخطب في موسم الحج في أمر مهم، فقال له عبد الرحمن بن عوف: «إن الموسم يجمع رعاع الناس وغوغاءهم، وإني أرى أن تمهل حتى تقدم المدينة... وتخلص لأهل الفقه»(٢)

١ رواه البخاري في كتاب فرض الخمس (٥٧)، باب ما كان النبي ﷺ يعطي المؤلفة قلوبهم (١٩)، انظر فتح الباري: ٦/ ٢٥١.

٢ رواه البخاري في صحيحه كتاب مناقب الأنصار، باب مقدم النبي المدينة، فتح الباري: ٧/ ٢٦٤.

Yaḥyā ibn Sa'īd al-Anṣāri – who saw the great Successors in Madinah like Sa'īd ibn al-Musayyab and a few of the young Companions like Anas ibn Mālik[1] – said, "I saw the *fuqahā'* of our land (Madinah) always performing *taslīm* after every two *rak'āt* of their daytime [voluntary prayers]."[2]

Az-Zuhri said, "If a dog salivated in a vessel of water and there is no other water for ablution except for this vessel, performing ablution with it is permissible." Sufyān said, "This is the epitome of *fiqh* because Allah said, '**...And [if you] find no water, then seek clean earth.**'[3] And this is considered water."[4]

The word *fuqahā'* was prevalent in Hadith literature, and in the statements of the Companions, the Successors and their Successors. It referred to the people with deep insight into the religion of Allah and who understand the connotations of the Book of Allah and the Sunnah of His Prophet (ﷺ).

The characteristics and qualities of the *fuqahā'* were manifest and well-known. The Prophet (ﷺ) alluded to some of these qualities in his sayings. For example, he said, "One of the signs of a man's *fiqh* is to lead a moderate life."[5]

He also said, "One of the signs of a man's *fiqh* is to say about that which he does not know, 'Allah knows best.'"[6]

1 Al-Bukhāri 1/391 and *Fatḥ al-Bāri* 3/49.
2 Reported by al-Bukhāri in *The Book on Optional Night Prayers, Chapter on the Offering of Supererogatory Prayers in Two*. See *Fatḥ al-Bāri* 3/48.
3 Sūrat an-Nisā' – Verse 43
4 Az-Zuhri means that it is permissible to perform ablution from a vessel of water with which a dog left bodily fluids in the case that a person has no other water except for this vessel. Az-Zuhri took the religious text at face value and believed that once a person found water, it is not permissible for him to perform *tayammum* (dry ablution). This concept does not seem correct because impure water is just like non-existent water.
5 Reported by Imām Aḥmad in his *Musnad* 5/194. The traceable version is weak, and the one from Abū al-Dardā' is sound.
6 Reported by Imām Mulim in his *Ṣaḥīḥ* from *The Book on the Hypocrites* no. 40 and Imām Aḥmād in his *Musnad* 1/381.

وقال يحيى بن سعيد الأنصاري- وكان قد أدرك كبار التابعين بالمدينة كسعيد ابن المسيب، ولحق قليلاً من صغار الصحابة كأنس بن مالك(١): «ما أدركت فقهاء أرضنا إلا يسلِّمون في كل ثنتين من النهار»(٢).

وقال الزهري: إذا ولغ الكلب في إناء ليس له وضوء غيره يتوضأ به، وقال سفيان: هذا الفقه بعينه، يقول الله تعالى: ﴿**فَلَمْ تَجِدُوا مَاءً فَتَيَمَّمُوا**﴾(٣)(٤)، وهذا ماء.

فكلمة الفقهاء كانت تتردد في الأحاديث وعلى ألسنة الصحابة والتابعين وأتباع التابعين دالة على أصحاب البصيرة النافذة في دين الله، الذين فهموا عن الله وعن رسول الله ﷺ.

وقد كانت سمات الفقهاء واضحة، وعلاماتهم بارزة، وقد دل الرسول ﷺ على شيء من صفاتهم في أحاديثه، كقوله:

«من فقه الرجل رفقه في معيشته»(٥)

وقوله: **«من فقه الرجل أن يقول لما لا يعلم الله أعلم»**(٦)

١ البخاري: ١/٣٩١، وفتح الباري: ٣/ ٤٩.
٢ هذا الأثر رواه البخاري في صحيحه في ترجمة باب ما جاء في التطوع مثنى مثنى من كتاب التهجد، انظر فتح الباري: ٣/ ٤٨.
٣ النساء: ٤٣.
٤ ومراد الزهري أنه يجوز الوضوء من الماء الذي ولغ فيه الكلب إذا لم يجد المتوضئ غير هذا الماء، وفقه الزهري أنه أعمل النص، فإن هذا المتوضئ، قد وجد الماء فلا يجوز له التيمم، وهذا الاستدلال فيه نظر؛ لأن الماء النجس كالمعدوم.
٥ أحمد في مسنده: ٥/١٩٤. ضعيف مرفوعًا، والموقوف على أبي الدرداء حسن.
٦ رواه مسلم في صحيحه، كتاب المنافقين/ ٤٠، وأحمد في مسنده: ١/ ٣٨١.

He also said, "One of the signs of a man's *fiqh* is to procure his [immediate] needs before he initiates his *ṣalāh*."[1]

He also said, "A man lengthening his prayer and shortening his sermon is indicative of his *fiqh*."[2]

As previously mentioned, the early generation of Muslims used the term *fiqh* to denote the entire religion, not just a specific aspect. According to them, the *faqīh* was the one who was concerned about the fundamentals before the detailed injunctions and was concerned with the actions of the heart before the actions of the limbs. For that reason, Imām Abū Ḥanīfah entitled his treatise on theology *al-Fiqh al-Akbar* (the Greatest *Fiqh*).[3]

In this era, *fiqh* was all-inclusive of creed, legal rulings and morals. 'Ubaydullāh ibn Mas'ūd clearly stated, "In the early times, *fiqh* referred to the knowledge of the Hereafter, knowing the nuances of the self, realizing the Hereafter and the pettiness of the life of this world. However, I am not saying that *fiqh* did not deal with the *fatāwā* (legal edicts) and practical rulings."[4]

1 Reported by al-Bukhāri in the *Book on Adhān* (*Call for Ṣalāh*) no. 42.
2 Reported by Imām Muslim in his *Ṣaḥīḥ* from *The Book on Friday* no. 47, ad-Dārimi in *The Book of Ṣalāh* no. 199 and Aḥmad 4/263.
3 In *The Encyclopedia of Jamāl 'Abdul an-Nāṣir* 1/9 and *Kashshāf Istilāḥ al-Funūn* 1/30, it was reported that when Abū Ḥanīfah was asked about *fiqh*, he said, "[It is] knowing the ins and outs of the self."
4 *At-Taqdīḥ 'Alā at-Tanqīḥ* by Ṣadr ash-Sharī'ah 1/78. These same words were stated by al-Ghazāli in *Iḥyā' 'Ulūm ad-Dīn* 1/32.

وقوله: «**من فقه المرء إقباله على حاجته حتى يقبل على صلاته**»(١)

وقوله: «**إن طول صلاة الرجل وقصر خطبته مئنّة من فقهه**»(٢).

وقد كان الفقه عند أهل الصدر الأول فقهاً شاملاً للدين كله، غير مختص بجانب منه، وقد كان الفقيه عندهم يعنى بالأصول قبل الفروع، ويعنى بأعمال القلوب قبل عمل الأبدان؛ ولذلك سمّى الإمام أبو حنيفة ورقات وضعها في العقيدة باسم «الفقه الأكبر»(٣)

فالفقه كان يشمل في ذلك العهد علم العقيدة، وأحكام الفروع، والأخلاق، وممن نص على هذا صدر الشريعة عبيد الله بن مسعود، قال: «اسم الفقه في العصر الأول كان مطلقاً على علم الآخرة، ومعرفة دقائق النفوس، والاطلاع على الآخرة وحقارة الدنيا، ولست أقول: إن الفقه لم يكون متناولاً الفتاوى والأحكام الظاهرة»(٤)

١ رواه البخاري في كتاب الأذان: ٤٢، في الترجمة.
٢ رواه مسلم في كتاب الجمعة/ ٤٧، والدارمي في كتاب الصلاة ١٩٩، وأحمد: ٤/ ٢٦٣.
٣ موسوعة جمال عبد الناصر: ١/ ٩، وفي كشاف اصطلاحات الفنون: ١/ ٣٠ أن أبا حنيفة سئل عن الفقه، فقال: «هو معرفة النفس ما لها وما عليها».
٤ كتاب التوضيح على التنقيح لصدر الشريعة: ١/ ٧٨، وقد قال مثل ذلك الغزالي في إحياء علوم الدين: ١/ ٣٢.

Similarly, Ibn 'Ābidīn said, "The *fuqahā'* are those who are knowledgeable regarding the rulings of Allah and are committed to practicing them. Limiting the term *fiqh* to [knowledge of] the detailed rulings is unprecedented. This is further supported by the saying of al-Ḥasan al-Baṣri,[1] 'A *faqīh* is one who shuns this worldly life and aspires for the Hereafter. He is the one who has a deep understanding of his religion, consistently worships his Lord, employs *wara'* (pious caution), abstains from [violating] the honor of the Muslims, refrains from [indulging in] their wealth and remains a sincere advisor to them.'"[2]

According to the terminology of the later generations: The later generations began using the term *fiqh* particularly for the science of Islamic Law. They limited it to imply knowledge of the practical legal rulings. Ṣadr ash-Sharī'ah 'Ubaydillāh ibn Mas'ūd said, "After the first generation passed, the science of *fiqh* was used to refer to the practical rulings that are derived from detailed evidences, either by generalization or analogy. Thus, they narrowed down the usage of the term *fiqh* while maintaining its original meaning."[3]

Al-Āmidi defined *fiqh* as "knowledge of the practical legislative rulings as derived from their detailed evidences."[4] He attributed this definition to ash-Shāfi'i.

Their definition of *Fiqh* is very precise, and it shows the keen perspective which the Muslim scholars had regarding the sciences of law. Below is a clarification of the elements of this definition:

1) ***Fiqh* is a science.** It covers a specific theme and has its own exclusive rules and principles. The *fuqahā'* treated it on this basis in their books, research and *fatāwā*. It is not merely a technique as some scholars claim.

1 Al-Ḥasan ibn Yasār al-Baṣri is one of the great scholars of the Successors. He was born on 21 A.H. and died on 110 A.H.
2 *Hāshyat Ibn 'Ābidīn* 1/26 & 1/33 – al-Maṭba'ah al-Miṣriyyah (1st Edition) 1272 A.H.
3 *At-Tawḍīḥ `Alā at-Tanqīḥ* 1/78.
4 *Al-Iḥkām fī Uṣūl al-Aḥkām* 1-5.

ويقول ابن عابدين: «المراد بالفقهاء: العالمون بأحكام الله تعالى اعتقاداً وعملاً؛ لأن تسمية علم الفروع فقهاً حادثة، ويؤيده قول الحسن البصري[١]: «إنما الفقيه المعرض عن الدنيا، الراغب في الآخرة، البصير بدينه، المداوم على عبادة ربه، الورع، الكاف عن أعراض المسلمين، العفيف عن أموالهم، الناصح لجماعتهم»»[٢].

(ب) الفقه في اصطلاح المتأخرين:

الفقه في اصطلاح المتأخرين معناه علم القانون الإسلامي، فقد خصه المتأخرون بعد الصدر الأول بالعلم بالأحكام الشرعية العملية، يقول صدر الشريعة: «بعد الصدر الأول اختص علم الفقه باستنباط الأحكام العملية من الأدلة التفصيلية بطريق العموم والشمول، أو بطريق الاستتباع، فتصرفوا فيه بالتخصيص، لا بالنقل والتحويل»[٣].

وقد عرف الآمدي الفقه بأنه: «العلم بالأحكام الشرعية العملية من أدلتها التفصيلية»[٤]، وقد عزاه الآمدي إلى الإمام الشافعي.

وتعريفهم للفقه في غاية الدقة؛ إذ إنه يظهر وجهة نظر علماء المسلمين الخاصة لعلم الحقوق، وفيما يلي إيضاح عناصر هذا التعريف:

أولاً: الفقه علم: فهو ذو موضوع خاص وقواعد خاصة، وعلى هذا الأساس درسه الفقهاء في كتبهم وأبحاثهم وفتاويهم، فهو ليس فناً كما ادعى بعض العلماء.

١ هو الحسن بن يسار البصري من كبار علماء التابعين، مولده سنة ٢١هـ ووفاته سنة ١١٠هـ.
٢ حاشية ابن عابدين: ١/ ٢٦، ١/ ٣٣، المطبعة المصرية، الأولى ١٢٧٢هـ.
٣ التوضيح على التنقيح: ١/ ٧٨.
٤ الإحكام في أصول الأحكام: ١- ٥.

2) *Fiqh* is the science of legal rulings. Legal rulings are those handed down through verbal transmission and taken from the religion itself. They are not based on simple common sense, such as knowing that this world was created or that one is half of two. They are also not rulings that can be merely based upon the human senses, such as the knowledge that fire burns. They are also not derived from linguistic jargon or complex grammatical rules.

A legal ruling is a rule given by the legislator on a certain issue. When this rule commissions the individual with a certain practice, it is called a *ḥukm taklīfi* (binding legal ruling). When this rule does not commission the individual [in and of itself], then it is called a *ḥukm waḍʿi* (declaratory law). Some examples are:

a) Repaying a debt is obligatory, and murder is prohibited. Obligation in the first case and prohibition in the second case are binding legal rulings because they enjoin performing an action (e.g. repaying a debt) and avoiding an action (e.g. murder) respectively.

b) One declaratory legal ruling is the fact that Sharia invalidates any contract drawn up by an insane person. Invalidity here is the declaratory legal ruling because it was declared as a result of an insane person's involvement in the contract, but does not prompt any particular action [unlike the *taklīfi*].

3) *Fiqh* is the science of practical legal rulings. The word 'practical' here means that *fiqh* rulings are related to issues practiced by people, such as acts of worship and daily transactions. Practical rulings, unlike creed, deal with the body rather than the heart.

4) *Fiqh* is derived from detailed evidences. This means that rulings do not belong to the science of *fiqh* unless they are based on the well-known sources of Sharia. A *faqīh* is one who traces back each legal ruling to its evidences. Islamic Law or *Fiqh* is not enacted by the state. Rather, it is a religious legislation that depends solely on religious texts.

ثانياً: الفقه العلم بالأحكام الشرعية، والأحكام الشرعية هي المتلقاة بطريق السمع المأخوذة من الشرع، دون المأخوذة من العقل، كالعلم بأن العالم حادث، وأن الواحد نصف الاثنين، أو الأحكام المأخوذة من الحس، كالعلم بأن النار محرقة، أو المأخوذة من الوضع والاصطلاح اللغوي، كالعلم بأن الفاعل مرفوع، والمفعول به منصوب.

والحكم الشرعي هو القاعدة التي نص عليها الشارع في مسألة من المسائل، وهذه القاعدة إما أن يكون فيها تكليف معين، فتسمى الحكم الشرعي التكليفي، وإما أن لا يكون فيها أي تكليف، فيقال لها الحكم الشرعي الوضعي.

مثاله: أداء الدَّيْن واجب، والقتل محرم، فالوجوب في الحالة الأولى، والتحريم في الحالة الثانية حكم شرعي تكليفي؛ لأن فيه تكليفاً بفعل هو أداء الدَّيْن، أو بالامتناع عن فعل وهو القتل.

ومثال الحكم الشرعي الوضعي أن الشرع نص على بطلان عقد المجنون، فالبطلان هو حكم شرعي وضعي؛ لأنه وضع نتيجة لعقد المجنون بدون أن يكلف فيه أي تكليف.

ثالثاً: الفقه العلم بالأحكام الشرعية العملية، وكلمة عملية تعني أن الأحكام الفقهية تتعلق بالمسائل العملية الناتجة من أفعال الناس في عباداتهم ومعاملاتهم اليومية، ويقابل الأحكام العملية الأحكام العقائدية، فإن تعلقها بالقلوب لا بأعمال الأبدان.

رابعاً: جاء في التعريف أن علم الفقه مكتسب من أدلة الأحكام التفصيلية، ومعنى ذلك أن الأحكام لا تعد من علم الفقه إلا إذا كانت مستندة إلى مصادر الشرع المعلومة أي إلى أدلة الشرع، والفقيه هو الذي يسند كل حكم من أحكام الشرع إلى دليله، فالقانون الإسلامي أو الفقه الإسلامي ليس وضعيّاً من صنع الدولة، بل هو تشريع ديني يستند إلى مصادر دينية.

Notes

This definition limits *fiqh* to rulings derived by considering the evidences. As for rulings adopted via *taqlīd* (blind imitation) without thorough consideration of the evidence, they do not belong to *fiqh*.

Detailed evidence refers to specific proofs from the Qur'an and Sunnah, such as Allah's saying,

"Prohibited to you are dead animals, blood, the flesh of swine,"[1] and the Prophet's (ﷺ) saying, "[Adorning] gold and silk has been made lawful for the females of my Ummah, and unlawful for its males."[2]

In contrast to the detailed evidence is the holistic evidence. The holistic evidence is the subject of research by the scholars of *Uṣūl al-Fiqh* (the Fundamentals of *Fiqh*), since they are concerned with the fundamental sources of evidence: the Book [of Allah], the authentic Sunnah, consensus, analogy and the like. Also, they focus on the implications of the genre of proofs in the Qur'an and Sunnah. For instance, of these formulated fundamentals is the following: a command implies obligation unless there is a textual connotation that indicates it being [merely] desirable. A prohibition implies unlawfulness unless there is a textual connotation that indicates it being [merely] undesirable.

Fiqh covers both decisive and speculative rulings.

This definition also shows that *fiqh* covers the practical rulings which are *qaṭ'i* (decisive) rulings in the religion which must be known, such as the obligation of the *ẓuhr* (noon) prayer and the prohibition of wine. It also covers the *ẓanni* (speculative) rulings such as whether or not touching a woman invalidates ablution, or whether it is obligatory to wipe over the entire head or just a part thereof when performing ablution.

1 Sūrat al-Mā'idah – Verse 3

2 See *Sunan an-Nasā'i* 5/437 and *Sunan at-Tirmidhi* 4/271. At-Tirmidhi said that it is *ḥasan-ṣaḥīḥ*.

والتعريف يجعل الفقه قاصراً على الأحكام التي تؤخذ من طريق النظر في الأدلة، أما الأحكام التي يتلقاها المقلدون من غير طريق النظر، فإنها لا تدخل في مفهوم الفقه.

ومرادهم بالأدلة التفصيلية آحاد الأدلة من الكتاب والسنة كقوله تعالى: ﴿**حُرِّمَتْ عَلَيْكُمُ الْمَيْتَةُ وَالدَّمُ وَلَحْمُ الْخِنْزِيرِ**﴾(١)، وقوله ﷺ: «**أحل الذهب والحرير على الإناث من أمتي، وحرم على ذكورها**»، رواه الترمذي والنسائي، وقال الترمذي: حسن صحيح(٢).

ويقابل الأدلة التفصيلية الأدلة الإجمالية، وهي محل نظر علماء أصول الفقه؛ حيث يبحثون في أصول الأدلة: الكتاب والسنة والإجماع والقياس... إلخ، كما يبحثون في جنس الأدلة في الكتاب والسنة كقولهم: الأمر يفيد الوجوب ما لم يصرفه صارف إلى الندب، والنهي يفيد التحريم ما لم يصرفه صارف إلى الكراهة.

شمول الفقه للأحكام القطعية والظنية:

والتعريف يدخل في الفقه الأحكام العملية المعلومة من الدين بالضرورة (القطعية)، كوجوب صلاة الظهر، وحرمة الخمر، والأحكام المظنونة على حد سواء، مثل مس المرأة هل ينقض الوضوء أم لا؟ وهل الواجب مسح الرأس جميعه في الوضوء أم بعضه؟ ونحو ذلك.

١ المائدة: ٣.

٢ انظر النسائي: ٤٣٧/٥، والترمذي: ٢٧١/٤.

Some other scholars, such as ar-Rāzi, had a different viewpoint. They believed that decisive rulings are not covered by *fiqh*.

Ibn al-Humām had the completely opposite view from that of ar-Rāzi; he limited *fiqh* to the decisive rulings while claiming that speculative rulings have no place in *fiqh*.

Both views could be refuted by the method which the *fuqahā'* wrote their books, since they included both decisive and speculative rulings therein. Furthermore, the decisive and speculative rulings are not agreed upon between all the Muslims. Rather, some scholars may have numerous proofs that make them believe that a particular ruling is decisive, while others do not have all those proofs. This is the case among the scholars, and hence, others will find more controversy on such issues.[1]

Comparison between Sharia and *Fiqh*

The technical definition of Sharia, according to the early predecessors, is identical to that of *fiqh*. For them, both *Fiqh* and Sharia cover all aspects of the religion including creed, rulings, and manners. Furthermore, the definitions of *Fiqh* and Sharia, according to the later generations, match. Both of them cover the practical rulings. However, the underlying difference between them, which should not be ignored, is that Sharia is the religion sent down by Allah whereas *Fiqh* is our understanding of this Sharia. If our understanding is correct, *Fiqh* is then in agreement with Sharia. On the other hand, if we misinterpret the truth sent down by Allah, this misunderstanding is not to be considered a representation of Sharia, but it still remains within the realm of *Fiqh*.

1 See *Majmū' al-Fatāwā* by Ibn Taymiyah 1/70.

وقد خالف بعض العلماء فذهبوا إلى أن الأحكام القطعية المجمع عليها لا تدخل في علم الفقه، ومن هؤلاء الرازي.

وناقض ابن الهمام طريقة الرازي فجعل الأحكام المظنونة غير داخلة في الفقه، وقصر الفقه على الأحكام القطعية.

ويرد على الفريقين صنيع الفقهاء على اختلاف مذاهبهم في كتبهم؛ حيث يوردون فيها الأحكام القطعية والظنية، ثم إن القطعية والظنية ليسا أمراً منضبطاً للمسلمين كلهم، فبعض العلماء تتوارد عليه الأدلة حتى يجزم بحكم ما، وآخر لا يكون عنده هذا العلم. هذا في العلماء، وغيرهم أشد تبايناً منهم[١].

مقارنة بين الشريعة والفقه:

التعريف الاصطلاحي للتشريع عند أهل الصدر الأول يطابق التعريف الاصطلاحي للفقه عندهم؛ إذ كل منهما كان يتناول الدين كله بعقائده وأحكامه وآدابه، وهو يطابقه في مدلوله الاصطلاحي عند المتأخرين؛ إذ كل منهما يطلق على الأحكام العملية، إلا أن بينهما فرقاً لا ينبغي أن يهمل، ذلك أن الشريعة هي الدين المنزل من عند الله، والفقه هو فهمنا لتلك الشريعة، فإذا أصبنا الحق في فهمنا كان الفقه موافقاً للشريعة من هذه الحيثية، وإذا أخطأ فقهنا الحق المنزل لم يكن هذا الفهم من الشريعة، ولم يخرج عن الفقه.

١ راجع مجموع فتاوى شيخ الإسلام ابن تيمية: ١/ ٧٠.

We can pinpoint the difference between the technical definition of *fiqh*, according to the later generations of scholars, and the general definition of Sharia in the following points:

1) *Fiqh* and Sharia converge and diverge on a number of points. In one way, *Fiqh* is more specific, and in another way, it is more general. Both *Fiqh* and Sharia apply to the rulings in which a *Mujtahid* reaches a judgement wherein he has agreed with the ruling enjoined by Allah.
• *Fiqh* differs from Sharia when it refers to a ruling wherein the *mujtahid* reaches an erroneous judgment.
• Sharia includes rulings related to doctrines, morals and [lessons learned from] the stories of the previous nations, while *Fiqh* does not.

2) Unlike *Fiqh*, Sharia is complete and all-inclusive. Sharia covers the broad-spectrum of fundamentals and principles that are mentioned in the Noble Quran and Prophetic Sunnah. Based on these principles, we derive rulings which cover every aspect of our lives. As for *Fiqh*, it is the opinions of *mujtahid* scholars derived from the Holy Qur'an and the Prophetic Sunnah.

3) Unlike *Fiqh*, Sharia is more general in applicability. Allah said in the Holy Qur'an,

"And We have not sent you, [O Muhammad], except as a mercy to the worlds."[1]

Such generality is vivid from the purport of Sharia, its ultimate objectives, and its texts which address all of humanity.

Fiqh is the working of the *mujtahid*. It may solve the problems of a society in the context of a specific time and place. However, that very same solution may not be applicable to the problems of another era or region. On the other hand, Sharia is constant and applicable to all eras and regions.

4) The rulings of Sharia are unquestionably true, whereas the understanding of the *fuqahā'* may be erroneous.

5) The rulings of Sharia are fixed and eternal.

1 Sūrat al-Anbiyā' – Verse 107

ويمكن أن نحدد الفرق بين الفقه بمعناه الاصطلاحي عند المتأخرين وبين الشريعة بمعناها الاصطلاحي العام في النقاط التالية:

١- النسبة بين الفقه والتشريع العموم والخصوص من وجه.

فيجتمع الفقه والتشريع في الأحكام التي أصاب المجتهد فيها حكم الله.

• ويفترق الفقه عن التشريع في الأحكام التي أخطأ فيها المجتهد.

• وتفترق الشريعة عن الفقه في الأحكام التي تتعلق بالناحية الاعتقادية والأخلاقية، وبقصص الأمم الماضية.

٢- الشريعة كاملة بخلاف الفقه، فالشريعة تتناول القواعد والأصول العامة المذكورة في الكتاب والسنة، ومن هذه القواعد والأصول نستمد أحكاما تشمل جميع أمور حياتنا، أما الفقه فهو آراء المجتهدين من علماء الأمة المأخوذة من الكتاب والسنة.

٣- الشريعة عامة بخلاف الفقه: **﴿وَمَا أَرْسَلْنَاكَ إِلاَّ رَحْمَةً لِّلْعَالَمِينَ﴾**(١)، وهذا العموم ملموس من واقع الشريعة ومقاصدها ونصوصها التي تخاطب البشر كافة.

والفقه الذي هو من استنباط المجتهد قد يعالج مشكلات المجتمع في زمن أو مكان بعلاج يمكن ألا يصلح لمشكلات زمان أو مكان آخر، بخلاف الشريعة الشاملة زماناً ومكاناً.

٤- أحكام الشريعة صواب لا خطأ فيها، وفهم الفقهاء قد يخطئ أحياناً.

٥- ثبات أحكام الشريعة وخلودها.

١ الأنبياء: ١٠٧.

Branches of Islamic *Fiqh* Topics

When the jurists compiled the Islamic Law into *Fiqh* books, they divided the topics of this law into two major sections: *'ibādāt* (acts of worship) and *mu'āmalāt* (transactions).

The most important topics covered in the acts of worship section are:

1) Ritual purity, which includes rulings related to water, impurities, ablution, ritual bathing, dry ablution, menstruation and post-partum bleeding
2) *Ṣalāh* (prayer)
3) *Zakāh* (charity)
4) Fasting
5) *I'tikāf* (seclusion in mosques for worship)
6) Funerals
7) Hajj and *'umrah*
8) Mosques, their merits and related rulings
9) Oaths and vows
10) Jihād
11) Food and beverages
12) Hunting and slaughtered animals[1]

The most important topics included in the transactions section are:

1) Marriage and divorce
2) Penalties, such as prescribed punishments, retribution and discretionary punishment
3) Sales
4) Loans
5) Mortgages
6) Watering
7) Sharecropping
8) Leasing and hiring
9) Transfer of payment

1 Many scholars include the last three topics in the section of transactions. Some would put the last two under a separate category, which is the section of religious etiquettes and customs.

أقسام موضوعات الفقه الإسلامي

عندما دوَّن الفقهاء القانون الإسلامي في مدونات سميت بكتب الفقه قسموا موضوعات هذا القانون إلى قسمين كبيرين هما قسم العبادات، وقسم المعاملات.

مباحث قسم العبادات: وأهم الموضوعات التي أدرجوها في هذا القسم هي:

١- الطهارة، وبحثوا فيها المياه والنجاسات والوضوء والغسل والتيمم والحيض والنفاس.
٢- الصلاة
٣- الزكاة
٤- الصيام
٥- الاعتكاف
٦- الجنائز
٧- الحج والعمرة
٨- المساجد وفضلها وأحكامها
٩- الأيمان والنذور
١٠- الجهاد
١١- الأطعمة والأشربة
١٢- الصيد والذبائح[1]

مباحث قسم المعاملات: وأهم الموضوعات التي أدرجوها في هذا القسم هي:

١- الزواج والطلاق.
٢- العقوبات (الحدود والقصاص والتعزيز).
٣- البيوع.
٤- القرض.
٥- الرهن.
٦- المساقاة.
٧- المزارعة.
٨- الإجارة.
٩- الحوالة.

١ كثير من الفقهاء يضع الثلاثة الأخيرة في قسم المعاملات. والبعض يجعل الأخيرين في قسم آخر، وهو الآداب الشرعية والعادات.

10) Preemption
11) Agency
12) Borrowing
13) Deposits for safekeeping
14) Misappropriation
15) Waifs and foundlings
16) Guarantorship
17) Bounty wages
18) Partnerships
19) Judiciary
20) Endowments
21) Gifts
22) Interdiction
23) Testaments or wills
24) Rulings of inheritance

The differences between acts of worship and transactions:

As mentioned previously, the majority of the *fuqahā'* divided legal rulings into acts of worship and transactions. They noticed tangible differences that caused them to differentiate between them:

1) There is a difference in terms of the original purpose of both. If the first and foremost aim of legal judgments is to seek nearness to Allah, give thanks to Him and seek the good reward in the Hereafter, then this type falls under acts of worship, such as praying, fasting, charity and pilgrimage. However, if the aim of the laws is to achieve a worldly benefit or to organize a relationship between two individuals, groups and the like, then this type is categorized under the section of transactions.

2) The jurists noticed that, in essence, the acts of worship are not logic-based. The texts simply came regarding them, either commanding or forbidding, and none grasps their ultimate reality but Allah. All we know about their wisdoms and objectives, which the texts stated or alluded to, are beyond being used for *qiyās* (analogy), nor has an effect on deeming matters permissible or invalid.

٠١- الشفعة.
١١- الوكالة.
٢١- العارية.
٣١- الوديعة.
٤١- الغصب.
٥١- اللقيط.
٦١- الكفالة.
٧١- الجعالة.
٨١- الشركات.
٩١- القضاء.
٠٢- الأوقاف.
١٢- الهبة.
٢٢- الحجر.
٣٢- الوصية.
٤٢- الفرائض.

الفرق بين العبادات والمعاملات:

عموم الفقهاء- كما قررنا من قبل- قسموا الأحكام الشرعية إلى عبادات ومعاملات، وقد لاحظوا فروقاً عدة جعلتهم يذهبون هذا المذهب:

الأول: اختلاف المقصود الأصلي لكل من العبادات والمعاملات.

فإذا كان الغرض الأول من الأحكام الشرعية التقرب إلى الله وشكره، وابتغاء الثواب في الآخرة، فإنهم يجعلون هذا النوع في قسم العبادات، كالصلاة والصوم والزكاة والحج، وإذا كان المقصود منه تحقيق مصلحة دنيوية، أو تنظيم علاقة بين فردين، أو جماعتين، فإنهم يضعون هذا النوع في قسم المعاملات.

الثاني: لاحظ الفقهاء أن الأصل في العبادات أنها غير معقولة المعنى، جاءت بها النصوص آمرة أو ناهية، لا يعلم حقيقتها إلا الله، وكل ما نعرفه من حكمها وعللها مما ورد به النص، أو عرف بالاستنباط، لا أثر له في قياس ولا إباحة ولا إلغاء.

Nothing more effectively proves their being strictly devotional matters than the fact that many of their elements are not understood by the mind. Even if one could grasp the wisdom behind them, this only occurs in a general sense.

As for customs, they usually carry some clear significance which the human mind can perceive many of their secrets. For this reason, when the wise people legislated during the absence of divine messages, their discretion led them to correctly legislate, and many of their legislations were later confirmed by Islam. Of course, there were instances when they did arrive at incorrect conclusions.

This fact is further supported by the legislative approach in transactions. It did not tend to delve into specific details, but rather came with holistic principles and general guidelines. Then it frequently expressed the justifications [for these guidelines] in order to help the jurists apply these principles in various times and environments. As for the acts of worship, the complete opposite took place; the Qur'an introduced them in general terms, and the Messenger (ﷺ) clarified their every detail.

3) While performing acts of worship, the worshipper must know beforehand that these acts were enjoined by Allah, for he needs to intend by them nearness to Allah, the Mighty and Majestic. This intention can only result after knowing that Allah was the One who enjoined this act upon him.

However, in the case of transactions, the intention of seeking nearness to Allah by them is not a condition of their validity. A person will not get rewarded by them except with that intention. This applies to the case of returning trusts and seized property, repaying debts and spending on one's wife. If these things are done just to avert the punishment of those in authority, the action will be valid without the right intention. The doer will not be asked to redo this act nor will he be liable for it in the Hereafter. This is because the rights have been fulfilled in the worldly life, and hence it will not be demanded of him a second time. However, he will not be rewarded unless he intends nearness to Allah with that act.

ولا أدل على أنها مقصورة على التعبد مما نراه فيها من أمور كثيرة يعجز العقل عن إدراكها، وإن أدركها فإنما يكون على وجه الإجمال لا التفصيل.

وأما العادات فالأصل فيها أنها معقولة المعنى، يدرك العقل كثيراً من أسرارها؛ لذلك نرى العقلاء في زمن الفترات استعملوا عقولهم في تشريعها، فأصابوا في الكثير منها، وإن كان التوفيق جانبهم في بعضها الآخر، ولما جاء الإسلام أقر مما كانوا يتعاملون به أموراً غير قليلة.

يرشدنا إلى ذلك أسلوب التشريع فيها، فهو لم يعمد إلى التفاصيل، بل جاء بالأصول الكلية والقواعد العامة، ثم أكثر من التعليل ليكون ذلك عوناً للفقهاء على التطبيق مهما تغير الزمن واختلفت البيئات، وأما العبادات فهي على العكس من ذلك، فالقرآن جاء بها إجمالاً، والرسول بيَّنها أكمل بيان.

الثالث: يشترط في التكليف بالعبادات العلم بأنه مأمور بها من الله تعالى؛ إذ لا بد للمكلف من نية التقرب بالعبادة إلى الله تعالى، وهذه النية لا تكون إلا بعد معرفة أن العبادة المتقرب بها إليه أمر منه جل وعلا.

وأما المعاملات فلا يشترط في صحة فعلها نية التقرب، ولكن لا أجر له فيها إلا بنية التقرب إلى الله تعالى، كرد الأمانة، والمغصوب، وقضاء الديون، والإنفاق على الزوجة، فمتى فعل شيئاً من هذه خوفاً من عقوبة السلطان ففعله صحيح دون النية، وتسقط المطالبة به، فلا يلزمه الحق في الآخرة بدعوى أن قضاءه في الدنيا غير صحيح لعدم نية التقرب، بل القضاء صحيح، والمطالبة ساقطة على كل حال، ولكن لا أجر إلا بنية التقرب.[١]

١ راجع في هذه المسألة كتابنا: مقاصد المكلفين: ٥٤، وكتاب المدخل في التعريف بالفقه الإسلامي لمحمد مصطفى شلبي: ١٥- ١٦.

The Inclusion of Secondary Man-made Laws under the Subject of Islamic *Fiqh*

The Divisions of Man-made Laws

Before explaining that Islamic law includes all the divisions of man-made law, I would like to make mention of the divisions of man-made law.

Man-made law is divided into two sections: public law and private law. This division is based on whether or not the state is a party in the legal relations governed by these legislations.

If the state, in its capacity as the holder of authority and sovereignty, is involved in the transaction regulated by a particular law, then the law is considered a public law. However, if the state is not a party in the aforementioned capacity and instead aims at achieving a private interest, then the law is considered a private law.

The Public Law

Public law is divided into two sections: external (foreign) law, which is also called international law, and internal (domestic) law which has four subdivisions.

The international law, is a set of rules that regulate the interrelations between countries and define their rights and obligations toward one another, whether at peace or at war.

Domestic public law has a set of rules that determine the entity of the state and regulate its relations with individuals in its capacity as the holder of authority and sovereignty. It has four subdivisions:

1) Constitutional law
2) Administrative law
3) Financial law
4) Criminal law

اشتمال موضوعات الفقه الإسلامي على فروع القوانين الوضعية

أقسام القانون الوضعي:

قبل أن نبين أن القانون الإسلامي مشتمل على جميع أقسام القانون الوضعي أحب أن أبين أقسام القانون الوضعي.

يقسم القانون الوضعي عند أهله إلى قسمين: القانون العام، والقانون الخاص، وهذا التقسيم مبني على أساس وجود الدولة أو عدم وجودها كطرف في العلاقات القانونية التي تحكمها تلك القواعد القانونية.

فإذا كانت الدولة طرفاً في العلاقة التي ينظمها القانون، باعتبارها صاحبة السلطة والسيادة سمي القانون قانوناً عامّاً، أما إذا لم تكن طرفاً بصفتها صاحبة السيادة والسلطان، وإنما تهدف إلى تحقيق مصلحة خاصة، سمي القانون خاصّاً.

القانون العام:

القانون العام قسمان: خارجي: ويسمى بالقانون الدولي، وداخلي: ويتفرع إلى أربعة فروع.

فالقانون الخارجي أو الدولي العام هو مجموعة القواعد التي تنظم علاقات الدول بعضها مع بعض، وتحدد حقوق كل منها وواجباتها؛ سواء في حالات السلم، أم في حالات الحرب.

والقانون العام الداخلي يحتوي على مجموعة القواعد التي تحدد كيان الدولة وتنظم علاقاتها بالأفراد بصفتها صاحبة السلطة والسيادة، ويتفرع إلى **أربعة فروع:**

١- القانون الدستوري.

٢- القانون الإداري.

٣- القانون المالي.

٤- القانون الجنائي.

Constitutional law: A group of rules that designate the governance system in the state, the general authorities within it, the jurisdiction of each authority, the interactions between these authorities and their relationship to the individuals governed therein. It further clarifies the political rights of individuals and the principles that guarantee their freedom.

Administrative law: A group of rules that clarify how the executive authority carries out its duties. This includes the types of services that the executive authority offers and the facilities that are employed to provide such services. It further demonstrates the relationship of the central authority to the provincial administrations and the municipal, local and rural councils. This relationship could either be centralized or decentralized. Administrative law demonstrates the administrative works and the required conditions of their validity along with the methods of monitoring them.

Financial law: The rules that govern the state's finances. It is therefore concerned with studying:

1) Public expenditures
2) Public revenues
3) Public loans
4) The state's budget

Criminal law: A group of rules that define crime specify the determined penalty for each crime and implement procedures that should be followed in pursuing, trying and punishing the criminal.

The Private Law

Private laws are a group of rules that regulate the relations in which the state is not a party in its capacity as the holder of authority and sovereignty. It therefore regulates the relationships between individuals as a whole or the relationships between individuals and the state, in which the state is treated as an ordinary individual.

فالقانـون الدسـتوري: هـو مجموعـة القواعـد التـي تبـين نظام الحكم في الدولة والسلطات العامة فيها، واختصاص كل سـلطة منهـا، وعلاقـة هـذه السـلطات بعضهـا ببعـض، وعلاقاتهـا مـع الأفـراد، كـما يبـين حقـوق الأفـراد السياسـية، ومـا يجـب لحرياتهـم مـن ضمانـات.

والقانـون الإداري: يضـم مجموعـة القواعـد التـي تبـين كيفيـة أداء السـلطة التنفيذيـة لوظائفهـا، فهـو يتنـاول أنـواع الخدمـات التـي تقـوم بهـا السـلطة التنفيذيـة والمرافـق التـي تقـوم بتقديـم تلـك الخدمـات، ويبـين علاقـات السـلطة المركزيـة بـالإدارات في الإقليـم والمجالـس البلديـة والمحليـة والقرويـة، فقـد تكـون العلاقـة مركزيـة وقـد تكـون لا مركزيـة، ويبـين القانـون الإداري الأعـمال الإداريـة والـشروط اللازمـة لصحتهـا، وطـرق الرقابـة عليهـا.

والقانون المالي: يتضمـن القواعـد التـي تحكـم ماليـة الدولـة، فهـو يعنى بدراسـة:

١- النفقات العامة.
٢- الإيرادات العامة.
٣- القروض العامة.
٤- ميزانية الدولة.

والقانـون الجنـائي: مجموعـة القواعـد التـي تحـدد الجرائـم، وتبـين العقوبـات المقـررة لـكل منهـا، والإجـراءات التـي تتبـع في تعقـب المتهـم ومحاكمتـه وتوقيـع العقـاب عليـه.

القانون الخاص:

ويريـدون بـه مجموعـة القواعـد التـي تنظـم العلاقـات التي لا تكـون الدولـة طرفـاً فيهـا بصفتهـا صاحبـة السـيادة والسـلطان، فهـو ينظـم العلاقـة بـين الأشـخاص بصفـة عامـة، أو بينهـم وبـين الدولـة باعتبارهـا شـخصاً يقـوم بأعـمال عاديـة.

It has many branches, which include civil law, commercial law, marine law, labor law, civil and commercial procedures laws and international private law.

Civil law: A group of rules that regulate all of the relations between individuals with the exception of those regulated by another branch of private law. Civil law is the basis of private law, from which all other laws branched off.

Civil law addresses two types of relationships:

1) Those pertaining to the family
2) Those pertaining to material interests, including everything that has to do with the individual's financial activities

Commercial law: A group of rules that regulate relationships resulting from commercial business.

Marine/Maritime law: A group of rules that regulate private relationships resulting from sea navigation.

Labor law: A group of rules that regulate the relationship between the employees and their employers.

Law of procedures: A group of rules that demonstrate the procedures to be taken in courts to protect the rights of individuals in matters of dispute.

International private law: A group of rules that regulate the relationships among citizens of different countries. It specifies jurisdiction and applicable law.[1]

ويتفرع إلى فروع كثيرة، هي: القانون المدني، والقانون التجاري، والقانون البحري، وقانون العمل، وقانون المرافعات: المدنية، والتجارية، والقانون الدولي الخاص.

فالقانون المدني: هو مجموعة القواعد التي تنظم العلاقات بين الأشخاص عدا ما يتناوله بالتنظيم فرع آخر من فروع القانون الخاص.

والقانون المدني هو أصل القانون الخاص، وبقية القوانين الأخرى الخاصة تفرعت منه.

والقانون المدني يتناول نوعين من العلاقات والروابط:

١- روابط الأحوال الشخصية.
٢- القواعد المتعلقة بالأحوال العينية، وهي تشمل كل ما يتصل بنشاط الشخص بالنسبة للمال.

والقانون التجاري: مجموعة القواعد التي تنظم العلاقات الناشئة من الأعمال التجارية.

والقانون البحري: مجموعة القواعد التي تنظم العلاقات الخاصة التي تنشأ بصدد الملاحة في البحار.

وقانون العمل: مجموعة القواعد التي تنظم العلاقة التي تنشأ بين العمال وأصحاب الأعمال.

وقانون المرافعات: مجموعة القواعد التي تبين الإجراءات الواجب اتباعها أمام المحاكم؛ وذلك للوصول إلى حماية الحقوق إذا ما تُنُوزِع فيها.

والقانون الدولي الخاص: مجموعة القواعد التي تنظم العلاقات ذات العنصر الأجنبي بين الأفراد، فهو يبين المحكمة المختصة، والقانون الواجب التطبيق(١).

---

1 *Al-Madkhal lil-'Ulūm al-Qānūniyyah* by Dr. Tawfīq Faraj: 35-66

١ المدخل للعلوم القانونية للدكتور توفيق فرج: ٣٥- ٦٦.

The place of these topics in the books of *Fiqh*:[1]

The international law or the public foreign law

Muslim jurists were deeply concerned with matters of international public law. They were indeed pioneers in this field. The writings of Imām Muhammad Ibn al-Ḥasan ash-Shaybāni (d. 189 AH), including *Kitāb as-Siyar al-Kabīr*,[2] prompted many contemporary scholars to credit him as the father of international law.

It is worth mentioning that the rules of international public law in Islamic Sharia were drawn originally from the Noble Qur'an itself, the hadiths of the Messenger of Allah (ﷺ), and the reports of the Companions. The most important rules of this law are:

1) The unity of mankind: The Islamic Sharia considers all people as one nation under the umbrella of humanity. It further stresses that their different nations and tribes are not meant for them to fight and dispute among each other; rather it is meant for them to recognize one another and cooperate for the spread of mutual compassion and the prevention of corruption. Superiority in virtue is only obtained through *taqwā* (piety and God-consciousness) as Allah said, **"O mankind, indeed, We have created you from male and female and made you peoples and tribes that you may know one another. Indeed, the most noble of you in the sight of Allah is the most righteous of you. Indeed, Allah is Knowing and Acquainted."**[3]

1 Refer to these books: *al-Qanūn ar-Rūmāni wash-Sharī'ah al-Islāmiyyah*: 101, *al-Madkhal* by Muhammad Mustafā Shalabi: 23, *al-Madkhal* by Madkūr: 4th ed., 51 and *al-Madkhal* by Muhammad Yūsuf Mūsā: 107.

2 The jurists named the section on international law *as-Siyar wal-Maghāzī*. The reason behind the name *as-Siyar* was mentioned by as-Sarkhasi in his book *al-Mabsūṭ*: 10/2. He said, "Know that the word *siyar* is the plural of *sīrah*. It was so called because it gives an account of the Muslims' conduct when dealing with the *mushrik* warriors, those who were given a pledge of safety by the Muslims, the *dhimmi*(s) (non-Muslims living in Muslim states), the apostates who are worse than the disbelievers, and the transgressors whose status is lower than the *mushrikīn*." It was named *maghāzi* because its rules are derived from the Prophet's *ghazawāt* (battles).

3 Sūrat al-Ḥujurāt – Verse 13

مواقع هذه الموضوعات في كتب الفقه(١):

القانون الدولي أو القانون العام الخارجي:

اهتم الفقهاء المسلمون بالمسائل التي هي موضوع القانون الدولي العام، وأبدعوا في ذلك، وقد كان لمؤلفات الإمام محمد بن الحسن الشيباني (المتوفى سنة ١٨٩هـ)، ومنها «كتاب السير الكبير»(٢)، أهمية خاصة في هذا المجال، حملت كثيراً من العلماء المعاصرين على اعتباره الأب للقانون الدولي.

والجدير بالذكر أن قواعد القانون الدولي العام في الشريعة الإسلامية ترجع في أصلها إلى القرآن الكريم نفسه، وإلى أحاديث الرسول ﷺ وآثار الصحابة، وأهم قواعد هذا القانون:

١- الوحدة الإنسانية: فقد اعتبرت الشريعة الإسلامية الناس جميعاً أمة واحدة تجمعها الإنسانية، وأكدت أن اختلافهم شعوباً وقبائل ليس للتقاتل والاختلاف، بل للتعارف والتعاون وتعميم المودة ومنع الفساد. والتفاضل إنما يكون بالتقوى: **﴿يَا أَيُّهَا النَّاسُ إِنَّا خَلَقْنَاكُم مِّن ذَكَرٍ وَأُنثَى وَجَعَلْنَاكُمْ شُعُوباً وَقَبَائِلَ لِتَعَارَفُوا إِنَّ أَكْرَمَكُمْ عِندَ اللهِ أَتْقَاكُمْ﴾**(٣).

١ راجع في هذا المبحث: كتاب القانون الروماني والشريعة الإسلامية: ١٠١، وكتاب المدخل لمحمد مصطفى شلبي: ٢٣، وكتاب المدخل لمدكور، الرابعة: ٥١، والمدخل لمحمد يوسف موسى: ١٠٧.

٢ يطلق الفقهاء على مباحث القانون الدولي اسم «السير والمغازي»، والسبب في تسميته بالسير وضحه السرخسي في كتابه المبسوط (١٠/ ٢)، فقال: «اعلم أن السير جمع سيرة، وبه سُمِّي هذا الكتاب؛ لأنه يبين فيه سيرة المسلمين في المعاملة مع المشركين من أهل الحرب، ومع أهل العهد منهم من المستأمنين وأهل الذمة، ومع المرتدين الذين هم أخبس الكفار بالإنكار بعد الإقرار، ومع أهل البغي الذين حالهم دون حال المشركين، وإن كانوا جاهلين، وفي التأويل مبطلين»، وسمي بالمغازي؛ لأن قواعده تُستقى من غزوات الرسول ﷺ.

٣ الحجرات: ١٣.

2) **Cooperation:** The Islamic Sharia considers cooperation an essential principle. It encourages it whenever it involves good deeds, and forbids it within the framework of sin and transgression. Allah, the Most High, said, **"And cooperate in righteousness and piety, but do not cooperate in sin and aggression..."**[1]

3) **Tolerance:** The Islamic Sharia calls for displaying dignified tolerance when dealing with individuals or communities. It also calls for repelling hostile attitudes by good ones, as Allay said, **"And not equal are the good deed and the bad. Repel [evil] by that [deed] which is better; and thereupon the one whom between you and him is enmity [will become] as though he was a devoted friend."**[2]

4) **The freedom of creed and self-determination:** The Islamic Sharia is established upon the principle of the freedom of creed; it therefore forbade compulsion in religion, as Allah said, **"There shall be no compulsion in [acceptance of] the religion."**[3]

The Islamic state should even offer shelter to whoever seeks it and protect them from being forced to give up their religion.

It equally established the principle of freedom in self-determination; therefore it made it incumbent on the fighters in the cause of Allah to call their enemies to Islam. If they refused, they would be obliged to pay the *jizyah* (poll tax). If they refused again, they were to be fought. However, the Sharia does not allow starting war prior to those steps.[4]

1 Sūrat al-Mā'idah – Verse 2
2 Sūrat Fuṣṣilat – Verse 34
3 Sūrat al-Baqarah – Verse 256
4 It is noteworthy to mention here that this was not the only way the Messenger dealt with others. There were many peace treaties sanctioned by him that did not involve any of the three choices mentioned here. Such decisions are left for the Muslim state to determine based on the circumstances and the nature of the struggle.

٢- التعاون: اعتبرت الشريعة الإسلامية التعاون مبدءً عامًّا أساسيًّا، وحثت عليه في مجال البر، ونهت عنه إذا هدف إلى الإثم والعدوان، قال تعالى: **﴿وَتَعَاوَنُوا عَلَى الْبِرِّ وَالتَّقْوَى وَلاَ تَعَاوَنُوا عَلَى الإِثْمِ وَالْعُدْوَانِ﴾**(١).

٣- التسامح: دعت الشريعة الإسلامية إلى التسامح غير الذليل مع الأفراد والجماعات، كما دعت إلى دفع العداوة بالتي هي أحسن: **﴿وَلاَ تَسْتَوِي الْحَسَنَةُ وَلاَ السَّيِّئَةُ ادْفَعْ بِالَّتِي هِيَ أَحْسَنُ فَإِذَا الَّذِي بَيْنَكَ وَبَيْنَهُ عَدَاوَةٌ كَأَنَّهُ وَلِيٌّ حَمِيمٌ﴾**(٢).

٤- حرية العقيدة وحرية تقرير المصير: قامت الشريعة على مبدأ حرية العقيدة؛ فمنعت الإكراه في الدين: **﴿لاَ إِكْرَاهَ فِي الدِّينِ﴾**(٣)، بل إن الدولة الإسلامية تحمي من يستظل بظلها، وتمنع من إجبارهم على ترك دينهم.

كما قامت على مبدأ الحرية في تقرير المصير؛ ولذلك ألزمت المجاهدين في سبيل الله بأن يدعوا أعداءهم إلى الإسلام، فإن أبوا فالجزية، فإن رفضوا قاتلوهم، ولم تجز القتال ابتداءً.

١ المائدة: ٢.
٢ فصلت: ٣٤.
٣ البقرة: ٢٥٦.

5) Justice: The Islamic Sharia calls for the institution of justice and to judge according to it in peace as well as in war. It obliges its followers to exercise justice with all people, as Allah stated, **"O you who have believed, be persistently standing firm in justice, witnesses for Allah, even if it be against yourselves..."**[1] Allah also said, **"And do not let the hatred of a people prevent you from being just. Be just; that is nearer to righteousness."**[2]

6) Reciprocity: The Islamic Sharia affirms the concept of reciprocity and the principle of identical repayment, which could be applied by confronting those who are likely to break their covenants, but only after informing them of our new stance regarding them.

The four types of domestic public law (constitutional, administrative, criminal, and financial) have been studied rigorously by the jurists; some in great detail and some in less detail.

As for the constitutional law which outlines governmental structures in a country, determines the authorities therein, allots each specialization its faculties, devises the cooperative and supervising mechanisms between its respective authorities, defines public freedoms and declares the rights of individuals before the state – all of this was studied under the banner of *imāmah* (leadership), *khilāfah* (caliphate), the *bay'ah* (pledge of allegiance) to the rulers, the conditions they should meet and the rights of the people over them. They also dealt with the concepts of justice, equality and *shūrā* (consultation).[3]

٥- العـدل: نـادت الشريعـة الإسـلامية بإقـرار العـدل والحكـم بـه في حـالات السـلم والحـرب، وألزمـت أتباعهـا بتحـري العـدل مـع كل النـاس: ﴿**يَـا أَيُّهَـا الَّذِيـنَ آمَنُـوا كُونُـوا قَوَّامِـينَ بِالْقِسْطِ شُـهَدَاءَ للهِ وَلَـوْ عَـلَى أَنْفُسِـكُمْ**﴾(١)، وقـال تعـالى: ﴿**وَلاَ يَجْرِمَنَّكُـمْ شَـنَآنُ قَـوْمٍ عَـلَى أَلاَّ تَعْدِلُـوا اعْدِلُـوا هُـوَ أَقْـرَبُ لِلتَّقْـوَى**﴾(٢).

٦- المعاملـة بالمثـل: أقـرت الشريعـة الإسـلامية مبـدأ المعاملة بالمثـل؛ فمـن ذلـك أننـا نواجـه الذيـن نخـشى منهـم نقـض العهـود بعـد إعلامهـم بذلـك.

والقانـون العـام الداخـلي بأنواعـه الأربعـة: الدسـتوري، والإداري، والجنـائي، والمـالي، بحثـه الفقهـاء مـا بـين موسـع ومضيـق.

أمـا القانـون الدسـتوري الـذي يحـدد شـكل الحكـم في الدولـة، ويبـين السـلطات العامـة فيهـا، ويـوزع الاختصاصـات بينهـا، ويحـدد علاقـات التعـاون أو الرقابـة بـين هـذه السـلطات، ويبـين الحريـات العامـة، وحقـوق الأفـراد قبـل الدولـة، فقـد بحثـه الفقهـاء في مبحـث الإمامـة والخلافـة والبيعـة، والـولاة وشروطهـم، وحقـوق النـاس عليهـم، وفي مباحـث العـدل والمسـاواة والشـورى(٣).

1 Sūrat an-Nisā' – Verse 135
2 Sūrat al-Mā'idah – Verse 8
3 There is a valuable printed book written by Abūl-A'lā al-Mawdūdi entitled *Tad īn ad-Dustūr al-Islāmi.*

١ النساء: ١٣٥.
٢ المائدة: ٨.
٣ هنـاك كتـاب قيـم مطبـوع لأبي الأعـلى المـودودي عنوانـه: «تدويـن الدسـتور الإسـلامي».

As for the administrative law which governs the activity of the executive authority, its protocol in carrying out its function and its guardianship of public facilities – this has been presented in the books of *Fiqh* under the title *as-Siyāsah ash-Shar'iyyah* or *al-Aḥkām as-Sulṭāniyyah*. Scholars authored independent works on the topic, such as *as-Siyāsah ash-Shar'iyyah* by Ibn Taymiyah, *al-Aḥkām as-Sulṭāniyyah* by Abū Ya'lā and *al-Aḥkām as-Sulṭāniyyah* by al-Māwardi.

As for criminal law, there is a sector of law compiled in specific chapters in *Fiqh* books entitled *al-Jinayāt* (criminal acts), *Ḥudūd* (prescribed penalties) and *Ta'zīrāt* (discretionary penalties). These chapters provide detailed information about the types of criminal acts and their respective penalties which are legislated by Islam. Certain criminal acts, for which no specific penalty is determined, are left to the discretion of the rulers and judges.

As for financial law, this issue was studied by the jurists in various places throughout the *Fiqh* books when discussing the topics of *zakāh*, *al-'ushr* (one-tenth given as taxes), *kharāj* (tax paid on the conquered lands), *jizyah* (poll tax), *rikāz* (extracted treasures), etc. Some books were specifically written about these issues, such as *Kitāb al-Kharāj* by Abū Yūsuf. This topic generally deals with studying the system of *Baytul-Māl* (state treasury), its revenues, deposited amounts and their channels of expenditure.

Private law and its branches

As for civil law, which regulates the transactions of the individuals, this is addressed in the transactions section of Islamic Jurisprudence, and covers all types of interpersonal affairs, whether those that pertain to the family or various transactions between people.

والقانون الإداري: وهو مجموعة القواعد التي تحكم نشاط السلطة التنفيذية في أداء وظيفتها، وقيامها على أمر المرافق العامة، فقد عرضت لها كتب الفقه بعنوان السياسة الشرعية أو الأحكام السلطانية، وقد ألَّف العلماء في هذا مؤلفات مستقلة، كالسياسة الشرعية لابن تيمية، والأحكام السلطانية لأبي يعلى، والأحكام السلطانية للماوردي.

والجنائي: مجموع في أبواب خاصة من كتب الفقه تحت عنوان: «الجنايات، وقطاع الطريق، والحدود والتعزيرات»، وفيها تفصيل لأنواع الجنايات، وتبيان للعقوبات التي قدرها الشارع لبعض الجنايات، والعقوبات التي تركها من غير تقدير مفوضة إلى أولي الأمر من الحكام والقضاة.

والقانون المالي: بحثه الفقهاء في مواضع متفرقة من كتب الفقه العامة عند الكلام على الزكاة، والعشر والخراج، والجزية والركاز وغيرها، وقد أُلِّف في هذا مؤلفات خاصة ككتاب الخراج لأبي يوسف، وهذا النوع بوجه عام يبحث في تنظيم بيت المال (خزانة الدولة) ببيان موارده والأموال التي توضع فيه، والوجوه التي تصرف فيها هذه الأموال.

القانون الخاص بفروعه:

القانون المدني المنظم للأحوال العينية هو قسم من المعاملات في الفقه الإسلامي التي تنظم الأحوال كلها؛ عينية كانت أو شخصية.

As for commercial law, the jurists studied its topics that were relevant to their times, such as partnerships, *muḍārabah* ventures[1] and bankruptcy. They left customs to decide the remainder of its components, for commerce then was not as complex as it is today. Rather, it was simple and straightforward.

Finally, there is the law of proceedings. This refers to a group of principles explaining the necessary actions and procedures to implement the civil and commercial laws. It covers lawsuits from the time they are filed until their verdict is carried out.

The jurists studied this law and its rulings in the chapters of lawsuits, judiciaries, and testimonies. Therein, they explained how a lawsuit is filed, the necessary steps that should be followed until it is judged and the difference between a legitimate lawsuit that may be heard and an illegitimate lawsuit that does not qualify to be heard in court.

Why didn't the jurists categorize Islamic *Fiqh* in the same manner that man-made laws are categorized?

In the past, the jurists were not interested in classifying *Fiqh* and dividing it into chapters as jurists of man-made law have done in modern times. They thought there was no benefit in categorizing it since there were no diversified courts whereby each would be specialized in deciding on a particular genre of claims. The process of claiming rights was almost identical throughout, for the same judge would decide on all the disputes presented to him. There was no difference between claims related to property, blood, honor or otherwise.

والقانون التجاري بحث الفقهاء فيه ما كانوا يحتاجون إليه في زمنهم في أبواب الشركات والمضاربة والتفليس، ثم جعلوا العرف حكماً فيما يجد فيها؛ لأن التجارة حينذاك لم تكن تشعبت وتعقدت صورها كما هي عليه الآن، بل كانت سهلة يسيرة.

وأخيراً نجد قانون المرافعات، وهو مجموعة القواعد التي تبين ما يجب اتخاذه من أعمال وإجراءات لتطبيق أحكام القانون المدني والتجاري، فهو يتبع الدعوى منذ رفعها إلى تنفيذ الحكم فيها.

هذا القانون بحث الفقهاء أحكامه في أبواب الدعوى والقضاء والشهادة، بينوا فيها كيفية رفع الدعوى، وما يجب اتخاذه من خطوات حتى تنتهي بالحكم فيها، والدعوى الصحيحة التي تسمع، والدعوى غير الصحيحة التي لا تسمع أمام القضاء.

لماذا لم يقسم الفقهاء الفقه كما قسمه رجال القانون الوضعي؟

لم يعن الفقهاء في العصور الماضية بتقسيم الفقه وتبويبه على النحو الذي قام به رجال القانون الوضعي في العصر الحديث لانعدام الفائدة المترتبة على هذا التقسيم في نظرهم؛ حيث لم يكن عندهم قضاء متنوع، يختص كل نوع منه بالفصل في دعاوى خاصة، ولم يكن هناك إجراءات مختلفة في إثبات الحقوق، فالقضاء موحد، والإجراءات تكاد تكون واحدة، والقاضي يحكم في كل نزاع يرفع إليه، لا فرق في ذلك بين ما يتعلق بالأموال، وما يتعلق بالدماء والأعراض وغيرها.

1 *Muḍārabah* is a partnership between an entrepreneur who invests his expertise and a capital provider who invests his wealth.

The Islamic Sharia is More Comprehensive than Man-made Law

The laws from which Muslims seek judgments are the Islamic Sharia and the *Fiqh* which sprouts from it. Yet, the Islamic Sharia is wider and more comprehensive than the concept of law as understood in Western societies.

Islamic law actually includes the topics covered by man-made laws and even extends to topics not covered by these laws. For this reason, the orientalist Nalino deemed that there is no perfect equivalent for the word *fiqh* in any of the Western languages. He said, "In *Fiqh*, the acts of worship are mentioned, in addition to a variety of things that we also have [in our laws]. For instance, there are [mention of] issues like *kharāj*, *zakāh* paid on minerals and the like. Also, it mentions family issues, personal statuses, inheritance and financial rights. Of them are *awqāf* (endowments), the ethics of judgeship, *ḥudūd* punishments and international laws in times of peace and war." Then he added, "In Islamic *Fiqh*, there are matters which the Western viewpoint considers an entirely religious affair, such as oaths, vows, ordinary slaughter (for food), ritual sacrifice of an animal, matters related to which foods and drinks are lawful and unlawful, matters related to land and sea game and matters of clothing and adornment."[1]

Some legal science researchers unjustifiably criticized Islamic law because of its comprehensive, all-inclusive nature. Their mistake stems from the fact that they used Western law as a standard against which all other laws and legislations are to be evaluated. We are confident that the faults they allegedly found with Islamic law actually embody one of the secrets behind its perfection. This is because the Islamic Sharia draws, for the Muslim individual and society, one harmonious course which decrees judgments that never conflict, and a system whose components are always in agreement. In this course, the Muslim submits to his Lord in all facets of his affairs and deeds.

1 *Hal lil-Qanūn ar-Rūmāni Ta`thīr `alā al-Fiqh al-Islāmi*: 11

الشريعة الإسلامية أوسع من القانون

القانـون الـذي يتحاكـم إليـه المسـلمون هـو الشريعـة الإسـلامية والفقـه المنبثـق عنهـا، ولكـن الشريعـة الإسـلامية أوسـع وأشـمل مـما يريـده الأوربيـون بالقانـون.

فالقانـون الإسـلامي يشـتمل عـلى الموضوعـات التـي تبحـث فيهـا القوانـين الوضعيـة، وموضوعـات أخـرى لم تتعـرض لهـا تلـك القوانـين؛ ولذلـك فـإن المسـتشرق «نالينـو» يـرى أنـه لا يوجـد في لغـات الغـرب مصطلـح يقابـل كلمـة «فقـه» مقابلة تامـة، ويقـول: «ففـي الفقـه تذكـر العبـادات، وهـي تشـتمل عـلى أشـياء منهـا مـا هـو عندنـا مـن الحقـوق العامـة كبعـض مسـائل الخـراج وزكاة المعـادن وغـير ذلـك، وتذكـر مسـائل الأسرة، والأحـوال الشـخصية، والوراثـة والحقـوق الماليـة، ومـن جملتهـا الأوقـاف، وآداب القـاضي، والحـدود (العقوبـات)، والسـير (قوانـين دوليـة في السـلم والحـرب)» ثـم يقـول: «ففـي الفقـه الإسـلامي يوجـد مـا هـو في نظـر الغـربي مـن المسـائل الدينيـة مثـل الأيمـان والنـذور، والذبائـح العاديـة (لـلأكل اليومـي)، والأضاحـي (القربـات)، ومسـائل مـا يحـل ويحـرم مـن الأكل والـشرب، ومسـائل صيـد الـبر والبحـر، واللبـاس والزينـة»[1].

لقـد عـاب بعـض الباحثـين في العلـوم القانونيـة القانـون الإسـلامي؛ إذ وجـدوا فيـه هـذا الشـمول والاتسـاع، وقـد كان خطؤهـم أنهـم جعلـوا القوانـين الغربيـة هـي القيـاس الـذي تقـاس بـه بقيـة القوانـين والشرائـع، ونحـن نوقـن أن هـذا الـذي عـدوه عيبـاً في القانـون الإسـلامي إنمـا هـو سر مـن أسرار كمالـه، ذلـك أن الشريعـة الإسـلامية ترسـم للفـرد المسـلم والمجتمـع المسـلم مسـاراً واحـداً لا تتعـارض أحكامـه، ولا تتضـارب جزئياتـه، يخضـع فيـه المسـلم لربـه في كل أمـوره وأعمالـه.

١ كتاب «هل للقانون الروماني تأثير على الفقه الإسلامي»: ١١.

The French orientalist Boscán was one of those who realized this in his article entitled *The Secret Behind the Development of the Islamic Fiqh and its Original Sources.* He says, "In principle, the Islamic Law covers the entire life of the believer and the entire life of the Muslim community. Beginning with the rulings of purification after using the toilet, answering the call of nature, performing prayer, it continues all the way until the guidelines of *jihād*, warfare, *zakāh*, while also addressing marriage, sales and bequests."[1]

According to Nalino, the failure to realize this difference between the Islamic law and the man-made law has led to dangerous confusion among the Western scholars.[2]

1 Ibid: 68
2 Ibid: 68

وممن تنبه إلى هذا المستشرق الفرنسي «بوسكه» في مقال له بعنوان «سر تكوُّن الفقه الإسلامي وأصل مصادره»، حيث يقول: «إن القانون الإسلامي يشمل من حيث المبدأ كل حياة المؤمن، وكل حياة الجماعة المسلمة، ابتداء من أحكام الاستنجاء وقضاء الحاجات الطبيعية، أو الصلاة، حتى قواعد الجهاد والحرب والزكاة، مارًا بالزواج والبيوع والوصايا»(١).

إن عدم إدراك هذا الفرق بين القانون الإسلامي والقانون الوضعي أوقع علماء الغرب ومن سار على نهجهم في لبس خطير كما يقول «نالينو»(٢).

١ المصدر السابق: ٦٨.
٢ المصدر السابق: ١٠.

Summary of Unit 1

This unit can be summarized in the following points:

1) In Arabic, the word *fiqh* denotes knowledge and understanding. According to the Arabs, it makes no difference whether the meaning intended to be understood is clear or ambiguous. In the understanding of the early scholars, the term *fiqh* referred to the entire religion. According to them, the bearer of *Fiqh* was the one more concerned with the fundamentals than the secondary issues and the deeds of the heart more than the deeds of the body. As for the later scholars, *fiqh* was a technical term that referred to the practical legal judgments that are derived from their detailed evidences. According to this usage, *Fiqh* includes both the definitive and speculative legal judgments.

2) The later scholars differentiated between *Fiqh*, in its technical sense, and the technical usage of Sharia, in many aspects. Of them, for instance, is that:

a) Unlike *Fiqh*, Sharia is complete, for *Fiqh* is essentially the opinions of *mujtahid* scholars, whereas Sharia is what has been revealed by Allah.

b) Unlike *Fiqh*, Sharia is general.

c) Sharia rulings are perfect and contain no mistakes, whereas the understanding of jurists may sometimes err.

d) *Fiqh* and Sharia converge and diverge on a number of points. In one way, *Fiqh* is more specific, and in another way, it is more general.

3) Legal judgments are divided into acts of worship and transactions. There are many differences between the two sections:

a) Acts of worship are meant for seeking nearness to Allah and giving thanks to Him. On the other hand, transactions are meant for achieving worldly benefits and regulating relationships between people.

خلاصة الوحدة

نخلص من دراسة هذه الوحدة إلى ما يلي:

١- يطلق الفقه في لغة العرب على الفهم والعلم، ولا فرق عند العرب في كون المعنى المراد فهمه واضحاً أو خفياً، وقد كان الفقه في اصطلاح أهل الصدر الأول شاملاً للدين كله، فقد كان الفقيه عنهم يعنى بالأصول قبل الفروع، وبأعمال القلوب قبل أعمال الأبدان، أما الفقه في اصطلاح المتأخرين فقد خص بالعلم بالأحكام الشرعية العملية المكتسب من أدلتها التفصيلية، والفقه يشمل الأحكام الشرعية القطعية، والأحكام الشرعية الظنية.

٢- يختلف الفقه بمعناه الاصطلاحي عن الشريعة بمعناها الاصطلاحي عند المتأخرين في عدة نقاط منها على سبيل المثال:

أ- أن الشريعة كاملة بخلاف الفقه لأن الفقه عبارة عن آراء المجتهدين من العلماء أما الشريعة فهي الوحي المنزل من عند الله سبحانه وتعالى.

ب- أن الشريعة عامة بخلاف الفقه.

ج- أحكام الشريعة صواب لا خطأ فيها، وفهم الفقهاء قد يخطئ أحياناً.

د- النسبة بين الفقه والتشريع هي العموم والخصوص من وجه.

٣- تنقسم الأحكام الشرعية إلى عبادات ومعاملات، وهناك عدة فروق بين القسمين منها:

أ- أن الغرض من العبادات هو التقرب إلى الله وشكره، أما الغرض من المعاملات فهو تحقيق المصلحة الدنيوية وتنظيم العلاقات بين الناس.

b) In essence, acts of worship are not influenced by logic, whereas transactions are originally based on logic.

c) Intending nearness to Allah is a prerequisite for validating the acts of worship, but it is not a requirement for the validity of transactions.

4) The Islamic Sharia includes all the sections of man-made law.

5) The scope of Islamic Sharia is much broader than that of man-made law. The Islamic Sharia includes topics which are covered by man-made laws, in addition to other topics which were not covered by these laws.

ب- الأصل في العبادات أنها غير معقولة المعنى، أما المعاملات فالأصل فيها معقولية المعنى.

ج- يشترط في صحة العبادات نية التقرب، ولا يشترط ذلك في صحة المعاملات.

٤- تشمل الشريعة الإسلامية جميع أقسام القانون الوضعي.

٥- الشريعة الإسلامية أوسع من القانون الوضعي، وذلك لأن الشريعة الإسلامية اشتملت على الموضوعات التي تبحث فيها القوانين الوضعية، وموضوعات أخرى لم تتعرض لها تلك القوانين.

Notes

Notes

UNIT 2

Fiqh in the Prophetic Era

Contents of Unit 2

- The excellence and virtue of the Prophet's era
- The way by which the Sharia was conveyed to the Messengers of Allah
- The Sources of the Islamic Sharia

Importance of Unit 2

The noblest era in history was the Prophet's era. In this era, the Qur'an was revealed to the Messenger of Allah ﷺ, and the Messenger of Allah ﷺ explained the Qur'an to the people via his statements and practices.

This unit will introduce us to the two forms of revelation: The Book and the *Sunnah*. Thus, we will understand what is meant by the Noble Qur'an, its unique characteristics, how Jibreel (Gabriel) used to descend with it upon the Messenger of Allah ﷺ and how Allah safeguarded it from the plots against it and any tampering of it. We shall also learn the great wisdom behind revealing it gradually upon the Messenger of Allah ﷺ.

Furthermore, we shall become acquainted with the Noble *Sunnah* of the Prophet, its types, its authoritativeness, and its status in relation to the Noble Qur'an. So let's get started.

Learning Objectives:

At the end of this lecture, students should be able to:

- Explain the status of the Noble Qur'an, its miraculous nature, and how Allah preserved it
- Explain the wisdom behind the Noble Qur'an being revealed in segments
- Mention the types of *Sunnah*, its authoritativeness, and its status in relation to the Noble Qur'an
- Compare between the Noble Qur'an and the *Qudsi* (Divine) Hadith
- Refute the false claims of those who deny the

الوحدة الثانية: الفقه في عصر النبوة

محتويات الوحدة الثانية

- فضل عصر النبوة ومكانته.
- الكيفية التي وصلت بها الشريعة إلى رسل الله.
- مصادر الشريعة الإسلامية.

أهمية دراسة الوحدة:

كان عصر النبوة هو أشرف العصور وأفضلها، ففيه نزل القرآن على رسول الله ﷺ، وبين رسول الله ﷺ القرآن للناس بأقواله وأفعاله.

وفي هذه الوحدة نتعرف على الوحيين: الكتاب والسنة، فنعرف المقصود بالقرآن الكريم، وخصائصه، وكيف كان ينزل به جبريل على رسول الله ﷺ، وكيف حفظه الله وصانه من كيد الكائدين وعبث العابثين، ونعرف الحكم الجليلة الرائعة من نزوله منجماً على رسول الله ﷺ.

ونتعرف أيضاً على السنة النبوية الشريفة، وأنواعها، وحجيتها، ومنزلتها من القرآن الكريم فهيا بنا لدراسة الوحدة.

الأهداف التعليمية:

يتوقع منك أيها الدارس الكريم بعد دراستك لهذه الوحدة أن تكون قادراً على أن:

- تُبين مكانة القرآن الكريم، وإعجازه، وحفظ الله تعالى له.
- تشرح الحكمة من نزول القرآن الكريم منجماً.
- تذكر أنواع السنة، وحجيتها، ومنزلتها من القرآن الكريم.
- تُقارن بين القرآن الكريم، والحديث القدسي.

authoritativeness of the *Sunnah*

• Answer those who denied the possibility of the Prophet ﷺ exercising *Ijtihād*

• تُفند مزاعم من ينكر حجية السنة.

• ترُد على من أنكر جواز اجتهاد النبي ﷺ.

Legislation During the Prophet's Era

In this chapter, we will discuss the following points:

1) The excellence and virtue of the Prophet's era

2) The condition of humanity at the advent of the Prophet's mission

التشريع في العهد النبوي

ونتناول فيه الحديث من خلال النقاط التالية:

١- فضل عصر النبوة ومكانته

٢- حالة البشرية على مشارف البعثة النبوية

The Excellence and Virtue of the Prophet's era

This era begins with the Prophet's mission which started 13 years before Hijrah and ends with the death of the Chosen Prophet ﷺ in Rabī` al-Awwal 11 H (8 June 632).

This is the best and the most perfect of all eras. In it, the legislation was not only sent down but perfected: "...This day those who disbelieve have despaired of [defeating] your religion; so fear them not, but fear Me. This day I have perfected for you your religion and completed My favor upon you..."[1] During this era, the religion of Allah was revealed to the Messenger ﷺ, and using it he shaped the character of the first generation, which later became the best of the Ummah and the most firmly established in Fiqh.

During this phase, the Sharia was perfectly understood and applied. Thus, the course followed by the Messenger ﷺ and his Companions has become the standard which we use to gauge every generation that succeeds them, in terms of the understanding and application of religion.

The orientalists, as well as those who followed them, were wrong in thinking that Islamic legislation, like other sciences, developed over time and that the era of the Prophet was merely its infancy. The Sharia was sent down complete and without deficiency. The Companions' *Fiqh* (proper understanding of religion) cannot be matched by any of those who came after them.

١- فضل عصر النبوة ومكانته

يبدأ هذا العصر بالبعثة النبوية قبل الهجرة بثلاثة عشر عاماً، وينتهي بوفاة المصطفى المختار ﷺ في ربيع الأول من السنة الحادية عشرة للهجرة.

وهذا العصر أفضل العصور وأكملها، ففيه نزل التشريع واكتمل: ﴿الْيَوْمَ أَكْمَلْتُ لَكُمْ دِينَكُمْ وَأَتْمَمْتُ عَلَيْكُمْ نِعْمَتِي وَرَضِيتُ لَكُمُ الإِسْلَامَ دِيناً﴾[1]، وفيه كان الرسول ﷺ يتلقى الوحي من ربه ويصوغ بدين الله ومنهجه الرعيل الأول، الذين أصبحوا أفضل الأمة وأفقهها وأعلمها.

وفيه فقهت الشريعة أفضل فقه، وطبقت أفضل تطبيق، وقد غدا ما كان عليه الرسول ﷺ وأصحابه في هذا العصر المقياس الذي نقيس به مدى ارتقاء بقية العصور اللاحقة فقهاً وتطبيقاً.

وقد أخطأ المستشرقون ومن حذا حذوهم في اعتبارهم أن التشريع نما عبر القرون كبقية العلوم، وأن عصر النبوة هو عصر الطفولة، إن الشريعة نزلت كاملة من غير نقصان، وفقه الصحابة لا يدانيه فقه أحد ممن جاء بعدهم.

1 Surat al-Mā'idah: 3

١ المائدة: ٣.

The Conditions of Humanity at the Advent of the Prophet's Mission

Before the Prophet's mission, humanity lived in complete ignorance and blind misguidance. It lived in the pitch-black darkness of shirk (polytheism) and ignorance. Our Messenger ﷺ once stated: "...And verily, when Allah looked to the people of the world, He despised them, the Arabs and the non-Arabs, except for some remnants from the People of the Book..."[1]

In that era, humanity strayed from its Lord and worshipped idols, stones, and fire instead of Him. As a result, their souls turned dark, their minds became bewildered, and the lights emanating from the hermitages and monasteries of the Jews and Christians were fading, incapable of properly illuminating those monasteries, let alone the outside world.

The laws of the *Tawrāh* (Torah) and Injīl (Gospel) lost their value before the Prophet's mission due to the distortion and alteration to which they were subjected. Consequently, they became incapable of directing humanity to the straight path.

The advocates of these two sets of legislation lost the credibility that qualified them to lead and inspire the human race. Our Lord, the Exalted and Glorified, informed us about this debased condition to which the carriers of the laws among the Children of Israel plummeted. Regarding this, Allah, the Exalted and Glorified, says: **"The example of those who were entrusted with the Torah and then did not take it on is like that of a donkey who carries volumes [of books]. Wretched is the example of the people who deny the signs of Allah."**[2]

1 Reported by Muslim in his [*Ṣaḥīḥ*], ḥadith no. 2865
2 Surat al-Jumu`ah: 5

٢- حالة البشرية على مشارف البعثة النبوية

لقد كانت البشرية قبيل البعثة النبوية تعيش في جهالة جهلاء وضلالة عمياء، تعيش في ظلمة دامسة من الشرك والجهل، وقد أخبرنا رسولنا ﷺ: «**أن الله نظر إلى أهل الأرض فمقتهم عربهم وعجمهم إلا بقايا من أهل الكتاب**»(١).

لقد تاهت البشرية في تلك الحقبة عن ربها ومعبودها، وعبدت من دونه الأصنام والأوثان والنيران؛ فأظلمت النفوس، واحتارت العقول، وكانت الأنوار التي تشع من غرفات الصوامع والأديرة التي يقطنها أحبار اليهود ورهبان النصارى خافتة، لا تكاد تضيء تلك الصوامع والأديرة، فضلاً عن أن تضيء عالم البشر.

لقد فقدت شريعة التوراة وشريعة الإنجيل قبيل البعثة النبوية خصائصها بسبب ما أصابهما من تحريف وتغيير، فأصبحتا غير صالحتين لإقامة الحياة الإنسانية على منهج سواء.

ورجال هاتين الشريعتين فقدوا المؤهلات التي ترفعهم إلى مستوى القيادة والريادة في عالم البشر، وقد أخبرنا ربنا تبارك وتعالى عن الحالة التي انحط إليها حملة شريعة بني إسرائيل، وفي ذلك يقول الله- عز وجل-: **﴿مَثَلُ الَّذِينَ حُمِّلُوا التَّوْرَاةَ ثُمَّ لَمْ يَحْمِلُوهَا كَمَثَلِ الْحِمَارِ يَحْمِلُ أَسْفَاراً بِئْسَ مَثَلُ الْقَوْمِ الَّذِينَ كَذَّبُوا بِآيَاتِ اللهِ﴾**(٢).

١ رواه مسلم في صحيحه، ورقمه: ٢٨٦٥.
٢ الجمعة: ٥.

Concerning the Jewish rabbis and Christian monks, He says: **"O you who have believed, indeed many of the scholars and the monks devour the wealth of people unjustly and avert [them] from the way of Allah..."**[1]

He also said about them: **"...And they were covered with humiliation and poverty and returned with anger from Allah [upon them]. That was because they [repeatedly] disbelieved in the signs of Allah and killed the prophets without right. That was because they disobeyed and were [habitually] transgressing."**[2]

The two superpowers at that time, the Persian and Roman empires, were plunged in every type of corruption; political corruption which was embodied in transgression and tyranny, spiritual corruption which was embodied in worshiping fire, stars, and human beings, moral corruption which eradicated values and virtues, and social corruption was embodied in the transgression and tyranny of the rulers against their people to the point of bloodshed, violation of sanctities, and seizing properties.

---

1 Surat at-Tawbah: 34
2 Surat al-Baqarah: 61

وقال في علماء اليهود وعباد النصارى: ﴿إِنَّ كَثِيراً مِّنَ الأَحْبَارِ وَالرُّهْبَانِ لَيَأْكُلُونَ أَمْوَالَ النَّاسِ بِالْبَاطِلِ وَيَصُدُّونَ عَن سَبِيلِ اللهِ﴾(١).

وقال فيهم: ﴿وَضُرِبَتْ عَلَيْهِمُ الذِّلَّةُ وَالْمَسْكَنَةُ وَبَآؤُوْا بِغَضَبٍ مِّنَ اللَّهِ ذَلِكَ بِأَنَّهُمْ كَانُواْ يَكْفُرُونَ بِآيَاتِ اللَّهِ وَيَقْتُلُونَ النَّبِيِّينَ بِغَيْرِ الْحَقِّ ذَلِكَ بِمَا عَصَواْ وَّكَانُواْ يَعْتَدُونَ﴾(٢).

وكانت الدولتان العظيمتان في ذلك الوقت- دولة الفرس ودولة الروم- غارقتين في شتى ألوان الفساد: الفساد المتمثل في الظلم والاستبداد، والفساد العقائدي المتمثل في عبادة النيران والكواكب والأفراد، والفساد الخلقي المدمر للقيم والفضائل، والفساد الاجتماعي المتمثل فيما لاقته الشعوب من ظلم الحكام وجورهم، والذي يصل إلى حد سفك الدماء، وهتك الحرمات، والاستيلاء على الأموال.

---

١ التوبة: ٣٤.
٢ البقرة: ٦١.

The conditions of the Arabian Peninsula were hardly any better. The Arabs changed the features of the religion which they inherited from their forefather Ismā`īl, the son of Ibrāhīm, peace be upon them. As a result, the various forms of idolatry became widespread; they began worshipping idols and statues, which left all of all of Arabia immersed in a state of abject ignorance. Under this ignorance, the Arabs lived in blind misguidance. Misguidance is the most appropriate description of the Arabs in this era, as the Most High said: "It is He who has sent among the unlettered a Messenger from themselves reciting to them His verses and purifying them and teaching them the Book and wisdom - although they were before in clear error." The definition of "misguidance" is to be misled from truth. Such misguidance was described as "evident" because it was deep and far-reaching from truth. The Qur'an described the conditions of the Arabs before Islam saying, "...And remember the favor of Allah upon you - when you were enemies and He brought your hearts together and you became, by His favor, brothers. And you were on the edge of a pit of the Fire, and He saved you from it..."[1]

Ja`far Ibn Abū Ṭālib, the head of the emigrant believers who moved to Abyssinia, described to the Najāshī (Negus) the misguidance that the Arabs were in before Islam saying, "O King! We were people of ignorance; we used to worship idols, eat carrion, commit immoralities, sever the ties of kinship, mistreat our neighbors, and the strong of us used to wrong the weak."[2]

Killing their own children for fear of poverty or shame, circling the Ka`bah in a state of nakedness, consuming usury, drinking wine, even raiding one another and plundering properties, spilling blood, and enslaving women and children were all manifestations of their misguidance.

1 Surat Āl-'Imrān – Verse 103
2 Reported by Aḥmad in his [*Musnad*]: 3/263-268 (1740) and 37/170-175 (22498) through Ibn Is~ḥāq with a *Ṣaḥīḥ Isnād* (sound chain of transmission)

ولم يكن الحال في الجزيرة العربية بأحسن من حال الأمم في خارجها، فقد غير العرب معالم الدين الذي ورثوه عن أبيهم إسماعيل بن إبراهيم- عليهما السلام- وانتشرت فيهم الوثنية بشتى صورها وألوانها، فعبدوا الأصنام والأوثان، وغطت سماء الجزيرة العربية جاهلية جهلاء، فعاش العرب في ظلها في ضلالة عمياء، والضلال أخص وصف يوصف به العرب في تلك الحقبة، قال تعالى: **﴿هُوَ الَّذِي بَعَثَ فِي الْأُمِّيِّينَ رَسُولاً مِّنْهُمْ يَتْلُو عَلَيْهِمْ آيَاتِهِ وَيُزَكِّيهِمْ وَيُعَلِّمُهُمُ الْكِتَابَ وَالْحِكْمَةَ وَإِن كَانُوا مِن قَبْلُ لَفِي ضَلَالٍ مُّبِينٍ﴾**[١]، والضلال الضياع عن الحق، ووصفه بالمبين للدلالة على شدة هذا الضلال وعمقه وإيغاله في البعد عن الصواب.

وقد وصف القرآن حال العرب قبل الإسلام فقال: ﴿وَاذْكُرُوا نِعْمَتَ اللهِ عَلَيْكُمْ إِذْ كُنْتُمْ أَعْدَاءً فَأَلَّفَ بَيْنَ قُلُوبِكُمْ فَأَصْبَحْتُمْ بِنِعْمَتِهِ إِخْوَاناً وَكُنْتُمْ عَلَى شَفَا حُفْرَةٍ مِّنَ النَّارِ فَأَنقَذَكُم مِّنْهَا﴾[٢].

ووصف جعفر بن أبي طالب أمير المهاجرين إلى الحبشة للنجاشي الضلال الذي كانت تعيشه العرب فقال: «أيها الملك، كنا قوماً أهل جاهلية نعبد الأصنام، ونأكل الميتة، ونأتي الفواحش، ونقطع الأرحام، ونسيء الجوار، ويأكل القوي منا الضعيف»[٣].

ومن ضلالهم قتلهم أبناءهم خشية الفقر أو العار، وطوافهم بالبيت عراة، وأكلهم الربا، وشربهم الخمر، وإغارة بعضهم على بعض، ناهبين الأموال، سافكين الدماء، سابين النساء والذرية.

١ الجمعة: ٢.
٢ آل عمران: ١٠٣.
٣ رواه أحمد في مسنده: ٣/ ٢٦٣- ٢٦٨ (١٧٤٠)، و٣٧/ ١٧٠- ١٧٥ (٢٢٤٩٨) من طريق ابن إسحاق بسند صحيح.

Methods of *Waḥy* (Revelation): How the Sharia reached the Messengers of Allah

The means by which the Divine Legislations reached the prophets and messengers of humanity is called *waḥy* (revelation). The Most High said: **"Indeed, We have revealed to you, [O Muhammad], as We revealed to Nûh (Noah) and the prophets after him..."**[1]

The Definition of *Waḥy*:

Linguistically, *waḥy* is to inform secretly.

Technically, *waḥy* denotes Allah informing His prophets and messengers of His words and legislations.

The Methods by which Allah Reveals to His Prophets and Messengers

Allah reveals to his prophets and messengers in two ways:

The First is by addressing them directly without an intermediary, but from behind a barrier, like the manner in which Allah addressed Mūsa ﷺ: **"...And Allah spoke to Mūsa (Moses) with [direct] speech"**[2] and: **"And when Mūsa arrived at Our appointed time and his Lord spoke to him..."**[3]

Another example is when Allah spoke to the Messenger Muhammad ﷺ on the occasion of al-Mi`rāj, when he was taken up to heaven and the five daily prayers were then enjoined.

The second is by Jibrīl (Gabriel) descending to the messengers and prophets of Allah, informing them of Allah's laws and words.

طريق الوحي: الكيفية التي وصلت بها الشريعة إلى رسل الله

الطريقة التي وصلت بها الشرائع الإلهية إلى الرسل والأنبياء من البشر تسمى بالوحي، قال تعالى: ﴿إِنَّا أَوْحَيْنَا إِلَيْكَ كَمَا أَوْحَيْنَا إِلَى نُوحٍ وَالنَّبِيِّينَ مِن بَعْدِهِ﴾(١)

تعريف الوحي لغة واصطلاحاً:

الوحي في اللغة: الإعلام في خفاء، وفي الاصطلاح: إعلام الله رسله وأنبياءه بشرعه وكلامه.

الطريق التي يوحى الله بها إلى رسله وأنبيائه

يوحي الله إلى رسله وأنبيائه بطريقين:

الأول: تكليم الله رسله وأنبياءه مباشرة بلا واسطة من وراء حجاب، كما كلم الله موسى عليه السلام: ﴿وَكَلَّمَ اللَّهُ مُوسَى تَكْلِيمًا﴾(٢)، وقال: ﴿وَلَمَّا جَاءَ مُوسَى لِمِيقَاتِنَا وَكَلَّمَهُ رَبُّهُ﴾(٣).

ومن ذلك تكليم الله رسوله محمداً ﷺ عندما عرج به إلى السماء، وفرض الله عليه الصلوات الخمس.

الثاني: أن ينزل جبريل عليه السلام على رسله وأنبيائه بشرعه وكلامه، فيبلغهم إياه على ما يريده الله تعالى.

1 Surat an-Nisā` - Verse 163
2 Surat an-Nisā`- Verse 164
3 Surat al-A`rāf - Verse 143

١ النساء: ١٦٣.
٢ النساء: ١٦٤.
٣ الأعراف: ١٤٣.

These two methods are mentioned in Allah's statement, **"And in no way is it feasible for a mortal that Allah should speak to Him, except by revelation or from behind a curtain, or that He should send a Messenger; then He reveals whatever He decides, by His permission. Surely He is Ever-Exalted, Ever-Wise."**[1]

Prophet Mūsa ﷺ wished to see Allah in this world, but Allah informed him that he would not be able to bear that in this worldly life: **"And when Mūsa arrived at Our appointed time and his Lord spoke to him, he said, 'My Lord, show me [Yourself] that I may look at You.' [Allah] said, 'You will not see Me, but look at the mountain; if it should remain in place, then you will see Me.' But when his Lord appeared to the mountain, He rendered it level, and Mūsa fell unconscious..."**[2]

How did Jibrīl descend upon the Messenger of Allah ﷺ?

According to the texts of the Qur'an and *Sunnah*, Jibrīl used to descend to the Prophet ﷺ in four ways:

The first: Angel Jibrīl would plant something into his heart that it is unquestionably from Allah, the Exalted and Glorified. It is related in [Ṣaḥīḥ Ibn Ḥibbān] that the Messenger of Allah ﷺ said, **"Verily, *ar-Rūḥ al-Qudus* (the Holy Spirit) casted into my heart that "no soul will ever die without taking in full its provision and term of life. So, fear Allah and beautify your requests."**[3]

---

1 Surat ash-Shūra - Verse 51

2 Surat al-A`rāf - Verse 143

3 This hadith was graded authentic by virtue of its corroborating reports. It was collected by Abu Nu`aym in [al-Ḥilyah] (10/26-27) from the hadih of Abu Umāmah. Its chain contains `Ufayr Ibn Ma`dān who is a weak narrator, but the other narrators are trustworthy. It was also related by al-Haythamī in [al-Majma`] (4/72), who attributed it to at-Tabarānī in [al-Kabeer] who graded it as *Ma`lūl* (defective) because `Ufayr Ibn Ma`dān was one of its narrators. However, there is a supporting report that was narrated by Jābir in the [Sunan] of Ibn Mājah (2144), Ibn Ḥibbān (3239) and (3241), and the [Musnad] of al-Ḥakim (2/4). Therefore, this hadith can be graded as

وهذان الطريقان هما المذكوران في قوله تعالى: ﴿وَمَا كَانَ لِبَشَرٍ أَن يُكَلِّمَهُ اللهُ إِلاَّ وَحْياً أَوْ مِن وَرَاءِ حِجَابٍ أَوْ يُرْسِلَ رَسُولاً فَيُوحِيَ بِإِذْنِهِ مَا يَشَاءُ إِنَّهُ عَلِيٌّ حَكِيمٌ﴾(١)، وقد رغب موسى عليه السلام أن يرى الله في الدنيا، فأعلمه الله أنه لا يطيق ذلك في الدنيا: ﴿رَبِّ أَرِنِي أَنظُرْ إِلَيْكَ قَالَ لَن تَرَانِي وَلَـكِنِ انظُرْ إِلَى الْجَبَلِ فَإِنِ اسْتَقَرَّ مَكَانَهُ فَسَوْفَ تَرَانِي فَلَمَّا تَجَلَّى رَبُّهُ لِلْجَبَلِ جَعَلَهُ دَكّاً وَخَرَّ موسَى صَعِقاً﴾(٢)، أما سماعه كلام الله من غير أن يراه فذاك ممكن، وقد وقع لموسى كثيراً.

كيف كان يتنزل جبريل على الرسول ﷺ؟

دلت النصوص من الكتاب والسنة أن جبريل عليه السلام كان يتنزل على النبي ﷺ بأربع طرق:

الأول: يقذف في روع النبي شيئاً لا يتمارى في أنه من عند الله- عز وجل- كما جاء في صحيح ابن حبان عن رسول الله ﷺ أنه قال: «إن روح القدس قذف في روعي أن نفساً لن تموت حتى تستكمل رزقها وأجلها، فاتقوا الله وأجملوا في الطلب»(٣).

---

١ الشورى: ٥١.

٢ الأعراف: ١٤٣.

٣ حديث صحيح بشواهده، أخرجه أبو نعيم في «الحلية»: ١٠/ ٢٦- ٢٧، من حديث أبي إمامة وفي مسنده عفير بن معدان، وهو ضعيف، وباقي رجاله ثقات، وأورده الهيثمي في = «المجمع»: ٤/ ٧٢، ونسبه للطبراني في «الكبير»، وأعله بعفير بن معدان، لكن له شاهد من حديث جابر عند ابن ماجه (٢١٤٤)، وابن حبان (٣٢٣٩) و(٣٢٤١)، والحاكم: ٢/ ٤، فيصح الحديث به، انظر: زاد المعاد، ط. مؤسسة الرسالة، ٧٧- ٧٨.

The second: Angel Jibrīl would be sent to the Messenger in his original form upon which Allah created him, whereby he ﷺ sees him with his very eyes. This rarely took place, for our Prophet Muhammad ﷺ did not see Jibrīl in his original form upon which Allah created him except twice.

The first time was three years after the advent of prophethood. In Ṣaḥīḥ al-Bukhāri, it was related, on the authority of Jābir Ibn `Abdillāh, that the Messenger of Allah ﷺ said, **"Once while I was walking, I heard a voice from the sky. I looked up and suddenly saw that Angel which had visited me in the cave of Ḥirā'; he was sitting on a chair between the sky and the earth. I became horrified by him, and returned and said: 'Wrap me!'"**[1]

The second encounter took place when the Prophet ﷺ was taken up to heaven. These two times were mentioned in Sūrat an-Najm in Allah's saying, **"Taught to him by one intense in strength - one of soundness. And he rose to [his] true form while he was in the higher [part of the] horizon. Then he approached and descended and was at a distance of two bow lengths or nearer. And he revealed to His Servant what he revealed. The heart did not lie [about] what it saw. So will you dispute with him over what he saw? And he certainly saw him in another descent at the Lote Tree of the Utmost Boundary - near it is the Garden of Refuge - when there covered the Lote Tree that which covered [it]. The sight [of the Prophet] did not swerve, nor did it transgress [its limit]."**[2]

The third: Angel Jibrīl would come to the Messenger ﷺ in his angelic form without him seeing him, but can only hear his voice, and remember what he casts into his heart.

authentic. See: [Zād al-Mi`ād] (77-78), ar-Risālah Foundation Edition.

1 [*Ṣaḥīḥ al-Bukhāri*] (4) and [*Muslim*] (1/143)
2 Surat an-Najm - Verses 5-17

الطريق الثاني: أن يوحي الملك إلى النبي والرسول وهو يراه عياناً على صورته التي خلقه الله عليها، وهذا قليل، فإن نبينا محمداً ﷺ لم ير جبريل عليه السلام على صفته التي خلقه الله عليها إلا مرتين:

الأولى: بعد البعثة بثلاث سنوات، ففي صحيح البخاري عن جابر بن عبد الله أن الرسول ﷺ قال: «**بينما أنا أمشي؛ إذ سمعت صوتاً من السماء، فرفعت بصري، فإذا الملك الذي جاءني بحراء جالس على كرسي بين السماء والأرض، فرعبت منه، فرجعت، فقلت: زملوني**»(١). والثانية: عندما عرج به إلى السماء.

وهاتان المرتان مذكورتان في سورة النجم في قوله تعالى: ﴿عَلَّمَهُ شَدِيدُ الْقُوَى ۞ ذُو مِرَّةٍ فَاسْتَوَى ۞ وَهُوَ بِالأُفُقِ الأعْلَى ۞ ثُمَّ دَنَا فَتَدَلَّى ۞ فَكَانَ قَابَ قَوْسَيْنِ أَوْ أَدْنَى ۞ فَأَوْحَى إِلَى عَبْدِهِ مَا أَوْحَى ۞ مَا كَذَبَ الْفُؤَادُ مَا رَأَى ۞ أَفَتُمَارُونَهُ عَلَى مَا يَرَى ۞ وَلَقَدْ رَآهُ نَزْلَةً أُخْرَى ۞ عِنْدَ سِدْرَةِ الْمُنْتَهَى ۞ عِنْدَهَا جَنَّةُ الْمَأْوَى ۞ إِذْ يَغْشَى السِّدْرَةَ مَا يَغْشَى ۞ مَا زَاغَ الْبَصَرُ وَمَا طَغَى﴾(٢).

الطريق الثالث: أن يأتي الملك إلى الرسول ﷺ بصفته الملائكية من غير أن يراه، ولكنه يسمع صوته، ويحفظ عنه ما ألقاه في قلبه.

١ صحيح البخاري (٤)، ومسلم: ١/١٤٣.
٢ النجم: ٥-١٧.

The fourth: Angel Jibrīl would take the form of a man and inform the Messenger of Allah ﷺ of what Allah has revealed to him.

These last two manners are mentioned in the hadith related in Ṣaḥīḥ al-Bukhāri on the authority of al-Ḥārith Ibn Hishām. It states that when `Ā`ishah (may Allah be pleased with her) asked the Messenger of Allah ﷺ about the forms in which revelation used to come to him, he said, "Sometimes it is [revealed] like the ringing of a bell, and this form of revelation is the hardest of all, but then this state passes after I have grasped what is inspired. Other times, the Angel comes to me in the form of a man, talks to me, and I grasp what he says."[1]

The hadith above indicates that Angel Jibrīl transmitted the revelation to the Messenger of Allah ﷺ in two manners:

The first manner: he would come to the Prophet ﷺ in his angelic form, which was the hardest on the Prophet ﷺ. The Messenger of Allah ﷺ described the voice of the Angel when he conveyed the revelation to him via the sounding of a bell (*ṣalṣalah*). The word "*ṣalṣalah*" originally alludes to the noise produced by iron bars when clanked against each other. Later on, it was used to denote any ringing sound. It was also said that it is a special sound that cannot be heard from the first time it is produced.[2]

The second manner: he would come to the Prophet ﷺ in the form of a man, which was easier on the Messenger of Allah ﷺ because he spoke to him in a human-like manner.

1 [*Ṣaḥīḥ al-Bukhāri*] (No. 2) and [*Muslim*] (4/1816)
2 *Fat-ḥ al-Bāri* (1/26), Dar-us-Salām Edition, Riyadh

والطريق الرابع: أن يتمثل له الملك رجلاً، فيكلم الرسول بما أوحاه الله إليه.

وهذان الطريقان مذكوران في حديث الحارث بن هشام الذي رواه البخاري في صحيحه، ففيه عن عائشة رضي الله عنها أن الحارث بن هشام رضي الله عنه سأل رسول الله ﷺ عن الكيفية التي يأتيه فيها الوحي، فقال: «**أحياناً يأتيني مثل صلصلة الجرس، وهو أشدُّه علي، فيُفْصَم عني وقد وعيت عنه ما قال، وأحياناً يتمثل لي الملك رجلاً، فيكلمني فأعي ما يقول**»(١).

فالحديث دل على أن إيحاء جبريل إلى الرسول ﷺ كان بطريقين:

الأول: أن يأتيه بصفته الملائكية، وقد كان هذا شديداً على الرسول ﷺ، وقد وصف الرسول ﷺ صوت الملك بالوحي في مثل هذه الحالة بصلصلة الجرس، والصلصلة في الأصل صوت وقوع الحديد بعضه على بعض، ثم أطلق على كل صوت له طنين، وقيل هو صوت متدارك لا يدرك في أول وهلة(٢).

الثاني: أن يتمثل له جبريل رجلاً، وقد كان هذا خفيفاً على الرسول ﷺ؛ لأنه كان يكلمه وهو في صفة البشر.

١ صحيح البخاري، حديث رقم (٢)، مسلم: ١٨١٦/٤.
٢ فتح الباري: ١/ ٢٦، طبعة دار السلام، الرياض.

Sources of the Islamic Sharia

Based on the aforementioned, we can conclude that the Sharia has only one source; the divine revelation. This is the source of all the legislations that descended upon the prophets and messenger of Allah, as the Most High said: **"Indeed, We have revealed to you, [O Muhammad], as We revealed to Nûh and the prophets after him..."**[1] However, what was revealed to our Messenger ﷺ is two types:

The first: the words of Allah which were recited to the Messenger of Allah ﷺ, whose recitation is an act of devotion, and which humanity has failed to produce anything like it, or even like a part of it. This is the Qur'an; its words and meanings are both from Allah.

The second: that which its meaning is from Allah. As for its words, they could be from Allah, like the Qudsi Hadith(s), or from the Messenger ﷺ, as we will explain later. This is the Sunnah. However, this does not necessitate that the Sunnah is entirely revelation; parts of it were decisions of the Prophet which were approved by Allah, and others were concepts which the Messenger ﷺ understood from the Qur'an. Again, this will be explained further *in-shā' Allāh.*

The 1st Source: The Noble Qur`an

I - The Definition of Qur'an:

The Noble Qur'an is the Book sent down from Allah to the Messenger of Allah ﷺ through Angel Jibrīl. It is the word of Allah, which is not created; it came first from Him and to Him it will return. The Messenger of Allah ﷺ, as well as the Companions, memorized it in its entirety. The Messenger of Allah ﷺ had it written on parchments, and the Companions had those after them memorize it, along with them writing it in *muṣ-ḥafs*. Thereafter, the trustworthy from each generation relayed it until it reached us via *mutawātir* chains of transmission, fully preserved from any addition or deletion.

مصادر الشريعة الإسلامية

ظهر لنا مما سبق أن للشريعة مصدراً واحداً هو الوحي الإلهي الرباني، وهو مصدر الشرائع كلها المنزلة على رسل الله وأنبيائه، كما قال تعالى: ﴿إِنَّا أَوْحَيْنَا إِلَيْكَ كَمَا أَوْحَيْنَا إِلَى نُوحٍ وَالنَّبِيِّينَ مِن بَعْدِهِ﴾(١)، ولكن الموحى به إلى رسولنا ﷺ قسمان:

الأول: كلام الله، المتلو على رسول الله، المتعبد بتلاوته، الذي أعجز الناس جميعاً أن يأتوا بمثله أو مثل شيء منه، وهذا هو القرآن لفظه ومعناه من الله.

الثاني: ما كان معناه من الله، أما لفظه فقد يكون من الله كالحديث القدسي، وقد يكون من الرسول ﷺ، كما سيأتي بيانه، وهذه هي السنة، وليس معنى ذلك أن جميع السنة وحي، فمنها اجتهاد أقره الله عليه، ومنها فقه فقهه الرسول ﷺ من القرآن، وسيأتي بيان ذلك إن شاء الله تعالى.

المصدر الأول: القرآن الكريم

أولاً: التعريف بالقرآن:

القرآن الكريم هو الكتاب المنزل على رسول الله من عند الله، حمله إليه جبريل، وهو كلام الله غير مخلوق، منه بدأ وإليه يعود، وقد حفظه الرسول ﷺ وحفظه أصحابه، وكتبه في الرقاع، وحفَّظه الصحابة لمن بعدهم، وكتبوه في المصاحف، ورواه من كل جيل عدوله، حتى وصل إلينا متواتراً محفوظاً من غير تزيد فيه ولا نقصان.

---

1 Surat an-Nisā' – Verse 163

١ النساء: ١٦٣.

The Qur'an is inimitable in its wording, and its recitation is an act of devotion. It is the basis of this religion, the honor of this *Ummah*, the cornerstone of its civilization, the overseer of its culture, the fountain of its legislations, the rectifier of its morals, and its guide to the straight path. Allah has taken it upon Himself to preserve this Qur'an: **"Indeed, it is We who sent down the Qur'an and indeed, We will be its guardian."**[1] Therefore, it was protected from vanishing, and even from the slightest alteration. As for the preservation of the *Tawrāh* (Torah) and the *Injīl* (Gospel), Allah consigned it to the Jewish rabbis and the Christian monks, but they failed to keep this trust: **"...as did the rabbis and scholars by that with which they were entrusted of the Scripture of Allah..."**[2]

Today, the Qur'an is printed in one volume with an average of 600 pages, each page has 15 lines. It has 114 Sūrah(s) of various lengths; after Sūrat al-Fātiḥah, which is comprised of five lines, the Sūrah(s) are ordered according to their length. The longer Sūrah(s) come first, then the shorter ones, some of which do not exceed a few lines.

II – What the Angel Jibrīl casted into the heart of the Messenger, as well as the Qudsī Hadith, are not Qur'an:

What the Angel casted into the heart of the Messenger ﷺ is not Qur'an, like his statement: **"Verily, ar-Rūḥ al-Qudus (the Holy Spirit) revealed unto my heart that "no soul will ever die without taking in full its provision and term of life. So, fear Allah and beauty your requests."**[3] Likewise, the translations of the Qur'an are not Qur'an, because a translation is what the translator understood from the Qur'an, while the Qur'an is both the wording and meaning.

---

1 Surat al-Ḥijr – Verse 9
2 Surat al-Mā`idah – Verse 44
3 Reported by Abu Nu›aym in *al-Hilyah* from Abu Umamah.

والقرآن معجز في لفظه، متعبد بتلاوته، وهو أصل هذا الدين، وعز هذه الأمة، وباني حضارتها، والمهيمن على ثقافتها، والمقيم لتشريعها، والمقوم لأخلاقها، والهادي لها إلى سواء السبيل، وقد تكفل الله بحفظ هذا القرآن: ﴿إِنَّا نَحْنُ نَزَّلْنَا الذِّكْرَ وَإِنَّا لَهُ لَحَافِظُونَ﴾(١)، فحُفِظ من الزوال والتغيير، أما حفظ التوراة والإنجيل فوكله الله إلى علماء اليهود وعباد النصارى، فضيعوا الأمانة: ﴿وَالرَّبَّانِيُّونَ وَالأَحْبَارُ بِمَا اسْتُحْفِظُوا مِن كِتَابِ اللهِ﴾(٢).

والقرآن الكريم يطبع في أيامنا هذه في مجلد واحد، وعدد صفحاته في المتوسط في الطبعات العادية ستمائة صفحة، في كل صفحة خمسة عشر سطراً، ويقسم إلى أربع عشرة ومائة سورة مختلفة الأطوال، فبعد سورة الفاتحة المكونة من خمسة سطور تتدرج السور في ترتيبها بوجه عام حسب طولها، فالسور الطويلة في البداية ثم القصيرة، وبعضها لا يتعدى سطراً واحداً.

ثانياً: ما قذفه الملك في روع الرسول والحديث القدسي ليس قرآناً:

وما قذفه الملك في روع الرسول ﷺ ليس قرآناً، كقوله ﷺ: «**إن روح القدس نفث في روعي أن نفساً لن تموت حتى تستكمل رزقها وأجلها، فاتقوا الله وأجملوا في الطلب**»(٣)، وترجمات القرآن ليست قرآناً؛ لأن المترجم هو ما فقهه المترجم من القرآن، والقرآن هو اللفظ والمعنى.

---

١ الحجر: ٩.
٢ المائدة: ٤٤.
٣ رواه أبو نعيم في الحلية من حديث أبي أمامة.

According to the correct view, both the wording and the meaning of the Qudsī Hadith come from Allah, like his saying, **"Allah, the Most High, said: `O My slaves, I have made oppression unlawful for Me, and made it between you unlawful as well, so do not oppress one another...'"**[1]

The difference between the Qur'an and the Qudsī Hadith is that the latter is not inimitable in its wording; its recitation is not an act of devotion, and it may not be *mutawātir*. As for the Qur'an, it is inimitable and must be *mutawātir*.

III – The Inimitability of the Qur'an

Allah gave our Messenger ﷺ many clear signs which proved his truthfulness, such as the splitting of the moon, the tasbīḥ (saying: *subḥān Allāh*) of pebbles in his hand, the water gushing forth from between his fingers, the increase of a small portion of food to the extent that it would be enough to feed a large number of people, etc. Nevertheless, the greatest sign that Allah gave him was the Qur'an; it is a magnificent sign that addresses the hearts and minds, and a sign that is stands permanently until the Day of Resurrection.

The art of speech and eloquence was the unique forte of the Arabs. They used to frequently hold gatherings to compete in poetry recitation and exhibit their literary feats. Just like all the previous generations, Allah gave them a sign which challenged them in what they mastered. They were mesmerized by His verses, to the degree that one of them would listen to a single *āyah* from the Book of Allah, and would then fall in prostration as a token of appreciation of its eloquence, despite the fact that faith had not yet entered his heart.

والحديـث القدسي لفظه ومعنـاه مـن اللـه- تبـارك وتعالى- على الصحيـح كقولـه ﷺ: «قـال اللـه تعـالى: يـا عبـادي، إني حرمـت الظلـم عـلى نفسي وجعلتـه بينكـم محرمـاً، فـلا تظالموا»(١)، والفـرق بينـه وبيـن القـرآن أنـه غير معجـز في لفظه، ولا متعبد بتلاوتـه، وقـد يكون متواتـراً، وقـد لا يكون متواتـراً، أمـا القـرآن فإنـه معجـز متواتـر ولابـد.

ثالثاً: إعجاز القرآن:

لقـد آتى اللـه رسولنـا ﷺ كثيراً مـن الآيات البينـات الدالة عـلى صدقـه، فمـن ذلـك انشقاق القمـر، وتسبيـح الحصى في يـده، ونبـع المـاء مـن بيـن أصابعـه، وتكثيره الطعام القليل حتـى يكفي الجمـع الكثير، وأعظـم مـا أعطـاه اللـه إيـاه القـرآن، وهـو آيـة باهـرة، تخاطب القلـوب والعقـول، كـما أنـه آيـة دائمـة إلى يـوم القيامـة.

وقـد كانـت البلاغـة والفصاحـة هـي البضاعـة التـي نبـغ العـرب فيهـا، فقـد أقامـوا المنتديـات للتبـاري في قـول الشـعر، حتـى أتـوا بالعجـب العجـاب، فجاءهـم اللـه بآيـة تبزهـم فيـما أتقنـوه وأحسنوه، فبهرتهـم آياتـه، حتـى إن الواحـد منهـم ليستمـع إلى آيـة مـن كتـاب اللـه، فيخـر سـاجداً لبلاغتهـا مـع أن الإيمـان لم يدخـل قلبـه بعـد.

---

1   Reported by Muslim in his [*Ṣaḥīḥ*] (No. 2577)

١ رواه مسلم في صحيحه ورقمه (٢٥٧٧).

Al-Walīd Ibn al-Mughīrah, one of the chiefs of Quraysh, once listened to the Messenger of Allah ﷺ while reciting the Qur'an, and was immediately shaken in the innermost of his soul. When he was asked to explain it, he responded,

"By Allah! No man among you is more well-versed in poetry and its styles, nor with the poetry of Jinn, than I am. By Allah! In no way do his statements resemble any of these things. By Allah! What he says has sweetness and is covered with beauty; its beginning is fruitful and its end is abundant with good. It is [bound] to surpass and not to be surpassed. It far exceeds other texts, and they are all inferior in quality." (Reported by al-Hākim)[1]

The Messenger of Allah ﷺ challenged his people, who were eloquent and fluent, to come up with the likes of the Qur'an, or even the likes of a single *Sūrah* of it, but they failed. Despite the strong enmity they had towards him, which could have driven them to make attempts to resist this Qur'an and therefore root out this religion, they found no way to do so.

If the Arabs were unable to produce the likes of the Qur'an, then others would be even less capable of doing so. History is a witness that the Qur'an is a miraculous sign, for no sensible individual has ever claimed to be capable of producing its likes. **"Indeed, those who disbelieve in the message after it has come to them... And indeed, it is a mighty Book. Falsehood cannot approach it from before it or from behind it; [it is] a revelation from a [Lord who is] Wise and Praiseworthy."[2] " And if you are in doubt about what We have sent down upon Our Servant [Muhammad], then produce a surah the like thereof and call upon your witnesses other than Allah, if you should be truthful. But if you do not - and you will never be able to - then fear the Fire, whose fuel is men and stones, prepared for the disbelievers."[3]**

---

1 Compiled by al-Ḥakim in [*al-Mustadrak*] (2/550-551) (3872) who graded it authentic according to the criteria of al-Bukhāri, and adh-Dhahabī agreed with him. It was collected by as-Suyūṭī in [*ad-Durr al-Manthūr*] (6/454, re: Surat al-Muddathir: 18) and he attributed it to Al-Ḥākim and Al-Bayhaqi in [*ad-Dalā`il*], on the authority of 'Ikrimah, on the authority of Ibn 'Abbās.

2 Surat Fuṣṣilat – Verses 41-42

3 Surat al-Baqarah – Verses 23-24

وقد استمع الوليد بن المغيرة أحد زعماء قريش إلى تلاوة الرسول ﷺ القرآن فهزه القرآن من أعماق نفسه، فلما سئل عن ذلك، قال مجيباً: «**والله ما منكم رجل أعلم بالأشعار مني، ولا أعلم برجزه ولا بقصيده، ولا بأشعار الجن، والله ما يشبه الذي يقول شيئاً من هذا، والله إن لقوله الذي يقوله حلاوة، وإن عليه لطلاوة، وإنه لمثمر أعلاه، مغدق أسفله، وإنه ليعلو ولا يعلى، وإنه ليحطم ما تحته**» رواه الحاكم[١].

وقد تحدى الرسول ﷺ قومه، وهم الفصحاء البلغاء، بأن يأتوا بمثل هذا القرآن، أو بمثل سورة منه، فعجزوا، ولم يستطيعوا ذلك، هذا مع شدة الخصومة، التي تدفعهم إلى معارضة القرآن لإبطال هذا الدين، ولكنهم لم يجدوا إلى ذلك سبيلاً.

وإذا كان العرب قد عجزوا عن الإتيان بمثل هذا القرآن فغيرهم أعجز، والتاريخ شاهد على أن القرآن آية معجزة، فلم يأت من يزعم أنه أتى بمثل القرآن: ﴿وَإِنَّهُ لَكِتَابٌ عَزِيزٌ $ لاَ يَأْتِيهِ الْبَاطِلُ مِن بَيْنِ يَدَيْهِ وَلاَ مِنْ خَلْفِهِ تَنزِيلٌ مِّنْ حَكِيمٍ حَمِيدٍ﴾[٢]، ﴿وَإِن كُنتُمْ فِي رَيْبٍ مِّمَّا نَزَّلْنَا عَلَى عَبْدِنَا فَأْتُوا بِسُورَةٍ مِّن مِّثْلِهِ وَادْعُوا شُهَدَاءَكُم مِّن دُونِ اللهِ إِن كُنتُمْ صَادِقِينَ $ فَإِن لَّمْ تَفْعَلُوا وَلَن تَفْعَلُوا فَاتَّقُوا النَّارَ الَّتِي وَقُودُهَا النَّاسُ وَالْحِجَارَةُ أُعِدَّتْ لِلْكَافِرِينَ﴾[٣].

---

١ أخرجه الحاكم في «المستدرك»: ٢/ ٥٥٠- ٥٥١، (٣٨٧٢) وصححه على شرط البخاري ووافقه الذهبي، وأورده السيوطي في «الدر المنثور»: ٦/ ٤٥٤ [المدثر: ١٨]، وعزاه للحاكم والبيهقي في الدلائل من طريق عكرمة عن ابن عباس.

٢ فصلت: ٤١-٤٢.

٣ البقرة: ٢٣-٢٤.

The challenge then became for all humankind, and even the Jinn as well: **"Say, 'If mankind and the jinn gathered in order to produce the like of this Qur'an, they could not produce the like of it, even if they were to each other assistants.'"**[1]

The Qur'an, with which Allah challenged humankind, has a style which "is not alien to the customary patterns of speech that the Arabs used. The Qur'an's words are structured of the letters of the Arabs, its sentences and verses are composed from its words, and its style of composition was congruent to the composition of the Arabs."[2] Yet, despite that, they were incapable of producing its likes.

IV – The Preservation of the Qur'an

Allah guaranteed His Messenger ﷺ that He would preserve the Qur'an from vanish and ruin: **"Indeed, it is We who sent down the Qur'an and indeed, We will be its guardian."**[3]

So, here is the Qur'an, fourteen centuries since its revelation, still as uncorrupt and pure as the first day it was revealed, despite the heinous plans devised against it and against the Islamic *Ummah*. The Qur'an is still alive, giving life to this *Ummah*, and guiding it to Allah's straight path.

وقد أصبح التحدي عالمياً للبشرية كلها، بـل للإنـس والجـن: ﴿قُـل لَّـئِنِ اجْتَمَعَتِ الإِنْسُ وَالْجِـنُّ عَـلَى أَن يَأْتُـوا بِمِثْلِ هَذَا الْقُـرْآنِ لاَ يَأْتُـونَ بِمِثْلِهِ وَلَوْ كَانَ بَعْضُهُـمْ لِبَعْضٍ ظَهِـيراً﴾[1].

إن القرآن الـذي تحدى بـه الله البشر جـرت أساليبه «عـلى معهـود العـرب في كلامهـا، فمـن حروفهـم ركبـت كلماتـه، ومـن كلماتـه ألفـت جملـه وآياتـه، وعـلى مناهجهـم في التأليـف جـاء تأليفـه»[2]، ومـع ذلـك عجـزوا عـن الإتيـان بمثله.

رابعاً: حفظ القرآن:

تعهد الله لرسوله ﷺ بحفظ كتابه مـن الـزوال والضياع: ﴿إِنَّا نَحْنُ نَزَّلْنَا الذِّكْرَ وَإِنَّا لَهُ لَحَافِظُونَ﴾[3].

وهـا هـو القرآن بعد تنزله بألف وأربعمائة عـام مـا يـزال غضّـاً طريّـاً لم يطرأ عليـه تغييـر ولا تحريـف، عـلى الرغـم مـن المؤامـرات الهائلـة التـي كيـد بهـا، وكيـدت بهـا الأمـة الإسـلامية، وبقـي حيّـاً يحيـي هـذه الأمـة، ويقيمهـا عـلى صراط اللـه المسـتقيم.

---

1 Surat al-Isrā - Verse 88
2 [an-Naba` al-`Aẓeem] by Muhammad ibn `Abdillāh Drāz (p. 83)
3 Surat al-Ḥijr – Verse 9

١ الإسراء: ٨٨.
٢ النبأ العظيم، لمحمد بن عبد الله دراز: ٨٣.
٣ الحجر: ٩.

One interesting point pertaining to the Most High, **"Indeed, it is We who sent down the Qur'an and indeed, We will be its guardian"**[1] is that some of the scholars speak in their books about the exerted efforts by which the Ummah has preserved the Qur'an. But nowadays, we have realized that it is the Ummah who is in need of the Qur'an to preserve it. Were it not for the Qur'an, this Ummah would have become extinct a long time ago. This fact is further supported by knowing that this Ummah will vanish and come to an end, by the end of time, once the Qur'an will be taken up. At that point, there will no longer be an Islamic Ummah which knows its religion, *'aqeedah* (creed), and Sharia – for the book that used to safeguard it has disappeared. From this, we can understand the degree of contempt and malice that the disbelieving missionaries, orientalists, and politicians harbor in their hearts against this Book which safeguards the Islamic Ummah, and thwarts the plots and strategies of its enemies. And indeed, Allah forever executes His plans.

ومـن لطيـف فقـه قولـه تعـالى: ﴿إِنَّـا نَحْـنُ نَزَّلْنَـا الذِّكْـرَ وَإِنَّـا لَـهُ لَحَافِظُـونَ﴾(١)، أن بعـض أهـل العلـم يتحدثـون في مؤلفاتهـم عـن الجهـود التـي حفظـت بهـا الأمـة القـرآن، ثـم ظهـر لنـا في هـذه الأيـام أن الأمـة هـي المحتاجـة إلى القـرآن ليحفظهـا، ولـولا القـرآن لزالـت مـن زمـن بعيـد، يدلنـا عـلى صحـة هـذا القـول أن الأمـة تـزول وتتـلاشى في آخـر الزمـان عندمـا يرفـع القـرآن، فـلا تبقـى أمـة إسـلامية تعـرف دينهـا وعقيدتهـا وشريعتهـا؛ لأن الكتـاب الـذي كان يحفظهـا زال، ومـن هنـا نعلـم مـدى الغـل والحقـد الـذي في قلـوب المنصريـن والمستشرقين والسياسـيين الكفـرة عـلى هـذا الكتـاب، الـذي يحفـظ أمـة الإسـلام، ويبطـل كيـد أعدائهـا ومكرهـم، واللـه غالـب عـلى أمـره.

The Companions used to guard the Messenger of Allah ﷺ, with his knowledge and approval. But when Allah revealed His statement, **"...And Allah will protect you from the people..."**[2] he ordered his guards to go home, as a way of showing trust in Allah's promise. Likewise, we firmly believe that Allah will guard His Book from distortion, and Allah is source of strength.

لقـد كان الصحابـة ﷺ يحرسـون رسـول اللـه ﷺ بعلمـه ورضـاه، فلـما أنـزل اللـه قولـه: ﴿وَاللَّهُ يَعْصِمُكَ مِنَ النَّاسِ﴾(٢)، أمـر حراسـه بالانطـلاق إلى منازلهـم، تصديقاً بوعـد اللـه، ونحـن نوقـن بـأن اللـه عاصـم كتابـه مـن التحريـف، وحافـظ لـه مـن الـزوال، واللـه المسـتعان.

How Did Allah Preserve His Book?

كيف حفظ الله كتابه؟

Allah preserved His Book through two ways:

حفظ الله كتابه بطريقين:

The first was documentation; thus the Qur'an is called: the Book. Allah the Almighty says: **"Alif, Lām, Mîm. This is the Book about which there is no doubt, a guidance for those conscious of Allah."**[3] **"And this [Qur'an] is a Book We have revealed [which is] blessed."**[4]

الأول: الكتابـة؛ ولذلـك سـمي هـذا القـرآن بالكتـاب، قـال تعـالى: ﴿الم ۞ ذَلِـكَ الْكِتَـابُ لَا رَيْـبَ فِيـهِ هُـدًى لِّلْمُتَّقِـينَ﴾(٣)، وقـال: ﴿وَهَـذَا كِتَـابٌ أَنْزَلْنَـاهُ مُبَـارَكٌ﴾(٤).

1 Surat al-Ḥijr – Verse 9
2 Surat al-Mā`idah – Verse 67
3 Surat al-Baqarah – Verses 1-2
4 Surat al-An`ām – Verse 155

١ الحجر: ٩.
٢ المائدة: ٦٧.
٣ البقرة: ١-٢.
٤ الأنعام: ١٥٥.

The second was memorizing; committing it to peoples' hearts. This took place via reciting it and listening to its recital; thus it was called the Qur'an (literally: the Oft-Recited). Allah, the Most High, says, **"...And this Qur'an was revealed to me that I may warn you thereby and whomever it reaches..."**[1] He ﷻ also said: **"So when the Qur'an is recited, then listen to it and pay attention that you may receive mercy."**[2]

The current Muṣḥaf identically matches the text dictated by the Messenger of Allah ﷺ, except that the latter was not initially written. The Messenger of Allah ﷺ used to receive the Waḥy (revelation) from Jibrīl, recite it to the Companions, and had them memorize it. The Messenger of Allah ﷺ appointed scribes for the Waḥy, including Abū Bakr, `Umar, `Uthmān, Zayd Ibn Thābit, Mu`āwyah Ibn Abū Sufyān, et al. Whenever a new *āyah* was revealed, he ordered those present, or the nearby scribes, to immediately write them down. They were written on the same materials which the Arabs used for writing, such as animal hides, parchments, stone sheets, and shoulder bones. These writings did not compose a complete copy of the Noble Qur'an in the same way today's Muṣ~ḥaf are arranged. These writings were dispersed between the Companions of the Messenger of Allah ﷺ.

However, the Qur'an, which was committed to memory, was completed in the manner known to us a short time before the death of the Messenger of Allah ﷺ. The Messenger of Allah ﷺ did not die until the arranged Qur'an was memorized. Ibn Mas`ūd, for example, used to pride himself in memorizing seventy Sūrah(s) which he took directly from the Prophet's mouth, and the [other] *Ḥuffāẓ* (memorizers) of the Qur'an were similarly known and distinguished.

1 Surat al-An`ām – Verse 19
2 Surat al-A`rāf – Verse 204

والثاني: الحفظ في الصدور، وهذا يتم عن طريق قراءته والاستماع لهذه القراءة؛ ولذلك سمي قرآناً، قال تعالى: **﴿وَأُوحِيَ إِلَيَّ هَذَا الْقُرْآنُ لِأُنذِرَكُم بِهِ وَمَن بَلَغَ﴾**(١)، وقال: **﴿وَإِذَا قُرِئَ الْقُرْآنُ فَاسْتَمِعُوا لَهُ وَأَنصِتُوا لَعَلَّكُمْ تُرْحَمُونَ﴾**(٢).

والمصحف موافق تماماً لما أملاه الرسول ﷺ إلا أنه لم يكن مكتوباً، فكان الرسول ﷺ يتلقى الوحي من جبريل، ثم يقرؤه على الصحابة ويُحفِّظهم إياه، وقد اتخذ الرسول ﷺ كُتَّاباً للوحي، منهم أبو بكر وعمر وعثمان وزيد بن ثابت ومعاوية بن أبي سفيان، فكلما أنزلت عليه آيات طلب ممن حضره من كتاب الوحي أو ممن كان قريباً منه كتابة تلك الآيات، فكانت تكتب على ما كان يكتب عليه العرب آنذاك مثل الرقاع أو قطع الجلد أو صفائح الحجارة وكسر الأكتاف...، ولكن لم تُكوِّن هذه المكتوبات نسخة كاملة من القرآن الكريم على الترتيب الذي عليه المصحف الآن، وتوزعت هذه المكتوبات عند صحابة الرسول ﷺ.

أما القرآن المحفوظ في الصدور فقد اكتمل على هذا النحو المعروف لدينا قرب وفاة الرسول ﷺ، ذلك أن الله كان يخبر رسوله بمكان الآيات التي تتنزل، ولم يُتوَف الرسول ﷺ إلا وقد اكتمل حفظ القرآن على هذا النحو المرتب عند جماعة من الصحابة، فابن مسعود كان يفخر بأنه حفظ سبعين سورة من فم الرسول ﷺ، وكان حَفَظَة كتاب الله معروفين ظاهرين.

١ الأنعام: ١٩.
٢ الأعراف: ٢٠٤.

V – The Wisdom Behind Sending Down the Qur'an Gradually:

Contrary to the previous divine scriptures, the Qur'an was not revealed to the Messenger of Allah ﷺ all at once. The *Tawrāh* (Torah) for example, the laws which were sent down to Mūsa, descended all at once as written in the Tablets. Allah the Almighty says, **"And We wrote for him on the tablets [something] of all things..."**[1] **"And when the anger subsided in Mûsa, he took up the tablets; and in their inscription was guidance..."**[2]

In fact, Allah sent down the Qur'an in fragments over a period of twenty-three years: **" And [it is] a Qur'an which We have separated [by intervals] that you might recite it to the people over a prolonged period. And We have sent it down progressively."**[3]

This method of revelation was due to a wisdom that Allah explained in His Book.

The wisdom behind sending down the Qur'an gradually:

1) Strengthening the heart of the Messenger of Allah ﷺ

2) The gradual presentation of judgments

3) Treating the incidents and problems that arose during the time revelation

We are going to deal with the above three reasons in detail.

Firstly: Strengthening the heart of the Messenger of Allah ﷺ:

Allah clearly stated this reason; when the disbelievers inquired about the reason that the Qur'an was sent down in separated parts, suggesting that it should be revealed as a whole at one time, Allah answered them saying, **"And those who disbelieve say, 'Why was the Qur'an not revealed to him all at once?' Thus [it is] that We may strengthen thereby your heart. And We have spaced it distinctly."**[4]

1 Surat al-A`rāf – Verse 145
2 Surat al-A`rāf – Verse 154
3 Surat al-Isrā' – Verse 106
4 Surat al-Furqān – Verse 32

خامساً: نزول القرآن منجماً والحكمة من وراء ذلك:

لم ينزل الله القرآن على الرسول ﷺ جملة واحدة كما أنزلت الكتب السماوية السابقة، فالتوراة، وهي الشريعة التي أنزلت على موسى أنزلت مرة واحدة مكتوبة في الألواح، قال تعالى: **﴿وَكَتَبْنَا لَهُ فِي الْأَلْوَاحِ مِن كُلِّ شَيْءٍ﴾**(١)، وقال: **﴿وَلَمَّا سَكَتَ عَن مُّوسَى الْغَضَبُ أَخَذَ الْأَلْوَاحَ وَفِي نُسْخَتِهَا هُدًى﴾**(٢).

لقد أنزل الله القرآن على رسوله مفرقاً على مدار ثلاثة وعشرين عاماً: **﴿وَقُرْآنًا فَرَقْنَاهُ لِتَقْرَأَهُ عَلَى النَّاسِ عَلَىٰ مُكْثٍ وَنَزَّلْنَاهُ تَنزِيلًا﴾**(٣)، وكان ذلك لحِكَم بيَّنها الله في كتابه، فمن ذلك تثبيت قلب الرسول ﷺ.

الحكمة من نزول القرآن منجماً:

نزل القرآن مفرقاً لحكم كثيرة، منها:

١- تثبيت قلب الرسول ﷺ.

٢- التدرج في تنزل الأحكام.

٣- مواجهة الواقعات والمشكلات التي تجد في عهد التنزيل.

وستتناول هذه الثلاث بشيء من التفصيل.

أولاً: تثبيت قلب الرسول ﷺ:

وقد نص الله على هذه الحكمة، فقد ذكر أن الكفار تساءلوا عن نزول القرآن مفرقاً، واقتراحهم نزوله جملة واحدة، ورد عليهم ببيان الحكمة في نزوله كذلك: **﴿وَقَالَ الَّذِينَ كَفَرُوا لَوْلَا نُزِّلَ عَلَيْهِ الْقُرْآنُ جُمْلَةً وَاحِدَةً كَذَٰلِكَ لِنُثَبِّتَ بِهِ فُؤَادَكَ وَرَتَّلْنَاهُ تَرْتِيلًا﴾**(٤).

١ الأعراف: ١٤٥.
٢ الأعراف: ١٥٤.
٣ الإسراء: ١٠٦.
٤ الفرقان: ٣٢.

The Qur'an used to descend upon the heart of the Messenger of Allah ﷺ as he carried out the mission of conveying the message to the people. This way, it would strengthen his heart, and soothe his agonies, while he faced the aggression of the unrelenting disbelievers. The Qur'an granted him insight regarding their doubts and requests, uncovered for him their plots, reassured him with the promises of victory and support, and aided him through this successive revelation in teaching his Companions and enabling them to learn their religion gradually, while simultaneously memorizing this Book. Whenever a group of verses were revealed, the Companions would memorize it, and then learn the knowledge, rulings, and instructions contained therein. They would then put them into practice step by step, and that could not have been accomplished with such perfection if the Qur'an was revealed all at once.

Second: The Gradual Legislation of Rulings

The Qur'an used to develop the souls of the Companions of the Messenger of Allah ﷺ, as well as their families and their society. It gradually progressed in legislating the rulings, little by little, so that these rulings would not overburden them. In this manner, the transformation of their lives, in accordance with the legislation and path of Allah, was eased.

This gradualism had two tracks:

The first track: gradual legislation of the rulings at large

The second track: gradual legislation of a single ruling

We will discuss each of these with a bit of detail.

لقـد كان القرآن يتنـزل عـلى قلـب الرسـول ﷺ وهـو يقوم بمهمتـه في إبـلاغ النـاس الرسالة، فيثبـت قلبـه، ويمسـح آلامـه، وهـو يواجـه عنـت الكفـار، وتطاولهـم عليـه، ويكشـف عـن بصيرتـه مـا يوردونـه مـن شبهات وتساؤلات، ويكشـف لـه عـن مؤامراتهـم، ويتـولى وعـده بالنصر والغلـب والتأييـد، ويعينـه بهـذا التنزيل المتلاحـق المتـوالي عـلى تربيـة أصحابـه، وتفقيههـم دينـه شـيئاً فشـيئاً، وتحفيظهـم هـذا الكتـاب، فكلمـا نزلت منـه آيات حفظوهـا وفقهـوا مـا فيهـا مـن علـم وأحـكام وتوجيهـات، وعملـوا بهـا شـيئاً فشـيئاً، ومـا كان هـذا ليتـم عـلى هـذه الصـورة الوافيـة لـو نـزل مـرة واحـدة.

ثانياً: التدرج في تشريع الأحكام:

كان القـرآن يبنـي نفـوس صحابـة رسـول اللـه وأسرهـم ومجتمعهـم، وكان يرتقـي بهـم في تشريـع الأحـكام شـيئاً فشـيئاً، حتى لا تثقـل عليهـم الأحـكام، وحتى يسـهل عليهـم أن يغـيروا حياتهـم وفق تشريـع اللـه ومنهجـه.

والتدرج أخذ مسارين:

الأول: التدرج في تشريع جملة الأحكام.

الثاني: التدرج في تشريع الحكم الواحد.

وسنتناول كل واحد من هذين بشيء من التفصيل.

Firstly: gradual legislation of the rulings at large

The Qur`anic rulings were gradually revealed via the verses of the Qur'an.

- On the Night of *al-Isrā`* (the Night Journey), which occurred one year before the *Hijrah*, the *Ṣalāh* (prayer) was prescribed.
- During the first year after the *Hijrah*, the *Adhān* (call to prayer) and fighting the disbelievers were legislated. Likewise, some marriage-related judgments were legislated such as *Ṣadāq* (dowry) and *Walīmah* (marriage banquet).
- During the second year after *Hijrah*, the *Ṣawm* (fasting), the prayer of the two 'Eid(s), the sacrificing of animals, and *Zakāh* were all legislated. In that same year, the *Qiblah* (direction of prayer) was changed and spoils of war were made lawful to the *Mujāhidīn* (fighters in the cause of Allah).
- In the third year, the rulings on inheritance, divorce, and shortening of prayer in times of travel and fear, were legislated.
- During the fourth year, the punishment for *Zinā* (illegal sexual intercourse) was instituted, Allah sent down the rulings on *Tayammum* (Dry Ablution) and slander, and prescribed Ḥajj (Pilgrimage).
- During the sixth year, Allah revealed the rulings on *Ṣulḥ* (reconciliation) and *Iḥṣār* (inability to reach the Sacred House). As well, the drinking of *Khamr* (alcohol) and gambling were prohibited.
- During the seventh year, the meat of domesticated donkeys was prohibited, while the judgments of *Muzāra`ah* (sharecropping) and al-*Musāqāh* (share-tenancy) were legislated.
- In the eighth year, the punishment for theft was enacted.
- In the ninth year, the case of *Li`ān* (mutual imprecation) was instituted and the disbelievers were prevented from entering Mecca.
- In the tenth year, usury was clearly prohibited.

أولاً: التدرج في تشريع جملة الأحكام:

تنزلت الأحكام القرآنية عبر الوحي بالقرآن شيئاً فشيئاً:

- ففي ليلة الإسراء قبل الهجرة بسنة فرضت الصلاة
- وفي السنة الأولى من الهجرة شرع الأذان والقتال، كما شرعت أحكام من النكاح كالصداق والوليمة
- وفي السنة الثانية شرع الصوم وصلاة العيدين ونحر الأضاحي، والزكاة، وحولت فيها القبلة، وأحلت الغنائم للمجاهدين
- وفي السنة الثالثة كان تشريع أحكام المواريث وأحكام الطلاق، وشرع قصر الصلاة في السفر وفي الخوف
- وفي السنة الرابعة شرعت عقوبة الزنا، وأنزل الله أحكام التيمم والقذف، وفرض الحج.
- وفي السنة السادسة بيّن الله أحكام الصلح والإحصار، وفيها حرم الله الخمر والميسر
- وفي السابعة حرمت الحمر الإنسية، وشرعت أحكام المزارعة والمساقاة
- وفي السنة الثامنة شرع حد السرقة
- وفي التاسعة شرع اللعان، ومنع الكفار من دخول مكة
- وفي العاشرة حرم الربا تحريماً لا خفاء به.

The Nature of Legislation in its Gradual Descent:

Those who studied the gradual legislation of the rulings at large divided it into two sections. This is because the Messenger of Allah ﷺ lived for 23 years after the mission, 13 of which he spent in Mecca and 10 years in al-Madinah al-Munawwarah. The incident of *Hijrah* of the Prophet was the milestone between these two eras. So whatever descended before the *Hijrah* belongs to the Meccan era and whatever descended after the *Hijrah* belongs to the Madīnan era. Accordingly, the Qur'an revealed before the *Hijrah* is called the `Meccan revelation` and the Qur'an revealed after the *Hijrah* is called the `Madīnan revelation` even if it was revealed in Mecca.

A study of the Qur`anic texts revealed in these two stages can make us well aware of the gradual methodology in each stage.

1. The nature of legislation in the Meccan era:

When studying the legislation in the Meccan era, we find that the legislations related to the practical aspects were few. At that point, the struggle with the disbelievers did not allow for detailed and secondary legislations. The legislation in that stage noticeably focused on the foundations of the religion and calling to them, such as belief in Allah, His messengers, and the Last Day. It also contained elements of enjoining morality such as justice, the performance of good deeds, the fulfillment of promises, forgiveness, fearing of Allah, and being grateful to Him. It further focused on shunning immoral behavior such as committing adultery, murder, burying female babies alive, cheating in measures and weights, and forbidding all acts akin to *Kufr* (disbelief) or conducive of it.

طبيعة التشريع في تنزلاته المتدرجة:

الدارسون للتدرج في جملة الأحكام الشرعية قسموها إلى قسمين، ذلك أن الرسول ﷺ عاش بعد البعثة النبوية ثلاثة وعشرين عاماً، قضى منها ثلاث عشرة سنة في مكة، وعشر سنوات في المدينة المنورة، والفاصل بين المرحلتين الهجرة النبوية، فما كان قبل الهجرة فهو المرحلة المكية، والقرآن الذي أنزل عليه يسمى بالقرآن المكي، وما بعد الهجرة فهو المرحلة المدنية، وما أنزل عليه في هذه المرحلة فهو القرآن المدني، حتى وإن أنزل في مكة فهو مدني.

ومن خلال دراسة النصوص القرآنية في كل من المرحلتين السابقتين نستطيع أن نتعرف إلى منهج التدرج في كل مرحلة منها.

١- طبيعة التشريع في المرحلة المكية:

من خلال دراسة التشريع في العهد المكي نجد أن التشريعات المتعلقة بالجانب العملي كانت قليلة، فالصراع مع الكفار في هذه المرحلة كان لا يسمح بتشريعات تفصيلية جزئية، والملاحظ أن التشريع في هذه المرحلة كان مركزاً على بيان أصول الدين، والدعوة إليها؛ كالإيمان بالله ورسوله واليوم الآخر، والأمر بمكارم الأخلاق؛ كالعدل والإحسان والوفاء بالوعد وأخذ العفو والخوف من الله وحده والشكر، وتجنب مساوئ الأخلاق؛ كالزنا والقتل ووأد البنات والتطفيف في الكيل والميزان والنهي عن كل ما هو كفر أو تابع للكفر.

Even the acts of worship legalized in Mecca, such as *Ṣalāh* and *Zakāh,* were not as detailed as the Madīnan period. In Mecca, the *Zakāh* only meant charity in its general sense and spending for charitable causes without specifying a particular amount or system for it.

If we carefully study the detailed legal rulings that were revealed in the Meccan era, we will find that they are related to some fundamental theological issues, such as the prohibition of sacrificing anything for other than Allah. In other instances, we find that they focused on fighting vices which were detrimental to human life.

If we refer to Sūrat al-An`ām, which is a Meccan *Sūrah,* we will find examples of the secondary detailed rulings that were revealed in the Meccan era. This included prohibiting the eating of animals which were sacrificed in the name of other than Allah, or instances in which Allah's name was not mentioned upon slaughter. It further detailed the animals whose meat is forbidden to eat, as is found in Allah's saying, **"And do not eat of that upon which the name of Allah has not been mentioned, for indeed, it is grave disobedience. And indeed do the devils inspire their allies [among men] to dispute with you. And if you were to obey them, indeed, you would be associators [of others with Him]."**[1] **"So eat of that [meat] upon which the name of Allah has been mentioned, if you are believers in His verses. And why should you not eat of that upon which the name of Allah has been mentioned while He has explained in detail to you what He has forbidden you, excepting that to which you are compelled."**[2] **"Say, 'I do not find within that which was revealed to me [anything] forbidden to one who would eat it unless it be a dead animal or blood spilled out or the flesh of swine - for indeed, it is impure - or it be [that slaughtered in] disobedience, dedicated to other than Allah...'"**[3]

1 Surat al-An`ām – Verse 121
2 Surat al-An`ām – Verse 118-119
3 Surat al-An`ām – Verse 145

حتى ما شرعه الله في مكة من عبادات كالصلاة والزكاة لم يكن على التفصيل والبيان الذي عرف في المدينة، فالزكاة كانت في مكة بمعنى الصدقة والإنفاق في سبيل الخير من غير أن يحدد لها جزء معين ولا نظام خاص.

والمتأمل في الأحكام التشريعية التفصيلية التي أنزلت في المرحلة المكية يلاحظ أنها تتعلق بالأصول العقائدية؛ كتحريم ما ذبح لغير الله، أو أنها تحارب الرذائل الخطيرة في الحياة الإنسانية.

وإذا رجعنا إلى سورة الأنعام- وهي سورة مكية- رأينا نماذج للأحكام التفصيلية الجزئية التي أنزلت في المرحلة المكية، فمن ذلك تحريم أكل الذبائح التي ذبحت بغير اسم الله، أو لم يذكر اسم الله عليها، وبيان المحرمات من الحيوان الذي لا يجوز أكله كقوله تعالى: ﴿**وَلَا تَأْكُلُوا مِمَّا لَمْ يُذْكَرِ اسْمُ اللهِ عَلَيْهِ وَإِنَّهُ لَفِسْقٌ وَإِنَّ الشَّيَاطِينَ لَيُوحُونَ إِلَى أَوْلِيَائِهِمْ لِيُجَادِلُوكُمْ وَإِنْ أَطَعْتُمُوهُمْ إِنَّكُمْ لَمُشْرِكُونَ**﴾(١)، وقوله: ﴿**فَكُلُوا مِمَّا ذُكِرَ اسْمُ اللهِ عَلَيْهِ إِن كُنتُم بِآيَاتِهِ مُؤْمِنِينَ ۞ وَمَا لَكُمْ أَلَّا تَأْكُلُوا مِمَّا ذُكِرَ اسْمُ اللهِ عَلَيْهِ وَقَدْ فَصَّلَ لَكُم مَّا حَرَّمَ عَلَيْكُمْ إِلَّا مَا اضْطُرِرْتُمْ إِلَيْهِ**﴾(٢)، وقوله: ﴿**قُل لَّا أَجِدُ فِي مَا أُوحِيَ إِلَيَّ مُحَرَّماً عَلَى طَاعِمٍ يَطْعَمُهُ إِلَّا أَن يَكُونَ مَيْتَةً أَوْ دَماً مَّسْفُوحاً أَوْ لَحْمَ خِنزِيرٍ فَإِنَّهُ رِجْسٌ أَوْ فِسْقاً أُهِلَّ**(٣) **لِغَيْرِ اللهِ بِهِ**﴾(٤)

١ الأنعام: ١٢١.
٢ الأنعام: ١١٨-١١٩.
٣ الإهلال: رفع الصوت، والمراد به ذكر غير اسم الله على الذبيحة.
٤ الأنعام: ١٤٥.

These verses presented some secondary practical rulings related to theological issues; the pre-Islamic Arabs used to sacrifice these animals, which Allah created, in the name of their false gods and idols, as a form of offering to them. On the other hand, they used to make lawful what Allah prohibited; so they were declaring things as either lawful or unlawful according to their own desires. As a result, the legislative aspect of faith was in complete chaos in their society.

This Nature of Legislation in the Madīnan era:

The legislation in the Meccan era was focused on explaining the fundamentals of religion. In the Madīnan era, the fundamentals of religion continued to be explained, accompanied by practical rulings in worship and social transactions. The verses that contained rulings that pertain to all human activities including devotion, such as *Ṣalāh*, *Zakāh*, *Ṣawm*, and Hajj; financial issues such as sales, leases, usurious transactions; criminal issues such as murder, theft, fornication/adultery, and highway robbery; family issues including marriage, divorce, and inheritance; international affairs such as wars, relations with the *Muḥāribīn* (non-Muslims at war with Muslims), the mutual treaties, and the spoils of war.

In all these previously mentioned cases, the Qur'an did not deal much with secondary details [of these practices] while often touching on major issues. The Messenger of Allah ﷺ used to expand on the brief accounts of the Qur'an, specifying and restricting texts as necessary. He even introduced new rulings not presented by the Qur'an. The reason that practical rulings were revealed in Madinah was the change of the Muslims` status. After the *Hijrah*, the Muslims formed a community and established a state which necessitated that legislations regulate their nascent society, build the character of its individuals, protect its families, and organize interrelations.

فهذه الأحكام العملية الجزئية تتعلق بالأمور العقائدية؛ حيث كانوا يتقربون بهذه الأنعام التي خلقها الله للأوثان والآلهة المزعومة، وكانوا يذبحونها باسم هذه الآلهة الباطلة، ومن جانب آخر هي تشريع لما لم يأذن الله به؛ إذ يحرمون ويحللون بأهوائهم، فقد كانوا يعيشون في فوضى في هذا الجانب.

٢- التشريع في المرحلة المدنية:

كان التشريع في المرحلة المكية منصباً على بيان أصول الدين، وفي المرحلة المدنية استمرت العناية بأصول الدين وتنزلت الآيات التي تبين الأحكام العملية وتوضحها، وقد تعرضت آيات الأحكام إلى جميع ما يصدر عن الإنسان من أعمال العبادات من صلاة وزكاة وصوم وحج، وإلى الأمور المدنية؛ كالبيع والإجارة والربا، وإلى الأمور الجنائية من قتل وسرقة وزناً وقطع طريق، وإلى نظام الأسرة من زواج وطلاق وميراث، وإلى الشئون الدولية؛ كالقتال وعلاقة المسلمين بالمحاربين، وما بينهم من عهود وغنائم الحرب.

والقرآن في هذا كله لا يتعرض كثيراً للتفاصيل الجزئية، إنما يتعرض غالباً للأمور الكلية، وقد كان الرسول ﷺ يبين ما في القرآن من إجمال، ويخصص ما يحتاج إلى تخصيص، ويقيد ما يحتاج إلى تقييد، وقد يأتي بأحكام لم يتعرض لها القرآن.

والسبب في تنزل الأحكام العملية في الفترة المدنية هو تغير وضع المسلمين، فقد شكل المسلمون بعد الهجرة مجتمعاً وكونوا دولة، فاحتاجوا إلى التشريعات التي يسير عليها المسلمون في مجتمعهم الجديد، وتبنى شخصية الفرد، وتحمى الأسرة، وتنظم العلاقات.

Secondly: gradual legislation of a single ruling

The gradual development of rulings was not restricted to the rulings at large; it was also reflected in individual judgments. An example of this is seen in the *Ṣalāh* for which two *rak`āt* were originally prescribed in every prayer. The Messenger of Allah ﷺ then migrated to Madinah and four *rak`āt* were prescribed in some prayers. Al-Bukhāri and Muslim narrated, on the authority of `Ā`ishah, who said, "Originally, two *rak`āt* were prescribed in every prayer. When the Prophet migrated [to Madinah] four *rak`āt* were enjoined, while the journey prayer remained unchanged (i.e. two *rak`āt*)."[1]

Aḥmad narrated in his [Musnad], on the authority of Mu`ādh Ibn Jabal, who said: "The prayer passed by three stages, as did the fasting. As for prayer, when the Prophet ﷺ came to Madinah, he prayed facing Bayt-ul-Maqdis (Jerusalem) for seventeen months. Then, Allah revealed, **"We have certainly seen the turning of your face, [O Muhammad], toward the heaven, and We will surely turn you to a qiblah (literally: their qiblah) with which you will be pleased."**[2] So Allah directed him to Mecca; this was one stage.

He then said: "People used to gather for prayer, and would inform one another of its time, until they were about to use a bell for this purpose. Then, a man form the Anṣār by the name of `Abdullāh Ibn Zayd Ibn `Abd Rabbih came to the Messenger ﷺ and said: 'O Messenger of Allah, I saw in a dream, and if say I was not asleep, it will be true, that while I was half awake and half asleep; I saw a man dressed in two green garments. He faced the *Qiblah* and said, `*Allāhu Akbar* (Allah is the greatest), *Ash-hadu Allā Elāha Illā Allāh* [I testify that there is no God but Allah]' (two times) until he finished the *Adhān*. Then, he waited for a while and said the like of what he had said before, adding `*Qad Qāmat aṣ-Ṣalāh* [The Prayer is Established]' (two times). The Messenger of Allah ﷺ said, **"Teach it to Bilāl so he may call the *Adhān* with it."**" So Bilāl was the first to proclaim this formula in *Adhān*. He (the narrator) further said: "`Umar Ibn al-Khaṭṭāb (may Allah be pleased with him) came and said: 'O Messenger of Allah! I have experienced that which he has experienced, but he preceded me.'" So these are two stages of development.

1 Reported by al-Bukhāri (4935) and Muslim (685). Also see [*Mishkāt al-Maṣābīḥ*] 1/425
2 Surat al-Baqarah – Verse 144

ثانياً: التدرج في تشريع الحكم الواحد:

لم يكن التدرج في التشريع قصراً على جملة الأحكام، بل تدرج أيضاً في تشريع الحكم الواحد، فالصلاة- مثلاً- فرضت ركعتين أولاً، ثم لما هاجر الرسول ﷺ فرضت أربعاً، روى البخاري ومسلم عن عائشة قالت: «**فرضت الصلاة ركعتين، ثم هاجر رسول الله ﷺ ففرضت أربعاً، وتركت صلاة السفر على الفريضة الأولى**»[١].

وروى أحمد في مسنده[٢] عن معاذ بن جبل قال: «أحيلت الصلاة ثلاثة أحوال، وأحيل الصيام ثلاثة أحوال، فأما أحوال الصلاة فإن النبي ﷺ قدم المدينة وهو يصلي سبعة عشر شهراً إلى بيت المقدس، ثم إن الله- عز وجل- أنزل عليه: ﴿**قَدْ نَرَى تَقَلُّبَ وَجْهِكَ فِي السَّمَاءِ فَلَنُوَلِّيَنَّكَ قِبْلَةً تَرْضَاهَا**﴾[٣]، فوجهه الله إلى مكة، هذا حول.

قال: وكانوا يجتمعون للصلاة، ويُؤْذِن بها بعضهم بعضاً، حتى نَقَسُوا، أو كادوا ينقسون[٤]، ثم إن رجلاً من الأنصار يقال له عبد الله بن زيد بن عبد ربّه أتى رسول الله ﷺ فقال: يا رسول الله، إني رأيت فيما يرى النائم، ولو قلت: إني لم أكن نائماً لصدقت، إني بينما أنا بين النائم واليقظان إذ رأيت شخصاً عليه ثوبان أخضران، فاستقبل القبلة، فقال: الله أكبر، أشهد أن لا إله إلا الله، مثنى مثنى، حتى فرغ من الأذان، ثم أمهل ساعة، ثم قال مثل الذي قال، غير أنه يزيد في ذلك: قد قامت الصلاة، مرتين، قال رسول الله ﷺ: «**علمها بلالاً، فليؤذن بها**»، فكان بلال أول من أذن بها، قال: وجاء عمر بن الخطاب رضي الله عنه فقال: يا رسول الله، قد طاف بي مثل الذي أطاف به، غير أنه سبقني، فهذان حولان.

١ أخرجه البخاري (٤٩٣٥)، ومسلم (٦٨٥)، وانظر مشكاة المصابيح: ١/٤٢٥.
٢ مسند الإمام أحمد: ٣٦/٤٣٦-٤٣٩ (٢٢١٢٤)، وفيه تمام تخريجه وتنقيده.
٣ البقرة: ١٤٤.
٤ أي: كادوا يضربون بالناقوس.

He (the narrator) then said: “At times, they would arrive to prayer after the Prophet (peace and blessings be upon him) had already performed a portion of it. A late comer would then ask the earlier ones how many *rak`āt* he missed, and would make them up, then enter the prayer with the other people.” He (the narrator) continued: “Then, Mu`ādh came and said: ‘If I come late to prayer, I will follow him in the very state that he is in, then I will make up the missed parts of prayer when he (the *Imām*, i.e. the Prophet ﷺ) finishes.’ Then, one day he (Mu`ādh) came late to prayer to find the Prophet had already started and finished performing a portion of it, so he just followed the Prophet ﷺ. When the Messenger of Allah ﷺ finished his prayer, Mu`ādh rose and made up the part of prayer he had missed. The Messenger of Allah ﷺ then said: **‘What Mu`ādh has done has become a *Sunnah* (established practice) for you, so follow its procedure.’”** These were the three stages.

As for the stages of fasting, when the Messenger of Allah ﷺ came to Madinah, he used to observe fast on three days from each month and on the Day of `Āshurā` (10th of Muharram). Then, Allah prescribed fasting and sent down His saying, **“ O you who have believed, decreed upon you is fasting as it was decreed upon those before you that you may become righteous - [fasting for] a limited number of days. And upon those who are able [to fast, but with hardship] - a ransom [as substitute] of feeding a poor person [each day]...”**[1] So, it was optional either to fast or feed needy people instead. Then, Allah the Almighty revealed the other verse: **“The month of Ramadan [is that] in which was revealed the Qur’an, a guidance for the people and clear proofs of guidance and criterion. So whoever sights [the new moon of] the month, let him fast it...”**[2] With that, Allah obligated the resident with no health issues to fast and exempted the ill and the traveler. The verse further explained that one who cannot fast due to old age can feed needy people in ransom. These were the two stages (of fasting).

1 Surat al-Baqarah – Verses 183-184
2 Surat al-Baqarah – Verse 185

قال: وكانوا يأتون الصلاة وقد سبقهم النبي ﷺ ببعضها، فكان الرجل يشير إلى الرجل إذا جاء: كم صلى؟ فيقول: واحدة أو اثنتين، فيصليهما، ثم يدخل مع القوم في صلاتهم، قال: فجاء معاذ، فقال: لا أجده على حال أبداً إلا كنت عليها، ثم قضيت ما سبقني، قال: فجاء وقد سبقه النبي ببعضها، قال: فثبت معه، فلما قضى رسول الله ﷺ صلاته، قام فقضى، فقال رسول الله ﷺ: «**قد سن لكم معاذ هكذا فاصنعوا**»، فهذه ثلاثة أحوال.

وأما أحوال الصيام فإن رسول الله ﷺ قدم المدينة فجعل يصوم من كل شهر ثلاثة أيام، وصام يوم عاشوراء، ثم إن الله فرض عليه الصيام، وأنزل الله تعالى: ﴿**يَا أَيُّهَا الَّذِينَ آمَنُوا كُتِبَ عَلَيْكُمُ الصِّيَامُ كَمَا كُتِبَ عَلَى الَّذِينَ مِن قَبْلِكُمْ**﴾(١)، إلى قوله: ﴿**وَعَلَى الَّذِينَ يُطِيقُونَهُ فِدْيَةٌ طَعَامُ مِسْكِينٍ**﴾(٢)، فكان من شاء صام، ومن شاء أطعم مسكيناً، فأجزأ ذلك عنه، ثم إن الله- عز وجل- أنزل الآية الأخرى: ﴿**شَهْرُ رَمَضَانَ الَّذِي أُنزِلَ فِيهِ الْقُرْآنُ هُدًى لِّلنَّاسِ وَبَيِّنَاتٍ مِّنَ الْهُدَى وَالْفُرْقَانِ فَمَن شَهِدَ مِنكُمُ الشَّهْرَ فَلْيَصُمْهُ**﴾(٣)، فأثبت الله صيامه على المقيم الصحيح، ورخص فيه للمريض والمسافر، وثبت الإطعام للكبير الذي لا يستطيع الصيام، فهذان حولان.

١ البقرة: ١٨٣.
٢ البقرة: ١٨٤.
٣ البقرة: ١٨٥.

He (the narrator) said: "They were allowed to eat and drink and have intercourse with their wives, so long as they did not sleep (at night). Once they slept (at night), they were no longer allowed to do so. Then, a man from the Anṣār, by the name of Ṣirmah, kept working all day until the night came upon him. When he went home, he prayed the Ishā` (night prayer) then went to bed. He didn't eat or drink until the morning and continued fasting the next day. The Messenger of Allah ﷺ saw him in extreme fatigue and asked him what the matter was, and so he told the Prophet ﷺ what had happened."

He (the narrator) said: "`Umar once had intercourse with his wife after he woke up (at night in Ramadan). He then went and told that to the Prophet ﷺ. In response, Allah sent down this verse: **"It has been made permissible for you the night preceding fasting to go to your wives [for sexual relations]. They are clothing for you and you are clothing for them. Allah knows that you used to deceive yourselves, so He accepted your repentance and forgave you. So now, have relations with them and seek that which Allah has decreed for you. And eat and drink until the white thread of dawn becomes distinct to you from the black thread [of night]. Then complete (literally: perfect) the fast until the sunset..."**[1] [2]

After stating this hadith, Ibn Kathīr said: "It was compiled by Abū Dāwūd in his [Sunan] and al-Ḥākim in his [*Mustadrak*], from the hadith of al-Mas`ūdī. He then said, "Al-Bukhāri and Muslim reported, from the hadith narrated by az-Zuhri, on the authority of `Urwah, from `Ā`ishah, who said: "Fast used to be observed on (the Day of) `Āshurā`, but when (fasting in) Ramadan was enjoined, it became optional to fast on that day." Al-Bukhāri narrated similar hadith(s) on the authority of Ibn 'Umar[3] and Ibn Mas'ūd[4].

1 Surat al-Baqarah – Verse 187
2 [*Sunan Abū Dāwūd*]: 506-507, [*Mustadrak al-Hākim*]: 2/274. It is also recorded in the [*Musnad*] of al-Imām Aḥmad: 36/436-439 (22124), and this wording is his. The complete takhrīj (referencing) and analysis of this hadith is found in it.
3 Ibn `Umar`s hadith is in [*Ṣaḥīḥ al-Bukhāri*] (4501) and so is the hadith of Ibn Mas`ūd (4503)
4 This was stated in [Tafsīr Ibn Kathīr]: 1/377 under the commentary on Allah`s saying, **"O you who have believed, decreed upon you is fasting..."** (Surat al-Baqarah – Verse 183)

قال: وكانوا يأكلون ويشربون، ويأتون النساء ما لم يناموا، فإذا ناموا امتنعوا، ثم إن رجلاً من الأنصار يقال له صِرْمة، ظل يعمل صائماً حتى أمسى، فجاء إلى أهله، فصلى العشاء، ثم نام، فلم يأكل ولم يشرب حتى أصبح، فأصبح صائماً، فرآه رسول الله ﷺ وقد جهد جهداً شديداً، فقال: «**ما لي أراك قد جهدت جهداً شديداً؟**» قال: يا رسول الله، إني عملت أمس، فجئت حين جئت، فألقيت نفسي فنمت، فأصبحت حين أصبحت صائماً.

قال: وكان عمر قد أصاب من النساء بعدما نام، فأتى النبي ﷺ فذكر له ذلك، فأنزل الله عز وجل: ﴿**أُحِلَّ لَكُمْ لَيْلَةَ الصِّيَامِ الرَّفَثُ إِلَى نِسَائِكُمْ هُنَّ لِبَاسٌ لَّكُمْ وَأَنْتُمْ لِبَاسٌ لَّهُنَّ عَلِمَ اللهُ أَنَّكُمْ كُنْتُمْ تَخْتَانُونَ أَنْفُسَكُمْ فَتَابَ عَلَيْكُمْ وَعَفَا عَنْكُمْ فَالآنَ بَاشِرُوهُنَّ وَابْتَغُوا مَا كَتَبَ اللهُ لَكُمْ وَكُلُوا وَاشْرَبُوا حَتَّى يَتَبَيَّنَ لَكُمُ الْخَيْطُ الأَبْيَضُ مِنَ الْخَيْطِ الأَسْوَدِ مِنَ الْفَجْرِ ثُمَّ أَتِمُّوا الصِّيَامَ إِلَى اللَّيْلِ**﴾(١)(٢)

قال ابن كثير بعد أن ساق هذا الحديث: وأخرجه أبو داود في سننه، والحاكم في مستدركه من حديث المسعودي به. ثم قال: «وقد أخرج البخاري ومسلم من حديث الزهري عن عروة عن عائشة أنها قالت: كان عاشوراء يصام، فلما نزل فرض رمضان، كان من شاء صام، ومن شاء أفطر»(٣)، وروى البخاري عن ابن عمر وابن مسعود(٤) مثله(٥).

١ البقرة: ١٨٧.
٢ سنن أبي داود: ٥٠٦-٥٠٧، ومستدرك الحاكم: ٢/ ٢٧٤، وهو في «مسند الإمام أحمد»: ٣٦/٤٣٦-٤٣٩ (٢٢١٢٤)، واللفظ له، وفيه تمام تخريجه وتنقيده.
٣ البخاري (٤٥٠٢)، ومسلم (١١٢٥).
٤ حديث ابن عمر في «صحيح البخاري»، (٤٥٠١)، وحديث ابن مسعود فيه أيضاً (٤٥٠٣).
٥ تفسير ابن كثير: ١/ ٣٧٧ ساقه عند تفسير قوله تعالى: ﴿يَا أَيُّهَا

The Gradual Prohibition of Khamr:

The Arabs were very fond of drinking *Khamr* (alcohol); they used to pride themselves in drinking it and serving it to their guests. One of their poets said:

When we drink it, it transforms us into kings,
And into lions who never fear confrontation.

When a nation falls so deeply in error that it turns a vice into a virtue, and an illness into a cure, its treatment becomes extremely difficult. Treatment is far easier when the offender admits his guilt and acknowledges the evil of what he is doing. For that reason, the Qur'an followed a unique approach in prohibiting *Khamr*.

In the beginning, it indirectly hinted to the evil of *Khamr* in Allah's saying, **"And from the fruits of the palm trees and grapevines you take intoxicant and good provision..."**[1] In this verse, Allah reminds his servants of His favors on them of the fruits from which they make intoxicants and good provision, which meant that intoxicants differ from good provision. Later, Allah revealed, **"They ask you about wine and gambling. Say, 'In them is great sin and [yet, some] benefit for people. But their sin is greater than their benefit...'"**[2] This verse changed the believers` attitude, who thought that drinking *Khamr* was a virtue. This was the most important aspect in treating their psychological attitude. Thereafter, the Muslims knew that drinking alcohol was not a merit and that the harms it brought outweighed its benefits. As a result, some Muslims gave up its consumption, while others kept drinking it. Then, Allah prohibited it at certain times until Muslims got used to giving it up partially: **"O you who have believed, do not approach prayer while you are intoxicated until you know what you are saying..."**[3] Upon that, they abstained from it at the times between prayers,

1 Surat an-Naḥl – Verse 67
2 Surat al-Baqarah – Verse 219
3 Surat an-Nisā' – Verse 43

التدرج في تحريم الخمر:

كان للعرب في شرب الخمر غرام شديد، يمدحون أنفسهم بشربها وتقديمها للضيوف، كما قال شاعرهم:

ونشربها فتتركنا ملوكاً أسداً لا ينهنها اللقاء

وعندما يصل الحال بأمّة أن تعدَّ الرذيلة فضيلة، والداء دواء فعند ذلك يصعب العلاج، ويكون العلاج أيسر بكثير عندما يكون مرتكب الجرم معتقداً بأنه جرم وفساد؛ ولذلك سلك القرآن في تحريم الخمر مسلكاً فذاً.

ففي البداية أشار إشارة خفية إلى ذم الخمر في قوله تعالى: ﴿وَمِن ثَمَرَاتِ النَّخِيلِ وَالأَعْنَابِ تَتَّخِذُونَ مِنْهُ سَكَراً وَرِزْقاً حَسَناً﴾(١)، فقد امتن الله على عباده بما أعطاهم إياه من تلك الثمرات التي يتخذون منها سَكَراً ورزقاً حسناً، فعد السكر غير الرزق الحسن، ثم أنزل الله قوله تعالى: ﴿يَسْأَلُونَكَ عَنِ الْخَمْرِ وَالْمَيْسِرِ قُلْ فِيهِمَا إِثْمٌ كَبِيرٌ وَمَنَافِعُ لِلنَّاسِ وَإِثْمُهُمَا أَكْبَرُ مِن نَّفْعِهِمَا﴾(٢).

وهذه الآية غيرت نفوس المؤمنين الذين كانوا يظنون أن شرب الخمر فضيلة، وهذا أهم جانب في علاج النفوس، فاعتقد المسلمون بعد ذلك أن تعاطي الخمر ليس فضيلة، وأن المضار التي تحويها الخمر أكثر من المنافع، وامتنع بعض المسلمين عن تعاطيها، واستمر آخرون في تناولها، ثم حرمها الإسلام في بعض الأوقات حتى يعتاد المدمنون تركها جزئياً: ﴿يَا أَيُّهَا الَّذِينَ آمَنُوا لاَ تَقْرَبُوا

الَّذِينَ آمَنُوا كُتِبَ عَلَيْكُمُ الصِّيَامُ﴾ [البقرة: ١٨٣].
١ النحل: ٦٨.
٢ البقرة: ٢١٩.

because otherwise they would not become sober in time for the next prayer. Then, Allah explicated prohibited it indefinitely, using an unequivocal injunction: **"O you who have believed, indeed, intoxicants, gambling, [sacrificing on] stone alters [to other than Allah], and divining arrows are but defilement from the work of Shaytān (Satan), so avoid it that you may be successful. Shaytān only wants to cause between you animosity and hatred through intoxicants and gambling and to avert you from the remembrance of Allah and from prayer. So will you not desist?"**[1]

Third: Legislation for an Occasion and for No Occasion:

The wisdom of the Qur'an being revealed in parts was to treat the problems that arose in the Prophet's era, and to answer the questions directed to the Messenger of Allah ﷺ.

Hence, some of the legislative verses were initially revealed without occasion, and not for the purpose of answering a question. This is demonstrated in Allah's saying, **"O you who have believed, decreed upon you is fasting as it was decreed upon those before you that you may become righteous - [fasting for] a limited number of days. So whoever among you is ill or on a journey [during them] - then an equal number of days [are to be made up]. And upon those who are able [to fast, but with hardship] - a ransom [as substitute] of feeding a poor person [each day]."**[2] **"Take, [O, Muhammad], from their wealth a charity by which you purify them and cause them increase, and invoke [Allah's blessings] upon them."**[3] Other similar examples are many, such as the verse that explains the channels of distributing *Zakāh* and enjoining Hajj.

1 Surat al-Mā`idah – Verse 90-91
2 Surat al-Baqarah – Verses 183-184
3 Surat at-Tawbah – Verse 103

الصَّلَاةَ وَأَنْتُمْ سُكَارَى﴾[١]، فامتنعوا عن شربها في الأوقات التي لا يفيق شاربها من سكره قبل وقت الصلاة التالية، ثم حرمها تحريماً قاطعاً لا شبهة فيه: **﴿يَا أَيُّهَا الَّذِينَ آمَنُوا إِنَّمَا الْخَمْرُ وَالْمَيْسِرُ وَالأَنصَابُ وَالأَزْلَامُ رِجْسٌ مِّنْ عَمَلِ الشَّيْطَانِ فَاجْتَنِبُوهُ لَعَلَّكُمْ تُفْلِحُونَ ۞ إِنَّمَا يُرِيدُ الشَّيْطَانُ أَن يُوقِعَ بَيْنَكُمُ الْعَدَاوَةَ وَالْبَغْضَاءَ فِي الْخَمْرِ وَالْمَيْسِرِ وَيَصُدَّكُمْ عَن ذِكْرِ اللهِ وَعَنِ الصَّلَاةِ فَهَلْ أَنْتُم مُّنتَهُونَ﴾**[٢].

ثالثاً: التشريع لمناسبة ولغير مناسبة:

من حكمة نزول القرآن مفرقاً، أنه كان يعالج المشكلات التي تقع في العهد النبوي، ويجيب على بعض الأسئلة التي توجه إلى الرسول ﷺ.

وعلى ذلك فإن بعض الآيات التشريعية أنزلت ابتداء من غير أن يكون حكماً لواقعة، ولا جواباً لسؤال، كقوله تعالى: **﴿يَا أَيُّهَا الَّذِينَ آمَنُوا إِذَا قُمْتُمْ إِلَى الصَّلَاةِ فَاغْسِلُوا وُجُوهَكُمْ وَأَيْدِيَكُمْ إِلَى الْمَرَافِقِ وَامْسَحُوا بِرُؤُوسِكُمْ وَأَرْجُلَكُمْ إِلَى الْكَعْبَينِ﴾**[٣]، وقوله: **﴿يَا أَيُّهَا الَّذِينَ آمَنُوا كُتِبَ عَلَيْكُمُ الصِّيَامُ كَمَا كُتِبَ عَلَى الَّذِينَ مِن قَبْلِكُمْ لَعَلَّكُمْ تَتَّقُونَ ۞ أَيَّاماً مَّعْدُودَاتٍ فَمَن كَانَ مِنكُم مَّرِيضاً أَوْ عَلَى سَفَرٍ فَعِدَّةٌ مِّنْ أَيَّامٍ أُخَرَ وَعَلَى الَّذِينَ يُطِيقُونَهُ فِدْيَةٌ طَعَامُ مِسْكِينٍ﴾**[٤]، وقوله: **﴿خُذْ مِنْ أَمْوَالِهِمْ صَدَقَةً تُطَهِّرُهُمْ وَتُزَكِّيهِم بِهَا﴾**[٥]، ومثل ذلك كثير من الآيات التي بينت مصارف الزكاة، وشرعت الحج.

١ النساء: ٤٣.
٢ المائدة: ٩٠-٩١.
٣ المائدة: ٦.
٤ البقرة: ١٨٣-١٨٤.
٥ التوبة: ١٠٣.

Of the legislative texts that followed this pattern is Allah's saying, **"Whoever comes to you while you are united and he wants to divide you or disunite your community, kill him."** (Reported by Aḥmad and Muslim).[1]

There is another group of rulings which is occasion-sensitive and was given in response to questions, such as Allah's saying, **"And they ask you about menstruation. Say, 'It is harm, so keep away from wives during menstruation.'"**[2] **"They ask you about the sacred month - about fighting therein. Say, 'Fighting therein is great [sin], but averting [people] from the way of Allah and disbelief in Him and [preventing access to] al-Masjid al-Haram and the expulsion of its people therefrom are greater [evil] in the sight of Allah. And trials are greater than killing.'"**[3]

When the Messenger of Allah ﷺ was asked about making *Wuḍū`* (ablution) with seawater, he answered: "Its water is pure and its dead (marine) creatures are lawful (to eat)."[4] When he ﷺ was asked about the possibility of using water in a faraway place from which beasts of prey and beasts of burden drink, he said, "If the water reaches [an amount of] two *Qullah*(s) (sing. *Qullah,* measure which is not definitely decided, however it denotes a big amount), it would not carry filth." (Reported by the Five Compilers)[5]

1 Reported by Muslim (1852), (60) and Aḥmad similar to it: 30/227 (18295)
2 Surat al-Baqarah – Verse 222
3 Surat al-Baqarah – Verse 217
4 Reported by Abū Dāwūd (83), Ibn Mājah (386), (3246) and at-Tirmidhi (69), who said it is a *ḥasan ṣaḥīḥ* (good authentic) hadith. It was also collected by an-Nasā`i (332) and (4350)
5 Reported by Aḥmad: 8/211 (4605), Abū Dāwūd (63), Ibn Mājah (517) and (518), at-Tirmidhi (67) and an-Nasā`i (52).

ومن النصوص التشريعية النبوية التي جاءت على هذا النحو قوله ﷺ: «**من أتاكم وأمركم جميع على رجل واحد، يريد أن يشق عصاكم، أو يفرق جماعتكم، فاقتلوه**» رواه أحمد ومسلم(١).

ويوجد قسم آخر من الأحكام شرع في مناسبة تستدعيه، فمن ذلك الأحكام التي وردت في إجابة سؤال كقوله تعالى: ﴿**وَيَسْأَلُونَكَ عَنِ الْمَحِيضِ قُلْ هُوَ أَذًى فَاعْتَزِلُوا النِّسَاءَ فِي الْمَحِيضِ**﴾(٢)، وقوله: ﴿**يَسْأَلُونَكَ عَنِ الشَّهْرِ الْحَرَامِ قِتَالٍ فِيهِ قُلْ قِتَالٌ فِيهِ كَبِيرٌ وَصَدٌّ عَن سَبِيلِ اللهِ وَكُفْرٌ بِهِ وَالْمَسْجِدِ الْحَرَامِ وَإِخْرَاجُ أَهْلِهِ مِنْهُ أَكْبَرُ عِنْدَ اللهِ وَالْفِتْنَةُ أَكْبَرُ مِنَ الْقَتْلِ**﴾(٣)، وسئل رسول الله ﷺ عن الوضوء بماء البحر، فقال: «**هو الطهور ماؤه الحل ميتته**»(٤)، وسئل ﷺ عن الماء الذي يكون بالفلاة من الأرض وما ينوبه من السباع والدواب، فقال: «**إذا بلغ الماء قلتين لم يحمل الخبث**» رواه الخمسة(٥).

١ أخرجه مسلم (١٨٥٢)، (٦٠)، وأحمد بنحوه: ٣٠/ ٢٢٧ (١٨٢٩٥).
٢ البقرة: ٢٢٢.
٣ البقرة: ٢١٦.
٤ أخرجه أبو داود (٨٣)، وابن ماجه (٣٨٦) و(٣٢٤٦)، والترمذي (٦٩)، وقال فيه: حسن صحيح، والنسائي (٣٣٢) و (٤٣٥٠).
٥ أخرجه أحمد: ٨/ ٢١١ (٤٦٠٥)، وأبو داود (٦٣)، وابن ماجه (٥١٧) و(٥١٨) والترمذي (٦٧)، والنسائي (٥٢).

This also includes the explanations given by the Qur'an, or the Messenger of Allah ﷺ, on incidents that had already occurred such as in the incident of *Ẓihār* in relation to Aws Ibn aṣ-Ṣāmit and his wife Khawlah bint Tha`labah, and her coming to the Messenger of Allah ﷺ and arguing with him; Allah therefore revealed His saying, **"Certainly has Allah heard the speech of the one who argues with you, [O Muhammad], concerning her husband and directs her complaint to Allah. And Allah hears your dialogue; indeed, Allah is Hearing and Seeing. Those who pronounce ẓihār (this is a pre-Islamic form of divorce in which the husband says to the wife, "Be as my mother's back.") among you [to separate] from their wives - they are not [consequently] their mothers. Their mothers are none but those who gave birth to them..."**[1]

The Prophet's *Sunnah* and its Sciences

I – The Definition of *Sunnah*

In its capacity as a source of legislation, it is defined as the statements, actions, and tacit approvals of the Messenger of Allah ﷺ.

The verbal *Sunnah* is represented in his saying, **"No two *witr* prayers are to be performed in one night."** (Reported by the Five Compilers, except Ibn Mājah)[2]

The practical *Sunnah* is exemplified in `Ā`ishah`s narration: "The Messenger ﷺ used to go to sleep. If he woke up, he would use *siwāk* (tooth stick), then make *Wuḍū`* (ablution), then offer eight *rak`āt* at the end of which he would sit [for *tashahhud*], and then make *Taslīm*. He would then offer the *witr* prayer in five *rak`āt* but would not sit (for *tashahhud*) or make Taslīm except in the fifth [*rak`ah*]."[3]

1 Surat al-Mujādalah – Verses 1-2
2 Ahmad: 26/222 (16296), Abū Dāwūd (1439), at-Tirmidhi (470) and an-Nasā`i (1679)
3 Reported by Ahmad: 41/402 (24921). Its *isnād* (transmission chain) is sound according to the criteria of the two shaykh(s) (i.e., al-Bukhāri and Muslim).

ومن هذا بيان الوقائع التي كانت تجد في ذلك العصر فينزل الوحي، أو يقول الرسول ﷺ القول بياناً لحكم تلك الوقائع، فمن ذلك مظاهرة أوس بن الصامت من زوجته خولة بنت ثعلبة ومجيئها إلى رسول الرسول ﷺ ومجادلتها له في هذا، فأنزل الله قوله جل وعلا: **﴿قَدْ سَمِعَ اللَّهُ قَوْلَ الَّتِي تُجَادِلُكَ فِي زَوْجِهَا وَتَشْتَكِي إِلَى اللَّهِ وَاللَّهُ يَسْمَعُ تَحَاوُرَكُمَا إِنَّ اللَّهَ سَمِيعٌ بَصِيرٌ ۞ الَّذِينَ يُظَاهِرُونَ مِنكُم مِّن نِّسَائِهِم مَّا هُنَّ أُمَّهَاتِهِمْ إِنْ أُمَّهَاتُهُمْ إِلَّا اللَّائِي وَلَدْنَهُمْ﴾**[١].

السنة النبوية وعلومها

أولاً: تعريف السنة:

السنة باعتبارها مصدراً تشريعيّاً هي: أقوال الرسول ﷺ وأفعاله وتقريراته.

فالقولية مثل قوله ﷺ: «**لا وتران في ليلة**»، رواه الخمسة إلا ابن ماجه[٢]

والسنة الفعلية مثل ما روته عائشة «**أن الرسول ﷺ كان يرقد فإذا استيقظ تسوك، ثم توضأ، ثم صلى ثماني ركعات يجلس في كل ركعتين ويسلم، ثم يوتر بخمس ركعات، ولا يجلس ولا يسلم إلا في الخامسة**»[٣].

١ المجادلة: ١-٢.
٢ أحمد: ٢٦/ ٢٢٢ (١٦٢٩٦)، وأبو داود (١٤٣٩)، والترمذي (٤٧٠)، والنسائي (١٦٧٩).
٣ أخرجه أحمد: ٤١/ ٤٠٢ (٢٤٩٢١) وإسناده صحيح على شرط الشيخين.

The tacit approval *Sunnah* can be represented in the hadith narrated by Abū Sa`īd al-Khudri and Jābir Ibn `Abdillāh, who said: "We traveled with the Messenger of Allah (may saws). The observer of the fast observed it, and the breaker of the fast broke it, but none of them found fault with one another."[1]

II – The Status of the *Sunnah* in Relation to the Qur'an[2]

The status of the authentic and confirmed *Sunnah* in relation to the Qur'an has many manifestations:

First: the *Sunnah* confirms the rulings brought by the Qur'an, such as the command to establish prayer, give *Zakāh*, observe *Tawḥīd*, and the forbiddance of committing *shirk*.

Second: the *Sunnah* introduces rulings that are inexplicitly referred to in the Book of Allah, such as the Prophet's forbiddance to eat the domesticated donkeys, or any animal of prey with a canine or a bird of prey with talons. The origin of this forbiddance is alluded to by Allah's saying, **"...and makes lawful for them the good things and prohibits for them the evil..."**[3] The Prophet ﷺ informed us that these types of meats fall under the prohibited `wicked things` and not of the good things.

Third: the *Sunnah* brings independent rulings which are not found in the Book of Allah, such as the Prophet's forbidding men to combine a woman and her maternal or paternal aunt in marriage.

Fourth: the *Sunnah* details what was mentioned in the Book of Allah in brief, ambiguous, general, or absolute terms. Thus, it elaborates what is outlined, clarifies what is ambiguous, specifies what is general, and restricts what is absolute. In this regard, the Lord of Might said, **"...And We revealed to you (the Prophet) the message that you may make clear to the people what was sent down to them..."**[4]

1 Reported by Muslim: 2/787, its number is (1117)
2 Refer to [ar-Risālah]: 91, [al-Muwāfaqāt]: 3/243, and [Irshād al-Fuḥūl] by ash-Shawkānī: 33.
3 Surat al-A`rāf – Verse 157
4 Surat an-Naḥl – Verse 44

ومثال السنة التقريرية، ما رواه أبو سعيد الخدري وجابر بن عبد الله قالا: «سافرنا مع رسول الله ﷺ، فيصوم الصائم، ويفطر المفطر، فلا يعيب بعضهم على بعض»(١).

ثانياً: منزلة السنة من القرآن(٢):

مقام السنة الصحيحة الثابتة عن الرسول ﷺ من القرآن على وجوه:

الأول: تقرير السنة للأحكام التي جاء بها القرآن؛ كالأمر بالصلاة والزكاة والصيام، والأمر بالتوحيد، والنهي عن الشرك، فهذه موافقة لكتاب الله، مقررة له.

الثاني: أن تأتي السنة بأحكام لها أصل في الكتاب؛ كنهي الرسول ﷺ عن أكل لحوم الحمر الأهلية، ونهيه عن أكل كل ذي ناب من السباع، وكل ذي مخلب من الطير، وأصل هذا التحريم راجع إلى قوله تعالى: ﴿**وَيُحِلُّ لَهُمُ الطَّيِّبَاتِ وَيُحَرِّمُ عَلَيْهِمُ الْخَبَائِثَ**﴾(٣)، فقد أعلمنا رسولنا ﷺ أن الحمر الأهلية وذوات الأنياب من السباع، والمخلب من الطير من الخبائث المحرمة، وليست من الطيبات.

الثالث: ذكر أحكام استقلت السنة ببيان حكمها، لم ترد في كتاب الله، مثل تحريم الرسول ﷺ الجمع بين المرأة وعمتها، والمرأة وخالتها في النكاح.

الرابع: بيان ما جاء في كتاب الله مجملاً أو مبهماً أو عامّاً أو مطلقاً، فتبين السنة المجمل، وتوضح المبهم، وتخصص العام، وتقيد المطلق، وفي ذلك يقول رب العزة: ﴿**وَأَنْزَلْنَا إِلَيْكَ الذِّكْرَ لِتُبَيِّنَ لِلنَّاسِ مَا نُزِّلَ إِلَيْهِمْ**﴾(٤).

١ رواه مسلم: ٢/ ٧٨٧، ورقمه (١١١٧).
٢ راجع في هذا الموضوع: الرسالة: ٩١، الموافقات: ٣/ ٢٤٣، وإرشاد الفحول للشوكاني: ٣٣.
٣ الأعراف: ١٥٧.
٤ النحل: ٤٤.

The command to establish prayer was given as absolute and general in **"And establish prayer..."**[1] The Prophet ﷺ elaborated on the number of prayers, the number of *rak`āt* in each prayer, its times, how to perform it, what is permissible in it, what is not, etc.

وقد جاء الأمر بالصلاة أمراً مطلقاً عامّاً ﴿وَأَقِيمُوا الصَّلَاةَ﴾(١)، فبين الرسول أعداد الصلوات، وعدد ركعات كل صلاة، وأوقاتها، وكيفياتها، وما يباح وما لا يباح فيها.

The Qur'an gave the order to pay *Zakāh* **"...and give zakāh..."**[2] but the Messenger of Allah ﷺ defined its amounts and conditions.

وأمر القرآن بالزكاة: ﴿وَآتُوا الزَّكَاةَ﴾(٢)، فبين الرسول ﷺ مقاديرها وشروطها.

The Qur'an ordered that the hand of a thief should be cut off, **"[As for] the thief, the male and the female, amputate their hands..."**[3] Then the Messenger of Allah ﷺ specified the spot of cutting in the hand and the amount of stolen money required to execute this penalty.

وأمر القرآن بقطع يد السارق: ﴿وَالسَّارِقُ وَالسَّارِقَةُ فَاقْطَعُوا أَيْدِيَهُمَا﴾(٣)، فبين الرسول مكان القطع، ومقدار المال الذي يجب فيه القطع.

The Prophet's clarification of the Qur'an includes his explanation of some Qur`anic texts which were ambiguous or difficult to understand. Some of the Companions, for example, could not understand the meaning of the word *"ẓulm"* (injustice) in Allah's saying, **"They who believe and do not mix their belief with injustice - those will have security, and they are [rightly] guided."**[4] The Messenger of Allah ﷺ then explained to them that the intended meaning of the word *"ẓulm"*, in this particular context, was *shirk* (associating others with Allah in worship) as deduced from Allah's saying, **"Indeed, association [with Allah] is great injustice."**[5]

ومن بيان الرسول ﷺ للقرآن توضيح المشكل أو الغامض منه على سامعه، فقد أشكل على الصحابة فقه الظلم الوارد في قوله تعالى: ﴿الَّذِينَ آمَنُوا وَلَمْ يَلْبِسُوا إِيمَانَهُمْ بِظُلْمٍ أُولَئِكَ لَهُمُ الْأَمْنُ وَهُمْ مُهْتَدُونَ﴾(٤)، فدلهم الرسول ﷺ على المعنى المراد، وأنه الشرك بدلالة قوله تعالى: ﴿إِنَّ الشِّرْكَ لَظُلْمٌ عَظِيمٌ﴾(٥).

1 Surat al-Baqarah – Verse 43
2 Surat al-Baqarah – Verse 43
3 Surat al-Mā`idah – Verse 38
4 Surat al-An`ām – Verse 82
5 Surat Luqmān – Verse 13

١ البقرة: ٤٣.
٢ البقرة: ٤٣.
٣ المائدة: ٣٨.
٤ الأنعام: ٨٢.
٥ لقمان: ١٣.

III – The Prophet's *Ijtihād* (Exercise of Discretion)

We have already mentioned that the sources of legislation in the Prophet's era were the Book of Allah and the *Sunnah* of His Messenger ﷺ. Now the question is: was the Messenger of Allah ﷺ warranted to give discretionary judgments on that which he received no revelation? The answer is that the entire *Ummah* is in agreement that it was permissible for our Prophet, as well as for all other Prophets (peace be upon them), to practice *Ijtihād* in the matters related to the worldly interests, strategies of wars, etc. This agreement was reported by Ibn Ḥazm and others. Our Prophet ﷺ exercised this *Ijtihād*. For example, he wanted to make peace with the Ghaṭafān tribe in return for giving them one-third of Madinah's yield of fruits and crops. In other instances, he advised the Companions not to pollinate the date palm-trees.

The scholars, however, differed over the prophet's exercise of *Ijtihād* (opinions based on discretion) with regard to legal judgments and religious affairs. The opponents of this view cited, in support, Allah's saying, **"Nor does he speak from [his own] inclination. It is not but a revelation revealed..."**[1]

They further argued that whenever the Messenger of Allah ﷺ was asked a question, he would wait for revelation to give the answer. This happened when a man came to the Prophet ﷺ daubed in perfume and making Ihram for '*Umrah* in a jubbah. He asked the Messenger of Allah ﷺ for the judgment of his *Ihram,* but the Messenger of Allah ﷺ looked at him for a while and gave him no answer. Then, the Messenger of Allah ﷺ received a revelation in which he was relieved and asked the people to fetch the questioner. When he came, the Messenger of Allah ﷺ informed him about the judgment according to the revelation he had received saying, **"As far as the perfume is concerned, wash it three times, and remove the jubbah too (as it was sewn), and do in *`Umrah* as you do in Ḥajj."** (Agreed Upon)[2]

1 Surat an-Najm – Verses 3-4
2 Reported by al-Bukhāri (1536) and Muslim (1180)

ثالثاً: اجتهاد الرسول ﷺ:

قلنا: إن مصادر التشريع في هذا العصر كتاب الله وسنة رسوله ﷺ؛ فهل يصدر عن الرسول ﷺ أحكام اجتهادية لم يُوحَ بها إليه؟ أجمعت الأمة على أنه يجوز لنبينا ولغيره من الأنبياء- عليهم الصلاة والسلام- الاجتهاد فيما يتعلق بمصالح الدنيا وتدبير الحروب ونحوها، حكى هذا الإجماع ابن حزم وغيره، وقد وقع هذا من نبينا ﷺ، فقد أراد أن يصالح غطفان على ثلث ثمار المدينة، ونصح الصحابة بترك تأبير النخل.

واختلفوا في حكم اجتهادهم ﷺ في الأحكام الشرعية والأمور الدينية، وقد استدل المانعون بقوله تعالى: **﴿وَمَا يَنطِقُ عَنِ الْهَوَى ۞ إِنْ هُوَ إِلاَّ وَحْيٌ يُوحَى﴾**[1]، واستدلوا بأن الرسول ﷺ كان إذا سئل ينتظر الوحي، كما فعل عندما جاءه رجل بعد الإحرام بالعمرة متضمخاً بطيب، مُحْرِماً في جبة، يسأل عن حكم إحرامه في حاله تلك، فنظر إليه الرسول ﷺ ولم يجبه، فجاءه الوحي، فلما سرّي عنه، التمس الرجل فجيء به، فأمره بالذي جاء به الوحي، فقال: «**أما الطيب الذي بك فاغسله ثلاث مرات، وأما الجبة فانزعها، ثم اصنع في العمرة كل ما تصنع في حجك**» متفق عليه[2].

١ النجم: ٣-٤.
٢ أخرجه البخاري (١٥٣٦)، ومسلم (١١٨٠).

This view was held by the Ẓāhiris. Whoever denied the application of *Qiyās* (analogy) rejected the application of *Ijtihād* in devotional matters. This is the view held by some Muʿtazilites, such as Abū ʿAli and Abū Hāshim.[1]

The majority of scholars held that the prophets were permitted to exercise *Ijtihād* in legal judgments and religious matters. They based their argument on the fact that Allah addressed His Prophet ﷺ in the same manner He addressed His servants, gave him examples, and ordered him to reflect and consider affairs. In fact, he was the greatest scholar in understanding the signs of Allah and the best to learn the lessons therein.

They also argued: If other members of the *Ummah* were unanimously permitted to exercise *Ijtihād*, despite the fact that they were subject to err, permitting the Prophet ﷺ, who was infallible, to exercise *Ijtihād* was probable for all the more reason.[2]

IV: The authoritativeness of the *Sunnah*[3]

The Qur'an indicated the authoritativeness of the *Sunnah* in Allah's saying, "**...And whatever the Messenger has given you - take; and what he has forbidden you - refrain from...**"[4] "**It is not for a believing man or a believing woman, when Allah and His Messenger have decided a matter, that they should [thereafter] have any choice about their affair. And whoever disobeys Allah and His Messenger has certainly strayed into clear error.**"[5] The related texts are numerous.

---

1 See: [Irshād al-Fuḥūl]: 255
2 [Irshād al-Fuḥūl]: 256, al-Bāb al-Ḥalabī ed. Egypt (1356 H./ 1937)
3 Refer to: [ar-Risālah] by ash-Shāfiʿi: 79, and [Tafsīr al-Qurṭubī]: 1/37
4 Surat al-Ḥashr – Verse 7
5 Surat al-Aḥzāb – Verse 36

وقد ذهب هذا المذهب الظاهرية، فكل من نفى القياس أحال التعبد بالاجتهاد، وهو مذهب بعض المعتزلة: أبو علي وأبو هاشم(١).

وأمر آخر ينبغي أن يلتفت إليه الباحث؛ هو أن بيان الرسول ﷺ عندما يصدر عن اجتهاد لا يصدر عن هوى؛ لأنه ﷺ إذا كان متعبداً بالاجتهاد وبالوحي لم يكن نطقاً عن الهوى، بل عن الوحي.

وكون الرسول ﷺ يسكت في بعض الأحيان عندما يسأل؛ فلأنه لم يظهر له الحكم، وذهب جمهور العلماء إلى أنه يجوز للأنبياء الاجتهاد في الأحكام الشرعية والأمور الدينية، واحتجوا على ما ذهبوا إليه بأنه سبحانه خاطب نبيه ﷺ كما خاطب عباده وضرب له الأمثال، وأمره بالتدبر والاعتبار، وهو أجل المفكرين في آيات الله، وأعظم المعتبرين.

وقالوا: إذا جاز لغيره من الأمة أن يجتهد بالإجماع مع كونه معرضاً للخطأ، فلأن يجوز لمن هو معصوم عن الخطأ بالأولى(٢).

رابعاً: حجية السنة(٣):

دل على حجية السنة القرآن في قوله تعالى: ﴿وَمَا آتَاكُمُ الرَّسُولُ فَخُذُوهُ وَمَا نَهَاكُمْ عَنْهُ فَانْتَهُوا﴾(٤)، وقوله: ﴿وَمَا كَانَ لِمُؤْمِنٍ وَلاَ مُؤْمِنَةٍ إِذَا قَضَى اللهُ وَرَسُولُهُ أَمْراً أَنْ يَكُونَ لَهُمُ الْخِيَرَةُ مِنْ أَمْرِهِمْ وَمَنْ يَعْصِ اللهَ وَرَسُولَهُ فَقَدْ ضَلَّ ضَلاَلاً مُبِيناً﴾(٥)، والنصوص في ذلك كثيرة.

---

١ انظر إرشاد الفحول: ٢٥٥.
٢ إرشاد الفحول: ٢٥٦، طبعة البابي الحلبي، مصر (١٣٥٦هـ- ١٩٣٧م).
٣ راجع: الرسالة للشافعي: ٧٩، تفسير القرطبي: ١/ ٣٧.
٤ الحشر: ٧.
٥ الأحزاب: ٣٦.

The Messenger of Allah ﷺ warned against those who reject his *Sunnah*; Abū Rāfi`, the freed slave of Allah's Messenger ﷺ, reported Allah's Messenger ﷺ as saying, **"I should not find anyone of you who is reclining on his couch and when a judgment of mine comes to him, either a command or prohibition, he says: I don't know this. I shall only follow what I find in the Book of Allah."**[1] What the Messenger of Allah ﷺ predicted has come true; a group of people appeared who call themselves the `Qur'anis' who claim that it is obligatory to apply the Qur'an to the exclusion of the *Sunnah*. They are liars; if they were really 'Qur'anic,' they would have responded to the Qur'an which commands them to apply the *Sunnah*.

The people of knowledge dismantled the wicked intentions these people hide under this claim. They only sought to play with the Book of Allah, yet when they found the *Sunnah*, which explains the Qur'an, to be a hindrance to their tampering, they aimed to demote the *Sunnah* as much as possible.

V: The Companions` Preservation of the *Sunnah* of the Messenger of Allah ﷺ:

The Messenger of Allah ﷺ used to urge his Companions to commit his *Sunnah* to memory and understand it in order to convey it to people. `Abdullāh Ibn `Amr Ibn al-`Ās (may Allah be pleased with them) said: the Messenger of Allah ﷺ said: **"Convey on my behalf, even if it is only an *ayah*, and relate traditions from the Banū Isrā`īl (Children of Israel), and there is no harm [in that], and the one who deliberately attributes a lie to me, let him reserve his seat in the Fire."**[2]

---

1 Reported by Abū Dāwūd (4605), at-Tirmidhi (2663), Ibn Mājah (13), and it was graded as *Ṣaḥīḥ* by Shaykh Aḥmad Shākir in his commentary on [ar-Risālah] by ash-Shāfi`i: 90
2 Compiled by Aḥmad: 11/25 (6486), al-Bukhāri (3461), and at-Tirmidhi (2669)

وقد حذرنا الرسول ﷺ من الذين يردون سنته، فعن أبي رافع مولى رسول الله ﷺ أن رسول الله ﷺ قال: «لا ألفين أحدكم متكئاً على أريكته يأتيه الأمر من أمري، مما أمرت به أو نهيت عنه، فيقول: لا أدري ما وجدنا في كتاب الله اتبعناه»[1].

وقد تحقق ما أخبر به الرسول ﷺ، فنشأ قوم يسمون أنفسهم بالقرآنيين، زعموا أن الواجب هو الأخذ بالقرآن دون السنة، وكذب هؤلاء، فلو كانوا قرآنيين حقَّاً، لاستجابوا للقرآن الذي يأمرهم بالأخذ بالسنة.

وقد كشف لنا أهل العلم عن المقاصد الخبيثة لهؤلاء فهم يريدون التلاعب بكتاب الله، ولكنهم وجدوا السنة بما فيها من بيان للقرآن عائقاً يحول دون مرادهم، فرأوا أنه لا بد من إبعاد السنة عن طريقهم، ليتمكنوا من تحقيق مقاصدهم.

خامساً: حفظ الصحابة سنة رسول الله ﷺ:

كان الرسول ﷺ يحث أصحابه على حفظ سنته وفهمها وتبليغها للناس، فعن عبد الله بن عمرو بن العاص- رضي الله عنهما- قال: قال رسول الله ﷺ: «بلّغوا عني ولو آية، وحدثوا عن بني إسرائيل ولا حرج، ومن كذب علي متعمدا فليتبوأ مقعده من النار»[2].

---

١ الحديث رواه أبو داود (٤٦٠٥)، والترمذي (٢٦٦٣)، وابن ماجه (١٣)، وصححه الشيخ أحمد شاكر في تعليقه على رسالة الشافعي: ٩٠.
٢ أخرجه أحمد: ١١/ ٢٥ (٦٤٨٦)، والبخاري (٣٤٦١)، والترمذي (٢٦٦٩).

The Messenger of Allah ﷺ used to speak elaborately, clearly, and deliberately so that the Companions could understand it, memorize it, and, subsequently, impart it to the people. Imām Aḥmad reported from `Ā`ishah, who said: "The words of Allah's Messenger ﷺ were elucidated, understood by everyone, and he would not pour them rapidly." Furthermore, the Messenger ﷺ invoked Allah for those who memorize his *Sunnah*, understand it, and then impart it to others. Ash-Shāfi`i and al-Bayhaqi narrated from Ibn Mas`ūd that the Messenger of Allah ﷺ said, **"May Allah illuminate a man who hears a saying from me, memorizes it, understands it, and then imparts it."** Abū Dāwūd and at-Tirmidhi collected it with the wording, **"May Allah brighten [the face of] a man who hears a tradition from us, then conveys it as he heard it. Perhaps, the recipient is more comprehending than the [original] hearer."** At-Tirmidhi said: it is a ḥasan ṣaḥīḥ (good and authentic) hadith.

The Companions were keen to preserve the *Sunnah* of the Messenger of Allah ﷺ. They used to keep his company hoping to memorize his words, observe his actions and conduct, and witness his judgments, decisions, and fatwa(s). Those who were present used to pass on knowledge to those who were absent. Al-Bukhāri narrated in his [Ṣaḥīḥ], on the authority of Ibn `Abbās, that the Commander of the Faithful `Umar Ibn al-Khaṭṭāb said, "I and an Anṣārī neighbor of mine from Banū Umayyah Ibn Zayd, who used to live in upper Madinah, used to visit the Prophet in turn. He used to go one day and I another day. When I went, I would bring him the news of what had happened that day regarding the divine revelation and other things, and when he went, he used to do the same for me."[1] So, `Umar and his Ansārī neighbor used to go by turns and attend the sessions of the Messenger of Allah ﷺ; therefore, they balanced between running their businesses and gaining knowledge from the Messenger of Allah ﷺ.

1 [Ṣaḥīḥ al-Bukhāri, Book of Grievances] (46), Chapter no. 25, hadith no. (2468). Also see [Fat-ḥ al-Bārī]: 5/114

وقد كان الرسول ﷺ يفصل كلامه تفصيلاً، ويتأنى في إلقائه كي يفهمه أصحابه الذين يسمعونه، ويحفظوه ويبلغوه الناس، روى الإمام أحمد، عن عائشة، قالت: **«كان كلام رسول الله ﷺ فصلاً، يفقهه كل أحد، لم يكن يسرده سرداً»**(١)، وقد دعا الرسول ﷺ للذين يحفظون سنته ويعونها ويبلغونها، روى الشافعي والبيهقي عن ابن مسعود أن رسول الله ﷺ قال: «نضر الله امرأ سمع مقالتي، فحفظها ووعاها وأداها»، وأخرجه أبو داود والترمذي بلفظ: **«نضر الله امرأ سمع منا شيئاً فبلغه كما سمعه، فرب مبلغ أوعى من سامع»**(٢)، وقال الترمذي: حسن صحيح.

وقد حرص الصحابة رضي الله عنهم على حفظ سنة رسول الله ﷺ، من أجل ذلك كانوا يلازمونه ويحفظون كلامه، ويراقبون أفعاله وتصرفاته، ويشهدون أحكامه وقضاياه وفتاويه، وكان الذي لم يشهد يتعلم من الذي كان شاهداً حاضراً، روى البخاري في صحيحه عن عبد الله بن عباس أن أمير المؤمنين عمر بن الخطاب قال: «إني كنت وجار لي من الأنصار في بني أمية بن زيد- وهي من عوالي المدينة- وكنا نتناوب النزول على النبي ﷺ، فينزل يوماً وأنزل يوماً، فإذا نزلت جئته من خبر ذلك اليوم من الأمر وغيره، وإذا نزل فعل مثله»(٣)، فعمر كان يتناوب مع جاره الأنصاري النزول من عوالي المدينة إلى مجالس رسول الله ﷺ، فيجمعون بين القيام بأعمالهم والتفقه من رسول الله ﷺ.

١ أخرجه أحمد: ٤١/ ٥٢٠ (٢٥٠٧٧)، إسناده حسن.

٢ أخرجه أبو داود (٣٦٦٠)، وابن ماجه (٢٣٠)، والترمذي (٢٦٥٦).

٣ صحيح البخاري، كتاب المظالم ٤٦، باب رقم ٢٥، رقم الحديث (٢٤٦٨)، انظر فتح الباري: ٥/ ١١٤.

VI: Recording the Prophetic *Sunnah*:

During the era of the Messenger of Allah ﷺ, the Arabs were illiterate. Those who mastered writing were only a handful of men in every tribe. However, the Arabs were gifted memorizers to an extent that one of them would hear a poem or a speech and then memorize it from its first recitation. Ibn `Abbās heard the poem of `Amr Ibn Abū Rabī`ah, which was made up of seventy lines, and memorized it the minute he heard it.[1]

In light of the aforementioned, and in order to prevent the *Sunnah* from getting mixed up with the Noble Qur'an, and so that the efforts put forth in recording would not distract the Companions from the other serious missions given to them, the Messenger of Allah ﷺ initially prevented his Companions from recording the *Sunnah*. Muslim narrated, on the authority of Abū Sa`īd al-Khudri, that the Messenger of Allah ﷺ said: **"Whoever wrote anything but the Qur'an, let him erase it."**[2] In the narration of at-Tirmidhi: "We sought the Prophet's permission to write [the *Sunnah*], but he did not permit us."[3]

Later, the Messenger of Allah ﷺ allowed some Companions to record his words and *Sunnah*. `Abdullāh Ibn `Amr Ibn al-Āṣ was one of these people; he said: "I used to write everything I heard from the Messenger of Allah ﷺ that I intended to memorize, but Quraysh forbade me. They said: 'Do you write everything you hear, even though Allah's Messenger is a human who talks when he is angry and when he is pleased (in different moods)?' I thus stopped writing. I then mentioned that to the Messenger of Allah ﷺ and he pointed with his finger to his mouth and said: **'Write! By He in whose Hand is my soul, nothing comes out from it except the truth.'"**[4]

1 [Difā` `Anil-Ḥadith an-Nabawi] (Defending the Prophet›s Hadith): 12
2 [Ṣaḥīḥ Muslim] (3004)
3 at-Tirmidhi (2665)
4 Abū Dāwūd (3646), [Jāmi` Bayān al-`Ilm]: 1/71

سادساً: تدوين السنة النبوية:

كان العرب في عهد الرسول ﷺ أمّة أُمِّيّة لا تكتب ولا تقرأ من كتاب، والذين يجيدون الكتاب أعداد قليلة في كل قبيلة، وكانوا مطبوعين على الحفظ، يسمع أحدهم القصيدة أو الخطبة فيحفظها عندما يسمعها لأول مرة، وقد استمع ابن عباس قصيدة عمر بن أبي ربيعة التي مطلعها:

أمن آل نعم أنت غاد فمبكر \\ غداة غد أم رائح فمهجر

وهي تقرب من سبعين بيتاً، فحفظها حين سمعها(١).

من أجل هذا، وحتى لا تختلط السنة بالقرآن الكريم، وكي لا تتوجه الجهود إلى التدوين فيشتغل الصحابة عن مهمات خطيرة نيطت بهم، نهي الرسول ﷺ أصحابه عن تدوين سنته(٢)، ولم يأذن لهم في بداية الأمر بتدوين شيء غير القرآن، روى مسلم عن أبي سعيد الخدري أن الرسول ﷺ قال: «**من كتب عني غير القرآن فليمحه**»(٣)، وفي رواية الترمذي: «استأذنا النبي ﷺ في الكتابة فلم يأذن لنا»(٤).

ثم أذن الرسول ﷺ لبعض الصحابة بتدوين كلامه وسنته، من هؤلاء عبد الله بن عمرو بن العاص، قال: كنت أكتب كل شيء أسمعه من رسول الله ﷺ أريد حفظه فنهتني قريش، وقالوا: أتكتب كل شيء تسمعه ورسول الله بشر يتكلم في الغضب والرضا؟ فأمسكت عن الكتاب، فذكرت ذلك لرسول الله ﷺ فأومأ بإصبعه إلى فيه فقال: «اكتب، فوالذي نفسي بيده ما يخرج منه إلا حق»(٥).

١ دفاع عن الحديث النبوي: ١٢.
٢ من الذين تحدثوا عن الحكمة في عدم كتابة السنة ابن حجر العسقلاني في هدي الساري، مقدمة فتح الباري: ٦.
٣ صحيح مسلم (٣٠٠٤).
٤ الترمذي (٢٦٦٥).
٥ أبو داود (٣٦٤٦)، وجامع بيان العلم: ١/ ٧١.

`Abdullāh Ibn `Amr Ibn Al-`Āṣ used to call the account he wrote about the Messenger of Allah ﷺ "aṣ-Ṣādiqah (The Truthful)." From aṣ-Ṣādiqah, `Amr Ibn Shu`ayb used to narrate, on the authority of his father, on the authority of his grandfather.

Of those who recorded hadith(s) in writing were: `Abdullāh Ibn Mas`ūd and Sa`d Ibn `Ubādah. Al-Ḥāfiẓ Ibn `Abdil-Barr narrated from Mis`ar, on the authority of Ma`in, who said: "'Abdur-Raḥmān Ibn `Abdullāh Ibn Mas`ūd showed me a book and swore by Allah it was handwritten by his father."[1]

Abū Shāh asked the Messenger of Allah ﷺ to write [something] for him, so the Messenger of Allah ﷺ said: **"Write for Abū Shāh."**[2]

On the authority of Ibrāhīm at-Taymi, who said: "My father talked to me and said, "Ali (may Allah be pleased with him) delivered a sermon on a pulpit made of bricks, while he was wearing a sword, to which an attached document was hanging; he said: 'By Allah, we have no book to read except Allah's Book and what this document contains.' He unrolled it and it contained what sort of camels are to be given as blood money, in addition to it saying: 'Madinah is a place of sanctuary – from `Ayr to such and such place, so whoever introduces a heresy in Islam, in it, will incur the curse of Allah, the angels, and all the people. Allah will not accept his obligatory or voluntary service on the Day of Resurrection.'"[3]

The transcription of the *Sunnah*, however, was only a partial, individual effort. More emphasis was placed on learning and memorizing the *Sunnah*. No individual Companion ever encompassed the whole *Sunnah*. However, the Companions in their totality memorized the entire *Sunnah*, though they varied as individuals in what amount of it they memorized.

1 [Jāmi` Bayān al-`Ilm]: 1/72
2 Al-Bukhāri (2434), Muslim (1355), Abū Dāwūd (2017) and at-Tirmidhi (2667)
3 [Ṣaḥīḥ Al-Bukhāri] (7300), and [Muslim] (1370)

وكان عبد الله بن عمرو بن العاص يسمي ما كتبه عن الرسول ﷺ: الصادقة[١].

ومن الصادقة كان يروي عمرو بن شعيب عن أبيه عن جده.

ومن الذين كتبوا شيئاً من الحديث: عبد الله بن مسعود، وسعد بن عبادة، فقد أخرج الحافظ ابن عبد البر عن مسعر، عن معن، قال: أخرج لي عبد الرحمن بن عبد الله بن مسعود كتاباً، وحلف لي أنه بخط أبيه بيده[٢].

وطلب الصحابي أبو شاه من الرسول ﷺ أن يكتب له، فقال الرسول ﷺ: «**اكتبوا لأبي شاه**»[٣].

وعن إبراهيم التيمي قال: حدثني أبي قال: «خطبنا علي رضي الله عنه على منبر من آجُرّ وعليه سيف فيه صحيفة معلقة فقال: والله ما عندنا من كتاب يقرأ إلا كتاب الله وما في هذه الصحيفة، فنشرها، فإذا فيها أسنان الإبل، وإذا فيها: المدينة حَرَم من عَير إلى كذا، فمن أحدث فيها حدثاً فعليه لعنة الله والملائكة والناس أجمعين، لا يقبل الله منه صرفاً ولا عدلاً»[٤].

ولكن المكتوب من السنة كان جهداً فردياً جزئياً، ولم تدون السنة كلها، وكان الاعتماد في حفظ السنة على الحفظ والاستظهار، ولم يكن واحد من الصحابة يحيط بسنة الرسول ﷺ جميعها، ولكن الصحابة في مجموعهم كانوا يحفظون جميع السنة، ثم هم متفاوتون في حفظهم لها.

١ طبقات ابن سعد: ٢/ ١٢٥ طبعة ليدن، وتأويل مختلف الحديث لابن قتيبة: ٩٣، وجامع بيان العلم: ١/ ٧٢.
٢ جامع بيان العلم: ١/ ٧٢.
٣ البخاري (٢٤٣٤)، ومسلم (١٣٥٥)، وأبو داود (٢٠١٧)، والترمذي (٢٦٦٧).
٤ صحيح البخاري (٧٣٠٠)، ومسلم (١٣٧٠).

Summary of Unit 2

This unit can be summarized in the following points:

1. The *waḥy* (revelation) is the means through which Allah informs His messengers and prophets of His laws and words. It may be directly imparted or transmitted though the Angel Jibrīl.
2. The Noble Qur'an is the word of Allah, revealed to the Messenger of Allah ﷺ; its recitation is worship, its text is inimitable, and it constitutes a cornerstone of religion. The Companions compiled it in one *muṣ-ḥaf*; and it has been preserved from alteration and distortion. It was revealed gradually to strengthen the heart of the Messenger of Allah ﷺ and to decide on newly emerging affairs.
3. The Prophet's *Sunnah* represents his sayings, actions, and tacit approvals; it explains and expounds the Qur'an; it is authoritative and, therefore, should be honored because it is a revelation similar to the Qur'an. The Companions and those who came after them preserved the *Sunnah* and committed it to writing.
4. Over a twenty-three year span, the Noble Qur'an followed a gradual approach in presenting its judgments in order to train the Companions to submit to Allah's orders.

The scholars unanimously agreed that *Ijtihād* was permissible to our Prophet ﷺ and to other previous prophets, with regard to worldly interests. However, they differed over the prophets` *Ijtihād* in legal judgments and religious affairs. According to the preponderant opinion, they were also permitted to exercise *Ijtihād* in legal judgments and religious affairs.

خلاصة الوحدة

نخلص من دراسة هذه الوحدة إلى ما يلي:

١- الوحي هو إعلام الله رسله وأنبياءه بشرعه وكلامه، وهو قد يكون بكلام الله مباشرة أو عن طريق مَلَك كجبريل عليه السلام.

٢- القرآن الكريم هو كلام الله تعالى المنزل على رسول الله ﷺ، المتعبد بتلاوته المعجز، وهو أصل الدين، وقد جمعه الصحابة في مصحف واحد، وقد حفظه الله من التبديل والتحريف، وقد أنزله الله منجماً ليثبت به قلب الرسول ﷺ، وليحكم به في القضايا.

٣- أن السنة النبوية هي أقوال الرسول ﷺ وأفعاله وتقريراته، وهي توضيح للقرآن الكريم وتبيين له، وهي حجة يجب العمل بها؛ لأنها وحي كالقرآن، وقد حفظها الصحابة- رضوان الله عليهم- ودونوها.

٤- أن القرآن الكريم نزل متدرجاً في بيانه للأحكام حتى يربي الصحابة على امتثال أوامر الله تعالى، وذلك على امتداد ثلاثة وعشرون عاماً .

أجمع العلماء على جواز الاجتهاد لنبينا ﷺ- ولغيره من الأنبياء- فيما يتعلق بمصالح الدنيا، واختلفوا بعد ذلك في اجتهاد الأنبياء في الأحكام الشرعية والأمور الدينية، والراجح هو قول من قال بجواز اجتهادهم في أمور الدين، وأحكام الشريعة.

Notes

Notes

UNIT 3

FIQH AT THE TIME OF THE COMPANIONS

(MAY ALLAH BE PLEASED WITH THEM)

Contents of Unit 3

- The Status and Virtue of the Companions
- The Companions' Care for the Noble Qur'an
- The Companions' Care for the Prophetic *Sunnah*
- The Companions` Differing; Why These Incidents Were Few
- The Sources of Legislation at the Time of the Companions
- The Jurist and Mufti Companions

Importance of Unit 3

The Companions of Allah's Messenger ﷺ were the best of this *Ummah* after its Prophet. Allah, the Glorified, chose them to accompany His Prophet ﷺ and carry his *da`wah* (call). Allah praised them in various places of the Noble Qur'an, like in *Surat* al-Fat-ḥ, al-Ḥadeed, al-Ḥashr, and elsewhere. In fact, He even praised them in the books that were revealed prior to the Qur'an, such as the *Tawrāh* (Torah) and *Injīl* (Gospel). Additionally, the Messenger of Allah ﷺ himself praised and spoke highly of them.

In this unit, you will learn about the virtue of the Companions, their status, their role in preserving and recording the Noble Qur'an, as well as their role in recording the noble Prophetic *Sunnah*. Then, you will learn about the sources of Islamic legislation at the time of the Companions, and their major jurists.

Learning Objectives:

At the end of this lecture, students should be able to:

1) Mention the Companions` status and virtue
2) Prove how much the Companions` cared about the Noble Qur'an and the honored *Sunnah* of the Prophet ﷺ

الوحدة الثالثة

الفقه في عصر الصحابة رضوان الله عليهم

محتويات الوحدة الثالثة

- مكانة الصحابة وفضلهم.
- عناية الصحابة بالقرآن الكريم.
- عناية الصحابة بالسنة النبوية.
- اختلاف الصحابة والسبب في قلته.
- مصادر التشريع في عصر الصحابة.
- فقهاء الصحابة أهل الفتيا.

أهمية دراسة الوحدة:

صحابة رسول الله ﷺ هم خير الأمة بعد نبيها، اختارهم الله سبحانه لصحبة نبيه، وحمل دعوته، وقد أثنى الله سبحانه عليهم في غير موضع في القرآن الكريم كسورة الفتح، والحديد والحشر وغيرها من السور، بل أثنى الله سبحانه عليهم في الكتب السابقة للقرآن، كالتوراة والإنجيل، وأثنى عليهم رسول الله ﷺ ومدحهم.

وفي هذه الوحدة تتعرف على فضل الصحابة ومكانتهم ودورهم في حفظ القرآن الكريم وتدوينه، ودورهم كذلك في تدوين السنة النبوية الشريفة، ثم تتعرف على مصادر التشريع في عصر الصحابة وأهم فقهائهم.

الأهداف التعليمية:

يتوقع منك أيها الدارس الكريم بعد دراستك لهذه الوحدة أن تكون قادراً على أن:

١- تذكر مكانة الصحابة وفضلهم.

٢- تُدلل على عناية الصحابة بالقرآن الكريم والسنة النبوية.

3) Compare the efforts of Abū Bakr and `Uthmān in preserving the Book of Allah

4) Mention which Companions of the Messenger of Allah ﷺ were proliferate in giving fatwa, those who moderately gave fatwa, and those who rarely gave fatwa

٣- تقارن بين عمل أبي بكر و عثمان في حفظ كتاب الله.

٤- تذكر صحابة رسول الله ﷺ المكثرين من الفتيا والمتوسطين والمقلين.

Fiqh at the Time of the Companions

The era of the Companions started with the death of the Messenger of Allah ﷺ and continued until the end of the time of *al-Khulafā` ar-Rāshidūn* (the Rightly-Guided Caliphs). Despite the fact that the Companions had a significant presence thereafter, they became relatively few in comparison to others, and their influence in managing the affairs of the state had diminished greatly.

الفقه في عصر الصحابة

ابتدأ عصر الصحابة بوفاة الرسول ﷺ، واستمر إلى نهاية عصر الخلفاء الراشدين، ومع أن الصحابة كان لهم وجود ظاهر بعد ذلك، إلا أنهم أصبحوا قليلي العدد بالنسبة إلى غيرهم، كما أن تأثيرهم في تسيير شؤون الدولة تناقص كثيراً.

Introduction: The Status of the Companions and their Role towards the Islamic Sharia

Firstly: Their Status and Virtue

The Companions were the ideal generation. The Messenger of Allah ﷺ cultured them himself, and the Qur'anic instructions continuously directed them; it treated the illnesses of the souls, purified the hearts, and elevated them to the zenith of glory. Ibn Mas`ūd said: "Those are the Companions of Muhammad ﷺ; they were the best of this *Ummah*, the purest at heart, the most profound in knowledge, the least in exaggeration. Allah chose them to be the Companions of His Prophet, and to establish His religion. So acknowledge their virtue, follow in their footsteps, and adhere to whatever of their manners and conduct you can, for they were upon the straight guidance."[1]

تمهيد: مكانة الصحابة ودورهم تجاه الشريعة الإسلامية:

أولاً: مكانة الصحابة وفضلهم:

أصحاب الرسول ﷺ هم الجيل المثالي، رباهم الرسول ﷺ، وكانت توجيهات القرآن تلاحقهم؛ تعالج أمراض النفوس، وتزكي القلوب، وترقى بهم إلى القمم السامقة، قال ابن مسعود: «أولئك أصحاب محمد ﷺ، كانوا أفضل هذه الأمة، أبرها قلوباً، وأعمقها علماً، وأقلّها تكلفاً، اختارهم الله لصحبة نبيه، ولإقامة دينه، فاعرفوا لهم فضلهم، واتبعوهم على أثرهم، وتمسكوا بما استطعتم من أخلاقهم وسيرهم، فإنهم كانوا على الهدى المستقيم»(١).

1 Collected by Abū `Umar Ibn `Abdil-Barr in [*Jāmi` Bayān al-`Ilm wa Faḍlih*]: 2/97. See: [*Jāmi` al-Uṣūl*]:1/292.

١ أخرجه أبو عمر ابن عبد البر في جامع بيان العلم وفضله: ٢/ ٩٧، وانظر جامع الأصول: ١/ ٢٩٢.

In the period following the Prophet's death, the Companions successfully lead their lives, in the Muslim community, according to the example of the Messenger of Allah ﷺ. The Messenger of Allah ﷺ himself foretold that this was going to happen. In the hadith narrated by Imām Ahmad, on the authority of Hudhayfah, who said that the Prophet ﷺ said, **"Prophethood will remain among you as long as Allah wills, then He will remove it. Then, there will be a *khilāfah* (caliphate) that follows the way of prophethood and that will remain as long as Allah wills, and then Allah will remove it..."**[1]

The Messenger of Allah ﷺ ordered that the way of the Rightly-Guided Caliphs should be followed in the hadith, **"It is incumbent upon you to follow my *Sunnah* (example), and the example of the rightly guided caliphs after me. Bite onto it with your molar teeth, and beware of the newly invented matters [in the religion]..."** (Narrated by Abū Dāwūd and at-Tirmidhi, who said: This hadith is *ḥasan* [good] and *ṣaḥīḥ* [authentic]).[2]

The caliphate continued for thirty years after the Messenger of Allah ﷺ; namely the rule of Abū Bakr, `Umar, `Uthmān, and `Ali. It came in a hadith: **"The caliphate after me will be thirty years."** This hadith was authenticated by Imām Aḥmad.[3]

Furthermore, of what indicates the virtue of the Companions is that Allah testified for them, was pleased with them, praised them in the Qur'an, and in His previous scriptures.

وقد استطاع الصحابة في الفترة التي تلت وفاة الرسول ﷺ أن يقيموا حياتهم في المجتمع الإسلامي وفق منهج الرسول ﷺ، وقد أخبر الرسول ﷺ بأن ذلك كائن، ففي الحديث الذي خرجه الإمام أحمد من حديث حذيفة رضي الله عنه عن النبي ﷺ قال: «**تكون النبوة فيكم ما شاء الله أن تكون، ثم يرفعها، ثم تكون خلافة على منهاج النبوة، فتكون ما شاء الله أن تكون، ثم يرفعها الله...**»(١).

وقد أمرنا الرسول ﷺ باتباع سنة الخلفاء الراشدين، ففي الحديث، «**عليكم بسنتي وسنة الخلفاء الراشدين المهديين من بعدي، عضوا عليها بالنواجذ، وإياكم ومحدثات الأمور...**»، رواه أبو داود والترمذي، وقال: حديث حسن صحيح(٢).

وقد استمرت الخلافة بعد الرسول ﷺ ثلاثين سنة، هي فترة حكم أبي بكر وعمر وعثمان وعلي، وفي الحديث: «**الخلافة بعدي ثلاثون سنة**»، وقد صحح الإمام أحمد هذا الحديث(٣).

ومما يدل على فضل الصحابة أن الله شهد لهم، ورضي عنهم، وأثنى عليهم في القرآن وفي كتبه السابقة.

---

1 *The* [*Musnad*] *of Imām Aḥmad*: 30/355 (18406). Its *Isnād* (chain of transmission) is *ḥasan* (good). Also see: [*Jāmi` al-`Ulūm wal-Ḥikam*]: 249
2 *The* [*Musnad*] *of Imām Ahmad*: 28/ 367-375 (17142), (17144), and (17145). Also see: [*Jāmi` al-`Ulūm wal-Ḥikam*]: 243; hadith no. (28)
3 *The* [*Musnad*] *of Imām Ahmad*: 36/ 248 (21919). Also see: [*Jāmi` al-`Ulūm wal-Ḥikam*]: 249

١ مسند الإمام أحمد: ٣٠/ ٣٥٥ (١٨٤٠٦)، وإسناد الحديث حسن، وانظر جامع العلوم والحكم: ٢٤٩.
٢ مسند الإمام أحمد: ٢٨/ ٣٦٧- ٣٧٥ (١٧١٤٢) و (١٧١٤٤) و (١٧١٤٥)، وانظر جامع العلوم والحكم: ٢٤٣ الحديث الثامن والعشرون.
٣ مسند الإمام أحمد: ٣٦/ ٢٤٨ (٢١٩١٩)، وانظر جامع العلوم والحكم: ٢٤٩.

Since the Companions had such as status, it is no wonder that they were the lanterns that dispersed darkness, the leaders of guidance, and the beacons of light that lit the way for those journeying towards their Lord, and a means of protection for this *Ummah* from error and deviance

وإذا كان للصحابة هذه المنزلة فلا عجب أن يكونوا مصابيح الدجى، وأعلام الهدى، ومنارات تضيء طريق السائرين إلى ربهم، وعصمة للأمة حال حياتهم من الضلال والزيغ.

Secondly: The Role of the Companions towards the Islamic Sharia:

ثانياً: دور الصحابة تجاه الشريعة الإسلامية:

The Companions maintained the religion of Allah; protecting it from being lost, conveying it to world, and duly striving for the cause of Allah. During the era of the rightly guided caliphs, the principle of *Shūrā* (consultation) was superbly practiced, and the Islamic Sharia was supreme in the Islamic *Ummah*; their affairs were managed by it, and their lives were guided through it. The jurist Companions made up the *Shūra* council; they would plan matters, and thus no command would ever be given except in compliance with the Islamic Sharia. They used to encourage the Muslims to gauge the rulers in light of the Islamic Sharia, and the texts of this Sharia were still fresh and free from alien interpretations and perverse explanations.

وقد قام الصحابة على دين الله، فحفظوه من الضياع، وبلغوه للعالمين، وجاهدوا في الله حق جهاده، وقد تحققت الشورى في أسمى مراتبها في عهد الخلفاء الراشدين، وكانت الشريعة الإسلامية هي المهيمنة على الأمة الإسلامية، وهي المصرفة لأمورهم، والقائدة لشؤونهم، وقد كان فقهاء الصحابة هم أصحاب الشورى، وبيدهم تدبير الأمور، فلم يكن يصدر أمر إلا إذا كان موافقاً للشريعة، وقد كانوا يشجعون المسلمين على مراقبة الحكام وفق مقاييس الشريعة، وكانت نصوص الشريعة غضة طرية لم تدخلها التأويلات والتمحلات المتكلفة.

The Companions encountered many difficult problems in their era. Following the death of the Messenger of Allah ﷺ, they differed over selecting who should succeed him, but this disagreement did not last for long. They promptly agreed to select the best of this *Ummah* after its Prophet (i.e. Abū Bakr). Another challenge was the Arab tribes turning into renegades and, as a result, busied the Companions with fierce wars against them. Then, the immense ordeal ensued whose victim was the Rightly-Guided Caliph; `Uthmān Ibn `Affān. Therein, the Companions were split into two groups, and several wars and tribulations took place. However, they all reunited again in *`Ām al-Jamā`ah* (the Year of Unity 41 AH).

وقد واجه الصحابة مشكلات جسام في عصرهم، فبعد وفاة الرسول ﷺ اختلفوا في الشخص الذي يكون خليفة للرسول ﷺ، ولم يطل الخلاف، فسرعان ما اجتمعت كلمتهم على خير هذه الأمة بعد نبيها، وارتد العرب عن الإسلام، فخاض الصحابة حرباً ضروساً ضد المرتدين، وذرت الفتنة الكبرى بقرنها، وراح ضحيتها الخليفة الراشد عثمان بن عفان، وانقسم الصحابة قسمين، وقامت فتن وحروب، ولكن الشمل التأم بعد ذلك في عام الجماعة.

On the legislative front, the companions faced a number of challenges as well:

First: the Companions feared losing any portion of the Qur'an – which is the foremost and greatest source of legislation – as a result of losing the memorizers who were martyred in the wars waged against the apostates.

Second: they were afraid that the *Ummah* would differ over the Qur'an in the same manner that the Jews and Christians did before.

Third: they were fearful of anything being falsely attributed to the *Sunnah* of the Messenger of Allah ﷺ.

Fourth: they were fearful of the Muslims deviating from the course set by their religion with regards to legislation.

Fifth: the Companions faced the various problems of everyday life, and they had to cope with them in light of Islam. They were tasked with addressing these issues within the framework of Islam; since this religion was sent down to oversee every aspect of life, and to direct it with the legislation of Allah.

Let us now explore how the Companions faced each of these issues.

وفي الجانب التشريعي واجه الصحابة عدة أمور:

الأول: خشية الصحابة من ذهاب شيء من القرآن- الأصل التشريعي الأول والأعظم- بسبب ذهاب حفظته في تلك الحروب التي خاضوها ضد المرتدين.

الثاني: خشيتهم من اختلاف الأمة في القرآن كما اختلف اليهود والنصارى من قبل، وبذلك يصبح لكل جماعة كتاب يزعمون أنه كتاب الله، ويكفرون من أخذ بغيره.

الثالث: خوفهم من الكذب في سنة الرسول ﷺ.

الرابع: خوفهم من أن يزيغ المسلمون عن المنهج الذي وضعه لهم دينهم في الجانب التشريعي.

الخامس: استقبل الصحابة مشكلات الحياة، وكان لزاماً عليهم أن يحكموها بالإسلام، بحيث يكون الإسلام إطاراً لها، ذلك أن هذا الدين أنزل ليهيمن على الحياة ويقودها بشرع الله.

وسنرى كيف واجه الصحابة كل واحدة من هذه القضايا.

The Companions' Care for the Noble Qur'an

Their Compilation of the Qur'an

The Messenger of Allah ﷺ left the Qur'an committed to memory as well as in written form. Those who memorized the Qur'an were many; of them memorized it all, and others memorized parts of it.

As for the writing of the Qur'an, it was carried out on parchments by certain Companions whom the Messenger of Allah ﷺ chose for this job. However, it was not written in the same order we have in today's *Muṣ-ḥaf*, because the Qur'an was revealed in light of occasions and events.

عناية الصحابة بالقرآن الكريم

تدوين الصحابة للقرآن

ترك الرسول ﷺ القرآن محفوظاً ومكتوباً، وقد كان الذين يحفظون القرآن كثيرين، بعضهم يحفظه كله، وآخرون يحفظون أجزاء منه.

أما المكتوب فهي الرقاع التي كان يأمر الرسول ﷺ من اختارهم لكتابة الوحي أن يكتبوه فيها، ولكنها لم ترتب حسب ترتيب المصحف الحالي بسبب تنزل القرآن حسب المناسبات والوقائع.

The Companions feared that the Qur'an would be lost with the death of its memorizers, and so Abū Bakr decided to collect the Qur'an after consulting with 'Umar Ibn al-Khaṭṭāb. The method they employed relied on both records; the memorized and written. They stipulated that the memorizers, from whom the Qur'an was collected, must have learned it directly from the Messenger of Allah ﷺ. As for the written, they relied on those portions of the Qur'an which the Messenger of Allah ﷺ ordered the scribes to write.

Regarding the collection of the Qur'an and its recording at the time of Abū Bakr, Zayd Ibn Thābit said, "Abū Bakr sent for me after the (heavy) casualties among the warriors [of the battle] of al-Yamāmah[1] (where a great number of *Qurrā`* (recitors) were killed). 'Umar was present with Abū Bakr, who said, "Umar has come to me and said, 'The people have suffered heavy casualties on the day of al-Yamāmah[2], and I am afraid that there will be more casualties among the *Qurrā`* (those who know the Qur'an by heart) at other battle-fields, whereby a large part of the Qur'an may be lost, unless you collect it. And I am of the opinion that you should collect the Qur'an.' Abū Bakr added, 'I said to `Umar: How can I do something which Allah's Messenger has not done?' 'Umar said (to me), `By Allah, this is a good thing.' 'Umar kept on pressing, trying to persuade me to accept his proposal, until Allah opened my heart to it and I had the same opinion as 'Umar.'" He said to Zayd, "You are a wise young man whom we do not suspect, and you used to write the Divine Revelation for Allah's Messenger – so investigate the Qur'an and collect it [in one manuscript]." Zayd said: "By Allah,

1 The Battle of al-Yamāmah took place between the Muslims and the Banū Ḥanīfah, who apostatized from Islam and were led by Mūsaylimah.

2 Around 40 to 50 Companions were martyred; the total number of casualties was around one thousand. See: [The History of aṭ-Ṭabarī; Years 11 and 12].

وقد خشي الصحابة من ذهاب القرآن بذهاب حفظته، فقرر أبو بكر جمعه بمشورة عمر بن الخطاب، وطريقة جمعه التي اختطوها تعتمد على الحفظ والكتابة، وكانوا يشترطون في الحفاظ الذين يأخذون منهم أن يكونوا قد تلقوها من الرسول ﷺ وعمدتهم في الكتابة تلك التي أمر الرسول ﷺ كتاب الوحي بكتابتها.

وقد حدثنا زيد بن ثابت عن جمع القرآن وتدوينه في عهد أبي بكر، قال: «أرسل إليّ أبو بكر الصديق رضي الله عنه مقتل أهل اليمامة(١)، فإذا عمر بن الخطاب عنده، قال أبو بكر: إن عمر أتاني مقتل أهل اليمامة، فقال: إن القتل استحرّ(٢) يوم اليمامة بقراء القرآن(٣)، وإني أخشى إن استحرّ القتل بالقراء في المواطن فيذهب كثير من القرآن، وإني أرى أن تأمر بجمع القرآن، قلت لعمر: كيف تفعل شيئاً لم يفعله رسول الله ﷺ؟ قال عمر: هذا والله خير، فلم يزل عمر يراجعني حتى شرح الله صدري لذلك، ورأيت في ذلك مثل الذي رأى عمر، وقال لزيد: إنك رجل شاب عاقل لا نتهمك، وقد كنت تكتب الوحي لرسول الله ﷺ فتتبع القرآن فاجمعه، قال زيد: فوالله لو كلفوني نقل جبل من الجبال ما كان أثقل عليّ مما أمرني به من جمع القرآن.

١ موقعة اليمامة، كانت بين المسلمين وبين بني حنيفة الذين ارتدوا بقيادة مسيلمة.

٢ استحر: اشتد وكثر.

٣ استشهد في معركة اليمامة من الصحابة نحو أربعمائة وخمسين، وجملة القتلى من المسلمين نحو ألف، انظر تاريخ الطبري حوادث سنتي ١١، ١٢.

if he (Abū Bakr) had ordered me to relocate one of the mountains, it would not have been harder for me than what he commanded me concerning the collection of the Qur'an. I said to both of them: 'How dare you do a thing which the Prophet has not done?' Abū Bakr said, `By Allah, it is [truly] a good thing.' I kept on arguing with him about it until Allah opened my heart to that which He had opened the hearts of Abū Bakr and 'Umar. So, I started locating Qur'anic material and collecting it from parchments, scapula, leaf-stalks of date palms, and from the hearts of men [who memorized it]. I found with Khuzaymah two verses from Sūrat at-Tawbah which I had not found with anybody else: **"There has certainly come to you a Messenger from among yourselves..."**[1] until the end of Surat at-Tawbah. The manuscript on which the Qur'an was collected remained with Abū Bakr till Allah decreed his death, and then with `Umar for the duration of his life, and finally it remained with Ḥafṣah, 'Umar`s daughter." [2]

The Companions Uniting the Ummah upon that Mus-haf

The collection of the Qur'an at the time of Abū Bakr was a great achievement through which Allah protected any portion of His Book from being lost. However, there remained another matter that was equally dangerous to the loss of the Qur'an; that being the *Ummah* differing over that *Muṣ-ḥaf*. This fear stemmed from the fact that the manuscript of the Qur'an existed in a single house in Madinah. As for the rest of the Islamic world, it did not contain a Qur'anic reference that the people could return to aside from what had been memorized by heart.

1 Surat at-Tawbah – Verse 128

2 Reported by al-Bukhāri in [Book: The Virtues of the Qur`an, Chapter: The Collection of the Qur`an] (4986), [*Fat-ḥul-Bārī*]: 9/10

قال زيد: قلت: كيف تفعلون شيئاً لم يفعله رسول الله ﷺ؟

قال: هو والله خير، فلم يزل أبو بكر يراجعني، حتى شرح الله صدري للذي شرح له صدر أبي بكر وعمر، فتتبعت القرآن أجمعه من العسب[١] واللخاف[٢] وصدور الرجال، حتى وجدت آخر سورة التوبة مع أبي خزيمة الأنصاري، لم أجدها مع أحد غيره: ﴿لَقَدْ جَاءَكُمْ رَسُولٌ مِّنْ أَنْفُسِكُمْ﴾[٣]، حتى خاتمة براءة، فكانت الصحف عند أبي بكر حتى توفاه الله، ثم عند عمر حياته، ثم عند حفصة بنت عمر[٤].

جمع الصحابة الأمّة على هذا المصحف

كان جمع القرآن على عهد أبي بكر عملاً عظيماً، حفظ الله به كتابه من أن يضيع شيء منه، ولكن بقي أمر آخر لا يقل خطورة عن ضياع شيء من القرآن؛ وهو أن تختلف الأمة في هذا الكتاب، ذلك أن الصحف التي كتبت كانت موجودة في بيت في المدينة المنورة، أما العالم الإسلامي فلم يكن فيه ما يرجع الناس إليه إلا المحفوظ في الصدور.

١ جمع عسيب وهو جريد النخل إذا نحي عنه خوصه.

٢ جمع لخفة وهي الحجارة البيض الرقاق العريضة.

٣ التوبة: ١٢٨.

٤ رواه البخاري في كتاب فضائل القرآن، باب جمع القرآن (٤٩٨٦)، فتح الباري: ٩/ ١٠.

This very danger became clearly manifest during the era of the Rightly-Guided Caliph, `Uthmān Ibn `Affān, for this is when the people differed over the recitation of the Qur'an and accused one another of inaccuracy. Once some of the Companions noticed this, they hurried to the Caliph in fear that the *Ummah* would differ regarding its Book just as the Jews and Christians differed over theirs. Thus, 'Uthmān sent for a group of the Companions, and demanded that they make a number of copies of the *Muṣ-ḥaf* that was collected at the time of Abū Bakr. Then, He distributed these copies throughout the Islamic world, and ordered the Companions to burn everything other than these standardized copies. These standardized copies then became the reference for the entire *Ummah,* and by that the dispute ended in its infancy.

In [Kitāb al-Maṣāḥif], Ibn Abi Dāwūd related, from Abū Qulābah, who said, "During the caliphate of `Uthmān, the teachers used to teach different recitations of the Qur'an. As a result, the students would meet one another and disagree [over which was correct], until the disagreement escalated to the teachers themselves, whereby each would deny the recitation of the other. When `Uthmān learned of this, he delivered a sermon and said, "If even you disagree, despite my being amongst you, the disagreement among the distant regions must be even more severe." [1]

'Uthmān was absolutely correct – may Allah have mercy upon him – for the regions more distant from Madinah had were far more in disagreement over the Qur'an. Imām al-Bukhāri reported in his [Ṣaḥīḥ], on the authority of Anas Ibn Mālik, that Ḥudhayfah Ibn al-Yamān came to `Uthmān after accompanying the people of Shām in their conquest of Armenia, and the people of Iraq in their conquest of Azerbai-

1 [*Kitāb al-Maṣāḥif*] by Ibn Abū Dāwūd: 1/203-204 (74). Also see: [Fat-ḥul-Bārī]: 9/18, the commentary on hadith no. (4987)

وقد ظهر هذا الخطر ماثلاً للعيان في عهد الخليفة الراشد عثمان بن عفان، فقد اختلف الناس في قراءة القرآن، وأخذ بعضهم يغلِّط بعضاً في القراءة، ورأى بعض الصحابة ذلك، فسارعوا إلى الخليفة وجلين من اختلاف الأمة في كتابها كما اختلف اليهود والنصارى، فأرسل عثمان إلى جماعة من الصحابة وطلب منهم أن ينسخوا عدة نسخ من المصحف الذي جمع في عهد أبي بكر، وأرسل إلى كل ناحية بنسخة، وأمر الصحابة بإحراق ما عدا هذه النسخ، وأصبحت هذه النسخ هي مرجع الناس، وبذلك قضى على ذلك النزاع والاختلاف في مهده.

أخرج ابن أبي داود في «كتاب المصاحف» من طريق أبي قلابة قال: «لما كان في خلافة عثمان جعل المعلم يعلِّم قراءة الرجل، والمعلم يعلم قراءة الرجل، فجعل الغلمان يلتقون فيختلفون، حتى ارتفع ذلك إلى المعلمين، حتى كفر بعضهم بقراءة بعض، فبلغ ذلك عثمان، فخطب، فقال: أنتم عندي تختلفون، فمن نأى من الأمصار أشد اختلافاً»(١).

وصدق- رحمه الله-، فقد كانت الأمصار البعيدة عن المدينة المنورة أشد اختلافاً في القرآن، روى البخاري في صحيحه عن أنس بن مالك، أن حذيفة بن اليمان قدم على عثمان، وكان يغازي أهل الشام في فتح أرمينية وأذربيجان مع أهل العراق، فأفزع حذيفة اختلافهم في القراءة، فقال حذيفة لعثمان: يا أمير المؤمنين، أدرك هذه الأمَّة قبل أن يختلفوا في الكتاب اختلاف اليهود والنصارى، فأرسل عثمان إلى حفصة: أن أرسلي إلينا بالصحف،

١ كتاب المصاحف لابن أبي داود: ١/ ٢٠٣- ٢٠٤ (٧٤)، وانظر فتح الباري: ٩/ ١٨، شرح الحديث رقم (٤٩٨٧).

jan. Ḥudhayfah was frightened by their differences in recitation, so he said to `Uthmān, "O chief of the Believers! Save this nation before they differ about the Book (Qur'an) just as the Jews and Christians did." So, 'Uthmān sent a message to Ḥafṣah saying, "Send us the manuscripts [of the Qur'an], so that we may copy them into the *Muṣ-ḥaf*(s), and then return them to you." Ḥafṣah sent them to `Uthmān, who then ordered Zayd Ibn Thābit, `Abdullāh Ibn az-Zubayr, Sa`īd Ibn al-Āṣ, and `Abdur-Raḥmān Ibn Ḥārith Ibn Hishām to copy these manuscripts into the *Muṣ-ḥaf*(s). Furthermore, 'Uthmān said to the three Qurashī men, "If you disagree with Zayd Ibn Thābit on any point in the Qur'an, then write it in the dialect of Quraysh, for the Qur'an was revealed in their tongue." They did so, and when they had written many copies of the manuscripts, `Uthmān returned the original manuscripts to Ḥafṣah, and sent one copy of what they had transcribed to every Muslim province, and ordered that all the other Qur'anic records, whether the fragments or whole copies, be burnt." [1]

With that, the Companions preserved the Qur'an from being lost – via additions to it or subtractions from it – and further preserved it from discrepancy with regards to its modes of recitation. All that was of the favors of Allah upon this *Ummah*, and of the preservation of His revealed religion which He promised to safeguard: **"Indeed, it is We who sent down the Qur'an and indeed, We will be its guardian."**[2]

The Companions' Care for the Prophetic Sunnah

Their Efforts in Preserving the Sunnah:
When the Messenger of Allah ﷺ died, his *Sunnah* was already committed to the memory of the Companions who were trustworthy, insightful, upright authorities. It suffices that they were praised by Allah and by the Messenger ﷺ.

1 [*Ṣaḥīḥ al-Bukhārī*, Book of Virtues, Chapter: The Collection of the Qur`ān] (4987). Also see: [Fat-ḥul-Bārī]: 9/11
2 Surat al-Hijr – Verse 9

ننسخها في المصاحف ثم نردها إليك، فأرسلت بها حصفة إلى عثمان، فأمر زيد بن ثابت، وعبد الله بن الزبير، وسعيد بن العاص، وعبد الرحمن بن الحارث بن هشام، فنسخوها في المصاحف، وقال عثمان للرهط القرشيين الثلاث: إذا اختلفتم في شيء من القرآن فاكتبوه بلسان قريش، فإنما نزل بلسانهم، ففعلوا، حتى إذا نسخوا الصحف في المصاحف، رد عثمان الصحف إلى حفصة، وأرسل إلى كل أفق بمصحف مما نسخوا، وأمر بما سواه من القرآن في كل صحيفة أو مصحف أن يحرق(١).

وبهذا حفظ الصحابة نص القرآن من الضياع- بنقص منه، أو تزيد فيه- وحفظوه من الاختلاف في طريقة قراءته، وذلك من توفيق الله لهذه الأمة، ومن الحفظ الذي تكفل به سبحانه لدينه الذي أنزله: ﴿إِنَّا نَحْنُ نَزَّلْنَا الذِّكْرَ وَإِنَّا لَهُ لَحَافِظُونَ﴾(٢).

عناية الصحابة بالسنة النبوية

جهودهم في حفظ السنة:

توفي الرسول ﷺ وسنته محفوظة في صدور أصحابه، وهم الثقات العدول أهل الضبط والبصيرة، وحسبهم ثناء الله عليهم، ومدح الرسول ﷺ لهم.

١ صحيح البخاري، كتاب فضائل القرآن، باب جمع القرآن (٤٩٨٧)، انظر فتح الباري: ١١/٩.
٢ الحجر: ٩.

The two Rightly-Guided Caliphs, Abū Bakr and `Umar, feared that the *Sunnah* of the Messenger of Allah ﷺ would be interpolated, rendering the second source of Sharia lost. This alteration taking place was imaginable in two ways:

First: mistakes and distortions unintentionally being introduced into the *Sunnah* due to forgetfulness, or due to a technical error during the receipt or conveyance of the narrations.

Second: fabricated and false narrations being intentionally inserted into the *Sunnah* by the enemies of Islam who integrated into Islamic communities with the aim of destroying the Muslims' religion. These types exist in every age, and it is enough to know that even Madinah was not free from the hypocrites during the Prophet's era.

In order to preserve the *Sunnah* from interpolation, lies, and confusion, the two Caliphs warned the Companions against excessively narrating the *Sunnah*. Furthermore, they used to verify whatever narration a Companion would report pertaining to the Messenger of Allah ﷺ.

Qabīṣah Ibn Dhu`ayb said: "A grandmother came to Abū Bakr asking him about her [right of] inheritance. He said to her: 'You have nothing in the Book of Allah and I know nothing [of inheritance] assigned to you in the Prophet's *Sunnah*; so go back until I ask the people.' When he asked the people, al-Mughīrah Ibn Shu`bah said, 'I witnessed the Messenger of Allah ﷺ when he assigned her (the grandmother) one-sixth [as a share of inheritance].' Abū Bakr said, 'Do you have any other witness with you?' Muhammad Ibn Maslamah al-Anṣārī stood up and said the like of what al-Mughīrah said; thus, Abū Bakr allotted her that [share]." [1]

Al-Bukhāri and Muslim narrated in their two [Ṣaḥīḥ(s)], on the authority of Abū Sa`īd al-Khudri, who said, "As I sat in one of the gatherings of the Anṣār in Madinah, Abū Mūsa came to us in a frightened state, so we said: 'What is with you?' He said, "Umar summoned me before him, so I came to his door, and greeted him thrice, but he did not respond

1 [*Al-Muwaṭṭa'*]: 458, Dār Ibn Ḥazm, Beirut, and [Musnad al-Imām Aḥmad]: 29/499 (17980) which has a complete takhrīj of the hadith

وقد خشي الخليفتان الراشدان أبو بكر وعمر على سنة الرسول ﷺ أن يدخل فيها ما ليس منها، فيضيع الأصل الثاني الذي قام عليه الدين، ووقوع هذا يتصور من وجهين:

الأول: أن يدخل الخطأ والتحريف إلى السنة من غير قصد بسبب النسيان، أو الخطأ في تحمل الرواية حين سماعها أو حين تبليغها.

الثاني: أن يدخل في السنة المكذوب والباطل إذا دخل في المجتمع الإسلامي أعداء الإسلام بغرض إفساد دين المسلمين، وهذا الصنف لا يخلو منه عصر، وحسبنا أن نعلم أن المدينة المنورة لم تخل من المنافقين في العهد النبوي.

وفي سبيل حماية السنة من الدخيل والكذب والتلبيس حذر الخليفتان الراشدان الصحابة من الإكثار من رواية السنة، ثم إنهما كانا يستوثقان إذا روى لهما أحد من الصحابة حديثاً عن الرسول ﷺ.

وعن قبيصة بن ذؤيب قال: جاءت الجدة إلى أبي بكر تسأله ميراثها، فقال لها: ما لك في كتاب الله شيء، وما علمت لك في سنة رسول الله ﷺ شيئاً، فارجعي حتى أسأل الناس، فسأل الناس، فقال المغيرة بن شعبة: حضرت رسول الله ﷺ أعطاها السدس، فقال أبو بكر رضي الله عنه: هل معك غيرك؟ فقام محمد بن مسلمة الأنصاري، فقال مثل ما قال المغيرة، فأنفذه لها أبو بكر رضي الله عنه(١).

وروى البخاري ومسلم في صحيحهما عن أبي سعيد الخدري، قال: كنت جالساً في المدينة في مجلس الأنصار، فأتانا أبو موسى فزعاً أو مذعوراً قلنا: ما شأنك؟ قال: إن عمر أرسل إلي أن آتيه، فأتيت بابه، فسلمت ثلاثاً، فلم يرد علي، فرجعت، فقال: ما منعك أن تأتينا؟ فقلت: إني

١ الموطأ: ٤٥٨، طبعة دار ابن حزم، بيروت، ومسند الإمام أحمد: ٢٩/ ٤٩٩ (١٧٩٨٠) وفيه تمام تخريجه.

to me, so I returned.' (When `Umar came to know about this,) he said [to Abu Musā], 'What stopped you from coming to us?' I replied, 'I came to your door and greeted thrice; they did not respond to me, so I returned, for Allah's Messenger said, **'If anyone of you asks permission to enter thrice, and permission is not given, then he should return.'** 'Umar said, 'Establish proof for this [narration], or else I will inflict pain upon you." Ubayy Ibn Ka`b said, 'None will go with him but the youngest person [as a witness].' Abū Sa`īd said, 'I am the youngest person.' He said, 'So, go with him.'" [1]

Here, you see how Abū Bakr and 'Umar were both keen to verify the narrations regarding the Messenger of Allah ﷺ, even though the narrators were the noble Companions.

'Ali Ibn Abi Ṭālib (may Allah be pleased with him) used to ask whoever narrates a hadith from the Messenger of Allah ﷺ to take an oath in order to verify his truthfulness.[2]

This effective method bore its fruits; it has not reached us that anyone has ever falsely attributed anything to the Messenger of Allah ﷺ during the time of the Rightly-Guided Caliphs. This goes back to their sound method, and because the major Companions were present in multitude, their prestige filled the hearts, and the liar was easily detected.

أتيتك، فسلمت على بابك ثلاثاً فلم يردوا عليَّ فرجعت، وقد قال رسول الله ﷺ: «**إذا استأذن أحدكم ثلاثاً، فلم يؤذن له، فليرجع**».

فقال عمر: أقم عليه البينة، وإلا أوجعتك، فقال أبي بن كعب: لا يقوم معه إلا أصغر القوم، قال أبو سعيد: فأنا أصغر القوم، قال: فاذهب به[1]، فأنت ترى كيف استوثق كل من أبي بكر وعمر في الرواية عن الرسول ﷺ مع كون الرواة من الصحابة الأخيار.

وقد كان علي بن أبي طالب رضي الله عنه يستحلف من يروي له حديثاً عن الرسول ﷺ، وذلك للاستيثاق من صدقه[2].

وقد أثمرت هذه الطريقة، فلم يبلغنا أن أحداً كذب على الرسول ﷺ في عهد الخلفاء الراشدين، وهذا راجع لهذا المنهج القويم، ولأن الصحابة الكبار موجودون بكثرة، وهيبتهم تملأ القلوب، ولأن الكاذب يسهل اكتشاف كذبه.

1 [*Ṣaḥīḥ al-Bukhārī*] (6245), [Ṣaḥīḥ Muslim] (2153) (33)
2 [*Musnad al-Imām Aḥmad*]: 1/179 (2)

١ صحيح البخاري (٦٢٤٥)، وصحيح مسلم (٢١٥٣) (٣٣).
٢ مسند الإمام أحمد: ١/ ١٧٩ (٢).

Recording the Prophetic *Sunnah*:

The *Sunnah* was not compiled at the time of the Messenger of Allah ﷺ, nor the time of the Companions, in comprehensive records. Al-Ḥāfiẓ Ibn Ḥajar attributed this to two reasons:

First: they were initially forbidden to do so, as was narrated in [Ṣaḥīḥ Muslim], fearing that the *Sunnah* might be confused with the Qur'an.

Al-Harawi compiled in the book [Dhamm al-Kalām], through az-Zuhri, who said: `Urwah Ibn az-Zubayr informed me that `Umar Ibn al-Khaṭṭāb wanted to record the *Sunan* and so he consulted the Companions of the Messenger of Allah ﷺ on this issue. The majority of the Companions consented, but 'Umar was still not sure what to do and waited for a whole month, seeking Allah's guidance, until one morning when Allah gave him the determination to make a decision. He said, "I've mentioned something to you about recording the *Sunan* that you already know. I then remembered the affairs of the People of the Scripture before you who recorded books alongside the book of Allah, but later fully dedicated themselves to these books and abandoned the book of Allah. By Allah, I will not confuse the Book of Allah with anything." So, he gave up the idea of recording the *Sunan*. [1]

Second: their perfect memories and great ability to memorize. The Companions, in general, did not know how to write. However, some individual Companions used to keep personal records for themselves. Among those who recorded the *Sunnah* was Ibn `Abbās who left behind, after his death, a camel-load of his writings. [2]

Ibn al-Qayyim reported, in his book [al-Qiyās fish-Shar` al-Islāmī (Analogy in Islamic legislation)], from at-Tirmidhi that Qatādah used to narrate hadith(s) from the sheet written by Sulaymān al-Yashkurī on the authority of Jābir Ibn `Abdullāh. [3] He also narrated that Abū Hurayrah eventually began to write down what he had memorized [of hadith(s)], lest he should forget them. Before that, he used to not write, and when he wrote, he began depending on his memory. [4]

---

1 [*Tanwīr al-Hawālik*]
2 [*At-Tabaqāt*]
3 [*Kitāb al-Qiyās*]: 108, as-Salafiyyah Edition (1375 H.)
4 [*Difā`an 'Anil-Hadith an-Nabawī*]: 15

تدوين السنة النبوية:

لم تدون السنن في عهد الرسول ﷺ وفي عهد الصحابة في مدونات جامعة، وقد أرجع الحافظ ابن حجر هذا لأمرين(١):

الأول: أنهم كانوا في ابتداء الحال قد نهوا عن ذلك، كما ثبت في صحيح مسلم؛ خشية أن يختلط بعض ذلك بالقرآن.

وقد أخرج الهروي في كتاب ذم الكلام من طريق الزهري قال: أخبرني عروة بن الزبير: أن عمر بن الخطاب ﷺ أراد أن يكتب السنن، واستشار فيها أصحاب رسول الله ﷺ، فأشار عليه عامتهم بذلك، فلبث عمر شهراً يستخير الله في ذلك شاكّاً فيه، ثم أصبح يوماً وقد عزم الله تعالى له، فقال: «إني كنت ذكرت لكم في كتابة السنن ما قد علمتم، ثم تذكرت، فإذا أناس من أهل الكتاب قبلكم قد كتبوا مع كتاب الله كتباً، فأكبوا عليها، وتركوا كتاب الله، وإني والله لا ألبس كتاب الله بشيء، فترك كتابة السنن»(٢).

الثاني: سعة حفظهم وسيلان أذهانهم، ولأن أكثرهم لا يعرفون الكتابة، ولكن لم يمنع هذا أن يوجد أفراد من الصحابة كانوا يكتبون السنة لأنفسهم، ومن الذين كتبوا من السنة ابن عباس ﷺ، فقد خلف بعد موته حمل بعير من كتابته(٣).

ونقل ابن القيم في كتاب القياس في الشرع الإسلامي عن الترمذي أن قتادة كان يحدث عن صحيفة سليمان اليشكري التي كتبها عن جابر بن عبد الله(٤)، وأبو هريرة صار يكتب من حفظه قبل أن ينساه، وكان قبل ذلك لا يكتب، فلما كتب أخذ يعتمد على حفظه(٥).

---

١ قواعد التحديث: ٧٠.
٢ تنوير الحوالك: ١/ ٤.
٣ الطبقات: ٥/ ٢١٦.
٤ كتاب القياس: ١٠٨، طبع السلفية (١٣٧٥هـ).
٥ دفاع عن الحديث النبوي: ١٥.

The Companions` Differing;

Why These Incidents Were Few

During the Prophet's era, the Companions never fell into a dispute which was left unresolved. The Messenger of Allah ﷺ used to decide on all disputes, and since his sayings were based on legislation, they had to be accepted and followed. Following the Prophet's death, disagreements were inevitable. Despite the knowledge and nobility of the Companions, they were not infallible, and thus when the Companions needed to exercise *Ijtihād*, that rendered divergent views on certain questions.

Their Disagreements Resulted From:

1) Emerging incidents that did not occur during the Prophetic era, which were triggered by the expansion of the Islamic state, and the multitudes of culturally diverse nations that embraced Islam. Each had their own customs, and this necessitated the exercise of *Ijtihād*.

2) The disparity between the Companions in their respective abilities to understand the texts

3) Hadith(s) reaching some of them and not others

4) The Companions' dispersal in different provinces after 'Uthmān permitted them to leave Madinah. Consequently, the Companions` knowledge dispersed throughout the Earth, but this made it difficult to access them for consultation whenever calamities arose.

The dispute that arose during the caliphate of 'Uthmān and led to his martyrdom; may Allah be pleased with him. This same dispute preoccupied the Companions during the caliphate of 'Ali. Although the essence of this dispute was the authority and caliphate, its effects extended to many other issues.

Why Their Disagreements Were Few:

The questions over which the Companions differed were very few. This is attributed to the following reasons:

اختلاف الصحابة والسبب في قلة اختلافهم

لم يختلف المسلمون في عصر النبي ﷺ في مسألة ما اختلافاً مستمراً لا يصير إلى اتفاق؛ لأن الرسول ﷺ كان يحسم كل اختلاف، وكان قوله تشريعاً يجب اتباعه والمصير إليه، وبعد وفاة الرسول ﷺ كان لا بد من أن يقع الخلاف؛ لأن الصحابي مهما أوتي من علم ليس معصوماً من الخطأ، وقد احتاج الصحابة إلى الاجتهاد، فتعارضت أقوالهم في بعض المسائل.

ويعود اختلافهم إلى ما يأتي:

١- وقوع حوادث، ونزول نوازل، لم تقع ولم تنزل في العهد النبوي، بسبب توسع رقعة الدولة الإسلامية، ودخول أمم كثيرة في الإسلام لها عادات وتقاليد مختلفة، وهذا يحتاج إلى اجتهاد.

٢- تفاوت الصحابة في فهم النصوص وفقهها.

٣- بلوغ الأحاديث لبعضهم وعدم بلوغها لآخرين.

٤- تفرق الصحابة في عهد عثمان وعلي في الأمصار بعد أن أذن لهم عثمان في الارتحال عن المدينة، مما أدى إلى انتشار علم الصحابة في الأمصار، كما أدى إلى صعوبة الرجوع إلى الصحابة في الملمات.

الاختلاف الذي ذر قرنه في خلافة عثمان، وانتهى باستشهاده رضي الله عنه، وقد شغل الصحابة في خلافة علي رضي الله عنه، وهو وإن كان خلافاً حول السلطة والخلافة، إلا أن آثاره امتدت إلى كثير من الأحكام.

السبب في قلة اختلافهم:

المسائل التي اختلفوا فيها كانت قليلة، وقليلة جداً، ويعود ذلك إلى عدة أمور:

First: the great *Fiqh* that the Companions enjoyed.

Second: they were trained by the teacher of humanity; they were taught and mentored by the Messenger of Allah ﷺ who taught them how to easily tackle such problems.

Third: the methodology which the Companions bound themselves to, which will be explained later.

The Sources of Legislation at the Time of the Companions

In this era, the sources of legislation were the Qur'an and *Sunnah,* in addition to a new source, *Ijtihād,* which they called *Ra'y* (literally: Opinion). If we track the situations where the Companions used the term *Ra'y,* we will find that this term incorporated other kinds of proofs which were later given distinct terms such as *Qiyās* (Analogy), *Istiḥsān* (Juristic Preference), and *Istiṣlāḥ* (Public Interest). It should be noted that they did not neglect the consideration of *'Urf* (Custom).

Examples of the Companions' Ijtihād:

We have already come across some examples of the Companions' *Ijtihād*. Other examples include:

1) Following the Messenger ﷺ's death, the Companions differed regarding the election of his successor. After the discussion that took place in the Saqīfat of Banū Sā'idah, they agreed to appoint Abū Bakr aṣ-Ṣiddīq.

2) Some of the Companions disagreed with Abū Bakr regarding his decision to fight against the withholders of Zakāh. Abū Bakr however drew an analogy between the case of the Zakāh withholder and the one who abandons prayer in that both should be fought.

3) Abū Bakr agreed with 'Umar to record and collect the Qur'an after the latter had feared the Qur'an would be lost due to the death of its memorizers.

4) 'Umar Ibn al-Khaṭṭāb gathered all Muslims to pray [tarāweeḥ] behind one Imām in Ramadan, whereas before each would pray separately in the masjid.

أولاً: الفقه العظيم الذي كان الصحابة يتمتعون به.

ثانياً: تدربهم على أيدي معلم البشرية، فقد تربوا على يدي الرسول ﷺ، فعلمهم كيف يواجهون مشكلات الحياة بيسر وسهولة.

ثالثاً: المنهج الذي أخذ الصحابة أنفسهم به، وسيأتي بيان هذا المنهج.

مصادر التشريع في عصر الصحابة

مصادر التشريع في هذا العصر الكتاب والسنة، والمصدر الجديد هو الاجتهاد، وقد كانوا يسمونه الرأي، وإذا تتبعنا مواضع استعمال الصحابة للرأي وجدنا هذه الكلمة شاملة لأنواع من الأدلة التي تميزت بأسماء خاصة فيما بعد؛ كالقياس والاستحسان والاستصلاح مع ملاحظة أنهم لم يهملوا العرف.

أمثلة لاجتهاد الصحابة:

مرت معنا أمثلة لاجتهاد الصحابة، وهذه بعض الأمثلة علاوة على ما تقدم:

١- بعد وفاة الرسول ﷺ اختلف الصحابة في الشخص الذي يلي أمر المسلمين، وبعد المحاورة التي وقعت في سقيفة بني ساعدة اتفقوا على تولية أبي بكر الصديق.

٢- خالف بعض الصحابة أبا بكر الصديق في قتال مانعي الزكاة، وقاس أبو بكر مانع الزكاة على تارك الصلاة في وجوب قتاله.

٣- وافق أبو بكر عمر بن الخطاب على كتابة المصحف وجمع القرآن بعد أن خشي عمر على ذهاب القرآن بذهاب حفظته.

٤- جمع عمر بن الخطاب المسلمين على إمام واحد في رمضان بعد أن كانوا يصلون أوزاعاً في المسجد.

After citing many examples of the *Ijtihād* of the Companions, Ibn al-Qayyim said, "The Companions judged the cases by referring to their counterparts and drawing similarities between them and their likes. They cross-referenced them to each other for judgments and by that opened the door of *Ijtihād* for scholars, making clear to them its way." [1]

The Mufti and Jurist Companions

Ibn al-Qayyim said, "Among the Companions of the Messenger of Allah ﷺ, those which I learned of them giving fatwa were one hundred and thirty-something, between men and women. The proliferate Companions were seven: `Umar Ibn al-Khaṭṭāb, `Ali Ibn Abi Ṭālib, `Abdullāh Ibn Mas`ūd, `Ā`ishah; the Mother of the Believers, Zayd Ibn Thābit, 'Abdullāh Ibn 'Abbās, and 'Abdullāh Ibn 'Umar.

Abū Muhammad Ibn Ḥazm said, 'The fatwa(s) given by each one of them would constitute a huge volume.'

The Companions about which a mediocre amount of fatwa(s) was reported were: Abū Bakr aṣ-Ṣiddīq, Umm Salamah, Anas Ibn Mālik, Abū Sa'īd al-Khudri, Abū Hurayrah, 'Uthmān Ibn 'Affān, `Abdullāh Ibn `Amr Ibn al-'Āṣ, 'Abdullāh Ibn Az-Zubayr, Abū Mūsa al-Ash'arī, Sa'd Ibn Abi Waqqāṣ, Salmān al-Fārisī, Jābir Ibn 'Abdillāh, and Mu'ādh Ibn Jabal. The fatwa(s) given by each of these thirteen Companions would make up a very small volume.

The rest of the Companions were scarce in fatwa; only one or two edicts were narrated about each of them."

Summary of Unit 3

This unit can be summarized in the following points:
1) The Companions of the Messenger of Allah ﷺ were the best generation ever; they made their lives subservient to the way of Allah and His Messenger. Allah praised them in many places of His Book and the Messenger of Allah ﷺ praised them in his *Sunnah*.

1 [*I'lām al-Muwaqqi`īn*]: 1/222-238

وقد ساق ابن القيم أمثلة كثيرة لاجتهاد الصحابة، ثم قال: «فالصحابة ﷺ مثلوا الوقائع بنظائرها وشبهوها بأمثالها، وردوا بعضها إلى بعض في أحكامها، وفتحوا للعلماء باب الاجتهاد، ونهجوا لهم نهجه، وبينوا لهم طريقه» [1].

فقهاء الصحابة أهل الفتيا

يقول ابن القيم: «الذين حفظت عنهم الفتوى من أصحاب رسول الله ﷺ مائة ونيف وثلاثون نفساً، ما بين رجل وامرأة.

والمكثرون منهم سبعة: عمر بن الخطاب، وعلي بن أبي طالب، وعبد الله بن مسعود، وعائشة أم المؤمنين، وزيد بن ثابت، وعبد الله بن عباس، وعبد الله بن عمر.

قال أبو محمد بن حزم: ويمكن أن يجمع من فتوى كل واحد منهم سفر ضخم.

والمتوسطون فيما روي عنهم من الفتيا: أبو بكر الصديق، وأم سلمة، وأنس بن مالك، وأبو سعيد الخدري، وأبو هريرة، وعثمان بن عفان، وعبد الله بن عمرو بن العاص، وعبد الله بن الزبير، وأبو موسى الأشعري، وسعد بن أبي وقاص، وسلمان الفارسي، وجابر بن عبد الله، ومعاذ بن جبل، فهؤلاء ثلاثة عشر يمكن أن يجمع من فتيا كل واحد منهم جزء صغير جداً.

والباقون مقلون جداً، لا يروى عن الواحد منهم إلا المسألة والمسألتان».

خلاصة الوحدة

نخلص من دراسة هذه الوحدة إلى ما يلي:

١- أصحاب رسول الله ﷺ هم الجيل المثالي، الذين أقاموا حياتهم وفق منهج الله ورسوله، وقد أثنى الله عليهم في غير موضع من كتابه، وأثنى عليهم رسول الله ﷺ في سنته.

١ إعلام الموقعين: ١/ ٢٢٢- ٢٣٨.

2) The Companions were in charge of the religion of Allah; they protected it from being lost or corrupted and conveyed it to the world. They played the greatest role in preserving the Noble Qur'an. They were scared that the Qur'an might be lost due to the death of its memorizers. After consulting 'Umar Ibn al-Khaṭṭāb, Abū Bakr decided to collect the Qur'an, and assigned this task to the noble Companion, Zayd Ibn Thābit, who carried it out efficiently.

3) The Companions had an equally important role in preserving the *Sunnah* of the Messenger of Allah ﷺ. The Two Rightly-Guided Caliphs, Abū Bakr and 'Umar, warned the Companions from narrating too many hadith(s), lest the *Sunnah* should be confused with alien sayings. Both of them used to verify whatever narration the Companions reported with regards to the Messenger of Allah ﷺ.

4) Although the Companions (may Allah be pleased with them) memorized the *Sunnah* of the Messenger of Allah ﷺ, it was not recorded at their time. They refrained from recording it as a precaution, fearing that it might be confused with the Qur'an, or that it would distract people from the Book of Allah.

5) The Companions differed on some rulings, but such cases of difference were few. There was not much dispute among the Companions because they enjoyed abundant knowledge and deep understanding.

٢- قام صحابة رسول الله ﷺ على دين الله، فحفظوه من الضياع، وبلغوه للعالمين، وكان لهم الدور الأعظم في حفظ القرآن الكريم، ذلك أنهم خشوا عليه من الضياع بسبب موت حملته، فقرر أبو بكر بمشورة عمر بن الخطاب أن يجمعوا القرآن الكريم، وأسندوا هذه المهمة إلى الصحابي الجليل زيد بن ثابت الذي قام بها خير قيام.

٣- وقد كان للصحابة أيضاً دور كبير في حفظ سنة رسول الله ﷺ، فحذر الخليفتان الراشدان أبو بكر وعمر الصحابة من الإكثار من رواية السنة، خشية أن يدخل في أحاديث رسول الله ﷺ ما ليس منها، وقد كان الخليفتان الراشدان يستوثقان إذا روى لهما أحد من الصحابة حديثاً عن رسول الله ﷺ.

٤- على الرغم من حفظ الصحابة - رضوان الله عليهم- على سنة رسول الله ﷺ إلا أن السنة لم تدون في عصرهم وذلك خشية أن يختلط شيء منها بالقرآن، وحذراً من أن ينشغل الناس بها عن كتاب الله تعالى.

٥- وقع خلاف بين صحابة رسول الله ﷺ في بعض الأحكام، إلا أنه كان خلافاً قليلاً، وترجع قلته إلى الفقه العظيم، والعلم الغزير الذي كانوا يتمتعون به.

Notes

Notes

Unit 4: Guiding Principles on How the Companions Learned the Legislations and Acted Upon Them

Contents of Unit 4

- **Principle 1:** The Companions restricting themselves to the blessed Sharia
- **Principle 2:** Their giving precedence to Sharia over personal opinion
- **Principle 3:** Their duly valuing personal opinion
- **Principle 4:** Not following whoever opposes the Sharia texts, no matter how high his status
- **Principle 5:** Recanting a personal opinion in favor of the proof
- **Principle 6:** The Companions` avoiding differences and argumentation
- **Principle 7:** Referring to the proper reference point for the ruling
- **Principle 8:** Verifying and deliberating in *Ijtihād*, and not hastening to give fatwa
- **Principle 9:** Frequent consultation of the people of knowledge, *Fiqh*, and discretion
- **Principle 10:** Avoiding questions which are disliked by the blessed Sharia

Importance of Unit 4

The Companions – may Allah be pleased with them – defined some guiding principles with regards to comprehending the Islamic legislation and acting upon it. These principles are of great importance, as they protect people from deviating from the straight path while dealing with *Fiqh* and the Sharia.

The Companions – may Allah be pleased with them – derived these principles from their proper understanding of the Book of Allah and the *Sunnah* of His Messenger ﷺ. The people of knowledge, in general, must be acquainted with these principles in order to remain firm upon the footsteps of the Companions of Allah's Messenger ﷺ. Thus, they will know how the Companions dealt with the Sharia texts, and with the new issues which did not occur at the time of the Messenger of Allah ﷺ. As well, they will know their stance on the issue of personal opinion, and in what fashion they dealt with disagreement.

الوحدة الرابعة

معالم هادية في تلقي الصحابة التشريع والعمل به

محتويات الوحدة الرابعة

- المعلم الأول: اقتصار الصحابة على الشريعة المباركة دون غيرها.
- المعلم الثاني: تقديمهم الشرع على الرأي.
- المعلم الثالث: تقدير الصحابة الرأي قدره.
- المعلم الرابع: عدم متابعة من خالف النص الشرعي مهما علت منزلته.
- المعلم الخامس: الرجوع عن الرأي إلى الدليل.
- المعلم السادس: تجنب الصحابة الاختلاف والجدل.
- المعلم السابع: طلب الحكم في مظانه.
- المعلم الثامن: التثبت والتروي في الاجتهاد وعدم التسرع بالفتيا.
- المعلم التاسع: الإكثار من مشاورة أهل العلم والفقه والرأي.
- المعلم العاشر: الابتعاد عن المسائل التي عابتها الشريعة المباركة.

أهمية دراسة الوحدة:

اختط الصحابة رضوان الله عليهم معالم هادية في تلقي التشريع والعمل به، وهذه المعالم لها أهمية كبيرة، إذ إنها تمنع من الانحراف عن الطريق المستقيم أثناء التعامل مع الفقه والشريعة.

وقد استمد الصحابة رضوان الله عليهم هذه المعالم من فقههم للكتاب والسنة. وأهل العلم عامة لا بد وأن يكونوا على دراية بهذه المعالم، حتى يكونوا دائماً على خطى أصحاب رسول الله ﷺ، فيعرفوا كيف كان الصحابة رضوان الله عليهم يتعاملون مع النصوص، ومع الحوادث والنوازل المستجدة التي لم تكن على عهد رسول الله ﷺ، وكيف كان موقفهم من قضية الرأي، وكيف كان حالهم عند الاختلاف.

Come; let us study this unit in order to learn – by Allah's permission – all these issues in detail.

Learning Objectives:

At the end of this lecture, students should be able to:

1) Differentiate between when opinions are praised and dispraised

2) Know how the Companions held the Sharia texts in high esteem and gave them precedence over everything else

3) Compare between the conduct of the companions in avoiding the issuance of fatwas, despite their immense knowledge, and that of some the people ascribed to knowledge who excitedly rush into issuing religious verdicts

4) Differentiate between when religious questions are praised and dispraised

Guiding Principles on How the Companions Learned the Legislations and Acted Upon Them

The Companions defined some guiding principles with regards to comprehending the Islamic legislation and acting upon it. Adhering to these principles prevents one from deviating from the correct path as far as the legislative aspect is concerned. The Companions derived such principles from their proper understanding of the Book of Allah and the *Sunnah* of His Messenger ﷺ.

These principles are of vital importance. They serve as beacons that guide the students of knowledge, and scholars, so that they do not lose track of the proper way to understand the blessed Sharia and act upon it. Ignorance of these principles by those involved in teaching and giving fatwa has caused much harm to the Muslims and deprived them of much good. It even evoked animosity and hatred in the *Ummah* whose religion enjoins upon it mutual love and solidarity.

هيا بنا لدراسة هذه الوحدة حتى تتعرف بمشيئة الله سبحانه على كل هذه التفاصيل.

الأهداف التعليمية:

يتوقع منك أيها الدارس الكريم بعد دراستك لهذه الوحدة أن تكون قادراً على أن:

١- تفرق بين الرأي المحمود، والرأي المذموم.

٢- تُبين مدى تعظيم الصحابة للنصوص الشرعية، وتقديمهم لها على ما سواها.

٣- تقارن بين سلوك الصحابة رضوان الله عليهم في تورعهم عن الفتيا، وخوفهم منها، مع رسوخهم في الفقه والعلم، وسلوك بعض المنتسبين للعلم الذين يفرحون بالفتيا ويتسابقون إليها.

٤- تفرق بين الأسئلة الممدوحة في الدين، والأسئلة المذمومة.

معالم هادية في تلقي الصحابة التشريع والعمل به

اختط الصحابة معالم هادية في الجانب التشريعي في تلقي التشريع والعمل به، ومراعاة هذه المعالم تمنع من الانحراف في المنهج الحق في الجانب التشريعي، وقد استمد الصحابة هذه المعالم من فقههم لنصوص الكتاب والسنة.

وهذه المعالم ذات أهمية كبيرة، فهي منارات تضيء لطلبة العلم والعلماء الطريق حتى لا ينحرفوا عن المسار الذي ينبغي أن يسلكوه وهم يتلقون هذه الشريعة المباركة ويعملون بها، والجهل بهذه المعالم من قِبَل بعض الذين تصدوا للفتيا والتعليم أضر بالمسلمين كثيراً، وحرم المسلمين خيراً كثيراً، وجلب العداوة والبغضاء للأمة التي أوجب عليها دينها التحاب والتآزر.

These principles can be considered a gauge that measures the adherence of the Muslims at large, and the people of knowledge in particular, to the way of the Messenger of Allah ﷺ and his Companions in the eras that followed them.

Principle 1: The Companions restricting themselves to the blessed Sharia

The Companions understood well that legislation is the exclusive right of Allah. Since the Sharia is from Allah, then it should be exclusively followed and all other contradicting legislations, traditions, and customs should be renounced. Allah obligated that His legislation be followed by whoever it reaches, and decreed that the servants have no choice in the matter: **"It is not for a believing man or a believing woman, when Allah and His Messenger have decided a matter, that they should [thereafter] have any choice about their affair. And whoever disobeys Allah and His Messenger has certainly strayed into clear error."**[1] When it comes to the Sharia of Allah, the motto of the Muslims is to listen and obey: **"The only statement of the [true] believers when they are called to Allah and His Messenger to judge between them is that they say, 'We hear and we obey.' And those are the successful."**[2]

These texts, and their likes, prohibit Muslims from following any legislation other than the divine legislation, be it an abrogated divine legislation or a man-made law. The adulterated legislations of the Torah, the revised legislations of the Evangel, as well as the French, English, and Roman laws, are all examples of paths opposing the path of Allah and His legislation. Allah says: **"And, [moreover], this is My path, which is straight, so follow it; and do not follow [other] ways, for you will be separated from His way. This has He instructed you that you may become righteous."**[3]

1 Surat al-Ahzāb – Verse 36
2 Surat an-Noor – Verse 51
3 Surat al-An'ām – Verse 153

وهذه المعالم تعتبر مقياساً لمدى استقامة المسلمين وأهل العلم على المنهج الذي كان عليه الرسول ﷺ وأصحابه في العصور التي جاءت بعد عصر النبوة والصحابة.

المعلم الأول: اقتصار الصحابة على الشريعة المباركة دون غيرها:

فقه الصحابة فقهاً قاطعاً أن التشريع حق الله وحده، وما دامت هذه الشريعة من عند الله فيجب اتباعها دون سواها، ونبذ ما عداها من الشرائع والعادات والأعراف التي تخالفها، وقد فرض الله على من علم شرعه اتباعه، وليس للعباد في ذلك خيار: **﴿وَمَا كَانَ لِمُؤْمِنٍ وَلَا مُؤْمِنَةٍ إِذَا قَضَى اللهُ وَرَسُولُهُ أَمْراً أَن يَكُونَ لَهُمُ الْخِيَرَةُ مِنْ أَمْرِهِمْ وَمَن يَعْصِ اللهَ وَرَسُولَهُ فَقَدْ ضَلَّ ضَلَالاً مُّبِيناً﴾**(١)، وشعار المسلمين تجاه شريعة الله السمع والطاعة: **﴿إِنَّمَا كَانَ قَوْلَ الْمُؤْمِنِينَ إِذَا دُعُوا إِلَى اللهِ وَرَسُولِهِ لِيَحْكُمَ بَيْنَهُمْ أَن يَقُولُوا سَمِعْنَا وَأَطَعْنَا وَأُولَئِكَ هُمُ الْمُفْلِحُونَ﴾**(٢).

فهذه النصوص وأمثالها تحرم على العباد اتباع تشريع غير التشريع الرباني، سواء أكانت شريعة سماوية منسوخة أم شريعة وضعية، فشريعة التوراة المغيرة وشريعة الإنجيل المبدلة، وشريعة القانون الفرنسي والإنجليزي والروماني، وغير ذلك من التشريعات، سبل مخالفة لسبيل الله وشريعته، والله يقول: ﴿وَأَنَّ هَذَا صِرَاطِي مُسْتَقِيماً فَاتَّبِعُوهُ وَلَا تَتَّبِعُوا السُّبُلَ فَتَفَرَّقَ بِكُمْ عَن سَبِيلِهِ﴾(٣)، وقد خط الرسول ﷺ لأصحابه خطّاً، ثم قال: «هذا سبيل الله»، ثم خط خطوطاً عن يمينه وعن شماله، وقال: «هذه سبل، على كل سبيل منها شيطان يدعو إليه» وقرأ: ﴿وَأَنَّ هَذَا صِرَاطِي مُسْتَقِيماً فَاتَّبِعُوهُ﴾(٤)، رواه أحمد والنسائي والدارمي(٥).

١ الأحزاب: ٢٦.
٢ النور: ٥١.
٣ الأنعام: ١٥٣.
٤ الأنعام: ١٥٣.
٥ مسند الإمام أحمد: ٧/ ٢٠٧- ٢٠٨ (٤١٤٢) وفيه تمام تخريجه، وانظر مشكاة المصابيح: ٥٩/١، وقال محقق المشكاة: «وإسناده حسن وصححه الحاكم وغيره».

In fact, the Messenger of Allah ﷺ drew a line then said, **"This is the way of Allah."** He then drew some lines to its right and left and said, **"These are (diverging) ways; on each of these ways there is a Shayṭān calling to it."** He then recited, **"And, [moreover], this is My path, which is straight, so follow it..."**[1] (Narrated by Aḥmad, an-Nasā'i and ad-Dārimi)[2]
These lines deviating from the correct path represent the various divergent ways. In today's world, they represent the deviant misguided legislations, and upon each of these paths is a devil calling to it. The Jews and Christians call to their abrogated and distorted faiths, the communists call to a legislation which is founded on disbelief and atheism; the devils of the East and West call to adopting man-made laws – those which permit the unlawful, forbid the lawful, and defy the rules of Allah.
The Messenger of Allah ﷺ was irate when he found 'Umar Ibn al-Khaṭṭāb consulting the Torah and admiring its contents. It was reported from ad-Dārimi, on the authority of Jābir, that 'Umar Ibn al-Khaṭṭāb came to the Messenger of Allah ﷺ with a copy of the Torah and said: "O Messenger of Allah! This is a copy of the Torah," but he ﷺ kept silent. As he began reading it, the face of the Messenger of Allah ﷺ was changing. Abū Bakr then said, "May your mother lose you! Can›t you see the face of the Messenger of Allah ﷺ?" Thereupon, 'Umar looked at the face of the Messenger of Allah ﷺ and said: "I seek refuge with Allah from the anger of Allah and the anger of His Messenger. We are content with Allah as [our] Lord, with Islam as [our] religion, and with Muhammad as [our] Prophet." The Messenger of Allah ﷺ then said: **"By the One in whose hand is the soul of Muhammad, if Moses appears to you and you follow him and abandon me, you will be misguided from the straight path. If he were alive and witnessed my prophethood, he would have followed me."** (Reported by ad-Dārimi)[3]

1 Surat al-An'ām – Verse 153
2 The [Musnad] of Imām Aḥmad: 7/207-208 (4142); there is its complete referencing. Also see: [Miskhāt al-Maṣābīh] 1/59. The authenticator of [al-Mishkāt] said: "Its *Isnād* (chain of transmission) is *Ḥasan*, and it was graded as *Ṣaḥīḥ* by al-Ḥākim and others.
3 [Sunan ad-Dārimi] (439). Also see: [Mishkāt al-Maṣābeeh] (1/68)

فهذه الخطوط المنحرفة عن الصراط هي السبل، وهي تمثل اليوم هذه الشرائع المنحرفة الضالة، وعلى رأس كل طريق داعية يدعو إليه، فشياطين اليهود يدعون إلى دينهم المنسوخ المحرف، وكذلك النصارى، وشياطين الشيوعيين يدعون إلى شرعة قامت على الكفر والإلحاد، وشياطين الغرب والشرق يدعون لتحكيم الشرائع التي وضعها البشر، التي تحل الحرام وتحرم الحلال، وتضاد حكم الله.

ولقد غضب الرسول ﷺ غضباً شديداً عندما جاءه عمر بالتوراة يستجيد ما فيها، فقد روى الدارمي عن جابر أن عمر بن الخطاب رضي الله عنه أتى رسول الله ﷺ بنسخة من التوراة، فقال: يا رسول الله، هذه نسخة من التوراة، فسكت، فجعل يقرأ ووجه رسول الله يتغير، فقال أبو بكر: «ثكلتك الثواكل»، ما ترى ما بوجه رسول الله ﷺ؟ فنظر عمر إلى وجه رسول الله ﷺ، فقال: أعوذ بالله من غضب الله وغضب رسوله، رضينا بالله رباً، وبالإسلام ديناً، وبمحمد نبيّاً. فقال رسول الله ﷺ: «**والذي نفس محمد بيده، لو بدا لكم موسى فاتبعتموه وتركتموني لضللتم عن سواء السبيل، ولو كان حيّاً وأدرك نبوتي لاتبعني**» رواه الدارمي(١).

١ سنن الدارمي (٤٣٩)، وانظر مشكاة المصابيح: ١/ ٦٨.

In the narration found in the [Musnad] of Aḥmad, and in [Shu'ab al-Eemān] by al-Bayhaqi, the hadith states: **"Are you doubting as the Jews and Christians doubted? Certainly, I have come to you with it plain and clear! Had Mūsā been alive today, he would have no choice but to follow me."**[1]

Principle 2: Their giving precedence to Sharia over personal opinion

A Muslim might find it cumbersome to apply Sharia in some situations, and as a result assume that his best interest lies in opposing the Qur'anic injunctions. As for Companions, they used to instruct people to accuse their discretion whenever it clashed with the religious texts. Sahl Ibn Ḥanīf said: "O people, recognize the flaw in your discretion, not in your religion. By Allah, had I been able to on the Day of Abū Jandal (i.e. the Day of Ḥudaybiyah), I would have rejected the command of Allah's Messenger ﷺ." (Reported by al-Bukhāri)[2]

In line with what Sahl touched upon, 'Umar said, "Beware of relying on discretion with regard to your religion." This was collected by al-Bayhaqi[3] in [al-Madkhal], in abridged form. It was also collected by aṭ-Ṭabarī and aṭ-Ṭabarānī[4] with a lengthier narration as thus: "When it comes to religion, you should find fault with [your] discretion, for I myself fell into rejecting the command of the Messenger of Allah ﷺ because of my *Ijtihād*-based discretion."[5]

Similarly, when 'Umar Ibn al-Khaṭṭāb was once delivering a sermon atop a pulpit, he said, "O people! When the *Ra'y* (opinion/discretion) comes from the Messenger of Allah ﷺ, it is correct because it is a guidance that Allah has shown to him. But when it comes from us, it is mere conjecture and preciosity."[6]

1 Compiled by Aḥmad: 23/349 (15156), and al-Bayhaqi in [Shu`ab al-Eemān] (177). In the comment he made on the hadith in [al-Mishkāt] (1/68), Sheikh Nāṣir-ud-Dīn al-Albāni said: "It contains Mujālid Ibn Sa`īd, who is weak, but I grade the hadith as *Ḥasan* because it has many other chains according to al-Lālakā`ī, al-Harawi, and others."
2 Al-Bukhāri: 6/2665 and Fat-h-ul-Bārī: 13/289 (7308)
3 Ibid: 13/289
4 Ibid
5 Ibid: 13/289
6 [Jāmi` Bayān al-`Ilm]: 2/64

وفي رواية عند أحمد في مسنده، والبيهقي في شعب الإيمان: **«أمتهوكون(١) أنتم كما تهوكت اليهود والنصارى؟! لقد جئتكم بها بيضاء نقية، ولو كان موسى حياً ما وسعه إلا اتباعي»(٢).**

المعلم الثاني: تقديمهم الشرع على الرأي:

قد يثقل على المسلم العمل بالنص في بعض المواقف، ويظن المرء أن الخير يتحقق بفعل مخالف لما أمر به القرآن، أو بترك لما أمر بفعله، وقد كان الصحابة يأمرون الناس بأن يتهموا رأيهم في مواجهة النصوص، فهذا سهل بن حنيف يقول: «يا أيها الناس اتهموا رأيكم على دينكم، لقد رأيتني يوم أبي جندل، ولو أستطيع أن أرد أمر رسول الله ﷺ لرددته» رواه البخاري(٣).

وقد أمر عمر بمثل قول سهل، ولفظه: «اتقوا الرأي في دينكم» أخرجه البيهقي(٤) في المدخل هكذا مختصراً، وأخرجه هو والطبري والطبراني(٥) مطولاً بلفظ: «اتهموا الرأي على الدين، فلقد رأيتني أرد أمر الرسول ﷺ برأيي اجتهاداً»(٦).

وخطب عمر بن الخطاب على المنبر فقال: «أيها الناس، إن الرأي إنما كان من الرسول ﷺ مصيباً؛ لأن الله كان يُريه، وإنما هو مِنَّا الظن والتكلف»(٧).

١ أي: متحيرون أنتم في دينكم.
٢ أخرجه أحمد: ٢٣/ ٣٤٩ (١٥١٥٦)، والبيهقي في شعب الإيمان (١٧٧)، وقال الشيخ ناصر الدين الألباني في الحديث في تعليقه على المشكاة: ١/ ٦٨: فيه مجالد بن سعيد وفيه ضعف، ولكن الحديث حسن عندي لأن له طرقاً كثيرة عند اللالكائي والهروي وغيرهما.
٣ البخاري: ٦/٢٦٦٥.وفتح الباري: ١٣/ ٢٨٩ (٧٣٠٨).
٤ المصدر السابق: ١٣/ ٢٨٩.
٥ المصدر السابق.
٦ المصدر السابق: ١٣/ ٢٨٩.
٧ جامع بيان العلم: ٢/ ٦٤.

Ibn 'Abbās – may Allah be pleased with him – said: "It is only the Book of Allah and the *Sunnah* of His Messenger ﷺ. Whoever speaks [concerning the religion] anything beyond that using his opinion, then I wonder if it would land in his good deeds or in his sins." [1]

The types of *Ra'y* (opinion/discretion) which the noble Companions warned against are the alien opinions that have no basis in the religion, or the rushed opinion wherein its giver does not tax himself with exerting the required effort to research it properly. The worst opinions are those given by those who know the texts, but act contrary to them, and then seek to misinterpret them and deny their apparent meanings so that they may qualify their corrupt views.

Principle 3: Their duly valuing personal opinion

The Companions needed to give opinion-based fatwa(s) for certain incidents that occurred during their time. However, they did not consider their opinions as authoritative as the texts of the religion; namely the Qur'an and *Sunnah*. Instead, they would emphasize that their judgment was mere opinion; meaning they are always subject to being correct and incorrect, and thus they did not impose their opinions on the other scholarly Companions.

Ibn Sirīn said: "Whenever Abū Bakr came across a case to which he could not find a solution either in the Qur'an or in the *Sunnah*, he would exercise personal judgment, and then say: 'This is my opinion; if it is right then it is from Allah, and if it is wrong then it is from me and from the Shayṭān.'"[2]

When a scribe of 'Umar Ibn al-Khaṭṭāb once wrote: "This is the decision of Allah and 'Umar," 'Umar objected by saying, "How evil is what you wrote! Rather, say: This is 'Umar's decision; if it is right, it is from Allah, and if it is wrong, it is from 'Umar."[3]

1 Ibid: 2/32
2 [I`lām al-Muwaqqi`īn]: 1/57
3 Ibid: 1/58

وقال ابن عباس t: «إنما هو كتاب الله وسنة رسوله ﷺ، فمن قال بعد ذلك شيئاً برأيه فما أدري أفي حسناته يجده أم في سيئاته»(١).

والرأي الذي حذر منه الصحابة الكرام هو الرأي المجرد الذي لا يستند إلى أصل من الدين، والرأي العجول الذي يبادر بالجواب غير مكلف صاحبه نفسه بالبحث عنه في مظانه، وأسوأ الآراء رأي الذين يعرفون النصوص، ويعملون بما يعارضها، ويتمحلون في تأويلها وإخراجها عن ظاهرها لتوافق آراءهم الفاسدة.

المعلم الثالث: تقدير الصحابة الرأي قدره:

احتاج الصحابة إلى الإفتاء بآرائهم في بعض النوازل التي وقعت في عصرهم، ولكنهم لم يجعلوا آراءهم ديناً يتبع بمنزلة الكتاب والسنة، فقد كانوا يصرحون بأنهم حكموا بهذا بالرأي، وأنه قابل للخطأ والصواب، ولم يكونوا يلزمون غيرهم من علماء الصحابة بالمصير إلى رأيهم.

يقول ابن سيرين: «إذا نزلت بأبي بكر قضية، فلم يجد لها في كتاب الله أصلاً، ولا في السنة أثراً اجتهد رأيه، ثم قال: هذا رأيي، فإن يكن صواباً فمن الله، وإن يكن خطأ فمني ومن الشيطان»(٢).

وكتب كاتب لعمر بن الخطاب: «هذا ما رأى الله ورأى عمر»، فقال عمر: «بئس ما قلت، قل: هذا ما رأى عمر، فإن يك صواباً فمن الله، وإن يكن خطأ فمن عمر»(٣).

١ المصدر السابق: ٢/ ٣٢.
٢ إعلام الموقعين: ١/ ٥٧.
٣ المصدر السابق: ١/ ٥٨.

When Ibn Mas`ūd was asked about a matter, he said, "I'll give my opinion on it; if it turns to be right, it is from Allah, but if it turns out to be wrong, it is from me and from the Shayṭān, and Allah and His Messenger are clear of it."[1]

'Umar Ibn Al-Khaṭṭāb once met a man and asked him, "What did you do?" He said, "'Ali and Zayd judged such and such." He (`Umar) said, "If I were in their place, I would have decided on such and such (other than what they decided)." The man said, "What prevents you, especially when you are in authority?" 'Umar said, "If I was to refer you to the Book of Allah or the *Sunnah* of His Prophet ﷺ, I would have done that. However, I would be referring you to an opinion, and opinions are shared [by all]." So, 'Umar did not repeal the judgment of 'Ali and Zayd. [2]

Principle 4: Not following whoever opposes the Sharia texts, no matter how high his status

The Companions never gave the opinion of anyone, regardless how high his status, precedence over the religious texts. For example, when Ibn 'Umar was asked about the *Mut'ah*[3] of Hajj, he recommended it. When the questioner said, "Are you going to view other than what your father viewed?" Ibn `Umar would clarify to him that 'Umar did not disagree with this. When people repeated the question over and over, he said, "Which is more deserving of being followed; the Book of Allah or 'Umar?" Another narration reads: "Is the command of the Messenger of Allah ﷺ more deserving of being followed or 'Umar? 'Umar did not view that!" [4]

1 Ibid: 1/60
2 Ibid: 1/68
3 When someone who intends to do Hajj makes Ihrām for 'Umrah first, then puts off his Ihrām, and then makes another Ihrām for Hajj.
4 Al-Bayhaqi narrated these two hadith(s) with a sound chain of transmission. See: [al-Majmū`] by an-Nawawī: 7/158. 'Umar (may Allah be pleased with him) did not forbid *Mut`ah* in Hajj to indicate that it was prohibited; rather he meant that the Ifrād Hajj was more preferable.

وقـال ابـن مسـعود في مسـألة سـئل عنهـا: «أقـول فيهـا برأيـي، فـإن يكـن صوابـاً فمـن اللـه، وإن يكـن خطـأ فمنـي ومـن الشـيطان، واللـه ورسـوله بريئـان»(١).

ولقـي عمـر بـن الخطـاب رجـلاً قـال: مـا صنعـت؟ قـال: قضى علـيٌّ وزيـد بكـذا، قـال: لـو كنـت أنـا لقضيـت بكـذا، قـال: فـما منعـك والأمـر إليـك؟ قـال: لـو كنـت أردك إلى كتـاب اللـه أو سـنة نبيـه ﷺ لفعلـت، ولكنـي أردك إلى رأي، والـرأي مشـترك، فلـم ينقـض مـا قالـه علـيٌّ وزيـد»(٢).

المعلم الرابع: عدم متابعة من خالف النص الشرعي مهما علت منزلته:

لم يكـن الصحابـة يقدمـون عـلى النصـوص قـول أحـد مهـما علـت منزلتـه، فهـذا ابـن عمـر يسـأل عـن متعـة الحـج(٣) فيأمـر بهـا، فيقـول لـه السـائل: أتخالـف أبـاك؟ فبـين للسـائل أن عمـر لم يـرد هـذا، فلـما أكـثروا عليـه، قـال: فكتـاب اللـه أحـق أن يتبـع أم عمـر؟ وفي روايـة: أمـر رسـول اللـه ﷺ أحـق أن تتبعـوا أم عمـر، إن عمـر لم يقـل ذلـك(٤).

١ المصدر السابق: ١/ ٦٠.
٢ المصدر السابق: ١/ ٦٨.
٣ متعـة الحـج: أن يحـرم مـن أراد الحـج بالعمـرة، ثـم يحـل مـن إحرامـه، ثـم يحـرم بالحـج.
٤ روى هذيـن الحديثـين البيهقـي بإسـناد صحيـح، المجمـوع للنـووي: ٧/ ١٥٨، وعمـر t لم ينـه عـن التمتـع مُحَرِّمـاً لـه، وإنمـا نهـى عنـه مفضِّـلاً الإفـراد.

When 'Urwah Ibn az-Zubayr said to Ibn 'Abbās, "How can you instruct people to perform 'Umrah in these ten [days] when there is no 'Umrah [prescribed] during these then?" Ibn 'Abbās replied, "Why don't you ask your mother about that first?" 'Urwah said, "Abu Bakr and 'Umar did not do that." Ibn 'Abbās said, "This is what causes your destruction! By Allah, I expect nothing but that Allah will punish you! I relate to you from the Prophet ﷺ and you relate to me from Abū Bakr and 'Umar?!" [1]

'Umar Ibn al-Khaṭṭāb disagreed with Abū Bakr aṣ-Ṣiddīq on several verdicts. While Abū Bakr did not differentiate between people with regard to grants, 'Umar did so upon becoming the caliph. 'Umar further opposed Abū Bakr on the issue of giving a share from *Zakāh* to the *Mu'allafat al-Qulūb* (those whose hearts are sought to be won over). Abū Bakr's opinion was to give them that share, and 'Umar's was to not give them, and eventually Abū Bakr conceded to 'Umar's opinion. On another occasion, Abū Bakr took the women of *Ahl ar-Riddah* (the apostate factions) as captives, while 'Umar opposed it. When he later became the caliph, he returned them to their families, except those who had given birth.

Another example is that while Abū Bakr allotted the lands conquered militarily to the conquerors, 'Umar made these lands endowments dedicated to the public interest of the Muslims.

Principle 5: Recanting a personal opinion in favor of the proof

When a judge passes a judgment, or a *Mujtahid* exercises *Ijtihād* on a given matter, then later discovers that the judgment of Allah's Messenger ﷺ was otherwise, he is obligated to concede to the judgment of Allah's Messenger ﷺ and recant his own judgment.

1 Narrated by al-Khaṭīb al-Baghdādī in the book of [al-Faqīh wal-Mutafaqqih]: 1/145.

وهـذا ابـن عبـاس t يقـول لـه عـروة بـن الزبـير: «تأمـر بالعمـرة في هـؤلاء العشر وليـس فيهـن عمـرة؟»، فيقـول لـه ابـن عبـاس: «أولا تسـأل أمـك عـن ذلـك؟»، فيقـول لـه عـروة: «فـإن أبـا بكـر وعمـر لم يفعـلا ذلـك»، فيقـول لـه ابـن عبـاس: «هـذا الـذي أهلككـم، والله مـا أرى إلا سـيعذبكم، إني أحدثكـم عـن النبـي ﷺ، وتحدثـوني بـأبي بكـر وعمـر»[1].

وقـد خالـف عمـر بـن الخطـاب أبـا بكـر الصديـق في عـدة مسـائل، فأبـو بكـر كان لا يفاضـل بـين النـاس في العطـاء، فلـما تـولى عمـر خالفـه في ذلـك، وخالفـه في حياتـه في إعطـاء المؤلفـة قلوبهـم، فأبـو بكـر رأى إعطاءهـم، وعمـر لم يـر ذلـك، ورجـع أبـو بكـر لـرأي عمـر في ذلـك، وسـبى أبـو بكـر نسـاء أهـل الـردة، ولم يـر عمـر ذلـك، فردهـن إلى أهلهـن في خلافتـه، إلا مـن ولـدت منهـن.

وقسـم أبـو بكـر الأراضي المفتوحـة عنـوة بـين الفاتحـين، وخالفـه عمـر فوقفهـا لمصالـح المسـلمين.

المعلم الخامس: الرجوع عن الرأي إلى الدليل:

إذا حكـم الحاكـم بحكـم، أو اجتهـد المجتهـد بـرأي في مسـألة مـا ثـم بلغـه نـص حكـم فيـه الرسـول ﷺ بخـلاف حكمـه، فإنـه يجـب عليـه أن يعـود إلى حكـم الرسـول ﷺ، ويبطـل حكمـه.

١ رواه الخطيب البغدادي في كتاب الفقيه والمتفقه: ١/ ١٤٥.

In his book [*al-Faqīh wal-Mutafaqqih*], al-Khaṭīb al-Baghdādī compiled a chapter entitled: "Instances wherein the Prophet's Companions, upon hearing and comprehending a Prophetic hadith, gave up their personal opinions in its favor." In it, he collected numerous incidents. Of them:

1) 'Umar used to say, "The blood money is for the blood-relatives of the deceased; a wife does not inherit any of the blood money of her slain husband." This continued until aḍ-Ḍaḥḥāk Ibn Sufyān (may Allah be pleased with him) said, "The Messenger of Allah ﷺ wrote to me that I should give a share of inheritance to the wife of Ashyam Aḍ-Ḍabbābī from the blood money of her husband." As a result, 'Umar retracted [his opinion].

2) Ibn al-Musayyab said, "'Umar Ibn al-Khaṭṭāb decided a certain amount of blood money for the injury of fingers. He was then informed about a letter that the Prophet ﷺ sent to Ibn Ḥazm in which he said, '**For every finger, ten camels (are due as blood money)**.' So, 'Umar applied this judgment and abandoned his first [judgment]."

3) Ubayy Ibn Ka'b narrated from the Messenger of Allah ﷺ that the *Ghusl* (ritual bathing) becomes incumbent only when seminal discharge is emitted: **"Water (bathing) is only necessitated by water (seminal discharge)."** Later, he retracted this opinion when he was informed that the Messenger of Allah ﷺ said something that abrogated his first hadith[1] to the effect that, **"When the two circumcised parts (private parts of male and female) meet [in sexual intercourse], *Ghusl* becomes mandatory."**

1 [Al-Faqīh wal-Mutafaqqih]: 1/139, [I'lām al-Muwaqqi'īn]: 2/283

وقد عنون الخطيب البغدادي في كتابه: «الفقيه والمتفقه» لهذه المسألة بقوله: «ذكر ما روي من رجوع الصحابة عن آرائهم التي رأوها إلى أحاديث النبي ﷺ إذا سمعوها ووعوها»، وساق تحته عدة وقائع منها:

١- كان عمر يقول: «الدية للعاقلة، لا ترث الزوجة من دية زوجها شيئاً، حتى قال الضحاك بن سفيان رضي الله عنه كتب إليَّ رسول الله ﷺ أن أورث امرأة أشيم الضبابي من دية زوجها»، فرجع عمر.

٢- عن ابن المسيب قال: قضى عمر بن الخطاب في الأصابع بقضاء، ثم أخبر بكتاب كتبه النبي ﷺ لابن حزم: «**في كل أصبع مما هنالك عشر من الإبل**»، فأخذ به، وترك أمره الأول.

٣- حديث أبي بن كعب أنه روى عن الرسول ﷺ حديثاً يفيد أن غسل الجنابة إنما يكون من الإنزال «الماء من الماء»، ثم رجع عن ذلك عندما بلغه أن الرسول ﷺ قال ما ينسخ حديثه الأول[1]: «**إذا التقى الختانان فقد وجب الغسل**».

١ الفقيه والمتفقه: ١/ ١٣٩، إعلام الموقعين: ٢/ ٢٨٣.

Principle 6: The Companions' avoiding differences and argumentation

The Companions understood the command of their Lord to adhere to the Book of Allah and the *Sunnah* of His Messenger, and His prohibition of them falling into dispute and disagreement concerning Allah's Religion: **"And hold firmly to the rope of Allah all together and do not become divided..."**[1] He (st) also said: **"...and do not dispute and [thus] lose courage and [then] your strength would depart..."**[2] He (st) also said: **"Indeed, those who have divided their religion and become sects - you, [O Muhammad], are not [associated] with them in anything..."**[3] He (st) also said: **"And do not be like the ones who became divided and differed after the clear proofs had come to them. And those will have a great punishment."**[4] Mālik Ibn Anas reported that the Messenger of Allah ﷺ said, **"I left with you two matters; if you hold fast to them, you will never go astray: the Book of Allah and the *Sunnah* of His Messenger."** (Reported by Mālik in his Muwaṭṭa')[5]

Similarly, the Messenger of Allah ﷺ warned against [futile] argumentation. Abū Umāmah reported that the Messenger of Allah ﷺ said, **"People never went astray after being guided, except that [futile] argumentation was cast among them."** Then, the Messenger of Allah ﷺ recited this verse: **"...They did not present the comparison except for [mere] argument. But, [in fact], they are a people prone to dispute."**[6][7]

---

1 Surat Āl-'Imrān – Verse 103
2 Surat al-Anfāl – Verse 46
3 Surat al-An'ām – Verse 159
4 Surat Āl-'Imrān – Verse 105
5 [Al-Muwaṭṭa'; the Book of Qadar; Chapter: The Prohibition of Following the Erroneous Opinions About Qadar] (3), [al-Mustadrak] by al-Ḥākim: 1/93 (318). Also see: [Jāmi` al-Uṣūl Min Aḥādīth ar-Rasūl]: 1/186
6 Surat az-Zukhruf – Verse 58
7 [Musnad al-Imām Aḥmad]: 36/493 (22164), Ibn Mājah (48), and at-Tirmidhi (3253), who said: This hadith is *Ḥasan Ṣaḥīh*. Also see: [Mishkāt al-Maṣabīḥ]: 1/63. In his commentary on the hadith, Sheikh Nāsir-ud-Dīn said: "Its *Isnād* (chain of transmission) is *Ṣaḥīḥ*."

المعلم السادس: تجنب الصحابة الاختلاف والجدال:

فقه الصحابة عن ربهم أمره إياهم بالاعتصام بكتاب الله وسنة رسوله ونهيهم عن الاختلاف والتنازع في دين الله: ﴿وَاعْتَصِمُوا بِحَبْلِ اللهِ جميعاً وَلاَ تَفَرَّقُوا﴾(١)، وقال: ﴿وَلاَ تَنَازَعُوا فَتَفْشَلُوا وَتَذْهَبَ رِيحُكُمْ﴾(٢)، وقال: ﴿إِنَّ الَّذِينَ فَرَّقُوا دِينَهُمْ وَكَانُوا شِيَعاً لَّسْتَ مِنْهُمْ فِي شَيْءٍ﴾(٣)، وقال: ﴿وَلاَ تَكُونُوا كَالَّذِينَ تَفَرَّقُوا وَاخْتَلَفُوا مِن بَعْدِ مَا جَاءَهُمُ الْبَيِّنَاتُ وَأُولَئِكَ لَهُمْ عَذَابٌ عَظِيمٌ﴾(٤)، وفي الحديث أن مالك بن أنس ﵁ بلغه أن رسول الله ﷺ قال: «تركت فيكم أمرين لن تضلوا ما تمسكتم بهما: كتاب الله وسنة رسوله» رواه مالك في موطئه(٥).

وحذر الرسول ﷺ من الجدال، فقد روي عن أبي أمامة قال: قال رسول الله ﷺ: «ما ضل قوم بعد هدى كانوا عليه إلا أوتوا الجدل»، ثم قرأ رسول الله ﷺ هذه الآية: ﴿مَا ضَرَبُوهُ لَكَ إِلاَّ جَدَلاً بَلْ هُمْ قَوْمٌ خَصِمُونَ﴾(٦)(٧).

---

١ آل عمران: ١٠٣.
٢ الأنفال: ٤٦.
٣ الأنعام: ١٥٩.
٤ آل عمران: ١٠٥.
٥ الموطأ، كتاب القدر، باب النهي عن القول بالقدر (٣)، والمستدرك للحاكم: ١/ ٩٣ (٣١٨)، وانظر جامع الأصول من أحاديث الرسول: ١/ ١٨٦.
٦ الزخرف: ٥٨.
٧ مسند الإمام أحمد: ٣٦/ ٤٩٣ (٢٢١٦٤)، وابن ماجه (٤٨)، والترمذي (٣٢٥٣)، وقال الترمذي: حسن صحيح، وانظر مشكاة المصابيح: ١/ ٦٣، وقال الشيخ ناصر الدين في تعليقه على الحديث: إسناده صحيح.

If the difference results from disparate understandings of the religious texts, or resultant of not being aware of the text, then the scholars should exert a sincere effort to learn the truth. In this case, such differences are not dispraised. Likewise, if debate is practiced in the fairest manner, with the aim of reaching the truth and refuting falsehood, then such a practice would be praised and rewardable.

Principle 7: Referring to the proper reference point for the ruling

The Companions stopped at nothing to reach a proper judgment; they used to seek it in its proper sources which, during their time, existed in the Companions' memories. We already know that the *Sunnah* of the Messenger of Allah ﷺ was preserved in the Companions' memories as a whole. However, not a single Companion collected the entire *Sunnah*. Obviously, no single Companion accompanied the Messenger of Allah ﷺ at every moment. A group of the Companions accompanied him at certain times, while another group enjoyed his company at other times. This was because they were busy carrying out tasks he ﷺ commissioned them with, such as military expeditions sent for Jihād, calling other people to Islam, and being sent as rulers to different areas throughout the Islamic state. For example, he sent 'Ali Ibn Abi Ṭālib, Mu`ādh Ibn Jabal, and Abū Mūsa al-Ash`arī to Yemen.

'Umar Ibn al-Khaṭṭāb said, regarding seeking permission three times, about which he did not know while others did, "This command of the Prophet ﷺ had remained hidden from me up until now due to [my] busyness in the markets."[1]

فإذا كان الاختلاف بسبب تفاوت العقول في فهم النصوص، أو بسبب عدم معرفة النص، فيجتهد العلماء في معرفة الحق، فهذا لا يعد من الخلاف المذموم.

وكذا الجدال إن كان بالتي هي أحسن لمعرفة الحق ودفع الباطل، فالآخذ به محمود مثاب.

المعلم السابع: طلب الحكم في مظانه:

لم يكن الصحابة يكتفون بعدم بلوغهم الحكم، بل كانوا يبحثون عن الحكم في مظانه، ومظان الحكم في وقتهم: محفوظات الصحابة، ونحن نعلم أن سنة الرسول ﷺ كانت محفوظة في صدور الصحابة في مجموعهم، ولم يجمع فرد من الصحابة السنة كلها، ذلك أنه من المعلوم بالضرورة أن الصحابة لم يكونوا يلازمون الرسول ﷺ كل الأوقات، بل يلازمه بعض الصحابة دون بعض، وذلك لانشغالهم في أمور كلفهم الرسول ﷺ بها كالسرايا التي كان يرسلها في الجهاد، وكالدعاة والولاة الذين كان يرسلهم إلى مختلف أنحاء الدولة الإسلامية، فقد أرسل علي بن أبي طالب ومعاذ بن جبل وأبا موسى الأشعري إلى اليمن.

وقد قال عمر بن الخطاب في أمر الاستئذان ثلاثاً حيث لم يعلمه وعلمه من دونه: «خفي عليَّ هذا من أمر النبي ﷺ، ألهاني الصفق بالأسواق»[1].

---

1 Reported by al-Bukhāri in his [Sahīh] (7353) in the book: [Adhering to the Book and Sunnah, Chapter: Refuting Tthose Who Said: The Prophet's ﷺ Judgments were Apparent], Fat-h-ul-Bārī: 13/321

١ الحديث رواه البخاري في صحيحه (٧٣٥٣) في كتاب الاعتصام بالكتاب والسنة، باب الحجة على من قال: إن أحكام النبي ﷺ كانت ظاهرة، فتح الباري: ١٣/ ٣٢١.

Abū Hurayrah explained why he memorized so many hadith(s) from the Messenger of Allah ﷺ, saying: "You claim that Abū Hurayrah transmits too many hadith from Allah›s Messenger (peace up upon him); know that our appointment is with Allah [to settle this dispute]. I was a poor man who stayed with Allah›s Messenger ﷺ being satisfied with bare subsistence, whereas the *Muhājireen* remained busy with transactions in the markets and the *Anṣār* had been engaged in looking after their properties. As for me, I attended the Messenger of Allah ﷺ saying one day: **"Who will spread his cloak until I finish speaking, then gathers it, and does not forget anything of what he heard from me?"** I spread the cloak I was wearing, and I swear by the One who sent him ﷺ with the truth, I never forgot anything that I heard from him."[1]

Principle 8: Verifying and deliberating in *Ijtihād*, and not hastening to give fatwa

The Companions (may Allah be pleased with them) used to be careful and meticulous when exercising *Ijtihād*. They never rushed to pass a judgment without deliberating repeatedly. When 'Abdullāh Ibn Mas`ūd was asked about a widow whose dead husband neither consummated the marriage nor fixed the dowry amount, people kept visiting him for a month before he said, "I say in this regard: she is entitled to receive a dowry equal to the dowries given to her female relatives, not more or less, in addition to her being entitled to inheritance, and obligated to observe the waiting period. If what I say is correct, it is from Allah, but if it is wrong, it is from me and from the Shayṭān, while Allah and His Messenger are clear of it." Some people from the Ashja` tribe, including al-Jarrāḥ and Abū Sinān, stood up and said, "Ibn Mas`ūd! We bear witness that the Messenger of Allah ﷺ decided on that very case amongst us regarding Barwa' bint Wāshiq and her husband Hilāl Ibn Murrah Al-Ashja`ī, and it was as you decided." Ibn Mas`ūd became extremely happy upon learning that his verdict conformed with the judgment of the Messenger of Allah ﷺ.[2]

---

1 Al-Bukhāri (7354)

2 [Musnad al-Imām Ahmad]: 7/308 (4276), Abū Dāwūd (2116), Ibn Mājah (1891), At-Tirmidhiyy (1145), An-Nasā`iyy: 6/121 (3354). It is a Sahīh hadith.

وبين أبو هريرة السبب في كثرة حفظه عن الرسول ﷺ فقال: «إنكم تزعمون أن أبا هريرة يكثر الحديث على رسول الله ﷺ، والله الموعد، إني كنت امرأً مسكيناً ألزم رسول الله ﷺ على ملء بطني، وكان المهاجرون يشغلهم الصفق بالأسواق، وكانت الأنصار يشغلهم القيام على أموالهم، فشهدت من رسول الله ﷺ ذات يوم قال: **«من يبسط رداءه حتى أقضي مقالتي ثم يقبضه، فلن ينسى شيئاً سمعه مني؟»**، فبسطت بردة كانت عليَّ، فوالذي بعثه بالحق ما نسيت شيئاً سمعته منه»(١).

المعلم الثامن: التثبت والتروي في الاجتهاد وعدم التسرع بالفتيا:

كان الصحابة ﵃ يتثبتون في اجتهادهم ولا يسارعون في الحكم ويرددون النظر، هذا عبد الله بن مسعود يسأل عن رجل تزوج امرأة، فمات عنها، ولم يدخل بها، ولم يفرض لها صداقاً، فاختلفوا إليه شهراً، أو قال: مرات، قال: «فإني أقول فيها: إن لها صداقاً كصداق نسائها لا وكس ولا شطط(٢)، وإن لها الميراث، وعليها العدة، فإن يك صواباً فمن الله، وإن يكن خطأ فمني ومن الشيطان، والله ورسوله بريئان». فقام ناس من أشجع فيهم الجراح وأبو سنان فقالوا: يا ابن مسعود نحن نشهد أن رسول الله ﷺ قضاها فينا في بروع بنت واشق، وإن زوجها هلال بن مرة الأشجعي كما قضيت، قال: ففرح عبد الله بن مسعود فرحاً شديداً حين وافق قضاء رسول الله ﷺ(٣).

---

١ البخاري (٧٣٥٤).

٢ الوكس: النقصان، والشطط: الزيادة.

٣ مسند الإمام أحمد: ٧/ ٣٠٨ (٤٢٧٦)، وأبو داود (٢١١٦)، وابن ماجه (١٨٩١)، والترمذي (١١٤٥)، والنسائي: ٦/ ١٢١ (٣٣٥٤)، وهو حديث صحيح.

This approach of Ibn Mas`ūd was the practice of all the other Companions. Ibn al-Qayyim (may Allah bestow mercy upon him) said, "The *Salaf* from among the Companions and Successors hated to rush into giving fatwa. Each one of them wished that he would be relieved by another who would bear that responsibility. However, once they felt that it became their individual responsibility, they would exercise *Ijtihād* to know its judgment from the Book, the *Sunnah*, and the sayings of the Rightly-Guided Caliphs."

'Abdullāh Ibn al-Mubārak said: Sufyān narrated to me from 'Aṭā` Ibn as-Sā`ib, from `Abdur-Raḥmān Ibn Abi Laylā, who said, "I witnessed a hundred and twenty of the Companions of the Messenger of Allah ﷺ (in the masjid); each *Muḥaddith* wished that one of his brothers (in Islam) would save him from having to narrate hadith, and each *Mufti* wished that one of his brothers would save him from having to give fatwa." [1]

Principle 9: Frequent consultation of the people of knowledge, *Fiqh*, and discretion

The Caliphs used to consult the people on the newly emerging issues for which they could find no judgment in the Book and *Sunnah*, and the books of *Sunnah* have transmitted to us the dialogues between 'Umar Ibn al-Khaṭṭāb, Abū Bakr, and Zayd Ibn Thābit in regard to collecting the Qur'an.

On another occasion, the Companions discussed the issue of fighting the apostates who would utter the *Shahādah* (testimony of faith) but withhold the *Zakāh*. Eventually though, they unanimously agreed that it was incumbent to fight them.

'Umar Ibn Al-Khaṭṭāb had a council of senior Companions whose advice he used to seek. He had included among them the young Ibn `Abbās, and when they objected to Ibn 'Abbās being preferred over others his age, 'Umar asked them a question that no one could answer but Ibn 'Abbās. `Umar`s intention was to show them how knowledgeable and firmly established in *Fiqh* Ibn 'Abbās was, and therefore prove his worthiness of being a Shūrā (council) member.

1 [Siyar A'lām an-Nubalā']: 4/263

وهـذا الـذي سـلكه ابـن مسـعود هـو المنهـج الـذي أخـذ بـه الصحابـة أنفسـهم، يقـول ابـن القيـم- رحمـه اللـه تعـالى-: «كان السـلف مـن الصحابـة والتابعيـن يكرهـون التسـرع في الفتـوى، ويـود كل واحـد منهـم أن يكفيـه إياهـا غيـره، فـإذا رأى أنهـا تعينـت عليـه بـذل اجتهـاده في معرفـة حكمهـا مـن الكتـاب والسـنة، وأقـوال الخلفـاء الراشـدين، ثـم أفتـى».

وقـال عبـد اللـه بـن المبارك: حدثنـي سـفيان بـن عطـاء بـن السـائب، عـن عبـد الرحمـن ابـن أبي ليـلى، قـال: «أدركـت عشريـن ومائـة مـن أصحـاب رسـول اللـه ﷺ أراه قـال في المسـجد، فـما كان منهـم محـدِّث إلا ود أن أخـاه كفـاه الحديـث، ولا مُفْـت إلا ود أن أخـاه كفـاه الفتيـا»(١).

المعلم التاسع: الإكثار من مشاورة أهل العلم والفقه والرأي:

كان الخلفـاء يشـاورون النـاس فيـما يجِـدُّ مـن قضايـا لا يجـدون لهـا حكـماً في الكتـاب والسـنة، وقـد نقلـت لنـا كتـب السـنة الحـوار الـذي جـرى بـين عمـر بـن الخطـاب وبـين أبي بكـر وزيـد بـن ثابـت في جمـع القـرآن.

وقـد ثـار نقـاش بـين الصحابـة حـول قتـال المرتديـن الذيـن منعـوا الـزكاة وهـم ينطقـون الشـهادتين، ثـم اتفقـوا عـلى وجـوب قتالهـم.

وعمـر بـن الخطـاب كان لـه جمـع يضـم كبـار الصحابـة يشـاورهم في أمـره، وقـد أدخـل في هـؤلاء ابـن عبـاس مـع صغـر سـنه، فلـما اعـترض مـن اعـترض عـلى تقديمـه ابـن عبـاس عـلى غـيره ممـن هـم في سـنه، سـألهم سـؤالاً لم يجـب عليـه إلا ابـن عبـاس، وغرضـه أن يدلهـم عـلى علمـه وفقهـه، واسـتحقاقه لأن يكـون مـن أهـل الشـورى.

١ سير أعلام النبلاء للذهبي: ٤/ ٢٦٣.

Of the issues in which ‘Umar sought consultation was the territories conquered by the Muslims. He sought to determine whether they should be distributed among the fighters or be left as endowment for the public treasury?

Al-Bukhāri (may Allah (st) bestow mercy on him) said in his [Ṣaḥīḥ]: “After the time of the Prophet ﷺ, the *Imām*(s) (leaders) used to consult the trustworthy scholars regarding the permissible matters in order to adopt the easiest decision. But, if the matter was clarified by the Book or *Sunnah*, they would look no further – in emulation of the Prophet ﷺ.

Abū Bakr, for example, decided to fight against the withholders of *Zakāh*. When ‘Umar opposed him saying, “How can you fight these people, while the Messenger of Allah ﷺ said, **‘I have been commanded to fight against people until they testify that there is no god but Allah, that Muhammad is the Messenger of Allah, establish the prayer, and pay the *Zakāh*. If they do that, their blood and properties are protected by me except when justified by law, and their affairs rest with Allah.’**?” Abū Bakr said, “By Allah, I will fight against those who separated what the Messenger of Allah ﷺ gathered together.” Then, ‘Umar followed Abū Bakr`s position. In this manner, Abū Bakr did not consider the advice of ‘Umar, because he already had relied on the judgment of the Messenger of Allah ﷺ in regards to those who separate between *Ṣalāh* and *Zakāh* and aim at altering the religion and its rulings – for the Prophet ﷺ said, **“Whoever changes his religion should be killed.”**

The *Qurrā’* (scholars of Qur’an) were those consulted in ‘Umar’s councils, whether they were old or young, and he was a strict observer of [the limits in] Allah’s Book.” [1]

1 [Sahīh al-Bukhāri; the Book of I‘tisām] no. (96), [Chapter: Allah`s saying: “…and their affair is [one of] consultation between them…” no. (28), after hadith no. (7368)

ومـن القضايـا التـي استشـار فيهـا عمـر أراضي البـلاد التـي فتحهـا المسـلمون، هـل تـوزع عـلى المقاتلـين، أم تـترك وقفـاً عـلى بيـت المـال؟

قـال البخـاري- رحمـه اللـه تعـالى- في صحيحـه: «وكانـت الأئمـة بعـد النبـي ﷺ يستشـيرون الأمنـاء مـن أهـل العلـم في الأمـور المباحـة ليأخـذوا بأسـهلها، فـإذا وضـح الكتـاب أو السـنة لم يتعـدوه إلى غـيره اقتـداء بالنبـي ﷺ.

ورأى أبـو بكـر قتـال مـن منـع الـزكاة، فقـال عمـر: كيـف تقاتـل النـاس وقـد قـال رسـول اللـه ﷺ: «**أمـرت أن أقاتـل النـاس حتـى يقولـوا: لا إلـه إلا اللـه، فـإذا قالـوا: لا إلـه إلا اللـه عصمـوا منـي دماءهـم وأموالهـم إلا بحقهـا، وحسـابهم عـلى اللـه**»، فقـال أبـو بكـر: واللـه لأقاتلـن مـن فـرق بـين مـا جمـع رسـول اللـه ﷺ، ثـم تابعـه بعـد عمـر، فلـم يلتفـت أبـو بكـر إلى مشـورة إذ كان عنـده حكـم رسـول اللـه ﷺ في الذيـن فرقـوا بـين الصـلاة والـزكاة وأرادوا تبديـل الديـن وأحكامـه. وقـال النبـي ﷺ: **«مـن بـدل دينـه فاقتلـوه»**

وكان القـراء أصحـاب مشـورة عمـر كهـولاً كانـوا أو شـباناً، وكان وقافـاً عنـد كتـاب اللـه»(١)

١ صحيـح البخـاري، كتـاب الاعتصـام ورقمـه (٩٦)، بـاب قولـه تعـالى: ﴿وَأَمْرُهُمْ شُورَىٰ بَيْنَهُمْ﴾، ورقمـه (28)، بإثـر الحديـث رقـم (7368).

In doing this, the Companions were treading the path of their Prophet ﷺ. Al-Bukhāri said, “On the Day of Uḥud, the Prophet ﷺ consulted his Companions on whether to stay in Madinah or to go out, and they decided to go out. When he wore his armor and was determined to go, they suggested that he stay in Madinah. However, he did not listen to them after he had already made up his mind. He said, **“It is not becoming of a Prophet, when he puts on his armor, to take it off until Allah gives His judgment.”**

When ‘Ā`ishah was slandered, the Prophet ﷺ consulted ‘Ali and Usāmah, and listened to their views, until the Qur’anic verses were revealed addressing the matter. Once that happened, at once he ﷺ flogged the slanderers without giving any attention to their disputes. Instead, he immediately proceeded to uphold what Allah had commanded of him.”[1]

Consultation is for when there is no text:

Consultation is only to be practiced for decisions regarding which the ruler or judge does not have a relevant text to rely upon. Whenever there exists a text pertaining to the subject in question, there is no plausible ruling except that which Allah had revealed.

وقد كان الصحابة في ذلك متبعين لنبيهم ﷺ، قال البخاري: «شاور النبي ﷺ أصحابه يوم أحد في المقام والخروج، فرأوا له الخروج، فلما لبس لأمته وعزم قالوا: أقم، فلم يمل إليهم بعد العزم، وقال: «**لا ينبغي لنبي يلبس لأمته، فيضعها حتى يحكم الله**».

وشاور علياً وأسامة فيما رمى به أهل الإفك عائشة، فسمع منهما حتى نزل القرآن، فجلد الرامين، ولم يلتفت إلى تنازعهم، ولكن حكم بما أمره الله»[١].

المشاورة فيما ليس فيه نص:

إنما تكون المشاورة في الحكم والقضاء فيما ليس عند الحاكم أو القاضي فيه نص، أما إذا وجد نص في المسألة فليس إلا الحكم بما أنزل الله تعالى.

1 Compiled by al-Bukhāri as a *Mu‘allaq* report following hadith no. (7368)

١ أخرجه البخاري تعليقاً بإثر الحديث رقم (٧٣٦٨).

Principle 10: Avoiding questions which are disliked by the blessed Sharia

The Messenger of Allah ﷺ said to his Companions: **"Avoid whatever I forbid you from, and do whatever I command of you to the best of your capacity. Indeed, that which doomed the people before you was their excessive questioning, and their objecting to their Prophets."** (Reported by al-Bukhāri and Muslim) [1]

The texts clarified to us when questions are forbidden by the Sharia, including:

1) Questions meant to stump and challenge
All the previous nations challenged their messengers with such questions, one example being the questions posed by the Children of Israel to Prophet Mūsa. It is for that reason that Allah dispraised the Children of Israel and warned this *Ummah* [of Islam] against imitating their same conduct with the Prophet Muhammad ﷺ: **"Or do you intend to ask your Messenger as Mūsa was asked before? And whoever exchanges faith for disbelief has certainly strayed from the soundness of the way."**[2]

Allah informed us about some of the questions they asked Prophet Mūsa ﷺ, and their likes given to Prophet Muhammad ﷺ: "The People of the Scripture ask you to bring down to them a book from the heaven. But they had asked of Mūsa [even] greater than that and said, 'Show us Allah outright,' so the thunderbolt struck them for their wrongdoing..."[3] The nonbelievers asked the Messenger of Allah ﷺ many similar questions: "And they say, 'We will not believe you until you break open for us from the ground a spring. Or [until] you have a garden of palm trees and grapes and make rivers gush forth within them in force [and abundance] or you make the heaven fall upon us in fragments as you have claimed or you bring Allah and the angels before [us] or you have a house of gold or you ascend into the sky. And [even then], we will not believe in your ascension until you bring down to us a book we may read.' Say, 'Exalted is my Lord! Was I ever but a human messenger?'"[4]

1 Reported by al-Bukhāri (7288) and Muslim (1337) who placed it after hadith no. (2357); the wording is for Muslim.
2 Surat al-Baqarah – Verse 108
3 Surat an-Nisā' – Verse 153
4 Surat al-Isrā' – Verses 90-93

المعلم العاشر: الابتعاد عن المسائل التي عابتها الشريعة المباركة:

قال الرسول ﷺ لأصحابه: «**ما نهيتكم عنه فاجتنبوه، وما أمرتكم به فأتوا منه ما استطعتم، فإنما أهلك الذين من قبلكم كثرة مسائلهم، واختلافهم على أنبيائهم**» رواه البخاري ومسلم(١).

وقد جاءت النصوص مبينة المواضع التي نهت الشريعة عن السؤال فيها، ومنها:

١- الأسئلة التي يقصد بها التعنت والتعجيز:

وكل الأمم واجهت رسلها بمثل هذا، ومن ذلك أسئلة بني إسرائيل لنبي الله موسى، وقد ذم الله بني إسرائيل بسبب ذلك، وحذر هذه الأمة أن تسلك مع نبيها هذا المسلك: ﴿أَمْ تُرِيدُونَ أَن تَسْأَلُوا رَسُولَكُمْ كَمَا سُئِلَ مُوسَى مِن قَبْلُ وَمَن يَتَبَدَّلِ الْكُفْرَ بِالإِيمَانِ فَقَدْ ضَلَّ سَوَاءَ السَّبِيلِ﴾(٢).

وقد أخبرنا الله ببعض الأسئلة التي ألقوها على موسى، وألقوا ما يشبهها على نبي الله محمد ﷺ: ﴿يَسْأَلُكَ أَهْلُ الْكِتَابِ أَن تُنَزِّلَ عَلَيْهِمْ كِتَاباً مِّنَ السَّمَاءِ فَقَدْ سَأَلُوا مُوسَى أَكْبَرَ مِن ذَلِكَ فَقَالُوا أَرِنَا اللهِ جَهْرَةً فَأَخَذَتْهُمُ الصَّاعِقَةُ بِظُلْمِهِمْ﴾(٣).

وقد سأل الكفار الرسول ﷺ شيئاً كثيراً من أمثال هذا، **﴿وَقَالُوا لَن نُّؤْمِنَ لَكَ حَتَّى تَفْجُرَ لَنَا مِنَ الأَرْضِ يَنبُوعاً $ أَوْ تَكُونَ لَكَ جَنَّةٌ مِّن نَّخِيلٍ وَعِنَبٍ فَتُفَجِّرَ الأَنْهَارَ خِلالَهَا تَفْجِيراً $ أَوْ تُسْقِطَ السَّمَاءَ كَمَا زَعَمْتَ عَلَيْنَا كِسَفاً أَوْ تَأْتِيَ بِاللهِ وَالْمَلآئِكَةِ قَبِيلاً $ أَوْ يَكُونَ لَكَ بَيْتٌ مِّن زُخْرُفٍ أَوْ تَرْقَى فِي السَّمَاءِ وَلَن نُّؤْمِنَ لِرُقِيِّكَ حَتَّى تُنَزِّلَ عَلَيْنَا كِتَاباً نَّقْرَؤُهُ قُلْ سُبْحَانَ رَبِّي هَلْ كُنتُ إَلاَّ بَشَراً رَّسُولاً﴾**(٤).

١ رواه البخاري (٧٢٨٨)، ومسلم (١٣٣٧)، وأورده بعد حديث رقم (٢٣٥٧)، واللفظ لمسلم.
٢ البقرة: ١٠٨.
٣ النساء: ١٥٣.
٤ الإسراء: ٩٠-٩٣.

2) Asking questions to mock and ridicule: Al-Bukhāri narrated in his [Ṣaḥīḥ], on the authority of Ibn ʻAbbās (may Allah be pleased with them), who said, "Some people used to mockingly ask the Messenger of Allah ﷺ: 'Who is my father?' Another man whose she-camel strayed would ask: 'Where is my she-camel?' In response, Allah revealed about this verse: **"O you who have believed, do not ask about things which, if they are shown to you, will distress you..."**[1]

3) Fussy questions about details whose mention may lead to new burdens: For example, the Children of Israel came to Mūsa asking him about the murderer of a slain person they had found, and regarding which two groups among them blamed each other for his death. So, he said **"...Indeed, Allah commands you to slaughter a cow..."**[2] They could have carried out Allah's command in a relatively short time by slaughtering any given cow. However, they began to seek minute details about the description of the cow which led them into hardship. The more questions they asked, the more the scope of choice became narrowed, because the cow whose detailed description was eventually stipulated was a rarity: **"... It is a cow which is neither old nor virgin, but median between that..."**[3] Then, **"...It is a yellow cow, bright in color - pleasing to the observers..."**[4] Then, **"...It is a cow neither trained to plow the earth nor to irrigate the field, one free from fault with no spot upon her."**[5]

4) Questions about the hidden, unseen matters: The knowledge of some of these matters is exclusively with Allah; He hasn't given its knowledge to any of His creation. One such question was that about the Hour: **"They ask you, [O Muhammad], about the Hour: when is its arrival? In what [position] are you that you should mention it? To your Lord is its finality."**[6] Some of these questioned matters are beyond the perception of the human mind, such as asking about the soul: **"And they ask you, [O Muhammad], about the soul. Say, 'The soul is of the affair of my Lord. And mankind have not been given of knowledge except a little.'"**[7]

---

1 Surat al-Mā'idah – Verse 101
2 Surat al-Baqarah – Verse 67
3 Surat al-Baqarah – Verse 68
4 Surat al-Baqarah – Verse 69
5 Surat al-Baqarah – Verse 71
6 Surat an-Nāzi'āt: 42-44
7 Surat al-Isrā': 85

٢- السؤال على وجه السخرية والاستهزاء:
روى البخاري في صحيحه(١) عن ابن عباس- رضي الله عنهما- قال: كان قوم يسألون رسول الله ﷺ استهزاء، فيقول الرجل: من أبي؟ ويقول الرجل تضل ناقته: أين ناقتي؟ فأنزل الله فيهم هذه الآية: ﴿يَا أَيُّهَا الَّذِينَ آمَنُوا لَا تَسْأَلُوا عَنْ أَشْيَاءَ إِن تُبْدَ لَكُمْ تَسُؤْكُمْ...﴾(٢)، الآية.

٣- الأسئلة التي يريد صاحبها التدقيق في الأمور، وتحديدها تحديداً مفصلاً قد يؤدي إلى زيادة التكاليف:
ومن أمثلة هذه الأسئلة أن بني إسرائيل جاؤوا موسى يسألونه عن قتيل لم يعرفوا قاتله، واتهمت فيه طائفتان، كل واحدة ترمي الأخرى به، فقال لهم: ﴿إِنَّ اللَّهَ يَأْمُرُكُمْ أَنْ تَذْبَحُوا بَقَرَةً﴾(٣)، وكانوا يستطيعون أن يحققوا أمر الله لهم في مدة وجيزة، بأن يأتوا ببقرة مهما كان لونها أو عمرها، سواء كانت سمينة أو ضعيفة، قارة في البيت أو تعمل في الحقل، ولكنهم، أخذوا يستفصلون عن ذلك كله استفصالاً جعل الأمر عليهم شديداً؛ لأن البقرة التي وصفت وحددت قليل وجودها: ﴿بَقَرَةٌ لَّا فَارِضٌ وَلَا بِكْرٌ عَوَانٌ بَيْنَ ذَٰلِكَ﴾(٤)، ﴿صَفْرَاءُ فَاقِعٌ لَّوْنُهَا تَسُرُّ النَّاظِرِينَ﴾(٥)، ﴿لَّا ذَلُولٌ تُثِيرُ الْأَرْضَ وَلَا تَسْقِي الْحَرْثَ مُسَلَّمَةٌ لَّا شِيَةَ﴾(٦).

٤- السؤال عن الأمور المغيبة المخفية:
وبعض هذه الأمور مما اختص الله بعلمه، ولم يطلع عليه أحداً من خلقه كالسؤال عن الساعة: ﴿يَسْأَلُونَكَ عَنِ السَّاعَةِ أَيَّانَ مُرْسَاهَا $ فِيمَ أَنتَ مِن ذِكْرَاهَا ۞ إِلَىٰ رَبِّكَ مُنتَهَاهَا﴾(٧)، وبعض هذه الأمور لا يطيق العقل الإنساني إدراك كنهه وحقيقته، كالسؤال عن الروح: ﴿وَيَسْأَلُونَكَ عَنِ الرُّوحِ قُلِ الرُّوحُ مِنْ أَمْرِ رَبِّي وَمَا أُوتِيتُم مِّنَ الْعِلْمِ إِلَّا قَلِيلًا﴾(٨).

---

١ صحيح البخاري (٤٦٢٢).
٢ المائدة: ١٠١.
٣ البقرة: ٦٧.
٤ البقرة: ٦٨.
٥ البقرة: ٦٩.
٦ البقرة: ٧١.
٧ النازعات: ٤٢-٤٤.
٨ الإسراء: ٨٥.

It was the Jews who asked about the soul, as was clearly stated in the hadith narrated by al-Bukhāri, on the authority of `Abdullāh Ibn Mas`ūd, who said: "As I accompanied Allah's Messenger ﷺ in a cultivable land in Madinah, while he was walking with the support of a staff, he passed by a group of Jews. Some of them said to the others: Ask him about the soul.' Others said: 'Don't ask him, so that he doesn't make you hear what you may not like.' Finally, one amongst them approached him and said: 'O Abul-Qāsim, tell us about the soul.' He ﷺ paused for a moment, and I realized he was receiving revelation, so I kept back until the revelation finished descending. Then, he ﷺ stood and said: **'And they ask you, [O Muhammad], about the soul...'**[1,2]

Also, gaining knowledge of some of the unseen matters, which results from these questions, could harm the person to know them, or could harm the people to discover them. Allah says, **"O you who have believed, do not ask about things which, if they are shown to you, will distress you..."**[3] With regards to the reason for this verse being revealed, al-Bukhāri narrated, on the authority of Anas Ibn Mālik, who said, "Once the people started asking Allah's Messenger questions, and they asked so many questions that he became angry, ascended the minbar, and said, **"You will not ask me anything today, except that I will make it clear to you."** I looked right and left, and found every man covering his face with his garment and weeping. Suddenly, there was a man who, whenever quarreling with the people, used to be called the son of a person other than his father. He said, 'O Messenger of Allah! Who is my father?' The Prophet ﷺ replied, **'Your father is Ḥudhāfah.'** And then `Umar got up and said, 'We accept Allah as [our] Lord, Islam as [our] religion, and Muhammad as [our] Messenger; we seek refuge with Allah from the tribulations.' The Messenger of Allah ﷺ said, **'I have never seen a day like today, in its good and its evil, for Jannah (Paradise) and the Hellfire were displayed in front of me until I saw them just beyond this wall.'"** When Qatādah would relate this hadith, he would mention the following verse: **"O you who have believed, do not ask about things which, if they are shown to you, will distress you..."**[4,5]

1 Surat al-Isrā`: 85
2 Reported by al-Bukhāri (7297) and Muslim (2794)
3 Surat al-Mā`idah – Verse 101
4 Surat al-Mā`idah – Verse 101
5 Ṣaḥīḥ al-Bukhāri (6362), Ṣaḥīḥ Muslim (2359)

والذين سألوا عن الروح هم اليهود، كما جاء ذلك صريحاً فيما رواه البخاري عن عبد الله بن مسعود قال: «كنت مع النبي ﷺ في حرث بالمدينة، وهو يتوكأ على عسيب، فمر بنفر من اليهود، فقال بعضهم: سلوه عن الروح، وقال بعضهم: لا تسألوه، لا يسمعكم ما تكرهون، فقاموا إليه، فقالوا: يا أبا القاسم، حدثنا عن الروح، فقام ساعة ينظر، فعرفت أنه يوحى إليه، فتأخرت عنه حتى صعد الوحي، ثم قام، ثم قال: ﴿وَيَسْأَلُونَكَ عَنِ الرُّوحِ﴾»(١) (٢).

وبعض هذه الأمور المغيبة التي يطلب المرء بالسؤال إظهارها، قد يسوؤه معرفته لها ومعرفة الناس إياها، والله يقول: ﴿يَا أَيُّهَا الَّذِينَ آمَنُوا لَا تَسْأَلُوا عَنْ أَشْيَاءَ إِن تُبْدَ لَكُمْ تَسُؤْكُمْ﴾(٣).

وقد روى البخاري سبب نزول هذه الآية عن أنس بن مالك قال: سألوا النبي ﷺ حتى أحفوه بالمسألة، فغضب فصعد المنبر، فقال: «لا تسألوني عن شيء إلا بينته لكم»، فجعلت أنظر يميناً وشمالاً، فإذا كل رجل لافٌّ رأسه في ثوبه يبكي، فإذا رجل، كان إذا لاحى الرجال يدعى إلى غير أبيه، فقال: يا نبي الله، من أبي؟ فقال: «حذافة»، ثم أنشأ عمر فقال: رضينا بالله رباً، وبالإسلام ديناً، وبمحمد ﷺ رسولاً، نعوذ بالله من سوء الفتن، فقال النبي ﷺ: «ما رأيت في الخير والشر كاليوم قط، إنه صورت لي الجنة والنار حتى رأيتهما وراء الحائط»، وكان قتادة يذكر عند هذا الحديث هذه الآية: ﴿يَا أَيُّهَا الَّذِينَ آمَنُوا لَا تَسْأَلُوا عَنْ أَشْيَاءَ إِن تُبْدَ لَكُمْ تَسُؤْكُمْ...﴾ (٤) (٥).

١ الإسراء: ٨٥.
٢ رواه البخاري (٧٢٩٧)، ومسلم (٢٧٩٤).
٣ المائدة: ١٠١.
٤ المائدة: ١٠١.
٥ صحيح البخاري (٦٣٦٢)، ومسلم (٢٣٥٩).

5) Questions that the *Shayṭān* casts into the heart:

On the authority of Anas Ibn Mālik, who reported Allah's Messenger ﷺ said, **"People will continue to ask themselves questions until they eventually say: 'Allah created all things, but who created Allah?'"** [1] According to the narration of al-Bukhāri and Muslim, **"Satan comes to one of you and says: 'Who created this? Who created that?' – until he eventually says: 'Who created your Lord? When he comes to that, one should seek refuge in Allah, and desist [from such thinking].'"**[2] In a variant narration by Muslim, **"He who finds himself confronted with such matters, let him say: 'I have believed in Allah.'"**[3]

The Messenger of Allah ﷺ only guided people to such an approach of treating these questions because the insinuations of *Shayṭān* never end; whenever you come with a proof, he will contrive tricks to get you more involved, wasting your time. One may never be secured from his trials permanently; therefore, the only way to repel him is to resort to Allah and seek His refuge: **"And if an evil suggestion comes to you from Shayṭān, then seek refuge in Allah. Indeed, He is Hearing and Knowing."**[4] This is what effectively distresses *Shayṭān* and makes him cry. In fact, it humiliates him and causes him to feel despised, for Allah is the source of strength.

٥- الأسئلة التي يوسوس بها الشيطان:

عن أنس بن مالك قال: قال رسول الله ﷺ: «**لن يبرح الناس يتساءلون حتى يقولوا: هذا الله خالق كل شيء، فمن خلق الله؟**»(١)، وفي رواية للبخاري ومسلم: «**يأتي الشيطان أحدكم يقول: من خلق كذا، من خلق كذا، حتى يقول: من خلق ربك؟ فإذا بلغه، فليستعذ بالله، ولينته**»(٢)، وفي لفظ لمسلم: «**فمن وجد من ذلك شيئاً فليقل آمنت بالله**»(٣).

وإنما أرشد الرسول ﷺ إلى هذا الأسلوب في معالجة مثل هذه الأسئلة؛ لأن وساوس الشيطان لا تنتهي، فكلما جئت بحجة فإنه يجد مسلكاً للمغالطة والاسترسال، فيضيع الوقت، وقد لا يسلم المرء من فتنته، فلا تدبير في دفعه أقوى من الالتجاء إلى الله، والاستعاذة بالله: ﴿وَإِمَّا يَنْزَغَنَّكَ مِنَ الشَّيْطَانِ نَزْغٌ فَاسْتَعِذْ بِاللَّهِ إِنَّهُ سَمِيعٌ عَلِيمٌ﴾(٤)، وهذا هو الذي يحزن الشيطان ويبكيه، ويجعله خاسئاً ذليلاً، والله المستعان.

1 Sahīh al-Bukhāri (7296), Sahīh Muslim (136)
2 Ṣaḥīḥ al-Bukhāri (3276), Ṣaḥīḥ Muslim (134) (214)
3 Ṣaḥīḥ Muslim (134) (212)
4 Surat al-A`rāf – Verse 200

١ صحيح البخاري (٧٢٩٦)، وصحيح مسلم (١٣٦).
٢ صحيح البخاري (٣٢٧٦)، صحيح مسلم (١٣٤) (٢١٤).
٣ صحيح مسلم (١٣٤) (٢١٢).
٤ الأعراف: ٢٠٠.

6) Pretentious questions about events that have not yet occurred:

Al-Qurṭubī (may Allah bestow mercy upon him) mentioned that Muslim narrated, on the authority of al-Mughīrah Ibn Shu`bah, that the Messenger of Allah ﷺ said: **"Verily Allah, the Glorious and Majestic, has forbidden for you: disobedience to [your] mothers, burying [your] daughters alive, withholding [the right of others] while demanding [yours]. And He disapproved three things for you: hearsay, excessive questioning, and wasting wealth."**[1] Many scholars said that **"excessive questioning"** means indulging in many *Fiqh* questions for pretension, exceeding the proper limits in discussing riddles, puzzles, and issues for which no revelation descended, in addition to stumping the questioned person and delving in fussy details. The *Salaf* (predecessors) hated all these things and regarded them pretentious. They used to say: "Whenever a new incident occurs, the one in charge of answering questions about it will be supported by Allah to find the answer." Mālik said: "I witnessed the people of this town when they had no knowledge other than the Book and *Sunnah*. Whenever a new issue arose, the ruler would gather the present scholars to discuss it, and then he would then implement the judgment they would conclude. But now, you ask too many questions while the Messenger of Allah ﷺ hated that."

Ibn Rajab said: "Many of the Companions used to hate questions about incidents which had not yet occurred, and they would refuse to answer them." 'Amr Ibn Murrah said: "'Umar came out to people and said: 'I forbid you to ask us about things which have not yet occurred, for we are busy enough with what is already taking place." Ibn 'Umar said: "Do not ask about things which have not yet happened, for I heard 'Umar (may Allah be pleased with him) say: 'The one who asks about things that have not yet occurred has been cursed.'"[2]

1 Ṣaḥīḥ Muslim (593) (12) following hadith no. (1715)

2 [Jāmi` al-'Ulūm wal-Ḥikam]: 1/245, ar-Risālah Foundation edition, an excerpt from the commentary on the ninth hadith.

٦- السؤال عما لم يقع تكلفاً وتنطعاً:

قال القرطبي- رحمه الله تعالى-: روى مسلم عن المغيرة بن شعبة عن رسول الله ﷺ قال: **«إن الله حرم عليكم عقوق الأمهات، ووأد البنات، ومنعاً وهات، وكره لكم قيل وقال وكثرة السؤال»**(١)، قال كثير من العلماء: المراد بقوله: «**وكثرة السؤال**» التكثير من المسائل الفقيه تنطعاً وتكلفاً فيما لم ينزل، والأغلوطات وتشقيق المولدات، وقد كان السلف يكرهون ذلك ويرونه من التكلف، ويقولون: إذا نزلت النازلة وُفِّقَ المسئول لها، قال مالك: أدركت أهل هذا البلد وما عندهم علم غير الكتاب والسنة، فإذا نزلت نازلة جمع الأمير لها من حضر من العلماء، فما اتفقوا عليه أنفذه، وأنتم تكثرون المسائل، وقد كرهها رسول الله ﷺ(٢).

وقال ابن رجب: «كان كثير من الصحابة يكرهون السؤال عن الحوادث قبل وقوعها، ولا يجيبون عن ذلك، قال عمرو بن مرة: خرج عمر على الناس فقال: أُحَرِّج عليكم أن تسألونا عما لم يكن، فإن لنا فيما كان شغلاً، وعن ابن عمر قال: لا تسألوا عما لم يكن، فإني سمعت عمر رضي الله عنه يقول: لُعِنَ السائل عما لم يكن»(٣).

١ صحيح مسلم (٥٩٣) (١٢) بإثر الحديث (١٧١٥).

٢ تفسير القرطبي: ٦/ ٣٣٦.

٣ جامع العلوم والحكم: ١/ ٢٤٥، طبعة مؤسسة الرسالة، ضمن شرح الحديث التاسع.

Occasions when questioning is commended:

Not every instance of asking questions about the religion is disliked. Allah, the Almighty, said, **"... So ask the people of the message if you do not know."**[1] Falling under that is posing questions about the rulings which Allah sent down for us to learn and understand. As well, it is acceptable to ask about the meanings of the Qur'an which a person cannot understand, or about the things which have actually occurred – for the servant needs to know its rulings in order to fulfill his duty to Allah and apply His laws.

For example, the Companions asked the Messenger of Allah ﷺ about the spoils of war, intercourse with wives during menstruation, intercourse with wives during the daytime in Ramadan, using seawater for *Wuḍū'* (ablution), what is lawful of the game and what is unlawful, the tools used for hunting, using utensils in which *khamr* (alcohol) was served, the *Zakāh* given by a well-off wife to her poor husband, and many other questions which the Messenger of Allah ﷺ never disapproved of or disliked. Of the questions in which the questioner is praised is when he wants to know what Allah has revealed in His Book. Asking about these things is allowable to seek elaboration on a verse that could be understood in two different ways and there is no clue as to which interpretation is more appropriate. The question could also be about something that the questioner does not know. In his *Tafsīr*, Ibn Kathīr commented on the verse, **"...But if you ask about them while the Qur'an is being revealed, they will be shown to you..."**[2] saying, "In other words, do not initiate the question about matters yourselves, or else they may come with a more burdensome ruling as a result of your pretensions... However, if the Qur'an addresses it holistically, then you asked for its detailed explanation, it would then be clarified for you since your need necessitated that [question]."[3]

1 Surat an-Nahl – Verse 43
2 Surat Al-Mā`idah: 101
3 Tafsīr Ibn Kathīr: 2/663

المواضع التي يحمد فيها السؤال:

ليس كل سؤال في الدين بمذموم، فقد قال تعالى: ﴿فَاسْأَلُوا أَهْلَ الذِّكْرِ إِن كُنتُمْ لَا تَعْلَمُونَ﴾(١)، ومن ذلك السؤال عن الأحكام التي أنزلها الله للتعلم والتفقه، والسؤال عما لم يفهمه المسلم من معاني كتاب الله، والسؤال عن النوازل التي وقعت، ويحتاج العبد إلى أن يعرف حكمها ليتقي ربه، ويعمل بشرعه.

فقد سأل الصحابة الرسول ﷺ عن الأنفال، وعن إتيان النساء في المحيض، وسألوه عن الذي واقع أهله في نهار رمضان، وعن التوضؤ بماء البحر، وسألوه عن الصيد ما يحلُّ منه وما لا يحل، وعن الآلة التي يصاد بها، وعن استعمال الأواني التي كان يشرب فيها الخمر، وعن زكاة المرأة الغنية لزوجها الفقير، وغير ذلك من الأسئلة، ولم يكن الرسول ﷺ يكره شيئاً من هذا.

ومن الأسئلة التي يحمد سائلها تلك الأسئلة التي يريد صاحبها أن يتعرف على ما أنزله الله في كتابه، ويكون السؤال عنها بالاستفصال عن آية تحتمل معنيين، ولا مرجح لأحدهما على الآخر، أو يكون بالاستفصال عن أمر خفي على السائل المراد منه، يقول ابن كثير في تفسير قوله: ﴿وَإِن تَسْأَلُوا عَنْهَا حِينَ يُنَزَّلُ الْقُرْآنُ تُبْدَ لَكُمْ﴾(٢)، «أي لا تسألوا عن أشياء تستأنفون السؤال عنها، فلعله قد ينزل بسبب السؤال تشديد وتضييق...، ولكن إذا نزل القرآن بها مجملة، فسألتم عن بيانها بينت لكم حينئذ لاحتياجكم إليها»(٣).

١ النحل: ٤٣.
٢ المائدة: ١٠١.
٣ تفسير ابن كثير: ٢/ ٦٦٣.

There are many examples to what was mentioned above. ʻĀʼishah once asked the Messenger of Allah ﷺ about the words of the Most High: **"And they who give what they give while their hearts are fearful because they will be returning to their Lord..."**[1] She said: "O Messenger of Allah! Are these the people who sin and are [hence] fearful?" He ﷺ said, **"No, rather they are those who pray and yet are fearful, fast and yet are fearful, charitable and yet are fearful – that it would not be accepted from them."**[2]

Another example is what al-Bukhāri narrated in his [*Ṣaḥīḥ*] about the revelation of: **"...And eat and drink until the white thread becomes evident to you from the black thread..."** However, the continuation: **"...at dawn..."** had not yet been revealed. Thus, some men, when intending to fast, used to tie their legs, one with white thread and the other with black thread and would keep on eating till they could distinguish one thread from the other. Then, Allah revealed **"...at dawn..."** whereupon they understood that what was meant was the night and the day.[3]

1 Surat Al-Muʼminūn: 60
2 Aḥmad narrated a hadith similar to it in [al-Musnad]: 42/156 (25263), Ibn Mājah (4198), at-Tirmidhi (3175), and al-Ḥākim in [al-Mustadark]: 2/393-394 (3486), who said: This hadith has a *Ṣaḥīḥ Isnād* (sound chain of transmission), but it was not compiled by al-Bukhāri and Muslim, and adh-Dhahabī agreed with him on that. See the complete *Takhrīj* and criticism of this hadith in [al-Musnad].
3 Reported by al-Bukhāri (1917) and Muslim (1091)

وهذا الذي بيناه هنا له أمثلة كثيرة، فهذه عائشة تسأل الرسول ﷺ عن قوله تعالى: ﴿وَالَّذِينَ يُؤْتُونَ مَا آتَوْا وَقُلُوبُهُمْ وَجِلَةٌ أَنَّهُمْ إِلَى رَبِّهِمْ رَاجِعُونَ﴾[١]، فتقول: يا رسول الله، أهم الذين يذنبون وهم مشفقون؟ فقال: «لا، بل هم الذين يصلون وهم مشفقون، ويصومون وهم مشفقون، ويتصدقون وهم مشفقون، ألا يتقبل منهم»[٢].

ومن ذلك ما رواه البخاري في صحيحه أنه أنزلت: ﴿وَكُلُوا وَاشْرَبُوا حَتَّى يَتَبَيَّنَ لَكُمُ الْخَيْطُ الأَبْيَضُ﴾[٣]، ولم ينزل «من الفجر»، وكان رجال إذا أرادوا الصوم ربط أحدهم في رجله الخيط الأبيض والخيط الأسود، ولم يزل يأكل حتى يتبين له رؤيتهما، فأنزل الله بعد: ﴿مِنَ الْفَجْرِ﴾[٤]، فعلموا أنه إنما يعني: الليل والنهار[٥].

١ المؤمنون: ٦٠.
٢ رواه بنحوه أحمد في المسند: ٤٢/ ١٥٦ (٢٥٢٦٣)، وابن ماجه (٤١٩٨)، والترمذي (٣١٧٥)، والحاكم في المستدرك: ٢/ ٣٩٣- ٣٩٤ (٣٤٨٦)، وقال: هذا حديث صحيح الإسناد ولم يخرجاه، ووافقه الذهبي، وانظر تمام تخريجه وتنقيده في المسند.
٣ البقرة: ١٨٧.
٤ البقرة: ١٨٧.
٥ الحديث رواه البخاري (١٩١٧)، ومسلم (١٠٩١).

Summary of Unit 4

Unit four can be summarized in the following points:

The Companions (may Allah be pleased with them) had some guiding principles with regards to how they dealt with the legislations they received, and uphold them with diligence. These principles included:

1) Following only Allah's Sharia and rejecting all other laws, traditions, and customs.
2) When there was a conflict between the Sharia and discretion, they would give priority to the Sharia and reject all the opposing personal opinions, even if they were seemingly good.
3) They applied discretion in the absence of a relevant text, but would not hold their personal opinions parallel to the Book and *Sunnah*. Rather, they viewed them as mere opinions which were subject to being correct and incorrect.
4) They would never give priority to anyone's opinion over the texts, no matter how high his status was.
5) They would willingly recant their discretionary judgments if they later discovered that they conflicted with the texts.
6) They avoided and disliked disagreement and argumentation.
7) They sought judgments in their proper places, from the appropriate sources.
8) They were exceptionally careful when exercising *Ijtihād* and giving fatwa; they took their time and never rushed in this practice.
9) The Caliphs used to consult the people of knowledge, *Fiqh*, and discretion.
10) They used to keep away from questions meant for obduracy and pretension.

خلاصة الوحدة

نخلص من دراسة هذه الوحدة إلى ما يلي:

أن الصحابة -رضوان الله عليهم- كانت لهم معالم في تلقي التشريع والعمل به ومنها:

١- أنهم كانوا يتبعون شريعة الله فقط، وينبذون ما عداها من الشرائع والأعراف والعادات.

٢- أنه إذا تعارض عندهم الشرع والرأي كانوا يقدمون الشرع وينبذون ما عارضه من الرأي مهما بدا صالحاً.

٣- أنهم كانوا إذا احتاجوا إلى الرأي عند عدم النص أخذوا به ولكن لا يجعلونه بمنزلة الكتاب والسنة، بل يرون أنه قابل للخطأ والصواب.

٤- أنهم ما كانوا يقدمون على النصوص قول أحد مهما علت منزلته.

٥- أنهم كانوا إذا حكموا بالرأي ثم ظهر لهم من النصوص ما يعارض هذا الرأي فإنهم يرجعون إلى النص ويدعون الرأي.

٦- أنهم كانوا يجتنبون الخلاف والجدال المذمومين.

٧- أنهم كانوا يطلبون الحكم في مظانه.

٨- أنهم كانوا يتثبتون في الاجتهاد والفتيا ولا يتسرعون.

٩- أن الخلفاء منهم كانوا يشاورون أهل العلم والفقه والرأي.

١٠- أنهم كانوا يبتعدون عن المسائل التي يقصد منها التعنت والتنطع.

Notes

Unit 5
Fiqh during the Era of the Successors

Contents of Unit 5

1) Virtue of the Successors
2) Wider dependence on opinions
3) Increase in differences among scholars
4) Rise of *Fiqh* schools
5) Wider narration of the Prophetic Sunnah
6) Prominent scholars among the Successors

Importance of Unit 5

The Successors are the best of the Muslim nation after the Prophet's Companions. Allah, the Glorified, praised them in the Holy Qur'an and so did the Prophet (ﷺ). As for the era of the Successors, it was characterized by some traits that made it different from the era of the Companions. These differences referred to the change of life and the calamities that afflicted the Muslim nation in the era of the Successors. Two great *Fiqh* schools rose in this era. They were Madinah's *Fiqh* school and Kufah's *Fiqh* school. Each had a good effect on the development of the Islamic *Fiqh*. Also, people elaborated on narrating the Prophetic Sunnah. In this unit, we are going to focus our attention on these topics and others.

Learning objectives

At the end of this unit, readers should be able to:

1) Identify the Successors and the era in which they lived
2) Explain how their widened dependence on opinions led to differences on many juristic issues
3) Show how *Fiqh* schools arose in Madinah and Kufah
4) Explain how the Successors were careful and diligent in narrating the Prophetic Sunnah

الوحدة الخامسة
الفقه في عصر التابعين

محتويات الوحدة الخامسة

١- فضل التـابعين.
٢- التوسع في الأخذ بالرأي.
٣- اتساع دائرة الاختلاف.
٤- تكوين المدارس الفقهية.
٥- التوسع في رواية السنة النبوية.
٦- أبرز علماء التابعين.

أهمية دراسة الوحدة:

التابعـون هـم أفضـل الأمـة بعـد صحابـة رسـول اللـه ﷺ، وقـد أثنـى عليهـم ربنـا جـل وعـلا في كتابـه، وأثنـى عليهـم رسـول اللـه ﷺ في أحاديثـه، وكان لهـذا العـصر - عـصر التابعـين- بعـض السـمات التـي اختلـف بهـا عـن عـصر الصحابـة، وذلـك نظراً لتغير الحـال عـما كان عليـه في عـصر الصحابـة، وظهـور النـوازل التـي لم تكـن في ذلـك العـصر، وقـد ظهـر في هـذا مدرسـتان كبيرتـان في الفقـه الإسـلامي هـما: مدرسـة المدينـة، ومدرسـة الكوفـة، وكان لـكل منهـما أثـر طيـب في النهـوض بالفقـه الإسـلامي، كـما حـدث في هـذا العـصر توسـع كبـير في روايـة السـنة النبويـة.

كل هـذه التفاصيـل وغيرهـا تعرفهـا بفضـل اللـه سـبحانه بعـد دراسـتك لهـذه الوحـدة.

الأهداف التعليمية:

يتوقـع منـك أيهـا الـدارس الكريـم بعـد دراسـتك لهـذه الوحـدة أن تكـون قـادراً عـلى أن:

١- تذكر من هم التابعون وفي أي عصر وجدوا.
٢- تُوضـح كيـف توسـعوا في الأخـذ بالـرأي وأدى ذلـك إلى الاختـلاف في كثـير مـن المسـائل.
٣- تُبين كيف تكونت المدارس الفقهية في المدينة والكوفة.
٤- تـشرح كيـف ظهـر الاهتـمام بالسـنة والإكثـار مـن روايـة الحديـث عـن الرسـول ﷺ.

5) Confirm the virtue of the Successors with respect to the protection of Islam as a religion
6) List the reasons behind the disparate scholarly views in the era of the Successors
7) Mention the reasons behind the widened narrating of the Prophetic Sunnah in the era of the Successors

The Era of the Successors

Preface: Virtue of the Successors

The Prophet's Companions (may Allah be pleased with them) were taught Islam and its laws at the hands of the Prophet (ﷺ) and followed the path to which he (ﷺ) guided them. Similarly, the Successors received the teachings of Islam through the Prophet's Companions who acquainted them with the application of Islam and its various sciences including *Fiqh* and *ijtihād* (independent reasoning). There is no doubt that the era of the Prophet's Companions was the best of all eras after the lifetime of the Prophet (ﷺ), for the Companions were the maintainers of the religion who kept the flag of Islam raised high. They are the undisputed forerunners of all the believers. The era of the Successors followed suit and was the best after the lifetime of the Prophet (ﷺ) and the era of the Companions (may Allah be pleased with them). It should be noted that some of the Prophet's Companions lived in the era of the Successors, but due to their small number, this period was named as the era of the Successors.

The era of the Successors started when al-Ḥusayn ibn 'Ali ibn Abū Ṭālib abdicated the caliphate to Mu'āwiyah ibn Abi Sufyān in the year 41 A.H. It concluded with the end of the Umayyad caliphate or during its last phases. Some of the Prophet's Companions even lived in that era as well, but they were very few.

٥- تُدلل على فضل التابعين وأثرهم في الحفاظ على الدين.

٦- تذكر أسباب اتساع الاختلاف في عصر التابعين.

٧- تُبين أسباب التوسع في رواية السنة في عصر التابعين.

عصر التابعين

تمهيد: فضل التابعين:

إذا كان الصحابة قد تربوا على يدي رسول الله ﷺ، وساروا على المنهج الذي اختطه لهم، فإن التابعين تربوا على أيدي صحابة الرسول ﷺ الذين نقلوا للتابعين هذا الدين، وعرفوهم بمنهج الإسلام في العلم والفقه والفتيا، وإذا كان عصر الصحابة خير العصور بعد عصر الرسول ﷺ؛ لأن الصحابة هم القائمون على أمر الدين، وهم سادات المؤمنين، فإن عهد التابعين خير العهود بعد عهدي الرسول والأصحاب؛ لأن الصحابة ما يزال لهم وجود في هذا العصر[1]، والذين خلفوهم فيه ساروا على نهجهم من بعدهم.

ويبدأ هذا العصر من تنازل الحسن بن علي بن أبي طالب عن الخلافة لمعاوية بن أبي سفيان في سنة ٤١هـ وينتهي بانتهاء الدولة الأموية أو قريباً من ذلك، وهذا الدور وإن ضم في أوائله جمعاً من الصحابة إلا أنهم كانوا قلة فيه.

---

١ في العصر السابق الشهرة والكثرة للصحابة، والتابعون الذين لهم الظهور معهم في العلم والفتوى قليلون، أما في هذا العصر فقد انعكس الأمر وصارت الغلبة والكثرة والشهرة للتابعين، لقلة الصحابة وموت كبارهم.

How did the Successors Acquire the *Fiqh* of the Companions?

The Muslim world was one nation with no borders between its countries. This gave way for the scholars among the Successors to move easily from one Muslim country to another and seek knowledge from the Prophet's Companions. One distinguished scholar from among the Successors, al-Ḥasan al-Baṣri, even met five hundred men from among the Prophet's Companions.

In addition, the Prophet's Companions were spread throughout the Muslim countries during the caliphate of 'Uthmān ibn 'Affān. As a result, the Companions would educate the people of those countries and maintain the prophetic tradition. 'Ali ibn Abi Ṭālib and Ibn Mas'ūd lived in Kufah. 'Umar ibn al-Khaṭṭāb, his son 'Abdullāh, and Zayd ibn Thābit all lived in Madinah. Abū Mūsa al-Ash'ari lived in Basrah. Mu'ādh ibn Jabal and Mu'āwiyah ibn Abi Sufyān lived in Syria. 'Abdullāh ibn 'Abbās lived in Mecca. 'Abdullāh ibn 'Amr ibn al-'Āṣ lived in Egypt. Hence, the teachings of Islam spread from those places to the whole world.[1]

As Ibn al-Qayyim stated, "Islam and its sciences spread around the world through Ibn Mas'ūd, Zayd ibn Thābit, 'Abdullāh ibn 'Umar and 'Abdullāh ibn 'Abbās."[2]

The Successors' Method of Deducing Juristic Rulings

The Successors followed in the Companions' footsteps when deducing juristic rulings, always first referring to the Holy Qur'an and the Prophetic Sunnah. If neccesary, they would seek the Companions' *ijtihād* (independent opinions) on such issues. If all of that did not suffice, they would resort to their own *ijtihād*, while taking into consideration the proper method of exercising *ijtihād* and its guidelines, as taught by the Qur'an and Sunnah and exemplified in the *ijtihād* of the Companions. However, we find that many new things surfaced during this era which we are going to discuss at length in the following sections.

1 *I'lām al-Muwaqqi'īn* 1/64
2 Ibid: 1/22

كيف نال التابعون فقه الصحابة:

كان العالم الإسلامي دولة واحدة يسهل التنقل بين أقطارها، فلا عوائق ولا حدود، فكان طلبة العلم يتنقلون في أقطار الدولة الإسلامية ويلتقون بصحابة رسول الله ﷺ، ويأخذون عنهم، وحسبنا أن نعلم أن أحد علماء التابعين- وهو الحسن البصري- التقى بخمسمائة من صحابة رسول الله ﷺ.

أضف إلى هذا أن الصحابة انتشروا في البلاد في خلافة عثمان بن عفان وسكنوها، ونشر كل واحد علمه في الديار التي حل بها، فعلي وابن مسعود أقاما في الكوفة، وعمر بن الخطاب وابنه عبد الله بن عمر، وزيد بن ثابت كانوا بالمدينة، وأبو موسى الأشعري كان بالبصرة، ومعاذ بن جبل ومعاوية بن أبي سفيان كانا بالشام، وعبد الله بن عباس كان بمكة، وعبد الله بن عمرو بن العاص كان بمصر، وعن هذه الأمصار انتشر العلم في الآفاق(١).

وعامة الدين والفقه والعلم- كما يقول ابن القيم- انتشر في هذه الأمة عن أصحاب ابن مسعود، وأصحاب زيد بن ثابت، وأصحاب عبد الله بن عمر، وأصحاب عبد الله بن عباس(٢).

منهج التابعين في التعرف على الأحكام:

سلك التابعون نهج الصحابة في التعرف على الأحكام، فقد كانوا يرجعون إلى الكتاب والسنة فيما يواجههم من نوازل، فإن لم يجدوا رجعوا إلى اجتهاد الصحابة، وإن لم يجدوا اجتهدوا رأيهم مراعين في ذلك المنهج الذي دلهم عليه الكتاب والسنة، والضوابط التي راعاها الصحابة في اجتهادهم, ولكننا نرى أموراً جدت في هذا العصر،

١ إعلام الموقعين: ١/ ٦٤.
٢ المصدر السابق: ١/ ٢٢.

Wider Dependence on Opinions

Some scholars among the Successors did not abide by this method and began to increasingly depend on *ijtihād*-based opinions. In fact, they began generating hypothetical juristic issues, and then deliberating their solutions and the rulings for them.

This group of scholars became known as *Ahl ar-Ra'y* or the People of Independent Reasoning. Most of them existed in Iraq, and their leader was Ibrāhīm ibn Yazīd an-Nakha'i, who was the instructor of Ḥammād ibn Abi Sulaymān (died 96 A.H.), who was the instructor of Imām Abū Ḥanīfah; may Allah bestow mercy upon his soul.

As a result, the jurists among the Successors who adopted the method of the Companions launched a campaign of criticism against this new method. They thought that this new method opposed the method of the Companions which was drawn out for us by the Noble Qur'an, and which the Prophet (ﷺ) himself applied. They believed that this new method would distract the Muslims from having the Qur'an and Sunnah as their primary references, and that it would preoccupy them with personal opinions.

Sufyān ibn 'Uyaynah said, "*Ijtihād*-based opinion is via consulting the people of knowledge, not for [just anyone] to state their opinion." Similarly, 'Umar ibn 'Abdil-'Azīz wrote to the people, "There is no one that has an opinion with [the presence of] a Sunnah of the Messenger of Allah [regarding the matter]."

Ibn Shihāb az-Zuhri used to say, "Let the Sunnah thrive; do not impede it with personal opinions." Similarly, 'Urwah ibn az-Zubayr used to say, "The Children of Israel remined upright [in their religion] until there rose among them a generation born of slavery who persuaded them to [over-depend on] personal opinions, which in turn led them astray."

وسنتناولها في المباحث التالية.

التوسع في الأخذ بالرأي

بعض العلماء خرج عن هذا المنهج عندما أكثروا من الاعتماد على الرأي، ولم يكتفوا بذلك، بل أخذوا يولدون المسائل، ويفرضون صوراً عقلية محتملة، ويضعون لها الحلول، ويفرضون لها الأحكام.

وقد عرف هؤلاء بأهل الرأي، وقد وجد أكثرهم في العراق، وزعيم هؤلاء إبراهيم بن يزيد النخعي شيخ حماد بن أبي سليمان المتوفى سنة ٦٩هـ وهذا شيخ الإمام أبي حنيفة- رحمه الله-.

وقد أثار فقهاء التابعين الذين فقهوا منهج الصحابة وساروا عليه، حرباً شعواء على هؤلاء، فقد رأوا أن هذه الطريقة مخالفة لطريقة الصحابة، التي اختطها لنا كتاب الله وبينها، وسار عليها رسول الله ﷺ، ورأوا أن هذا باب شر يصرف المسلمين عن العناية بالكتاب والسنة، ويشغلهم بآراء الرجال.

قال سفيان بن عيينه: اجتهاد الرأي هو مشاورة أهل العلم، لا أن يقول برأيه، وكتب عمر بن عبد العزيز إلى الناس: أنه لا رأي لأحد مع سنة سنها رسول الله ﷺ.

وكان ابن شهاب الزهري يقول: دعوا السنة تمضي لا تعرضوا لها بالرأي، وكان عروة بن الزبير يقول: ما زال أمر بني إسرائيل معتدلاً حتى نشأ فيهم المولدون أبناء سبايا الأمم، فأخذوهم بالرأي، فأضلوهم[1].

١ المصدر السابق: ١/ ٧٧- ٧٩.

Increased Differing

The sphere of differences between the scholars widened during the era of the Successors. This was due to several reasons, such as:

1) Increased dependence on personal opinions which was just recently alluded to.

2) Seditions implanted among the Muslims which disunited them and caused them to fight against one another. In light of these events, sects emerged that held legislative beliefs which opposed those of the earlier generations of this *Ummah,* such as the Khawārij and the Mu'tazilah.

3) The Prophetic Sunnah was scattered throughout the Muslim world due to the fact that the Prophet's Companions had themselves become scattered; each land possessed a portion of the Sunnah. It is known that the Prophetic Sunnah had not yet been collected in one book. As a result, the people of each country would take the Prophetic Sunnah from the Companions living with them. Since it was impossible for a Companion to know all of the Prophetic Sunnah, the scholars of each locale would give *fatwa* based on whatever Prophetic tradition reached them and then employ *ijtihād* for whatever had not reached them, and thus differed because of that.

4) Within the Muslim State, each of the recently conquered countries had different customs and traditions. These differences led to differences between the jurists, since a scholar takes into consideration the customs and circumstances of his land as long as they do not conflict with the laws of Islam.

The Rise of *Fiqh* Schools

Many *Fiqh* schools came into existence in the era of the Successors – the most famous of which were the Madinah *Fiqh* School and the Kufah *Fiqh* School.

اتساع دائرة الخلاف

اتسعت دائرة الاختلاف في هذا العصر، ويرجع هذا إلى عدة أسباب، منها:

١- الإكثار من الاعتماد على الرأي الذي أشرت إليه قبل قليل.

٢- الفتن التي هبت على الدولة الإسلامية الفتية، وفرقت المسلمين، ومزقت وحدتهم، وسفكت دماءهم، وقد ظهرت في هذه الأثناء فرق تبنت أحكاماً تشريعية خالفت بها سلف الأمة؛ كالخوارج والمعتزلة.

٣- تفرق السنة في أقطار الدولة الإسلامية، فكان كل بلد عنده من سنة رسول الله ﷺ نصيب، فقد علمنا أن السنة لم تدون ولم تجمع في كتاب، وكانت موزعة في صدور الصحابة، فلما تفرق الصحابة في الآفاق أخذ أهل كل ناحية عن الصحابي الذي في قطرهم علمه، وكان أهل الفتوى يرجعون في كل ناحية إلى ما عندهم من سنة رسول الله ﷺ، ويجتهدون فيما لا يعلمونه، فيختلفون بسبب ذلك.

٤- كان لأهل البلاد المفتوحة عادات وتقاليد مختلفة، وهذا الاختلاف يؤدي إلى اختلاف الفقهاء؛ لأن الفقيه يراعي أحوال بلده وظروفه ما دامت غير مخالفة للشرع.

تكوين المدارس الفقهية[1]

تعددت المدارس الفقهية في عصر التابعين وأشهرها مدرستان: مدرسة المدينة، ومدرسة الكوفة.

---

١ سيأتي الحديث عن المدارس الفقهية بتفصيل في عصر التدوين والأئمة المجتهدين.

Madinah's *Fiqh* School

The Prophet (ﷺ) took Madinah as his second motherland after he (ﷺ) emigrated from Mecca. Madinah was the headquarters of the first Islamic state, its capital even after Islam spread far and wide, and in its shade lived the Muhājirūn[1] and the Anṣār.[2] Even after Kufah became the capital of the Muslim caliphate, Madinah continued to be the center of religious knowledge, as its scholars were the inheritors of the Prophetic knowledge and its people were an extension of the first Muslim community.

There were many who followed the method of the Prophet's Companions in Madinah. The most famous of them were known as the seven jurists:

1) Sa'īd ibn al-Musayyib, died in 94 A.H.
2) 'Urwah ibn az-Zubayr, died in 94 A.H.
3) Abū Bakr ibn 'Abdur-Rahmān ibn al-Hārith ibn Hishām al-Makhzūmi, died in 94 A.H.
4) 'Ubaydullāh ibn 'Abdillāh ibn 'Utbah ibn Mas'ūd, died in 98 A.H.
5) Khārijah ibn Zayd ibn Thābit, died in 99 A.H.
6) Al-Qāsim ibn Muhammad ibn Abi Bakr, died in 107 A.H.
7) Sulaymān ibn Yassār, died in 107 A.H.

مدرسة المدينة:

كانت المدينة المنورة موطن الرسول ﷺ بعد هجرته، وهي مقر الدولة الإسلامية الأولى، وعاصمة الدولة الإسلامية بعد انتشار الإسلام، عاش في أكنافها المهاجرون والأنصار، وبعد انتقال عاصمة الخلافة منها بقيت لها الزعامة الدينية، فقد كان علماؤها ورثة العلم النبوي، وكان أهلها امتداداً للمجتمع الإسلامي الأول.

والذين حملوا الراية بعد الصحابة وساروا على نهجهم في المدينة المنورة كثيرون، أشهرهم الفقهاء السبعة، وهم:

١- سعيد بن المسيب المتوفى سنة (٤٩هـ).

٢- عروة بن الزبير المتوفى سنة (٤٩هـ).

٣- أبو بكر بن عبد الرحمن بن الحارث بن هشام المخزومي المتوفى سنة (٤٩هـ).

٤- وعبيد الله بن عبد الله بن عتبة بن مسعود المتوفى سنة (٨٩هـ).

٥- خارجة بن زيد بن ثابت (٩٩هـ).

٦- والقاسم بن محمد بن أبي بكر (٧٠١هـ).

٧- وسليمان بن يسار (٧٠١هـ).

وهؤلاء هم الذين كان يطلق عليهم الفقهاء السبعة، وهم الذين قيل فيهم:

إذا قيل من في العلم سبعة أبحر
روايتهم عن العلم ليست خارجة
فقل هم عبيد الله عروة قاسم
سعيد أبو بكر سليمان خارجة

1 Those who migrated from Mecca to Madinah.
2 The citizens of Madinah who sheltered and sponsored the Muhājirūn.

Kufah's *Fiqh* School

After Kufah had become a Muslim city, a group of scholars from among the Prophet's Companions relocated there, such as Ibn Mas'ūd, Abū Mūsa al-Ash'ari, Sa'd ibn Abi Waqqās, 'Ammār ibn Yāsir, Ḥudhayfah ibn al-Yamān and Anas ibn Mālik. The number of Companions moving to Kufah increased when Caliph 'Uthmān ibn 'Affān gave the Muslims permission to move throughout the Muslim lands and establish new residences. Their numbers further increased when the Muslims fought one another after the murder of the Rightly-guided Caliph 'Uthmān ibn 'Affān. The number of Companions who lived there reached three hundred, and thus 'Ali ibn Abi Ṭālib made it the headquarters for his caliphate. After the Companions, numerous great scholars upheld the sciences in Kufah, including 'Alqamah ibn Qays an-Nakha'i (born in 62 A.H.), al-Aswad ibn Yazīd an-Nakha'i and Abū Maysarah 'Amr ibn Sharāhīl al-Hamadāni. This school of *Fiqh* was led by Ibn Abi Laylā, Ibn Shubrumah, the judge Sharīk and Abū Ḥanīfah.

Widened Narration of the Prophetic Sunnah

The widened narration of the Prophetic Sunnah began at the end of the Companions' era. We previously mentioned how the rightly-guided caliphs limited the narration of the Prophetic Sunnah and how this method effectively protected the Sunnah from any fabricated hadith(s) being admitted into it. However, the Companions did not continue like this; they began to abundantly narrate the Prophetic Sunnah at the end of the era of the rightly-guided caliphs. Thereafter, the floodgates of narrating, rehearsing hadith(s) and traveling to do so were opened wide.

مدرسة الكوفة:

انتقل إلى الكوفة بعد تمصيرها مجموعة من الصحابة، منهم ابن مسعود وأبو موسى الأشعري، وسعد بن أبي وقاص، وعمار بن ياسر، وحذيفة بن اليمان، وأنس بن مالك، وازداد عدد الصحابة فيها بعد أن أذن عثمان بن عفان للصحابة بالخروج إلى الأمصار، ثم ازداد عددهم بعد وقوع الفتنة ومقتل الخليفة الراشد عثمان بن عفان، وقد بلغ عدد الصحابة الذين حلوا بها أكثر من ثلاثمائة صحابي، وقد جعلها علي بن أبي طالب مقر خلافته، وقد قام بأمر علماء الكوفة بعد الصحابة جماعة من العلماء، منهم: علقمة بن قيس النخعي (٦٢هـ)، والأسود بن يزيد النخعي، وأبو ميسرة عمرو بن شراحيل الهمداني، وانتهت رياسة هذه المدرسة إلى ابن أبي ليلى، وابن شبرمة، وشريك القاضي، وأبي حنيفة كما سيأتي معنا[1].

التوسع في رواية السنة النبوية

التوسع في الرواية بدأ في آخر عهد الصحابة

رأينا كيف حد الخلفاء الراشدين من رواية السنة النبوية، وكيف أثمرت تلك الطريقة في حفظ السنة من أن يدخل فيها المكذوب.

ولكن لم يستمر الصحابة على هذه الحال، فقد أخذوا يكثرون من التحديث في أواخر عصر الخلفاء الراشدين، ثم انفتح الباب على مصراعيه في التحديث بالسنة وروايتها والرحلة في سبيل ذلك في هذا العهد.

١ انظر إعلام الموقعين لابن القيم: ١/ ٢٧، ومفاتيح الفقه الحنبلي: ١/ ٤.

This was not limited to the Successors. Rather, even the younger Companions who lived until this era would take part in this practice. They would visit one another to learn the hadith(s) of the Messenger of Allah (ﷺ). In fact, a Companion would travel a month long journey and traverse far distances in order to reach another Companion and collect a single hadith from him.

In the biography of ʻAbdullāh ibn Unays, Ibn Hajar said that Jābir ibn ʻAbdillāh al-Anṣāri (may Allah be pleased with him) said, "I was informed about a hadith on the law of *qisās* (equal retaliation) whose narrator lived in Gaza, so I traveled to him a distance of one month."[1]

In *Ṣaḥīḥ al-Bukhāri,* Imām al-Bukhāri reported that Jābir ibn ʻAbdillāh traveled for a month to Gaza to narrate a hadith from ʻAbdullāh ibn Unays. Imām al-Bukhāri reported the hadith with no chains of transmission. In his commentary on that hadith, the verifier of the book *Jāmiʻ al-Uṣūl* said, "Imām al-Bukhāri mentioned this hadith in the section on virtues of seeking knowledge, and in his book *al-Adab al-Mufrad*. Also, Imām Ahmad and Imām Abū Yaʻlā reported it in their books of hadith, from ʻAbdullāh ibn Muhammad ibn ʻAqīl, that he heard Jābir ibn ʻAbdillāh saying, 'I was told that a man heard a hadith from the Prophet (ﷺ), so I bought a camel and traveled for a month reach that man. When I arrived there, I found that this man was ʻAbdullāh ibn Unays. Upon that, I ordered the doorman to inform him that ʻAbdullāh that Jābir wanted him. ʻAbdullāh ibn Unays asked, 'Jābir ibn ʻAbdillāh?' I replied, 'Yes, it is me.' So, he came out and embraced me. I told him I was informed that he heard a hadith from the Prophet (ﷺ) that I had not known, and I desired to know it before I die. Upon that, ʻAbdullāh ibn Unays said, 'I heard Allah's Messenger (ﷺ) saying, 'The people would be assembled on the Day of Resurrection naked…'"[2]

1 *Difāʻ ʻan as-Sunnah an-Nabawi* 9
2 Reported by Imām al-Bukhāri in his *Ṣaḥīḥ* in *muʻallaq* form before hadith no. (78) and in *al-Adab al-Mufrad* (970), was collected by Imām Ahmad in *al-Musnad* 25/431-435 (16042), and its complete referencing is there. See *Jāmiʻ al-Uṣūl* 8/10.

ولم يتوقف هذا على التابعين، بل فعل هذا صغار الصحابة الذين كانوا أحياء في هذا العصر، فقد كان يأتي بعضهم بعضاً ليسمع حديث رسول الله ﷺ، وكان الصحابي يمضي الأيام الطويلة ويقطع المسافات الشاسعة كي يصل إلى صحابي آخر ليسمع منه حديثاً بلغه أنه يحفظه، أورد الحافظ ابن حجر العسقلاني في ترجمة عبد الله بن أنيس من كتاب الإصابة عن الإمامين أحمد والبخاري وغيرهما أن الصحابي ابن الصحابي جابر بن عبد الله الأنصاري- رضي الله عنهما- قال: بلغني حديث في القصاص وصاحبه بغزة، فرحلت إليه مسيرة شهر[١].

وفي صحيح البخاري عن جابر بن عبد الله- رضي الله عنهما- أنه رحل مسيرة شهر إلى عبد الله بن أنيس في حديث واحد، وقد أخرجه البخاري بدون إسناد، وقال محقق جامع الأصول في تعليقه على الحديث: ذكره البخاري تعليقاً في كتاب العلم، وأخرجه أيضاً في كتابه الأدب المفرد، وأحمد وأبو يعلى في مسنديهما من طريق عبد الله بن محمد بن عقيل: إنه سمع جابر بن عبد الله يقول: بلغني عن رجل حديث سمعه من رسول الله ﷺ، فاشتريت بعيراً، ثم شددت عليه رحلي، فسرت إليه شهراً، حتى قدمت الشام، فإذا عبد الله بن أنيس، فقلت للبواب: قل له جابر على الباب، فقال: ابن عبد الله، قلت: نعم، فخرج فاعتنقني، فقلت: حديث بلغني عنك أنك سمعته من رسول الله ﷺ، فخشيت أن أموت قبل أن أسمعه، فقال سمعت رسول الله ﷺ يقول: «يحشر الناس يوم القيامة عراة...» الحديث[٢].

١ دفاع عن الحديث النبوي: ٩.
٢ علقه البخاري في صحيحه قبل الحديث رقم (٧٨)، وأخرجه في الأدب المفرد (٩٧٠)، وهو في مسند الإمام أحمد: ٢٥/ ٤٣١- ٤٣٥ (١٦٠٤٢) وفيه تمام تخريجه، وانظر: جامع الأصول: ٨/ ١٠.

Abū Dāwūd and at-Tirmidhi reported that Qays ibn Kathīr said, "I was sitting with Abū ad-Dardā' in the mosque of Damascus. A man came to him and said, 'O Abū ad-Dardā', I have come to you from the city of Allah's Messenger (ﷺ) for a hadith that I have heard you relate from Allah's Messenger (ﷺ). I have come for no other purpose. He said, 'I heard Allah's Messenger (ﷺ) say, 'Whoever travels on a road in search of knowledge, Allah will place him on a road to Paradise. Indeed, the angels will lower their wings for the seeker of knowledge, out of pleasure [for what he seeks]. Indeed, the scholar is sought forgiveness for by the inhabitants of the heavens and the earth and even by the fish in oceans. The superiority of the scholar over the devout worshipper is like that of the moon, on the night when it is full, over the rest of the stars. The scholars are the heirs of the prophets, and the prophets have not left for inheritance a dinār or dirham, but rather they left knowledge; whoever takes it has certainly taken an abundant share.'"[1]

Reasons behind the Spread of the Prophetic Sunnah

The spread of the Prophetic Sunnah was for the following reasons:

The Companions initially feared that if people were preoccupied with the Prophetic Sunnah, they would neglect the Holy Qur'an. When the Holy Qur'an had become memorized in the hearts of the Muslims, the impediment that had once prevented them from extensively narrating the Prophetic Sunnah was removed.

The Prophet (ﷺ) had foretold many of the seditions and calamities that would afflict the Muslim community, and so the Prophet's Companions began narrating these hadith(s) which exposed such seditions and clarified the points of confusion.

When recent developments and events that required juristic rulings and explanations took place, only the memorizers of the Prophetic Sunnah carried the juristic rulings and explanations for these issues.

1 Reported by Imām Ahmad in *al-Musnad* 36/45-46 (21715), Abū Dāwūd (3641), Ibn Mājah (223) and at-Tirmidhi (2682). It is also in *Sunan ad-Dārimi* (347) and *Ṣaḥīḥ Ibn Ḥibbān* (88). It is a *ḥasan* hadith.

وروى أبو داود عن قيس بن كثير قال: كنت جالساً مع أبي الدرداء في مسجد دمشق، فجاءه رجل، فقال: يا أبا الدرداء، إني جئتك من مدينة الرسول ﷺ، لحديث بلغني أنك تحدثه عن رسول الله، ما جئت لحاجة، وفي رواية الترمذي: قدم رجل المدينة على أبي الدرداء وهو بدمشق، فقال: ما أقدمك يا أخي؟ قال: حديث بلغني أنك تحدثه عن رسول الله ﷺ، قال: أما جئت لحاجة؟ قال: لا، قال: أما قدمت لتجارة؟ قال: لا، قال: ما جئت إلا في طلب هذا الحديث، قال: فإني سمعت رسول الله ﷺ يقول: «من سلك طريقاً يبتغي فيه علماً، سلك الله به طريقاً إلى الجنة، وإن الملائكة لتضع أجنحتها رضاً لطالب العلم، وإن العالم ليستغفر له من السماوات ومن في الأرض، حتى الحيتان في الماء، وفضل العالم على العابد كفضل القمر على سائر الكواكب، وإن العلماء ورثة الأنبياء، وإن الأنبياء لم يورثوا ديناراً ولا درهماً، إنما ورثوا العلم، فمن أخذ به أخذ بحظ وافر»(1).

أسباب شيوع رواية الحديث:

يمكننا أن نعيد شيوع رواية الحديث إلى عدة أسباب:

كان الصحابة يخافون على القرآن إذا اشتغل الناس بالسنة، فلما استقر الأمر وأمن العلماء على القرآن زال المانع الذي يمنعهم من الإكثار من الرواية.

كثير من الفتن التي ظهرت، كان الرسول ﷺ قد أخبر عنها وبينها، فكان الصحابة يروون هذه الأحاديث التي تكشف الفتنة وتزيل الشبهة.

جدت أحداث ونوازل تستدعي بيان الحكم، وهذا البيان موجود عند حَفَظَة الحديث.

١ أخرجه أحمد في المسند: ٣٦/ ٤٥- ٤٦ (٢١٧١٥)، وأبو داود (٣٦٤١)، وابن ماجه (٢٢٣)، والترمذي (٢٦٨٢)، وهو في سنن الدارمي (٣٤٧)، وصحيح ابن حبان (٨٨)، وهو حديث حسن.

The Companions (may Allah be pleased with them) spread the Prophetic Sunnah to avoid the sin of withholding knowledge.

Effects of the Widespread Narration of the Prophetic Sunnah

The increased narration of the Prophetic Sunnah had resulted in some people narrating about the Messenger (ﷺ) while being either inaccurate or dishonest. Consequently, there were inauthentic hadith(s) that were incorrectly attributed to the Prophetic Sunnah. In fact, some heretics even deliberately forged hadith(s) in the name of the Prophet (ﷺ) as an attempt to corrupt Islam. As a result, the Muslim scholars exerted great efforts to discern the honest, trustworthy narrators from those who could not be trusted to relay the Prophetic Sunnah.

Prominent Scholars among the Successors

The seven jurists mentioned earlier were the most authoritative scholars from among the Successors in Madinah. The most authoritative jurists in Mecca were 'Aṭā' ibn Abi Rabāḥ, Ṭāwūs ibn Kaysān, Mujāhid ibn Jabr, 'Amr ibn Dinār and 'Ikrimah, the servant of Ibn 'Abbās.

The most authoritative jurists from among the Successors in Basrah were al-Ḥasan al-Baṣri, Muhammad ibn Sirīn and Ka'b ibn Sur al-Azdi.

As for the other parts of the Muslim world, such as Kufah, Yemen and Egypt, there were well-versed jurists who were well grounded in *Fiqh* and were resorted to for issuing *fatwa*(s) and educating the people.[1]

1 See *I'lām al-Mużwaqqi'īn* 1/24-28.

التأثم من كتمان العلم.

أثر شيوع الرواية في الحديث:

وكان من أثر شيوع رواية الحديث أن حدَّث أقوام عن الرسول ﷺ لم يكونوا أهل ضبط وعدالة، فدخل في حديث الرسول ﷺ ما ليس منه، بل تعمد أقوام من الزنادقة الكذب في حديث الرسول ﷺ لإفساد دين الإسلام، فاحتاج العلماء إلى البحث عن الرواة الصادقين الحفظة العدول، والنظر في حال الرواة.

أبرز علماء التابعين

وأفقه علماء التابعين في المدينة الفقهاء السبعة الذين سبق ذكرهم، وأفقه أهل مكة عطاء بن أبي رباح، وطاوس بن كيسان، ومجاهد بن جبر، وعمرو بن دينار، وعكرمة مولى ابن عباس.

ومن فقهاء التابعين في البصرة الحسن البصري، ومحمد بن سيرين، وكعب بن سُوْر الأزدي.

وكان في البلاد الأخرى كالكوفة واليمن ومصر علماء فقهوا العلم وتصدوا للفتيا والتعليم[1].

١ راجع إعلام الموقعين: ١/ ٢٤- ٢٨.

Conclusion: Virtue of the Three Eras

Without question, the time of the Prophet, the era of the Companions and the era of the Successors were the best of all eras in the history of Islam. ʻAbdullāh ibn Masʻūd narrated that the Prophet (ﷺ) said, "The best of my *Ummah* is my generation, then those that follow them, and then those who follow them. Then, there will come people whose testimony precedes their oath, and their oath precedes their testimony."[1]

Also, ʻĀ'ishah (may Allah be pleased with her) narh rated, "A man asked the Prophet (ﷺ), 'Which generation is the best?' He (ﷺ) answered, 'The people of my generation are the best, then those who follow them, and then those who follow them.'"[2]

Since those three eras were the best Muslim generations of all, their scholars and jurists, along with their methods, were also the best of all.

خاتمة: فضل الأعصار الثلاثة

أفضل العصور هي العصور الثلاثة السابقة: عصر الرسول ﷺ، ثم عصر الصحابة، ثم عصر التابعين: في الصحيحين عن عبد الله بن مسعود قال: قال رسول الله ﷺ: «خير أمتي القرن الذين يلونني، ثم الذين يلونهم، ثم الذين يلونهم، ثم يجيء قوم تسبق شهادة أحدهم يمينه، ويمينه شهادته»[١]، وفي صحيح مسلم عن عائشة- رضي الله عنها- قالت: سأل رجل رسول الله ﷺ: أي الناس خير؟ قال:«القرن الذي أنا فيه، ثم الثاني، ثم الثالث»[٢]، وإذا كانت هذه خير القرون فإن علماءها أفضل علماء الأمة، وفقهاءها أفضل الفقهاء، وطريقة العلماء والفقهاء في تلك العصور أفضل الطرق.

---

1 Collected by al-Bukhāri (2652), Muslim (2533), (210), and the wording is his. It is also in *Musnad Aḥmad* 6/76 (3594) wherein the locations of these hadith(s) are mentioned.
2 *Ṣaḥīḥ Muslim* (2536), *Musnad Aḥmad* 42/132 (25233)

١ أخرجه البخاري (٢٦٥٢)، ومسلم (٢٥٣٣) (٢١٠) واللفظ له، وهو في مسند أحمد: ٦/ ٧٦ (٣٥٩٤) وفيه ذكر مواضع أحاديث هذا الباب.
٢ صحيح مسلم (٢٥٣٦)، وهو في مسند أحمد: ٤٢/ ١٣٢ (٢٥٢٣٣).

Summary of Unit 5

The Successors were taught Islam at the hands of the Prophet's Companions (may Allah be pleased with them). The Companions acquainted the Successors with the various sciences of Islam, which included *Fiqh* and giving *fatwa*, which they themselves learned from the Messenger (ﷺ).

The Successors would refer to the Qur'an and Sunnah to deduce the juristic rulings for the issues they faced. If they could not find a ruling therein, they would exercise independent reasoning or *ijtihād*, and naturally this led to differences among the Successors on juristic rulings.

Some jurists who were distinguished in their dependence on Hadith were given the name *Ahl al-Ḥadīth* (the People of Hadith). Other jurists who were known to give greater dependence on *ijtihād* and independent reasoning, though at times referred to the hadith, were given the name *Ahl ar-Ra'y* (the People of Independent Reasoning).

Unlike the era of the Prophet's Companions (may Allah be pleased with them), the circle of differences widened in the era of the Successors.

خلاصة الوحدة

نخلص من دراسة هذه الوحدة إلى ما يلي:

أن التابعين هم الذين تربوا على أيدي الصحابة- رضوان الله عليهم- ونهلوا منهم العلم والفقه والفتيا التي أخذوها من الرسول ﷺ.

كان التابعون يرجعون إلى الكتاب والسنة، فإذا لم يجدوا حكماً في المسألة أخذوا بالرأي- وهو الاجتهاد- مما أدى إلى اختلافهم في أحكام المسائل.

تميز الفقهاء بين مكثر من رواية الحديث والاعتماد عليه حتى سُمُّوا أهل الحديث، وبين مقل من رواية الحديث معتمداً على الاجتهاد والرأي؛ فسُمُّوا أهل الرأي.

اتسعت دائرة الاختلاف في هذا العصر- عصر التابعين- عما كان عليه الحال في عصر صحابة رسول الله ﷺ.

Notes

Notes

Unit 6
The Era of Compilation and Mujtahid Imām(s)

Contents of Unit 6

- Compiling the Prophetic Sunnah
- Introducing *Fiqh* schools
- The *Ahl al-Ḥadīth Fiqh* school
- The *Ahl ar-Ra'y Fiqh* school
- The *Ẓāhiri Fiqh* school

Importance of Unit 6

The rightly-guided caliph 'Umar ibn 'Abdil-'Azīz commanded Ibn Shihāb az-Zuhri to compile the Prophetic Sunnah. Ibn Shihāb complied with the caliph's orders and collected the Sunnah of Allah's Messenger (ﷺ). Through that decision, 'Umar ibn 'Abdil-'Azīz had opened the door for the scholars to collect the hadith(s) of the Messenger of Allah (ﷺ). As a result, the famous compilations of the Prophetic Sunnah were trasncribed, such as the *Muwaṭṭa'* of Imām Mālik, the *Musnad* of Imām Ahmad, *Ṣaḥīḥ al-Bukhāri, Ṣaḥīḥ Muslim, Sunan Abi Dāwūd, Sunan at-Tirmidhi* and *Sunan Ibn Mājah.*

During this era – wherein the Sunnah was compiled – the approaches of various *Fiqh* schools came into existence. The *Fiqh* schools of *Ahl al-Ḥadīth, Ahl ar-Ra'y* and *Ahl aẓ-Ẓāhir* all appeared then. Each of these *Fiqh* schools had a vital role in the rise of Islamic *Fiqh*.

Let us now discuss the details in this unit.

Learning Objectives

Dear reader, after studying this unit, you are expected to be capable of:

1) Explaining how the Prophetic Sunnah was compiled, and knowing the most famous books of Hadith

2) Draw a comparison between the three *Fiqh* schools: *Ahl al-Ḥadīth, Ahl ar-Ra'y* and *Ahl aẓ-Ẓāhir*

الوحدة السادسة
عصر التدوين والأئمة المجتهدين

محتويات الوحدة السادسة

- تدوين السنة النبوية.
- التعريف بالمدارس الفقهية.
- مدرسة أهل الحديث.
- مدرسة أهل الرأي.
- مدرسة أهل الظاهر.

أهمية دراسة الوحدة:

أمر الخليفه الراشد عمر بن عبد العزيز ابنَ شهاب الزهري أن تدون السنة النبوية، ونفذ ابن شهاب أمر الخليفة فجمع سنة رسول الله ﷺ، وبذلك يكون عمر بن عبد العزيز قد فتح الباب أمام أهل العلم لجمع أحاديث رسول الله ﷺ فكتبت دواوين السنة المشهورة: موطأ مالك، ومسند أحمد، وصحيح البخاري، وصحيح مسلم، وسنن أبي داود، وسنن الترمذي، وسنن ابن ماجه.

وفي هذا العصر - عصر تدوين السنة - تبلورت اتجاهات المدارس الفقهية: مدرسة أهل الحديث، ومدرسة أهل الرأي ومدرسة أهل الظاهر، وكان لكل مدرسة دور في النهوض بالفقه الإسلامي.

هيا بنا لنتعرف على التفاصيل من خلال دراستنا لهذه الوحدة.

الأهداف التعليمية:

يتوقع منك أيها الدارس الكريم بعد دراستك لهذه الوحدة أن تكون قادراً على أن:

١- تُبين كيف تم تدوين سنة رسول الله ﷺ، وأشهر دواوين السنة.

٢- تُقارن بين المدارس الفقهية الثلاثة: مدرسة أهل الحديث، ومدرسة أهل الرأي، ومدرسة أهل الظاهر.

3) Refute the supporters of the *Ẓāhiri Fiqh* school, who reject *qiyās* (analogical deduction) under the pretext that the juristic rulings are unjustifiable

The Era of Compilation and *Mujtahid Imām*(s): Preface: The Status of Knowledge and *Fiqh* in this Era

This era began as the Umayyad dynasty began withering away and reached its peak when the Abbasid dynasty was flourishing toward supremacy of the Islamic state. The conclusion of this era was when this Abbasid dynasty subdivided into smaller states halfway through the 4th century A.H. The scholars of this era had inherited the revealed texts that were transmitted to them via the Companions and Successors, in addition to inheriting the *Fiqh* (understanding) of the Companions and Successors itself.

They had received the Qur'an via both a written and oral transmission. As for the Sunnah, its narrations had become widespread in the far corners of the Muslim world, and thus, the scholars journeyed throughout the world to collect and compile the Prophetic Sunnah. Before this era had ended, the Sunnah was compiled, the science of *jarh* and *ta'dīl* (impugnment and validation of the narrators) was established and the principles of the hadith sciences were codified. Despite that, there still remained a degree of discrepancy among some with regard to discerning the authentic from the inauthentic hadith(s). As a result, a large group of scholars focused their efforts to distinguish sound hadith(s) from false ones. They filtered out the authentic and clarified the authenticity of each hadith the scholars would quote or the people would transmit between themselves. However, such attempts did not completely do away with the weak hadith(s) that were widespread between the people or sometimes even quoted as proof by the scholars in their books or mentioned by the preachers in their sermons.

٣- تُفند دعوى الظاهرية الذين ينفون القياس بدعوى أن الأحكام غير معللة.

عصر التدوين والأئمة المجتهدين

تمهيد: الحالة العلمية في هذا العصر وموقع الفقه فيها:

ابتدأ هذا العصر وشمس الأموية تؤذن بالمغيب، واكتمل وازدهر وشمس الدولة العباسية تتألق في سماء الأمة الإسلامية، وتوقف وانتهى عندما تجزأت الخلافة العباسية في منتصف القرن الرابع، وقد ورث علماء هذا العصر علم الوحي الذي نقله إليهم الصحابة والتابعون كما ورثوا فقه الصحابة والتابعين.

وقد تلقوا القرآن مكتوباً محفوظاً، أما السنة فقد انتشرت رواياتها في مختلف الأمصار، ورحل العلماء يجوبون الأقطار ويدونون السنة، ولم ينته هذا العصر حتى دونت السنة، ووضع علم الجرح والتعديل، وقواعد مصطلح الحديث، إلا أن الحديث اختلط فيه الصحيح بالضعيف؛ لذا اتجه جمع كبير من العلماء لتخليص الحديث مما شابه، فجردوا الصحيح، وبينوا حال الأحاديث التي يرويها العلماء، ويتناقلها الناس، إلا أن ذلك لم يقض على الأحاديث الضعيفة التي انتشرت بين الناس، واحتج بها العلماء في كتبهم، والوعاظ في خطبهم.

The scholars of this era inherited the methodology taught by the Prophet (ﷺ) and adopted by the Companions and the Successors. Many jurists adopted this method when it came to determining the juristic rulings for the contemporary events and incidents they encountered.

Since the scholars varied in knowledge, in the amount of the Sunnah they each memorized, in the amount of *Fiqh* they learned from the Companions and the Successors and in their disparate degrees of adherence to the methodology of the Companions which they established [for later scholars], there arose some differences in the fundamentals, as well as in the methods of deducing the juristic rulings.

Each of these methods eventually became a *madhhab* (juristic approach), wherein each had its own fundamentals, branches, scholars and adherents. The scholars of these *madhhab*(s) differed among themselves regarding certain fundamental principles, such as the proof value of the actions of the Madinan people, the proof value of *qiyās* (analogical deduction), the proof value of *istiḥsān* (juristic preference) and the like. Naturally, differing over these juristic principles led to differing in the specific juristic branches that are formulated based on them. A wide range of debates and intellectual exchanges began taking place between the scholars of these various *madhhab*(s), and this was further encouraged by the concern which the caliphs had for the sciences, especially *Fiqh*, and their participation in them through sponsoring these debates and forums.

What widened the gap of differences even further was that some scholars of *Fiqh* began preoccupying themselves with hypothetical juristic matters. Nevertheless, these differences were regulated and contained by the proofs and evidences. The scholars of this era rejected *taqlīd* (blind following), considered the evidences, denounced stubborn fanaticism and would accept the truth from wherever it came.

وورث أهل هذا العصر المنهج الذي بينه الرسول ﷺ، وسار عليه الصحابة والتابعون، وقد فقه كثير من الفقهاء هذا المنهج وساروا عليه في تعرفهم على أحكام الوقائع والنوازل.

وبما أن العلماء كانوا يتفاوتون في حفظ سنة الرسول ﷺ والعلم بفقه الصحابة والتابعين، ويتفاوتون في الالتزام بمنهج الصحابة الذي قَعَّدوه وأَصَّلُوه، فقد حدث اختلاف في بعض الأصول، وفي طريقة استخلاص الأحكام.

وقد تحددت هذه المناهج في مذاهب لكل منها أصوله وفروعه وعلماؤه وأتباعه، واختلف علماء هذه المذاهب فيما بينهم حول بعض الأصول كحجية عمل أهل المدينة والقياس والاستحسان ونحو ذلك، والاختلاف في الأصول أدى إلى اختلاف في الفروع، وكثر الجدال بين علماء هذه المذاهب، وعقدت المناظرات والمساجلات، وشجع على هذا اهتمام الخلفاء بالعلوم وخاصة علم الفقه، ومشاركتهم في هذه العلوم، ورعايتهم لهذه المناظرات والمداولات.

وقد ساعد اشتغال بعض العلماء بالفقه الفرضي في توسيع شقة الخلاف، ولكن الخلاف كان محكوماً بالدليل والبرهان، فقد كان العلماء في هذا العصر يرفضون التقليد، وينظرون في الدليل، وينهون عن التعصب، ويأخذون الحق ممن جاء به.

Many of the sciences were compiled in this era, the most important of them being the Sunnah and the sciences of *Fiqh*: the *Fiqh* of the Qur'an, the *Fiqh* of the Sunnah, the *Fiqh* of the Companions and the Successors, and the *Fiqh* of the *Mujtahid Imām*(s) and their various *madhhab*(s).

The main characteristics of this era, in terms of legislations, were:

1) Compiling the Prophetic Sunnah
2) Compiling the *Fiqh* issues
3) Development of the *Fiqh* schools

We will now dicuss these characteristics in detail.

Compiling the Prophetic Sunnah: The early stages of compiling the Sunnah

We previously discussed the Sunnah being partially recorded during the lifetime of the Messenger (ﷺ), the era of the Companions (may Allah be pleased with them) and the era of the Successors. In addition, we have learned why the Sunnah was not compiled during these earlier stages.

In summation, al-Harawi said, "The most common way of narrating the Sunnah was that people would memorize and dictate the hadith(s) of the Prophet (ﷺ). Aside from that, there was only *Kitāb aṣ-Ṣadaqāt* and a few other documents that a researcher would only find after rigorous investigation."[1] Thereafter, the need arose for the Sunnah to be documented in writing; Islam had spread, the Muslim territories increased, the conquests continued, the Companions dispersed throughout the lands, most of them passed away, their followers were scattered everywhere, accuracy was becoming scarce, and thus the Sunnah being lost became a legitimate fear. For these reasons, the scholars were in need of compiling the Hadith and preserving it through writing. Undoubtedly, writing is the ideal means of safeguarding information, as Ibn al-Athīr said, "Indeed, the mind could become oblivious, the attention could be distracted, the memory could falter, while the pen preserves and does not forget."[2]

1 *Tanwīr al-Ḥawālik 'alā Muwaṭṭa' Mālik* 1/4, *Qawā'id at-Taḥdīth* 71
2 *Jāmi' al-Uṣūl* 1/40

وقد دونت العلوم في هذا العصر، ومن أهم ما دون علم السنة، وعلم الفقه: فقه الكتاب والسنة، وفقه الصحابة والتابعين، وفقه الأئمة المجتهدين على اختلاف مذاهبهم، وأهم سمات هذا العصر في الجانب التشريعي:

١- تدوين السنة النبوية.

٢- تدوين المسائل الفقهية.

٣- المدارس الفقهية.

وسنتناول هذه السمات في كالآتي:

تدوين السنة

بدايات التدوين:

تحدثنا عن تدوين السنة في عصر الرسول ﷺ وعصر الصحابة وعصر التابعين، ورأينا كيف أن السنة لم تدون، وتعرفنا على أسباب ذلك.

وقد بقيت الطريقة السائدة في رواية السنة كما يقول الهروي: «إنهم كانوا يؤدونها لفظاً، ويأخذونها حفظاً، إلا كتاب الصدقات والشيء اليسير الذي يقف عليه الباحث بعد الاستقصاء»(١)، فلما انتشر الإسلام، واتسعت البلاد وتفرقت الصحابة في الأقطار، وكثرت الفتوح، ومات معظم الصحابة، وتفرق أصحابهم وأتباعهم، وقل الضبط، وبعد العهد، وخشي ذهاب السنة ودروسها، احتاج العلماء إلى تدوين الحديث، وتقييده بالكتابة، فالكتابة هي الأصل في الحفظ كما يقول ابن الأثير: «فإن الخاطر يَغْفُل، والذهن يغيب، والذِّكر يهمل، والقلم يحفظ ولا ينسى»(٢).

١ تنوير الحوالك على موطأ مالك: ١/ ٤، وقواعد التحديث: ٧١.
٢ جامع الأصول: ١/ ٤٠.

When the rightly-guided caliph 'Umar ibn 'Abdil-'Azīz realized that the Prophetic Sunnah was in danger – and he, may Allah bestow mercy on him, was a man of great insight in the religion of Allah – he commanded that the Sunnah be compiled. He knew that the scholars among the Companions and the Successors did not compile the Sunnah for a wisdom particular to their times, while that wisdom did not exist in his time, so the *fatwa* changed due to the changed times. It was mentioned in the *Muwaṭṭa'* of Imām Mālik, on the authority of Muhammad ibn al-Ḥasan, that the rightly-guided caliph 'Umar ibn 'Abdul-'Azīz wrote to Abū Bakr ibn Muhammad ibn 'Amr ibn Ḥazm, ordering him to write down all the hadith(s) reported about the Prophet (ﷺ) and his Companions, 'Umar and others, lest the Sunnah be lost or the scholars pass away.[1] This was also narrated by Imām al-Bukhāri as a *mu'allaq* report in *aṣ-Ṣaḥīḥ*.[2] Similarly, Abū Nu'aym reported in his book *Tāreekh Aṣbahān* that 'Umar ibn 'Abdil-'Azīz wrote to his provinces, "Find the hadith(s) of the Messenger of Allah (ﷺ) and collect them."[3]

Ibn 'Abdil-Barr collected in his book *at-Tamhīd*, on the authority of Ibn Wahb, that he heard Imām Mālik say, "'Umar ibn 'Abdil-'Azīz would write to his subjects everywhere, teaching them the Sunnah and the matters of *Fiqh*. In addition, he would write to the people of Madinah, asking them about their affairs and ordering them to act upon the Sunnah that they knew well. He would also write to Abū Bakr ibn 'Amr ibn Ḥazm ordering him to collect the Sunnah and send it to him. However, 'Umar (may Allah be pleased with him) passed away before Ibn Ḥazm sent him the books [of the Sunnah] that he had written."[4] Ibn Ḥajar explained that it was Ibn Shihāb az-Zuhri who collected the Sunnah, at the orders of 'Umar ibn 'Abdil-'Azīz.[5] As for Abū Bakr ibn 'Amr ibn Ḥazm, he was 'Umar's governor over Madinah.

1 *Muwaṭṭa' Mālik* – the narration of Muhammad ibn al-Ḥasan; 427-428, hadith no. (936) and *Sunan ad-Dārimi* (491-492)

2 Narrated by al-Bukhāri, as a *mu'allaq* report, in his *Ṣaḥīḥ; the Book of Knowledge* after hadith no. (99).

3 *Fatḥ al-Bāri* 1/257 – under the chapter *How Knowledge is Removed*. See *Tanwīr al-Hawālik 'alā Muwaṭṭa' Mālik* 1/4.

4 *Tanwīr al-Ḥawālik 'alā Muwaṭṭa' Mālik* 1/4. See the adjacent treatise: 403 – printed by Dār al-Bashā'ir al-Islāmiyyah.

5 Ibid, and see *Qawā'id at-Taḥdīth* 70.

فلما رأى الخليفة الراشد عمر بن عبد العزيز الخطر الذي يتهدد سنة رسول الله ﷺ، وكان- رحمه الله- من ذوي البصيرة في دين الله، أمر بتدوين السنة، فإنه كان يعلم أن علماء الصحابة والتابعين عزفوا عن تدوين السنة لحكمة وجدت في زمانهم، وزالت تلك الحكمة في زمانه، فتغيرت الفتوى بتغير الزمان، ففي موطأ مالك برواية محمد بن الحسن أن عمر بن عبد العزيز كتب إلى أبي بكر بن محمد بن عمرو بن حزم أن انظر ما كان من حديث رسول الله ﷺ أو سنته أو حديث عمر أو نحوه فاكتبه لي، فإني خفت دروس العلم وذهاب العلماء(١)، علقه البخاري في صحيحه(٢)، وأخرج أبو نعيم في تاريخ أصبهان أن عمر بن عبد العزيز كتب إلى الآفاق انظروا حديث رسول الله ﷺ فاجمعوه(٣).

وأخرج ابن عبد البر في التمهيد من طريق ابن وهب قال: سمعت مالكاً يقول: كان عمر بن عبد العزيز يكتب إلى الأمصار يعلمهم السنن والفقه، ويكتب إلى المدينة يسألهم عما مضى، وأن يعملوا بما عندهم، ويكتب إلى أبي بكر بن عمر ابن حزم أن يجمع السنن، ويكتب إليه بها، فتوفي عمر وقد كتب ابن حزم كتباً قبل أن يبعث بها إليه(٤)، وقد أفاد ابن حجر أن الذي قام بتدوين السنة بأمر عمر بن عبد العزيز هو ابن شهاب الزهري(٥)، وأبو بكر بن عمرو بن حزم كان والي عمر على المدينة.

١ موطأ الإمام مالك، رواية محمد بن الحسن: ٤٢٧- ٤٢٨، حديث رقم (٩٣٦)، وسنن الدارمي (٤٩١) و(٤٩٢).

٢ علقه البخاري في صحيحه، كتاب العلم، باب كيف يقبض العلم، بإثر الحديث رقم (٩٩).

٣ فتح الباري: ١/ ٢٥٧، ط. دار السلام، باب كيف يقبض العلم، وانظر: تنوير الحوالك على موطأ مالك: ١/ ٤.

٤ تنوير الحوالك على موطأ مالك: ١/ ٤، وانظر الرسالة المستطرفة: ٤٠٣، طبعة دار البشائر الإسلامية.

٥ المصدر السابق، وانظر قواعد التحديث: ٧٠.

Although the Sunnah was not completely compiled in the era of 'Umar ibn 'Abdil-'Azīz due to the shortness of his caliphate, and although the books compiled by Ibn Shihāb az-Zuhri were not preserved, 'Umar had paved the way for the compilation of the Sunnah. Before him, the scholars had feared doing so because of the texts(s) forbidding that the hadith(s) be written, as well as the previous caliphs' abstention from doing so. Certainly, 'Umar ibn 'Abdil-'Azīz introduced a good practice in transcribing the Sunnah, for this opened the door for the hadith(s) to be collected and compiled.

The Most Important Compilations of Hadith

The compilations of Hadith that were composed in this era are the absolute most important books of the Sunnah. These are the primary books in the science of Hadith, and they are many, but we will mention the most famous of them:

1) The *Muwaṭṭa'* by Imām Mālik ibn Anas

Imām Mālik was one of the four Imām(s) of *Fiqh*. He was born in 93 A.H. and died in 179 A.H. His book of Hadith is the oldest compilation that has reached us. He collected in it what he considered authentic hadith(s), Qur'anic *tafsīr* and Islamic history. Also, he gathered therein some views of the Companions, Successors and Imām(s) before him.

2) The *Musnad* by Imām Aḥmad ibn Ḥanbal

Imām Aḥmad ibn Ḥanbal was also one of the four Imām(s) of *Fiqh*. His book is one of the greatest books of Hadith, for it contains 27,647 hadith(s).[1] It was given the name *al-Musnad* because Imām Aḥmad organized its hadith(s) based on their *isnād* (chain of transmission). He would gather all the hadith(s) narrated by each Companion together in one section. The number of Companions he narrated from in his book reached 904 Companions.

1 According to the numbering found in the publication supervised by Shaykh Shu'ayb al-Arna'ūt, and was printed into 50 volumes by Mu'assasat ar-Risālah in Beirut (1993/1413 A.H).

وإذا كانت السنة لم تدون في عهد عمر لقصر خلافته، ولم تحفظ الكتب التي دونها ابن شهاب الزهري- فإن عمر قد فتح الطريق للتدوين بعد أن كان العلماء يهابون ذلك لما صح عندهم من نهي الرسول ﷺ عن كتابة الحديث، ولعزوف الخلفاء الراشدين عن ذلك، لقد سن عمر بن عبد العزيز للمسلمين كتابة السنة، ففتح الباب لجمع الأحاديث وتدوينها.

أمهات دواوين السنة:

دواوين السنة التي دونت في هذا العصر هي أهم كتب السنة بإطلاق، وهي الكتب الأصول في علم الحديث، وهي كثيرة، ولكننا نذكر أشهرها:

الأول: كتاب الموطأ للإمام مالك بن أنس أحد الأئمة الأربعة، ولد عام (٣٩) للهجرة، وتوفي عام (٩٧١) وهو أقدم مصنف في الحديث وصل إلينا، وقد جمع فيه ما صح عنده من حديث وتفسير وتاريخ، وذكر بعض أقوال الصحابة والتابعين والأئمة قبله.

الثاني: المسند للإمام أحمد بن حنبل، أحد الأئمة الأربعة، وهذا الكتاب من أعظم كتب الحديث، فقد بلغت أحاديثه (٧٤٦٧٢) حديثاً[1].

وقد سمي بالمسند؛ لأن الإمام أحمد رتب أحاديثه على المسانيد، وأورد أحاديث كل صحابي في موضع واحد، وعدد الصحابة الذين لهم مسانيد في كتابه (٩٠٤) صحابياً.

١ وفق الترقيم للطبعة التي أشرف عليها الشيخ شعيب الأرنؤوط وصدرت عن مؤسسة الرسالة بيروت (١٤١٣هـ- ١٩٩٣م)، في خمسين مجلداً مع الفهارس.

3) *Al-Jāmiʿ aṣ-Ṣaḥīḥ* by Imām Abū 'Abdillāh Muhammad ibn Isma'īl ibn al-Mughīrah ibn Bardazbah al-Bukhāri

Imām al-Bukhari was the *Ḥāfiẓ* of Islam, and without dispute one of the absolute greatest Imām(s). He was born in 194 A.H. and died in 256 A.H. In his book, he compiled the most authentic, most widespread traditions of the Messenger (ﷺ) while making sure to exclude the weak hadith(s). He did not limit his collecting to particular subjects; rather he collected hadith(s) pertaining to a wide spectrum of subjects, and from them, he inferred his views on matters of *Fiqh* and the *sīrah* (the Prophet's Biography). Needless to say, this book attained a degree of prominence and acceptance that can never be surpassed.

The number of hadith(s) narrated in *Ṣaḥīḥ al-Bukhāri* – including the repetitions, the *muʿallaq* (chainless) reports and the alternate chains – is approximately 7,563 hadith(s), according to the recent numbering by Muhammad Fu'ād 'Abdil-Bāqi.

The number of hadith(s) with complete chains – after excluding the repetitions – is approximately 4,000 hadith(s).[1]

4) *Al-Jāmiʿ aṣ-Ṣaḥīḥ* by Imām Muslim ibn al-Ḥajjāj ibn Muslim al-Qushayri an-Naysabūri

Imām Muslim was one of the greatest memorizers of hadith. The scholars of his age, and those after them, all attested to his mastery of this science. He was born in 204 A.H. in Naysabūr and died in 261 A.H.

Imām Muslim compiled many books, the most famous of which is this book in which he followed the method of Imām al-Bukhāri in his book *aṣ-Ṣaḥīḥ*. Thus, he only narrated in this book the hadith(s) he considered authentic. However, Imām al-Bukhāri used to put the different narrations of the same hadith in different sections, while Imām Muslim compiled all the narrations of the same hadith together in one section. Essentially, *al-Jāmiʿ aṣ-Ṣaḥīḥ* includes 3,033 distinct hadith(s) and its total number of hadith narrations is about 12,000.

1 *Hady as-Sāri Muqaddimat Fatḥ al-Bāri* 665 – printed by Dār as-Salām

الثالث: الجامع الصحيح لأبي عبد الله محمد بن إسماعيل بن المغيرة بن بردزبة البخاري (٤٩١- ٦٥٢هـ)، حافظ الإسلام، وإمام الأئمة الأعلام، جمع في كتابه أحاديث رسول الله ﷺ الصحاح المستفيضة المتصلة دون الأحاديث الضعيفة، ولم يقتصر في جمعه على موضوعات معينة، بل جمع الأحاديث في جميع الأبواب، واستنبط منها الفقه والسيرة، وقد نال من الشهرة والقبول درجة لا يرام فوقها.

وقد بلغت أحاديث البخاري بالمكرر سوى المعلقات والمتابعات (٣٦٥٧) حديثاً حسب ترقيم محمد فؤاد عبد الباقي لأحاديث البخاري.

وعدد أحاديث البخاري سوى المكرر من الأحاديث المتصلة قرابة أربعة آلاف(١).

الرابع: الجامع الصحيح لمسلم بن الحجاج بن مسلم القشيري النيسابوري، أحد أئمة الحديث وحفاظه، اعترف علماء عصره ومن بعدهم له بالتقدم والإتقان في هذا العلم، ولادته في نيسابور في سنة (٤٠٢هـ)، ووفاته في سنة (١٦٢هـ).

صنف الإمام مسلم كتباً كثيرة، وأشهرها صحيحه، وقد تأسى في تدوينه بالبخاري- رحمه الله- فلم يضع فيه إلا ما صح عنده، وقد جمع مسلم في صحيحه روايات الحديث الواحد في مكان واحد، والبخاري فرق الروايات في مواضع مختلفة.

وعدة أحاديثه الأصول (٣٣٠٣) حديثاً، وجملة أحاديثه اثنا عشر ألفاً.

١ هدي الساري مقدمة فتح الباري: ٦٦٥، ط. دار السلام.

5) The *Sunan* by Abū Dāwūd Sulaymān ibn al-Ash'ath as-Sijistāni

He was one of the great memorizers of the Prophetic Sunnah. He was born in 202 A.H. and died in 275 A.H. His book *as-Sunan* contains 5,274 hadith(s).

In this book, Abū Dāwūd focused his efforts on collecting the hadith(s) quoted as evidence by the jurists and by the scholars from all over the Muslim community.

This book contains hadith(s) that are traceable to the Messenger (ﷺ), in addition to statements narrated from the Companions, as well as statements attributed to the scholars of the Successors.

6) *Al-Jāmi' aṣ-Ṣaḥīḥ*, more commonly known as *as-Sunan*, by Abū 'Isā Muhammad ibn 'Isā ibn Sawrat at-Tirmidhi

Imām at-Tirmidhi was born in 209 A.H. and died in 279 A.H. He was keen on compiling all the hadith(s) related to juristic rulings just as Imām Abū Dāwūd had done. However, he clarified the sound hadith(s) from the weak ones, and mentioned the juristic positions adopted by the Companions, the Successors and the jurists of the Muslim world.

The total number of hadith(s) that he narrated in his book is 3,956.

7) The *Sunan* by 'Abdullāh ibn Shu'ayb ibn 'Ali ibn Bahr ibn Sinān an-Nasā'i

Imām an-Nasā'i was born in 215 A.H. in Nasā', a famous town in Khurasan, and died in 302 A.H. in ar-Ramlah, Palestine.

In *as-Sunan*, Imām an-Nasā'i compiled the hadith(s) related to juristic rulings, and the number of hadith(s) therein is 5,758 hadith(s).

الخامس: السنن لأبي داود سليمان بن الأشعث السجستاني أحد الحفاظ لأحاديث الرسول ﷺ، ولد في سنة (٢٠٢هـ)، وتوفي في سنة (٢٧٥هـ).

جمع في كتابه هذا جملة من أحاديث رسول الله ﷺ، فقد بلغت أحاديثه (٤٧٢٥) حديثاً.

وقد وجه أبو داود همه في هذا الكتاب إلى جمع الأحاديث التي استدل بها الفقهاء، ودارت فيهم، وبنى عليها الأحكام علماء الأمصار.

والكتاب فيه الأحاديث المرفوعة إلى الرسول ﷺ، والأحاديث الموقوفة على الصحابة، والمنسوبة إلى علماء التابعين.

السادس: الجامع الصحيح للترمذي وهو المشهور باسم السنن لأبي عيسى محمد بن عيسى بن سورة الترمذي (٢٠٩- ٢٧٩هـ)، وقد عني بجمع أحاديث الأحكام كما فعل أبو داود، ولكنه بيَّن الحديث الصحيح من الضعيف، وذكر مذاهب الصحابة والتابعين وفقهاء الأمصار.

ومجموع الأحاديث التي رواها في كتابه: (٣٩٥٦) حديثاً.

السابع: السنن لأبي عبد الله بن شعيب بن علي بن بحر بن سنان النسائي، ولد سنة (٢١٥هـ) بنساء، وهي بلدة مشهورة بخراسان، وتوفي في مدينة الرملة بفلسطين في سنة (٣٠٢هـ).

وقد جمع النسائي في كتابه أحاديث الأحكام، وعدد أحاديثه: (٥٧٥٨) حديثاً.

8) The *Sunan* by Muhammad ibn Yazīd ibn Mājah ar-Rab'i[1] al-Qazwīni

Imām Ibn Mājah was born in 209 A.H. and died in 273 A.H. He was keen on collecting the various hadith(s) of the Messenger (ﷺ). Muhammad Fu'ād 'Abdul-Baqi, the verifier of the book *as-Sunan,* said, "The total number of hadith(s) included in *Sunan Ibn Mājah* is 4,341, but the book is not comparable to *Ṣaḥīḥ al-Bukhāri* and *Ṣaḥīḥ Muslim,* nor the three *Sunan* of Abū Dāwūd, at-Tirmidhi and an-Nasā'i. This is because it contains a number of weak hadith(s), as well as some false reports."

Fiqh Schools

Preface: Introduction to *Fiqh* Schools

Fiqh schools first began appearing in the previous era, but it was during this era – the era of compilation – that their respective juristic approaches began developing into full maturity. Each of them resembled an independent approach within the Islamic *Ummah,* with its own leaders and followers. The scholars of each approach had set certain principles that distinguished their method in *Fiqh* from the others, and this is how the *Fiqh* schools first developed.

A *Fiqh* school is not a physical institution for studying *Fiqh,* but rather a method produced by a jurist and supported by the followers of that jurist. Therefore, it denotes an approach and methodology that distinguishes one group of jurists from another.

As we discussed, *Fiqh* schools were initially named after the cities where they arose; the city of Madinah was home for the school of *Ahl al-Ḥadīth,* and Kufah was home for the school of *Ahl ar-Ra'y.* Thereafter, each of these two schools of *Fiqh* moved beyond its homeland and became a movement that had a following throughout the Muslim lands. Thus, the school of Madinah became the *Ahl al-Ḥadīth* school, and the school of Kufah became the *Ahl ar-Ra'y* school. Every scholar whose views we have come across used to restrict the classification of *Fiqh* schools to these two.

1 Note: He is titled ar-Rab'i because of allegiance, not ancestry.

الثامن: السنن لمحمد بن يزيد بن ماجه الربعي بالولاء القزويني (٩٠٢- ٣٧٢هـ)، وقد عني ابن ماجه بجمع سنن الرسول ﷺ، قال محقق الكتاب محمد فؤاد عبد الباقي(١): جملة أحاديث السنن لابن ماجه (١٤٣٤) حديثاً، وليس لهذا الكتاب رتبة الصحيحين، ولا السنن الثلاثة لأبي داود والترمذي والنسائي؛ لأن فيه عدداً من الأحاديث الضعيفة، وفيه بعض الأحاديث الواهية أو المنكرة.

المدارس الفقهية(٢)

تمهيد: التعريف بالمدارس الفقهية:

بدأ ظهور المدارس الفقهية في العصر السابق، وفي هذا العصر- عصر التدوين- تبلورت الاتجاهات الفقهية، وشكل كل منها تياراً في الأمة الإسلامية، له زعماؤه وأتباعه، ووضع علماء كل اتجاه أصولاً ومعالم ميزت طريقهم عن غيره، وبذلك تكونت المدارس الفقهية.

ولا يراد بالمدرسة الفقهية بناء يتدارس فيه الفقه، ولكن يقصد بها طريقة ينتهجها الفقيه، فيأخذها عنه غيره، ويتابعونه عليها، وبذلك تصبح تياراً ومسلكاً، يعرفون بها دون غيرهم.

وقد نسبت المدارس في بداية الأمر إلى المدائن التي نشأت فيها كما سبق بيانه، فالمدينة المنورة هي مهد مدرسة أهل الحديث، والكوفة مهد مدرسة أهل الرأي، ثم خرجت كل واحدة من المدرستين من مهدها، فشكّلت تياراً له أتباعه في مختلف ديار الإسلام، فعرفت مدرسة أهل المدينة بمدرسة أهل الحديث، ومدرسة الكوفة باسم مدرسة أهل الرأي، وكل من اطلعنا على قوله من أهل العلم رأيناه يقصر المدارس الفقهية على هاتين المدرستين.

١ سنن ابن ماجه: ٢/ ١٥١٩.

٢ راجع كتابنا: المذاهب والمدارس الفقهية.

However, we find that the *Ẓāhiri* school – the followers of Dāwūd aẓ-Ẓāhiri – had some distinct principles which makes us class them as an independent *Fiqh* school. Consequently, our view is that there are three primary schools of *Fiqh*:

1) The *Fiqh* school of *Ahl al-Ḥadīth*
2) The *Fiqh* school of *Ahl ar-Ra'y*
3) The *Fiqh* school of *Ahl aẓ-Ẓāhir*

ولكننا نرى الظاهريين أتباع داود الظاهري قد استقلوا ببعض الأصول، مما يجعلنا نعدهم مدرسة مستقلة، وبذلك تصبح المدارس الفقهية في نظرنا ثلاث مدارس:

١- مدرسة أهل الحديث.

٢- مدرسة أهل الرأي.

٣- مدرسة أهل الظاهر.

The *Fiqh* School of *Ahl al-Ḥadīth*

I. The Birth and Development of this School

The *Fiqh* school of *Ahl al-Ḥadīth* first appeared in Madinah. Initially, it was known as the Madinah *Fiqh* School, for Madinah was the cradle of the Prophetic Sunnah and the earliest residence of the jurists. It was home for the offspring of the Companions; those who actually lived with the Prophet (ﷺ), memorized the hadith(s) from him, disseminated it, and emulated his every action and decision. Thus, it was only natural that the jurists of this school be influenced by the earliest jurists from among the Companions, as well as the scholars among the Successors who lived in Madinah and emulated the Companions.

The scholars among the Successors who represented this school of *Fiqh* were many, the most famous of them being the seven well-known jurists. They had laid the foundations of the first school of *Fiqh*, and inculcated the people to act upon the Islamic principles which they drew from the Noble Qur'an.

The leadership of this *Fiqh* school was assumed by Imām Mālik ibn Anas (may Allah bestow mercy upon him). Ibn Taymiyah says, "Imām Mālik was the best to lead the *Fiqh* school of Madinah due to his mastery of both the Prophetic narrations and juristic opinions. None from his generation, nor the following generations, had juristic talent equivalent to his. Furthermore, the admiration he enjoyed in the hearts of the Muslims – the layman and the scholar alike – was not hidden from anyone that possessed the slightest glimpse of knowledge."

مدرسة أهل الحديث[1]

أولاً: مهد مدرسة الحديث وامتدادها:

كان مهد مدرسة الحديث في أول نشأتها بالحجاز، وفي المدينة المنورة بالذات، وعرفت بمدرسة المدينة؛ لأنها مهد السنة، ومأوى الفقهاء، وبها سلالة الصحابة الذين عاصروا الرسول ﷺ، وحفظوا عنه الحديث وتناقلوه، واقتدوا به في أفعاله وتصرفاته، فكان من الطبيعي أن يتأثر فقهاء هذه المدرسة بفقهاء الصحابة الأوائل، وعلماء التابعين الذين استوطنوا المدينة، ونهجوا نهج الصحابة.

وعلماء التابعين الذين كانوا يمثلون مدرسة المدينة كثيرون، وأشهرهم الفقهاء السبعة، وقد كونوا المدرسة الفقهية الأولى، ووضعوا الأسس الأولى للمنهج الفقهي، وعملوا على نفاذ الحياة بأسرها- ومنها الحياة التشريعية- على القواعد الدينية والخلقية، التي استمدوها من القرآن الكريم[2].

وقد انتهت رياسة مدرسة المدينة إلى الإمام مالك- رحمه الله تعالى- يقول ابن تيمية: «مالك أقوم الناس بمذهب أهل المدينة رواية ورأياً، فإنه لم يكن في عصره ولا بعده أقوم بذلك منه، كان له من المكانة عند أهل الإسلام- الخاص والعام- ما لا يخفى على من له بالعلم أدنى إلمام»[3].

١ راجع كتابنا: المذاهب والمدارس الفقهية.

٢ مناهج الاجتهاد في الإسلام، لمحمد سلام مدكور: ١٠٠، نشرته جامعة الكويت.

٣ صحة عمل أهل المدينة لشيخ الإسلام ابن تيمية.

His book *al-Muwaṭṭa'* included his methodology in *Fiqh* which he acquired from those scholars before him – those who themselves acquired it from the Prophet's Companions (may Allah be pleased with them).

II. The Status of the First *Fiqh* School

The Madinah *Fiqh* school's status was highly respected by the rulers and the subjects alike. The Umayyad caliphs used to prefer the scholars of Ḥijāz (the Arabian Peninsula) and their juristic opinions over the scholars of Syria and their juristic opinions. Similarly, al-Manṣūr, al-Mahdi and ar-Rāshīd, who were the best of the Abbasid caliphs, would give the scholars of Ḥijāz and their juristic opinions preference over those of Iraq. Once the caliphs resorted to the juristic opinions of scholars from places other than Madinah, the caliphate began to collapse and innovations began spreading all over the Muslim world. As mentioned by Ibn Taymiyah, the other Muslim lands were dependent on the knowledge of the scholars of Madinah. They never considered themselves equal in knowledge to the scholars of Madinah. Syrian scholars like al-Awzā'i, Egyptian scholars like al-Layth ibn Sa'd, and the scholars from Basrah like Ayūb, Ḥammād ibn Zayd and 'Abdur-Raḥmān ibn Mahdi, were all obvious followers of the scholars of Madinah and their classical opinions, and would hold them in very high esteem.[1]

As Ibn Taymiyah said regarding the juristic approach in Madinah during the eras of the Companions, Successors and those who succeeded them, "It was the most correct of all the *Fiqh* methods that existed in the different Muslim cities, whether in the East or West, and both in the fundamentals and the branches [of *Fiqh*]."[2] Elsewhere, Ibn Taymiyah also said, "As for the generations praised by the Prophet (ﷺ), the *Fiqh* method adopted by the scholars of Madinah during those generations was the most correct of all methods. This was because they would imitate the Prophet (ﷺ) in all that was narrated about him more than any other scholars. Scholars from other places were inferior to them with respect to their knowledge of the Sunnah and with regard to its practice. For this reason, no scholar of Islam ever held that scholars of any locale agreeing by consensus should be taken as a religious proof except the consensus of the scholars of Madinah."[3]

1 Ibid: 26
2 Ibid: 17
3 Ibid: 20

وقد ضمن الإمام مالك كتابه «الموطأ» ذلك المنهج الذي تلقاه عمن قبله، وقد تلقاه أولئك عن الصحابة.

ثانياً: مكانة مدرسة الحديث الأولى وهي المدينة:

لقد كان لمدرسة المدينة مكانة كبيرة عند الحكام والمحكومين، فخلفاء بني أمية كانوا يرجحون علماء الحجاز وقولهم على أهل الشام وقولهم، وكذلك كان المنصور والمهدي والرشيد- وهم سادات خلفاء بني العباس- يرجحون علماء الحجاز وقولهم على علماء أهل العراق، وعندما وجد فيهم مَنْ عَدَلَ إلى الآراء المشرقية كثر الإحداث فيهم وضعفت الخلافة(١).

كما يذكر ابن تيمية أن سائر أمصار المسلمين كانوا منقادين لعلم أهل المدينة، لا يعدُّون أنفسهم أكفاءهم في العلم، كأهل الشام ومصر، مثل الأوزاعي ومن قبله ومن بعده من الشاميين، ومثل الليث بن سعد ومن قبله، ومن بعده من المصريين، وتعظيمهم لعمل أهل المدينة، واتباعهم لمذاهبهم القديمة ظاهر بيِّنٌ، وكذلك علماء أهل البصرة؛ كأيوب، وحماد بن زيد، وعبد الرحمن بن مهدي وأمثالهم(٢).

وكان مذهب أهل المدينة في زمن الصحابة والتابعين وتابعيهم كما يقول ابن تيمية: «أصح مذاهب أهل المدائن الإسلامية شرقاً وغرباً في الأصول والفروع»(٣)، ويقول ابن تيمية في موضع آخر: «في القرون التي أثنى عليها الرسول ﷺ كان مذهب أهل المدينة أصح مذاهب أهل المدائن، فإنهم كانوا يتأسون بأثر رسول الله ﷺ أكثر من سائر الأمصار، وكان غيرهم من أهل الأمصار دونهم في العلم بالسنة النبوية واتباعها، ولهذا لم يذهب أحد من علماء الإسلام إلى أن إجماع أهل مدينة من المدائن حجة يجب اتباعها غير المدينة»(٤).

١ المصدر السابق: ٣٢.
٢ المصدر السابق: ٢٦.
٣ المصدر السابق: ١٧.
٤ المصدر السابق: ٢٠.

III. The Madinan *Fiqh* Method Became Widespread

From the time of the rightly-guided caliphs onward, the scholars of Madinah continuously journeyed to the Muslim states to spread their religious knowledge, and 'Umar ibn 'Abdil-'Azīz would regularly send questions to the scholars of Madinah and ask them for religious edicts.

Similarly, Abū Ja'far al-Manṣūr asked the scholars of Ḥijāz to go to Iraq and spread their religious knowledge there. Thus, Hishām ibn 'Urwah, Muhammad ibn Is-ḥāq, Yaḥyā ibn Sa'īd al-Anṣāri, Rabī'ah ibn Abi 'Abdir-Raḥmān, Ḥanẓalah ibn Abi Sufyān al-Jumaḥi, 'Abdul-'Azīz ibn Abi Salamah al-Mājishūn and others went to Iraq to spread the teachings of Islam. Abū Yūsuf used to attend their study circles and learn the hadith(s) from them, and he was of those who narrated many hadith(s) from the scholars who came to Iraq from Ḥijāz.

People from every corner of the Muslim world journeyed to Madinah to learn at the hands of Imām Mālik. The people of Ḥijāz, Syria and Iraq learnt *al-Muwaṭṭa'* from Imām Mālik, and of the youngest who learned at his hands was Imām ash-Shāfi'i.[1]

In addition, some of the disciples of Abū Ḥanīfah traveled to Madinah and learnt *Fiqh* from Imām Mālik. Ibn Taymiyah mentions some of the specific juristic questions which Abū Yūsuf had asked Imām Mālik.

1 Ibid: 36

ثالثاً: انتشار مذهب أهل المدينة:

لم يـزل علـماء أهـل المدينـة منـذ عهـد الخلفـاء الراشـدين يخرجـون إلى مختلـف أمصـار المسـلمين؛ لنـشر العلـم، وقـد كان عمـر بـن عبـد العزيـز يرسـل إلى علـماء المدينـة يسـألهم ويسـتفتيهم.

وطلـب أبـو جعفـر المنصـور مـن علـماء الحجـاز أن يذهبـوا إلى العـراق، وينـشروا فيـه العلـم، فقـدم عليهـم هشـام بـن عـروة، ومحمـد بـن إسـحاق، ويحيـى بـن سـعيد الأنصـاري، وربيعـة بـن أبي عبـد الرحمـن، وحنظلـة بـن أبي سـفيان الجمحـي، وعبـد العزيـز بـن أبي سـلمة الماجشـون، وغـير هـؤلاء، وكان أبـو يوسـف يختلـف في مجالـس هـؤلاء ويتعلـم منهـم الحديـث، وأكـثر عمـن قـدم مـن الحجـاز(١).

وقـد رحـل النـاس مـن فجـاج الأرض إلى الإمـام مالـك، فقـد أخـذ «الموطـأ» عـن الإمـام مالـك أهـل الحجـاز والشـام والعـراق، ومـن أصغـر مـن أخـذ عنـه الشـافعي(٢).

وقـد رحـل تلاميـذ الإمـام أبي حنيفـة إلى الإمـام مالـك، وأخذوا عنـه العلـم، وقـد ذكـر ابـن تيميـة مسـائل سـأل عنهـا أبـو يوسـف الإمـام مالـك(٣).

١ المصدر السابق: ٢٦.
٢ المصدر السابق: ٣٦.
٣ المصدر السابق: ٢٥.

IV. The Rise of the *Ahl al-Ḥadīth Fiqh* School in Baghdad

The *Ahl al-Ḥadīth* school did not remain confined to Madinah, nor to Ḥijāz. Rather, the scholars that upheld it and called for it lived in all parts of the Muslim world. However, the people of Madinah who lived during the lifetime of Imām Mālik were the most precise in upholding the principles of this school. After the death of Imām Mālik and his like in Ḥijāz, Baghdad became the most distinguished place for this school of *Fiqh*. This is because it was taken as residence by scholars who spread the Sunnah and clarified the true teachings of Islam, such as Aḥmad ibn Ḥanbal, Abū 'Ubayd and other jurists of *Ahl al-Ḥadīth*. Ever since, the Sunnah thrived there in both the fundamental and secondary matters of Islam, and from there the Sunnah radiated from Baghdad to the other Muslim lands. In turn, many great scholars appeared in the East, such as Isḥāq ibn Ibrāhīm ibn Rāhuyah, 'Abdullāh ibn al-Mubārak and their disciples. Hadith scholars from Madinah also traveled to the western Muslim lands and spread the Prophetic Sunnah there. As a result, there existed more Islamic knowledge at that time in Baghdad, Khurasān and the western Muslim lands than there was in Ḥijāz and Basrah.

V. The Most Famous Scholars of the *Ahl al-Ḥadīth Fiqh* School

The leadership of this *Fiqh* school was assumed by Imām Mālik, Imām ash-Shāfi'i, Imām Aḥmad and Imām Sufyān ath-Thawri. Ash-Shihristāni said, "Ahl al-Ḥadīth were the people of Ḥijāz, namely the companions of Mālik ibn Anas, the companions of Muhammad ibn Idrīs ash-Shāfi'i, the companions of Sufyān ath-Thawri and the companions of Dāwūd ibn 'Ali al-Asfahāni."[1]

1 *Al-Milal wan-Niḥal* 1/206 by ash-Shihristāni

رابعاً: ظهور مدرسة أهل الحديث في بغداد:

لم تبق مدرسة أهل الحديث محصورة في إطار المدينة المنورة، ولا في إطار الحجاز، بل كان العلماء المنادون بها والقائمون عليها موجودين في كل قطر، ولكن أهل المدينة كانوا إلى عهد الإمام مالك أقوم بها من غيرهم، وبعد موت الإمام مالك وأمثاله من علماء الحجاز برزت بغداد من بين المدائن كأبرز معقل لأهل الحديث؛ لأنه قد سكن بها من أفشى السنة، وأظهر حقائق الإسلام، مثل أحمد بن حنبل، وأبي عبيد، وأمثالهما من فقهاء أهل الحديث، وظهرت بها السنة في الأصول والفروع منذ ذلك الوقت، وانتشرت السنة منها إلى الأمصار، وظهر في المشرق علماء أعلام، أمثال إسحاق بن إبراهيم بن راهويه وأصحابه، وأصحاب عبد الله بن المبارك، وصار إلى المغرب من علم أهل المدينة ما نقل إليهم من علماء الحديث، فصار في بغداد وخراسان والمغرب من العلم ما لا يكون مثله إذ ذاك بالحجاز والبصرة[١].

خامساً: أشهر علماء أهل الحديث:

آلت زعامة مدرسة أهل الحديث إلى الأئمة: مالك، والشافعي، وأحمد، وسفيان الثوري، يقول الشهرستاني: «أصحاب الحديث هم أهل الحجاز، هم أصحاب مالك بن أنس، وأصحاب محمد بن إدريس الشافعي، وأصحاب سفيان الثوري، وأصحاب داود بن علي الأصفهاني»[٢].

١ راجع المصدر السابق: ٣٢.

٢ الملل والنحل، للشهرستاني: ١/ ٢٠٦.

In his book *al-Madkhal,* al-Bayhaqi narrated that Yaḥyā ibn Muhammad al-Anbāri said, "The People of Hadith are five groups: the Māliki(s), the Shāfi'i(s), the Hanbali(s), the Rāhuyah(s) and the Khuzaymi(s)."[1] By the term Rāhuyah(s), he is referring to the companions of Imām Isḥāq ibn Rāhuyah, and by the term Khuzaymi(s), he is referring to the companions of Imām Muhammad ibn Isḥāq ibn Khuzaymah. Both were of the greatest scholars of Hadith.

Ash-Shihristāni and Yahya ibn Muhammad did not mean to confine scholars of Hadith to these few aforementioned scholars, but they intended that those were the most famous scholars of Hadith who had disciples during the lifetime of ash-Shihristāni. In fact, Imām Mālik, Imām ash-Shāfi'i and Imām Aḥmad ibn Ḥanbal still have disciples until today, whereas other scholars do not.

Many of the famous scholars of Hadith who had disciples during the second and third centuries after *Hijrah* were well-known. In the second century, the most famous of them were Yaḥyā ibn Sa'īd al-Qaṭṭān, Wakī' ibn al-Jarrāḥ, Sufyān ath-Thawri, Sufyān ibn 'Uyaynah, Shu'bah ibn al-Ḥajjāj, 'Abdur-Raḥmān ibn Mahdi, al-Awzā'i and al-Layth ibn Sa'd."[2]

VI. The Reason Behind Naming Them *Ahl al-Ḥadīth*

Ash-Shihristāni said, "They were named scholars of Hadith because they were keen with collecting the Prophetic hadith(s), spreading such reports, and deducing the juristic rulings directly from the revealed texts. They would not resort to analogical deduction, whether explicit or implicit, for any juristic question as long as there were religious texts dealing with the question." Furthermore, they disdained hypothetical discussions, feared giving *fatwa,* and would not exercise *ijtihād* unless it was necessary.

1 *I'lām al-Muwaqqi'īn* 2/284

2 *Al-Ḥadīth wal-Muḥaddithūn* 387 by Abū Zahrah. See *Mafātīḥ al-Fiqh al-Ḥanbali* 1/55.

ونقل البيهقي في كتابه «المدخل» عن يحيى بن محمد العنبري قوله: «طبقات أصحاب الحديث خمسة: المالكية، والشافعية، والحنبلية، والرهاوية، والخزمية»[١]، ومراده بالرهاوية أصحاب الإمام إسحاق بن راهويه، وبالخزمية أتباع محمد بن إسحاق بن خزيمة، وكانا من كبار علماء الحديث.

وليس مراد الشهرستاني ويحيى بن محمد أن أهل الحديث محصورون في هؤلاء، بل مراده أن هؤلاء هم أهل الحديث الذين لهم أتباع في عصر الشهرستاني، ولا يزال لمالك والشافعي وأحمد أتباع إلى اليوم، وقد انقرض من عداهم.

أما أهل الحديث المشهورون الذين لهم أتباع في هذا القرن الثاني والثالث فهم كثير، وأشهرهم في القرن الثاني الهجري: يحيى بن سعيد القطان، ووكيع بن الجراح، وسفيان الثوري، وسفيان بن عيينة، وشعبة بن الحجاج، وعبد الرحمن بن مهدي، والأوزاعي، والليث بن سعد[٢].

سادساً: السبب في تسميتهم بأهل الحديث:

يقول الشهرستاني: «وإنما سموا بأصحاب الحديث؛ لأن عنايتهم بتحصيل الأحاديث ونقل الأخبار وبناء الأحكام على النصوص، ولا يرجعون إلى القياس الجلي والخفي ما وجدوا خبراً أو أثراً»[٣]، وكانوا يكرهون الخوض بالرأي، ويهابون الفتيا والاستنباط إلا لضرورة لا يجدون منها بداً.

١ إعلام الموقعين: ٢/ ٢٨٤.

٢ الحديث والمحدثون لأبي زهرة: ٣٨٧، وانظر مفاتيح الفقه الحنبلي: ١/ ٥٥.

٣ الملل والنحل للشهرساني: ١/ ٢٠٦.

The *Ahl al-Ḥadīth* school was the vanguard in compiling the Prophetic Sunnah. The scholars of Hadith suffered immensely on route to collecting the Prophetic hadith(s) and documenting them. As a result, they successfully collected the Sunnah, filtered between the authentic and inauthentic hadith(s), compiled them into collections and collected with them the views of the jurists, in each land, from among the Companions and the Successors. Also, they authored works on the narrators of hadith, and set the rules and criteria through which the credibility of the narrators could be determined. With that, they laid the foundation for the science of *musṭalaḥ* (hadith terminology) and *al-jarḥ wat-ta'dīl* (narrator evaluation).

VII. The Principles of *Ahl al-Ḥadīth* in Deducing Juristic Rulings

Ahl al-Ḥadīth scholars would not imitate any one man in all his juristic views. Instead, we find them following a clear method to reach the correct juristic rulings through the hadith(s) and reports available to them. Ad-Dahlawi explained the fundmantal principles of this methodology, saying:

1) When there is a Qur'anic text on a juristic question, no one is allowed to resort to any other texts. When the Qur'anic text carries the potential of many juristic implications, then the Sunnah decides which meaning is intended by it.

2) When no ruling is found in the Qur'an on a juristic matter, they resort to the Sunnah of the Messenger of Allah (ﷺ) without differentiating between the hadith(s) well-known to the jurists and others. They do not stipulate that the hadith be narrated by people of a certain place, by a certain group of narrators or transmitted in a certain way. Likewise, they do not stipulate that the hadith be acted upon by the Companions (may Allah be pleased with them) or the Successors. The only thing they stipulate is that the hadith be authentic. Whenever the hadith is found to be authentic, they follow nothing else; they dimiss consideration of the Companions' views and the opinions of the *Mujtahid Imām*(s) whenever they contradict an authenticated hadith.

ومدرسة أهل الحديث كان لها فضل السبق إلى تدوين السنة، وقد كابد علماء الحديث في سبيل جمع الحديث وتدوينه الشيء الكثير، وقد جمعوا السنة، وخلصوها مما شابها، ودونوها، وجمعوا مع السنة آثار فقهاء كل بلد من الصحابة والتابعين، ودونوا المدونات التي تبحث في رجال الحديث، ووضعوا القواعد والضوابط التي يحكم بها على عدالة الرجال، وبذلك دُوِّن فن مصطلح الحديث، والجرح والتعليل.

سابعاً: أصول أهل الحديث في بيان الأحكام:

لم يكن من طريقة أهل الحديث أن يقلدوا رجلاً بعينه في كل ما يذهب إليه؛ ولذلك نجدهم اتبعوا منهجاً واضحاً للتوصل إلى الحكم الصحيح، من خلال ما وجدوه من الأحاديث والآثار، وقد بيَّن الدهلوي أصول هذا المنهج ومعالمه[1]:

١- إذا وجدوا في المسألة قرآناً ناطقاً، فإنهم لا يجيزون التحول منه إلى غيره، فإذا كان القرآن محتملاً لوجوه، فالسنة قاضية عليه.

٢- فإذا لم يجدوا حكم المسألة في كتاب الله، فإنهم يأخذون بسنة رسول الله ﷺ، ولا يفرقون في هذا بين السنة المستفيضة الدائرة بين الفقهاء وغير المستفيضة، ولا يشترطون مجيء الحديث من رواية أهل بلد أو أهل بيت أو بطريقة خاصة، كما أنهم لا يشترطون عمل الصحابة بالحديث، أو عمل التابعين، كل ما يشترطونه هو صحة الحديث.ومتى صح الحديث فلا يتبعون خلافه، فلا اعتبار للآثار، ولا لآراء المجتهدين، إذا خالفت الحديث.

١ الإنصاف في أسباب الاختلاف للدهلوي: ٤٧.

3) Whenever they exhausted their efforts in search of a hadith but could not find a hadith pertaining to a particular juristic matter, they turned to the views of the Companions and the Successors without differentiating between certain people or certain places. If the majority of the caliphs and jurists had agreed on a matter, this became the chosen view. If they differed, they would adopt the view of the most pious, most knowledgeable, most precise or most distinguished in a particular subject. If two views are found that are equally strong, then this becomes a matter wherein there are two [valid] opinions.

٣- وإذا أفرغوا جهدهم في تتبع الأحاديث، ولم يجدوا في المسألة حديثاً، أخذوا بأقوال جماعة من الصحابة والتابعين، ولا يتقيدون بقوم دون قوم، ولا بلد دون بلد، فإن اتفق جمهور الخلفاء والفقهاء على شيء فهو المتبع، وإن اختلفوا أخذوا بحديث أعلمهم علماً، أو أورعهم ورعاً، أو أكثرهم ضبطاً، أو ما اشتهر عنهم، فإن وجدوا شيئاً يستوي فيه قولان، فهي مسألة ذات قولين.

4) If they are incapable of applying that, they employ the general principles of the Qur'an and Sunnah and reflect on what they imply and allude to. Then, they compare it to other cases that resemble it in the Qur'an and Sunnah, and from there build their opinion. While doing that, they do not depend on the fundamentals of *Fiqh*, but rather on what is essentially understood and satisfies the heart.

٤- فإن عجزوا عن ذلك تأملوا في عمومات الكتاب والسنة وإيماءاتهما، واقتضاءاتهما، وحملوا نظير المسألة عليها في الجواب، إذا كانتا متقاربتين بادي الرأي، لا يعتمدون في ذلك على قواعد من الأصول، ولكن على ما يخلص إلى الفهم، ويثلج به الصدر.

VIII. Mistakes Some Adherents of *Ahl al-Ḥadīth* Fell Into[1]

Ahl al-Ḥadīth continued following the methodology of the first generation – that which was drawn out for them by the Prophet (ﷺ) and his Companions. However, some adherents of this school deviated from this approach and began busying themselves with matters that were never before entertained by the vanguard scholars of this school. Imam al-Khaṭṭābi, who is an adherent of this school, said in regards to the condition of many during his time who were considered *Ahl al-Ḥadīth*, "The majority of *Ahl al-Ḥadīth* are engrossed in collecting narrations, their multiple chains of transmission and pursuing the rare hadith(s) that are usually fabricated or reversed. They give no care to the contents [of the hadith], nor try to understand its meaning, nor extract its implications or the juristic rulings found therein. At times, they may even criticize the jurists under the claim that they have deviated from the Sunnah."[2]

1 This section was added into the English version with permission of the original author.
2 *Ma'ālim as-Sunan* 1/6

While describing the *Ahl al-Ḥadīth* scholars of his time, Ibn 'Abdil-Barr said, "This group merely narrated the hadith and collected it, having been content with exhausting its efforts in collecting what it does not understand. They are satisfied with being ignorant of what they carry, and as a result collected the worthy and the unworthy, the authentic and inauthentic, and the true and false reports, all in one book and sometimes even on the same page. You find them believing a matter and its opposite, all while not realizing their contradiction. They preoccupied themselves with memorizing instead of studying and considering. Thus, their tongues relay knowledge while their hearts are void of understanding. Their greatest aims are in discovering a rare manuscript or an unknown narrator. You find them oblivious to matters that a person could hardly fend without, such as basic knowledge about prayer, fasting, *zakāh* and Hajj."[1]

The *Fiqh* School of *Ahl ar-Ra'y*

مدرسة أهل الرأي

I. The Intended Meaning Behind ***Ahl ar-Ra'y***

أولاً: المراد بأهل الرأي:

The term *ra'y* denotes having knowledge of a matter, though that knowledge is presumptious. The jurists used this as a technical term that refers to considering and deliberating matters that no specific text addresses. There are many instances when the Companions (may Allah be pleased with them) used the term *ra'y* in reference to their *ijtihād* – matters wherein the general interests are considered, *qiyās* (analogical deduction) is exercised and juristic preference is employed.

المـراد بالـرأي العلـم بالـشيء عـلى سـبيل الظـن، وقـد خصـه الفقهـاء بالنظـر وإعـمال الفكـر في الوقائـع التـي لم يـرد بهـا نـص، وكثـيراً مـا اسـتعمل الصحابـة كلمـة رأي في اجتهاداتهـم، التـي ظهـر أنهـا مبنيـة عـلى اعتبـار المصلحـة، أو قائمـة عـلى أسـاس مـن القيـاس أو الاستحسـان ونحوهـما.

The title *Ahl ar-Ra'y* refers to those who excessively depended on *ra'y* (independent reasoning) and *qiyās* in determining the legislated rulings. However, this does not imply that they did not depend on the Qur'an and Sunnah.

والمـراد بأهـل الـرأي الذيـن أكـثروا مـن اسـتعمال الـرأي والقيـاس في بيـان الأحـكام الشرعيـة، وليـس المـراد أنهـم لم يكونـوا يعتمـدون عـلى الكتـاب والسـنة.

As said by ash-Shihristāni, "The *Ahl ar-Ra'y*

1 *Jāmi' Bayān al-'Ilm* 1/208

school of jurists were the people of Iraq, such as Imām Abū Ḥanīfah an-Nu`mān ibn Thābit and his disciples. Of his disciples were Muhammad ibn al-Ḥasan, Abū Yūsuf Ya'qūb ibn Ibrāhīm ibn Muhammad al-Qāḍi, Zafr ibn al-Hudhayl and al-Ḥasan ibn Ziyād al-Lu'lu'i."[1]

II. The Reason Behind Naming Them ***Ahl ar-Ra'y***

Ash-Shihristāni said, "They were known as *Ahl ar-Ra'y* because they were most keen on finding the proper analogical deduction and the underlying meanings behind the juristic rulings, all in order to extract other rulings based on that. At times, they may even give clear analogies preference over *āḥād* [prophetic] reports. Imām Abū Ḥanīfah once said, 'We taught this [method of] independent reasoning as best we could. Whoever is capable of other than this, then for them is [the right to] their opinion, and for us is our opinion.'"[2]

Clearly, this *Fiqh* school did not give as much care to the revealed texts as the first school. Instead, they delved deep into *ra'y*, in addition to extensively considering the hypothetical scenarios that have not yet taken place.

III. The Mistakes of *Ahl ar-Ra'y*

Ibn al-Qayyim listed five mistakes made by the scholars of *Ahl ar-Ra'y*. Of them, we will suffice with mentioning three:[3]

وأصحاب الرأي كما يقول الشهرستاني: «هم أهل العراق، أصحاب أبي حنيفة النعمان بن ثابت، ومن أصحابه: محمد بن الحسن، وأبو يوسف يعقوب بن إبراهيم بن محمد القاضي، وزفر بن الهذيل، والحسن بن زياد اللؤلؤي»[١].

ثانياً: السبب في تسميتهم بأهل الرأي:

يقول الشهرستاني: «وإنما سموا أصحاب الرأي؛ لأن أكثر عنايتهم بتحصيل وجه القياس، والمعنى المستنبط من الأحكام، وبناء الحوادث عليها، وربما يقدمون القياس الجلي على آحاد الأخبار، وقد قال أبو حنيفة: علمنا هذا رأي أحسن ما قدرنا عليه، فمن قدر على غير ذلك، فله ما رأى، ولنا ما رأينا»[٢].

ولم تعن هذه المدرسة بالنصوص عناية المدرسة الأولى، وتوسعوا في الرأي، كما توسعوا في النظر في المسائل الفرضية التي لم تقع بعد.

ثالثاً: أخطاء أهل الرأي:

أحصى ابن القيم أخطاءهم فكانت خمسة، نكتفي بذكر ثلاثة منها[٣]:

1 *Al-Milal wan-Niḥal* 1/207
2 Ibid
3 *I'lām al-Muwaqqi'īn* 1/390

١ الملل والنحل: ١/ ٢٠٧.
٢ المصدر السابق.
٣ إعلام الموقعين: ١/ ٣٩٠.

1. *Their Assumption that the Revealed Texts Do Not Tackle Every Incident*

Ibn al-Qayyim wrote an entire chapter proving that the revealed texts comprehensively tackle every ruling, and that they do not leave the scholars greatly dependent on *ra'y* and *qiyās*.[1] In that chapter, he listed many issues over which the righteous *salaf* (predecessors) differed, exercised their independent reasoning and *qiyās*, although there were revealed texts that addressed these questions. Correct *qiyās* should not be taken as an independent evidence, but rather as a secondary method of asserting rulings for matters which the revealed texts did not tackle.

An example of this is them differing about the one who steals the shrouds of the dead and whether his hand should be cut off. The correct logic is that he is a thief, and thus falls under the statement of the Most High, **"[As for] the thief, the male and the female, amputate their hands..."**[2] Another example is sufficing with the Prophet's statement, "All intoxicants are *khamr* (wine),"[3] and not resorting to *qiyās* to prohibit other intoxicants.

2. *Opposing Many Revealed Texts using Ra'y and Qiyās*

Ibn al-Qayyim listed a multitude of incidents wherein *Ahl ar-Ra'y* ignored hadith(s) on a matter and determined its ruling based on *qiyās*. Of these incidents was their neglecting the hadith pertaining to naked women, the hadith that that an unmarried fornicator be exiled for one year, the hadith that speaking during prayer by a forgetful or ignorant person does not annul it, the hadith that a *luqaṭah* (waif) should be given to whoever claims it and gives a full description of it, the hadith on a goat whose udders have been tied up, and other hadith(s) which these scholars dismissed based on *ra'y* and *qiyās*.[4]

الأول: ظنهم قصور النصوص عن بيان جميع الحوادث:وقد عقد ابن القيم فصلاً كبيراً، بيَّن فيه شمول النصوص للأحكام، وأنها مغنية عن الرأي والقياس(١)، وقد ساق فيه مسائل كثيرة اختلف فيها السلف الصالح، وقالوا فيها برأيهم، وأعملوا فيها القياس، مع أن النصوص قد بينتها، والقياس الصحيح شاهد أو تابع، وليس مستقلاً في إثبات حكم من الأحكام لم تدل عليه النصوص.

ومن أمثلة ذلك اختلافهم في النباش الذي يسرق أكفان الموتى، هل تقطع يده؟ والصحيح أنه سارق داخل في قوله تعالى: ﴿**وَالسَّارِقُ وَالسَّارِقَةُ فَاقْطَعُوا أَيْدِيَهُمَا**﴾ [المائدة: ٨٣]، ومن ذلك الاكتفاء بقوله ﷺ: «**كل مسكر خمر**» عن إثبات التحريم بالقياس في الاسم أو الحكم.

الثاني: معارضة كثير من النصوص بالرأي والقياس:

وقد أورد ابن القيم فيضاً من النصوص ترك فيها القياسيون الأحاديث وأخذوا بالرأي والقياس، فمن ذلك تركهم حديث العرايا، وحديث تغريب الزاني غير المحصن، وحديث عدم إبطال كلام الناسي والجاهل للصلاة، وحديث دفع اللقطة إلى من جاء فوصف وعاءها ووكاءها وعفاصها، وحديث المصراة، وغير ذلك من الأحاديث التي تركوها بالرأي والقياس(٢).

---

1 Ibid: 1/392
2 Sūrat al-Ma'idah – Verse 38
3 Reported by al-Bukhāri.
4 *I'lām al-Muwaqqi'īn* 1/274

١ المصدر السابق: ١/ ٣٩٢.
٢ المصدر السابق: ١/ ٢٧٤.

3. Their Belief that Many Sharia Rulings Contradict Sound Qiyās

Ibn al-Qayyim allotted an extensive chapter to refuting this claim of theirs, wherein he quotes a long chapter from his instructor Ibn Taymiyah. Therein, he presents many examples in which the people of *qiyās* claimed that a [textual] ruling contradicts sound *qiyās*, and then counters their arguments and establishes that these examples are actually in complete agreement with sound *qiyās*. Of what they believed to be contrary to sound *qiyās* was *muḍārabah*, sharecropping and treewatering because they consider them to be a form of waging, for they involve work in exchange for a compensation. However, the compensated person and the return amount are supposed to be specified in waging. They claim that since the work and profit are not specified in such contracts, they oppose the *qiyās*. He then explained how they were mistaken, since such contracts are a form of partnership, and not one of pure compensation in which both the return and the compensated person must be determined. This is because partnerships do not fall under ordinary compensations, even though they involve a shade of compensation.[1]

The *Fiqh* School of *Ahl aẓ-Ẓāhir*

I. The Intended Meaning Behind ***Ahl aẓ-Ẓāhir***

This *Fiqh* school is the polar opposite of the *Ahl ar-Ra'y* school. *Ahl ar-Ra'y* were excessive in their usage of *ra'y*, and *Ahl aẓ-Ẓāhir* went to the extreme of rejecting it altogether. This school is attributed to Dāwūd ibn 'Ali ibn Khalaf.[2] He was originally from Esfahan, was born in Kufah, but lived in Baghdad. He was well-known as Dāwūd aẓ-Ẓāhiri. He was born in 200 A.H. or a few years later and died in 270 A.H.

1 *I'lām al-Muwaqqi'īn* 1/432

2 See his biography in *Tārīkh Baghdād* 8/369-375 – printed by Dār as-Sa'ādah in 1931, *Tahdhīb al-Asmā' wal-Lughāt* 1/182 – printed by Dār at-Tibā'ah al-Munīriyyah in Egypt, *Ṭabaqāt ash-Shāfi'iyyah al-Kubrā* 2/42-48 by Tāj ad-Dīn as-Subki – printed by al-Ḥusayniyyah al-Miṣriyyah and *at-Tadhkirah* 2/572-573 by al-Ḥāfiẓ adh-Dhahabi – printed by Dār Iḥyā' 'Ulūm at-Turāth al-'Arabi in Beirut (4th Edition).

الثالث: اعتقادهم في كثير من الأحكام الشرعية أنها على خلاف القياس:

وقد بين ابن القيم بطلان ما ذهبوا إليه في مبحث طويل، نقل فيه عن شيخه شيخ الإسلام ابن تيمية فصلاً كبيراً، ضرب فيه كثيراً من الأمثلة التي قال أهل القياس: إنها مخالفة للقياس، وقد ناقشهم فيها، وبين أنها موافقة للقياس.

ومما ظنوه مخالفاً للقياس: المضاربة، والمساقاة، والمزارعة؛ لأنها عندهم من جنس الإجارة؛ لأنها عمل بعوض، والإجارة يشترط فيها العلم بالعوض والمعوّض، فلما رأوا العمل والربح في هذه العقود غير معلومين، قالوا: هي على خلاف القياس، وبين أنهم غلطوا في هذا؛ فإن هذه العقود من جنس المشاركات لا من جنس المعاوضات المحضة، التي يشترط فيها العلم بالعِوَض والمعوَّض، والمشاركات جنس غير جنس المعاوضات، وإن كان فيها شوب المعاوضة[1].

مدرسة أهل الظاهر

أولاً: المراد بأهل الظاهر:

هذه المدرسة تقابل مدرسة أهل الرأي، فأهل الرأي توسعوا في الأخذ بالرأي، وأهل الظاهر غلوا في رفضه ورده، وتنسب هذه المدرسة إلى داود بن علي بن خلف[2] الأصبهاني الأصل، الكوفي المولد، البغدادي الدار، الشهير بداود الظاهري، المولود في سنة ٢٠٠هـ أو بعدها بقليل، المتوفى في سنة ٢٧٠هـ.

١ المصدر السابق: ١/ ٤٣٢.

٢ انظر ترجمته في تاريخ بغداد: ٨/ ٣٦٩- ٣٧٥، مطبعة السعادة سنة ١٩٣١م؛ وتهذيب الأسماء واللغات للنووي: ١/ ١٨٢، دار الطباعة المنيرية، مصر؛ وطبقات الشافعية الكبرى لتاج الدين السبكي: ٢/ ٤٢- ٤٨، المطبعة الحسينية المصرية؛ وتذكرة الحافظ للذهبي، ٢/ ٥٧٢- ٥٧٣، دار إحياء علوم التراث العربي، بيروت، الطبعة الرابعة.

Dāwūd learnt *Fiqh* at the hands of Abū Thawr, a disciple of Imām ash-Shāfi'i, and Is-ḥāq ibn Rāhuyah, who was one of the great scholars of *Ahl al-Ḥadīth*. He learned from many of the famous jurists of his time. Dāwūd held Imām ash-Shāfi'i in great esteem and adopted his principles in *Fiqh*. However, he later drew for himself an independent method in which he relied on the *ẓāhir* (literal) meanings of the texts and on *ijmā'* (scholarly consensus), while rejecting the usage of other evidences, such as *qiyās* (analogical deduction). The reason for his denial of *qiyās* was that rulings had no *'illah* (comprehendible justification), and that Allah legislated a Sharia solely on the basis of His authority, not on the basis of detectable wisdoms and effective causes.

وقد تفقه داود على أبي ثور تلميذ الإمام الشافعي، وإسحاق بن راهويه، وهو إمام من أئمة أهل الحديث، وأخذ عن الفقهاء الأعلام في وقته، وكان داود معظماً للإمام الشافعي، آخذاً بأصوله، ثم اختط لنفسه طريقاً، خالف فيه غيره من فقهاء الإسلام، وطريقته تتمثل في الاعتماد على ظاهر النصوص والإجماع، ونفي الأصول الأخرى التي اعتمد عليها غيره من العلماء كالقياس، والسبب الذي جعله ينفي القياس هو دعواه أن الأحكام غير معللة، وأن الله شرع ما شرع من أحكام بمحض المشيئة المجردة عن الحكمة والتعليل.

The scholars of this school realized the pitfall that *Ahl ar-Ra'y* fell into with regard to the texts of the Sharia, wherein they gave precedene to *ra'y* over the revealed texts on many occasions. *Ahl aẓ-Ẓāhir* realized that this was due to their neglecting to memorize, rehearse and properly understand the revealed texts. Thus, Dāwūd's stance was a reaction to those who went to extremes in the usage of *ra'y*. However, he himself ended up going to another extreme by rejecting the usage of *qiyās* altogether.[1] He advocated that texts are not to be rationalized, and limited his method strictly to the literal understandings of the texts.

لقد رأى أهل الظاهر ما جناه الرأي على النصوص الشرعية بحيث قُدِّم الرأي على النص في كثير من الأحكام، بسبب إهمال النصوص حفظاً وفقهاً ودراسة، فكان موقف داود ردة فعل للذين تطرفوا بالأخذ بالرأي، فجاء موقفه تطرفاً في الجانب الآخر، فمنع الأخذ بالقياس[(1)]، وقال بعدم تعليل النصوص، وقصر منهجه على الأخذ بظاهر النصوص.

His method led people to care greatly for memorizing, studying, understanding and teaching the religious texts. However, they stopped at its literal, apparent meanings, and did not dive into the depths of its implications.

وقد أدى منهجه هذا إلى الاعتناء بالنصوص حفظاً ومدارسة وفقهاً وتعليماً إلا أنهم وقفوا عند ظاهرها، ولم يغوصوا في أعماقها.

1 Before Dāwūd aẓ-Ẓāhiri, this method was advocated by Ibrāhīm ibn Sayyār an-Naẓām al-Mu'tazili, and many Mu'tazili scholars followed him in this *fiqhi* approach. Of them was Ja'far ibn Ḥarb, Ja'far ibn Mubashir and Muhammd ibn 'Abdillāh al-Iskāfi. See *Jāmi' Bayān al-'Ilm* 2/78 by Ibn 'Abdil-Barr.

١ سبق إبراهيم بن سيار النظام المعتزلي داود الظاهري إلى هذا القول، وتابعه معتزلة أئمة في الاعتزال على قوله، منهم جعفر بن حرب، وجعفر بن مبشر، ومحمد بن عبد الله الإسكافي، انظر جامع بيان العلم لابن عبد البر: ٢/ ٧٨.

II. The Mistakes of ***Ahl aẓ-Ẓāhir***

The approach adopted by the scholars of *Ahl aẓ-Ẓāhir* had very serious consequences. It implies that the Sharia gives different verdicts for similar cases and similar verdicts for matters that are inherently different. This is because – as you should now know – they believe that Allah does not forbid a matter for its harm, nor enjoins a matter for its benefit.[12] Ibn al-Qayyim argues that they are mistaken in this regard for four reasons.[3] Of them, we will suffice with mentioning three:

1. Rejecting Sound Qiyās[4]

They reject sound analogical deduction, even when the *'illah* (effective cause) is expressly stated in the text, whereby it is clearly understood that this should be generalized to any applicable context. For example, no rational person would doubt that the Prophet (ﷺ) saying "Indeed, Allah and His Messenger forbid you [to eat] the meat of donkeys, for it is an impure thing"[5] is equivelant to him saying that you are forbidden from [eating] every impure thing.

1 One of the overly literal views of *Ahl aẓ-Ẓāhir* is that it is not lawful for the one who urinates in still water that does not flow to perform ablution from this water based on the hadith forbidding that. However, they permit for other than the urinator to bathe and perform ablution from this same water. Similarly, they differentiate between urinating directly into water, urinating in a vessel and then pouring it into water, and urinating beside water and then it flows into the water. Of all those scenarios, they only forbade performing ablution from water in which one urinates directly. See *al-Majmū'* by an-Nawawi.

2 *I'lām al-Muwaqqi'īn* 2/34, 149

3 Ibid: 1/377

4 See *al-Iḥkām fī Uṣūl al-Aḥkām* 2/977 by Ibn Ḥazm

5 Reported by Imām al-Bukhāri.

ثانياً: أخطاء أهل الظاهر:

لقد أدى هذا المنهج بأهل الظاهر إلى نتائج خطيرة، فقد جوزوا ورود الشريعة بالفرق بين المتساويين، والجمع بين المختلفين؛ لأنهم- كما عرفت- يقرون أن الشارع ينهى عن الشيء لا لمفسدة، ويأمر به لا لمصلحة(١) (٢)، وقد خطأهم ابن القيم من أربعة أوجه(٣)، نكتفي بذكر ثلاثة منها:

أحدها: رد القياس الصحيح(٤)، ولاسيما المنصوص على علته التي يجري النص عليها مجرى التنصيص على التعميم، فلا يشك عاقل أن قوله ﷺ: «**إن الله ورسوله ينهيانكم عن لحوم الحمر، فإنها رجس**» بمنزلة قوله: ينهيانكم عن كل رجس.

١ من ظاهرية أصحاب الظاهر أنهم لا يجوزون لمن بال في الماء الدائم الذي لا يجري أن يتوضأ منه عملاً بالحديث الذي ينهى عن ذلك، ولكنهم يجوزون لغير البائل أن يتوضأ منه ويغتسل، كما فرقوا بين البول في الماء مباشرة، والبول في إناء ثم صبه بالماء أو بوله بجانب الماء بحيث يجري البول إلى الماء، فلم يحرِّموا التوضؤ إلا على الماء الذي يتبول فيه مباشرة. انظر المجموع للنووي.

٢ إعلام الموقعين: ٢/ ٣٤، ١٤٩.

٣ المصدر السابق: ١/ ٣٧٧.

٤ انظر الإحكام في أصول الأحكام لابن حزم: ٢/ ٩٧٧.

Similarly, the Messenger (ﷺ) saying with regard to the cat "It is not impure; it is of those who [freely] roam about among you"[1] is equivelant to him saying whatever freely roams among you is not impure. Similarly, when a person says to another, "Do not eat this kind of food because it is poisoned," this means he forbids him to eat this sort of food. Also, when a person says to another, "Do not have this drink because it is intoxicating," this means he forbids him to have any intoxicants. Similarly, when a person says to another, "Do not marry this woman because she is unfaithful," this means he forbids him to marry any woman who is unfaithful.

2. Poorly Understanding the Religious Texts

Many of the juristic rulings were in fact alluded to by the texts, yet they did not understand these implications from them. This is because they confined the text to its literal meanings, without considering what they indirectly imply, allude to, subtely hint at and what was customarily understood by its [original] audience. For instance, they did not understand that the Most High saying [about parents] **"...say not to them [so much as], 'fie' and do not repel them"**[2] implied the impermissibility of beating, cursing or humiliating them. Ibn Ḥazm said, "No Arab ever understood that the word 'fie' refers to killing or beating. Hence, if nothing was ever revealed except this verse [regarding parents], then nothing but the statement 'fie' would have been prohibited."[3]

وقوله في الهر: «**ليست بنجس؛ إنها من الطوافين عليكم والطوافات**» بمنزلة قوله: كل ما هو من الطوافين عليكم والطوافات، فإنه ليس بنجس، ولا يستريب عاقل في أن من قال لغيره: لا تأكل هذا الطعام؛ فإنه مسموم، نهي عن كل طعام كذلك، وإذا قال: لا تشرب هذا الشراب؛ فإنه مسكر، نهي له عن كل مسكر، ولا تتزوج هذه المرأة فإنها فاجرة، نهي له عن كل امرأة فاجرة.

الثاني: تقصيرهم في فهم النصوص؛ فكثير من الأحكام دلت عليها النصوص، ولم يفهموا دلالتها عليها، وسبب هذا أنهم حصروا الدلالة في مجرد ظاهر اللفظ دون إيمائه وإشارته وتنبيهه وعرفه عند المخاطبين، فلم يفهموا من قوله تعالى: ﴿فَلَا تَقُل لَّهُمَا أُفٍّ وَلَا تَنْهَرْهُمَا﴾[1]، ضرباً ولا سبّاً ولا إهانة، يقول ابن حزم في الآية: «ما فهم أحد قط في لغة العرب ولا العقل أن قول: «أف» يعبر به عن القتل والضرب، ولو لم يأت إلا هذه الآية ما حَرُم إلا قول «أف» فقط»[2].

1 Reported by Imām al-Bukhārī.
2 Sūrat al-Isra' – Verse 23
3 *Mulakhaṣ Ibṭāl al-Qiyās* 9

١ الإسراء ٢٣.
٢ ملخص إبطال القياس: ٩.

Certainly, this is a strange phenomena, and thus Imām adh-Dhahabi commented on this statement of Ibn Ḥazm's by saying, "O you! With such rigidity and its likes, you open the door to being ridiculed and set yourself up for being a laughing stock. Rather, there is none among the Arabs, nor even the non-Arabs, nor anyone sensible and in their right mind except that they understand that the prohibition to say 'fie' to one's parents implies that everything above it is even greater in prohibition. Can any rational person understand anything but that? Isn't this clearly an example of alluding to the greater using that which is lesser? This is of the matters that are understood in the languages of the Arabs, non-Arabs, Turks and all of humanity alike. Clearly, someone saying, 'Do not scold your parents' implies the unlawfulness of cussing at them, supplicating against them, beating them until they beg for mercy and choking them to death – all by greater virtue."

Then, he struck an example to further clarify this point and said, "Were a man to say to his wife, 'If you talk to men, I will beat you,' and then she goes off and commits adultery with men without speaking a single word to them, there is no doubt that she has been disobedient. In fact, she has fallen into a greater disobedience by doing so, and is more deserving of beaing beaten than someone who just spoke with men."

3. Believing that a Muslim's Contracts, Transactions and Stipulations are all Invalid unless Evidence Arises that Proves their Validity

According to them, unless there is a textual evidence that proves the legality of a transaction, this transaction is rendered invalid. As a result, they baselessly declared many transactions between the people to be invalid. The majority of jurists have the opposite opinion; all transactions are legal except those prohibited and deemed invalid by a revealed text. This is obviously the correct opinion, for deeming something invalid entails it being prohibited and sinful, and we know that nothing is prohibited except what Allah and His Messenger prohibited, and nothing is sinful except what Allah and His Messenger deemed sinful. In the same manner, there is no obligation except what Allah obligated, and nothing unlawful except what Allah deemed unlawful, and nothing in the religion except what Allah legislated.

In acts of worship, everything is prohibited except what was legislated by a revealed text. As

وهذه ظاهرة عجيبة، وقد علق الحافظ الذهبي على كلام ابن حزم هذا قائلاً: «يا هذا، بهذا الجمود وأمثاله جعلت على عرضك سبيلاً، ونصبت نفسك أعجوبة وضحكة، بل يقال لك: ما فهم أحد من عربي ولا نبطي، ولا عاقل ولا واع أن النهي عن قول: «أف» للوالدين، إلا وما فوقها أولى بالنهي منه، وهل يفهم ذو حس سليم إلا هذا؟! وهل هذا إلا من باب التنبيه بالأدنى على الأعلى، وبالأصغر على الأكبر، بل مثل هذا مما أمن فيه حفظ اللسان العربي، بل العجمي، والتركي وجميع خطاب بني آدم، وهل إذا قال: «لا تنهر والديك» إلا والنهي عن شتمهما، أو لعنهما، أو ضربهما حتى يستغيثا، أو خنقهما حتى يموتا بطريق الأولى؟!».

وضرب مثالاً يوضح هذا: «فإن الرجل إذا قال لزوجته: لا تكلمي الرجال أضربك، فذهبت وزنت مع الرجال ولم تكلمهم كلمة، كانت عاصية له قطعاً، بل كانت أشد عصياناً بذلك، وأحق بالضرب وأولى من أن لو كلمت الرجال قط».

الثالث: اعتقادهم أن عقود المسلمين وشروطهم ومعاملاتهم كلها على البطلان، حتى يقوم الدليل على الصحة، فإذا لم يقم عندهم دليل على صحة شرط أو عقد أو معاملة استصحبوا بطلانه، فأفسدوا بذلك كثيراً من معاملات الناس، وعقودهم وشروطهم بلا برهان من الله بناء على هذا الأصل، وجمهور الفقهاء على خلاف هذا، وأن الأصل في العقود والشروط الصحة إلا ما أبطله الشارع أو نهى عنه، وهذا القول هو الصحيح، فإن الحكم ببطلانها حكم بالتحريم والتأثيم، ومعلوم أنه لا حرام إلا ما حرمه الله ورسوله، ولا تأثيم إلا ما أثَّم اللهُ ورسولُهُ به فاعلَه، كما أنه لا واجب إلا ما أوجبه الله، ولا حرام إلا ما حرمه الله، ولا دين إلا ما شرعه الله.

for transactions, they are all valid except those disqualified by a revealed text.

The difference between the two is that Allah, the Glorified, is not to be worshipped except with the acts He legislated on the tongues of His Messengers. This is because acts of worship are His exclusive right, and hence they must be performed solely on His terms which He has legislated and accepted. As for transactions, stipulations and interpersonal agreements, they are all consented unless their invalidity is clearly established in the texts.

For this very reason, Allah condemned the polytheists for opposing these two fundamental principles – namely forbidding what He did not forbid and seeking nearness to Him through acts which He never legislated.

On a similar note, when Allah is silent about a matter, wherein he does not state its permissibility or prohibition, this is considered consent from Him and it becomes impermissible to invalidate it or deem it unlawful. This is because the lawful is whatever Allah permitted, the unlawful is whatever He forbade, and whatever He was silent about entails consent from Him.

Comparing the Three *Fiqh* Schools

The scholars of *Ahl aẓ-Ẓāhir* did well in caring for the revealed texts of the Sharia. They dedicated themselves with studying, rehearsing and becoming knowledgable of these texts, but erred in their stopping at the literal, apparent meanings of the texts and refusing to understand them correctly.

فالأصل في العبادات البطلان، حتى يقوم دليل على الأمر، والأصل في العقود والمعاملات الصحة، حتى يقوم دليل على البطلان والتحريم.

والفرق بينهما أن الله- سبحانه- لا يُعبد إلا بما شرعه على ألسنة رسله، فإن العبادة حقه على عباده، وحقه الذي أحقه هو، ورضي به، وشرعه.

وأما العقود والشروط والمعاملات، فهي عفو حتى يحرمها، ولهذا نعى الله سبحانه على المشركين مخالفة هذين الأصلين، وهو تحريم ما لم يحرمه، والتقرب إليه بما لم يشرِّعه، وهو سبحانه لو سكت عن إباحة ذلك وتحريمه، لكان عفواً لا يجوز الحكم بتحريمه وإبطاله، فإن الحلال ما أحله الله، والحرام ما حرمه، وما سكت عنه، فهو عفو.

موازنة بين المدارس الثلاث:

أحسن أهل الظاهر في الاعتناء بالنصوص الشرعية حفظاً ومدارسة وتفقهاً، ولكنهم أخطؤوا في وقوفهم عند ظاهر النصوص، وقَصَّروا في فهمها.

The scholars of *Ahl ar-Ra'y* did well by not stopping at the literal meanings of the revealed texts, but rather dove beneath their surface to discern the reasoning behind these rulings. By doing that, they widened the scope in which these texts could be used – by recognizing the implications of the texts, the subtle gestures therein, what the language entails and by drawing analogies between resembling cases. However, they erred in the area where *Ahl aẓ-Ẓāhir* excelled, namely in being less concerned with the revealed texts than the analogies that can be made based on these texts. More specifically, they did not exhaust their efforts in pursuing the hadith(s) for collection, nor in discerning the authentic from the inauthentic among them.

Ibn al-Qayyim describes the condition of this school, saying, "The scholars of *ra'y* and *qiyās* did not give due attention to the revealed texts, and believed that they were not sufficient for all the juristic rulings. The zealots among them claimed that they were not even sufficient for 1% of the juristic rulings. As a result, they were overly dependent on juristic reasoning and analogy to deduce these ruings, adopted the approach of *qiyās ash-shabah*,[1] made claims about the reasoning behind certain rulings that the Sharia never confirmed, and made rulings contingent upon certain factors which the Sharia never legislated. This forced them to infer view that directly conflicted with both the texts and sound *qiyās*. This led to many inconsistencies in their views. At times, they would give precedence to the texts, and other times give precedence to the *qiyās*. Other times, you find them differentiating between the famous texts and the less famous ones. All that led them to assume that many of the legislated rulings were themselves contradictory to sound *qiyās*."[2]

1 *Qiyās ash-shabah*, which means an analogy of resemblance, is a method wherein two cases are claimed to have the same ruling solely based on the fact that they resemble one another, irrespective of whether or not that resemblance has any influence on the ruling at hand. For example, the brothers of Yūsuf (as) said, **"If he steals – a brother of his has stolen before."** [Surah Yūsuf – Verse 77] They used his brother's theft as evidence that he too could have stolen.

2 *I'lām al-Muwaqqi'īn* 1/39

وأهـل الـرأي أحسـنوا؛ إذ لم يقفـوا عنـد ظاهـر النـص، بـل غاصـوا في أعـماق النصـوص، واسـتخلصوا علـل الأحـكام، ووسـعوا دلالـة النـص، فنظـروا في إشـارته وإيمائـه، وقاسـوا النظـير عـلى النظـير، والشـبيه عـلى الشـبيه، ولكنهـم أسـاؤوا فيـما أحسـن فيـه أهـل الظاهـر، فلـم يعتنـوا بالنصـوص عنايتهـم بالعلـل والقيـاس، ولم يبذلـوا جهدهـم في طلبهـا، ومعرفـة الصحيـح والضعيـف مـن الأحاديـث.

يقـول ابـن القيـم واصفـاً حـال هـذه المدرسـة: «وأهـل الـرأي والقيـاس لم يعتنـوا بالنصـوص، ولم يعتقدوهـا وافيـة بالأحكام، ولا شـاملة لهـا، وغلاتهـم عـلى أنهـا لم تـفِ بعـشر معشـارها، فوسـعوا طريـق الـرأي والقيـاس، وقالـوا بقيـاس الشـبه[١]، وعلقـوا الأحـكام بأوصـاف لا يعلـم أن الشـارع علقهـا بهـا، واسـتنبطوا عللاً لا يعلـم أن الشـارع شرع الأحـكام لأجلهـا، ثـم اضطرهـم ذلـك إلى أن عارضـوا بـين كثـير مـن النصـوص والقيـاس، ثـم اضطربـوا، فتـارة يقدمـون القيـاس، وتـارة يقدمـون النصـوص، وتـارة يفرقـون بـين النـص المشـهور وغـير المشـهور، واضطرهـم ذلـك أيضـاً إلى أن اعتقـدوا في كثـير مـن الأحـكام أنهـا شرعـت عـلى خـلاف القيـاس»[٢].

١ قيـاس الشـبه هـو: الجمـع بـين الأصـل والفـرع بمجـرد الشـبه مـن غـير علـة تجمـع بينهـما، كقـول إخـوة يوسـف: ﴿إِن يَسْرِقْ فَقَدْ سَرَقَ أَخٌ لَّهُ مِن قَبْلُ﴾ [يوسـف: ٧٧]، فقـد اسـتدلوا عـلى سرقتـه بكـون أخـاه قـد سرق مـن قبـل.

٢ إعلام الموقعين: ١/ ٣٩.

As for *Ahl al-Ḥadīth,* it was the best of the three schools, for it treaded the middle path between the two aforementioned schools. That is because it inherited the knowledge of the Companions and the Successors who exercised the merits of these two schools and avoided their pitfalls. Like *Ahl aẓ-Ẓāhir,* the scholars of *Ahl al-Ḥadīth* gave great care to the revealed texts and ascertaining the sound hadith(s) from the weak ones. Furthermore, they invested great effort in understanding the texts, extracting the rulings from them and applying these texts to particular situations. At the same time, they excelled like *Ahl ar-Ra'y* by not sufficing with the literal meanings of the texts. Instead, they considered the expressed and implied meanings of these texts, in addition to recognizing their hints and gestures. They did not ignore the apparent reasoning behind the rulings, but while not overlooking the texts and resorting to *qiyās* unless that was actually necessary.

Imām ash-Shāfi'i, may Allah bestow mercy upon him, said, "We judge based on consensus, and then based on analogy which is weaker than the former, but it is a necessary practice. This is because analogical deduction is unlawful when the [relevant] text exists. The matter is just like the permissibility of purifying via *tayammum* (dry ablution) during travel when water is absent. Purification through it is not valid when the water is present, but rather only permissible during need." Furthermore, it has been reported by Imām Aḥmad that Imām ash-Shāfi'i said, "*Qiyās* is only [practiced] during times of necessity."[1]

1 *Fatḥ al-Bāri* 13/291, *I'lām al-Muwaqqi'īn* 1/23,27

أما مدرسة أهل الحديث فقد توسطت بين المدرستين السابقتين، ذلك أنها وارثة علم الصحابة والتابعين، فقد أخذت من كل مدرسة محاسنها، وتجنبت مساوئها، فقد عنيت بما عني به أهل الظاهر، لقد عنيت بالنصوص عناية كبيرة، وشغلت بغربلة الأحاديث والتعرف على الصحيح والضعيف، واجتهدت في فقه النصوص، واستنباط الأحكام منها، وتطبيق هذه النصوص على الوقائع، وأحسنت فيما أحسن فيه أهل الرأي؛ إذ لم يقفوا عند ظاهر النص، فنظروا في منطوق النص ومفهومه، كما نظروا في إشارته وإيمائه، ولم يهملوا علل الأحكام، ولكنهم لم يتعدوا النصوص إلى الرأي إلا عند الاضطرار، حيث لا يجدون نصّاً بعد الطلب والتحرِّي.

يقول الشافعي- رحمه الله تعالى-: «ونحكم بالإجماع، ثم القياس، وهو أضعف من هذا، ولكنها منزلة ضرورة؛ لأنه لا يَحِلُّ القياس والخبر موجود، كما يكون التيمم طهارة في السفر عند الإعواز من الماء، ولا يكون طهارة إذا وجد الماء، إنما يكون طهارة عند الإعواز»(١)، وقد روى الإمام أحمد عن الشافعي قوله: «القياس عند الضرورة»(٢).

١ الرسالة للشافعي: ٥٩٩.
٢ فتح الباري: ١٣/ ٢٩١، إعلام الموقعين: ١/ ٢٣، ٢٧.

Summary of Unit 6

1) 'Umar ibn 'Abdul-'Azīz commanded that the Prophetic Sunnah be compled after the reason for not writing it down no longer applied. He charged Ibn Shihāb az-Zuhri with the task of compiling the Prophetic Sunnah.

2) The Prophetic Sunnah was compiled in a number of famous works, such as the *Muwaṭṭa'* of Imām Mālik, the *Musnad* of Imām Aḥmad, the *Ṣaḥīḥ* of Imām al-Bukhāri, the *Ṣaḥīḥ* of Imām Muslim, the *Sunan* of Imām Abū Dāwūd, the *Sunan* of Imām at-Tirmidhi, the *Sunan* of Imam an-Nasā'i and the *Sunan* of Imām Ibn Mājah.

3) During this era of compilation, three distinct *Fiqh* schools appeared. Each of them embodied an independent approach within the scholarship of Islamic law, and each had its own founders and followers. These three schools of *Fiqh* were:

a) The school of *Ahl al-Ḥadīth*. This school was founded in the Prophet's noble city, Madinah, and thus it was initially titled the school of Madinah. It was ultimately led by Imām Mālik ibn Anas, may Allah bestow mercy upon him. The primary concern of the scholars of this school was the collection of hadith(s), narrating the Prophetic reports, and basing the juristic rules on the revealed texts. They would not resort to *qiyās*, whether obvious or subtle, so long as a hadith or view of the Companions existed.

b) The school of *Ahl ar-Ra'y*. This school was found in the lands of Iraq, and thus it was initially titled the school of Kufah. Its most famous scholar was Imām Abū Ḥanīfah an-Nu'mān ibn Thābit. They were called *Ahl ar-Ra'y* because of their excessive dependence on independent reasoning and analogy to deduce the juristic rulings. However, this does not mean that they would not depend on the Qur'an and Sunnah whatsoever.

c) The school of *Ahl aẓ-Ẓāhir*. This school is attributed to Dāwūd ibn 'Ali ibn Khalaf, who was born in 200 A.H. The followers of this school believed that the text-based rulings could not be rationalized, and thus limited their approach to the literal, apparent meanings of these texts.

خلاصة الوحدة

نخلص من دراسة هذه الوحدة إلى ما يلي:

١- أمر الخليفة الراشد عمر بن عبد العزيز بتدوين السنة، بعد زوال العلة المانعة من ذلك، وأسند هذه المهمة إلى ابن شهاب الزهري.

٢- أشهر دواوين السنة هي: موطأ مالك، ومسند أحمد، وصحيح البخاري، وصحيح مسلم، وسنن أبي داود، وسنن الترمذي، وسُنن النسائي، وسُنن ابن ماجه.

٣- ظهر في عصر التدوين ثلاث مدارس فقهية، شكَّل كل منها تياراً في الأمة الإسلامية وصار له زعماؤه وأتباعه، وهذه المدارس هي:

أ- مدرسة أهل الحديث: نشأت هذه المدرسة بالمدينة النبوية الشريفة، ولذا سميت بمدرسة المدينة، وانتهت رياسة المدرسة إلى الإمام مالك بن أنس، وكان أكثر اهتمام أصحاب هذه المدرسة بتحصيل الأحاديث، ونقل الأخبار، وبناء الأحكام على النصوص، ولا يرجعون إلى القياس الجلي الخفي، ما وجدوا خبراً أو أثراً.

ب- مدرسة أهل الرأي: نشأت هذه المدرسة بأرض العراق، ولهذا سميت بمدرسة الكوفة، وأشهر أئمتها: الإمام أبو حنيفة النعمان بن ثابت، وسموا بأهل الرأي؛ لأنهم أكثروا من استعمال الرأي والقياس في بيان الأحكام الشرعية، وليس المراد أنهم لم يكونوا يعتمدون على الكتاب والسنة.

ج- مدرسة أهل الظاهر: تنسب هذه المدرسة إلى داود بن علي بن خلف المولود سنة ٢٠٠هـ وقد ذهب أصحاب هذه المدرسة إلى عدم تعليل النصوص، وقصروا منهجهم على الأخذ بظواهر النصوص.

Notes

Notes

Unit 7
Introducing the *Madhhab*(s) of *Fiqh*

Contents of Unit 7

- Introducing the *Madhhab*(s) of *Fiqh*
- The Imām(s)' Correction of Their *Madhhab*(s)
- *Madhhab* Terminology

Importance of this Unit

During the era of the Successors and the *Mujtahid Imām*(s), a great number of scholars excelled in the study of the Sharia sciences. Many of those scholars were qualified to exercise *ijtihād* (independent reasoning) in the absolute sense, and thus they concocted their own methods of deducing the juristic rulings. Each of them had students and disciples who would adopt their methods in deducing the rulings, and from here the renowned *madhhab*(s) were born. Several of these historical *madhhab*(s), or major schools of *Fiqh*, still exist until today. Others have vanished and no longer have any followers. Each of these remaining *madhhab*(s) has its own fields of study, terms that are particular to it and phases wherein it developed and/or was refined. In this unit, we are going to delve with a bit of detail into these *madhhab*(s) and the matters particular to these legendary *Fiqh* schools.

Learning Objectives

By the end of this unit, readers should be able to:

1) Explain the rise of the *Fiqh Madhhab*(s) and their respective fields of focus

2) Recognize the greatness of these celebrated Imām(s) and jurists who would not hesitate in recanting their views whenever they realized that the truth was otherwise

3) Explain the terms pertaining to *madhhab*(s)

الوحدة السابعة: مقدمة للحديث عن المذاهب الفقهية

مقدمة للحديث عن المذاهب الفقهية

محتويات الوحدة السابعة

- التعـريف بالـمذاهــب.
- تصحيح الأئمة لمذاهبهــم.
- المصطلحات التي تحكي المذهب والاختلاف فيه.

أهمية دراسة الوحدة:

نبـغ في عـصر التابعـين وعـصر الأئمـة المجتهديـن، مجموعـة كبـيرة مـن العلـماء الذيـن أكبـوا عـلى دراسـة علـوم الشريعـة، وكثـير مـن هـؤلاء العلـماء بلـغ مرتبـة الاجتهـاد المطلـق وقـد اختـط بعـض العلـماء طريقـة سـلكوها في التعـرف عـلى الأحـكام، وأصبـح لـكل منهـم تلاميـذ وأتبـاع يتبنـون طريقتـه، والمذاهـب الفقهيـة التـي عرفهـا التاريـخ بعضهـا بـاقٍ إلى يومنـا هـذا، وبعضهـا قـد انقرضـت ولم يبـق لهـا أتبـاع، وهـذه المذاهـب الباقيـة لـكل منهـا مجـال يعمـل فيـه المذهـب، واصطلاحـات خاصـة بـه، ومراحـل تطـور وتصحيـح مـر بهـا، وفي هـذه الوحـدة نتعـرض بـشيء مـن التفصيـل لهـذه الأمـور التـي تخـص المذاهـب الفقهيـة.

الأهداف التعليمية:

يتوقـع منـك أيهـا الـدارس الكريـم بعـد دراسـتك لهـذه الوحـدة أن تكـون قـادراً عـلى أن:

١- تُوضـح نشـأة المذاهـب الفقهيـة، والدائـرة التـي تعمـل فيهـا هـذه المذاهـب.

٢- تستشـعر عظمـة وجلالـة قـدر العلـماء الأئمـة الأعـلام، حيـث إنهـم لم يكونـوا يـترددون في الرجـوع عـن أقوالهـم وآرائهـم، إذا ظهـر أن الحـق بخلافهـا.

٣- تذكر المصطلحات الخاصة بالمذاهب.

Introducing the *Madhhab*(s)

I. The Development of *Madhhab*(s)

During the era of the Successors and the *Mujtahid* Imām(s), a boom of great scholars surfaced in the Muslim world. The lands of the Islamic state were replete with religious sciences and outstanding scholars who mastered these sciences – many of which had reached the degree of exercising *ijtihād muṭlaq*, which means independent reasoning in its absolute sense.

Some of them adopted methods for themselves to deduce juristic rulings and had disciples and followers who adopted their methods which would become known as *madhhab*(s) (schools of thought).

Some of these historical *madhhab*(s) are still in existence, such as the *Fiqh* schools founded by Imām Abū Ḥanīfah, Imām Mālik, Imām ash-Shāfi'i and Imām Aḥmad. On the other hand, there are some *madhhab*(s) that have vanished and no longer have followers, such as the schools founded by Imāms al-Layth ibn Sa'd, Dāwūd aẓ-Ẓāhiri, Ibn Jarīr aṭ-Ṭabari, Ibn Khuzaymah and Isḥāq ibn Rāhuyah.

In present times, whoever studies the remaining *madhhab*(s) will find that each schools has its own marvelous juristic system, comprised of its writings, fundamentals, principles and scholars. Moreover, each *madhhab* has roots that extend all the way back to its first founder. The founders of the *madhhab*(s) were celebrated scholars that learned under the tutelage of the scholars before them, and inherited from them what they themselves had memorized and understood from the Prophet's inheritance – the revealed sciences. During the era of these great Imām(s), the Muslim lands overflowed with knowledge and scholars, and in this atmosphere, the sciences of Sharia were sought by the sharpest minds, the purest souls, and the most ambitious members of society. Thus, the scholars of Sharia were the highest tier of citizens, and enjoyed the loftiest status in the Muslim communities.

التعريف بالمذاهب

أولاً: نشأة المذاهب وتكوُّنها:

نبغ في عصر التابعين وعصر الأئمة المجتهدين مجموعة كبيرة من العلماء، وكانت الأمصار في الدولة الإسلامية تزخر بالعلم والعلماء، وكثير من هؤلاء العلماء بلغوا مرتبة الاجتهاد المطلق.

وقد اختط بعض هؤلاء العلماء الأخيار طريقة سلكوها في التعرف على الأحكام، وأصبح لكل منهم تلاميذ وأتباع يتبنون طريقته، وقد عرفت هذه الطرق بالمذاهب.

والمذاهب الفقهية الباقية إلى اليوم هي مذهب الإمام أبي حنيفة، والإمام مالك، والإمام الشافعي، والإمام أحمد، وهناك مذاهب انقرض أتباعها؛ كمذهب الليث بن سعد، وداود الظاهري، وابن جرير الطبري، وابن خزيمة، وإسحاق بن راهويه.

ومن ينظر اليوم في المذاهب الفقهية الباقية فإنه يجد أن لكل مذهب بناء فقهيّاً هائلاً له مؤلفاته وقواعده وأصوله وعلماؤه، وجذور كل مذهب تمتد إلى صاحب المذهب ومؤسسه.

ومؤسسو المذاهب علماء أعلام؛ تربوا على أيدي العلماء الذين سبقوهم، وأخذوا عنهم ما حفظوه وفقهوه من ميراث النبوة؛ وقد كانت البلاد الإسلامية في عصر الأئمة تموج بالعلم والعلماء، وقد استقطبت العلوم الشرعية أصحاب العقول الراجحة، والنفوس الزاكية، والهمم العالية، فالعلماء بالشريعة كانوا هم أصحاب المكانة العالية المرموقة في المجتمعات الإسلامية.

The minds of the great Imām(s) were enlightened by the Qur'an and Sunnah, and its guidance protected them from being restricted to the blind following which later prevented many minds from seeking the deeper meanings of the Qur'an and Sunnah. As a result, the latter were barred from correctly handling the contemporary issues of their times which the Muslims faced.

As for these renowned Imām(s), may Allah be pleased with them, they ascended with what they learned of the revealed texts to lofty stations. They fine-tuned their *madhhab*(s), set fundamentals for them and left reservoir of resources to aid those after them in ascertaining the truth and understanding the texts.

The celebrated Shāfi'i jurist, Abū Shāmah, said, "Imām ash-Shāfi'i built his *madhhab* upon a formidable foundation. This is because he based it on the Book of Allah, the Sunnah of His Messenger, sound *ijtihād* which was taught by the Qur'an and Sunnah, and striking the closest resemblance to what already existed in the Qur'an and Sunnah."

In truth, all the celebrated Imām(s) founded their schools upon this methodology which was described by Abū Shāmah.

Their *madhhab*(s) were embodied in their views that they recorded in their books, dictated to their students or given as responses to those who asked them for *fatwa*(s) and were recorded by their disciples.

The disciples of these Imām(s) played a major role in collecting, preserving and transmitting the knowledge of their teachers. Were it not for them, their *madhhab*(s) would have withered away and been lost. This is clearly highlighted in the example of the legendary Hadith scholar and jurist from Egypt, al-Layth ibn Sa'd (may Allah bestow mercy upon him). Many scholars regarded him superior to Imām Mālik, but his companions did not preserve his juristic views. The great Imām ash-Shāfi'i, may Allah bestow mercy upon him, said, "Al-Layth was superior in *Fiqh* to Mālik, but his disciples did not retain his *madhhab*."[1]

1 *Mukhtasar al-Mu'ammal fī ar-Radd ilā al-Amr al-Awwal* 3/37 by Abū Shāmah

وقد تفتحت عقول الأئمة على أنوار الوحي من الكتاب والسنة من غير أن يعزلها عنه ظلمات التقليد التي منعت العقول فيما بعد من الغوص في الكتاب والسنة وهي تواجه المسائل والمستجدات والقضايا التي تعرض للمسلمين في ذلك العصر.

لقد سما الأئمة- رضوان الله عليهم- بما علموه من عالم الوحي إلى درجات راقية، وأحكموا مذاهبهم وقعَّدوها، وتركوا لمن بعدهم ثروة علمية تعين من وراءهم على معرفة الحق، كما تعينهم على فقه النصوص.

يقول العلامة أبو شامة الفقيه الشافعي: «بنى الشافعي مذهبه بناء محكماً، وذلك أنه كان اعتماده على كتاب الله وسنة رسوله، والنظر الصحيح من الاجتهاد الراجع إلى الكتاب والسنة، وترجيح أشبه المذاهب بالكتاب والسنة»[١]، وكل الأئمة أحكموا مذاهبهم على هذا النهج الذي ذكره أبو شامة.

وقد تمثلت مذاهبهم في أقوالهم التي دونوها في كتبهم، أو أملوها على تلامذتهم، أو أجابوا بها من سألهم واستفتاهم، وقد حملها عنهم أصحابهم وتلامذتهم.

وجاء أصحاب الأئمة من بعدهم، فكان لهم دور كبير في استيعاب علوم أئمتهم، وحفظها ونقلها، ولولاهم لضاعت مذاهبهم وتلاشت، واعتبر بهذا بعالم مصر المحدِّث الفقيه الليث بن سعد- رحمه الله- فإن جمعاً من أهل العلم يقدمونه على الإمام مالك، ولكن أصحابه لم يحفظوا فقهه، يقول الإمام الشافعي- رحمه الله تعالى-: «الليث أفقه من مالك، إلا أن أصحابه لم يقوموا به»[٢].

١ مختصر كتاب «المؤمل في الرد إلى الأمر الأول» لأبي شامة- مجموعة الرسائل المنيرية: ٣/ ٣٧.

٢ تاريخ الإسلام للذهبي: ١/ ٣٠٧، حوادث: ١٧١- ١٨٠، تهذيب الأسماء واللغات للنووي: ٢/ ٧٤.

The role of the Imām(s)' disciples was not confined to transmitting the views of their Imām(s) and transcribing what they heard from them. Rather, the first generation of each *madhhab* enjoyed sound minds, a forte for critical thinking and an ability to analyze and deduce for themselves. For that reason, many of these disciples would have their own *ijtihād* and would not hesitate in disagreeing with their Imām(s) upon realizing that the truth was other than their view.

One example that illustrates this is the Ḥanafi *madhhab*, wherein the students and companions of Imām Abū Ḥanīfah collaborated with the Imām in establishing and developing the *madhhab*. Ḥanafi records mention that the companions of Abū Ḥanīfah that authored the books with him were forty men. When they would disagree with one another on a matter, they would refer it back to him for judgment. They would leave the matter three days for deliberation, and then finally write it in their records.[1]

It appears that this record wherein the Fiqh rulings were written, after exhaustive *ijtihād* by Abū Ḥanīfah and his companions, represents the bae sis for the works of *Fiqh* that the companions of Abū Ḥanīfah authored after him.

Even the authoritative books in the Ḥanafi *madhhab* did not restrict themselves to the views of Abū Ḥanīfah. Rather, the official view of the *madhhab* could be that of Abū Ḥanīfah, Abū Yūh suf, Muhammad ibn al-Ḥasan, Zufar, al-Ḥasan ibn Ziyād or others. This will be discussed in detail later.

1 Introduction of *Nasb-ur-Rayah* 1/38. These statements are reported from Asad ibn al-Furāt and Ishāq ibn Ibrāhīm and others.

ولم يقتصر دور أصحاب الأئمة وتلامذتهم على نقل أقوال أئمتهم واستيعاب ما سمعوه منهم، فقد كان الرعيل الأول من أهل كل مذهب أصحاب عقول راجحة، قادرة على النظر والاستنباط؛ ولذلك فإن كثيراً منهم كانوا يزاحمون أئمتهم في الاجتهاد، ولم يكونوا يتحرجون من مخالفة أئمتهم إذا تبين لهم أن الحق في خلاف قولهم.

واعتبر في هذا بالمذهب الحنفي، فإن أصحاب الإمام أبي حنيفة وتلامذته شاركوا الإمام في تأصيل المذهب وإنضاجه، فمدونات الحنفية تذكر أن أصحاب أبي حنيفة الذين دونوا معه الكتب كانوا أربعين رجلاً، كانوا يختلفون عنده في جواب المسألة، فيأتي هذا بجواب، وهذا بجواب، ثم يرفعونها إليه، ويسألونه عنها، فيأتي بالجواب عن كثب، وكانوا يقيمون في المسألة ثلاثة أيام، ثم يكتبونها في الديوان(١).

ويبدو أن هذا الديوان الذي كتبت فيه مسائل الفقه التي تمخض عنها اجتهاد أبي حنيفة وأصحابه تمثل أصول المدونات الفقهية التي دونها أصحاب أبي حنيفة من بعده.

والكتب المعتمدة عند الحنفية لا تقصر المذهب على أقوال أبي حنيفة، فقد يكون المذهب قول أبي حنيفة، وقد يكون قول أبي يوسف، أو محمد بن الحسن، أو قول زفر، أو الحسن بن زياد، وسيأتي بيان هذا وتوضيحه.

١ انظر: مقدمة نصب الراية: ١/ ٣٨، وهذه الأقوال منقولة عن أسد بن الفرات، وإسحاق بن إبراهيم، والموفق المكي وغيرهم.

II. The Definition of the Term *Madhhab*

In the Arabic language, a *madhhab* is a path that is traveled on or a passageway that is used. It is also used in reference to a matter that a person journeys toward, whether that matter is tangible or intangible. Shaykh Ahmad as-Sawi says, "In origin, a *madhhab* is the place of travel, like the physical roadways."[1] In *Lisān al-'Arab*, it says, "The *madhhab* is the washroom because it is gone to by necessity, similar to a belief that is arrived at [by compelling reasons]."[2]

The Arabs say, "You treaded the *madhhab* of so and so," meaning you followed their ways. They also say, "He followed a virtuous *madhhab*," meaning mode of conduct.

The *madhhab* of any people is their standard that is particular to them, whether in regard to beliefs, conduct, laws or otherwise.

However, a matter is not considered the *madhhab* of a person unless it is particular to him or her. For example, we cannot say that eating, drinking and sleeping are the *madhhab* of any particular person or group. Likewise, scholars do not use the term *madhhab* except in reference to an approach that was developed after much consideration, was clearly drawn out, was given definitive parameters and based on sound principles. In *al-Mu'jam al-Wasīṭ*, it says, "Scholars use the term *madhhab* in reference to a group of views, theories and philosophies that are fused together in a synchronized manner."[3]

In the science of *Fiqh*, its scholars use the term *madhhab* in reference to a specific juristic approach that was adopted by a *mujtahid* jurist. Based on this approach, the jurist adopted a number of rulings in the smaller branches of *Fiqh*.

1 *Hāshiyat Aḥmad as-Sawy 'alā Sharh as-Saghīr lid-Dardīr* 1/16
2 *Lisān al-'Arab* 1/1081
3 *Al-Mu'jam al-Wasīt* 1/317 by Ibrāhīm Anīs and others

ثانياً: المذهب لغة واصطلاحاً:

المذهـب في لغـة العـرب: الطريـق الـذي يذهـب فيـه؛ أي يُسـار فيـه، ويمـر منـه، ويطلـق أيضـاً عـلى الـشيء الـذي يذهـب إليـه الإنسـان، سـواء أكان حسـيّاً أو معنويّـاً، يقـول الشيـخ أحمـد الصـاوي: «المذهـب في الأصـل محـل الذهـاب، كالطريـق المحسوسـة»(١)، وجـاء في لسـان العـرب أن «المذهـب المتوضأ؛ لأنـه يذهـب إليـه، والمعتقـد الـذي يذهـب إليـه»(٢).

«وتقـول العـرب: ذهـب مذهـب فـلان: قصـد قصـده وطريقتـه»(٣)، ويقولـون أيضـاً: «ذهـب فـلان مذهبـاً حسـناً»(٤).

والمذهــب في اصطـلاح كل قـوم: الطريقـة التـي اختطهـا شـخص أو مجموعـة؛ سـواء أكانـت في مجـال الاعتقـاد، أم السـلوك، أم الأحـكام، أم غيرهـا.

ولا يكـون الأمـر مذهبـاً لشـخص مـا، إلا إذا كان طريقـة اختـص بهـا دون غـيره؛ فـالأكل والشرب والنـوم ليـس مذهبـاً يختـص بفـرد أو مجموعـة، ولا يطلـق المذهـب عنـد أصحـاب العلـم والمعرفـة إلا عـلى منهـج يكـون بعـد تأمـل ونظـر، واختـط صاحبـه خطـة واضحـة المعـالم، بيِّنـة الأبعـاد، تقـوم عـلى أصـول وقواعـد، ففـي المعجـم الوسـيط: «المذهـب عنـد العلـماء مجموعـة مـن الآراء والنظريـات العلميـة والفلسـفية، ارتبـط بعضهـا ببعـض ارتباطـاً يجعلهـا وحـدة متسـقة»(٥).

ويطلـق المذهـب عنـد علـماء الفقـه عـلى المنهـج الفقهـي الـذي سـلكه فقيـه مجتهـد، اختـص بـه مـن بـين الفقهـاء، أدى بـه إلى اختيـار جملـة مـن الأحـكام في مجـال علـم الفـروع.

١ حاشية أحمد الصاوي على الشرح الصغير للدردير: ١/ ١٦.
٢ لسان العرب: ١/ ١٠٨١.
٣ القاموس المحيط: ١١٠، والمصباح المنير: ٢١١.
٤ لسان العرب: ١/ ١٠٨١.
٥ المعجـم الوسيـط، لإبراهيـم أنيـس وآخـرون: ١/ ٣١٧، دار إحيـاء الـتراث العـربي، الثانيـة.

While defining the Māliki *madhhab*, al-Qarāfi said, "The Māliki *madhhab* comprises the detailed *ijtihād*-based juristic rulings that are particular to it, alongside the causes of these rulings, conditions, hindrances and arguments that were used as the reason for arriving at them."[1]

يقـول القـرافي في سـياق تعريفـه مذهـب مالـك: «مذهـب مالـك مـا اختـص بـه مـن الأحـكام الشرعيـة الفروعيـة الاجتهاديـة، ومـا اختـص بـه مـن أسـباب الأحـكام والـشروط والموانـع والحجـاج المثبتـة لهـا»(١).

Ad-Dardīr defined it with his statement, "The *madhhab* of Mālik, for instance, is a term that denotes his conclusions in the *ijtihād*-based rulings that he exhausted his efforts in deducing."[2]

وعرفـه الدرديـر بقولـه: «مذهـب مالـك مثـلاً عبـارة عـما ذهـب إليـه مـن الأحـكام الاجتهاديـة التـي بـذل وسـعه في تحصيلهـا»(٢).

III. Each *Madhhab*'s Field of Study

ثالثاً: الدائرة التي يعمل المذهب فيها:

Upon considering these definitions, you will clearly notice that the arena wherein the *Fiqh Madhhab*(*s*) work is that of the detailed branches of *Fiqh*.

وإذا أنـت تأملـت في هـذه التعريفـات تجـد أن المجـال الـذي يعمـل فيـه المذهـب الفقهـي هـو الأحـكام الشرعيـة الفرعيـة.

As for differing in terms of creed, this is a matter that divides the Muslim *Ummah* into sects. The Imām(s) of the Sunni *Fiqh Madhhab*(s) all followed the same methodology in terms of creed; their creed is that of *Ahl as-Sunnah wal-Jamā'ah*. Those who opposed them were factions that deviated from this orthodox creed, such as the *Khawārij* and the *Mu'tazilah*. Thus, there are no *madhhab*(s) among *Ahl as-Sunnah* in terms of creed, just as the Companions were all upon a single methodology in terms of creed but differed on some detailed rulings in *Fiqh*.

فالاختـلاف في العقيـدة يقسـم الأمـة إلى فِـرَق، فعلـماء المذاهـب الفقهيـة السـنية كلهـم أتبـاع منهـج واحـد في الاعتقـاد، فعقيدتهـم هـي عقيـدة أهـل السـنة والجماعـة، ومخالفوهـم فِـرَق انحـرف بهـا المسـار كالخـوارج والمعتزلـة، فـلا مذاهـب بـين علـماء أهـل السـنة في مجـال الاعتقـاد، والصحابـة جميعـاً عـلى طريقـة واحـدة في الاعتقـاد، ولكنهـم اختلفـوا في بعـض أحـكام مسـائل الفـروع.

1 *Al-Ihkām fī Tamyīz al-Fatāwā 'anil-Ahkām* 220
2 *Hāshiyat ad-Dasūqi 'alā Sharḥ al-Kabīr* 1/19

١ الإحكام في تمييز الفتاوى عن الأحكام: ٢٢٠.
٢ حاشية الدسوقي على الشرح الكبير: ١/ ١٩.

A researcher must also be acquainted with the fact that not all branches of *Fiqh* can be included under the term *Fiqhi Madhhab*(s). This is because some rulings are not open for dispute due to the decisive evidences (in transmission and implication) that enjoin them. For example, the obligation of the five obligatory prayers, the obligation of the fasting in Ramadan, the obligation of paying *zakāh*, *ẓuhr* prayer being four *rak'ah*(s), *maghrib* prayer being three *rak'ah*(s) and so on. These are indisputable juristic rulings, and thus cannot be attributed to any school of *Fiqh*. It cannot be said, for instance, that *ẓuhr* prayer is four *rak'ah*(s) according to the *madhhab* of Abū Ḥanīfah, or that fasting Ramadan is obligatory in the *madhhab* of Mālik, or that wine is unlawful in the *madhhab* of ash-Shāfi'i. No *madhhab* can be said to have a distinct view on any of these, for they are all in agreement on such rulings. For this same reason, matters of consensus are also among those which cannot be attributed to a single *madhhab*, even if the evidence for this matter is a speculative proof. Hence, a woman marrying her paternal aunt's husband or her maternal aunt's husband is unlawful by the consensus of *Ahl as-Sunnah*, even though its proof is a singular (*āḥād*) hadith.

Regarding this, al-Qarāfi said, "It cannot be said that this ruling is the *madhhab* of Mālik or ash-Shāfi'i unless it was particular to them, for this is what is ordinarily meant when attributing something to a particular individual."[1]

Similarly, ad-Dardīr said in *Sharḥ al-Kabīr*, "The rulings which the Legislator enjoined definitively in the Qur'an or Sunnah are not to be considered from the *madhhab* of any *mujtahid* scholar."[2]

This is what is meant by a *madhhab*, and this is the arena wherein it can correctly be said, "The *madhhab* of so and so on the matter is..." This is also the arena wherein *taqlīd* (blind following) is permissible so long as a person is not a scholar.

1 *Al-Ihkām fī Tamyīz al-Fatāwā 'anil-Ahkām* 199
2 *Ash-Sharḥ al-Kabīr* 1/9

وينبغي للباحث أيضاً أن ينتبه إلى أن مسائل الفروع ليست كلها مما يصح أن يدخل في إطار ما يسمى بالمذهب الفقهي، فالأحكام التي لا مجال للاختلاف فيها؛ لكون أدلتها قطعية الدلالة، قطعية الثبوت، مثل وجوب الصلوات الخمس، ووجوب شهر رمضان، ووجوب الزكاة، وكون صلاة الظهر أربعاً، والمغرب ثلاثاً ونحو ذلك لا يصح أن تنسب إلى مذهب شخص بعينه، فلا يقال: مذهب أبي حنيفة أن صلاة الظهر واجبة، ومذهب مالك أن صوم رمضان واجب، ومذهب الشافعي أن الخمر حرام، فلا خصوصية لواحد منهم بواحد من هذه، فإن مذهبهم جميعاً في هذه مذهب واحد؛ ولذا فإن المسائل المجمع عليها لا يصح أن تنسب إلى مذهب رجل بعينه، وإن كان دليلها ظني الثبوت، أو ظني الدلالة، فنكاح المرأة على عمتها، أو على خالتها متفق على تحريمه عند أهل السنة، ودليله خبر آحاد.

وفي هذا يقول القرافي- رحمه الله-: «لا يقال: هذا مذهب مالك أو الشافعي إلا فيما يختص به؛ لأنه ظاهر اللفظ في الإضافة والاختصاص»[١].

وقال الدردير في شرحه الكبير: «الأحكام التي نص الشارع عليها في القرآن أو في السنة لا تعد من مذهب أحد من المجتهدين»[٢].

هذا هو المراد بالمذهب، وهذه هي الدائرة التي يصح أن يقال: إن مذهب فلان فيها كذا، وهي الدائرة التي يجوز فيها التقليد إذا لم يكن المرء عالماً.

١ الإحكام في تمييز الفتاوى عن الأحكام: ١٩٩.
٢ الشرح الكبير: ١/ ٩.

Fourth: Not Everything in the *Madhhab* can be Attributed to the Imām of that *Madhhab*

It should be known that each *madhhab* contains the *ijtihād*-based views of its Imām, in addition to all the views given by the scholars of that *madhhab*. Hence, it is not permissible to attribute all these views to the founder of that *madhhab*.

Some researchers and jurists, in each *madhhab*, attributed the views given by the students, followers and companions of the founding Imām(s) to the Imām(s) themselves. This is neither fair nor correct, for the *madhhab* of each scholar is what he viewed and personally arrived at. Hence, whoever attributes rulings to a scholar that he never viewed has certainly transgressed.

For example, it can be said that the Shāfiʿī *madhhab* on this matter is such and such, whereby the speaker does not mean that was the view of ash-Shāfiʿī himself. Rather, he only meant that this was the authoritative view among the Shāfiʿī scholars. This is a matter of terminology, and there is no harm in being lenient with terminology in such cases.

The authoritative view in a *madhhab* could be the view expressly stated by the Imām himself, or not stated by him but attributed to him by analogy of his other views, or taken from the alluded or inferred implications of his words, or taken from the views of his companions or students, or stated by one of the scholars of his *madhhab* who disagreed with him, or it might be that nothing was ever reported from the Imām concerning that matter.

Of what proves the impermissibility of attributing everything in a madhhab to its Imām is:

1) It is impermissible, religiously and logically, to attribute to the Imām what he did not say, or what was said by another, or what he was silent about, or what was misunderstood from his words.

رابعاً: ليس كل ما في المذهب يجوز أن ينسب لإمام المذهب:

مـما ينبغي أن يتنبه إليه أن كل مذهب يضم أقوال إمام المذهب واجتهاداته، كما يضم جميع الأقوال والاجتهادات التـي ذهب إليها علماء المذهب، ولا يجوز أن تنسب كل هـذه الأقوال إلى مؤسس المذهب.

إن بعـض الباحثـين وبعـض الفقهـاء في كل مذهـب نسـب كثـيراً مـن أقـوال أصحـاب الأئمـة وتلامذتهـم وأتباعهـم إلى الأئمـة، وهـذا ليـس عـدلاً ولا صواباً، فمذهب العالـم مـا قالـه وذهـب إليـه، ومـن قـوّل عالمـاً مـا لم يقلـه، ونسـب إليـه أحكامـاً لم تصـدر عنـه، فقـد ظلـم وجـار.

نعـم، قـد يقـال: المذهب الشافعي في هـذه المسألة كذا، ولا يريـد القائـل أن الشافعي قـد قال ذلـك وأفتـى بـه، وإنمـا يريـد أن هـذا الحكـم هـو المعتمد في الفتوى عند الشافعية، وهـذه مسـألة اصطلاحية، ولا مشاحَّة في الاصطلاح.

إن العمـدة في المذهـب قـد يكـون قـولاً للإمـام نـصَّ عليـه، وقـد لا يكـون نـصَّ عليـه، وإنمـا نسـب إليـه قياسـاً على قولـه، أو أخـذ مـن إشـارته أو إيمائه، وقـد يكـون قـولاً لصاحـب أو تلميـذ مـن أصحـاب إمـام المذهـب أو تلامذتـه، أو قالـه أحـد علمـاء مذهبـه مخالفـاً لمـا نص عليـه، وقـد لا يؤثـر عـن الإمـام في ذلـك قـول أو حكـم.

ويـدل لعـدم جـواز نسـبة كل مـا في المذهـب مـن أقـوال للأئمـة أمـور:

١- لا يجـوز شرعـاً ولا عقـلا أن ينسـب إلى الإمـام قـول لم يقلـه، أو قالـه غـيره، أو سـكت عليـه، أو فهـم مـن كلامـه خطأً.

2) Each *madhhab* contains many contradictory views that were held by various jurists from that *madhhab*. How then can all these views be attributed to the same Imām when they contradict one another?

3) The companions of each Imām, who were qualified to perform *ijtihād*, did not adopt all the opinions of the Imām on every detailed ruling. Rather, they were people of critical thinking and independent research, and thus one cannot attribute their views to the Imām when it concluded from their variant *ijtihād*.

4) Many mistakes took place in transmitting the views of the Imām(s), making analogies based on their views, and applying their principles. Yet, many jurists still attributed all these judgments to the Imām. As well, many later jurists filled the *madhhab* with views that are inconsistent with the fundamentals drawn out by the Imām of that *madhhab* and his principles which he previously judged by. This was particularly true regarding the rulings based on hypothetical situations – many of which were scenarios that would never actually happen.

The Imām(s)' Correction of Their *Madhhab*(s)

Undoubtedly, these great Imām(s) were constantly correcting and refining their views throughout their academic journeys. This is because the Imām(s) were human beings; they were correct at times and mistaken at others, and their command of the sciences continued maturing as their lives went on. Every day, they learned new things that they had not known before, and they were far more pious than to insist upon wrong after discovering that the truth was otherwise.

Abū Shāmah mentioned that al-Buwayṭi heard Imām ash-Shāfi'i saying, "I withheld no effort in writing these books, but surely mistakes will be found in them, for Allah – the Most High – says, **'If it had been from [any] other than Allah, they would have found within it much contradiction.'**[1] Therefore, whatever you find in these books of mine that oppose the Qur'an or Sunnah, then I have hereby recanted it."[2]

1 Sūrat an-Nisā' – Verse 82
2 *Al-Mu'ammal fī ar-Radd ilā al-Amr al-Awwal* 3/33

٢- يضم كل مذهب أقوالاً كثيرة متعارضة متناقضة لمجتهدي المذهب، فكيف يمكن أن تنسب إلى إمام المذهب كل تلك الأقوال مع تعارضها واختلافها.

٣- لم يكن أصحاب الإمام ومجتهدو مذهبه يتابعون الإمام في كل ما ذهب إليه في مسائل الفروع، فإنهم كانوا أصحاب نظر اجتهادي مستقل في كثير من الأحيان، فلا يجوز أن تنسب أقوالهم إلى إمام مذهبهم مع اختلاف الاجتهاد.

٤- كثر الخطأ في نقل أقوال الأئمة، والقياس على أقوالهم، والتخريج على قواعدهم، وعد كثير من الفقهاء كل ذلك مذهباً لإمام المذهب، وحشا كثير من المتأخرين المذهب بأقوال لا تنطبق على أصول إمام المذهب، ولا قواعده ومسائله، خصوصاً المسائل التي بنوا أحكامها على فرض الوقوع، وكثير منها من قبيل المستحيل.

تصحيح الأئمة لمذاهبهم

لا شك أن الأئمة أثناء مسيرتهم العلمية كانوا دائمي التصحيح والتنقيح لمذاهبهم، فالأئمة بشر، يصيبون ويخطئون، وكلما امتد بهم العمر قويت ملكتهم العلمية، وحازوا علماً لم يطلعوا عليه من قبل، وهم كانوا أورع وأتقى من أن يقيموا على خطأ تبين لهم صوابه.

ذكر أبو شامة أن البويطي سمع الشافعي يقول: «لقد ألفت هذه الكتب، ولم آل فيها جهداً، ولابد أن يوجد فيها الخطأ؛ لأن الله تعالى يقول: ﴿**وَلَوْ كَانَ مِنْ عِندِ غَيْرِ اللَّهِ لَوَجَدُوا فِيهِ اخْتِلَافًا كَثِيرًا**﴾[١]، فما وجدتم في كتبي هذه مما يخالف الكتاب والسنة فقد رجعت عنه»[٢].

١ النساء: ٨٢.
٢ المؤمل في الرد إلى الأمر الأول: ٣/ ٣٣.

Abū Shāmah reported that Imām Mālik said, "I am but a human being; I am correct at times and incorrect at others. So look at my opinion; whatever agrees with the Qur'an and Sunnah, accept it, and whatever does not agree with the Qur'an and Sunnah, disregard it."[1]

Commenting on these statements by the Imām(s), Abū Shāmah said, "And that is what must be presumed about all the Imām(s)."[2]

In fact, some of the Imām(s) themselves have shown us how they would correct and revise their *madhhab*(s), and we have learned of their final opinions. We have seen other Imām(s) that left behind troves of narrations with multiple *ijtihād*-based edicts, and very rarely did they elucidate their preference from between these multiple views.

Of the first type was Imām ash-Shāfi'i (may Allah bestow mercy upon him). He transcribed his views himself, and explained his fundamentals upon which he built his *madhhab*. He did not stop there, but rather he later revised and corrected his own *madhhab*. Thus, his new *madhhab* which he compiled in Egypt represents the revisions and corrections of his old *madhhab*.

For this reason, a multitude of Shāfi'i imām(s) have stated the necessity of adopting the latter views of ash-Shāfi'i, and the impermissibility of attributing the old views to Imām ash-Shāfi'i. Al-Juwaini said, "The old views are not to be considered the *madhhab* of ash-Shāfi'i, for he recanted them in his new *madhhab*, and that which is recanted cannot still be considered the *madhhab* of the recanter."[3]

Imām an-Nawawi said, "Every juristic matter wherein an old and new opinion are reported about Imām ash-Shāfi'i (may Allah bestow mercy upon him), then the newer edict is the correct one, and the one that should be followed, for the older views were retracted."[4]

For this reason, Ibn al-Qayyim criticized the jurist scholars of each *madhhab* who give edicts based on the older views of their Imām(s), saying, "Many times, the followers of an Imām give edicts based on their Imām's old views, which he himself recanted, and this [error] exists in every *madhhab*."[5]

---

1 Ibid
2 Ibid
3 *Al-Burhān* 2/1366 by al-Juwayni
4 *Al-Majmū'* 1/66
5 *I'lām al-Muwaqqi'īn* 4/302

ونقل أبو شامة عن مالك قوله: «إنما أنا بشر أخطئ وأصيب، فانظروا في رأيي، فكل ما وافق الكتاب والسنة فخذوا به، وما لم يوافق الكتاب والسنة فاتركوه»(١).

وعقب أبو شامة على هذين القولين لهذين الإمامين بقوله: «وذلك الظن بجميع الأئمة»(٢).

وقد وجدنا من الأئمة من دلنا على مساره في تصحيحه لمذهبه وتنقيحه إياه، وعرفنا بالذي صار إليه في آخر أمره، ووجدنا من الأئمة من ترك لنا ثروة علمية فيها الروايات والأقوال في المسائل الاجتهادية، وقلما نجده بين اختياره فيما تعددت فيه عنه الأقوال.

فمن الصنف الأول الإمام الشافعي- رحمه الله تعالى- فإنه دوَّن مذهبه بنفسه، وبيَّن لنا قواعده وأصوله التي بنى عليها مذهبه، ولم يكتف بذلك، بل أعاد تصحيح مذهبه وتنقيحه، فمذهبه الجديد الذي دونه في مصر، يمثل تصحيحاً وتنقيحاً لمذهبه القديم.

وقد تواترت الأقوال عن أئمة الشافعية في وجوب المصير إلى أقوال الشافعي في مذهبه الجديد، وعدم جواز عدّ القديم مذهباً للشافعي، يقول الجويني: «لا تحسب الأقوال القديمة من مذهب الشافعي، فإنه رجع عنها جديداً، والمرجوع عنه لا يكون مذهباً للراجع»(٣).

وقال النووي: «كل مسألة فيها قولان للشافعي- رحمه الله-: قديم وجديد، فالجديد هو الصحيح، وعليه العمل؛ لأن القديم مرجوع عنه»(٤).

وقد وجه ابن القيم اللوم للمفتين من علماء المذاهب الذين يفتون بالأقوال القديمة من أقوال أئمتهم، وفي ذلك يقول: «أتباع الأئمة يفتون كثيراً بأقوال أئمتهم القديمة، التي رجعوا عنها، وهذا موجود في سائر الطوائف»(٥).

---

١ المصدر السابق.
٢ المصدر السابق.
٣ البرهان للجويني: ٢/ ١٣٦٦.
٤ المجموع: ١/ ٦٦.
٥ إعلام الموقعين: ٤/ ٣٠٢.

Why it is Difficult to Determine the Correct View of a *Madhhab*

Imām ash-Shāfi'i made it easy for those after him to know the correct opinions of his *madhhab,* and this is by checking his new views. In fact, the book of ash-Shāfi'i that contained his old juristic opinions were not preserved, and nothing remains of them except scattered pages in the books of other scholars. Thus, one cannot find any printed book today that contains his old *madhhab*.

As for the other Imāms, their *madhhab* is embodied in the views reported about them via their students and companions. However, this would include what they did and did not recant. At times though, these Imām(s) may allude to what view they prefer based on their *ijtihād*, such as them saying about one of the two views "This is more beloved to me" or "This is more worthy" or "...more resembling of the truth." Other times, these Imām(s) may leave a subtle indication as to their preference, such as branching out on one of the two views and not the other. His branching out on a view is indicative of its strength in his eyes, and thus it was worthy of him basing other rulings on it.[1]

Al-Mirdāwi said, "The Imām's opinion can be expressly stated or gestured at, such as when we say 'He gestured or hinted to it' or 'His words implied' or 'He was silent about it' and the likes."[2]

The juristic matters for which these Imām(s) clearly determined the correct choice of their *madhhab* are far less than those wherein the correct stance has not been narrated.

1 *Al-Maḥṣūl* 5/392 by ar-Rāzi; *al-Baḥr al-Muḥīṭ* 6/120 by az-Zarkashi
2 *Al-Inṣāf* 12/241

السبب في صعوبة معرفة الصحيح من المذاهب:

سهَّل الإمام الشافعي- رحمه الله تعالى- بتصحيحه مذهبه على من بعده معرفة الصحيح من مذهبه، وذلك برجوع الباحث إلى مذهبه الجديد، بل إن كتب الإمام الشافعي التي تمثل مذهبه القديم لم تحفظ، ولم يبق منها إلا صفحات متناثرة في كتب أهل العلم؛ ولذلك لم نجد له في أيامنا كتاباً مطبوعاً من كتبه التي تمثل قديم مذهبه.

أما غيره من الأئمة، فإن ما حفظ عنه أصحابه وتلامذته من أقواله ومروياته يمثل مذهبه، ما رجع عنه وما لم يرجع عنه، وقد يشير الواحد من الأئمة إلى ما صار إليه اجتهاده من الأقوال التي رويت عنه؛ كأن يقول في أحد القولين: هذا أحب إليَّ، أو يقول: هذا أولى، وبالحق أشبه.

وقد ينبه على هذا تنبيهاً خفيّاً، كأن يذكر قولين، ويفرع على أحدهما، ولا يفرع على الآخر، فإن تفريعه على أحدهما يدل على قوته عنده، وأن المفرع عليه أقوى عنده من القول الذي لم يفرع عليه[1].

يقول المرداوي: «كلام الإمام قد يكون صريحاً أو تنبيهاً، كقولنا: أومأ إليه، أو أشار إليه، أو دل كلامه عليه، أو توقف فيه، ونحو ذلك»[2].

والمسائل التي حدد فيها الإمام صحيح مذهبه قليلة جداً بجانب ما لم ينص عليه من الأقوال والروايات من المسائل.

١ المحصول للرازي: ٥/ ٣٩٢، البحر المحيط للزركشي: ٦/ ١٢٠.
٢ الإنصاف: ١٢/ ٢٤١.

This is why it is difficult, and sometimes impossible, to distinguish the latter opinions from the former in any *madhhab* except for that of Imām ash-Shāfi'i. Amidst illustrating the difficulty of navigating to the correct views of Imām Aḥmad, due to abundant narrations in his *madhhab*, aṭ-Ṭūfi says, "The book *Zād al-Musāfir* by Abū Bakr and *al-Jāmi' al-Kabīr* by al-Khallāl collected a vast number of Imām Aḥmad's views, but without distinguishing which view he chose last in his life. At best, al-Khallāl would sometimes say, 'This was a former opinion of Aḥmad which he recanted.' However, such cases are quite few in comparison to those wherein his preference remained unknown."

Madhhab Terminology

There are certain terms used by the jurists of the *madhhab*(s), and the seeker of knowledge must become acquainted with these terms in order to properly understand the words of the jurists. Ignorance of the technical usage of these terms, within the context of *madhhab*(s), could lead to much confusion in understanding the intent of its scholars. In this unit, our focus will not be to present the various terms of each *madhhab*, but rather to become familiar with the terms used by the jurists to indicate the *ijtihād* of their Imām(s), the more famous views of that *madhhab* and the stronger views of the *madhhab*.

These terms are, for the most part, universal in usage between the *madhhab*(s), and this is because they are used here for their original linguistic meanings.

Let us discuss the most important of these terms. Of them are:

Naṣṣ

In *Fiqh* books, this term denotes the Imām's exact statement. It entails that the Imām of this *madhhab* expressly stated this view in clear terms, for the words *naṣṣ* and *manṣooṣ 'alayh* mean that which is explicit in its meaning.[1]

1 *Mughni al-Muḥtāj* 1/12; *al-Inṣāf* 1/9 by al-Mirdāwi

ولذا فإن معرفة المتقدم والمتأخر من مذاهب الأئمة غير الشافعي فيها صعوبة، وقد تبلغ هذه الصعوبة درجة الاستحالة أحياناً، يقول الطوفي مبيناً صعوبة تصحيح مذهب الإمام أحمد بسبب تعدد الروايات وكثرتها في مذهبه: حوى كتاب «زاد المسافر» لأبي بكر، و«الجامع الكبير» للخلال، علماً جمّاً من علم الإمام أحمد t من غير أن يُعلم منه في آخر حياته الإخبار بصحيح مذهبه في تلك الفروع، غير أن الخلال يقول في بعض المسائل: هذا قول قديم لأحمد رجع عنه، لكن ذلك يسير بالنسبة إلى ما لم يُعلم حاله منها.

المصطلحات التي تحكي المذهب والاختلاف فيه

هناك مصطلحات يطلقها الفقهاء في كل مذهب، ولابد لطالب العلم من التعرف على هذه المصطلحات، حتى يفقه عن فقهاء المذاهب مرادهم، وحتى لا يقع في الخطأ لعدم معرفته بمصطلحات المذاهب التي يعبرون بها عن مذاهبهم، وليس مرادنا في هذا المبحث أن نعرض لكل المصطلحات في المذاهب المختلفة، وإنما مرادنا ذكر المصطلحات التي يستعملها الفقهاء لذكر المذهب أو التي تبين الراجح منه والمشهور أو التي تحكي اجتهادات فقهاء المذهب، وتبين القوي والضعيف من ذلك كله.

وهذه المصطلحات متقاربة في المذاهب كلها، والسبب في ذلك أنهم لم ينقلوها عن معانيها المرادة بها لغة إلى معنى اصطلاحي خاص، بل قصدوا منها معانيها اللغوية.

وسنعرض لأهم هذه المصطلحات، فمن ذلك:

١- النص:

يرد في كتب المذاهب قولهم: نص عليه، أو المنصوص عليه، ومرادهم من ذلك أن إمام المذهب نص على هذا القول بعبارة صريحة واضحة، ومعنى النص أو المنصوص عليه الصريح في معناه[١].

١ مغني المحتاج: ١/ ١٢، الإنصاف للمرداوي: ١/ ٩.

Qawl/Riwāyah

In *Fiqh* books, the terms *qawl* (view; literally: saying) and *riwāyah* (narration) refer to the *ijtihād*-based edicts that have been reported about the Imām of this *madhhab*. It is possible that the Imām may have one view, two views or even more on a single matter. Also, the views of an Imām could be taken from what was narrated about him, from his edicts, from what he dictated or from what he authored himself. It should be noted that jurists of the Shāfi'i *Fiqh* school use the word *qawl* whereas the jurists of other *Fiqh* schools use the word *riwāyah* instead. The secret behind this is that Imām ash-Shāfi'i recorded most of his juristic views himself, while the other Imām(s) were reported about via others.[1]

Wujūh

In Fiqh books, the term *wujūh* (directions) refer to the opinions deduced by the companions of Imām ash-Shāfi'i based on the general fundamentals of the Shāfi'i *madhhab*. In other words, they are the conclusions of their respective *ijtihād*(s) in light of the principles of their *madhhab* and without violating the parameters of that *madhhab*.[2]

Imām an-Nawawi said, "The *wujūh* of the companions of ash-Shāfi'i, who followed his *madhhab*, are the rulings extracted based on his principles, but at times using an independent *ijtihād* other than that of the Imām himself."[3]

This definition of the term *wujūh* is not restricted to the Shāfi'i *madhhab*. Rather, it is used in all *madhhab*(s). Muhammad ibn Abil-Fatḥ al-Ba'li al-Ḥanbali said, "In juristic terms, *wujūh* are the rulings reported about the disciples of a *Mujtahid Imām*, either those who met him or those after them, that were based on the principles of that Imām. Thus, it is said, 'This is a *wajh* (pl. *wujūh*) in the *madhhab* of Aḥmad, Imām ash-Shāfi'i and the likes, even when it disagrees with the Imām's view but is supported by evidences."[4]

In summation, *qawl* and *riwāyah* refer to the Imām of the *madhhab*, while *wujūh* refers to the Imām's disciples and companions.[5]

1 See *al-Majmū'* 1/65; *al-Maṭla' 'alā Abwāb al-Muqni'* 46.
2 *Muqaddimat Kitāb al-Wasīṭ* 1/238
3 *Al-Majmū'* 1/65; *Mughni al-Muḥtāj* 1/12
4 *Al-Maṭla' 'alā Abwāb al-Muqni'* 460
5 *Al-Majmū'* 1/65

٢ - الأقوال والروايات:

يريدون بالأقوال والروايات ما صدر عن إمام المذهب من اجتهادات، وقد يكون للإمام في المسألة قول واحد، أو قولان، أو أكثر من ذلك.

وأقوال الإمام تؤخذ من مروياته وفتاويه وأماليه وتآليفه.

ومما ينبغي أن ينبه إليه أن فقهاء الشافعية يستعملون «الأقوال»، بينما يستعمل فقهاء المذاهب الأخرى: الروايات، والسر في ذلك أن الشافعي دوَّن غالب فقهه بنفسه، بينما أئمة المذاهب الآخرون روي عنهم فقههم بطريق النقل(١).

٣ - الوجوه:

الوجوه: هي الآراء التي استنبطها أصحاب الشافعي المنتسبون إليه من الأصول العامة للمذهب بتخريجها على ضوء القواعد التي رسمها لهم الإمام الشافعي، وبعبارة أخرى هي: ما أدى إليه اجتهادهم على ضوء قواعد المذهب، ولا يخرج عن نطاق المذهب(٢).

ويقول النووي: «الأوجه لأصحاب الشافعي المنتسبين إلى مذهبه، يخرجونها على أصوله، ويستنبطونها من قواعده، ويجتهدون في بعضها، وإن لم يأخذوه من أصله»(٣).

وليس هذا التعريف للوجوه قصراً على مذهب الشافعي، بل عام في المذاهب كلها، وفي ذلك يقول محمد بن أبي الفتح البعلي الحنبلي: «الوجه في اصطلاح الفقهاء: الحكم المنقول في المسألة لبعض أصحاب الإمام المجتهدين فيه، ممن رآه فمن بعدهم، جارياً على قواعد الإمام، فيقال: وجه في مذهب أحمد، والإمام الشافعي، أو نحوهما، وربما كان مخالفاً لقواعد الإمام إذا عضده الدليل»(٤).

وخلاصة القول أن الأقوال والروايات هي لإمام المذهب، والأوجه لأصحاب الإمام(٥).

١ راجع في هذا: المجموع: ١/ ٦٥، المطلع على أبواب المقنع: ٤٦.
٢ مقدمة كتاب الوسيط: ١/ ٢٣٨.
٣ المجموع: ١/ ٦٥، وانظر مغني المحتاج: ١/ ١٢.
٤ المطلع على أبواب المقنع: ٤٦٠.
٥ المجموع: ١/ ٦٥.

Madhhab

In *Fiqh* books, jurists intend by *madhhab* the preponderant view of choice in their estimate. This could be the view of the Imām or any of his disciples.

Takhrīj

In *Fiqh* books, the term *takhrīj* (extraction) refers to the analogies that are built on the Imām's views. Aṭ-Ṭūfi said, "*Takhrīj* can be based on the general principles of the Imām, the revealed texts or the sound mind. This is because, in essence, *takhrīj* is to build a secondary ruling on a primary ruling, by way of analogy, due to a relevant resemblance between them. For instance, *takhrīj* is practiced on the principle of "being obligated beyond capacity" in many rulings of *Fiqh* and *Uṣūl al-Fiqh* alike.[1]

Ṣaḥīḥ (correct), Ḍa'īf (weak) and the likes

In *Fiqh* books, the jurists of each *madhhab* use many terms when discussing the different views within that *madhhab*. These terms serve to clarify the strength of each view, and/or the likelihood of it being correct, and what is stronger and more prominent in the *madhhab*.

By doing so, they aid the mufti in choosing a view, and thus the Ḥanafi scholars used to call them, "the mufti's guidelines."

These terms were laid down for the people of *taqlīd* within each *madhhab*, in the era when the *Mujtahid Imām*(s) became few and the people of *taqlīd* became plenty. Hence, arising with this new age was a need for these terms in order to discern the stronger view of each *madhhab*.[2]

Of these terms is their telling of differences by saying the matter has two positions, or two narrations, or two *wujūh* (viewpoints). By that, they only mean to explain that there is a difference of opinion on the matter, not to assert with these terms that one of these views is the preponderant one.[3]

1 Mukhtaṣar ar-Rawḍah 3/644
2 See Ḥāshiyat Ibn ʿĀbidīn 1/69.
3 *Al-Inṣāf* 1/4 by al-Mirdāwi

٤ - المذهب:

يريد فقهاء المذهب بالمذهب القول الراجح المفتى به عندهم، وقد يكون قول الإمام أو قول أصحابه[١].

٥ - التخريج:

التخريج هو القياس على قول الإمام، يقول الطوفي: التخريج يكون من القواعد الكلية للإمام، أو الشرع، أو العقل؛ لأن حاصله أنه بناء فرع على أصل بجامع مشترك، كتخريجنا على قاعدة تكليف ما لا يطاق فروعاً كثيرة في أصول الفقه وفروعه[٢].

٦ - الصحيح والضعيف والأصح والأظهر والأقوى ونحو ذلك:

يستعمل الفقهاء في كل مذهب ألفاظاً كثيرة تحكي الخلاف في قوة المذهب، وتبين الصحيح والضعيف فيه، أو ما هو أصح وأظهر.

وهذه الألفاظ علامات تدل المفتي على ما يفتي به؛ ولذا فإن علماء الحنفية يسمونها برسم المفتي.

وقد وضعت هذه الألفاظ لأهل التقليد من أتباع المذهب بعد أن قلَّ المجتهدون، وكثر المقلدون، واحتاجوا في فتاويهم أن يفتوا بالقول الصحيح أو الراجح الذي عليه الفتوى في كل مذهب من المذاهب[٣].

ومن هذه الألفاظ قولهم في حكاية الاختلاف: فيه قولان، أو روايتان، أو وجهان، ويريدون بمثل ذلك حكاية الخلاف فحسب، وليس مرادهم الترجيح بهذه الألفاظ[٤].

١ المجموع: ١/ ٦٥.
٢ مختصر الروضة: ٣/ ٦٤٤.
٣ راجع: حاشية ابن عابدين: ١/ ٦٩.
٤ الإنصاف للمرداوي: ١/ ٤.

وإذا أرادوا بيـان صحيـح القـول أو الروايـة أو الوجـه أو ضعيفها أطلقـوا لفـظ الصحيـح والضعيف.

وإذا كان في المذهـب روايتـان أو قولان أو وجهان صحيحان أحدهما أصح من الآخـر، قالوا في بيـان أقواهما: الأصح والأظهر(١).

فالأصح والأظهـر صيغتـا تفضيـل، تـدل كل واحـدة منهـما عـلى الصحـة والظهـور، مـع رجحـان صحـة أحدهـما أو ظهـوره(٢).

وإذا أطلـق علـماء مذهـب مـن المذاهـب في مسـألة مـا قولهـم: «المذهـب أو عـلى المذهـب» فيريـدون بـه الراجـح في حكايـة المذهـب(٣)، وإذا قالـوا: الأشـهر فهـو القـول أو الوجـه الـذي يزيـد شـهرة عـلى القـول الآخـر لشـهرة ناقلـه، أو مكانتـه عـن المنقـول عنـه، أو اتفـاق الـكل عـلى أنـه منقـول عنـه.

ويريـدون بالمشـهور القـول أو الوجـه الـذي اشـتهر بحيـث يكـون مقابلـه رأيـاً غريبـاً.

When they wished to denote the correctness of a view, narration or the likes, they would use the terms *ṣaḥīḥ* (correct) and *ḍa'īf* (weak).

If the *madhhab* contains two correct *qawl*(s), *riwāyah*(s) or *wujūh*, and one was more correct than the other, they would call it *asaḥ* (more correct) or *aẓhar* (more prominent).[1]

Asaḥ and *aẓhar* are both comparative tenses; both entailing that all matters are correct, but among them is what is more correct and more prominent.[2]

When the scholars of a *madhhab* say regarding a juristic matter, "The view of the *madhhab* is..." they mean that the preponderant view of that *madhhab* is such and such.[3] When they say, "The more popular view..." they are referring to the *qawl*, *riwāyah* or *wajh* that is more famous due to the fame of its reporter, or his nearness to the source that was reported from, or because they agreed that this reported opinion was indeed his.

When they say *mashūr* (popular), they mean the position or viewpoint that became popular making the counter position *gharīb* (odd).

١ مقدمة وسيط الغزالي: ١/ ٢٣٤.
٢ المرجع السابق: ١/ ٢٣٩.
٣ مغني المحتاج: ١/ ١٢، مقدمة وسيط الغزالي: ١/ ٢٤٠.

1 *Muqadimat al-Wasīt* 1/234 by al-Ghazāli
2 Ibid: 1/239
3 *Mughni al-Muhtāj* 1/12; *Muqadimat al-Wasīt* 1/240 by al-Ghazāli

Summary of Unit 7

1) The founding *Imām*(s) of the *madhhab*(s) drew methods for themselves that they adopted to deduce legal opinions. These methods are known as the *madhhab* or major *Fiqh* schools.

2) Linguistically, a *madhhab* is a path that is journeyed upon. Conventionally, it denotes the method that an individual or group chooses to follow, whether in theology, spirituality, legal rulings or otherwise.

3) The arena wherein the *Fiqh madhhab*(s) work is that of the detailed rulings in *Fiqh*.

4) It is not permissible to ascribe every legal opinion in the *madhhab* to the founding Imām of that *madhhab*.

5) Throughout their lifelong pursuit of knowledge, the great Imām(s) were constantly correcting and refining their *madhhab*(s).

6) There are various terms used by jurists of every *madhhab*. The meanings of these terms are similar in all of the *madhhab*(s).

خلاصة الوحدة

نخلص من دراسة هذه الوحدة إلى ما يلي:

١- اختط العلماء الأعلام أئمة المذاهب طريقة سلكوها في التعرف على الأحكام، وقد عرفت هذه الطرق بالمذاهب.

٢- المذهب في لغة العرب: الطريق الذي يذهب فيه. وفي اصطلاح كل قوم: الطريقة التي اختطها شخص أو مجموعة؛ سواء أكانت في مجال الاعتقاد، أو السلوك، أو الأحكام، أو غيرها.

٣- المجال الذي يعمل فيه المذهب الفقهي هو الأحكام الشرعية الفرعية.

٤- لا يجوز أن ينسب كل ما في المذهب لإمام المذهب.

٥- كان الأئمة الأعلام -أثناء سيرتهم العلمية- دائمي التصحيح والتنقيح لمذاهبهم.

٦- هناك بعض المصطلحات التي يطلقها الفقهاء في كل مذهب، وهذه المصطلحات متقاربة في المذاهب كلها.

NOTES

Notes

Unit 8
The Four *Mujtahid* Imām(s) and their *Madhhab*(s)
Contents of Unit 8

1) Imām Abū Ḥanīfah
2) Imām Mālik
3) Imām ash-Shāfi'i
4) Imām Aḥmad ibn Ḥanbal

Importance of this Unit

Allah, the Glorified and High, destined that four *madhhab*(s) in particular survive and continue while others have vanished and no longer have any followers. These four *madhhab*(s) are the Ḥanafi *madhhab*, the Māliki *madhhab*, the Shāfi'i *madhhab* and the Hanbali *madhhab*. Each of these four *madhhab*(s) has its own vanguards who established it, its own fundamentals which the founding Imām of this *madhhab* chose for deducing rulings, and its own terms which are particular to it. Let us now begin with the unit and become more acquainted with these details.

Learning objectives

By the end of this unit, readers should be able to:

- Discuss the four *madhhab*(s) which the whole Muslim nation has approved, as well as the Imāms of these *madhhab*(s), their fundamentals and the terms particular to each *madhhab*.
- Draw a comparison between the fundamentals of the four *madhhab*(s).

Imām Abū Ḥanīfah

I. Lineage

He is an-Nu'mān ibn Thābit ibn Zawṭi al-Kufi. He was a merchant of silk cloth. His grandfather, Zawṭi, was from KAbūl and was a bondsman of the family of Taymullah ibn Tha'labah before being emancipated. His father, Thābit, was born Muslim, and it was said that he was never a bondsman. Thābit went to 'Ali ibn Abi Ṭālib when he was still young, and 'Ali (may Allah be pleased with him) supplicated that Allah bless him and his offspring.

الوحدة الثامنة
الأئمة الأربعة ومذاهبهم
محتويات الوحدة الثامنة

١- الإمـام أبو حنيفــة.
٢- الإمـام مــالك.
٣- الإمـام الشــافعي.
٤- الإمـام أحمد بن حنبــل.

أهمية دراسة الوحدة:

كتـب اللـه سـبحانه وتعـالى البقـاء والاسـتمرار لأربعـة مذاهـب فقهيـة، ومـا عداهـا فقـد تـلاشى واندثـر فلـم يبـق لهـا أتبـاع، وهـذه المذاهـب هـي: المذهـب الحنفـي، والمذهـب المالـكي، والمذهـب الشـافعي، والمذهـب الحنبـلي، وكل مذهـب مـن هـذه المذاهـب لـه رجالـه الذيـن قـام عـلى أكتافهـم، ولـه أصولـه التـي ارتضاهـا إمـام المذهـب للتعـرف عـلى الأحـكام، ولـه مصطلحاتـه الخاصـة بـه.
هيـا بنـا لدراسـة هـذه الوحـدة؛ لنتعـرف عـلى هـذه التفاصيل.

الأهداف التعليمية:

يتوقـع منـك أيهـا الـدارس الكريـم بعـد دراسـتك لهـذه الوحــدة أن تكـون قـادراً عـلى أن:

- تذكر المذاهب الأربعة التي تلقتها الأمة بالقبول، وأئمتها، وأصولها، والمصطلحات الخاصة بكل منها.
- تقارن بين أصول المذاهب الأربعة.

الإمام أبو حنيفة

أولاً: نسبه وعصره:

هـو النعـمان بـن ثابـت بـن زوطـي الكـوفي، كان خـزَّازاً يبيـع الخـز، وكان جـده زوطـي مـن أهـل كابـل مملـوكاً لبنـي تيـم الله بـن ثعلبـة، فأعتـق، وولـد أبـوه ثابـت عـلى الإسـلام، وقيـل: هـو مـن الأحـرار، ومـا وقـع عليـه رق قـط، وذهـب ثابـت إلى عـلي بـن أبي طالـب وهـو صغـير، فدعـا لـه بالبركـة فيـه وفي ذريتـه.

Abū Ḥanīfah was born in the year 80 A.H. and died in Baghdad in the year 150 A.H. He was buried in the graveyard of al-Khayzarān in Baghdad where his grave is well-known.[1]

Adh-Dhahabi said about him, "He was the esteemed Imām, the jurist of Islam, and the scholar of Iraq... He was born in the year 80 A.H. during the lifetime of the Prophet's younger Companions. He met Anas ibn Mālik when he visited Kufah, although it has not been confirmed that he reported anything from any of them."[2]

Ibn Kathīr said about him, "Abū Ḥanīfah an-Nu'mān was the jurist of Iraq, one of the great Imām(s) of Islam, one of the premier scholars, and one of the four *Mujtahid Imām*(s) whose *madhhab* is still followed. He was the first of them to pass away, as he had lived to witness the era of the Companions (may Allah be pleased with them)."[3]

Abū Ḥanīfah was from the generation that succeeded the Successors. There is no doubt that he lived in the same age as some of the Prophet's Companions (may Allah be pleased with them), such as Anas ibn Mālik in Basrah, 'Abdullāh ibn Abi Awfā in Kufah, Sahl ibn Sa'd as-Sa'īdi in Madinah and Abū aṭ-Ṭufayl 'Amir ibn Wāthilah in Mecca. However, he did not personally meet any of them. Some of his companions claimed that he met some of the Companions and narrated hadith(s) from them, but this claim was denied by those specialized in hadith transmission, such as Ibn Khalkān.

II. His Teachers and Disciples

Abū Ḥanīfah narrated from a number of the Successors, such as al-Ḥakam, Hammād ibn Abi Sulaymān, 'Amir ash-Sha'bi, 'Ikrimah, 'Aṭā', Qatādah, az-Zuhri, Nāfi' the bondsman of Ibn 'Umar and Abū Isḥāq as-Sabee'i.[4]

1 *Al-Ikmāl fī Asmā' ar-Rijāl* 3/790 by al-Khatīb at-Tabrīzi
2 *Siyar A'lām an-Nubalā'* 6/390 by adh-Dhahabi
3 *Al-Bidāyah wan-Nihāyah* 10/107
4 *Al-Bidāyah wan-Nihāyah* 10/107, *al-Ikmāl* and *Mishkāt al-Masābīḥ* 3/790

ولد أبو حنيفة سنة ثمانين، ومات ببغداد سنة خمسين ومائة، ودفن بمقابر الخيزران، وقبره معروف ببغداد[١].

قال فيه الذهبي: «الإمام، فقيه الملة، عالم العراق،... ولد سنة ثمانين في حياة صغار الصحابة، ورأى أنس بن مالك لما قدم عليهم الكوفة، ولم يثبت له حرف عن واحد منهم»[٢].

قال فيه ابن كثير: «الإمام أبو حنيفة النعمان... فقيه العراق، وأحد أئمة الإسلام، والسادة الأعلام، وأحد الأركان العلماء، وأحد الأئمة الأربعة، أصحاب المذاهب المتبوعة، وهو أقدمهم وفاة؛ لأنه أدرك عصر الصحابة»[٣].

وأبو حنيفة من أتباع التابعين، ولا شك أنه أدرك زمن بعض الصحابة، منهم أنس بن مالك بالبصرة، وعبد الله بن أبي أوفى بالكوفة، وسهل بن سعد الساعدي في المدينة، وأبو الطفيل عامر بن واثلة بمكة، ولم يلق أحداً منهم، ويزعم أصحابه أنه لقي جماعة من الصحابة، وروى عنهم، ولم يثبت ذلك عند أهل النقل، كما في ابن خلكان.

ثانياً: شيوخه وتلامذته:

روى أبو حنيفة عن جماعة من التابعين منهم: الحكم، وحماد بن أبي سليمان، وعامر الشعبي، وعكرمة، وعطاء، وقتادة، والزهري، ونافع مولى ابن عمر، وأبو إسحاق السبيعي[٤].

١ الإكمال في أسماء الرجال، للخطيب التبريزي، مطبوع في ذيل مشكاة المصابيح: ٣/ ٧٩٠.
٢ سير أعلام النبلاء للذهبي: ٦/ ٣٩٠.
٣ البداية والنهاية: ١٠/ ١٠٧.
٤ البداية والنهاية: ١٠/ ١٠٧، والإكمال، انظر مشكاة المصابيح: ٣/ ٧٩٠.

Abū Ḥanīfah's most famous disciple who would spread his *madhhab* was Abū Yūsuf Ya'qūb ibn Ibrāhīm ibn Sa'd al-Anṣāri, who was better known as al-Qāḍi Abū Yūsuf. Abū Yūsuf was born in 113 A.H. and died in 182 A.H in Kufah. He studied *Fiqh* at the hands of Abū Ḥanīfah, and then traveled to Madinah where he met Imām Mālik and learned a great deal. Abū Yūsuf recanted many of his juristic views after acquiring the knowledge of the people of Ḥijāz. He worked as a judge during the Abbasid caliphate, and was instrumental in spreading the Ḥanafi *madhhab*. He authored many books, though none remain except *ar-Radd 'alā Siyar al-Awzā'i* and *al-Kharāj*, which he was commanded to write by the Muslim caliph Harūn ar-Rashīd.

Another of his disciples was Muhammad ibn al-Ḥasan ash-Shaybānī. He was born in Wasit in 132 A.H. and died in ar-Rayy in 189 A.H. He studied under Abū Ḥanīfah for a short time, and continued studying at the hands of Abū Yūsuf. Later, he traveled to Madinah where he stayed for a period of time, learning *Fiqh* at the hands of Imām Mālik and also reporting Prophetic hadith(s) from him. He was the one credited with documenting the Ḥanafi *madhhab* and spreading it far and wide.

Other disciples were Zufar ibn al-Hudhayl (born in 110 A.H. and died in 158 A.H.) and al-Ḥasan ibn Ziyād al-Lu'lu'i (born in 133 A.H. and died in 204 A.H.).[1]

III. The Fundamentals of Abū Hanīfah's Madhhab

1. *Depending on Qur'an, the Sunnah and the Companions' views*

Numerous sayings were reported from Abū Ḥanīfah that illustrate the fundamentals upon which he built his *madhhab*. Of these reports was his statement, "If I find the ruling in the Book of Allah, I take it. If not, then I resort to the Sunnah of the Messenger of Allah (ﷺ). If I cannot find in the Book of Allah or in the Sunnah of the Messenger of Allah (ﷺ), I take from the views of the Companions. I take whichever of their views I wish and abandon whichever of their views I wish, but do not select from other than their views. In the case that there are no views except from Ibrāhīm, ash-Sha'bi, Ibn Sirīn, 'Aṭā' or Sa'īd ibn al-Musayyib, I exercise my own *ijtihād* just as they did."[2]

1 Ibid
2 *Tārīkh Baghdād* 13/368 and *al-Intiqā'* 143 by Ibn 'Abdil-Barr

وأشهر تلامذة أبي حنيفة الذين نشروا مذهبه أبو يوسف: يعقوب بن إبراهيم بن سعد الأنصاري، الشهير بالقاضي أبو يوسف (٣١١- ٢٨١هـ)، مولده، ووفاته بالكوفة، تفقه على أبي حنيفة، ورحل إلى المدينة، واجتمع بالإمام مالك، وأخذ عنه العلم، ورجع عن كثير من أقواله بعد اطلاعه على علم أهل الحجاز، تولى القضاء في الدولة العباسية، وكان له أثر كبير في نشر المذهب الحنفي، ألّف كثيراً من الكتب، ولم يبق منها إلا كتاب «الرد على سير الأوزاعي»، وكتاب «الخراج» الذي كتبه بتكليف من هارون الرشيد.

ومن تلامذته: محمد بن الحسن الشيباني، ولد بواسط عام ٢٣١هـ وتوفي بالري عام ٩٨١هـ أدرك أبا حنيفة، وتتلمذ عليه فترة قصيرة، ودرس على أبي يوسف، ورحل إلى المدينة، ومكث بها مدة، وتفقه على الإمام مالك، وأخذ عنه الحديث، وهو الذي دوّن فقه المذهب الحنفي ونشره.

ومن تلامذته أيضاً: زفر بن الهذيل (٠١١- ٨٥١هـ)، والحسن بن زياد اللؤلؤي (٣٣١- ٤٠٢هـ)(١).

ثالثاً: قواعد مذهبه:

١- اعتماده على الكتاب والسنة وأقوال الصحابة:

نقلت عن الإمام أبي حنيفة أقوال تدل على الأصول التي بنى عليها مذهبه، فمن ذلك أنه قال: آخذ بكتاب الله إذا وجدت فيه الحكم، وإلا فسنة رسول الله ﷺ، فإن لم أجد في كتاب الله ولا سنة رسول الله ﷺ أخذت بقول أصحابه، آخذ بقول من شئت منهم، وأدع قول من شئت، ولا أخرج عن قولهم إلى غيرهم، فأما إذا انتهى الأمر إلى إبراهيم، والشعبي، وابن سيرين، وعطاء، وسعيد بن المسيب، فإني أجتهد كما اجتهدوا(٢).

١ المصادر السابقة.
٢ تاريخ بغداد: ١٣/ ٣٦٨، والانتقاء لابن عبد البر: ١٤٣.

Abū Ḥanīfah's View of Āḥād Hadith(s)[1]

خبر الواحد عند أبي حنيفة:

Imam Abū Ḥanīfah stipulated a number of conditions for accepting an *āḥād* report. They were:

اشترط الإمام أبو حنيفة للأخذ بخبر الواحد شروطاً:

1) It should not be opposed by its narrator. If its narrator himself opposes it, then one must act upon his view and not his narration, for he would not have opposed his own narration unless he found a defect in it, on the basis of evidence [he knew].

الأول: أن لا يخالفه راويه، فإن خالفه فالعمل بما رأى، لا بما روى؛ لأنه لا يخالف مرويه إلا وقد اطلع على قادح استند فيه لدليل.

2) It should not pertain to a matter that is unavoidable (*'umoom al-balwa*), for unavoidable circumstances necessitate that the rulings regarding them be well known. Therefore, if such matters are reported via *āḥād* chains of transmission, then that itself is a defect in it.

الثاني: أن لا يكون مما تعم به البلوى، فإن عموم البلوى يوجب اشتهاره أو توافره، فإذا رُوي آحاداً فهو علة قادحة عنده.

3) It should not oppose sound *qiyās*, and its narrator must be one of the jurists. The *āḥād* hadith which opposes sound *qiyās* is not accepted when this *qiyās* is based on a *'illah* (effective cause) that is established though a report that is stronger than the *āḥād* report, and this *'illah* is definitely present in the case addressed by the *aḥād* report. As for when the *'illah* is merely presumed to exist in the case addressed by the *āḥād* report, then Abū Ḥanīfah neither accepts nor rejects such a hadith. On the other hand, Abū Ḥanīfah does accept the *āḥād* report which opposes sound *qiyās* if the *qiyās*'s *'illah* is not found in the case addressed by the *āḥād* hadith.[2]

الثالث: أن لا يخالف القياس، وأن يكون راويه فقيهاً، فإن خالف القياس، ولم يكن راويه فقيهاً، فالحديث المعارض لا يقبل إذا عرفت العلة بنص راجح على الخبر، ووجدت العلة قطعاً في الفرع، ويتوقف الإمام أبو حنيفة إذا وجدت العلة ظنّاً في الفرع، ويقبل الحديث المخالف للقياس إذا لم توجد في الفرع(١).

1 Note: *Āḥād* (single) reports are narrations that have been transmitted by people whose number does not reach that of *mutawātir* reports. *Mutawātir* (consecutive) reports are narrations that have been transmitted by such a large number of people that they could not have possibly agreed upon a lie altogether.

2 *Al-Fikr as-Sāmi*

١ الفكر السامي.

When these conditions are fulfilled in an *āḥād* hadith, it is accepted and preferred over sound *qiyās*, even if its chain of narration is weak. In such cases, neither its particular chain of transmission, nor its agreement or disagreement with the people of Madinah, are taken into consideration. Regarding this, Ibn al-Qayyim says in his book *al-I'lām*, "The companions of Abū Ḥanīfah – may Allah bestow mercy upon him – unanimously agree that Abū Ḥanīfah's *madhhab* holds that a weak hadith is given preference over *qiyās*. Abū Ḥanīfah built his *madhhab* upon this fundamental principle, and thus he preferred the hadith regarding boisterous laughing [breaking *wudu'*] over *qiyās* and *ra'y*. In addition, he preferred the the hadith on the permissibility of performing *wudu'* with the wine of dates, despite its weakness, over *qiyās* and *ra'y*. Also, he adopted the hadith that forbids cutting the hands of a thief that stole less than ten dirhams, although the hadith is weak. He also adopted the hadith that the maximum length for menses is ten days, despite the hadith being weak. Additionally, he adopted the hadith that stipulates being in a city for Friday prayer to be valid, despite it being weak."[1]

In case these conditions are not fulfilled in the hadith, he regards it as a *shādh* (odd) and *qiyās* is exercised. In these cases, the hadith is rejected, even if it were authentic and even if everyone in Madinah acted upon it.

This was the method followed regarding the hadith of *al-muṣarrāh* (the animal whose udders were tied up to appear full). Both al-Bukhari and Muslim narrate that the Prophet (ﷺ) said, "Do not tie up the udders of camels and sheep. Whoever buys one, the choice is his [even] after milking it; if he wishes, he may keep it, and if he wishes, he may return it along with one *ṣā'* of dates." Abū Ḥanīfah viewed that returning dates in exchange for the [consumed] milk opposes sound *qiyās*, namely that the likes or value of what was consumed should be returned, not a different commodity.

1 *I'lam al-Muwaqqi'īn* 1/81

فإذا توفرت هذه الشروط في خبر الواحد فإنه يأخذ به، ولو كان ضعيف السند، ويقدمه على القياس، ولا يلتفت لسنده الخاص، ولا لكونه على وفق عمل أهل المدينة أو خلافهم، وعلى هذا يحمل كلام ابن القيم في الإعلام: «وأصحاب أبي حنيفة- رحمه الله- مجمعون على أن مذهب أبي حنيفة أن ضعيف الحديث أولى عنده من القياس»، وعلى ذلك بنى مذهبه، كما قدَّم حديث القهقهة على القياس والرأي، وقدَّم حديث الوضوء بنبيذ التمر في السفر مع ضعفه على الرأي والقياس، ومنع قطع السارق بسرقة أقل من عشرة دراهم، والحديث فيه ضعف، وجعل أكثر الحيض عشرة أيام، والحديث فيه ضعف، وشرط في إقامة الجمعة المصر، والحديث فيه كذلك»(١).

فإذا لم تتوفر تلك الشروط في الحديث اعتبر الحديث شاذاً، وذهب إلى القياس، وترك الحديث، ولو صحيحاً، أو عمل به أهل المدينة أجمع.

وقد فعل ذلك في حديث المصراة، والحديث في الصحيحين: «لا تصروا الإبل والغنم، فمن ابتاعها بعد فهو بخير النظرين بعد حلبها: إن شاء أمسك، وإن شاء ردها وصاعاً من تمر»، فأبو حنيفة يرى أن رد التمر بدل اللبن مخالف للقياس فيما يضمن به المتلف من مثله أو قيمته.

١ إعلام الموقعين: ١/ ٨١.

2. *Using Qiyās Liberally*
Among the fundamental principles of Imām Abū Ḥanīfah is exercising *qiyās* liberally, except in *ḥudūd* (prescribed punishments), *kaffārāt* (expiations) and numerical figures fixed by Sharia. What is meant by *qiyās* is *takhrīj* (extraction of) the *manāṭ* (*'illah* / effective cause) of each case. As for *tahqīq* (verifying) and *tanqīh* (isolating) that *manāṭ* in new cases, that can be practiced by the *mujtahid* jurists and others alike.
The reason why Abū Ḥanīfah was liberal in exercising *qiyās* is because he had not collected as many hadith(s) as the other Imām(s). This is due to the fact that he lived before the other Imām(s), and his strict rules in accepting hadith(s) because of the widespread lying and tribulations in Iraq.
3. *Using Istiḥsān Liberally*
The *madhhab* of Imām Abū Ḥanīfah is known for being liberal in practicing *istiḥsān* (juristic preference). It was confirmed that Abū Ḥanīfah said, "I sometimes practice *istihsān* in place of *qiyās*." The like was confirmed about his disciple Muhammad ibn al-Ḥasan as well. When they would find a view from the Companions that opposed *qiyās*, they would abandon the *qiyās* and follow the Companions' view or return to the broader principles for deducing the ruling; this is what was known as *ra'y* among the earlier generations.[1]
4. *Loopholing*
Another fundamental of Abū Ḥanīfah's *madhhab* is loopholing, which they call escaping overly restrictive circumstances. Basically, it is the dismissal of a legislated ruling or replacing it with another ruling. Most scholars criticized Abū Ḥanīfah for accepting the practice of loopholing. In fact, some of *Ahl ar-Ra'y* themselves rejected this method, in addition to Imām al-Bukhari refuting it on many occasions and even allotting a book in his *al-Jāmi' aṣ-Ṣaḥīḥ* to addressing it.

1 Al-Fikr as-Sāmi 1/359

٢- توسع الإمام أبي حنيفة في القياس:

من قواعد الإمام أبي حنيفة الأخذ بالقياس والتوسع فيه في غير الحدود، والكفارات، والتقديرات الشرعية، والمراد بالقياس هو تخريج المناط، أما تحقيق المناط وتنقيحه، فهما مبذولان للمجتهد وغيره.

والسبب في توسع الإمام أبي حنيفة في القياس أنه أقل من غيره من الأئمة في رواية الحديث؛ لتقدم عهده على عهد بقية الأئمة، ولتشدده في رواية الحديث بسبب فشو الكذب في العراق وكثرة الفتن.

٣- التوسع في الاستحسان:

من مذهب الإمام أبي حنيفة التوسع في الاستحسان، وقد ثبت عنه أنه قال: أستحسن وأدع القياس، وكذا ثبت عن صاحبه محمد بن الحسن، وذلك أنه إذا وجد أثراً يخالف القياس يترك القياس، ويعمل بالأثر، أو يرجع إلى أصول عامة، وهو ما يعرف عند الأقدمين بالرأي[1].

٤-الحيل:

من أصول مذهب أبي حنيفة الحيل، ويسمونه المخارج من المضايق، وهو التحيل على إسقاط حكم شرعي، أو قلبه إلى حكم آخر، وقد عاب سائر العلماء على أبي حنيفة أخذه بالحيل، ورد مذهبه في هذا بعض من يقول بالرأي، ورد عليه البخاري كثيراً، وعقد للحيل كتاباً في جامعه الصحيح.

١ الفكر السامي: ١/ ٣٥٩.

IV. Compiling the Madhhab of Abū Ḥanīfah & the Ḥanafi Jurists

We previously mentioned that forty men from among Abū Ḥanīfah's companions shared in establishing the *madhhab* with him. However, these records that documented the rulings that were agreed upon between Abū Ḥanīfah and his companions did not reach us.

Fortunately, the companions of Abū Ḥanīfah did report to us his personal juristic views. These opinions were collected by the primary compiler of the Ḥanafi *madhhab*, Muhammad ibn al-Ḥasan ash-Shaybāni. The earliest books on Ḥanafi *Fiqh* were all his authoring, and they were the views he narrated directly from Abū Ḥanīfah or through Abū Yūsuf. Sometimes, he would finish one of these books, and then first submit it to Abū Yūsuf for verification.

It should be noted that the early books written by Muhammad ibn al-Ḥasan did not confine the Ḥanafi *madhhab* to the opinions of Abū Ḥanīfah. Rather, it would sometimes include the opinions of several of his companions. Their views were listed alongside those of the Imām, and thus the *madhhab* during that period represented all these views collectively.

Ḥanafi jurists divide the juristic issues reported from Abū Ḥanīfah and his companions into two categories: fundamental cases and rare cases.

As for the **fundamental cases**, they are also called the "popular narrations." These are the cases wherein an opinion is narrated from the founding Imām(s) of the *madhhab*, namely Abū Ḥanīfah, Abū Yūsuf and Muhammad ibn al-Ḥasan. Zufr and al-Ḥasan ibn Ziyād may also be included here, along with others who heard directly from the Imām, but the apparent narration is almost always referring to the view of at least one of these three.

رابعاً: تدوين مذهب أبي حنيفة ودواوين مذهب الحنفية:

ذكرنا من قبل أن الإمام أبا حنيفة شاركه في وضع المذهب أربعون رجلاً من أصحابه، إلا أن هذا الديوان الذي سجل فيه ما اتفق عليه أبو حنيفة وأصحابه لم يصل إلينا.

وقد نقل إلينا أصحاب الإمام أبي حنيفة فقهه، وقام بتدوين ذلك الفقه مدون كتب المذهب محمد بن الحسن الشيباني، فالمدونات الأولى كلها من وضعه وتأليفه، سواء مما رواه بنفسه عن أبي حنيفة أو مما رواه عن أبي يوسف، وقد كان أحياناً يضع المؤلَّف، ثم يقوم بعرضه على أبي يوسف.

ونلحظ أن كتب المذهب الأولى التي وضعها محمد بن الحسن لم تجعل المذهب قصراً على قول أبي حنيفة، بل أشركت معه عدداً من أصحابه، وضعت أقوالهم بجانب قوله، فالمذهب في تلك الفترة مجموع تلك الأقوال.

وقد قسم علماء الحنفية المسائل الفقهية التي رويت عن أبي حنيفة وأصحابه إلى قسمين: القسم الأول أطلقوا عليه مسائل الأصول، والقسم الثاني: أطلقوا عليه مسائل النوادر.

فمسائل الأصول: وتسمى عندهم أيضاً بظاهر الرواية، وهي المسائل التي رويت عن أصحاب المذهب، وهم أبو حنيفة وأبو يوسف ومحمد، وقد يلحق بهم زفر والحسن بن زياد وغيرهما ممن أخذ عن الإمام، لكن الغالب الشائع في ظاهر الرواية أن يكون قول الثلاثة أو قول بعضهم.

NOTES

The books collecting these "popular narrations" are six, and they have all been written by Muhammad ibn al-Ḥasan ash-Shaybāni. They are *al-Mabsūṭ, az-Ziyādāt, al-Jāmi' as-Saghīr, as-Siyar as-Saghīr, al-Jāmi' al-Kabīr* and *as-Siyar al-Kabīr.*

They were named the "popular narrations" because they were reported by Muhammad ibn al-Ḥasan via a trustworthy chain of transmission. Therefore, they are confirmed about him either with a *mutawātir* or *mashhūr* chain.[1]

When Ḥanafi jurists use the word *al-Aṣl* (the primary), they are referring to the book *al-Mabsūṭ* by Muhammad ibn al-Ḥasan. They called it this because it was the first of his six books on the popular narrations. After it, he wrote *al-Jāmi' as-Saghīr,* then *az-Ziyādāt,* and finally *as-Siyar al-Kabīr.*

As for the **rare cases**, these are the juristic rulings that were opined by the scholars of the *madhhab* but not in the books of "popular narrations." Some of these books were also written by Muhammad ibn al-Ḥasan, such as the book entitled *al-Hārūniyāt.* It was given this name because it was written during the caliphate of Harūn ar-Rashīd. He also wrote a book entitled *al-Kaysāniyyāt* which was narrated via Shu'ayb ibn Sulaymān al-Kaysāni. A third book was *ar-Raqqiyāt,* referring to the city of ar-Raqqah. Therein, he collected the juristic rulings that were presented to Muhammad ibn al-Ḥasan during his term as the judge of ar-Raqqah.

A third category of books in Ḥanafi *Fiqh* are composed of *fatāwā* (edicts) and *wāqi'āt* (incidents). Basically, these are all the cases for which rulings were independently deduced by later Ḥanafi jurists, after they were posed with them, and could not find a narration addressing them by the earlier jurists of the *madhhab.*

1 *Hāshiyat Ibn 'Ābidīn* 1/69 and *Sharḥ 'Uqūd Rasm al-Mufti* 1/16 by Ibn 'Ābidīn

وكتب ظاهر الرواية المسماة بالأصول ستة كتب، ألفها جميعاً محمد بن الحسن، وهي: المبسوط، والزيادات، والجامع الصغير، والسير الصغير، والجامع الكبير، والسير الكبير.

وسميت بظاهر الرواية؛ لأنها رويت عن محمد بن الحسن برواية الثقات، فهي ثابتة عنه، إما متواترة، أو مشهورة عنه(١).

وإذا أطلق علماء الحنفية الأصل فإنهم يريدون به كتاب المبسوط لمحمد، سمي بذلك لأنه أول مؤلفاته من كتب ظاهر الرواية الست، ثم صنف بعده الجامع الصغير، ثم الكبير، ثم الزيادات، وآخرها تصنيفاً السير الكبير، وفي ذلك يقول ابن عابدين(٢):

واشتهر المبسوط بالأصل وذا // لسبقه الستة تصنيفاً كذا
الجامع الصغير بعده فما // فيه على الأصل لذا تقدما
وآخر الستة تصنيفاً ورد // السير الكبير فهذا المعتمد

ومسائل النوادر هي المسائل المروية عن أصحاب المذهب في غير كتب ظاهر الرواية، وبعض هذه الكتب ألفها محمد بن الحسن كالهارونيات، سميت بذلك لأنه أملاها في دولة هارون الرشيد، والكيسانيات نسبة إلى راويها شعيب بن سليمان الكيساني، والرقيات نسبة إلى مدينة الرقة، وهي تمثل المسائل التي عرضت على محمد بن الحسن وهو قاضي مدينة الرقة، جمعت في كتاب سمي بالرقيات.

الفتاوى والواقعات: هناك قسم ثالث من المؤلفات يضاف إلى القسمين الأولين عند علماء الحنفية يسمى بالفتاوى والواقعات.

وهي مسائل استنبطها المجتهدون المتأخرون لما سئلوا عنها، ولم يجدوا فيها رواية عن أهل المذهب المتقدمين.

١ حاشية ابن عابدين: ١/ ٦٩، وشرح المنظومة المسماة: بعقود رسم المفتي لابن عابدين: ١/ ١٦، مجموع رسائل ابن عابدين.
٢ شرح عقود رسم المفتي: ١/ ١٨- ١٩، حاشية ابن عابدين: ١/ ٧٠.

The works of many jurists fall under this third category; among them are the companions of Abū Yūsuf, the companions of Muhammad ibn al-Ḥasan and many others who succeeded them and compiled in a similar fashion. Their respective biographies can be found in *Ṭabaqāt al-Ḥanafiyyah*.

Al-Ḥākim ash-Shāheed merged the six books of "popular narrations" written by Muhammad ibn al-Ḥasan into one compilation, known as *al-Kāfi*. It is one of the authoritative sources for citing the Ḥanafi *madhhab* as was said by the great scholar, Ibrāhīm al-Bīri, who narrated this from Ibn ʿĀbidīn.

The book *al-Kāfi* was then explained by the great scholar Shamsuddin as-Sarkhasi, who died in 490 A.H. This book is known by the followers of the Ḥanafi *madhhab* as *Mabsūṭ as-Sarkhasi*. Ibn ʿAbidīn reported that the great scholar aṭ-Ṭarsūsi said that he never acted upon any view that contradicts what exists in *Mabsūṭ as-Sarkhasi*, nor depended on any other book [for *Fiqh*], nor based a *fatwa* on anything but it.

V. Terms Used in Ḥanafi Fiqh

We have already mentioned some terms used by the Ḥanafi jurists in their books. In addition to those, some other important terms are:

***Al-Imām al-Aʿẓam* (the Greatest Imām):** When mentioned in absolute terms, this refers to the founder of the *madhhab* Imām Abū Ḥanīfah.

The Three Imām(s): This refers to Abū Ḥanīfah, Abū Yūsuf and Muhammad.

The Two Shaykh(s): This refers to Abū Ḥanīfah and Abū Yūsuf.

The Two Parties: This refers to Abū Ḥanīfah and Muhammad.

The Two Companions: This refers to Abū Yūsuf and Muhammad.

وهؤلاء كثيرون، منهم أصحاب أبي يوسف وأصحاب محمد، وجاء بعدهم كثير نسجوا على منوالهم، وموضع معرفتهم كتب طبقات الحنفية[١].

وقد جمع الحاكم الشهيد كتب ظاهر الرواية الستة في كتاب واحد سماه بكتاب «الكافي»، وكتاب الكافي- كتاب معتمد في نقل المذهب كما يقوله العلامة إبراهيم البيري فيما نقله عنه ابن عابدين[٢].

وقام بشرح الكافي شمس الأئمة السرخسي المتوفى سنة أربعمائة وتسعين، وهذا الكتاب هو المشهور عند الحنفية بمبسوط السرخسي، ,قد نقل ابن عابدين عن العلامة الطرسوسي أنه لا يعمل بما خالف كتاب مبسوط السرخسي، ولا يركن إلا إليه، ولا يعول في الفتوى إلا عليه[٣].

خامساً: مصطلحات الفقه الحنفي:

ذكرنا جملة من مصطلحات الحنفية في مؤلفاتهم، وهناك مصطلحات أخرى منها:

«الإمام الأعظم»: يريدون به عند إطلاقه صاحب المذهب أبا حنيفة.

وإذا قالوا: «أئمتنا الثلاثة» أرادوا بهم أبا حنيفة وأبا يوسف ومحمد.

وإذا أطلقوا «الشيخين» أرادوا بهما أبا حنيفة وأبا يوسف.

ويريدون «بالطرفين» أبا حنيفة ومحمد.

و«بالصاحبين» أبا يوسف ومحمداً.

١ المصدران السابقان.

٢ شرح عقود رسم المفتي: ١/ ٢٠.

٣ المصدر السابق.

***Aṣ-Ṣadr al-Awwal* (the First Era):** When mentioned in absolute terms, this refers to the first three generations of Muslims: the Companions, the Successors and the generation that succeeded them.

ويريدون «بالصدر الأول» عند إطلاقهم إياه أهل القرون الثلاثة من الصحابة والتابعين وأتباعهم.

***As-Salaf* (the Predecessors):** They use this in reference to the earliest Ḥanafi jurists that end with Muhammad ibn al-Ḥasan.

و«السلف» عندهم فقهاء الحنفية إلى محمد بن الحسن.

***Al-Khalaf* (the Successors):** They use this in reference to the early Ḥanafi jurists that came after Muhammad ibn al-Ḥasan and ended with Shams al-A'immah al-Halwāni (d. 456 A.H.). The latter jurists are those from Shams al-A'immah until Hāfiẓ ad-Dīn al-Bukhāri (d. 693 A.H.).

ومرادهم «بالخلف» من بعد محمد إلى شمس الأئمة الحلواني المتوفى ٦٥٤هـ والمتأخرون من بعد شمس الأئمة إلى حافظ الدين البخاري المتوفى سنة ٣٩٦هـ

***Al-Ustādh* (the Teacher):** This refers to 'Abdullāh ibn Muhammad ibn Ya'qūb as-Sabdhamuni (d. 340 A.H).

وإذا أطلقوا «الأستاذ» أرادوا به عبد الله بن محمد بن يعقوب السبذموني المتوفى سنة ٠٤٣هـ

***Burhān al-Islām* (he Proof of Islam):** This refers to Riḍā ad-Dīn as-Sarkhasi (d. 544 A.H.).

و«برهان الإسلام» رضى الدين السرخسي المتوفى سنة ٤٤٥هـ

***Burhān al-A'immah* (the Proof of Imām(s)):** This refers to 'Ali ibn 'Abdil-'Azīz ibn 'Umar ibn Māzah, who they also call *Ṣadr al-A'immah.*

ويطلقون «برهان الأئمة» على عبد العزيز بن عمر بن مازه، وقد يطلقون عليه الصدر الكبير.

***Tāj ash-Sharī'ah* (the Crown of Islamic Law):** This refers to Maḥmūd ibn Aḥmad ibn 'Ubaydullāh ibn Ibrāhīm (d. 673 A.H.).

و«تاج الشريعة» عندهم محمود بن أحمد بن عبيد الله بن إبراهيم المتوفى سنة ٣٧٦هـ

***Ṣadr ash-Sharī'ah* (the Vanguard of Islamic Law):** This refers to 'Ubaydullāh ibn Mas'ūd, and this Mas'ūd is the son of *Tāj ash-Sharī'ah* (d. 673 A.H.). 'Ubaydullāh ibn Mas'ūd was known as the younger *Ṣadr ash-Sharī'ah* or the second of them.

وإذا أطلق «صدر الشريعة» عندهم عنوا به عبيد الله بن مسعود بن تاج الشريعة المتوفى سنة ٧٤٧هـ ويسمى بصدر الشرعية الأصغر أو الثاني.

***Ṣadr ash-Sharī'ah al-Akbar* (The Greatest Vanguard of Islamic Law):** This refers to Aḥmad ibn Jamal ad-Dīn 'Ubaydullāh ibn Ibrāhīm al-Maḥbūbi, which makes this Aḥmad the father of *Tāj ash-Sharī'ah*. Thus, he is also known as the first *Ṣadr ash-Sharī'ah*.

أما «صدر الشريعة الأكبر» أو «الأول» فهو أحمد بن جمال الدين عبيد الله بن إبراهيم المحبوبي والد تاج الشريعة.

Imām Mālik ibn Anas

I. Lineage

He is Abū 'Abdillāh Mālik ibn Anas ibn Mālik ibn Abi 'Āmir al-Aṣbahi, from the family of Ḥimyar ibn Saba' al-Akbar, descending from the family of Yashjub ibn Qaḥṭān.[1]

He was born in 95 A.H. and died in 179 A.H. in Madinah. He died at either 84 years of age, or at 90 years according to the records of al-Wāqidi.[2]

Al-Khaṭib at-Tabrīzi said about him, "He is the scholar of the scholars, and the instructor of the Imām(s)."[3] Imām Mālik was brought up in a house of knowledge, for his great grandfather, Abū 'Āmir, was a celebrated Companion who participated in all the battles alongside the Prophet (ﷺ), with the exception of the Battle of Badr. Others say he was of the earliest of the Successors. Mālik's grandfather, who was also named Mālik, was a great scholar of the Successors and one of the four men who carried the body of the caliph 'Uthmān (may Allah be pleased with him) to his grave under the cover of the night. The paternal uncle of Imām Mālik, Abū Suhayl Nāfi' ibn Mālik ibn 'Āmir, was also one of the greatest scholars and nobles of the Successors. Imām Mālik narrated hadith(s) from his uncle in his book *al-Muwaṭṭa'*. He may have also reported hadith(s) from his father, through his grandfather, in books other than *al-Muwatta'*.[4]

Imām Mālik became outstandingly skilled in the narration and verification of Hadith. He also had become versed in the *Fiqh* of the Qur'an and Sunnah, and inherited the knowledge of his predecessors from among the Companions and Successors. Thus, he was of the most celebrated Imām(s) in both sciences, *Fiqh* and Hadith.

1 *Jāmi' al-Uṣūl* 1/180
2 Ibid. For a more elaborate biography of Imām Mālik, see *Siyar A'lām an-Nubalā'* 8/48.
3 *Al-Ikmāl fī Asmā' ar-Rijāl*; *al-Mishkāh* 3/787
4 *Al-Fikr as-Sāmi* 1/376

الإمام مالك بن أنس

أولاً: نسبه وعصره:

هو أبو عبد الله مالك بن أنس بن مالك بن أبي عامر الأصبحي، من بني حمير بن سبأ الأكبر، ثم من بني يشجب بن قطحان(١).

ولد سنة خمس وتسعين من الهجرة، ومات بالمدينة سنة تسع وسبعين ومائة، وله أربع وثمانون سنة، وقال الواقدي: مات وله تسعون سنة(٢).

قال فيه الخطيب التبريزي: «هو شيخ العلماء، وأستاذ الأئمة»(٣)، كان بيت الإمام مالك بيت علم، فجده الأعلى أبو عامر صحابي جليل، شهد المشاهد كلها مع رسول الله ﷺ خلا بدراً، وقيل: إنه تابعي مخضرم، وجده الأسفل مالك من كبار علماء التابعين، وهو أحد الأربعة الذين حملوا عثمان إلى قبره ليلاً، وعم الإمام وهو أبو سهيل: نافع بن مالك بن أبي عامر من جلة علماء التابعين وسادتهم، روى عنه في «الموطأ»، وربما روى مالك عن أبيه عن جده في غير «الموطأ»(٤).

تبحّر الإمام مالك في رواية الحديث وضبطه، والتفقه في الكتاب والسنة، وتلقى علم سلفه من الصحابة والتابعين، فكان إماماً في الحديث، إماماً في الفقه.

١ جامع الأصول: ١/ ١٨٠.
٢ المصدر السابق: وإن شئت التوسع في الاطلاع على ترجمة الإمام مالك، فعليك بسير أعلام النبلاء: ٨/ ٤٨.
٣ الإكمال في أسماء الرجال، انظر المشكاة: ٣/ ٧٨٧.
٤ الفكر السامي: ١/ ٣٧٦.

II. His Teachers and Disciples

Imām Mālik is a scholar from the generation following the Successors. He acquired knowledge directly from Muhammad ibn Shihāb az-Zuhri, Yaḥya ibn Sa'īd al-Anṣāri, Nāfi' the bondsman of 'Abdullāh ibn 'Umar, Muhammad ibn al-Munkadir, Hishām ibn 'Urwah ibn az-Zubayr and others.[1]

As for Imām Mālik's disciples, there are too many to count. Of them was ash-Shāfi'i, Muhammad ibn Ibrāhīm ibn Dinār, Abū Hishām al-Mughīrah ibn 'Abdur-Rahmān al-Makhzūmi and countless others.[2] These disciples were the teachers of al-Bukhāri, Muslim, Abū Dāwūd, at-Tirmidhi, Aḥmad ibn Ḥanbal, Yaḥya ibn Ma'īn and other renowned scholars of Hadith.[3]

III. The Fundamentals of Mālik's Madhhab

Imām Mālik (may Allah bestow mercy upon him) inherited the knowledge of the people of Ḥijāz at large and the people of Madinah in particular. Ibn Taymiyah said, "There is no doubt that Imām Mālik was the best to lead the *Fiqh* school of Madinah due to his mastery of both the Prophetic narrations and juristic opinions. None from his generation, nor the following generations, had juristic talent equivalent to his. Furthermore, the admiration he enjoyed in the hearts of the Muslims – the layman and the scholar alike – was not hidden from anyone that possessed the slightest glimpse of knowledge."[4]

He added, "It was said that Mālik reported most of the hadith(s) of *al-Muwaṭṭa'* from Rabī'ah, who narrated them from Sa'īd ibn al-Musayyib, who narrated them from 'Umar, who was a primary source of hadith."[5]

Ibn al-Madīni said, "Imām Mālik would frequently adopt the views of Sulaymān ibn Yasār, and Sulaymān ibn Yasār would adopt the views of 'Umar ibn al-Khaṭṭāb."[6]

1 *Jāmi' al-Usūl* 1/180
2 *Jāmi' al-Usūl* 1/181
3 *Jāmi' al-Usūl* 1/181
4 *Ṣiḥḥat 'Amal Ahl al-Madīnah* 33
5 Ibid: 29
6 *Ad-Dībāj al-Mudhahhab* by Ibn Farhūn and *al-Fikr as-Sāmi* 1/384

ثانياً: شيوخه وتلاميذه:

الإمام مالك من علماء أتباع التابعين أخذ العلم عن محمد بن شهاب الزهري، ويحيى بن سعيد الأنصاري، ونافع مولى عبد الله بن عمر، ومحمد بن المنكدر، وهشام بن عروة بن الزبير، وخلق كثير غيرهم(١).

وأخذ العلم عنه خلق كثير لا يحصون كثرة منهم: الشافعي، ومحمد بن إبراهيم بن دينار، وأبو هشام المغيرة بن عبد الرحمن المخزومي، وغير هؤلاء ممن لا يحصى عدده(٢)، وهؤلاء مشايخ البخاري، ومسلم، وأبي داود، والترمذي، وأحمد بن حنبل، ويحيى بن معين، وغيرهم من أئمة الحديث(٣).

ثالثاً: قواعد مذهب الإمام مالك:

ورث الإمام مالك- رحمه الله تعالى- علم أهل الحجاز عامة والمدينة خاصة، يقول ابن تيمية- رحمه الله-: «لا ريب عند أحد أن مالكاً ﷺ أقوم الناس بمذهب أهل المدينة رواية ورأياً، فإنه لم يكن في عصره ولا بعده أقوم بذلك منه، كان له من المكانة عند أهل الإسلام- الخاص منهم والعام- ما لا يخفى على من له بالعلم أدنى إلمام»(٤).

وقال أيضاً: «يقال: إن مالكاً أخذ جل «الموطأ» عن ربيعة، وربيعة عن سعيد بن المسيب، وسعيد بن المسيب عن عمر، وعمر محدث»(٥). وقال ابن المديني: «كان مالك يذهب إلى قول سليمان بن يسار، وسليمان بن يسار يذهب إلى قول عمر بن الخطاب»(٦).

١ جامع الأصول: ١/ ١٨٠.
٢ جامع الأصول: ١/ ١٨١.
٣ المصدر السابق: ١/ ١٨١.
٤ صحة عمل أهل المدينة: ٣٣.
٥ المصدر السابق: ٢٩.
٦ الديباج المذهب لابن فرحون، وانظر الفكر السامي: ١/ ٣٨٤.

Imām Mālik had not written down the fundamentals of his *madhhab,* the principles upon which he deduced rulings or his method of *ijtihād.* He did, however, mention some of them and hint at others.

Based on those he mentioned, hinted at, extracted by the jursists of his *madhhab* by studying his views or by his opinions that are recorded in *al-Muwaṭṭa'*, the core fundamentals of Mālik's *madhhab* are: the Qur'an, the Sunnah, scholarly consensus, consensus of the people of Madinah, *qiyās,* the views of the Companions, public interests, customs, *sadd adh-dharā'i'* (precautionary measures), *istiḥsān* (juristic preference) and *istiṣḥāb* (circumstantial consideration).[1]

IV. Mālik's View on the Practices of the People of Madinah

Historic debates took place between Imām Mālik and the adherents of his *madhhab,* and between many of the other scholars and Imām(s) regarding the practices of the people of Madinah. Imām Mālik (may Allah bestow mercy upon him) viewed that, "When the people of Madinah unanimously agree on something, this is regarded as undisputable consensus even if others oppose it."[2]

Based on this, the Māliki *madhhab* gives precedence to the practices of the people of Madinah, when they are unanimously agreed upon, over *qiyās* and authentic *āḥād* hadith(s).[3] Whoever reads the book of Imām al-Layth ibn Sa'd (may Allah bestow mercy upon him) becomes certain that the scholars did not interpolate this as one of the practices of Imām Mālik, and that his *madhhab* is in fact to consider their practices as a proof and evidence.[4]

والإمام مالك لم يدون أصول مذهبه وقواعده في الاستنباط ومناهجه في الاجتهاد، وإن كان قد صرح ببعضها، وأشار إلى بعض آخر.

وجماع أصول مذهب مالك، بناء على ما صرح به، أو أشار إليه، أو استنبطه فقهاء مذهبه من الفروع المنقولة عنه، والآراء المدونة في موطئه هي: الكتاب، السنة، الإجماع، إجماع أهل المدينة، القياس، قول الصحابي، المصلحة المرسلة، العرف والعادات، سد الذرائع، الاستحسان، الاستصحاب[١].

رابعاً: عمل أهل المدينة عند مالك:

احتدم الجدل بين الإمام مالك- رحمه الله- وأتباع مذهبه، وبين كثير من العلماء والأئمة في عمل أهل المدينة، فذهب الإمام مالك- رحمه الله تعالى- إلى أنه «إذا أجمع أهل المدينة على شيء صار إجماعاً مقطوعاً عليه، وإن خالفهم فيه غيرهم»[٢]، وهم يذهبون في هذا إلى تقديم عمل أهل المدينة المجمع عليه على القياس وأخبار الآحاد الصحيحة[٣]، ومن طالع كتاب الإمام الليث بن سعد- رحمه الله- علم أن العلماء لم يتقوّلوا على الإمام مالك، وأن مذهبه اعتبار عملهم حجة ودليلاً[٤].

---

1 *Al-Imām Mālik* 258 by Abū Zahrah, *al-Madārik* 578 by al-Qādi 'Iyād and *ad-Dībāj al-Mudhahhab* 66 by Ibn Farḥūn
2 *Al-Muswaddah* 331 by Ibn Taymiyah
3 *Al-Fikr as-Sāmi* 1/388
4 To learn more about this matter, review our book *al-Madāris wal-Madhāhib al-Fiqhiyyah* 115.

١ الإمام مالك لأبي زهرة: ٢٥٨، والمدارك للقاضي عياض: ٥٧٨، والديباج المذهب لابن فرحون: ٦٦.
٢ المسودة لابن تيمية: ٣٣١.
٣ الفكر السامي: ١/ ٣٨٨.
٤ للتوسع في هذه المسألة راجع كتابنا: المدارس والمذاهب الفقهية: ١١٥.

V. Compiling the Madhhab of Mālik & the Māliki Jurists

Imām Mālik wrote *al-Muwaṭṭa'*, a book in which he collected hadith(s), the legal opinions of the Companions and Successors, as well as which views he concluded were strongest. We have already mentioned above the method he followed in writing his book and deducing his views.

When teaching, Imām Mālik followed a method of inculcation that was void of any discussion or debate with his students. His disciples would simply write down all the hadith(s), Companions' reports, and legal opinions they had heard from Imām Mālik regarding the legal cases presented to him. He would only give legal opinions to actual cases that took place and was averse to hypothetical cases.

The legal opinions of Imām Mālik are not confined to those in *al-Muwaṭṭa'*. His disciples would also hear his legal opinions from him directly, memorize them and spread them to the far corners of the Muslim world.

The most famous book on Māliki *Fiqh, after al-Muwaṭṭa'*, is *al-Mudawwanah* by Saḥnūn. Principally, *al-Mudawwanah* is based on the book *al-Asadiyyah*, referring to Asad ibn al-Furāt who died in 213 A.H.

Asad ibn al-Furāt met Imām Mālik and learned *al-Muwaṭṭa'* in its entirety from him. He then went to Iraq where he met Abū Ḥanīfah's disciples and learned the basics of Ḥanafi *Fiqh* from them. He then brought these Ḥanafi views to Ibn al-Qāsim, seeking to know Mālik's views on these cases.[1]

'Abdur-Rahmān ibn al-Qāsim was one of those who accompanied Imām Mālik and studied under him for a long time. He accompanied Mālik for twenty years, during which he memorized his legal opinions. According to some reports, it was said that he memorized three hundred skins filled with the opinions held by Imām Mālik.[2]

1 *Al-Fikr as-Sāmi* 2/95 and *Muqaddimat Ibn Khaldūn* 806
2 *Al-Fikr as-Sāmi* 1/439

خامساً: تدوين مذهب مالك ودواوين مذهب المالكية:

دون الإمام مالك كتابه «الموطأ»، وهو كتاب خلط فيه الحديث بفقه الصحابة والتابعين، وما تبين له وذهب إليه، وقد بينا منهجه الذي سار عليه في تأليفه وفقهه.

وكان الإمام مالك في تدريسه ينهج الطريقة الإلقائية الخالية من المناقشة والجدال مع تلامذته، وكان تلامذته يدونون ما يروي لهم من أحاديث وآثار، وما يقوله من فتاوى في المسائل التي تعرض عليه، وكان لا يُجيب إلا على المسائل الواقعة، وينفر من الفقه الافتراضي.

وفقه مالك ليس مقصوراً على «المَوَطَّأ»؛ فقد تلقى تلامذته عنه فقهه وحفظوه ونقلوه إلى مختلف أصقاع العالم الإسلامي.

وأشهر الكتب في الفقه المالكي بعد «الموطأ» كتاب «المدونة» لسحنون، وأصل المدونة هو كتاب الأسدية، نسبة إلى أسد بن الفرات المتوفى سنة ٢١٣هـ.

أدرك أسد بن الفرات الإمام مالك وأخذ عنه الموطأ، ثم ارتحل إلى العراق، فالتقى هناك بتلامذة الإمام أبي حنيفة، وتفقه بهم، وأخذ فقه الحنفية مجرداً، وحمله إلى ابن القاسم، ليقول له ما يراه مالك في تلك المسائل(١).

وعبد الرحمن بن القاسم من الذين صحبوا مالكاً طويلاً ولازموه، فقد صحبه عشرين سنة، وحفظ عنه مسائله، يقال: إنه حفظ عنه ثلاثمائة جلد من مسائله(٢).

١ الفكر السامي: ٢/ ٩٥، مقدمة ابن خلدون: ٨٠٦.
٢ الفكر السامي: ١/ ٤٣٩.

Asad ibn al-Furāt recorded the responses Ibn al-Qāsim gave to those cases he presented to him. Then, Asad returned to Qayrawān, where he worked as a judge, spread these opinions there and named his book *al-Asadiyyah.*[1]

Many Māliki jurists did not approve this method adopted by Asad ibn al-Furāt in his book *al-Asadiyyah,* for it applied the views of Imām Mālik to those of the Ḥanafi *madhhab,* and Imām Mālik (may Allah bestow mercy upon him) used to reject entertaining hypothetical *Fiqh* which the Ḥanafi *madhhab* became known for. From another angle, Māliki *Fiqh* – just like Shāfi'i and Ḥanbali *Fiqh* – used to depend on the texts of the Qur'an and Sunnah when deducing legal rulings and would cite the evidences alongside every ruling; this is clear to whoever examines how Mālik constructed his book *al-Muwaṭṭa'*. As for the works of the Ḥanafi *madhhab,* they contain bare rulings; the evidences were not mentioned by the founders of the *madhhab* at the time of compilation.

Asad ibn al-Furāt wanted the Māliki *madhhab* to become like the Ḥanafi *madhhab,* for he had become infatuated with studying Ḥanafi *Fiqh.* Thus, he journeyed during the lifetime of Mālik to Iraq, and studied under Muhammad ibn al-Ḥasan who was the direct disciple of Abū Ḥanīfah. His aim was that the Māliki jurists develop answers for the [hypothetical] cases existent in Ḥanafi *Fiqh.*

1 *Muqaddimat Ibn Khaldūn* 806 and *al-Fikr as-Sāmi* 1/439

وقد دوَّن أسد بن الفرات إجابات ابن القاسم في المسائل التي عرضها عليه، وعاد بها إلى القيروان حيث كان يعمل قاضياً هناك، ونشرها في تلك الديار، وسمي مؤلفه بالأسدية(١).

ولم يرتض كثير من فقهاء المالكية المنهج الذي سلكته الأسدية حيث إنزلت آراء مالك على فقه الحنفية، فالإمام مالك- رحمه الله- كان يرفض الفقه الفرضي التقديري الذي عرف به الحنفية، ومن جهة أخرى فإن الفقه المالكي مثله في ذلك مثل الفقه الشافعي والحنبلي، كان يعتمد النصوص من الكتاب والسنة ويبني عليها الأحكام، ويقرن الأحكام بأدلتها، وهذا ظاهر فيما قام به الإمام مالك في موطئه، بينما كانت مدونات الفقه الحنفي فقهاً مجرداً خلت من ذكر الأدلة عند تدوينها على يد مؤسسي المذهب.

لقد أراد أسد بن الفرات أن يكون للمالكية فقه كفقه الحنفية، وقد أغرم أسد بدراسة الفقه الحنفي، فرحل في حياة مالك إلى العراق، ولازم محمد بن الحسن صاحب أبي حنيفة، فأراد من فقهاء المالكية أن يجيبوا على مسائل الفقه الحنفي.

١ مقدمة ابن خلدون: ٨٠٦، الفكر السامي: ١/ ٤٣٩.

Asad returned with his *Fiqh* book to Tunisia, and the Māliki jurists noticed that the method upon which this book was based differed from the methods adopted by Imām Mālik. Rather, they noticed that the detailed rulings themselves differed from those viewed by the Māliki jurists. One of these jurists was 'Abdus-Salām ibn Sa'īd at-Tanūkhi, also known as Saḥnūn. He returned Asad's record to Ibn al-Qāsim and suggested to him that he reconsider its contents and to verify whether or not it actually conformed with what had been narrated about Imām Mālik. Ibn Khaldūn reported that Ibn al-Qāsim recanted the legal views documented in *al-Asadiyyah,* and that Saḥnūn recorded whatever Ibn al-Qāsim dictatied to him, either pertaining to his revised views or his previous views which officially retracted. Then, Ibn al-Qāsim sent a message with Saḥnūn requesting that Asad remove from *al-Asadiyyah* all that he recanted and to follow the records of Saḥnūn. Asad refused this request, and so the people abandoned his book and followed the book by Saḥnūn which is named *al-Mudawwanah.* Another of its names is *al-Mukhṭalatah* – meaning that which is mixed – because some of its cases were placed in other than their chapter of relevance. Thus, Saḥnūn filtered his book *al-Mudawwanah* from what flawed it, and reinfused it with the actual approach of Imām Mālik in his *Fiqh*.

Since then, *al-Mudawwanah* has been regarded as the primary source of Māliki *Fiqh* after *al-Muwaṭṭa'*. The Māliki jurists allotted great care to this book, to the degree that commentaries for it were written, its hadith(s) were rigorously verified and its text was abridged. This book is regarded as a main reference for all Māliki jurists everywhere, including Andalusia, Morocco, Iraq and Egypt.

عـاد أسـد بالمدونـة إلى تونـس، ولاحـظ فقهـاء المالكيـة، المنهج الـذي بنيـت عليـه المدونـة المخالفـة لمنهجيـة الإمـام مالـك، بـل لاحظـوا أن بعـض الفـروع تختلـف عـما عليـه الفتـوى عندهـم، وكان مـن هـؤلاء عبـد السـلام بـن سـعيد التنوخـي الملقـب بسـحنون، فحمـل المدونـة مـرة أخـرى وعـاد بهـا إلى ابـن القاسـم، واقـترح عليـه إعـادة النظـر فيهـا، والتدقيـق في ذكـر فقـه الإمـام مالـك بحسـب المـروي عنـه، وقـد ذكـر ابـن خلـدون أن ابـن القاسـم رجـع عـن كثـير مـن المسـائل التـي دونهـا في «الأسـدية»، وأن سـحنون كتـب مـا أمـلاه عليـه ابـن القاسـم ودونـه، وأثبـت مـا رجـع عنـه منهـا، وكتـب ابـن القاسـم مـع سـحنون، إلى أسـد مطالبـاً إيـاه بـأن يمحـو مـن أسـديته مـا رجـع عنـه، وأن يأخـذ بكتـاب سـحنون، فأنـف مـن ذلـك، فـترك النـاس كتابـه واتبعـوا مدونة سـحنون ويسـمى كتابـه المدونـة، كـما يسـمى المختلطـة؛ لأن بعـض المسـائل وضعـت في غـير الأبـواب المناسـبة لهـا[1]، وبذلـك صفـى سـحنون المدونـة مـما شـابها، وأعـاد إليهـا صيغـة الإمـام مالـك في فقهـه.

وأصبحـت المدونـة هـي الكتـاب الأول عنـد فقهـاء المالكيـة بعـد «الموطـأ»؛ ولـذا فـإن علـماء المالكيـة إذا أطلقـوا اسـم الكتـاب انـصرف عندهـم إلى المدونـة، وقـد اعتنـى بهـا فقهـاء المالكيـة عنايـة كبـيرة، فكانـت مـدار بحثهـم، وتناولوهـا بالروايـة وبالـشرح والاختصـار، وهـي عمـدة عندهـم عـلى اختـلاف بلادهـم، فهـي عمـدة عنـد الأندلسـيين والمغاربـة كـما هـي عمـدة عنـد العراقيـين والمصريـين.

---

١ مقدمة ابن خلدون: ٨٠٧.

The great Andalusian jurist 'Abdul-Malik ibn Habīb as-Sulami wrote the book *al-Wāḍihah fī al-Fiqh was-Sunan* in which he relied on the Prophetic hadith(s), particularly those mentioned in the book *al-Muwaṭṭa'*, and thoroughly explained them. He also included other hadith(s) and sayings of the Companions and Successors. 'Abdul-Mālik followed the same method in his book that Imām Mālik followed in *al-Muwaṭṭa'*, and then added atop all that: the views of Imām Mālik, the views of the Māliki scholars who studied under him and those after them. Finally, he included his own independent conclusions that are scattered throughout the book.

The book *al-Wāḍihah* was a source of pride for the scholars of the Māliki *madhhab*, and remained that way until *al-'Atabiyyah* was written.

Muhammad ibn Aḥmad al-'Atabi al-Andalusi wrote the book *al-'Atabiyyah*, which is also known as *al-Mustakhrajah*. The Andalusian scholars relied mainly on this book and turned away from *al-Wāḍihah* and others. In this book, al-'Atabi recorded the views of Imām Mālik and those of his most knowledgable disciples. Al-'Atabi included therein all that has been narrated about Imām Mālik, but without verifying or cross-referencing with other narrations. For this reason, his book was replete with weak narrations and inconsistent rulings.

In his book *al-Bayān wat-Tahṣil*, Ibn Rushd pointed out which narrations of *al-'Atabiyyah* were actually authentic.

Muhammad ibn Ibrāhīm al-Iskandari, who was known as Ibn al-Mawwāz, wrote a book that became known as *al-Mawwāziyyah*. It is the greatest book ever produced by the Mālikis, was the most correct in its rulings and was most comprehensive and extensive in its discourse.

ودوَّن عالم الأندلس الكبير عبد الملك بن حبيب السلمي كتاب «الواضحة في الفقه والسنن»، وقد اعتمد فيها على أحاديث الرسول ﷺ، وخاصة: «الموطأ»، وقد أفرده بالشرح، وتناول غيره من الأحاديث، كما اعتمد أقوال الصحابة والتابعين، وطريقته في واضحته كطريقة مالك في موطئه، وضمت إلى هذا كله فقه مالك وفقه علماء المالكية من تلامذة الإمام فمن بعدهم، وللمؤلف اجتهادات واضحة منثورة في كتابه.

وقد كانت الواضحة مفخرة علماء المالكية ومرجعهم حتى ظهور العتبية.

وألف محمد بن أحمد العتبي الأندلسي كتاب «العتبية» أو «المستخرجة»، وقد اعتمد عليها علماء الأندلس وهجروا الواضحة وغيرها، وقد دون العتبي فيها آراء مالك، وآراء تلامذته الأعلام من بعده، وقد حفظ العتبي في مؤلفه المسمى باسمه مرويات الإمام مالك، إلا أنه لم يمحص هذه الروايات، ولم يقارنها بالمرويات الأخرى، ولذا كثرت فيها الروايات المطروحة والمسائل الغريبة الشاذة.

وقد ميز صحيح روايات العتبية، ابن رشد في كتابه «البيان والتحصيل».

ودون محمد بن إبراهيم الإسكندري المعروف بابن المواز مؤلفاً عرف بنسبته إليه، فقد سمي بـ «الموازية»، وهو أجل كتاب ألفه المالكيون وأصحه مسائل، وأبسطه كلاماً وأوعبه.

The judge Isma'īl ibn Isḥāq, who was one of the Māliki jurists of Iraq, wrote the book *al-Mabsūṭ*. This book illustrates the methods followed by the Māliki jurists of Iraq in both *Fiqh* and compilation.

When the Māliki jurists use the term *Dīwān* (pl. *Dawāwīn*), this refers to the seven books mentioned above: *al-Mudawwanah, al-Wāḍihah, al-'Atabiyyah, al-Mawwāziyyah, al-Asadiyyah, al-Mabsūṭ* and *al-Majmū'*. They use the term *al-Ummahāt* (the primaries) in reference to the first four books mentioned above. In reality, the *Dīwān*(s) are actually six because *al-Mudawannah* is the revised version of *al-Asadiyyah* after it was brought back to Ibn al-Qāsim.

VI. Terms Used in Māliki Fiqh

This is a summary of terms in the Māliki *madhhab*, taken from the introduction of *Masā'il lā Yu'dhar fīhā bil-Jahl* by Shaykh Ibrāhīm al-Mukhtar Aḥmad 'Umar al-Jabarti az-Zayla'i. Therein, he states that he collected these terms from the book *Mawahib al-Jalīl* by al-Ḥaṭṭab, from the introduction of *Hāshiyat al-'Adawi 'alal-Kharshi*, and *Ḥāshiyat* ad-Dasuqi 'alā Sharḥ *al-Kabīr*, from *ad-Dībāj* by Ibn Farḥūn, from *Nafḥ aṭ-Ṭīb* by al-Muqri, and from other books on the Māliki *madhhab*. By learning these terms, the student becomes familiar with the expressions used by the scholars of that *madhhab*.

Here are some recurrent terms in Māliki *Fiqh*:

The People of Madinah: This term refers to the followers of Imām Mālik – namely Ibn Kinānah, Ibn al-Mājishun, Mutarrif, Ibn Nāfi', Ibn Maslamah and their peers.

The Egyptians: This term refers to Ibn al-Qāsim, Ashhab, Ibn Wahb, Aṣbagh ibn al-Faraj, Ibn 'Abdil-Hakam and their peers.

The Iraqis: This term refers to the judge Isma'īl ibn Isḥāq, the judge Abūl-Ḥasan ibn al-Qaṣṣār, Ibn al-Jallāb, the judge 'Abdul-Wahhāb, the judge Abūl-Faraj, Shaykh Abū Bakr al-Abhuri and their peers.

وألف القاضي إسماعيل بن إسحاق أحد فقهاء مالكية العراق كتاب «المبسوط»، وكتابه هذا يظهر طريقة فقهاء مالكية العراق في الفقه والتدوين.

وإذا أطلق فقهاء المالكية اسم الدواوين، فإنهم يطلقونها على هذه المؤلفات السبعة التي ذكرناها، وهي: المدونة، والواضحة، والعتبية، والموازنة، والأسدية، والمبسوطة، والمجموعة.

وإذا أطلقوا الأمهات، فإنهم يريدون بها الأربع الأولى من الدواوين، والحق أن الدواوين ستة؛ لأن الأسدية هي المدونة بعد إعادة ابن القاسم النظر فيها.

سادساً: اصطلاحات المالكية:

هذه نبذة من اصطلاحات المالكية لخصتها من كلام الشيخ إبراهيم المختار أحمد عمر الجبرتي الزيلعي في مقدمته لكتاب «مسائل لا يعذر فيها بالجهل»[1]، وصرح أنه جمعها من ديباجة «مواهب الجليل» للحطاب، ومن مقدمة حاشية العدوي على الخرشي، وحاشية الدسوقي على الشرح الكبير، والديباج لابن فرحون، ونفح الطيب للمقري، وغير ذلك من كتب المذهب، ليكون الطالب على بصيرة من عبارات علماء مذهبه.

يريد المالكية بالمدنيين من أتباع مالك: ابن كنانة، وابن الماجشون، ومطرف، وابن نافع، وابن مسلمة، ونظرائهم.

ويطلقون المصريين ويريدون بهم: ابن القاسم، وأشهب، وابن وهب، وأصبغ بن الفرج، وابن عبد الحكم، ونظائرهم.

وعندما يطلقون العراقيين في مدوناتهم يشيرون بهم إلى: القاضي إسماعيل بن إسحاق، والقاضي أبي الحسن بن القصار، وابن الجلاب، والقاضي عبد الوهاب، والقاضي أبي الفرج، والشيخ أبو بكر الأبهري، ونظائرهم.

---

١ مسائل لا يعذر فيها بالجهل على مذهب مالك، دار الغرب الإسلامي، بيروت، لبنان، ط. الثانية (١٤٠٦هـ- ١٩٦٨م).

The Moroccans: This term refers to Shaykh Ibn Abū Zayd, Ibn al-Qābisi, Ibn al-Lubād, al-Bāji, al-Lakhmi, Ibn Muḥriz, Ibn 'Abdil-Barr, Ibn Rushd, Ibn al-'Arabi, Sanad al-Makhzumi, Ibn Shablūn and Ibn Sha'bān.

The Twin Pair: The term refers to Ashhab and Ibn Nāfi' due to the fact that the former was blind, as said by al-'Adawi. However, the earlier Māliki jurists would use this term in reference to Imām Mālik and Ibn 'Uyaynah, as Imām ash-Shāfi'i said, "Imām Mālik and Ibn 'Uyaynah are the twin pair. Were it not for them, the knowledge of Ḥijāz would have been lost."

The Two Brothers: This term refers to Muṭarrif and Ibn al-Mājishun due to the fact that they both agreed upon so many legal opinions.

The Two Judges: This term refers to the judge Ibn al-Qaṣṣār and the judge 'Abdul-Wahhāb.

The Two Muhammad(s): The term refers to Ibn al-Mawwāz and Ibn Saḥnūn. Ibn 'Arafah said that the term refers to Ibn al-Mawwāz and Ibn 'Abdul-Hakam.

The Four Muhammad(s): This term refers to the two from Qarawān: Ibn 'Abdūs and Ibn Saḥnūn, and the two from Egypt: Ibn 'Abdul-Hakam and Ibn al-Mawwaz, who all lived in the same era.

The Imām: This term refers to al-Mazari.

The Shaykh: This term refers to 'Ali ibn Abi Zayd.

أما المغاربة فيشيرون بهم إلى: الشيخ ابن أبي زيد، وابن القابسي، وابن اللباد، والباجي، واللخمي، وابن محرز، وابن عبد البر، وابن رشد، وابن العربي، والقاضي سند المخزومي، وابن شبلون، وابن شعبان.

والقرينان في مدونات المالكية: أشهب، وابن نافع، فقرن أشهب مع ابن نافع لعدم بصره كما ذكره العدوي، وكان المتقدمون يطلقون القرينان على الإمام مالك، وابن عيينة، من ذلك قول الإمام الشافعي: مالك وابن عيينه القرينان، لولاهما لذهب علم الحجاز.

والأخوان: مطرف، وابن الماجشون، وسُمِّيا بذلك لكثرة ما يتفقان عليه.

والقاضيان: القاضي ابن القصار، والقاضي عبد الوهاب.

والمحمدان: ابن المواز، وابن سحنون، وعند ابن عرفة: ابن المواز، وابن عبد الحكم.

والمحمدون أربعة: وهم الذين اجتمعوا في عصر واحد من أئمة مذهب مالك ما لم يجتمع مثلهم في زمان، اثنان قرويان: ابن عبدوس، وابن سحنون، واثنان مصريان: ابن عبد الحكم، وابن المواز.

والإمام في الفقه عندهم: المازري، ويطلق الشيخ عندهم على ابن أبي زيد.

Agreement: This term refers to the agreement by the jurists of the Māliki *madhhab.*

Consensus: This term refers to the consensus of all the scholars.

The Majority: This term refers to the majority of the four *Mujtahid Imām* (s): Mālik, Abū Ḥanīfah, ash-Shāfi'i and Aḥmad ibn Ḥanbal.

*Terms used by Imām Mālik in **al-Muwaṭṭa'**:*
Imām Mālik (may Allah bestow mercy upon him) relieved us of having to investigate and debate the intended meanings behind his choice of terms, for he himself clarified what he meant when using these terms.

Imām Mālik said, "Throughout the book, whenever I said 'my opinion,' this usually is not my [personal] opinion in reality. Rather, it denotes what I heard from many scholars and virtuous imām (s) who truly feared Allah, the Most High. When they were too numerous [to list], I would just say 'my opinion' if this opinion of theirs was an opinion of the Companions which they adopted, and so I subsequently adopted it from them. Hence, this opinion is one that has been inherited by one generation after another until our time.

As for 'an opinion,' this denotes the opinion of a group of preceding imām (s).

As for 'the agreed upon matter,' this denotes the opinion that has been agreed upon by the scholars and jurists and not differed over whatsoever.

As for 'our practice' or 'in our land,' this denotes what the people [of Madinah] have been practicing and basing their rulings upon, and is common knowledge among the scholars and the ignorant alike.

As for 'some scholars,' this denotes a scholarly view that I prefer.

At times, there were matters I did not hear [a ruling for] from them, and so I exercised *ijtihād* and compared it to the views of those I met. I practice this until it appears to be the truth, or close to it, without violating the methods of the people of Madinah. Even though I did not hear this in particular [from them], I still did not adopt a personal view until after performing *ijtihād*, considering the Sunnah, comparing [my view] with the views of the former scholars, and with our [local] practices that have been followed since the Messenger of Allah (ﷺ) and the rightly-guided caliphs. Therefore, I have in fact followed their views and not veered from them."[1]

1 *Ad-Dībāj al-Mudhahhab* 25 by Ibn Farḥun

والمراد بالاتفاق اتفاق أهل المذهب، وبالإجماع إجماع العلماء، وإذا قالوا الجمهور عنوا بهم الأئمة الأربعة

مصطلحات مالك في موطئه:

بيَّن الإمام مالك- رحمه الله تعالى- مراده من بعض ألفاظه التي عبر بها في كتابه الموطأ، فأغنانا بذلك عن الاجتهاد والاختلاف في تحديد مراده من تلك الألفاظ.

فقال مالك: «أما أكثر ما في الكتاب «فرأيي» فلعمري ما هو برأيي، ولكنه سماع من غير واحد من أهل العلم والفضل والأئمة المُهتدَى بهم الذين أخذت عنهم، وهم الذين كانوا يتقون الله تعالى، فكثر علي، فقلت: «رأيي»، وذلك رأيي إذ كان رأيهم رأي الصحابة الذين أدركوهم عليه، وأدركتهم أنا على ذلك.

فهذا وراثة توارثناها قرناً عن قرن إلى زماننا، وما كان «رأياً» فهو رأي جماعة من تقدم من الأئمة، وما كان فيه «الأمر المجتمع عليه»، فهو ما اجتمع عليه من قول أهل الفقه والعلم لم يختلفوا فيه، وما قلت: «الأمر عندنا» فهو ما عمل به الناس، وجرت به الأحكام، وعرفه الجاهل، والعالم، وكذلك ما قلت فيه: «ببلدنا»، وما قلت فيه: بعض أهل العلم، فهو شيء أستحسنه من قول العلماء.

وأما ما لم أسمع منهم، فاجتهدت ونظرت على مذهب من لقيته، حتى وقع ذلك موقع الحق أو قريباً منه، حتى لا يخرج عن مذهب أهل المدينة وآرائهم، وإن لم أسمع ذلك بعينه فما نسبت الرأي إليَّ إلا بعد الاجتهاد مع السنة، وما مضى عليه عمل أهل العلم المقتدى بهم، والأمر المعمول عندنا به- منذ لدن- رسول الله ﷺ والأئمة الراشدين مع من لقيت، فذلك رأيهم ما خرجت إلى غيره»[1].

١ الديباج المذهب لابن فرحون: ٢٥.

Imām ash-Shāfi'i

I. Lineage

He is Imām Abū 'Abillāh Muhammad ibn Idrīs ibn al-'Abbās ibn 'Uthmān ibn Shāfi' ibn as-Sā'ib ibn 'Ubayd ibn 'Abd Yazīd ibn Hāshim ibn al-Muttalib ibn 'Abd Manāf ibn Quṣay al-Qurashi al-Muṭṭtalibi al-Ḥijāzi al-Makki. His lineage meets with the Prophet Muhammad (ﷺ) in his forefather 'Abd Manaf.

Imām ash-Shāfi'i was born in Gaza, though some reports said he was born in 'Asqalan. Both Gaza and 'Asqalan are of the holy lands which Allah has blessed, as they are both not far from Jerusalem. He was taken to Mecca when he was two years of age, and passed away in Egypt. He was born in 150 A.H., the same year as Imām Abū Ḥanīfah's death, and died in 204 A.H.

His grandfather as-Sā'ib embraced Islam on the Day of Badr. He fought as a pagan against the Muslims in the Battle of Badr, in which he was carrying the flag of Banu Hāshim, and was taken captive by the Muslim army. He ransomed himself and then embraced Islam.

II. His Teachers and Disciples

Imām ash-Shāfi'i first acquired the knowledge of the people of Hijāz. He learned *Fiqh* at the hands of Muslim ibn Khalid az-Zinji.[1] Then, he journeyed to Imām Mālik and accompanied him for a long period, during which he studied *al-Muwaṭṭa'* from Mālik himself. Imām Mālik said to him, "Fear Allah and avoid sins, for you will become something special." He then headed to Iraq, debated with Muhammad ibn al-Ḥasan and became well-known in Iraq and elsewhere. People from the farthest horizons came to benefit from his knowledge: both the young and old, and even the greatest scholars of *Fiqh*, Hadith, and otherwise – such as Aḥmad ibn Ḥanbal, Abū Thawr, al-Ḥusayn ibn 'Ali al-Karābisi, al-Ḥārith ibn Shūrayḥ al-Baqqāl, az-Za'farāni and others.[2]

1 Ibid: 10/252
2 Ibid: 10/252

الإمام الشافعي

أولاً: نسبه وعصره:

هو الإمام أبو عبد الله محمد بن إدريس بن العباس بن عثمان بن شافع بن السائب بن عبيد بن عبد يزيد بن هاشم بن المطلب بن عبد مناف بن قصي القرشي المطلبي الحجازي المكي، يلتقي مع رسول الله ﷺ في عبد مناف.

ولد الشافعي بغزة، وقيل: بعسقلان، وهما من الأراضي المقدسة التي بارك الله فيها، فإنهما على نحو مرحلتين من بيت المقدس، ثم حمل إلى مكة وهو ابن سنتين، وتوفي بمصر، وكانت ولادته في سنة ١٥٠هـ وهي السنة التي توفي فيها الإمام أبو حنيفة، ووفاته في سنة ٢٠٤هـ.

أسلم جده السائب في يوم بدر، وكان قد شهد بدراً مشركاً، وكان حامل راية بني هاشم، فأسر، وفدى نفسه، وأسلم.

ثانياً: شيوخه وتلامذته:

أخذ الشافعي علم أهل الحجاز، فقد أخذ الفقه عن مسلم بن خالد الزنجي[١]، ورحل إلى الإمام مالك ولزمه، وقرأ عليه «الموطأ»، وقال له الإمام مالك: «اتق الله، واجتنب المعاصي، فإنه سيكون لك شأن»، ورحل إلى العراق، وناظر محمد بن الحسن، واشتهر الشافعي في العراق، وفي الآفاق، وعظم قدره، وارتفعت مرتبته، عكف عليه للاستفادة الصغار والكبار، والأئمة والأحبار من أهل الحديث والفقه وغيرهم، مثل أحمد بن حنبل، وأبو ثور، والحسين بن علي الكرابيسي، والحارث بن شريح البقال، والزعفراني وغيرهم[٢].

١ المصدر السابق: ١٠/ ٢٥٢.
٢ المصدر السابق: ١٠/ ٢٥٢.

III. The Fundamentals of Shāfiʿī's Madhhab

Imām ash-Shāfiʿī (may Allah bestow mercy upon him) had an exceptional mind, sharp intellect and deep insight. He had the capacity to collect various sciences from the jurists of Islam. He acquired the knowledge of Ḥijāz and mastered their *Fiqh*, memorized the Qur'an and much of the Sunnah, interacted with *Ahl ar-Ra'y* and considered their methods. After maturing in knowledge and intellect, he was able to draw out a unique method through which one can correctly arrive at the juristic rulings.

Initially, Imām ash-Shāfiʿī followed the Māliki *madhhab* but later he developed his own distinct *madhhab* after traveling through the lands of Islam, meeting the scholars and debating them. He authored his book *al-Hujjah* in Iraq, and its views are known as those of "ash-Shāfiʿī's old *madhhab*." It earned this name because ash-Shāfiʿī recanted some of his views that are written there upon settling in Egypt. In Egypt, he authored his book *al-Umm*, which represents his "new *madhhab*." He also authored his book *ar-Risālah* in Iraq, and it is considered the first book ever written on the science of *Uṣūl al-Fiqh* (the fundamentals of jurisprudence). For this reason, Imām ash-Shāfiʿī is regarded as the father of *Uṣūl al-Fiqh*.

Imām ash-Shāfiʿī mentions the fundamentals of his *madhhab* and his methods of deduction in his books. For instance, he writes in *ar-Risālah*, "No one can ever say that something is lawful or unlawful except by way of knowledge; knowledge means being informed through the Qur'an, Sunnah, scholarly consensus or *qiyās*."[1]

Part of his *madhhab* was not giving precedence to any evidence over the Qur'an and Sunnah. He says in *al-Umm*, "Nothing can be resorted to, aside from the Qur'an and Sunnah, whenever they are present."[2]

---

1 *Ar-Risālah* 39 and similar words on p. 58
2 *Kitāb al-Umm* 7/346

ثالثاً: أصول مذهبه:

كان الشافعي- رحمه الله- ذا عقل ثاقب وفكر راجح وبصيرة نيرة، وقد استطاع أن يستوعب علوم فقهاء الإسلام، فقد أخذ علم أهل الحجاز وفقههم، وحفظ الكتاب والسنن، وخالط أهل الرأي، ونظر في طريقتهم، واستطاع بعد نضوجه العلمي أن يضع منهجاً فذّاً للطريقة التي ينبغي أن يسار عليها في التوصل إلى الأحكام.

وقد كان الشافعي على مذهب مالك في بداية أمره، ولكنه استقل بمذهب عرف به بعد رحلاته في الأمصار الإسلامية، ومقابلته للعلماء، ومناظرته لهم، وقد ألّف كتاب «الحجة» في العراق، وهو ما يسمى بمذهب الشافعي القديم، وسمي بذلك لأنه رجع عن بعض أقواله فيه عندما استقر بمصر، وفي مصر ألّف كتابه «الأم»، وهو يمثل مذهبه الجديد، وألّف كتابه «الرسالة» في العراق، ويعد كتاب «الرسالة» أول كتاب يؤلف في علم «أصول الفقه»؛ ولذلك فإنه يعد واضع علم أصول الفقه.

والإمام الشافعي ذكر أصول مذهبه ومنهجه في الاستنباط في كتبه، ففي كتابه الرسالة يقول: «ليس لأحد أبداً أن يقول في شيء حل ولا حرم إلا من جهة العلم، وجهة العلم الخبر في الكتاب أو السنة أو الإجماع أو القياس»(١).

وهو يرى تقدم الكتاب والسنة على بقية الأدلة، قال في «الأم»: «لا يصار إلى شيء غير الكتاب والسنة وهما موجودان»(٢).

---

١ الرسالة: ٣٩، وقريب منه في: ٥٨.
٢ كتاب الأم: ٧ /٣٤٦.

He would also accept the *āḥād* reports as proof so long as the narrators are trustworthy and credible. He did not stipulate that it pertain to matters that are avoidable like the Ḥanafis, nor that it agree with the practices of the people of Madinah like the Mālikis. All he stipulated was the authenticity of the chain and nothing else.

Unlike Abū Ḥanīfah and Mālik, ash-Shāfi'i restricted the usage of hadith(s) with *mursal* (incomplete) chains. He stipulated that it be corroborated with another proof, such as being through a narrator that only reports from trustworthy narrators. For this reason, ash-Shāfi'i accepted all the *mursal* hadith(s) reported by Sa'īd ibn al-Musayyib since this condition was met with him. In his book *al-Umm*, Imām ash-Shāfi'i said, "I pay no attention to incomplete chains, except those narrated by Sa'īd ibn al-Musayyib."[1]

Ash-Shāfi'i would take the apparent meanings of the Qur'an and Sunnah; he would not leave the literal interpretation unless evidence arose indicating that the text meant otherwise.

Also, Imām ash-Shāfi'i did not accept *istiḥsān* (juristic preference) as one of his fundamentals, and allotted a chapter in his book *al-Umm* to refuting the principle of *istiḥsān*.[2]

Another principle rejected by ash-Shāfi'i was taking into consideration *al-maṣāliḥ al-mursalah* (public interests) and the practices of the people of Madinah. As for the proof of consensus, Imām ash-Shāfi'i held a different view from the prominent one in *Uṣūl al-Fiqh* regarding the definition of consensus. In his eyes, actual consensus is only that which deals with "the obligatory acts that none can be ignorant about, such as the *ṣalāh*, *zakāh* and prohibiting the unlawful."[3]

As for *aḥād* reports over which no disagreement is known, ash-Shāfi'i does not permit that this be considered a matter of consensus because not knowing [of the disagreement] is not itself an evidence; perhaps they disagreed and he was unaware. Imām ash-Shāfi'i said in this respect, "We believe that they did not differ in whatever we did not know they differed over."[4]

1 Ibid: 7/267
2 Ibid: 7/244
3 Ibid: 7/144
4 Ibid

وهو يحتج بخبر الواحد ما دام راويه ثقة عدلاً، ولا يشترط في خبر الواحد الشهرة فيما تعم به البلوى كما قال الأحناف، ولا أن يوافق عمل أهل المدينة، كما قال مالك، فهو يشترط صحة السند فقط.

ولا يطلق العمل بالمرسل كما فعل أبو حنيفة ومالك، بل قيده بشرط أن يؤيده دليل آخر، كأن يقول راويه لا يرسل إلا عن ثقة؛ ولذلك قبل مراسيل سعيد بن المسيب كلها، لتوافر هذا الشرط فيها، وفي هذا يقول في كتابه «الأم»: «ليس المنقطع بشيء ما عدا منقطع ابن المسيب»(١).

وهو يأخذ بظاهر الكتاب والسنة، لا يعدل عن هذا الظاهر، إلا إذا دل الدليل على أن المراد بالنص غيره.

ولم يجعل الإمام الشافعي من أصوله الاستحسان، وقد عقد في كتابه «الأم» كتاباً بين فيه إبطال القول بالاستحسان(٢).

ومما رفضه الشافعي القول بالمصالح المرسلة، وعمل أهل المدينة، والإجماع الذي يراه الشافعي حجة ليس هو الإجماع الذي اشتهر في كتب الأصوليين، فالإجماع الذي يصح عنده هو الذي يكون «في الفرض الذي لا يسع جهله من الصلوات والزكاة وتحريم الحرام»(٣).

أما أخبار الآحاد التي لا يعلم فيها خلاف، فلا يجيز الشافعي أن يقال فيه: هذا إجماع؛ لأن عدم العلم ليس دليلاً، فقد يكون الناس اختلفوا وهو لا يدري، والذي يقوله الشافعي في هذا المقام: «لا نعلمهم اختلفوا فيما لا نعلمهم اختلفوا فيه»(٤).

١ المصدر السابق: ٧/ ٢٦٧.
٢ المصدر السابق: ٧/ ٢٤٤.
٣ المصدر السابق: ٧/ ١٤٤.
٤ المصدر السابق.

Also, Imām ash-Shāfi'i gave the views by the Companions precedence over *qiyās*. When there is an opinion by a Companion that is not opposed by another [Companion], this opinion is adopted without hesitation, and when the Companions differed among themselves on an opinion, he chooses from their views. In his "new *madhhab*," Imām ash-Shāfi'i said when discussing the inheritance of the brother and grandfather, "This is an opinion we have taken form Zayd ibn Thābit, from whom we have taken most [of the rulings] on inheritance." He also said, "Were it not for the report narrated about Abū Bakr (may Allah be pleased with him), *qiyās* would have – in my view – entailed killing the monk." Hence, he ignored *qiyās* because the view of a Companion existed on the matter. Ar-Rabi' said about Imām ash-Shāfi'i, "He never opposed the Qur'an, the Sunnah or the opinion of the Companions. In fact, he deemed that which opposed the Companions' views to be an innovation in the religion."[1]

As for *qiyās*, Imām ash-Shāfi'i viewed that it can only be resorted to when there is a necessity. To him, it was like eating the flesh of a dead animal; it can only be resorted to when there exists no other option. Ibn Ḥajar al-'Asqalani said, "In conclusion, exercising *ra'y* is only [allowed] when there is no text that exists, and this is exactly what Imām ash-Shāfi'i alluded to in the narration collected by al-Bayhaqi, with an authentic chain, that Aḥmad ibn Ḥanbal said, 'I heard ash-Shāfi'i saying, '*Qiyās* can only be resorted to when absolutely necessary.'"[2]

1 *I'lām al-Muwaqqi'īn* 1/85
2 *Fatḥ al-Bāri* 13/291 and *I'lām al-Muwaqqi'īn* 1/70

والإمام الشافعي يقدم قول الصحابي على القياس، وإذا قال الصحابي قولاً لم يخالفه فيه غيره لم يعدوه، وإذا اختلفوا تخير من أقوالهم، «وقد قال في مذهبه الجديد في كتاب الفرائض في ميراث الجد والإخوة: وهذا مذهب تلقيناه عن زيد بن ثابت، وعنه أخذنا أكثر الفرائض، وقال: القياس عندي قتل الراهب لولا ما جاء عن أبي بكر ﵁، فترك صريح القياس لقول الصديق، وقال في رواية الربيع عنه: ما خالف كتاباً أو سنة أو أثر بعض أصحاب النبي ﷺ، فجعل ما خالف الصحابي بدعة»[١].

والقياس عند الشافعي يعمل به للضرورة، فهو عنده كأكل الميتة لا يجوز تناولها، وهو يجد سعة في غيرها، يقول ابن حجر العسقلاني: «والحاصل أن المصير إلى الرأي يكون عند فقد النص، وإلى هذا يومئ قول الشافعي فيما أخرجه البيهقي بسند صحيح إلى أحمد بن حنبل: سمعت الشافعي يقول: «القياس عند الضرورة»[٢].

١ إعلام الموقعين: ١/ ٨٥.
٢ فتح الباري: ١٣/ ٢٩١، إعلام الموقعين: ١/ ٧٠.

IV. Compiling the Madhhab of ash-Shāfi'i and the Shafi'i Jurists

We previously mentioned that Imām ash-Shāfi'i himself authored his *madhhab* and then revised and rewrote it while in Egypt.

In the introduction of his verification of *ar-Risālah,* the great scholar and verifier Shaykh Aḥmad Shākir said, "Imām ash-Shāfi'i wrote many books; some of which he wrote himself and taught to people, and others he dictated to his disciples. Counting these books is difficult, and many of them have been lost. He authored in Mecca, and in Baghdad, and in Egypt."

Of his books which are still circulated between the scholars is what he wrote in Egypt – namely the book *al-Umm* in which ar-Rabi' combined several books by ash-Shāfi'i. Ar-Rabi' gave the book this name after hearing these books directly from ash-Shāfi'i, and whatever he did not hear directly he pointed out. He also pointed out whatever he found in ash-Shāfi'i's handwriting and did not hear from him; this is known to the scholars who read the books *al-Umm, Ikhtilāf al-Ḥadīth* and *ar-Risālah.* These two other books are also narrated by ar-Rabi' from Imām ash-Shāfi'i, though he did not include them in the book *al-Umm.*[1]

Of the most authoritative books in Shafi'i *Fiqh* is *al-Mukhtaṣar* by al-Muzani (75 – 164 A.H.). The Shāfi'i jurists held this work in very high esteem, and the students of knowledge would invest much in learning it. As mentioned by adh-Dhahabi, *al-Mukhtasar* filled the lands to the point that it was an inseperable part of a bride's wedding gifts.[2]

In *al-Mukhtaṣar,* al-Muzani summarized all the books of ash-Shāfi'i, from both his old and new *madhhab,* and then added his own independent judgments and opinions.[3]

1 *Ar-Risālah* 9
2 *Siyar A'lām an-Nubalā'* 12/493
3 *Muqaddimat al-Ḥāwi* 1/67 by Dr. Maḥmūd Matraji

رابعاً: تدوين مذهب الشافعي ودواوين مذهب الشافعية:

ذكرنا من قبل أن الشافعي دوَّن مذهبه بنفسه، ثم أعاد تدوينه بعد تمحيصه وتدقيقه مرة أخرى بمصر.

يقول العلامة المحقق الشيخ أحمد شاكر في مقدمة تحقيقه لرسالة الشافعي: «ألف الشافعي كتباً كثيرة، بعضها كتبه بنفسه وقرأه على الناس أو قرؤوه عليه، وبعضها أملاه إملاء، وإحصاء هذه الكتب عسير، وقد فقد كثير منها، فألف في مكة، وألف في بغداد، وألف في مصر».

«والذي في أيدي العلماء من كتبه الآن ما ألفه في مصر، وهو كتاب «الأم» الذي جمع فيه الربيع بعض كتب الشافعي، وسماه بهذا الاسم، بعد أن سمع منه هذه الكتب، وما فاته سماعه بين ذلك، وما وجده بخط الشافعي ولم يسمعه بينه أيضاً، كما يعلم ذلك أهل العلم ممن يقرؤون كتاب «الأم»، وكتاب «اختلاف الحديث» وكتاب «الرسالة» وهما مما روي الربيع عن الشافعي منفصلين، ولم يدخلهما في كتاب «الأم»(١).

ومن المؤلفات المعتمدة في فقه الشافعية: مختصر المزني (١٧٥- ٢٦٤هـ)، وقد نال هذا الكتاب حظوة عند علماء الشافعية، وكان موضع اهتمام طلبة العلم، وامتلأت البلاد بمختصره كما يقول الذهبي، وكانت العروس يوضع في جهازها مختصر المزني(٢).

وقد اختصره من سائر كتب الشافعي من القديم والجديد، وأدخل فيه اجتهاداته وأحكامه(٣).

١ الرسالة: ٩.
٢ سير أعلام النبلاء: ١٢/ ٤٩٣.
٣ مقدمة الحاوي، د. محمود مطرجي: ١/ ٦٧.

Many books were written to explain *al-Mukhtaṣar*, and they were listed by the verifier of the book *al-Ḥ*āwi by al-Māwardi. The book *al-Ḥawi* is one of many works explaining *al-Mukhtaṣar*, and it was authored by Abūl-Ḥasan 'Ali ibn Muhammad ibn Ḥabīb al-Māwardi (364 – 450 A.H.).[1]

This book focuses on the views of ash-Shāfi'i and points out which view belongs to his old or new *madhhab*. He always mentions the opinions of Imām Abū Ḥanīfah, Imām Mālik and Imām Aḥmad and whether they agree with the Shāfi'i *madhhab* or not. However, he always defends the Shāfi'i position whenever the other Imām(s) disagreed with him on a matter. Then, he mentioned the views given by ash-Shāfi'i's companions. When they had two different opinions, he would analyze the two and then champion that which he believed to be correct.

V. Terms Used in Shāfi'i Fiqh

Old & New: Imām ash-Shāfi'i had two *madhhab*(s) in *Fiqh*, an old version and a new one. The old version represents his views in Iraq before his relocation to Egypt. This version is recorded in his book *al-Ḥujjah*, which was narrated about him via al-Ḥasan ibn al-Ḥasan, better known as az-Za'farāni.

As for the new version, these are his views after he traveled to Egypt. This version is found within his book *al-Umm*, which was narrated about him via his disciple Ismā'īl ibn Yaḥyā al-Muzani.

The Judge: The Shāfi'is use this term in reference to Ḥusayn ibn Muhammad ibn Aḥmad al-Marwazi.

The Two Judges: This term refers to 'Ali ibn Muhammad ibn Ḥabīb al-Māwardi and 'Abdul-Wāḥid ibn Ismā'īl ar-Rawyāni.

Imām al-Ḥaramayn: This term refers to 'Abdullāh ibn Yūsuf ibn 'Abdullāh al-Juwayni.

1 Ibid

وقد كثرت شروحه وتعددت، وقد ذكر هذه الشروح محقق كتاب الحاوي للماوردي(١).

وبين يدي وقت كتابة هذه السطور أحد شروحه، وهو كتاب الحاوي للماوردي: وهو أبو الحسن علي بن محمد بن حبيب الماوردي (٣٦٤- ٤٥٠هـ).

وقد شرح به مذهب الشافعي، ذاكراً فيه أقواله، مع بيان الجديد والقديم منهما، ثم يذكر أقوال الأئمة أبي حنيفة ومالك، وأحمد الموافقة والمخالفة للمذهب، وهو دائم الانتصار لمذهب الشافعي فيما خالفوه فيه.

ثم يتبع ذلك بذكر أقوال الأصحاب، وإن كان لهم وجهان ذكرهما، ويخطئ ما يراه خاطئاً، ويصوب ما يراه صواباً.

خامساً: مصطلحات فقهاء الشافعية:

القديم والجديد: للشافعي مذهبان، القديم وهو ما قاله بالعراق قبل انتقاله إلى مصر، وقد ضمنه كتابه الحجة الذي رواه عنه الحسن بن الحسن المعروف بالزعفراني.

والجديد: ما صار إليه في مصر بعد رحيله إليها، وقد ضمنه كتابه الأم الذي رواه عنه تلميذه إسماعيل بن يحيى المزني.

ويطلق الشافعية القاضي على حسين بن محمد بن أحمد المروزي.

ويطلقون مصطلح: القاضيان على الماوردي: وهو علي بن محمد بن حبيب الماوردي، والروياني: وهو عبد الواحد بن إسماعيل الروياني.

ويطلقون إمام الحرمين على عبد الله بن يوسف بن عبد الله الجويني.

١ المصدر السابق.

Shaykh al-Islām: This term refers to Shaykh Zakariyyā al-Anṣari.

***Al-Mukhtaṣar*:** This term refers to al-Muzani's book, which is his abridgment of the books written by ash-Shāfi'i.

Imām Aḥmad ibn Ḥanbal

I. His Lineage and Status

He is Imām Aḥmad ibn Muhammad ibn Ḥanbal Abū 'Abdillāh ash-Shaybāni, the Imām of *Ahl as-Sunnah*. Ash-Shāfi'i said about him, "I departed from Iraq, leaving behind no man better, more pious or more learned than Aḥmad ibn Ḥanbal."[1]

Yaḥyā ibn Ma'īn said about him, "Imām Aḥmad had unique characteristics that I never found [combined] in any other scholar. He was a narrator of Hadith, a *ḥafiẓ* (superb memorizer), a scholar, a pious man, an ascetic and a man of sharp intellect."[2]

Imām Aḥmad was born in Baghdad in Rabi' al-Awwal, 164 A.H. His father died when Aḥmad was three years old, and so his mother took care of him. He died on Friday, the 12th of Rabi' al-Awwal, 241 A.H. at the age of 77.[3]

II. The Fundamentals of Aḥmad ibn Ḥanbal's Madhhab[4]

Imām Aḥmad built his *madhhab* on five main principles:

1st Principle: Relying on the Texts and Ignoring Whatever Opposes Them

If a relevant text is found, Imām Aḥmad would give his opinion based on it and would not acknowledge anything or anyone that opposes it. For this reason, he ignored the view of 'Umar regarding al-Mabtutah in light of the hadith of Fātimah bint Qays on the matter, and ignored his view regarding *tayammum* for the sexually impure in light of the hadith of 'Ammār and ignored his view regarding applying perfume before *iḥrām* due to the hadith of 'A'ishah on the matter being authentic.

---

1 *Al-Ikmāl fī Asmā' ar-Rijāl* 3/797 and *al-Bidāyah wan-Nihāyah* 10/335

2 *Al-Bidāyah wan-Nihāyah* 10/336

3 *Al-Bidāyah wan-Nihāyah* 10/326

4 This section is taken from *I'lām al-Muwaqqi'īn* 1/29,33. Also, see *al-Madkhal* 41 by Ibn Badrān.

ويطلقون شيخ الإسلام على الشيخ زكريا الأنصاري.

ويطلقون المختصر على كتاب المزني الذي اختصره من مؤلفات الشافعي[١].

الإمام أحمد بن حنبل

أولاً: مكانته وفضله وعلمه:

هو الإمام أحمد بن محمد بن حنبل أبو عبد الله الشيباني، إمام أهل السنة، يقول فيه الشافعي: «خرجت من العراق، فما تركت رجلاً أفضل، ولا أعلم، ولا أورع، ولا أتقى من أحمد بن حنبل»[٢].

وقال يحيى بن معين فيه: «كان في أحمد خصال ما رأيتها في عالم قط: كان محدِّثاً، وكان حافظاً، وكان عالماً، وكان ورعاً، وكان زاهداً، وكان عاقلاً»[٣].

ولد الإمام أحمد في مدينة بغداد في ربيع الأول من سنة أربع وستين ومائة، وتوفي والده وهو ابن ثلاث سنين، فكفلته أمه، وتوفي الإمام أحمد يوم الجمعة، الثاني عشر من ربيع الأول من سنة إحدى وأربعين ومائتين، وله من العمر سبع وسبعون سنة[٤].

ثانياً: أصول مذهبه[٥]:

بنى الإمام أحمد مذهبه على خمسة أصول:

الأصل الأول: الاعتماد على النص وعدم الالتفات إلى ما خالفه:

فإذا وجد النص أفتى بموجبه، ولم يلتفت إلى ما خالفه، ولا من خالفه كائناً من كان؛ و لهذا لم يلتفت إلى خلاف عمر في المبتوتة لحديث فاطمة بنت قيس، ولا إلى خلافه في التيمم للجنب لحديث عمار بن ياسر، ولا إلى خلافه في استدامة المحرم الطيب الذي تطيب به قبل إحرامه، لصحة حديث عائشة في ذلك.

---

١ راجع المجموع: ١/ ٧٠.

٢ الإكمال في أسماء الرجال، انظر مشكاة المصابيح: ٣/ ٧٩٧، والبداية والنهاية: ١٠/ ٣٣٥.

٣ البداية والنهاية: ١٠/ ٣٣٦.

٤ البداية والنهاية: ١٠/ ٣٢٦.

٥ هذا المبحث مأخوذ من إعلام الموقعين: ١/ ٢٩، ٣٣، وانظر المدخل لابن بدران: ٤١.

Imām Aḥmad would not give anything preference over an authentic hadith. He would not allow for any established practice, opinion, *qiyās* or view by a Companion to challenge the authority of a Prophetic hadith. Even when there is no known difference of opinion – and as a result many people consider it a matter of consensus – he still does not allow it to override the authority of an authentic hadith.

2nd Principle: *Fatwa(s) Given by the Companions*
If he finds an opinion by a Companion that has no known opposition by another Companion, Imām Aḥmad would consider it the only acceptable view. At the same, he would not say that this is a matter of consensus. Instead, out of pious caution, he would say, "I do not know of anything to challenge it" or the similar.

3rd Principle: *When the Companions Differed, He Adopted the Closest View to the Qur'an and Sunnah*
When the Companions (may Allah be pleased with them) had different views, Imām Aḥmad would choose the nearest of their views to the Qur'an and Sunnah, and would not select from other than their views. If he could not discern the strongest view, then he would mention the various opinions without choosing decisively between them. Isḥāq ibn Ibrāhīm ibn Hāni' said, "Abū 'Abdillāh Aḥmad ibn Ḥanbal was asked, 'What should a man do when asked by his people regarding a matter in which there is a difference of opinion?' He replied, 'He should give his fatwa based on whatever agrees with the Qur'an and Sunnah. If it does not [clearly] agree with the Qur'an and Sunnah, he should not adopt it.' It was said to him, 'Should it even be answered?' He said, 'No.'"

4th Principle: *Acting Upon Weak and Mursal Hadith(s)*
However, it must be noted that a weak hadith which Aḥmad accepted would not be *matrūk* (rejected), as we will discover in the pages to come.

ولم يكن يقدم على الحديث الصحيح عملاً ولا رأياً ولا قياساً ولا قول صاحب، ولا عدم علمه بالمخالف الذي يسميه كثير من الناس إجماعاً، ويقدمونه على الحديث الصحيح.

الأصل الثاني: ما أفتى به الصحابة:

فإنه إذا وجد لبعضهم فتوى لا يعرف له مخالف منهم فيها لم يعدها إلى غيرها، ولم يقل: إن ذلك إجماع، بل من ورعه في العبارة يقول: لا أعلم شيئاً يدفعه، أو نحو هذا.

الأصل الثالث: إذا اختلف الصحابة أخذ ما كان أقرب إلى الكتاب والسنة:

إذا اختلف الصحابة تخير من أقوالهم ما كان أقربها إلى الكتاب والسنة، ولم يخرج عن أقوالهم، فإن لم يتبين له موافقة أحد الأقوال حكى الخلاف فيها، ولم يجزم بقول، قال إسحاق بن إبراهيم بن هانئ في مسائله: قيل لأبي عبد الله: يكون الرجل في قومه، فيسأل عن الشيء فيه اختلاف؟

قال: يفتي بما وافق الكتاب والسنة، وما لم يوافق الكتاب والسنة أمسك عنه.

قيل له: أفيجاب عليه؟ قيل: لا.

الأصل الرابع: الأخذ بالمرسل والحديث الضعيف:

وليس المراد بالضعيف الذي يأخذ به أحمد المتروك كما سيأتي بيانه.

5th Principle: Qiyās

When there is a matter for which Imām Aḥmad had no text, nor view of a Companion, nor a weak or *mursal* report, he resorted to the fifth principle: *qiyās*. He only used it when necessary, as he was the one who said in *Kitāb al-Khallāl*, "I asked ash-Shāfi'i about *qiyās*, and he said, 'It can only be resorted to when absolutely necessary.'"

These five principles are the basis of his fatwa(s), and upon them Imām Ahmad built his *madhhab*.

Ibn al-Qayyim held that these five principles were essentially four; the Qur'an, the Sunnah, the views of the Companions and *qiyās*.

However, Imām Aḥmad did not limit himself to these four or five principles, and this is clearly illustrated to whoever learns the fundamentals of Ḥanbali *fiqh*.[1]

In reality, the fundamentals of Imām Aḥmad, through which he deducing his juristic opinions, are: the Qur'an, the Sunnah, consensus, the views of the Companions, *qiyās, istisḥab, al-maṣāl-lih al-mursalah* and *sadd adh-dharā'i'*.

III. Compiling the Madhhab of Imām Ahmad & the Ḥanbali Jurists

Imām Aḥmad ibn Ḥanbal was averse to writing books on specific juristic rulings and opinions. This is because he wanted Muslims to place more importance on the revealed texts, such as the Qur'an and Sunnah, and plant in their hearts an attachment to the revelation. He occupied himself with collecting the Sunnah, the views of the Companions and the Book of Allah, and did not author a single book on *Fiqh*. The most he every wrote was a treatise on prayer; he wrote it to an imām that he once prayed behind that could not perform prayer properly. This treatise was later published and became widespread. Aside from that, his companions documented his words and opinions, and spread them far and wide.

1 See *al-Kawkab al-Munīr* which is known as *al-Mukhtasar at-Tahrīr* 382-389 by al-Fatūhi. Also, see *al-Muswaddah fī Usūl al-Fiqh* 450-455 by Ibn Taymiyyah. Also, *see al-Fikr as-Sāmi* 3/19.

الأصل الخامس: القياس:

إذا لم يكن عند الإمام أحمد في المسألة نص، ولا قول صحابي، ولا أثر مرسل أو ضعيف عدل إلى الأصل الخامس، وهو القياس، فاستعمله للضرورة، وقد قال في كتاب الخلال: سألت الشافعي عن القياس، فقال: إنما يصار إليه عند الضرورة.

فهذه الأصول الخمسة هي أصول فتاويه، وعليها مدارها.

وهذا الذي اعتبره ابن القيم خمسة هو في الحقيقة أربعة، وهي: الكتاب، والسنة، وقول الصحابي، والقياس.

ثم إن الإمام أحمد لم يقتصر على أربعة، ولا على خمسة، كما هو مبين في أصول فقه الحنابلة[1].

فأصول الاستنباط عند الإمام هي: الكتاب، والسنة، والإجماع، وقول الصحابي، والقياس، والاستصحاب، والمصالح المرسلة، وسد الذرائع.

ثالثاً: تدوين مذهب أحمد ودواوين مذهب الحنابلة:

كان الإمام أحمد يكره وضع الكتب التي تشتمل على التفريع والرأي، وما ذلك إلا ليتوفر الالتفات إلى النقل، ويزرع في القلوب التمسك بالأثر، وقد شغل وقته في جمع السنة والأثر وتفسير كتاب الله تعالى، ولم يؤلف كتاباً في الفقه، وكان غاية ما كتبه فيه رسالة في الصلاة، كتبها إلى إمام صلى وراءه، فأساء في صلاته، وهي رسالة قد طبعت ونشرت، وقد كتب أصحابه كلامه وفتاويه وانتشرت في الآفاق.

١ راجع: شرح الكوكب المنير، المسمى بمختصر التحرير للفتوحي: ٣٨٢- ٣٨٩، والمسودة في أصول الفقه لابن تيمية: ٤٥٠- ٤٥٥، الفكر السامي: ٣/ ١٩.

Then came Aḥmad ibn Muhammad ibn Harūn, better known as Abū Bakr al-Khallāl. He dedicated himself to collecting the religious knowledge of Aḥmad Ibn Ḥanbal. He journeyed through the lands to meet Ibn Ḥanbal's companions and disciples and documented what he narrated about Imām Aḥmad with its chains of transmission. He compiled multiple books from that, of them being the book *al-Jāmi'* which exceeds twenty volumes. This book is regarded as the primary source of the Ḥanbali *madhhab*. Also, Abū Dāwūd Sulaymān ibn al-Ash'ath, the famous compiler of *as-Sunan*, narrated from him a number of juristic matters, which came to be called *Masā'il al-Imām Aḥmad* by Abū Dāwud.

Similarly, Abūl-Qāsim 'Amr ibn Abi 'Ali al-Ḥusayn al-Khiraqi, who died in 324 A.H., wrote a concise book on the *madhhab* of Aḥmad entitled *Mukhtaṣar al-Khiraqi*. This book became so famous that many of the Hanbali jurists explained it, and three hundred different explanations for it were eventually written.

IV. Terms Used in Ḥanbali Fiqh

The Judge: This term refers to greatest scholar of his time, Muhammad ibn al-Ḥusayn ibn Muhammad ibn Khalaf ibn Aḥmad ibn al-Farā', more famously known as Abū Ya'lā. As for the later Ḥanbali jurists, such as the authors of *al-Iqnā'*, *al-Muntahā* and those after them, they use this term in reference to 'Alā' ad-Dīn 'Ali ibn Sulaymān al-Mirdāwi, the author of *al-Inṣāf*.

***Al-Munaqqiḥ* (the Revisor):** This term refers to al-Mirdāwi, as he revised the book *al-Muqni'* into his book *at-Tanqīḥ al-Mushbi'*.

The Shaykh: Later jurists use this term in reference to Shaykh Muwaffaq ad-Dīn Ibn Qudamah. Some also use it in reference to Shaykh al-Islām Ibn Taymiyah, while others refer to him as "the Imām."

ثم جاء أحمد بن محمد بن هارون أبو بكر الخلال، فصرف عنايته إلى جمع علوم أحمد بن حنبل، فطاف في البلاد للاجتماع بأصحاب أحمد، وكتب ما روي عنه بالإسناد، وصنف كتباً في ذلك، منها كتاب «الجامع»، ويقع في أكثر من عشرين مجلداً، وهذا الكتاب هو الأصل لمذهب أحمد، وقد روي بعض «مسائل الإمام أحمد» أبو داود سليمان بن الأشعث صاحب السنن.

وصنف أبو القاسم عمر بن أبي علي الحسين الخرقي المتوفى سنة ٤٢٣هـ- كتاباً مختصراً في فقه أحمد سمي بـ «مختصر الخرقي» وقد اشتهر هذا الكتاب، وشرحه كثير من فقهاء المذهب، وقد زادت شروحه على ثلاثمائة شرح.

رابعاً: مصطلحات الفقه الحنبلي:

إذا أطلق الحنابلة لفظ «القاضي» أرادوا به علامة زمانه: محمد بن الحسين بن محمد بن خلف بن أحمد بن الفراء الملقب بأبي يعلى، والمتأخرون كصاحب الإقناع والمنتهى ومن بعدهما يطلقون لفظ «القاضي» على علاء الدين علي بن سليمان المرداوي صاحب الإنصاف.

ويلقبون المرداوي بـ «المنقح»؛ لأنه نقح «المقنع» في كتابه «التنقيح المشبع».

وإذا أطلق المتأخرون «الشيخ» أرادوا به الشيخ موفق الدين ابن قدامة، وبعضهم يطلقه مريداً به شيخ الإسلام ابن تيمية، وقد يطلقون عليه اسم «الإمام».

The Two Shaykh(s): This term refers to Muwaffaq and Majd ad-Dīn 'Abdus-Salām ibn Taymiyah.

Ash-Shāriḥ (the Explainer): This term refers to 'Abdur-Rahmān ibn Abi 'Amr, the nephew of Muwaffaq, who explained the book *al-Muqni'*.

Taqi ad-Dīn & Shaykh al-Islām: This term refers to Aḥmad ibn 'Abdul-Ḥalīm ibn Taymiyah.

Al-Fatāwā (the Edicts): This term is used specifically in reference to the book *al-Fatāwā* by Ibn Taymiyah.

If you wish to learn more about the terms in Ḥanbali *Fiqh,* refer to the priceless book *Musṭalaḥ*āt al-*Fiqh al-Ḥanbali* which was compliled by Dr. Sālim 'Ali an-Naqi and the book *al-Madkhal ilā Madhhab Aḥmad* by Ibn Badrān.

وإذا قالوا: «الشيخان» أرادوا بهما الموفق ومجد الدين عبد السلام بن تيمية.

ويطلقون «الشارح» ويريدون به عبد الرحمن بن أبي عمر بن أخي الموفق شارح «المقنع».

ويطلقون «تقي الدين» و«شيخ الإسلام» على شيخ الإسلام أحمد بن عبد الحليم بن تيمية.

وإذا قالوا: «الفتاوى» قصدوا فتاويه دون غيرها.

وإذا شئت أن تطلع على مصطلحات الفقه الحنبلي في الأعلام والمدونات وطرق الدلالة على المذهب فعليك بالكتاب القيم الجامع في هذا الموضوع الذي دونه الدكتور سالم علي النقي بعنوان «مصطلحات الفقه الحنبلي»، ولابن بدران إلمامة بهذا الموضوع في كتابه «المدخل إلى مذهب أحمد»[1].

---

١ ص: ٢٠٢-٢١٣.

Summary of Unit 8

1) Imām Abū Ḥanīfah: He is an-Nu'mān ibn Thābit ibn az-Zawṭi al-Kufi. He was born in 80 A.H. and died in 150 A.H. He is the founder of the Ḥanafi *Madhhab* in which he depends on the Qur'an, the Sunnah, the Companions' views, *qiyās*, juristic preference and loopholing.

2) Imām Mālik: He is Mālik ibn Anas ibn Mālik ibn Abi 'Āmir al-Aṣbaḥi. He was born in 95 A.H. and died in 179 A.H. He is the founder of the Māliki *madhhab* in which he relied on the Qur'an, the Sunnah, consensus, the consensus of the people of Madinah, *qiyās,* the Companions's views, *al-maṣāliḥ al-mursalah,* customs and traditions, *sadd adh-dharā'i',* juristic preference and *istisḥāb.*

3) Imām ash-Shāfi'i: He is Abū 'Abdillāh Muhammad ibn Idrīs ibn al-'Abbās ibn 'Uthmān ibn Shāfi' ibn as-Sā'ib ibn 'Ubayd ibn 'Abd Yazīd ibn Hāshim ibn 'Abd Manaf ibn Quṣay al-Qurashi. He was born in Gaza in 150 A.H. and died in 204 A.H. He is the founder of the Shāfi'i *madhhab* in which he relied on the Qur'an, the Sunnah, consensus, the Companions' views and *qiyās.*

4) Imām Aḥmad ibn Ḥanbal: He is Aḥmad ibn Muhammad ibn Ḥanbal Abū 'Abdillāh ash-Shaybāni. He is the Imām of *Ahl as-Sunnah.* He was born in Baghdad in 164 A.H. and died in 241 A.H. He is the founder of the Ḥanbali *madhhab,* in which he depended on the Qur'an, the Sunnah, the Companions' views (especially the view closest to the Qur'an and Sunnah), *qiyās, istisḥāb, al-masāliḥ al-mursalah* and *sadd adh-dharā'i'.*

خلاصة الوحدة

نخلص من دراسة هذه الوحدة إلى ما يلي:

١- الإمام أبو حنيفة هو: النعمان بن ثابت بن زوطي الكوفي، ولد سنة ثمانين، وتوفي سنة خمسين ومائة، وهو الذي أسس المذهب الحنفي، وقد اعتمد في مذهبه على: الكتاب، والسنة، وأقوال الصحابة، والقياس، والاستحسان، والحيل.

٢- الإمام مالك هو: مالك بن أنس بن مالك بن أبي عامر الأصبحي، ولد سنة خمس وتسعين، ومات سنة تسع وسبعين ومائة، وهو مؤسس المذهب المالكي، وقد اعتمد في مذهبه على: الكتاب، والسنة، والإجماع، وإجماع أهل المدينة، والقياس، وقول الصحابي، والمصلحة المرسلة، والعرف، والعادات، وسد الذرائع، والاستحسان، والاستصحاب.

٣- الإمام الشافعي هو: أبو عبد الله محمد بن إدريس بن العباس بن عثمان بن شافع بن السائب بن عبيد بن عبد يزيد بن هاشم بن عبد مناف بن قصي القرشي، ولد بغزة سنة خمسين ومائة، وتوفي سنة أربع، ومائتين، وهو مؤسس المذهب الشافعي، وقد اعتمد في مذهبه على الكتاب، والسنة، والإجماع، وقول الصحابي، والقياس.

٤- الإمام أحمد هو: أحمد بن محمد بن حنبل أبو عبد الله الشيباني، إمام أهل السنة، ولد في بغداد سنة أربع وستين ومائة، وتوفي سنة إحدى وأربعين ومائتين، وهو مؤسس المذهب الحنبلي، وقد اعتمد في مذهبه على القرآن والسنة، وفتاوي الصحابة (فإذا اختلفوا أخذ من أقوالهم ما كان أقرب إلى الكتاب والسنة)، والقياس، والاستصحاب، والمصالح المرسلة، وسد الذرائع.

Notes

Unit 9

The Era of *Taqlīd* (Imitation) and Stagnation

Note:

The heading of this unit does not refer to a major regression in the study of *Fiqh*. Rather, this heading refers to the fact that, in comparison to the previous era which was robust with breakthroughs in *Fiqh*, this era was not. Nonetheless, this era still witnessed a wide spectrum of contributions in *Fiqh*, as well as the appearance of new *Mujtahid Imām*(s), but they were relatively few in comparison to the imitating majority. Hence, this heading was given to describe the majority of this era's jurists, not the exceptional minority.

Contents of Unit 9

1) The Definition of *Taqlīd* and its Danger
2) The Prophetic Sunnah & its Collections in the Era of *Taqlīd*

Importance of this Unit

The Muslim world was profuse with religious knowledge. It was abundant with scholars who had inherited the sciences of their predecessors, analyzed the world around them through the scope of the Book of Allah and the Sunnah of His Messenger (ﷺ), and gauged matters in light of these guidelines that they mastered. Thereafter, the zeal for knowledge began dwindling greatly, and the Muslims began limiting themselves radically by entering the abyss of *taqlīd* (imitation). The more time progressed, the more *taqlīd* increased and the more the Muslims distanced themselves from the light of knowledge. Many of the imitators of the *madhhab*(s) began neglecting the books written by the founding *Imām*(s) of their *madhhab* and began limiting themselves to the books of that *madhhab*'s later scholars. These later works were abridged books, commentaries and explanations. Once these replaced the original works, it was inevitable that the *Fiqh* of this era would weaken and gradually dissipate.

الوحدة التاسعة

عصر التقليد والجمود

ملحوظة:

هذا العنوان لا يعني تخلف الفقه تخلفاً كبيراً وجموده، ولكن المقصود من هذا العنوان هو قياس حالة الفقه بالعصر السالف في الازدهار العام للفقه، ولكن هذه الفترة قد شهدت تنوعاً في العطاء الفقهي، وأيضاً ظهور مجتهدين، ولكنهم قليل بالنسبة للكثير المقلد، فأصبح العنوان يطلق على غالب الفقهاء وليس القليل منهم.

محتويات الوحدة التاسعة

١- تعريف التقليد وخطورته.

٢- السنة النبوية في عصر التقليد ومدوناتها.

أهمية دراسة الوحدة:

كان العالم الإسلامي يزخر بالعلم والعلماء الذين كانوا يستوعبون علوم سلفهم، ثم ينظرون إلى الحياة من خلال كتاب الله وسنة رسوله ﷺ، وفق المعايير التي تلقوها، والضوابط التي فقهوها، ثم بعد ذلك خمدت حركة العلم بصورة كبيرة، وضيّق المسلمون على أنفسهم، وحصروا أنفسهم في نطاق محدود، وذلك بدخولهم في ظلمات التقليد، وكلما تقادم الزمان في هذا العصر ازداد التقليد وبعد المسلمون عن نور العلم، وقد ترك كثير من مقلدي المذاهب النظر في كتب الإمام الذي يقتدون به، وقصروا النظر على كتب متأخري المذهب، من المختصرات والحواشي والشروح، وهذا دليل ضعف الفقه أو انحلال قوته.

As for the Prophetic Sunnah, its preservation and study did not stop in this era. This period continued to witness scholars who were keen to narrate the collections of hadith with chains of transmission that traced back to its collector. In this era, scholars also undertook the mission of gathering the Sunnah into all-inclusive collections. Additionally, some scholars dedicated themselves to authoring books on the juristic explanations of these hadith(s) in this era.

Let us now study this unit in order to fully grasp all of these details and more.

Learning objectives

By the end of this unit, readers should be able to:

- Define *taqlīd* and identify its danger
- Draw a comparison between the study of *Fiqh* in this era and the era of the first generation of Muslims
- Show the status of the Prophetic Sunnah in this era

The Definition of *Taqlīd* and its Danger

The Definition of Taqlīd

The scholars' definitions of *taqlīd* are all similar. Some have defined it as "the acceptance of an opinion without knowing its evidence." Others said, "In Sharia, *taqlīd* is settling for a view with no proof supporting it." In other words, the *muqallid* (imitator) considers his imām's view to be the ultimate proof, irrespective of whether it is correct in light of the Sunnah or whether it is incorrect and has been disproven by the verses and hadith(s).[1]

أما السنة النبوية في هذا العصر فلم تتوقف العناية بها، فقد وجد في هذا العصر من يحرص على رواية كتب السنة بالإسناد إلى مدونيها، واشتغل العلماء في هذا العصر بتجميع السنة على صعيد واحد في مصنفات مستوعبة، كما صنف أيضاً في هذا العصر مدونات التفسير الفقهي وشروح الأحاديث الفقهية.

هيا بنا لدراسة هذه الوحدة لنتعرف على كل هذه التفاصيل وغيرها.

الأهداف التعليمية:

يتوقع منك أيها الدارس الكريم بعد دراستك لهذه الوحدة أن تكون قادراً على أن:

- تعرف معنى التقليد وخطورته.
- تُقارن بين حال الفقه في هذا العصر، وحاله في الصدر الأول.
- تُبين حال السنة النبوية في هذا العصر.

تعريف التقليد وخطورته

تعريف التقليد:

تعريفات العلماء للتقليد متقاربة، فقد عرفه بعضهم بأنه: أخذ للقول من غير معرفة بدليله، وقال آخرون: التقليد في الشرع: الرجوع إلى قول لا حجة لقائله عليه، فالمقلد يعتبر قول إمامه حجة مطلقة؛ سواء أكانت أقواله صواباً موافقة للسنة، أم خطأ قد جاءت الآيات والأحاديث بضدها(١).

---

1 I'lām al-Muwaqqi'īn 2/179 and Jāmi' Bayān al-'Ilm 2/143. Also, see al-Mustasfā 2/387 by al-Ghazāli.

١ إعلام الموقعين: ٢/ ١٧٩، جامع بيان العلم: ٢/ ١٤٣، وانظر المستصفى للغزالي: ٢/ ٣٨٧.

The Danger of Taqlīd and the Muslims' Condition in this Era

خطورة التقليد وحال المسلمين في هذا العصر:

When fresh water is left to sit for a long time, its color and taste become altered and subsequently becomes no longer usable. In fact, it becomes harmful to whoever drinks from it or washes with it. The same applies for the human being when he becomes shackled, his ideas and mind are chained, and his creativity and independent reasoning are suppressed. Such events pollute the human mind and make his life miserable, and this is exactly what took place in this era.

الماء عندما يركد ويطول مكثه يأسن، فيتغير لونه وطعمه، ويصبح غير صالح، بل يضر متعاطيه والمغتسل منه، وكذلك الحياة الإنسانية إذا كبلتها القيود، وحجر فيها على الأفكار والعقول، وحورب الإبداع والاجتهاد فإنها تأسن ويشقى الإنسان بعد ذلك بنفسه وعقله، وهذا ما حصل في هذا العصر.

Initially, the Muslim world was profuse with religious knowledge. It was abundant with scholars who had inherited the sciences of their predecessors, analyzed the world around them through the scope of the Book of Allah and the Sunnah of His Messenger (ﷺ) and gauged matters in light of these guidelines that they mastered. Sadly, this wide world of knowledge eventually became stagnant. After once being like a rapidly flowing river whose water continuously refreshed itself, it suddenly became placid and inactive. In the past, the Islamic lifestyle was one that was governed by Islam. Whenever a complication arose, the scholars of every previous era would consider such problems and find that Islam had a solution for them. But when the Muslims limited themselves without reason and ignored the dynamic nature of the Sharia, they caused their own misfortune.

العالم الإسلامي الذي كان يزخر بالعلم والعلماء الذين كانوا يستوعبون علوم سلفهم، ثم ينظرون إلى الحياة من خلال كتاب الله وسنة رسوله ﷺ، وفق المعايير التي تلقوها، والضوابط التي فقهوها، هذا العالم الواسع خمدت فيه حركة العلم، فكان كنهر جار متدفق يتجدد ماؤه، فإذا به يكاد يتوقف عن الجريان، كانت الحياة الإسلامية في الماضي محكومة بالإسلام، يمضي الأحياء، وتَجِدُّ لهم المعضلات والمشكلات، وينظر علماء كل عصر إلى مشكلاتهم فيجدون لها في دين الإسلام حلاً، فلما ضيق المسلمون على أنفسهم، وحصروا أنفسهم في نطاق محدود، حجروا على أنفسهم واسعاً، وجَنَوْا على أنفسهم.

The Abbasid caliphate became decrepit midway through the 4th *hijri* century. On top of breaking into smaller states, they were afflicted with another tragedy that was embodied in this stagnation and *taqlīd* that the Muslims fell into. With the passage of time, the scene became eerier and the Muslims drowned farther into *taqlīd*. Until this very day, we are still suffering from the effects of this era.

لقد هرمت الخلافة العباسية في منتصف القرن الرابع الهجري، وتمزقت أوصالها، وأصبحت الدولة دولاً، وصاحب هذا البلاء بلاء آخر تمثل في هذا الجمود وذلك التقليد الذي أصاب المسلمين، وكلما امتد الزمان وطالت الأيام ازدادت ظلمة الليل وأغرق المسلمون في التقليد، وما زلنا إلى يومنا هذا نرزح تحت وطأة عصر التقليد.

The more time progressed, the more *taqlīd* increased and the more the Muslims distanced themselves from the light of knowledge. Many of the imitators of the *madhhab*(s) began neglecting the books written by the founding *Imām*(s) of their *madhhab*, and began limiting themselves to the books of that *madhhab*'s later scholars. Ibn al-'Arabi spoke in his book *al-'Awāsim min al-Qawāṣim* about the backwardness of the sciences in Andalusia during his age, wherein he said, "And the condition remained like this; the sciences died except in the hearts of a select few. For generations, knowledge had vanished and ignorance had surfaced – all by the decree of Allah. The scholars that came would blindly follow the scholars that [recently] passed until it reached a point that the views of Mālik and his senior companions were not even considered any longer."[1]

The Mālikis have confined themselves to *Mukhtaṣar al-Khalīl* and its explanations since the 8th *hijri* century onward. Al-Hajawi said, "Since the age of al-Khalīl until now, the Muslims' minds have increasingly become dull, their wills have diminished and their ideas have become numb due to overly relying on abridged works and detailed rulings [without their sources]. They sufficed with *al-Khalīl* and its explanations to the extent that Nāṣir al-Laqqāni said, 'We are mere followers of al-Khalīl, so if he goes astray, we will go astray as well.' Similarly, Aḥmad as-Sudāni said, 'This is the greatest proof that *Fiqh* has deteriorated; the Muslims from Egypt to the ocean have become Khalili and no longer Māliki.'"[2] [3]

Al-Hajawi then explained that if he was to write a biography of al-Khalīl and ignore the Māliki jurists after him, this would not be unfair to them since most of those jurists were no more than copies of al-Khalīl. He then said, "Since the age of al-Khalīl, *Fiqh* has gradually weakened and reached the brink of extinction."[4]

1 Al-Fikr as-Sāmi 2/177
2 Al-Fikr as-Sāmi 2/245
3 Al-Khalīl died in the year 676 A.H.
4 Al-Fikr as-Sāmi 2/245

وكلما تقادم الزمان في هذا العصر ازداد التقليد وابتعد المسلمون عن نور العلم، وقد ترك كثير من مقلدي المذاهب النظر في كتب الإمام الذي يقتدون به، وقصروا النظر على كتب متأخري المذهب، وقد تحدث ابن العربي في «العواصم من القواصم» عن تدني العلم ببلاد الأندلس في عصره، فقال: «وبقيت الحال هكذا، فماتت العلوم إلا عند آحاد الناس، واستمرت القرون على موت العلم وظهور الجهل، وذلك بقدر الله، وجعل الخلف منهم يتبع السلف حتى آلت الحال إلى أن لا ينظر في قول مالك وكبراء أصحابه»(١).

ثم إن المالكية عكفوا على مختصر خليل وشروحه منذ القرن الثامن الهجري يقول الحجوي: «من زمن خليل إلى الآن زادت العقول فترة، والهمم ركوداً، وتخدرت الأفكار بشدة الاختصار والإكثار من الفروع التي لا يحاط بها والصور النادرة، فاقتصروا على خليل وشروحه، حتى قال الناصر اللقاني: إنما نحن خليليون إن ضل ضللنا، قال أحمد السوداني: وذلك دليل دروس الفقه وذهابه، فقد صار الناس من مصر إلى المحيط خليليين لا مالكية»(٢) (٣).

ثم بيّن الحجوي أنه لو اقتصر على ترجمة خليل دون من جاء بعده من فقهاء المالكية فإنه لا يكون ظالماً لهم؛ لأن غالبهم تابعون له، ثم يقول: «فمن زمن خليل إلى الآن تطور الفقه إلى طور انحلال القوى، وشدة الضعف، والخرف الذي ما بعده إلا العدم»(٤).

١ الفكر السامي: ٢/ ١٧٧.
٢ الفكر السامي: ٢/ ٢٤٥.
٣ توفي الخليل سنة ٦٧٦هـ.
٤ الفكر السامي: ٢/ ٢٤٥.

This epidemic in *Fiqh* did not only apply to the lands where the Māliki *madhhab* was prominent. Rather, this was the case throughout the lands of Islam. The earlier Shāfi'i jurists, for instance, dedicated themselves to studying the books written by Imām ash-Shāfi'i and thus benefitted themselves and others a great deal. This is because such books are profuse with knowledge, correct usage of evidence, coherence of [classical] opinions and consideration of the revealed texts. Secondarily, Shāfi'i jurists would study the abridged work of al-Muzani, for it followed the same format as the books of Imām ash-Shāfi'i. Shāfi'i jurists in the age of *taqlīd*, however, neglected the classical books and focused on the books of Shaykh Abū Isḥāq ash-Shirāzi and Shaykh Abū Ḥāmid al-Ghazāli. People became infatuated with studying the books of these two jurists, and such zealotry developed for them that a learned scholar in this era would consider their words as sacred as the texts of the Qur'an and Sunnah, as said by Abū Shāmah ash-Shāfi'i (may Allah bestow mercy upon him).[1] With the passage of time, jurists veered farther and farther from the wholesome books of knowledge. Eventually, the Shāfi'i jurists began clinging to books like *Mukhtaṣar Abū Shujā'*, which is an extremely concise abridgment of the Shāfi'i *madhhab*. This book was abridged to the point that its vocabulary needed to be explained – a matter that led ash-Shirbini to write a commentary on it. He named this commentary *al-Iqnā' fī Ḥal Alfāẓ Abū Shujā'*, which basically means "A Decoding of the Terms of Abū Shujā'." Then, ash-Shabrawi came and added footnotes on the commentary written by ash-Shirbini.[2]

ولم يكن هذا حال الفقه في الديار التي انتشر فيها المذهب المالكي فحسب، بل كان هذا حال جميع الديار الإسلامية، فالمتقدمون من فقهاء الشافعية كانت عنايتهم بمؤلفات الشافعي، فاستفادوا وأفادوا، لما فيها من علم غزير، وحسن استدلال، وتوجيه للأقوال، وعناية بالنصوص، ثم اعتنوا بمختصر المزني، وهو على نمط كتب الشافعي، ولكن فقهاء الشافعية في عصر التقليد أهملوا كتب المتقدمين، وعنوا بكتب الشيخين أبي إسحاق الشيرازي وأبي حامد الغزالي، فقد أكب الناس على الاشتغال بها، وكثر المتعصبون لمؤلفات هذين الفقيهين، حتى صار المتبحر يرى نصوصهما كنصوص الكتاب والسنة على حد قول أبي شامة الشافعي- رحمه الله-(١)، وكلما تقادم الوقت ابتعد الفقهاء عن الكتب العلمية المتينة، حتى صارت عناية المتأخرين من فقهاء الشافعية بمثل كتاب مختصر أبي الشجاع، وهو مختصر في فقه الشافعية بلغ الغاية في الاختصار، ولشدة اختصاره احتاجت ألفاظه إلى حل، فوضع الشربيني شرحاً له سماه الإقناع في حل ألفاظ أبي الشجاع، ثم جاء الشبراوي ووضع حاشية على شرح الشربيني(٢).

1 Mukhtasar al-Mu'ammil 3/53
2 The book al-Mukhtasar is printed along with its commentary and footnotes. It was first published in the year 1289.

١ مختصر المؤمل- مجموعة الرسائل المنيرية: ٣/ ٣٥.
٢ والمختصر مطبوع مع الشرح والحاشية، وطبعته الأولى في سنة ١٢٨٩.

Ibn Qudāmah wrote the book *al-Muqni'* on the *Fiqh* of Imām Aḥmad ibn Ḥanbal. In this book, Ibn Qudamah mentioned two narrations to help readers become accustomed to the practice of preferring one narration over another. This book was then abridged by Sharaf ad-Dīn Abūn-Najā (d. 960 A.H.) in his book *Zād al-Mustaqni'*. Many Ḥanbali jurists focused their attention on this concise book, and a commentary on it was later written by Mansūr ibn Yūnus al-Bahūti in which he would only mention the preponderant views.[1]

This first to author an abridged work on Ḥanafi *Fiqh* was at-Tahāwi (d. 321 A.H.). Then, al-Karkhi (d. 340 A.H.) wrote another, and then his disciple al-Jassās ar-Razi (d. 370 A.H.) wrote another, and then Abūl-Ḥasan al-Qaduri wrote yet another. The Ḥanafis continued writing abridged works, competed in doing so, and ultimately abandoned the books of their earliest jurists. In his famous book *Ḥāshiyat Ibn 'Ābidīn*, Ibn 'Ābidīn complained of the severe condensation of the book that was explained in *ad-Durr al-Mukhtār* and its mysterious, riddle-like phrasing.[2]

The Prophetic Sunnah & its Collections in the Era of *Taqlīd*

The Prophetic Sunnah in the Era of Taqlīd

The scholarly care for the Prophetic Sunnah did not cease in this era. Certainly, many jurists were ignorant of the Sunnah and incapable of discerning which hadith(s) were authentic and which were weak. Subsequently, the most circulated *Fiqh* books were filled with weak and fabricated hadith(s). However, there were some jurists that allotted attention to the Sunnah, including a group of scholars that dedicated special care to the Sunnah and its collections. In this era, there existed those who were keen to narrate the Sunnah collections with chains of transmission tracing back to their compilers. In the following section, we are going to suffice with discussing two types of books containing the Prophetic Sunnah:

1 Zād al-Mustaqni' was printed along with its explanation. It was printed by Muhibb ad-Dīn al-Khatīb, the owner of al-Maktabah as-Salafiyyah in Cairo.

2 Hāshiyat Ibn 'Abidīn 1/2

وألف ابن قدامة كتاب المقنع في فقه الإمام أحمد بن حنبل، وأطلق فيه روايتين، ليتعود قارئه ترجيح الروايات، واختصره بعد ذلك شرف الدين أبو النجا المتوفى في سنة ٩٦٠هـ في كتابه زاد المستقنع، وقد تركزت عناية كثير من الحنابلة بهذا المختصر، وقد شرح المختصر هذا منصور بن يونس البهوتي، والتزم فيه الاقتصار على المذهب الراجح(١).

وأول من ألف مختصرا في فقه الأحناف الطحاوي المتوفى سنة ٣٢١هـ ثم ألف الكرخي المتوفى سنة (٣٤٠هـ) مختصراً، ثم تلميذه الجصاص الرازي المتوفى في سنة (٣٧٠هـ)، ثم أبو الحسن القدوري المتوفى في سنة (٤٢٨هـ)، وتتابع الأحناف في تأليف المختصرات وتنافسوا في ذلك، وتركت كتب فقهائهم الأوائل، وقد اشتكى ابن عابدين في شرحه المشهور بحاشية ابن عابدين من شدة اختصار الكتاب الذي يشرحه «الدر المختار» وبلوغه حد الإلغاز(٢).

السنة النبوية في عصر التقليد ومدوناتها

السنة النبوية في عصر التقليد

لم تتوقف العناية بالسنة النبوية في هذا العصر، فإذا كان كثير من الفقهاء قد جهل السنة ولم يستطع أن يميز بين صحيحها وضعيفها، فامتلأت الكتب الفقهية المتداولة بالأحاديث الضعيفة والموضوعة- فإن بعض الفقهاء كانت لهم عناية بالسنة، وهناك طائفة من أهل العلم عنيت بالنسبة وكتبها عناية خاصة، فقد وجد في هذا العصر من يحرص على رواية كتب السنة بالإسناد إلى مدونيها، وسنكتفي في هذا المبحث بالحديث عن نوعين من أنواع التأليف في السنة النبوية.

١ وقد طبع الزاد وشرحه، طبعه محب الدين الخطيب صاحب المكتبة السلفية- القاهرة.

٢ حاشية ابن عابدين: ١/ ٢.

1) All-Inclusive Compilations of the Sunnah
2) Compilations Narrating the Hadith(s) found in the Commonly Circulated *Fiqh* Books

Compilations of Hadith in this Era:
I. All-Inclusive Compilations of the Sunnah

In the previous era, the primary collections of hadith were compiled and finalized. As for the scholars of this later era, they dedicated themselves to collecting the Sunnah into comprehensive, all-inclusive works. Of these books are:

1) *Jāmi' al-Usūl fī Ahādith ar-Rasūl*
This book was compiled by Majd ad-Dīn Abūs-Sa'ādāt al-Mubārak ibn Muhammad ibn 'Abdil-Karīm ibn 'Abdil-Wahid ash-Shaybāni al-Jazari al-Mūṣili, also known as Ibn al-Athīr, who was born in 544 A.H and died in 606 A.H.

In this book, Ibn al-Athīr compiled the most reliable six books of hadith: *al-Muwaṭṭa'* by Imām Mālik, *Ṣaḥīḥ al-Bukhāri* by Imām al-Bukhāri, *Ṣaḥīḥ Muslim* by Imām Muslim, *as-Sunan* by Abū Dāwūd, *as-Sunan* by at-Tirmidhi and *as-Sunan* by an-Nasā'i.

2) *Mishkāt al-Masābīh*
This book was compiled by Abū 'Abdillāh ibn Muhammad ibn 'Abdillāh al-Khaṭib at-Tabrīzi. He was a scholar of the eighth *hijri* century, and his book collected the hadith(s) narrated in the most famous books of hadith, such as: *Ṣaḥīḥ al-Bukhāri, Ṣaḥīḥ Muslim, al-Muwaṭṭa'* by Mālik, *al-Umm* by ash-Shāfi'i, *Musnad Aḥmad, Sunan at-Tirmidhi, Sunan Abū Dāwūd, Sunan an-Nasā'i, Sunan Ibn Mājah, Sunan ad-Dārimi, Sunan ad-Dāraquṭni, Sunan al-Bayhaqi* and *at-Tajrīd liṣ-Ṣiḥāḥ as-Sittah* by Razīn.

3) *Jami' al-Jawāmi'*
Also known as *al-Jami' al-Kabīr*, this book was compiled by Jalal ad-Dīn 'Abdur-Raḥmān ibn Abi Bakr as-Suyūṭi, who was born in 849 A.H. and died in 911 A.H.

In this book, Imām as-Suyūṭi had intended to collect all the hadith(s) of the Messenger of Allah (ﷺ), thus he collected from 71 different books of hadith.

الأول: المصنفات المستوعبة للسنة.
الثانية: المؤلفات التي خرَّج أصحابها فيها كتب الفقه المتداولة.

مدونات السنة في هذا العصر
أولاً: تدوين المصنفات المستوعبة للأحاديث:

انتهت عهود الرواية والتدوين الأساسي في جوامع ومصنفات وسنن ومسانيد في العصر السابق، واشتغل العلماء في هذا العصر بتجميع السنة على صعيد واحد في مصنفات مستوعبة، ومن هذه المصنفات:

١- جامع الأصول في أحاديث الرسول:
صنفه مجد الدين أبو السعادات المبارك بن محمد بن محمد بن عبد الكريم بن عبد الواحد الشيباني الجزري ثم الموصلي المعروف بابن الأثير، ولد في سنة (٥٤٤هـ)، وتوفي في سنة (٦٠٦هـ).

وقد جمع ابن الأثير في كتابه هذا أحاديث الكتب الستة المعتمدة في الحديث، وهي: الموطأ، وصحيح البخاري، وصحيح مسلم، وسنن أبي داود، وسنن الترمذي، وسنن النسائي.

٢- مشكاة المصابيح:
مؤلفه أبو عبد الله محمد بن عبد الله الخطيب التبريزي من علماء القرن الثامن الهجري، وقد جمع فيه الأحاديث الواردة في كتب الحديث، مثل: صحيح البخاري، وصحيح مسلم، وموطأ مالك، والأم للشافعي، ومسند أحمد، وسنن الترمذي، وسنن أبي داود، وسنن النسائي، وسنن ابن ماجه، وسنن الدارمي، وسنن الدارقطني، وسنن البيهقي، والتجريد للصحاح الستة لرزين.

٣- جمع الجوامع:
«جمع الجوامع» أو «الجامع الكبير» مؤلفه جلال الدين عبد الرحمن بن أبي بكر السيوطي، ولد السيوطي عام (٨٤٩هـ)، وتوفي سنة (٩١١هـ).

وقد قصد السيوطي أن يجمع فيه جميع حديث رسول الله ﷺ، وقد جمع فيه أحاديث واحد وسبعين كتاباً من كتب الحديث[1].

١ انظر أسماء هذه الكتب في ضعيف الجامع الصغير: ١/ ٣١.

4) *Al-Jāmiʿ as-Saghīr and its Supplement*

The compiler of *al-Jāmiʿ aṣ-Ṣaghīr* was also Imām as-Suyūṭi; it is essentially a more concise version of the former *al-Jāmiʿ al-Kabīr*.

Shaykh Nāṣir ad-Dīn al-Albāni said, "The book *al-Jāmiʿ aṣ-Ṣaghīr min Ḥadīth al-Bashīr an-Nadhīr* by al-Ḥāfiẓ as-Suyūṭi is one of the most compres hensive and beneficial books of hadith, in addition to being of the easiest to handle and one of the best organized..."[1]

As-Suyūti arranged the hadith(s) of his book alphabetically and added a supplement to its end which he arranged in the same fashion and named *Ziyādat al-Jāmiʿ*. Shaykh Yūsuf an-Nabhāni fused the original book and its supplement together, arranged the new compilation and named it *al-Fatḥ al-Kabīr fī Dumm az-Ziyādah ilā al-Jāmiʿ aṣ-Ṣaghīr*.

Shaykh al-Albāni then came and verified this great book, differentiated between its authentic and weak hadith(s) and printed it in two volumes. He named the first *Ṣaḥīḥ al-Jāmiʿ aṣ-Ṣaghīr wa Ziyādatuh* and the second *Ḍaʿīf al-Jāmiʿ aṣ-Ṣaghīr wa Ziyādatuh*.[2]

II. Books of Juristic Commentaries on the Qur'an and Sunnah

These compilations deal with the Qur'anic verses and the Prophetic hadith(s) that entail juristic rulings on matters of practice. In other words, these are the books that discuss the meanings of verses and hadith(s) which explain how to perform certain practices. These verses and hadith(s) are what the jurists erected the Islamic *Fiqh* science upon, since the definition of *Fiqh* is, "Knowledge of the practical legislated rulings that are derived from the detailed evidences."[3]

1 Ibid: 1/28

2 The two books were printed by al-Maktab al-Islāmi. Its first publication was in 1388 A.H./1969 A.D. Each of the two books is comprised of six parts, and the number of hadith(s) in Sahīh al-Jāmiʿ as-Saghīr wa Ziyādatuh is 8058 and the number of hadith(s) in Daʿīf al-Jāmiʿ as-Saghīr wa Ziyādatuh is 6469.

3 *Jamiʿ al-Jawāmiʿ* 2/42

٤- الجامع الصغير وزيادته:

مؤلف كتاب «الجامع الصغير» هو السيوطي مؤلف «الجامع الكبير»، وقد أخذ «جامعه الصغير» من «الجامع الكبير».

وقد قال فيه الشيخ ناصر الدين الألباني: «الجامع الصغير من حديث البشير النذير، للحافظ السيوطي، من أجمع كتب الحديث مادة وأغزرها فائدة، وأقربها تناولاً، وأسهلها ترتيباً...»(١).

وقد رتب السيوطي كتابه هذا على حروف المعجم، وقد وضع له ذيلاً سماه «زيادة الجامع»، رتبه كترتيبه، وقد قام الشيخ يوسف النبهاني بضم «الزيادة» إلى «الجامع» ومزج أحدهما بالآخر، ورتبهما ترتيباً لا بأس به، وسماه «الفتح الكبير في ضم الزيادة إلى الجامع الصغير»(٢).

ثم جاء الشيخ ناصر الدين الألباني فحقق هذا الكتاب العظيم، وفصل بين الأحاديث الصحيحة والأحاديث الضعيفة، وطبعه في كتابين، سمي الأول: «صحيح الجامع الصغير وزيادته»، وسمي الثاني: «ضعيف الجامع الصغير وزيادته»(٣).

ثانياً: تصنيف مدونات التفسير الفقهي وشروح الحديث الفقهية:

المراد بالمصنفات في التفسير الفقهي وشروح الحديث الفقهية العلم المعروف بآيات الأحكام وأحاديث الأحكام.

ونعني بآيات الأحكام وأحاديث الأحكام نصوص الكتاب والسنة التي تشتمل على الأحكام العملية، أي: المتعلقة بكيفية العمل، وهذه الآيات والأحاديث هي التي أقام عليها الفقهاء بناء علم الفقه الإسلامي، فقد عرف الفقهاء الفقه الإسلامي بأنه: «العلم بالأحكام الشرعية العملية المكتسب من الأدلة التفصيلية»(٤).

١ ضعيف الجامع: ١/ ٤.

٢ المصدر السابق: ١/ ٢٨.

٣ وقد طبع الكتابين المكتب الإسلامي، وطبعته الأولى مؤرخة بتاريخ (١٣٨٨هـ- ١٩٦٩م)، وكل واحد من الكتابين يتألف من ستة أجزاء، وعدد أحاديث صحيح الجامع الصغير وزيادته (٨٠٥٨) حديثاً، وعدد ضعيف الجامع الصغير وزيادته (٦٤٦٩) حديثاً.

٤ جمع الجوامع: ٢/ ٤٢.

The "detailed evidences" referred to in this definition are these verses and hadith(s) which are known as the verses pertaining to rulings and the hadith(s) pertaining to rulings.

Early Muslim scholars paved the way for us by writing books in which they explained the Qur'anic verses pertaining to rulings. Of these books are:

Aḥkām al-Qur'ān by Aḥmad ibn 'Ali ar-Rāzi al-Ḥanafi, better known as al-Jaṣṣāṣ (305 – 370 A.H.)

Aḥkām al-Qur'ān by Abūl-Ḥasan 'Ali ibn Muhammad ash-Shāfi'i, better known as Ilkiyā al-Hirrāsi (450 – 504 A.H.)

Aḥkām al-Qur'an by Abū Bakr Muhammad ibn 'Abdillāh al-Mu'āfiri al-Andalusi al-Māliki, better known as Ibn al-'Arabi (468 – 543 A.H.)

Al-Jāmi' li Āyāt al-Aḥkām by Abū 'Abdillāh ibn Muhammad ibn Aḥmad al-Anṣāri al-Khazraji al-Māliki, better known as al-Qurṭubi, who died in 671 A.H.

This last book is the best of them, as it not only explains the Qur'anic verses pertaining to juristic rulings but also explains the rest of the Qur'an as well. Moreover, being Māliki did not drive him to stubbornly follow their views in all matters. Instead, he investigated the evidences until he arrived at whatever he believed was correct, regardless of whose view it was. His fairness drove him to even defend those who were roughly criticized by Ibn al-'Arabi al-Māliki for having different views, and would at times blame him for harsh expressions he used in reference to the Muslim scholars who merely held different opinions.[1]

والأدلة التفصيلية المذكورة في التعريف هي هذه الآيات والأحاديث المعروفة بآيات الأحكام وأحاديث الأحكام.

وقد مهد لنا علماؤنا الأوائل الطريق عندما قام جمع من العلماء بوضع مؤلفات فسروا فيها آيات الأحكام، ومن هذه المؤلفات:

٣- كتاب أحكام القرآن لأحمد بن علي الرازي الحنفي المشهور بالجصاص (٣٠٥- ٣٧٠هـ).

٤- كتاب أحكام القرآن لأبي الحسن علي بن محمد الشافعي المشهور بإلكيا الهراسي (٤٥٠- ٥٠٤هـ).

٥- وكتاب أحكام القرآن لأبي بكر محمد بن عبد الله المعافري الأندلسي المالكي المشهور بابن العربي (٤٦٨- ٥٤٣هـ).

٦- وكتاب الجامع لآيات الأحكام لأبي عبد الله محمد بن أحمد الأنصاري الخزرجي المالكي المشهور بالقرطبي المتوفى سنة ٦٧١هـ.

وهذا الأخير هو أفضلها؛ فهو لم يكتف بتفسير آيات الأحكام، بل فسر القرآن كله، ومع أنه مالكي فإنه لا يتعصب لمذهبه، بل يمشي مع الدليل حتى يصل إلى ما يرى أنه الصواب أياً كان قائله، وقد دفعه إنصافه أن يقف موقف الدفاع عمن يهاجمهم ابن العربي من المخالفين، مع توجيه اللوم إليه أحياناً على ما يصدر منه من عبارات قاسية في حق علماء المسلمين، الذاهبين إلى ما لم يذهب إليه(١).

1 At-Tafsīr wal-Mufassirīn 2/428 by adh-Dhahabi

١ التفسير والمفسرون للذهبي: ٢/ ٤٢٨.

Books of Juristic Explanations of Prophetic Hadith(s)
Comprehensive works of hadith were compiled which collected everything that came from the Messenger (ﷺ). They did not differentiate between hadith(s) pertaining to creed, juristic rulings, morals, exhortation, stories or events. Of them was *Ṣaḥīḥ al-Bukhāri, Ṣaḥīḥ Muslim, Musnad al-Imām Aḥmad, al-Muwaṭṭa'* by Imām Mālik, *al-Musnad* by aṭ-Ṭayālisi and many others.

Aside from these, some scholars compiled works on the Sunnah-based rulings in particular, such as Abū Dāwūd, at-Tirmidhi, Ibn Mājah, ad-Dārimi and others. These great scholars had intended to only collect the hadith(s) pertaining to juristic rulings, but did not fully abide by these guidelines and ended up including others as well.

Another group of scholars did in fact compile the hadith(s) pertaining to juristic rulings and then arranged these compilations based on the various subjects in *Fiqh*.

The most important of these compilations are:

1) *'Umdat al-Ahkām*
It was compiled by Shaykh 'Abdul-Ghani ibn 'Abdil-Wāḥid ibn 'Ali ibn Rafi' al-Jammā'ili al-Maqdisi ad-Dimashqi, also known as Taqi ad-Dīn. He was the greatest *ḥāfiẓ* (hadith expert) of his time. He was born in 541 A.H. and died in 600 A.H.

Shaykh 'Abdul-Ghani excelled in many branches of religious sciences, though his greatest focus was Hadith. Shaykh 'Ali ibn Muhammad al-Hindi, the verifier of the book Ḥāshiyat al-'Uddah 'alā I*ḥkām al-Aḥkām,* said that *'Umdat al-Aḥkām* is the most concise, most authentic and oldest book of hadith pertaining to juristic rulings.[1]

1 Muqadimmat Hāshiyat al-'Uddah 1/4

المؤلفات في أحاديث الأحكام وشروحها:

ألفت في الأحاديث كتب جامعة تجمع كل ما صدر عن الرسول ﷺ من حديث، لا فرق بين أحاديث العقائد والأحكام والأخلاق والمواعظ والقصص والأخبار، ومن ذلك صحيح البخاري، وصحيح مسلم، ومسند الإمام أحمد، وموطأ مالك، ومسند الطيالسي، وغيرها كثير.

وخص جمع من العلماء أحاديث السنن بالتأليف، كالسنن لكل من أبي داود والترمذي والنسائي وابن ماجه والدارمي وغيرهم.

وهؤلاء العلماء الفضلاء اتجهوا إلى جمع أحاديث الأحكام، ولكنهم لم يلتزموا بذلك التزاماً تامّاً، فقد أدخلوا فيها غيرها.

ثم جاءت طائفة أخرى عنيت بجمع أحاديث الأحكام دون غيرها، ورتبوا هذه المؤلفات على أبواب الفقه، وسنذكر أهم هذه المؤلفات.

١- كتاب عمدة الأحكام

ومؤلفه هو الشيخ عبد الغني بن عبد الواحد بن علي بن رافع الجماعيلي المقدسي ثم الدمشقي الملقب بتقي الدين، كان حافظ عصره، ولد سنة إحدى وأربعين وخمسمائة وتوفي في سنة ستمائة للهجرة النبوية.

نبغ الشيخ في علوم كثيرة، ولكن عنايته كانت في الحديث أكثر وأعظم، وكتابه كما يقول محقق كتاب حاشية العدة على إحكام الأحكام الشيخ علي بن محمد الهندي: «أوجز كتب الأحكام وأصحها وأقدمها»(١).

١ مقدمة حاشية العدة: ١/ ٤.

Shaykh Aḥmad Shākir, the verifier of the book *Iḥkām al-Aḥkām*, said in the introduction of that book, "In this book, Shaykh 'Abdul-Ghani compiled all the hadith(s) that the *Fiqh* chapters are centered around, those of them with the highest caliber of authenticity, like those agreed upon by Imām al-Bukhāri and Imām Muslim. From there came the book *'Umdat al-Aḥkām* which can be understood by the student of knowledge, the beginner and the intermediate alike. At the same time, the well-versed researcher can hardly do without it."[1]

According to Shaykh 'Ali ibn Muhammad al-Hindi, the verifier of the book *Ḥāshiyat al-'Uddah 'alā Iḥkām al-Aḥkām*, the number of hadith(s) narrated in the book *'Umdat al-Aḥkām* is 419 hadith(s). As for Shaykh Aḥmad Shākir, he mentioned that the number of hadith(s) reported in this book are 427, though he mentioned in the introduction to his book that the hadith(s) narrated in *'Umdat al-Aḥkām* are more than 500 hadith(s).

2) *Ihkām al-Ahkām*

In this book, the great scholar and judge Taqi ad-Dīn Abūl-Futūḥ Muhammad ibn 'Ali ibn Wahb al-Miṣri al-Qushayri, better known as Ibn Daqīq al-'Īd, explained *'Umdat al-Aḥkām*. He was born in 625 A.H. and died in 702 A.H.

Imām Ibn Daqīq al-'Īd (may Allah bestow mercy upon him) was exceptionally skillful at identifying defects in the chains of hadith, as well as extracting the rulings of Sharia from its sources – namely the Book of Allah and the Sunnah of His Messenger (ﷺ). Atop that, he was notably skillful in the related sciences as well.[2]

وقال محقق كتاب: «إحكام الأحكام» الشيخ أحمد شاكر في مقدمته لذلك الشرح: جمع الشيخ عبد الغني في هذا الكتاب الأحاديث التي هي: أصول الأبواب أو جلها، فكان مما يحفظ ويقتنى، واقتصر فيه على أحاديث من أعلى أنواع الصحيح، مما اتفق على إخراجه الشيخان: البخاري ومسلم في صحيحيهما، فكان كتابه هذا: «عمدة الأحكام»، وكان كتاباً قريباً لطالب العلم المبتدي والمتوسط، ثم لا يستغني عنه المنتهي والمتبحر(١).

ومجموع أحاديث الكتاب تسعة عشر وأربعمائة حديثاً، وفق إحصاء محقق كتاب «حاشية العدة على إحكام الأحكام» الشيخ علي بن محمد الهندي، أما الشيخ أحمد شاكر فإنه بلغ ترقيمه أحاديث الكتاب إلى سبعة وعشرين وأربعمائة حديث، وإن نص في مقدمته هو على أن أحاديثه تزيد على الخمسمائة حديث.

٢- إحكام الأحكام شرح عمدة الأحكام:

هذا الكتاب شرح فيه الإمام العلامة القاضي تقي الدين أبو الفتح محمد بن علي بن وهب المصري القشيري المعروف بابن دقيق العيد، المولود في سنة خمس وعشرين وستمائة والمتوفى سنة اثنتين وسبعمائة للهجرة كتاب «عمدة الأحكام» السابق ذكره.

والإمام ابن دقيق العيد- رحمه الله- «جمع بين التقدم في معرفة علل الحديث وحسن الاستنباط للأحكام والمعاني الشرعية من مصادرها في كتاب الله- جل وعز- وسنة رسوله- صلوات الله وسلامه عليه- مع المشاركة في جميع العلوم التي تتصل بذلك»(٢).

---

1 Muqaddimat Ihkām al-Ahkām: p. 7-8 by Ibn Daqīq al-'Īd and verified by Ahmad Shākir

2 Hāshiyat 'Uddat al-Ahkām 1/5 by Muhibb ad-Dīn al-Khatib

١ مقدمة إحكام الأحكام لابن دقيق العبد لأحمد شاكر: ص٧، ٨ مع تقديم وتأخير وشيء من التصرف.

٢ محب الدين الخطيب كتاب حاشية عدة الأحكام: ١/ ٥.

3) *Al-Hāshiyah*

The great Yemeni scholar Shaykh Muhammad ibn Isma'īl al-Amīr aṣ-Ṣan'āni wrote a commenā tary on Ibn Daqīq al-'Īd's book *Iḥkām al-Aḥkām*, which was an explanation of *'Umdat al-Aḥkām*. He named his book *al-'Uddah 'alā Iḥkām al-Aḥkām*.

Aṣ-Ṣan'āni was one of the great scholars of Yemen. Aside from *al-Ḥāshiyah*, he wrote a book entitled *Subul as-Salām* in which he explains the book *Bulugh al-Marām* by Ibn Ḥajar al-'Asqalāni.

He was born in 1099 A.H. in the city of Kaḥlān, and then moved to San'ā' in 1110 A.H. He died in 1182 A.H. after living his life as a skilled veteran in the sciences of Hadith and in defense of the Sunnah.

The book *al-Ḥāshiyah* is printed in four volumes, under the care of Muḥibb ad-Dīn al-Khaṭib, and verified by 'Ali ibn Muhammad al-Hindi.[1]

4) *Bulugh al-Marām*

This book was compiled by "Amīr al-Mu'minīn fil-Ḥadith"[2] Abūl-Faḍl Aḥmad ibn 'Ali ibn Muhammad al-'Asqalāni al-Miṣri, better known as Ibn Ḥajar al-'Asqalāni.

He was born in 773 A.H. and both his parents died when he was a child. He had mastered the science of Hadith and serviced it greatly. He died in 852 A.H. and the number of hadith(s) in his book reached 1,477 hadith(s).[3]

5) *Subul as-Salām*

This book is an explanation on the aforementioned *Bulugh al-Marām* that was written by Shaykh al-Ḥusayn ibn Muhammad al-Maghribi. Then, Shaykh Muhammad ibn Isma'īl, best known as aṣ-Ṣan'āni, abridged this explanation.

1 Printed by al-Maktabah as-Salafiyyah in Cairo.

2 In Hadith terminology, this term is used as a title to any person who has extensive knowledge of most hadith(s), whereby only a few hadith(s) escaped his knowledge.

3 See Ibn 'Affān's print of the explanation of Subul as-Salām, Cairo, 1st Edition (1420 A.H./2000 AD).

٣- حاشية الصنعاني على إحكام الأحكام:

وضع علامة اليمن الشيخ محمد بن إسماعيل الأمير الصنعاني حاشية على إحكام الأحكام شرح عمدة الأحكام لابن دقيق العيد، سماه بـ«العدة على إحكام الأحكام».

والصنعاني أحد أعلام اليمن، وهو شارح بلوغ المرام لابن حجر العسقلاني الذي اشتهر باسم «سبل السلام».

ولد في مدينة كحلان سنة (١٠٩٩)، وانتقل إلى مدينة صنعاء سنة (١١١٠)، وتوفي سنة: (١١٨٢)، وكان له باع طويل في علم الحديث ونصرة السنة.

والحاشية مطبوعة في أربع مجلدات كبار بعناية محب الدين الخطيب، وتحقيق علي بن محمد الهندي[(١)].

٤- كتاب بلوغ المرام:

هذا الكتاب من تأليف أمير المؤمنين في الحديث أبو الفضل، أحمد بن علي بن محمد العسقلاني المصري المشتهر بابن حجر العسقلاني.

ولد- رحمه الله- سنة (٧٧٣) ومات أبواه وهو صغير، وقد بلغ في علم الحديث الغاية، وكانت له فيه النهاية، وتوفي سنة (٨٥٢هـ)، وقد بلغت أحاديث الكتاب (١٤٧٧) حديثاً[(٢)].

٥- سبل السلام شرح بلوغ المرام:

شرح الشيخ الحسين بن محمد المغربي كتاب «بلوغ المرام» السابق الذكر، وقد اختصر هذا الشرح الشيخ العلامة محمد بن إسماعيل المشتهر بالصنعاني صاحب كتاب العدة الذي سبق ذكره.

١ طبعة السلفية القاهرة (١٣٧٩هـ).

٢ انظر طبعة دار ابن عفان لشرحه سبل السلام، القاهرة، الأولى (١٤٢٠هـ- ٢٠٠٠م).

It has been predestined for this abridgment to become wide-spread. As for the commentary itself written by al-Maghribi, had it not been mentioned in the introduction to the abridgement by aṣ-Ṣan'āni, it would not have been known at all.

Aṣ-Ṣan'āni explained his method in abridging this explanation, and his modification to *Bulugh al-Marām*, by saying, "This is a light explanation of *Bulugh al-Marām*, which was authored by the great scholar Shaykh al-Islām Aḥmad ibn 'Ali ibn Ḥajar (may Allah station him in the lands of peace). I abridged it from the explanation of the great scholar and judge Sharaf ad-Dīn al-Ḥusayn ibn Muhammad al-Maghribi. I limited myself to merely decoding its terms and clarifying their meanings – seeking by that the pleasure of Allah. Additionally, I simplified it for the readers and students by omitting the various views and differences of opinion unless that was directly relevant to the evidences. Also, I avoided being detrimentally brief or overwhelmingly long, though I added a load of useful lessons aside from those in the original. I ask Allah to make it of the most beneficial things [for me] on the Appointed Day, for He is sufficient for me, and the best Disposer of my affairs, and upon Him we rely in the beginning and the end."[1]

6) *Al-Muntaqā min al-Akhbār fil-Ahkām*

This book was compiled by the great Imām and Ḥāfiẓ Abūl-Barakāt Majd ad-Dīn 'Abdus-Salām ibn 'Abdillāh ibn Muhammad ibn al-Khaḍir ibn Taymiyah, the grandfather of Shaykh al-Islām Ibn Taymiyah. He selected the material of this book from his larger book *al-Ahkām al-Kubrā*.

The number of hadith(s) in this book is 5029, according to the numbering of its publisher, Muḥibb ad-Dīn al-Khaṭib.

وقد قدر لهذا الشرح أن ينتشر، ويطبق ذكره الآفاق، أما أصله، وهو شرح المغربي، فلولا إشارة الصنعاني إليه في مقدمة كتابه لما عرف له ذكر.

وقد بين الصنعاني منهجه في اختصاره لذلك الشرح وفعله فيه فقال: «هذا شرح لطيف على «بلوغ المرام» تأليف الشيخ العلامة، شيخ الإسلام: أحمد بن علي بن حجر، أحله الله دار السلام، اختصرته من شرح القاضي العلامة شرف الدين: الحسين بن محمد المغربي، مقتصراً على حل ألفاظه، وبيان معانيه، قاصداً بذلك وجه الله، ثم التقريب للطالبين والناظرين فيه، مُعْرِضاً عن ذكر الخلافات والأقاويل، إلا أن يدعوا إليه ما يرتبط به الدليل، ومتجنباً للإيجاز المُخِلِّ والإطناب المُمِلِّ، وقد ضممت إليه زيادات جمة على ما في الأصل من الفوائد، والله أسأل أن يجعله في المعاد من خير العوائد، فهو حسبي ونعم الوكيل، وعليه في البداية والنهاية التعويل»[١].

٦- كتاب المنتقى من الأخبار في الأحكام:

ألف هذا الكتاب الإمام الحافظ أبو البركات مجد الدين عبد السلام بن عبد الله بن محمد بن الخضر بن تيمية جد شيخ الإسلام ابن تيمية، وقد انتقى هذا الكتاب من كتابه الكبير الذي سماه «الأحكام الكبرى».

وقد بلغت أحاديث «المنتقى» حسب ترقيم ناشره محب الدين الخطيب (٥٠٢٩) حديثاً.

1 *Subul as-Salām* 31

١ سبل السلام: ٣١.

The great scholar ash-Shawkāni, who wrote the explanation for this book, described this book by saying, "The book entitled *al-Muntaqā min al-Akhbār fil-Aḥkām* is matchless; no other imām has ever composed anything like it. It collects a brilliant selection of the purified Sunnah that no other book has collected, and it almost entirely encompasses every hadith on juristic rulings. Furthermore, it contains a multitude of juristic lessons, which are implied by the hadith(s), that would normally take lifespans to collect. Eventually, this book became a vital resource for many scholars in their search for evidence, especially in this age and these lands."[1]

7) *Nayl al-Awṭār*

This book is an explanation of *al-Muntaqā* that was written by Abū 'Abdillāh Muhammad ibn 'Ali ibn Muhammad ash-Shawkāni aṣ-Ṣan'āni, the greatest scholar of Yemen at his time. He was born in 1172 A.H. and died in 1250 A.H.

Imām ash-Shawkāni was a scholar in Hadith, *tafsīr*, *fiqh* and *uṣūl al-fiqh*. In addition, he was a historian, literarian and grammarian, who gravitated to being the chief judge of Yemen.

The book *Nayl al-Awṭār* was distinguished in the following aspects:

- The author references each hadith and shows its grade, whether authentic or weak, alongside mentioning the views of the Hadith scholars on it.
- The author mentions the linguistic and technical definitions for the words in each hadith.
- The author deduces the juristic rulings and its evidences without stubbornness or bias.
- The author mentions the views of the Companions, the Successors and the scholarly views from all eight *madhhab*(s): the four *Mujtahid Imām*(s), the Ẓāhiri *madhhab*, the Twelver Shiites, the Zaydi sect and the Ibāḍi sect.
- The author relies on the holistic fundamental principles and explains how applying them results in each detailed ruling.[2]

1 Nayl al-Awtār 1/5, printed by Dār al-Khayr (Beirut & Damascus), 1st Edition (1416 A.H. /1996 AD)

2 The introduction to Nayl al-Awtār by Dr. Wahbah az-Zuhayli.

وقد وصف هذا الكتاب شارحه العلامة الشوكاني فقال: «الكتاب الموسوم بالمنتقى من الأخبار في الأحكام لم ينسج على بديع منواله، ولا حرر على شكله ومثاله أحد من الأئمة الأعلام، قد جمع من السنة المطهرة ما لم يجتمع في غيره من الأسفار، وبلغ إلى غاية في الإحاطة بأحاديث الأحكام، تتقاصر عنها الدفاتر الكبار، وشمل من دلائل المسائل جملة نافعة تفنى دون الظفر ببعضها طوال الأعمار، وصار مرجعاً لجلة العلماء عند الحاجة إلى طلب الدليل، لا سيما في هذه الديار وهذه الأعصار»[1].

٧- نيل الأوطار شرح منتقى الأخبار:

وقد شرح «المنتقى» أبو عبد الله محمد بن علي بن محمد الشوكاني ثم الصنعاني عالم اليمن في عصره ولد في (١١٧٢هـ) وتوفي في سنة (١٢٥٠هـ).

وقد كان الشوكاني محدثاً مفسراً فقيهاً مجتهداً أصوليّاً مؤرخاً أديباً نحويّاً، وقد وصل إلى درجة قاضي قضاة اليمن.

ويتميز كتاب نيل الأوطار بالمزايا التالية:

- تخريج الحديث وبيان درجته من صحة وضعف، وأقوال أئمة الحديث فيه.
- إيضاح معاني ألفاظ الحديث لغة واصطلاحاً شرعيّاً.
- استنباط الأحكام الشرعية وأدلتها من غير تعصب ولا تعسف.
- إيراد أقوال الصحابة والتابعين ومذاهب علماء الأمصار وأئمة المذاهب الثمانية «الأربعة والإمامية والزيدية الظاهرية والإباضية».
- الاعتماد على القواعد الأصولية والشرعية الكلية، وبيان كيفية تطبيق الأحكام الشرعية الفرعية عليها[2].

١ نيل الأوطار: ١/ ٥، طبعة دار الخير، بيروت ودمشق، الأولى (١٤١٦هـ-١٩٩٦م).

٢ نيل الأوطار: المقدمة للدكتور وهبة الزحيلي.

8) *Ṣafwat al-Aḥkām*

This book was written by a contemporary scholar, Professor Qahṭān 'Abdur-Raḥmān ad-Dawri, who depended on the books *Nayl al-Awṭār* and *Subul as-Salām* to author his book.[1]

The Hadith(s) that Qualify as Evidence for Juristic Rulings

For a hadith to qualify as evidence for a ruling, it is stipulated that this hadith be authentic, irrespective of whether this ruling pertains to creed, morals or practice.

An authentic hadith is, as defined by Ibn Kathīr, "a hadith with a complete chain that is comprised entirely of credible, upright narrators, and is not *shādh*[2] (odd) nor *ma'lul* (defective).[3]"[4]

Similarly, Imam an-Nawawi defined it as, "that which its chain is complete with credible, upright transmitters and does not bear any *shudhudh* (irregularity) or *'illah* (defect)."[5]

1 Printed by Dār al-Furqān (Amman, Jordan).
2 A shādh (odd) hadith is that which has a chain of trustworthy narrators, but its text contradicts a resembling hadith whose narrators are more trustworthy.
3 A ma'lul (defective) hadith is that which has an apparently sound chain, but a hidden defect is discovered that affects its degree of authenticity.
4 Al-Bā'ith al-Hathīth Sharh Ikhtisār 'Ulūm al-Hadīth li Ibn-Kathīr 19 by Ahmad Shākir, printed by Dār al-Fikr
5 Tadrīb ar-Rāwi fī Sharh Taqrīb an-Nawāwi 26 by as-Suyūti. This was printed by Dār al-Kutub al-'Ilmiyyah, Beirut (1st Edition, 1417 A.H./1996 AD).

٨- كتاب صفوة الأحكام من نيل الأوطار وسبل السلام:

مؤلف هذا الكتاب عالم معاصر هو الأستاذ قحطان عبد الرحمن الدوري(١).

وقد اعتمد في تأليفه على كتاب نيل الأوطار وكتاب سبل السلام.

الأحاديث التي يحتج بها في الأحكام:

يشترط في الأحاديث التي يحتج بها في الأحكام أن تكون صحيحة، لا فرق بين الأحكام العقائدية أو الأخلاقية أو العملية.

والحديث الصحيح كما عرفه ابن كثير هو: «الحديث المسند الذي يتصل إسناده بنقل العدل الضابط إلى منتهاه، ولا يكون شاذاً ولا معللاً»(٢).

وقال النووي في حده: «هو ما اتصل سنده بالعدول الضابطين من غير شذوذ ولا علة»(٣).

١ طبع في دار الفرقان، عمان- الأردن.
٢ «الباعث الحثيث شرح اختصار علوم الحديث لابن كثير» لأحمد شاكر: ١٩، دار الفكر.
٣ تدريب الراوي في شرح تقريب النواوي للسيوطي: ٢٦، دار الكتب العلمية، بيروت، الأولى (١٤١٧هـ- ١٩٩٦م).

Based on this definition, a hadith is not authentic if there exists any sort of disconnect in its chain of narrators, such as it being *munqaṭi'* (severed),[1] *mu'ḍal* (problematic)[2] or *mursal* (loose).[3] Also, a hadith is not authentic when a narrator in its chain is not trustworthy, such as someone who is unknown, or his reputation is unknown, or is known to be indecent. Also, a hadith is not authentic when the credibility of one of its narrators is flawed, such as him having a weak memory or being lax and having many mistakes. Additionally, a hadith is not authentic when a trustworthy transmitter opposes with his narration someone more trustworthy than him. Furthermore, a hadith is not authentic when a consequential defect is discovered in its transmission.[4]

The Impermissibility of Using Fabricated Hadith(s) as Evidence

Hadith scholars and others are unanimously agreed that citing a *mawḍū'* (fabricated) hadith as evidence is not permissible.

A *mawḍū'* hadith is that which is forged and dishonestly attributed to the Messenger of Allah (ﷺ).

Obviously, whatever is falsely attributed to the Messenger of Allah (ﷺ) is not part of the religion of Allah, and lying on behalf of Allah and/or His Messenger (ﷺ) is of the greatest crimes. The Most High says, **"So who is more unjust than one who lies about Allah and denies the truth when it has come to him?"**[5]

1 A munqaṭi' (severed) hadith is that which has a disconnect in its narrators, but after the generations of the Companions and Successors.

2 A mu'dal (problematic) hadith is that which two or more narrators are missing from its chain. Hence, it becomes very problematic to judge the authenticity when two disconnects exist or one disconnect that is two generations long.

3 A mursal (loose) hadith is that which its content is not ascribed by the Successor to a particular narrator from among the Companions. Since the Succesor, by definition, is someone that never met the Prophet (ﷺ), this entails a form of disconnect in the chain.

4 See Qawā'id at-Tahdīth min Funūn Mustalah al-Hadīth 79 by Jamal ad-Dīn al-Qāsimi, verified by Muhammad Bahjah al-Bitār ('Īsā al-Bābi al-Halabi, Cairo).

5 Sūrat az-Zumar - Verse 32

فخرج من الصحيح ما لم يكن متصل الإسناد بأن يكون مقطوعاً بأي وجوه الانقطاع، ومنه المنقطع والمعضل والمرسل، وخرج بالعدل من لم يكن مستور العدالة، فلا يقبل ما نقله مجهول عيناً أو حالاً أو المعروف بالضعف، وخرج بالضابط من لم يكن حافظاً متيقظاً، فلا تقبل رواية المغفل كثير الخطأ، وخرج بالشذوذ ما يرويه الثقة مخالفاً من هو أوثق منه، وخرج بالعلة ما فيه أسباب خفية قادحة، فخرج الشاذ والمعلل(١).

عدم جواز الاحتجاج بالموضوع:

اتفق أهل العلم من المحدثين وغيرهم على عدم جواز الاحتجاج بالحديث الموضوع في الأحكام.

والموضوع من الحديث هو: «المختلق المصنوع»(٢) المكذوب على رسول الله ﷺ.

والمكذوب على رسول الله ﷺ ليس من دين الله، والكذب على الله وعلى رسوله من أعظم الجرائم: ﴿فَمَنْ أَظْلَمُ مِمَّن كَذَبَ عَلَى اللهِ﴾(٣).

١ راجع قواعد التحديث من فنون مصطلح الحديث، لجمال الدين القاسمي، تحقيق محمد بهجة البيطار: ٧٩، عيسى البابي الحلبي، القاهرة.

٢ علوم الحديث لابن الصلاح: ٩٨، وتنزيه الشريعة لابن عراق الكناني: ١/ ٥.

٣ الزمر: ٣٢.

The Impermissibility of Using Weak Hadith(s) as Evidence for Rulings

Just as it is not permissible to cite fabricated hadith(s) as evidence, it also is not permissible to cite weak hadith(s) as evidence. A weak hadith is any hadith in which the conditions of authenticity are not all met.[1]

Similarly, other scholars defined a weak hadith as, "Any hadith which lacks one of the conditions for acceptance. There are degrees of weak hadith, some being weaker than others, and the worst of them being the fabricated hadith."[2]

The "Weak" Hadith(s) Which the Scholars Accept as Evidence

The impermissibility of using weak hadith(s) as evidence may appear problematic since it has been reported that Imām Abū Ḥanīfah, Imām Aḥmad ibn Ḥanbal and others accepted weak hadith(s) and preferred them over *ra'y* and *qiyās* when deducing rulings.

1 See al-Shadhā al-Fayyāh min 'Ulūm Ibn Salāh 1/133 by Shaykh Burhān ad-Dīn al-Abnāsi.

2 Mu'jam 'Ulūm al-Hadīth 141 by Dr. 'Abdur-Rahmān ibn Ibrahīm al-Khamīsi. Printed by Dār al-Andalus, Jeddah (1st Edition, 1421 A.H./2000 AD).

لا يجوز الاحتجاج بالضعيف من الحديث في الأحكام:

وكما لا يجوز الاحتجاج بالموضوع من الحديث، فإنه لا يجوز الاحتجاج بالضعيف أيضاً، ويعرف الحديث الضعيف من النظر في الحديث الصحيح «فكل حديث لم تجتمع فيه صفات الحديث الصحيح فهو ضعيف»[١].

وقالوا في تعريفه أيضاً: «هو الحديث الذي فقد شرطاً من شروط القبول، وهو أنواع بعضها أضعف من بعض، وشرها الموضوع»[٢].

مراد أهل العلم بالضعيف الذي يجوز الاحتجاج به:

يشكل على ما ذكرته من عدم جواز الاحتجاج بالضعيف في الأحكام ما عُزي إلى الإمام أبي حنيفة وأحمد وغيرهما أنهما يأخذان بالحديث الضعيف في الأحكام ويقدمانه على الرأي والقياس.

١ راجع: الشذا الفياح من علوم ابن الصلاح للشيخ برهان الدين الأبناسي: ١/ ١٣٣، مكتبة الرشد، الرياض، الطبعة الأولى (١٤١٨هـ-١٩٩٨م)، وقال في التعريف: «ما لم تجتمع فيه شروط الصحيح ولا الحسن».

٢ معجم علوم الحديث، د. عبد الرحمن بن إبراهيم الخميسي: ١٤١، دار الأندلس، جدة، الأولى (١٤٢١هـ- ٢٠٠٠م).

وقد بين شيخ الإسلام ابن تيمية- رحمه الله تعالى- أنه ليس مرادهما بالضعيف المتروك، لكن المراد به «الحسن»؛ كحديث عمرو بن شعيب عن أبيه، عن جده، وحديث إبراهيم بن مسلم العبدي، أبو إسحاق الكوفي المعروف بالهجري، وأمثالهما ممن يُحَسِّنُ الترمذي حديثه أو يصححه، وكان الحديث في اصطلاح من قبل الترمذي: إما صحيح وإما ضعيف، والضعيف نوعان: ضعيف متروك، وضعيف ليس بمتروك، فتكلم أئمة الحديث بذلك الاصطلاح، فجاء من لا يعرف اصطلاح الترمذي، فسمع قول بعض الأئمة: «الحديث الضعيف أحب إليَّ من القياس»، فظن أنه يحتج بالحديث الذي يضعفه مثل الترمذي، وأخذ يرجح طريقه من يرى أنه أتبع للحديث الصحيح، وهو من المتناقضين الذين يرجحون الشيء على ما هو أولى بالرجحان منه إن لم يكن دونه[١].

Shaykh al-Islām Ibn Taymiyah (may Allah bestow mercy upon him) explained that these were not *matrūk* (rejected) which they cited, but rather they were *ḥasan* (good) hadith(s).[1] Some examples of this are the hadith(s) narrated by ʻAmr ibn Shuʻayb, from his father, from his grandfather, or the hadith(s) narrated by Ibrāhīm ibn Muslim al-ʻAbdi, from Abū Isḥāq al-Kūfi, who is better known as al-Hijri, and other hadith(s) which at-Tirmidhi would deem *ḥasan* or authentic. Before the time of Imām at-Tirmidhi, a hadith was either graded authentic or weak, and the weak was subdivided into acceptable and *matrūk* (unacceptable). However, when scholars of hadith began using these terms differently, people came along that were unaware of this change. As a result, when some Imām(s) said, "A weak hadith is more desirable to me than *qiyās*," it was wrongly understood that these Imām(s) accepted hadith(s) deemed weak by at-Tirmidhi and his likes as evidence for juristic rulings. Subsequently, these people adopted the juristic views of those who only depended on clearly authentic hadith(s), and rejected worthier views because they thought its supporting evidence was unacceptable.[2]

وقال ابن القيم في «إعلام الموقعين»:

«أخذ الإمام أحمد بالمرسل والحديث الضعيف، إذا لم يكن في الباب شيء يدفعه، وهو الذي رجحه على القياس، وليس المراد بالضعيف عنده الباطل، ولا المنكر، ولا ما في روايته متهم، بحيث لا يسوغ الذهاب إليه والعمل به، بل الحديث الضعيف عنده قسيم الصحيح، وقسم من أقسام الحسن، ولم يكن يقسم الحديث إلى صحيح وحسن وضعيف، بل إلى صحيح وضعيف، وللضعيف عنده مراتب، فإذا لم يجد في الباب أثراً يدفعه، ولا قول صاحب، ولا إجماعاً على خلافه، كان العمل به عنده أولى من القياس، وليس أحد من الأئمة إلا وهو موافقه على هذا الأصل من حيث الجملة، فإنه ما منهم أحد إلا وقدم الحديث الضعيف على القياس»[٢].

In his book *Iʻlām al-Muwaqqiʻīn*, Ibn al-Qayyim said, "Imām Aḥmad would accept weak and *mursal* hadith(s) if no other hadith contradicted them, and he would also prefer it over *qiyās*. For him, weak hadith(s) differ from those that are *bāṭil* (invalid), *munkar* (denied) and those with chains containing a suspicious narrator. To him, weak hadith(s) are the counterpart of authentic hadith(s), and the *ḥasan* hadith falls under the former. He would not divide the hadith(s) into authentic, *ḥasan* and weak. Instead, he would merely divide them into authentic and weak, but considered the weak to have several degrees. Thus, whenever he did not come across another report which rejected the [*ḥasan*] hadith, nor a Companion's view on the matter, nor a consensus proving the opposite, he would prefer acting upon it over resorting to *qiyās*. Every *Mujtahid Imām*(s) agrees on this principle, in general at least, as they all would give weak hadith(s) preference over *qiyās*."[3]

١ منهاج السنة النبوية: ٤/ ٣٤١.
٢ إعلام الموقعين: ١/ ٣١.

1 A hasan (good) hadith is that which fulfills the conditions of an authentic hadith, except that the precision of its narrator(s) may be of a slightly less caliber than those of an authentic chain.
2 Minhāj as-Sunnah an-Nabawiyyah 4/341
3 Iʻlām al-Muwaqqiʻīn 1/31

Summary of Unit 9

1) In the era of stagnation and scholarly imitation, most people were interested in studying abridgements, commentaries and footnotes, and neglected the books of the early jurists, even the books by the founding Imām(s) of their *madhhab*(s).

2) Despite the fact that it was an era of imitation and stagnation, the peoples' care for the Prophetic Sunnah never vanished. For this reason, this era witnessed the production of comprehensive collections of the Sunnah, such as *Jāmi' al-Uṣūl* fī Aḥādith ar-Rasūl, *Mishkāt al-Maṣābīh*, *Jāmi' al-Jawāmi'* and *al-Jāmi' aṣ-Ṣaghīr* and its supplement.

3) Books on the juristic *tafsīr* of the Qur'an came into existence, such as *Aḥkām al-Qur'ān* by al-Jaṣṣāṣ, *Aḥkām al-Qur'ān* by Ibn al-'Arabi and *al-Jāmi' li Aḥkām al-Qur'ān* by al-Qurṭubi.

4) Collections of juristic hadith(s) were also produced, such *'Umdat al-Ahkām, Bulugh al-Marām* and its commentary *Subul as-Salām,* and *Muntaqā al-Akhbār* and its commentary *Nayl al-Awṭār*.

5) Scholars unanimously agreed upon the impermissbility of accepting weak hadith(s) as evidence for juristic rulings.

6) Weak hadith(s) can be divided into two subcategories:

- *Matrūk* (unacceptable) weak hadith(s): these cannot be used as evidence for establishing jurisitic rulings.
- *Maqbūl* (acceptable) weak hadith(s): these can be used as evidence for establishing juristic rulings according to some great jurists, such as Imām Abū Ḥanīfah and Imām Aḥmad.

خلاصة الوحدة

نخلص من دراسة هذه الوحدة إلى ما يلي:

١- عكف أكثر الناس في عصر التقليد على دراسة المختصرات وشروحها وحواشيها، وأهملوا النظر في كتب الأولين، حتى كتب الإمام الذي يقتدون به.

٢- لم تتوقف العناية بالسنة في هذا العصر -عصر التقليد- فظهرت المصنفات المستوعبة للأحاديث، مثل: جامع الأصول في أحاديث الرسول، ومشكاة المصابيح، وجمع الجوامع، والجامع الصغير وزيادته.

٣- ظهرت مصنفات التفسير الفقهي (وهو العلم المعروف بـ «آيات الأحكام») مثل: أحكام القرآن للجصاص، وأحكام القرآن لابن العربي، والجامع لأحكام القرآن للقرطبي.

٤- ظهرت أيضاً مصنفات «أحاديث الأحكام» مثل: عمدة الأحكام، وبلوغ المرام وشرحه «سبل السلام»، ومنتقى الأخبار، وشرحه «نيل الأوطار».

٥- اتفق أهل العلم على عدم جواز الاحتجاج بالحديث الموضوع في الأحكام.

٦- الأحاديث الضعيفة تنقسم إلى قسمين:

- ضعيف متروك: وهذا لا يجوز الاحتجاج به في الأحكام.
- ضعيف غير متروك: وهذا قد احتج به بعض العلماء، مثل أبي حنيفة والإمام أحمد.

Notes

Unit 10
The Compilation of *Fiqh* in the Era of *Taqlīd* and Stagnation

Contents of Unit 10

1) Compiling *Fiqh* Books Based on *Madhhab*
2) Compiling *Fiqh* Books Based on Evidence and the Classical Views
3) Compiling Books on the Principles of *Fiqh*

Importance of this Unit

The jurists of the four *madhhab*(s) continued compiling all different kinds of *Fiqh* books in this era. Despite the phenomena of *taqlīd* and intellectual stagnation that afflicted *Fiqh* in this age, there still existed some jurists who compiled a number of juristic books that followed the methods of the earliest generations. These works contained mention of the evidences, the views of the classical scholars of various lands and the views of the great Imām(s). Of these books is *al-Muhallā, al-Mughni, al-Majmū'* and others.

In this era, scholars also authored books on the science of *al-qawā'id al-fiqhiyyah* (the principles of *Fiqh*). Some examples are *al-Ashbāh wan-Naẓā'ir* by as-Suyūṭi, *Qawā'id al-Aḥkām fī Masāliḥ al-Anām* by al-'Izz ibn 'Abdis-Salām, and many others.

Come – let us now study this unit in order to fully understand, by Allah's favor, these details.

Learning objectives

By the end of this unit, readers should be able to:

1) Mention the most important texts compiled in this era and their commentaries
2) Draw a comparison between these texts and their commentaries and between the compilations that were based on the evidences
3) Explain how compiling the principles the *Fiqh* began and the most important books written on this subject

الوحدة العاشرة
التدوين الفقهي في عصر التقليد والجمود

محتويات الوحدة العاشرة

١- التدوين الفقهي المذهبي.
٢- المدونات الفقهية التي عنيت بالدليل وفقه الأوائل.
٣- تدوين علم القواعد الفقهية.

أهمية دراسة الوحدة:

استمر فقهاء المذاهب الأربعة في هذا العصر في تدوين المؤلفات الفقهية عامة، وعلى الرغم من حالة الجمود والتقليد التي أصابت الفقه في هذا العصر، فإن بعض الفقهاء دونوا مجموعة من الكتب الفقهية ساروا فيها على منهج الأوائل، حيث ذكروا فيها الأدلة، وأقوال السلف وعلماء الأنصار، وأقوال أصحاب المذاهب الفقهية، وذلك مثل كتاب المحلى، والمغني، والمجموع، وغيرها من الكتب.

وقد دون العلماء أيضاً في هذا العصر مصنفات في علم «القواعد الفقهية» مثل «الأشباه والنظائر» للسيوطي، و «قواعد الأحكام في مصالح الأنام» للعز بن عبد السلام، وغير ذلك كثير.

هيا بنا لدراسة هذه الوحدة حتى تتعرف بفضل الله سبحانه على هذه التفاصيل.

الأهداف التعليمية:

يتوقع منك أيها الدارس الكريم بعد دراستك لهذه الوحدة أن تكون قادراً على أن:

١- تذكر أهم المتون التي صنفت في هذا العصر وشروحها.

٢- تقارن بين هذه المتون وشروحها، وبين المدونات الفقهية التي عينت بالدليل.

٣- تشرح كيف بدأ تدوين علم القواعد الفقهية، وأهم المصنفات التي كتبت فيه.

Compiling *Fiqh* Books Based on *Madhhab*

In this era, the jurists of the four *madhhab*(s) continued compiling a wide spectrum of *Fiqh* books in general and abridged texts and their commentaries in particular. In this unit, we will discuss a number of these compilations that were produced during this period.

I. Juristic Compilations on the Ḥanafi *Madhhab*

Ḥanafi jurists compiled their most authorized source texts in this era, such as *al-Wiqāyah, Muhktaṣar al-Qadūri* and *al-Kanz*. Some may also add *al-Mukhtār* and *Majma' al-Baḥrayn* to this category.

As for *al-Wiqayah,* its full title is *Wiqāyat ar-Riwāyah fī Masā'il al-Hidāyah.* This book was compiled by Tāj ash-Sharī'ah Maḥmūd ibn Ṣadr ash-Sharī'ah Aḥmad ibn 'Ubaydillāh Jamal ad-Dīn al-'Ibādi al-Maḥbubi al-Bukhāri, who died in 673 A.H. His book *al-Wiqāyah* is an abdrigment of the book *al-Hidāyah.* He abridged it for his grandson, Ṣadr ash-Sharī'ah 'Ubaydullāh ibn Mas'ūd ibn Maḥmūd. This grandson explained the book, then abridged it and named it *an-Niqāyah.*[1]

As for *Mukhtaṣar al-Qadūri,* it was compiled by Abūl-Ḥusayn Aḥmad ibn Muhammad ibn Ja'far al-Qadūri. As-Sam'āni said in his book *Kitāb al-Ansāb,* "He was of the people of Baghdad. He was an honest jurist that gravitated to being the leading Ḥanafi scholar of his time, and enjoyed a lofty repute until he died in 428 A.H. in Baghdad."[2]

The book *Mukhtaṣar al-Qadūri* is the most famous and frequently used book in the Ḥanafi *madhhab.* When Ḥanafis say "*al-Kitāb* (the Book)," this book is the first that comes to mind. Throughout this work, al-Qadūri would mention the preponderant view from among the various "popular narrations."

1 *An-Nāfi' al-Kabīr Sharḥ al-Jāmi' aṣ-Ṣaghīr* 23 by Abūl-Ḥasanāt al-Kufawi
2 Ibid: 24

التدوين الفقهي المذهبي

استمر فقهاء المذاهب الأربعة في هذا العصر في تدوين المؤلفات الفقهية عامة، والمتون والشروح خاصة، وسنتناول في هذه الوحدة شيئاً من المدونات في هذا العصر.

أولاً: المدونات الفقهية في المذهب الحنفي:

ألف الحنفية في هذا العصر المتون المعتمدة عندهم، وهي:

الوقاية، ومختصر القدوري، والكنز، ومنهم من يضيف إليها كتابين آخرين هما: المختار، ومجمع البحرين.

أما كتاب **الوقاية**، فهو المسمى بـ: «وقاية الرواية في مسائل الهداية» للإمام تاج الشريعة محمود بن صدر الشريعة أحمد بن عبيد الله جمال الدين العبادي المحبوبي البخاري المتوفى سنة (٦٧٣)، اختصره من «الهداية» وألفه لحفيده صدر الشريعة عبيد الله بن مسعود بن محمود، الذي شرحه، ثم اختصره وسماه «النقاية»[١].

وأما «**مختصر القدوري**»: فهو لأبي الحسين أحمد بن محمد بن جعفر القُدوري «بالضم» قال السمعاني في «كتاب الأنساب»: كان من أهل بغداد، فقيهاً صدوقاً، انتهت إليه رياسة أصحاب مذهب أبي حنيفة، وارتفع جاهه، مات في رجب سنة ثمان وعشرين وأربعمائة ببغداد[٢].

ومتن القدوري أكثر المتون استعمالاً وانتشاراً عند الحنفية، وإذا أطلق الكتاب عندهم انصرف إلى هذا المختصر، وقد التزم القدوري في مختصره بذكر الراجح من مختلف ظاهر الرواية.

١ النافع الكبيرشرح الجامع الصغير، لأبي الحسنات الكفوي: ٢٣.
٢ المصدر السابق: ٢٤.

As for *Kanz ad-Daqā'iq*, it was compiled by Abūl-Barakāt Ḥāfiẓ ad-Dīn 'Abdullāh ibn Aḥmad ibn Maḥmūd an-Nasafi. He is attributed to the city of Nasaf in Sind, and was a virtuous imām that had no peer in his age. He was simply unmatched in both the principle and detailed matters of *Fiqh*.

As for *al-Mukhtār lil-Fatwā*, it was compiled by Abūl-Faḍl Majd ad-Dīn 'Abdullāh ibn Maḥmūd ibn Mawdūd ibn Maḥmūd al-Mawṣili. He was a great jurist and scholar, one that was well-versed in the *madhhab*. He was uniquely talented in the fundamental and detailed matters alike, and had committed the famous *fatwa*(s) of the Imām(s) to memory. He was born in Mawṣil in 599 A.H. and died in Baghdad in 683 A.H. He compiled the book *al-Mukhtār lil-Fatwā* while he was a young man, and then explained it in another book named *al-Ikhtiyār li-Ta'līl al-Mukhtār*.

As for the book *Majma' al-Baḥrayn*, it was compiled by Muẓaffar ad-Dīn Aḥmad ibn 'Ali ibn Taghlab as-Sā'āti al-Ba'labki. He was originally from Ba'labak, but was raised in Baghdad where his father was a famous clockmaker. He became known for his knowledge of grammar and syntax, and for his skill in watchmaking. He was raised in Baghdad and overachieved every expectation, eventually becoming the undisputed imām of his age in the Sharia sciences. He was renowned for his credibility, precision and excellent memory. The scholars of his age attested to the fact that he was one of a kind in his field. He died in 694 A.H. In the book *Majma' al-Baḥrayn*, he combined both *Mukhtaṣar al-Qadūri* and the text by an-Nasafi.

The Fiqh Books which Focused on the Evidences and the Books on Comparative Fiqh

Many of the juristic works within the Ḥanafi *madhhab* focused on verifying the actual views of their *madhhab* and which of them were strongest, without considering the evidences of the rulings. In fact, some of these works took the books which included the evidences for each ruling and abridged them by omitting these evidences. A few exceptional cases did exist – compilations that included the evidences and how they were used to extract the ruling. Of these was *Badā'i' aṣ-Ṣanā'i'* by al-Kāsāni, *Fatḥ al-Qadīr* by Ibn al-Humām and *al-Lubāb fil-Jam' Bayn as-Sunnah wal-Kitāb* by 'Ali ibn Zakariyyā al-Anṣāri al-Khazraji.

وأما «**كنز الدقائق**»: فهو لأبي البركات حافظ الدين عبد الله بن أحمد بن محمود النسفي، نسبة إلى مدينة «نسف» من بلاد «السند» في بلاد «ما وراء النهر»، كان إماماً فاضلاً، عديم النظير في زمانه، فقيد المثيل في الأصول والفروع[1].

وأما «**المختار للفتوى**» فهو لأبي الفضل مجد الدين عبد الله بن محمود بن مودود بن محمود الموصلي، كان شيخاً فقيهاً عارفاً بالمذهب، ومن أفراد الدهر في الفروع والأصول، حافظاً لمسائل مشاهير الفتاوى، ولد بالموصل سنة تسع وتسعين وخمسمائة، وتوفي في بغداد سنة ثلاث وثمانين وستمائة، صنف «المختار للفتوى» في عنفوان شبابه، ثم شرحه وسماه «الاختيار لتعليل المختار»[2].

وأما «**مجمع البحرين**»: فهو لمظفر الدين أحمد بن علي بن تغلب الساعاتي البعلبكي أصلاً والبغدادي منشأ، وأبوه هو الذي عمل الساعات المشهورة ببغداد، واشتهر بعلم النحو والهيئة وعمل الساعات، وابنه هذا نشأ ببغداد، وبلغ رتبة الكمال، وصار إمام العصر في العلوم الشرعية، كان ثقة حافظاً متقناً، أقر له شيوخ زمانه بأنه فارس جواد في ميدانه، وكانت وفاته سنة أربع وتسعين وستمائة[3]، جمع في هذا الكتاب بين مختصر القدوري، ومنظومة النسفي.

الكتب التي عنيت بأدلة الأحكام وكتب الفقه المقارن:

كثير من المؤلفات الفقهية الحنفية عنيت بتحقيق المذهب وبيان القول الصحيح أو الراجح فيه، من غير التفات إلى أدلة الأحكام، بل إن بعض المؤلفات تعمد إلى كتب الفقه التي تذكر الأحكام بأدلتها فتختصرها بحذف تلك الأدلة، إلا أن بعض المدونات اعتنت بذكر الأدلة، وبيان طرق الاستدلال، ووجه دلالة الأدلة على الأحكام، ومن هذه المؤلفات «بدائع الصنائع» للكاساني، و«فتح القدير» لابن الهمام، و «اللباب في الجمع بين السنة والكتاب» لعلي بن زكريا الأنصاري الخزرجي.

١ المصدر السابق.
٢ المصدر السابق: ٢٥.
٣ المصدر السابق: ٢٥.

II. Juristic Compilations on the Māliki *Madhhab*

One of the major books on the Māliki *madhhab* compiled during this era was *adh-Dhakhirah* by al-Qarāfi. This work was an encyclopedia of knowledge pertaining to the Māliki *madhhab*. In its introduction, the author himself mentions that between original works and commentaries, he gathered from over forty books to produce this compilation.[1]

This compilation collected what existed in the five major works that Mālikis everywhere relied upon – namely *al-Mudawwanah* by Saḥnūn, *al-Jawāhir ath-Thamīnah fī Madhhab 'Ālim al-Madinah* by Jalal ad-Dīn ibn Najm ibn Shas, *at-Talqīn* by the judge 'Abdul-Wahhāb ibn Naṣr al-Baghdadi, *at-Tafrī'* by Ibn Jallāb, and *ar-Risālah* by Ibn Abi Zayd al-Qayrawāni.

It appears that these books were the most famous in Māliki *Fiqh* at that time.

Abū 'Umar 'Uthmān ibn Abi Bakr, who was known as Ibn al-Ḥājib, compiled an abridged work on Māliki *Fiqh* known as *Mukhtaṣar Ibn al-Ḥājib*. This book became exceptionally popup lar and became the prime focus of the Mālikis. *Mukhtaṣar Ibn al-Ḥājib* is the abridgment of the book *at-Tahdhīb* by al-Barad'i, and *at-Tahdhīb* is the abridgment of the book *al-Mukhtaṣar* in which Ibn Abi Zayd abridged the book *al-Mudawwanah*.[2]

Then, Khalīl ibn Isḥāq al-Kurdi (d. 776 A.H.) came and radically abridged the already abridged work of Ibn al-Ḥājib. From that point, the Mālikis set their sights on this new work; they memorized it, studied it, wrote explanations and commentaries for it, and abandoned the other books because of it. Over sixty explanations and commentaries were written on this book altogether.[3]

1 *Adh-Dhakirah* 1/36
2 *Muqaddimat Ibn Khaldūn* 808
3 *Al-Fikr as-Sāmi* 2/398

ثانياً: المدونات الفقهية في المذهب المالكي:

من الكتب الكبار التي دونت في مذهب المالكية في هذا العصر كتاب «الذخيرة للقرافي» (٦٢٦- ٦٨٤)، فإنه حوى علماً جمّاً في مذهب المالكية، فإن مؤلفه كما يقول في مقدمته جمع له من تصانيف المذهب نحو أربعين تصنيفاً ما بين شرح وكتاب مستقل(١).

وقد جمع فيه بين الكتب الخمسة التي عكف عليها المالكيون شرقاً وغرباً، وهو يريد بالكتب الخمسة: المدونة لسحنون، والجواهر الثمينة في مذهب عالم المدينة لجلال الدين بن نجم بن شاس، والتلقين للقاضي عبد الوهاب بن نصر البغدادي، والتفريع لابن جلاب، والرسالة لابن أبي زيد القيرواني.

ويبدو أن هذه الكتب هي المشهورة عند المالكية في ذلك الوقت.

وقد ألف أبو عمر عثمان بن أبي بكر المعروف بابن الحاجب المتوفى سنة ٦٤٦هـ مختصراً في فقه المالكية عرف بمختصر ابن الحاجب، وقد علا ذكره وانتشر، وشغل به المالكية عن غيره، وهذا المختصر هو اختصار لكتاب التهذيب للبرادعي، وتهذيب البرادعي هو اختصار لمختصر ابن أبي زيد الذي اختصر به المدونة(٢).

ثم جاء خليل بن إسحاق الكردي المتوفى سنة ٧٦٧هـ فاختصر مختصر ابن الحاجب، وبالغ في اختصاره، واشتغل المالكية بهذا الكتاب حفظاً ومدارسة، ووضعوا عليه الشروح والحواشي، وهجروا غيره، وقد زادت الشروح والحواشي التي وضعت عليه على الستين(٣).

١ الذخيرة: ١/ ٣٦.
٢ مقدمة ابن خلدون: ٨٠٨.
٣ الفكر السامي: ٢/ ٣٩٨.

The most reviewed explanations on this book are *Sharḥ al-Ḥattāb* and *Sharḥ al-Mawwāq*. Other famous explanations are *Sharḥ az-Zarqāni, Sharḥ al-Kharashi, Sharḥ ar-Rahūni* and the explanation written by Aḥmad ibn Aḥmad ad-Dardīr named *ash-Sharḥ aṣ-Ṣaghīr 'alā Aqrab al-Masālik ilā Madhhab Mālik.* The footnotes on this last book were written by Shaykh Aḥmad ibn Muhammad aṣ-Ṣāwi.[1]

Ad-Dardīr also had another commentary named *ash-Sharḥ al-Kabīr* in which Muhammad 'Arafah ad-Dasūqi wrote the footnotes. This book was later printed, along with its footnotes, margins and verifications by Shaykh 'Ulaysh.[2]

III. Juristic Compilations on the Shāfi'i *Madhhab*

One of the greatest books compiled in this era on the Shāfi'i *madhhab* was *Nihāyat al-Maṭlab fī Dirāyat al-Madhhab* by Imām al-Ḥaramayn al-Juwayni. Ibn Khalkan said regarding it, "Nothing has ever been authored like it in Islam."

The verifier of *al-Wasīṭ* says that *Nihāyat al-Maṭlab* is the summary of the Shāfi'i *madhhab*; Imam al-Ḥaramayn extracted it from books of Imām ash-Shāfi'i like *al-Umm, ar-Risālah* and others. He also extracted it from the books of his disciples, such as *Mukhtaṣar al-Muzani, Mukhtaṣar al-Buwayṭi* and others. He also extracted from the works of notable scholars who were skilled in determining which view was stronger, in addition to the contributions of Imam al-Ḥaramayn himself. He had included his own deductions, determinations of the "stronger view" and applications of established rulings onto new cases. These contributions were strictly based on the Book of Allah, the Sunnah of His Messenger ﷺ, the legitimate evidences, the views of the other Imām(s) which he cited and his articulate discussions with them.[3]

1 Printed by Dār al-Ma'ārif, Egypt (1392 A.H.)
2 Printed by Dār Iḥyā' al-Kutub al-'Arabiyyah, Cairo
3 Al-Wasit by al-Ghazali: 1/243

وأكثر شروحه تحريراً شرح الحطاب، وشرح المواق، ومن الشروح التي وضعت عليه شرح الزرقاني، وشرح الخرشي، والرهوني، وشرحه أحمد بن أحمد الدردير، المتوفى سنة ١١٩٣هـ شرحاً سماه «الشرح الصغير على أقرب المسالك إلى مذهب مالك»، وعليه حاشية العلامة الشيخ أحمد بن محمد الصاوي(١).

وللدردير شرح آخر سماه بالشرح الكبير، وقد وضع عليه محمد عرفة الدسوقي حاشية، وقد طبع الكتاب والحاشية، وبهامشه تقريرات الشيخ عليش(٢).

ثالثاً: التدوين الفقهي في مذهب الشافعية:

ومن الكتب الكبار التي ألفت في مذهب الشافعية في هذا العصر كتاب «نهاية المطلب في دراية المذهب» لإمام الحرمين، قال فيه ابن خلكان: «ما صنف في الإسلام مثله».

ونهاية المطلب- كما يقول محقق كتاب الوسيط خلاصة للفقه الشافعي استخلصه إمام الحرمين من كتب الإمام الشافعي ككتاب «الأم» و«الرسالة» وغيرهما، ومن كتب أصحابه كمختصر المزني، والبويطي، وغيرهما، ومن كتب أصحاب الوجوه والترجيحات، بالإضافة إلى ما جادت به قريحة إمام الحرمين من استنباطات وترجيحات، وتفريعات، معتمداً على كتاب الله وسنة رسوله، والأدلة المعتبرة، وما ذكره من آراء لأئمة المذاهب الآخرين، ومناقشاته القوية البليغة معهم»(٣).

١ طبعة دار المعارف، مصر (١٣٩٢هـ-).
٢ طبعة دار إحياء الكتب العربية، القاهرة.
٣ الوسيط للغزالي: ١/ ٢٤٣.

Al-Ghazāli, who was the student of al-Juwayni, abridged his teacher's book *Nihāyat al-Maṭlab fī Dirāyat al-Madhhab* into his own book *al-Basīṭ*. Despite that, it still came out to be eight volumes, which drove him to abridge it further into his book *al-Wasīṭ*, and then consolidate it further into his book *al-Wajīz*. This final book *al-Wajīz* was explained by 'Abdul-Karīm ibn Muhammad ar-Rāfi'i (d. 623A.H.) in his book *Fatḥ al-'Azīz Sharḥ al-Wajīz*.

Due to the length of *Fatḥ al-'Azīz Sharḥ al-Wajīz*, an-Nawawi abridged it into his book *Rawḍat aṭ-Ṭālibīn wa 'Umdat al-Muḥaqiqīn*. Al-Ghazāli had a fourth book on Shāfi'i *Fiqh* called *al-Khulaṣah* that was also radically abridged.

Another very important book in the Shāfi'i *madhhab* is *al-Muhadhab* by Abū Isḥāq ash-Shirāzi. An-Nawawi had begun writing a detailed explanation of *al-Muhadhab* in his book *al-Majmū'*, but he died before completing it.[1]

Together, an-Nawawi and ar-Rāfi'i had verified and presented the Shāfi'i *madhhab* in their books. The most important book by ar-Rāfi'i was *al-Muḥarrar*, which he took from al-Ghazāli's book *al-Wajīz*.

Then, an-Nawawi abridged the book *al-Muḥarrar* by ar-Rāfi'i into his book *al-Minhāj* due to gargantuan size of the former.

After an-Nawawi and ar-Rāfi'i, a group of Shāfi'i scholars followed their footsteps and depended on their compilations. Since then, the works of those scholars became regarded by the Shāfi'i jurists as the most reliable sources on their *madhhab*.

For instance, Muhammad ash-Shirbini al-Khaṭib composed an explanatory text for the book *al-Minhāj* by an-Nawawi, which was an abridged version of *al-Muḥarrar* by ar-Rāfi'i, and titled it *Mughni al-Muḥtaj ilā Ma'rifat Ma'āny Alfāẓ al-Minhāj*.

1 *Al-Majmū'* 1/3

وقد قام الغزالي تلميذ الجويني باختصار كتاب شيخه «نهاية المطلب في دراية المذهب» في كتابه «البسيط»، ومع ذلك فإنه جاء في ثمانية مجلدات، مما دعاه إلى اختصاره في كتابه «الوسيط»، ثم اختصر «الوسيط» في كتابه «الوجيز»، وقد قام بشرح الوجيز عبد الكريم بن محمد الرافعي المتوفى سنة ٦٢٣هـ في كتابه الموسوم بـ«فتح العزيز شرح الوجيز».

وقد قام باختصار فتح العزيز النووي في كتابه: «روضة الطالبين وعمدة المحققين» بسبب طوله واتساعه، وللغزالي كتاب رابع في غاية الاختصار في الفقه الشافعي هو كتاب «الخلاصة».

وفي الغزالي وكتبه الأربعة يقول أبو حفص عمر بن عبد العزيز بن يوسف الطرابلسي شعراً[١]:

هذب المذهب حبر	أحسن الله خلاصه
ببسيط ووسيط	ووجيز وخلاصه

ومن الكتب التي كان للشافعية بها عناية كتاب: «المهذب» لأبي إسحاق الشيرازي، وقد شرحه النووي شرحاً موسعاً في كتابه «المجموع» لكنه توفي قبل إتمامه له[٢].

وقد حرر الرافعي والنووي مذهب الشافعية، وأهم كتب الرافعي «المحرر»، وقد أخذه من كتاب «الوجيز» للغزالي.

وقد اختصر النووي كتاب «المحرر» للرافعي في كتاب «المنهاج» ودعاه إلى اختصاره طوله وكبر حجمه.

وجاء من بعد الرافعي والنووي جمع من علماء الشافعية ساروا مسارهم، واعتمدوا على مدوناتهم، وأصبحت مؤلفاتهم العمدة عند الشافعية.

فمحمد الشربيني الخطيب وضع شرحاً ضافياً على متن المنهاج للنووي المختصر من محرر الرافعي سماه «مغني المحتاج إلى معرفة معاني ألفاظ المنهاج».

١ انظر مقدمة الوسيط: ١/ ٢٠٥.
٢ المجموع للنووي: ١/ ٣.

Al-Minhāj was also explained by al-Jammāl ar-Ramli in his book *Nihāyat al-Muḥtaj* by Ibn Ḥajar al-Makki in his book *Tuḥfat al-Muḥtaj Sharḥ al-Minhaj,* and by Zakariyyā al-Anṣāri in his book *al-Manhaj.*

The two aforementioned books by ar-Ramli and Ibn Ḥajar which explained an-Nawawi's *al-Minhāj* are essentially the greatest authority for Shāfi'i scholars when verifying the stance of the *madhhab* on a particular matter.

IV. Juristic Compilations on the Ḥanbali *Madhhab*

In this era, the Ḥanbalis authored volumes of explanatory works pertaining to *Mukhtaṣar al-Khiraqi.* There were over 300 distinct explanations written on this book. The most famous ones are:

1) *Al-Mughni* by Shaykh Muwaffaq ad-Dīn Ibn Qudāmah al-Maqdisi

2) The explanation by al-Qāḍi Abū Ya'lā Muhammad ibn al-Ḥusayn ibn al-Farā'

Shaykh Muwaffaq (may Allah bestow mercy upon him) was indeed the expert on this *madhhab.* Jurists from within and beyond the Ḥanbali *madhhab* recognized his unique status, and his compilation became the greatest authority in Ḥanbali *Fiqh.* Not only was he a man of great knowledge but also an exemplar educator. He authored several books – each being suitable for a student of knowledge of a different academic level.

Aside from *al-Mughni,* Shaykh Mūwaffaq compiled three other books: *al-'Umdah, al-Muqni'* and *al-Kāfi.*

Shaykh Muwaffaq took into consideration four degrees of students while compiling his works. His book *al-'Umdah* was written for beginners. He limited its content to the authoritative opinions in the *madhhab,* and this book was later explained by Shaykh al-Islām Ibn Taymiyah (may Allah bestow mercy upon him).

Then, Shaykh Muwaffaq compiled his book *al-Muqni'* to suit those who were more advanced, but not yet intermediates. For this reason, he kept it void of the evidences and arguments. He made the book moderate in length by citing the various narrations reported about Imam Aḥmad. This way, the reader is given the opportunity to work one's mind and become accustomed to discerning which is correct.

وشرحه أيضاً الجمال الرملي في كتابه «نهاية المحتاج»، وابن حجر المكي في كتابه «تحفة المحتاج شرح المنهاج»، واختصر «منهاج» النووي زكريا الأنصاري في كتابه «المنهج».

وكتابا الرملي وابن حجر المكي اللذان شرحا منهاج النووي عمدة علماء الشافعية في تحقيق المذهب.

رابعاً: المدونات الفقهية في مذهب الحنابلة:

أكثر الحنابلة في هذا العصر من التأليف في مختصر الخرقي، وقد زادت شروحه على ثلاثمائة شرح كما سبق بيانه.

وأفضل هذه الشروح وأشهرها شرحان:

الأول: المغني للشيخ موفق الدين بن قدامة المقدسي.

الثاني: شرح القاضي أبي يعلى محمد بن الحسين بن الفراء.

والشيخ الموفق- رحمه الله- شيخ المذهب بحق، وقد عرف فقهاء الحنابلة وغيرهم قدره، فمؤلفاته أصبحت العمدة في فقه المذهب الحنبلي، وكما كان رجل علم، فإنه رجل تربية، وقد ألف عدة مؤلفات راعى فيها المستوى العلمي لطلبة العلم.

ألف الشيخ الموفق ثلاثة كتب غير المغني هي: «العمدة، والمقنع، والكافي».

راعى الموفق في مؤلفاته أربع طبقات: فصنف «العمدة» للمبتدئين، وقد اقتصر فيه على المعتمد في المذهب، وقد شرحه شيخ الإسلام ابن تيمية- رحمه الله تعالى-.

ثم ألف الموفق «المقنع» لمن ارتقى عن درجتهم، ولم يصل إلى درجة المتوسطين؛ فلذلك جعله عرياً عن الدليل والتعليل، وجعله وسطاً بين التقصير والتطويل، غير أنه يذكر الروايات عن الإمام أحمد، ليجعل لقارئه مجالاً إلى كدِّ ذهنه، ليتمرن على التصحيح.

Shaykh Muwaffaq compiled his book *al-Kāfi* for intermediate students of knowledge. In it, he mentioned many of the evidences so that its reader can climb to the level of performing *ijtihād* within the *madhhab*, for it shows the evidences, entices one to analyze them and to not take anything for granted.

Then, the author compiled *al-Mughni* for the advanced students. In this stage, the reader becomes acquainted with different narrations, the differences among the Imām(s), many of their respective proofs and what arguments are in their favor and which are against them. This way, anyone with the potential to be a jurist can practice the performance of *ijtihād* in the absolute sense once one becomes qualified to do so.[1] We will discuss this particular book further in a forthcoming discussion.

Books Explaining al-Muqni'

After Shaykh Muwaffaq had compiled his book *al-Muqni'*, much attention was given to this book by the scholars and students of the Ḥanbali *madhhab*. They explained it, taught it, memorized it, wrote commentaries on it and made modifications to it. The reason behind it receiving such attention was that the Ḥanbali scholars saw this book to be ideal in its knowledge, compilation and arrangement.

The first to write an explanation for *al-Muqni'* was Shaykh Muwaffaq's nephew 'Abdur-Raḥmān ibn Abi 'Umar Muhammad ibn Aḥmad ibn Qudāmah al-Maqdisi, who died in 682 A.H. This explanation could very well be considered the work of Shaykh Muwaffaq himself, since Shaykh 'Abdur-Raḥmān simply took *al-Mughni* and rearranged to match the arrangement of *al-Muqni'*. Therefore, we can consider that this explanation of *al-Muqni'*, which was known as *ash-Sharḥ al-Kabīr*, is actually *al-Mughni* after its rearrangement. Thus, the text and the explanation can be considered the work of one scholar, Shaykh Muwaffaq.

1 *Al-Madkhal* 221 by Ibn Badrān

وصنف الشيخ الموفق «الكافي» للمتوسطين، وذكر فيه كثيراً من الأدلة لتسمو نفس قارئه إلى درجة الاجتهاد في المذاهب حينما يرى الأدلة، وترتفع نفسه إلى مناقشتها، ولم يجعلها قضية مسلمة، ثم ألف «المغني» لمن ارتقى درجة عن المتوسطين، وهناك يطلع قارئه على الروايات، وعلى خلاف الأئمة، وعلى كثير من أدلتهم، وعلى ما لهم وما عليهم من الأخذ والرد، فمن كان فقيه النفس حينئذ مرن نفسه على الاجتهاد المطلق، إن كان أهلاً لذلك وتوافرت فيه شروطه[1]، وسنخص هذا الكتاب بمزيد من البحث في بحث قادم.

شروح المقنع:

بعد تأليف الموفق للمقنع أصبح مدار اهتمام علماء المذهب وطلابه، فقد تناولوه بالشرح والتدريس، والحفظ والإضافة والتعليق، والسبب في هذا الاهتمام الكبير أن الكتاب حاز المواصفات المثلى في نظر أهل العلم من الحنابلة علماً وتصنيفاً وترتيباً.

وأول من وضع شروحاً على «المقنع» ابن أخي الشيخ الموفق عبد الرحمن بن أبي عمر محمد بن أحمد بن قدامة المقدسي المتوفى سنة ٦٨٢هـ وهذا الشرح كأنما هو من وضع الشيخ الموفق، فإن الشيخ عبد الرحمن قصد إلى كتاب عمه «المغني»، فأعاد ترتيبه على وفق ترتيب «المقنع»، وبذلك يكون الشرح الكبير للمقنع هو «المغني» بعد إعادة ترتيبه وفق ترتيب «المقنع»، فكأنما المتن والشرح هما من وضع عالم واحد هو الشيخ الموفق.

١ المدخل لابن بدران: ٢٢١.

Another marvelous explanation of *al-Muqni'* is the book *al-Mubdi' fī Sharḥ al-Muqni'* by Burhān ad-Dīn Abū Isḥāq Ibrāhīm ibn Muhammad ibn 'Abdillāh ibn Muhammad ibn Mufliḥ ad-Dimashqi, who died in 884 A.H.

The author of this book followed a liberal approach in his explanation. He mentioned the evidences from the Qur'an and Sunnah with a brief referencing for the hadith(s). He reported the scholarly views from among the Companions, the Successors and those after them. He mentioned the official view of the [Ḥanbali] *madhhab*. He collected the multiple narrations of Imām Aḥmad on each case, and he relayed the views of the other major Ḥanbali scholars.[1]

Another book composed to explain *al-Muqni'* was *al-Inṣāf* fī Ma'rifat ar-Rājiḥ *min al-Khilāf 'alā Madhhab Aḥmad*. This book was compiled by the great scholar, verifier and reviver of the Ḥanbali *madhhab* 'Alā' ad-Dīn Abūl-Ḥasan 'Ali ibn Sulaymān al-Mirdāwi, who died in 885 A.H.

In the introduction of his book, after praising *al-Muqni'*, he stated that his aim in authoring *al-Inṣāf* was "to clarify the correct, the famous, the acted upon and the strongest view of the *madhhab*, in addition to what views most Ḥanbali scholars championed and would not abandon."[2]

Then, the author of *al-Inṣāf* abridged *al-Muqni'* in his book *at-Tanqīḥ al-Mushbi' fī Taḥrir Aḥkām al-Muqni'*. In it, he verified the general narrations reported in *al-Muqni'* and the various *wujūh* within the *madhhab*. He also stipulated certain conditions for these rulings and explained the obscure rulings and words. Moreover, he made certain exceptions which the *madhhab* viewed were excluded from the general terms of these rulings. Due to all this, *at-Tanqīḥ* became a rectification for most books on this *madhhab*.

1 *Al-Mubdi' Sharḥ al-Muqni'* 1/4 (Introduction)
2 *Al-Inṣāf* 1/3

ومن شروح «المقنع» المبدعة كتاب «المبدع في شرح المقنع» لبرهان الدين أبي إسحاق: إبراهيم بن محمد بن عبد الله بن محمد بن مفلح الدمشقي المتوفى سنة ٨٨٤هـ.

«وقد سلك المؤلف بهذا الشرح مسلك التحرر، وذكر الأدلة من الكتاب والسنة، مع تخريج موجز للأحاديث، ونقل أقوال العلماء من الصحابة والتابعين فمن بعدهم، والمفتى به من المذهب، ومختلف روايات مسائل الإمام أحمد، وأقوال علماء المذهب الحنبلي»(١).

ومن المؤلفات الموضوعة على «المقنع» كتاب: «الإنصاف في معرفة الراجح من الخلاف على مذهب أحمد» للعلامة المحقق مجدد المذهب الحنبلي علاء الدين أبي الحسن علي بن سليمان المرداوي المتوفى سنة ٨٨٥هـ.

وصرح في مقدمة مصنفه بعد ثنائه على كتاب «المقنع» أن مقصده من وراء تأليف «الإنصاف» هو «بيان الصحيح من المذهب والمشهور والمعمول عليه والمنصور، وما اعتمده أكثر الأصحاب، وذهبوا إليه، ولم يعرجوا على غيره، ولم يعولوا عليه»(٢).

ثم اقتضب منه كتابه المسمى «التنقيح المشبع في تحرير أحكام المقنع»، (مطبوع)، فصحح فيه الروايات المطلقة في «المقنع»، وما أطلق فيه من الوجهين أو الأوجه، وقيد ما أخل به من الشروط، وفسر ما أبهم فيه من حكم أو لفظ، واستثنى من عمومه ما هو مستثنى على المذهب... فصار كتابه تصحيحاً لغالب كتب المذهب(٣).

١ المبدع شرح المقنع (المقدمة): ١/ ٤.
٢ الإنصاف: ١/ ٣.
٣ المدخل لابن بدران: ٢٢٢.

It is worth mentioning that students of knowledge can find, in the introduction and conclusion of al-Mirdāwi's book *al-Inṣāf*, the technical terms used in both *al-Muqni'* and *al-Inṣāf* and the way by which these views were verified. By doing that, he provides an excellent summary of the terms used in Ḥanbali *Fiqh*, which is vital for a student of knowledge's insight and enables one to understand the *madhhab*, its terms and how to investigate the views of the Ḥanbali *madhhab*.

One of the useful and comprehensive books on Ḥanbali *Fiqh* is *Muntahā al-Irādah fī al-Jam' bayn al-Muqni' ma'at-Tanqīḥ waz-Ziyādah* by Ibn an-Najjār, who is better known as al-Fatuḥi, who died in 972 A.H. This book became an authority on the *madhhab* for a long time. Students of knowledge dedicated themselves to this book for a long time and abandoned other books because of it. The majority of this book was taken from *al-Furū'* by Ibn Mufliḥ.

The famous texts that are authorities on the Ḥanbali *madhhab* are three, as per Ibn Badrān. The oldest of them is *Mukhataṣar al-Khiraqi*, and it continued to be the most preferred book of the Ḥanbalis. They kept studying, explaining and memorizing it until al-Muwaffaq authored *al-Muqni'* and its popularity skyrocketed. This continued until al-Mirdāwi compiled *at-Tanqīḥ al-Mushbi'*.

Compiling *Fiqh* Books Based on Evidence and the Classical Views

Despite the state of stagnation and *taqlīd* that plagued the *Fiqh* of this era, there were still some jurists who compiled a number of juristic books that followed the approach of the earliest generations. These works, in truth, are of the greatest juristic works centered around views of the *salaf* (predecessors), the scholars of each land and the views of the great Imām(s). These books focused on their views and their evidences, along with differentiating between the authentic and weak evidences and between the weaker and stronger of their views without bias. The most famous of these compilations that reached us were *al-Muḥallā* by Ibn Ḥazm, *al-Mughni* by Ibn Qudāmah, *al-Majmū'* by an-Nawawi and the books of Ibn Taymiyah, especially *al-Fatāwā*.

ومـما يحسـن أن ينبـه طلبـة العلـم عليـه أن المـرداوي في مقدمة كتابه «الإنصاف» وخاتمتـه ذكر المصطلحات الواردة في كتـاب «المقنع» وكتـاب «الإنصاف» وطريقـة تحقيـق المذهـب، وهـو بذلك يضع خلاصـة جيـدة لمصطلحـات الفقه الحنبلـي، التـي تبصـر طالب العلم، وتعرفه بالمذهب ومصطلحاته، وطرق التعريـف إلى المذهب عنـد الحنابلـة.

ومـن الكتـب المفيـدة الجامعـة في مذهـب الحنابلـة كتـاب «منتهـى الإرادات في الجمـع بيـن المقنـع مـع التنقيـح وزيـادات» لابـن النجـار الشـهير بالفتوحـي المتوفـى سـنة ٩٧٢هـ وقـد أصبـح عمـدة المذهـب زمنًـا، وعكـف عليـه طلاب العلم وهجروا مـا عـداه، وكان غالب استمداده مـن كتـاب الفـروع لابـن مفلـح.

والمتـون المشـتهرة التـي هـي العمـدة في المذهـب الحنبلـي ثلاثـة كمـا يقول ابـن بـدران، أقدمهـا مختصـر الخرقـي، وقـد بقـي هـو الكتـاب الأول عنـد الحنابلـة، تناولـوه بالدراسـة والـشـرح والحفـظ حتـى ألـف الموفـق «المقنـع»، فطـارت شـهرته في الآفـاق، وبقـي كذلـك حتـى ألـف المـرداوي «التنقيـح المشـبع».

المدونات الفقهية التي عنيت بالدليل وفقه الأوائل

عـلى الرغـم مـن حالـة الجمـود والتقليـد التـي أصابـت الفقـه في هـذا العـصر، فـإن بعـض الفقهـاء، دونـوا مجموعـة مـن الكتـب الفقهيـة سـاروا فيهـا عـلى منهـج الأوائـل، وهـذه المدونـات تعـد- بحـق- مـن أعظـم المدونـات الفقهيـة التـي تُعنَـى بذكـر أقوال السلف وعلمـاء الأمصار وأقوال أصحاب المذاهـب، وهـي تعنـى بأقوالهـم، كـما تعنـى بأدلتهـم، وتبيـن الصحيـح والضعيـف مـن الأدلـة، وتبيـن الراجـح مـن الأقـوال، وتنصـف في الترجيـح، وأشـهر هـذه المدونـات التـي وصلـت إلينا: المحلى لابـن حـزم، والمغنـي لابـن قدامـة، والمجمـوع للنـووي، وكتـب ابـن تيميـة، وخاصـة فتاويـه.

We will give a short synopsis of the first three books: *al-Muḥallā, al-Mughni* and *al-Majmū‘*.

Al-Muḥallā

Its author was Abū Muhammad ‘Ali ibn Aḥmad ibn Sa‘īd ibn Ḥazm al-Andalusi. He was born in Cordoba in 384 A.H. and died in Aunbah, a coastal village west of Andalusia.

Ibn Ḥazm was one of the unique scholars who mastered the sciences of Sharia, the Arabic language and its literature, philosophy and medicine. Furthermore, he was a scholar in the study of other religions as well.

Ibn Ḥazm was one of the scholars of *Ahl aẓ-Ẓāhir* – those who paid great attention to the revealed texts via memorizing, studying and teaching them. These scholars rejected *taqlīd, qiyās* and attributing *‘illah*(s) (effective causes) for the revealed texts. Shaykh Muhammad Muntaṣir al-Kittāni said about Ibn Ḥazm, “He lead one of the *madhhab*(s) within *Ahl as-Sunnah wal-Jamā‘ah* that had its own fundamental rules, principles and aims. This *madhhab* also had its own books, treatise and compilations, long, medium and short. It also had its students, followers, supporters and preachers from both the earlier and later generations.”[1]

However, the followers of Ibn Ḥazm, who were known as the “Ḥazmis,” eventually became extinct, but his book remained, and it continued influencing the generations – with varying degrees – until today.

Ibn Ḥazm had his own independent views. He refused to accept any view without being convinced that the evidence was in its favor. His qualifying for *ijtihād*, in its absolute sense, in *Fiqh* and the sciences of Islam, was a matter acknowledged by many scholars. Of them were his contemporaries, students and those who came after from all over the world, like al-Ḥumaydi, the historian ‘Abdul-Wāḥid al-Marākishi, al-Ḥāfiẓ adh-Dhahabi and others.[2]

1 *Mu‘jam Fiqh Ibn Ḥazm* 17, prepared by Muhammad al-Muntaṣir al-Kittāni, Lajnat Mawsū‘at al-Fiqh al-Islāmi bi-Kulliyyat ash-Sharī‘ah, Damascus and printed by Dār al-Fikr, Damascus

2 Ibid: 17

وسنعطي نبذة موجزة عن الكتب الثلاثة الأولى: المحلى، والمغني، والمجموع.

١- المحلى:

مؤلفه هو أبو محمد علي بن أحمد بن سعيد بن حزم الأندلسي، ولد بقرطبة في سنة ٣٨٤هـ وتوفي في «أونبة» قرية في غربي الأندلس على خليج البحر المحيط في عام ٤٥٦هـ.

وقد كان ابن حزم من العلماء الأفذاذ الذين أحاطوا بعلوم الشريعة، وعلوم اللغة العربية وآدابها، وعلوم الفلسفة، وعلم الطب، وكان عالماً بالأديان الأخرى.

وابن حزم من فقهاء أهل الظاهر الذين يعنون بالنصوص عناية كبيرة حفظاً ومدارسة وتدريساً، ويرفضون التقليد ويحرمونه، كما يرفضون القياس والتعليل للنصوص، ويذكر الشيخ محمد المنتصر الكتاني أن ابن حزم كان «صاحب مذهب من مذاهب أهل السنة والجماعة له أصوله وقواعده، ومبادئه وأهدافه، وله كتبه ورسائله ومدوناته، مطولة ووسيطة ومختصرة، وله التلاميذ والأتباع والأنصار، والدعاة بين القدامى والمحدثين»[١].

ولكن أتباع ابن حزم الذين كانوا يسمون بالحزميين انقرضوا، وبقيت كتبه التي خلفها تؤثر في الأجيال من بعده بنسب متفاوتة.

وابن حزم صاحب رأي مستقل يأبى أن يأخذ قولاً ما لم يقم عليه دليل وبرهان، وقد اعترف لابن حزم بالاجتهاد المطلق في الفقه وعلوم الإسلام طائفة من العلماء، فيهم معاصروه وتلاميذه، ومن جاء بعدهم مشرقاً ومغرباً، كالحميدي وعبد الواحد المؤرخ المراكشي، والحافظ الذهبي وغيرهم[٢].

١ معجم فقه ابن حزم، إعداد محمد المنتصر الكتاني: ١٧، لجنة موسوعة الفقه الإسلامي بكلية الشريعة، دمشق، طبع دار الفكر- دمشق.

٢ المصدر السابق: ١٧.

Al-Muḥallā was one of four books wherein Ibn Ḥazm recorded his opinions and methodology. These books were: *al-Īṣāl* which was the longest one, *al-Khiṣāl* which was the intermediate one, *al-Muḥallā* which was shorter than *al-Khiṣāl*, and *al-Mujallā* which was the shortest one.

Al-Īṣāl was a unique juristic encyclopedia. Its author wrote this book into 24 large volumes with tightly packed lines of small font. Al-Ḥumaydi mentions that Ibn Ḥazm reported in his book *al-Īṣāl* the juristic views of the Companions, the Succesors and the great Muslim *Imām*(s) that followed them. Alongside that, he listed the proofs of each group and the actual authenticity – or lack thereof – for each hadith cited on the matter.[1] However, no known manuscript is known to have survived of this great work.

In the introduction of his book *al-Muhallā*, Ibn Ḥazm said that he restricted himself in this book to the fundamental proofs without being overly thorough. It could be easily digested this way by the students and beginners, and a stepping stone towards comprehending the arguments, discovering the different views and authenticating the evidences leading to the determination of the correct opinions in matters of disagreement. This book also served to familiarize the student with the Qur'anic rulings, most of the hadith(s) confirmed about the Messenger of Allah (ﷺ) and how to sift between these hadith(s) and those which are not authentic. Additionaly, it introduces the student to the trustworthy narrators, how to discern between them and others, how to recognize invalid *qiyās*, its flaws and the contradictions of those who viewed it.[2]

1 *Mu'jam Fiqh Ibn Ḥazm* 24 (Introduction)
2 *Al-Muḥallā* 1/2 by Ibn Ḥazm (al-Maktab at-Tujāri, Beirut)

وكتاب «المحلى» واحد من أربعة كتب لابن حزم دون فيها فقهه ومذهبه، وهي: الإيصال، وهو أكبرها، والخصال، أوسطها، والمحلى يليهما، والمجلى، أصغرها.

والإيصال موسوعة فقهية لم يكتب مثلها، وقد كتبه مؤلفه في أربعة وعشرين مجلداً كبيراً بخط دقيق متقارب، وقد ذكر الحميدي أن ابن حزم أورد في كتابه الإيصال أقوال الصحابة والتابعين ومن بعدهم من أئمة المسلمين في مسائل الفقه، والحجة لكل طائفة وعليها، والأحاديث الواردة في ذلك من الصحيح والسقيم وبيان ذلك كله، وتحقيق القول فيه[١]، ولكن هذا المؤلف العظيم لا تعرف له نسخة مخطوطة اليوم.

أما المحلى فإنه كما يقول مؤلفه في مقدمة كتابه «اقتصر فيه على قواعد البراهين بغير إكثار، ليكون مأخذه سهلاً على الطالب والمبتدئ ودرجاً إلى التبحر في الحجاج ومعرفة الاختلاف وتصحيح الدلائل المؤدية إلى معرفة الحق مما تنازع فيه الناس، والإشراف على أحكام القرآن، والوقوف على جمهرة السنن الثابتة عن رسول الله ﷺ، وتمييزها مما لم يصح، والوقوف على الثقات من رواة الأخبار، وتمييزهم من غيرهم، والتنبيه على فساد القياس، وتناقضه، وتناقض القائلين به»[٢].

١ معجم فقه ابن حزم (المقدمة): ٢٤.
٢ المحلي لابن حزم: ١/ ٢، المكتب التجاري، بيروت.

Ibn Ḥazm codified his juristic discussions and arranged each separately. Every case was a distinct matter that was chaptered with its own evidence, comparison and discussion. The cases in this book were 2,308 in number, although some were contained in a single line, others were a page, others were a number of pages and some even exceeded 30 pages. In total, *al-Muḥallā* was 11 volumes long and contained 4,388 pages.

وابـن حـزم قنـن قضايـا الفقـه، ودونهـا مسـائل، كل مسـألة قضيـة قائمـة بنفسـها، أدلـة ومقارنـة ومناقشـة، وقـد بلـغ عـدد مسـائله «٢٣٠٨» مسـألة، منهـا مـا هـو في أسـطر، وصفحـة، وصفحـات، ومنهـا مـا هـو في عـشر صفحـات، وفي عشريـن صفحـة، وفي ثلاثـين، وفي أكـثر مـن ثلاثـين.

والمحلى في أحد عشر مجلداً، يشتمل على (٤٣٨٨) صفحة.

Al-Muḥallā was the last book written by Ibn Ḥazm. He died (may Allah bestow mercy upon him) before finishing it, so his son al-Faḍl Abū Rāfi' finished this work by taking from his father's larger book *al-Īṣāl* and summarizing its elaborate discussions. The original portion of *al-Muḥallā*, which was written by Ibn Ḥazm, ends on volume 10, page 401. The number of cases summarized by Abū Rāfi' were 285.[1] Ibn Ḥazm's style in *al-Muḥallā* was to say "Issue: ..." and then say "Abū Muhammad said..." referring to himself. He would also say, "'Ali said..." as this was his name. Then, he would state his view and support it with a verse, with a hadith for which he mentions the entire chain of transmission or by reporting a consensus on the issue at hand. At times, he may cite all three or he may select from whatever of these proofs is available for the issue.

والمحـلى آخـر مؤلفـات ابـن حـزم، مـات- رحمـه اللـه-، ولمـا يتمـه بعـد، فأتمـه ولـده الفضـل أبـو رافـع مـن كتـاب والـده الكبـير الإيصـال مختـصراً منـه مسـائله وملخصـاً لهـا، وينتهـي المحـلى كـما ألفـه ابـن حـزم عنـد آخـر المسـألة (٢٠٢٣) في الصفحـة (٤٠١) مـن المجلـد العـاشر، وعـدد المسـائل التـي لخصهـا أبـو رافـع (٢٨٥) مسـألة[1]، وطريقـة ابـن حـزم في المحـلى أن يقـول: مسـألة، ثـم يقـول: قـال أبـو محمـد وهـي كنيتـه، أو قـال عـلي وهـو اسـمه، ويعنـي بذلـك نفسـه، ويذكـر فقهـه، ثـم يسـتدل عليـه بآيـة، أو حديـث، ويسـوقه بسـنده إلى النبـي ﷺ، وقـد يذكـره مـن طـرق مختلفـة متعـددة، وكلهـا مسـندة، وقـد يسـتدل بالإجـماع، وقـد يسـتدل بآيـة وحديـث وإجـماع في المسـألة الواحـدة، وقـد يقتـصر عـلى الموجـود منهـا في الاسـتدلال لتلـك المسـألة.

Besides his own juristic views, he used to mention the views of the Companions, the Successors, those who succeeded them, until the views of the three *Imāms*: Abū Ḥanīfah, Mālik and ash-Shāfi'i. He would sometimes add the views of their major disciples as well, provided that they were not of those who drowned in *taqlīd*. He did not mention the views of Aḥmad, except in rare cases, because according to the scholars of Andalusia, Imām Aḥmad was only a scholar in Hadith. At times, Ibn Ḥazm may mention the views of those who came after the three *Imām*(s) until the middle of the fifth *hijri* century.

ثـم يذكـر في المسألة مع فقهـه: فقـه الصحابـة، والتابعـين، ومـن تبعهـم، إلى فقـه الثلاثـة: أبي حنيفـة، ومالـك، والشـافعي، وقـد يذكـر فقـه بعـض كبـار أصحابهـم، ممـن لم يسـتهلك في التقليـد، ولا يذكـر فقـه أحمـد إلا نـادراً، إذ أحمـد عنـد الأندلسـيين إمـام في الحديـث فقـط، وقـد يذكـر فقـه مـن جـاء بعـد الثلاثـة إلى منتصـف القـرن الخامـس.

1 *Mu'jam Fiqh Ibn Ḥazm* 28 (Introduction)

١ معجم فقه ابن حزم (المقدمة): ٢٨.

Ibn Ḥazm used to trace all these views, via their chain of transmitters, back to those who said them. Based on that, he used to confirm, deny, evaluate, accept, reject and compare between his views and those he quoted. He would discuss their proofs in a brilliantly scientific fashion and with an eloquence that the jurists of Andalusia were known for in their books.

Ibn Ḥazm was harsh in his criticism of those who opposed him due to his stern personality. He was especially rough when discussing the views of the Ḥanafis and Mālikis. This harshness at times reached the degree of him considering the opposing views as being outright foolish. As a result, many people became averse to Ibn Ḥazm and his views, and many scholars even refused to benefit from his jurisprudence because of his attitude.

Al-Mughni

Its author was Muwaffaq ad-Dīn Abū Muhammad ʻAbdullāh ibn Aḥmad ibn Qudamah al-Maqdisi ad-Dimashqi. He was born in 541 A.H. and died in 620 A.H.

Al-Muwaffaq excelled in many sciences. Ibn al-Ḥājib said about him, "He is the supreme *imām* and the mufti of the *Ummah*. Allah conferred upon him a great favor, a marvelous mind and perfect knowledge. The lands buzzed with his mention, and the eras were void of his likes. He mastered the textual and logical sciences. As for the textual, namely the science of Hadith, he was at the forefront of this subject matter. As for the science of *Fiqh*, he was the shining knight in this field. He was the most qualified of those who give *fatwa* and had authored many vast compilations, and I doubt that human history will witness his like."[1]

وكل تلك الآراء والمذاهب يوردها بسنده منه إلى قائليها، فيصحح، ويضعف، ويعدل، ويجرح، ويقبل، ويرفض، ويقارن بين فقهه وفقه غيره من جميع من ذكر، ويناقش أدلتهم وحججهم بلغة علمية أدبية، في بيان وإيضاح رائعين اشتهر بهما فقهاء الأندلس في كتبهم للفقه.

وابن حزم شديد الوطأة على مخالفيه في الرأي بسبب حدة في مزاجه، وأشد ما يكون عنفاً عندما يناقش الحنفية والمالكية، وتصل الحدة إلى درجة عالية من القسوة تجعله يسفه رأي المخالف، وقد حصل من كثير من الناس نفرة تجاه ابن حزم وفقهه، وتحامى عن الانتفاع بفقهه كثير من العلماء من أجل ذلك.

٢- المغني:

مؤلفه هو موفق الدين أبو محمد عبد الله بن أحمد بن قدامة المقدسي ثم الدمشقي المولود في سنة ٥٤١هـ والمتوفى في سنة ٦٢٠هـ.

نبغ الموفق في علوم كثيرة قال فيه ابن الحاجب: «هو إمام الأئمة، ومفتي الأمة، خصه الله بالفضل الوافر، والخاطر العاطر، والعلم الكامل، طنت بذكره الأمصار، وضنت بمثله الأعصار، قد أخذ بمجامع الحقائق النقلية والعقلية، فأما الحديث فهو سابق فرسانه، وأما الفقه فهو فارس ميدانه، أعرف الناس بالفتيا، وله المؤلفات الغزيرة، وما أظن الزمان يسمح بمثله»[1].

1 *Al-Mughni* 1/4 (Introduction)

١ المغني (المقدمة): ١/ ٤ مكتب الرياض الحديثة، الرياض.

Abū Shāmah said, "I was informed by more than one person that Imām Abūl-'Abbās Aḥmad ibn Taymiyah said, 'No one has entered Syria, after al-Awzā'i, who was more knowledgeable than Shaykh Muwaffaq (may Allah bestow mercy upon him).'"[1]

Aḍ-Ḍiyā' said, "He – may Allah bestow mercy upon him – was a great *imām* in the sciences of the Qur'an and its interpretation, and a great *imām* in the sciences of Hadith and its problems. He was a unique *imām* in *Fiqh*, unmatched by his contemporaries. He was also a great *imām* in the science of different opinions and was the greatest scholar of his time in subject of inheritance. He was also a great *imām* in *Uṣūl al-Fiqh*, an expert in mathematics and an expert in astronomy."[2]

He authored many books on numerous sciences. The number of his compilations reached 47 distinct works.[3] The greatest and most famous of his books was *al-Mughni*. He explained the *madhhab* of Imām Aḥmad and his preferred views in this book, both the controversial issues and matters of scholarly disagreement. He did not limit himself to just that, but also mentioned the views of every *madhhab*'s founding *Imām* and made brief references to their proofs for these views. Whenever possible, he would also ascribe the narrations he reports to their proper references, namely the books of the great *Imām*(s) of Hadith. He based most of this on *ash-Sharḥ al-Mukhtaṣar* by Abūl-Qāsim 'Umar ibn al-Ḥusayn ibn 'Abdillāh al-Khiraqi.[4]

'Izz ad-Dīn ibn 'Abdis-Salām said about this book, "I did not accept for myself be a mufti until I had a copy of *al-Mughni*."[5] He also said, "I have never seen a book of knowledge in Islam like *al-Muhallā*, *al-Mujallā* and *al-Mughni*."[6]

1 Ibid: 1/5
2 Ibid: 1/6
3 Find their names in the introduction of *al-Mughni* 1/26-36.
4 Taken from the words of al-Muwaffaq in *al-Mughni* 1/2 with slight modification.
5 *Al-Mughni* 1/11 (Introduction)
6 Ibid

وقال أبو شامة: «وبلغني من غير وجه عن الإمام أبي العباس أحمد بن تيمية- رحمه الله- أنه قال: ما دخل الشام بعد الأوزاعي أفقه من الشيخ الموفق- رحمه الله»[١].

وقال الضياء: «كان- رحمه الله- إماماً في القرآن وتفسيره، إماماً في علم الحديث ومشكلاته، إماماً في الفقه، أوحد زمانه فيه، إماماً في علم الخلاف، أوحد زمانه في الفرائض، إماماً في أصول الفقه، إماماً في النحو، إماماً في الحساب، إماماً في النجوم السيارة والمنازل»[٢].

صنف مصنفات كثيرة في علوم عدة، وقد بلغت تصانيفه (٤٧) مصنفاً[٣]، وأعظم مصنفاته وأشهرها كتاب «المغني»، وقد «شرح في كتابه هذا مذهب الإمام أحمد واختياره، وبين في كثير من المسائل ما اختلف فيه مما أجمع عليه»، ولم يكتف بذلك، بل «ذكر ما ذهب إليه إمام كل مذهب من المذاهب، وأشار إلى أدلة بعض أقوالهم على سبيل الاختصار، وعزا ما أمكنه عزوه من الأخبار، إلى كتب الأئمة من علماء الآثار، وبنى ذلك على شرح مختصر «أبي القاسم عمر بن الحسين بن عبد الله الخرقي»[٤].

قال عز الدين بن عبد السلام في هذا الكتاب: «ما طابت نفسي بالفتيا حتى صار عندي نسخة من المغني»[٥]، وقال أيضاً: «ما رأيت في كتب الإسلام في العلم مثل المحلى والمجلى وكتاب المغني»[٦].

١ المصدر السابق: ١/ ٥.
٢ المصدر السابق: ١/ ٦.
٣ انظر أسماءها في مقدمة المغني: ١/ ٢٦- ٣٦، الطبعة الأولى (١٤٠٦هـ- ١٩٨٦م)، دار هجر.
٤ من كلام الموفق في المغني بشيء من التصرف، المغني: ١/ ٢.
٥ المغني (المقدمة): ١/ ١١.
٦ المصدر السابق.

The value of this book is clearly noticeable to whoever looks through it thoroughly, thinks deeply about it, reflects on its style, understands its method, realizes the depths of its ideas and discusses its proofs.

Al-Majmū' Sharḥ al-Muhaẓab

Its author is Abū Zakariyyā Yaḥyā ibn Sharaf an-Nawawi ad-Dimashqi. He was born in 631 A.H. and died in 676 A.H.

An-Nawawi (may Allah bestow mercy upon him) was of impeccable strength in the science of Hadith, its narrators and distinguishing between the authentic and weak among them. He authored multiple books on this science, from which many people benefited, and which scholars across the board approved of. Of them was his valuable explanation of *Ṣaḥīḥ Muslim,* his books *Riyāḍ aṣ-Ṣāliḥīn* and *al-Azkar*. He also had great contributions in the sciences of the Arabic language.

As for *Fiqh,* he reached its very peak, and thus is considered one of the greatest authorities on Shāfi'i *Fiqh* and of the most credible verifiers of their *madhhab*. Of his books in this regard was *Rawḍat aṭ-Ṭālibīn,* which consists of eleven volumes.

An-Nawawi (may Allah bestow mercy upon him) authored *al-Majmū'* as an explanation for *al-Muhadhab* that was compiled by Abū Isḥāq ash-Shirāzi. Imām an-Nawawi intended to make this explanation a comprehensive encyclopedia of *Fiqh* but decided otherwise after beginning its compilation. This is because when he was still completing the chapter on menstruation, he realized that the book was already three large volumes. This convinced him that "continuing in this manner would elicit boredom in the reader and subsequently lessen its benefit due to its length and the inability of most to acquire a personal copy of it. For this reason, he abandoned this format and made it moderately elaborate."[1]

وتبدو قيمة الكتاب لمن سبر غوره، وأمعن النظر فيه، وتأمل أسلوبه، وعرف طريقته، وأدرك عمق فكرته، وناقش أدلته.

٣- المجموع شرح المهذب:

مؤلفه هو أبو زكريا يحيى بن شرف النووي الدمشقي ولد في سنة ٦٣١هـ، وتوفي في سنة ٦٧٦هـ.

كان النووي- رحمه الله تعالى- حافظاً للحديث وفنونه ورجاله وصحيحه وضعيفه، وله في ذلك تصانيف انتفع الناس بها كثيراً، وتلقاها العلماء بالقبول، منها شرحه القيم على صحيح مسلم، ورياض الصالحين، والأذكار.

وله في اللغة باع طويل، ومؤلفات نافعة.

أما الفقه فقد بلغ فيه الغاية، فإنه يعد حجة في فقه الشافعية، وهو من المشهود لهم بتحقيق المذهب، ومن كتبه فيه كتاب «روضة الطالبين» وهو في أحد عشر مجلداً.

وقد ألف النووي- رحمه الله- «المجموع» شارحاً فيه كتاب «المهذب» لأبي إسحاق الشيرازي، وقد أراد أن يكون هذا الشرح موسوعة فقهية مستوعبة، ولكنه عدل عن ذلك بعد أن سار فيه شوطاً، فإنه لم يكد ينتهي من كتاب الحيض حتى بلغ الكتاب ثلاث مجلدات كبار، فرأى «أن الاستمرار على هذا المنهاج يؤدي إلى سآمة مطالعه، ويكون سبباً إلى قلة الانتفاع به لكثرته، والعجز عن تحصيل نسخة منه، فترك ذلك وعدل عن هذه الطريقة وسلك منهجاً وسطاً»(١).

1 *Al-Majmū'* 1/6, printed by al-Maktabah as-Salafiyyah (Madinah)

١ المجموع للنووي: ١/ ٦، طبعة المكتبة السلفية، المدينة المنورة.

The author (may Allah bestow mercy upon him) invested great care in explaining *al-Muhadhab* by interpreting the verses and hadith(s) it contained, and by discussing the Companions' reports, the *fatwa*(s) and the poetry found therein. In addition, he would explain whether the hadith(s) cited as proof were authentic, weak, accepted or rejected, and would reference each hadith to the Hadith book that collected it. Also, when the compiler of *al-Muhadhab* would cite a weak hadith as proof, he would point out its weakness, and then report the authentic hadith(s) – if they existed – that could serve as proof in its place.

وقد اعتنى المؤلف- رحمه الله تعالى- بشرح كتاب المهذب، ففسر ما ورد فيه من آيات وأحاديث، وتكلم على ما ورد فيه من آثار وفتاوى وأشعار، وبيَّن من الأحاديث المستدل بها الصحيح والضعيف، والمقبول والمردود، وعزا الأحاديث إلى الكتب التي أخرجتها، وإذا احتج المصنف بحديث ضعيف بيَّن ضعفه، ثم أورد من الأحاديث الصحيحة ما يصلح شاهداً إن وجد.

He would also elaborate on the uncommon terms found in the book, and the names of ash-Shāfi'i's disciples, the other scholars or the narrators and transmitters, either briefly or in detail, depending on whether the matter is consequential in that context.

وبيَّن ما وقع في الكتاب من ألفاظ اللغات وأسماء الأصحاب وغيرهم من العلماء والنقلة والرواة مبسوطاً في وقت ومختصراً في وقت بحسب الحاجة والمواطن.

He went to great lengths in clarifying the rulings in simple terms. He would identify which of the author's positions was a matter of agreement between the Shāfi'i jurists, which were viewed by the majority, which were viewed by him alone and which were opposed by a majority of the Shāfi'i jurists.

وقد بالغ في إيضاح الأحكام بعبارة سهلة، فبين ما ذكره المصنف واتفق عليه فقهاء الشافعية، أو جمهورهم، كما بين ما انفرد به أو خالفه فيه معظم فقهاء الشافعية.

In *al-Majmū'*, an-Nawawi included all the views and *wujūh* in the Shāfi'i *madhhab*. He would not leave out any view, *wajh* or report – even if it were weak – except that he mentioned it. Then, he would defend out the preponderant view, explain the flaw in the weak view and highlight the clearly mistaken view. He would not hesitate in declaring that someone was mistaken, even if he was one of the greatest scholars.

وقد استوعب الأقوال والوجوه في مذهب الشافعية، فلم يترك قولاً ولا وجهاً ولا نقلاً ولو كان ضعيفاً إلا ذكره، وبين رجحان الراجح، وضعف الضعيف، وزيف الزائف، ولم يهب من تغليط الغالط ولو كان من أكابر العلماء.

One of the excellent things done by an-Nawawi in his book was that he would reference each view to the books of those who held it. One example of that was the views of Imām ash-Shāfi'i (may Allah bestow mercy upon him).

ومن الأمور التي أحسن النووي فيها في كتابه هذا أنه كان يرجع في نقل الأقوال إلى كتب أصحابها، ومن ذلك أقوال الإمام الشافعي- رحمه الله تعالى.

Of the most important things an-Nawawi focused on in this book was mentioning the views of the *salaf* and their proofs. As for the other scholarly positions, most were taken from the books *al-Ishrāf* and *al-Ijmā'* by Ibn al-Mundhir, and the books authored by the disciples of the great *Imām*(s). Very rarely did he cite what the Shāfi'i jurists reported about other *madhhab*(s), because some of these reports which exist in the Shāfi'i books about others are denied by those *madhhab*(s) to whom they are attributed.

An-Nawawi introduced his book with a wholesome 72 page introduction. In it, he spoke a bit about the life of Imām ash-Shāfi'i and the author of the book. Then, he talked about the virtues of knowledge, its branches and those who qualify for this virtue. He also talked about the etiquette of the scholar and the student, rulings related to the mufti and the one seeking a *fatwa*, and the parameters of a *fatwa* and its etiquette. Another valuable section of his introduction discussed hadith, consensus, the views of the Companions and similar.

It was not destined for an-Nawawi to complete this precious book, as Allah chose to bring him to His company before its completion. He finished the section on usury, in the chapter of trade, shortly before his death. That portion of his book amounted to nine volumes.[1] Thereafter, Taqi ad-Dīn Abūl-Ḥasan 'Ali ibn 'Abdil-Kāf as-Subki attempted to complete it, and his contribution to this book increased it to 11 volumes in total, but he also died before completing it.

ومن أهم ما اعتنى به النووي ذكر مذاهب السلف بأدلتها، وأكثر ما نقله من مذاهب العلماء من كتاب الإشراف والإجماع لابن المنذر، ومن كتاب أصحاب أئمة المذاهب، ولم ينقل مما نقله فقهاء الشافعية عن غيرهم من الفقهاء إلا القليل؛ لأنه وقع في كتب الشافعية نقول عن المذاهب الأخرى ينكرها أصحاب المذاهب المنسوبة إليهم(١).

وقد قدم لكتابه بمقدمة ضافية بلغت (٧٢) صفحة، وقد ذكر فيها طرفاً من أخبار وأحوال الشافعي- رحمه الله- ، ومصنف الكتاب، ثم تحدث عن فضل العلم، وبين أقسامه، وذكر مستحقي فضله، وتكلم على آداب العالم والمتعلم، وأحكام المفتي والمستفتي وصفة الفتوى وآدابها، وذكر فصولاً هامة تتعلق بالحديث والإجماع وأقوال الصحابة، ونحو ذلك.

ولم يقدر للنووي- رحمه الله- أن يتم هذا السفر النفيس، فاختاره الله إلى جواره قبل أن ينهي مراده منه، وعندما وافاه الأجل كان قد انتهى إلى «باب الربا» من كتاب البيوع، وقد جاء هذا المقدار من الكتاب في تسعة مجلدات(٢)، وقد قام بإتمامه تقي الدين أبو الحسن علي بن عبد الكافي السبكي، وقد بلغت التكملة أحد عشر مجلداً، ولكنه أيضاً توفي قبل أن يتمه.

1 Printed by al-Maktabah as-Salafiyyah in Madinah. In the footnotes of this book, the publisher printed two other books; the first was *Fatḥ al-'Azīz Sharḥ al-Wajīz* by Imām ar-Rāfi'i, and the second was the referencing of the hadith(s) used by ar-Rāfi'i in his book, which was entitled *Takhiṣ al-Ḥabīr* by Ibn Ḥajar. In the past and present, a number of jurists tried to complete the work of as-Subki in explaining *al-Majmū'*. Of them was the great scholar, 'Īsā ibn Yūsuf Manūn (d. 1376 A.H.) and Shaykh Muhammad Najīb al-Mutī 'i (d. 1406 A.H.). The version completed by al-Mutī'i was published into 20 volumes, the last eight volumes being the work of al-Mutī'i which completes the book *al-Majmū'*.

١ المجموع: ١/ ٥.

٢ طبعة المكتبة السلفية بالمدينة المنورة، وقد طبع الناشر مع الكتاب في الحاشية كتابين، الأول: كتاب فتح العزيز شرح الوجيز للإمام الرافعي، والثاني: تخريج أحاديث كتاب الرافعي هذا المعروف باسم «تلخيص الحبير لابن حجر».

وسعى عدد من الفقهاء قديماً وحديثاً إلى إتمام عمل السبكي في شرحه للمجموع، منهم العلامة عيسى بن يوسف منون (توفي سنة ١٣٧٦هـ)، والشيخ محمد نجيب المطيعي (توفي سنة ١٤٠٦هـ)، والطبعة التي بتكملة المطيعي تقع في عشرين جزءاً، الثمانية الأخيرة منها للمطيعي، وبها يتم كتاب المجموع للنووي.

The Benefit of These Types of Compilations

These types of juristic works are of great benefit to the scholar and students of knowledge. We can summarize their benefit in the following points:

1) The first beneficial feature of these types of works is that they are books of comparative *Fiqh* and the *Fiqh* of Islam at large. They were concerned with the views of the Companions and Successors and the numerous narrations within the *madhhab*(s) to which they belong. Hence, these works are records containing the views of the jurist Compansions and the *Imām*(s) among the Successors who recorded their views by themselves, such as ath-Thawri, al-Awzā'i and al-Layth, or those whose views were transmitted via memory, such as Abū Laylā and Ibn Shubrumah. These books were also concerned with mentioning the views of the four great *Imām*(s), and the views of the other great scholars who were known for their prowess in *Fiqh* and *ijtihād*. Hence, each of these works is truly a juristic encyclopedia in the fullest sense of the word.

2) For the most part, these types of works discuss the disparate views without obdurance, and without bias in their interpretation of the evidences; they support whatever they perceive as having stronger evidence. For that reason, reading any one of these books suffices the reader from having to refer to many different books, referring to the books of evidences or referring to the matters of consensus and the matters of juristic controversy.

3) For the most part, these books present the rulings along with their evidences. By doing that, the people of knowledge can read the proofs for these rulings and in turn possess insight on the matters of their religion, and that is how Allah described the Messenger (ﷺ) and his followers, **"Say, 'This is my way; I invite to Allah with insight, I and those who follow me.'"**[1]

1 Surah Yūsuf – Verse 108

فائدة هذا النوع من المؤلفات:

هـذا النـوع مـن المؤلفـات الفقهيـة مفيـد فائـدة كبـيرة للعلـماء وطلبـة العلـم، ويمكننـا إيجـاز هـذه الفوائـد في النقـاط التاليـة:

أولاً: أول ميـزة لهـذا النـوع مـن المؤلفـات أنهـا كتـب في الفقـه المقـارن، وفقـه الإسـلام العـام، فهـي تهتـم بذكـر مذاهـب الصحابـة والتابعـين، كـما تهتـم بروايـات المذهـب الـذي ينتمـي كل منهـا إليـه، ولذلـك فإنهـا سـجل لأقـوال فقهـاء الصحابـة وأئمـة التابعـين الذيـن دونـوا أقوالهـم بأنفسـهم، كالثـوري، والأوزاعـي، والليـث، أو تنوقلـت عنهـم بطريـق الحفـظ، كابـن أبي ليـلى، وابـن شـبرمة، وتهتـم أيضـاً بذكـر مذاهـب الأئمـة الأربعـة وغيرهـم ممـن عرفـوا بالفقـه والاجتهـاد، فـكل واحـد منهـا موسـوعة فقهيـة بـكل مـا تحملـه هـذه الكلمـة مـن معنـى.

ثانيـاً: يناقـش هـذا النـوع مـن المؤلفـات الآراء دون تعصـب، ودون أن يتكلـف توجيـه الأدلـة نحـوه في معظـم مـا كتبـوه، ويرجحـون مـا يـرون قـوة دليلـه، ولذلـك فـإن مطالعـة أي كتـاب مـن هـذه الكتـب يغنـي عـن مراجعـة الكتـب المختلفـة، ومراجعـة كتـب أدلـة الأحـكام ومراجعـة مسـائل الإجـماع والخـلاف.

ثالثـاً: هـذه الكتـب تسـوق الأحـكام بأدلتهـا في كثـير مـن الأحيـان، وبهـذا يتمكـن أهـل العلـم مـن الاطـلاع عـلى أدلـة الأحـكام فيكونـون عـلى بصـيرة مـن دينهـم، ويكونـون كـما وصـف اللـه رسـوله وأتباعـه بقولـه: **﴿قُـلْ هَـٰذِهِ سَـبِيلِي أَدْعُـو إِلَى اللـهِ عَـلَى بَصِـيرَةٍ أَنَـا وَمَـنِ اتَّبَعَنِـي﴾**(١).

١ يوسف: ١٠٨.

4) When the researcher learns the *Fiqh* views of any *madhhab* along with the evidences for these views, one is rescued from being shackled by the Qur'anically condemned *taqlīd* and intellectual stagnation. Knowing the evidences enables one to climb toward being adherent to a position based on conviction and not merely a blind follower. This is essential because the scholars stipulate this insight-based conviction for anyone who disseminates knowledge in the name of the religion.

In the introduction of his book *al-Majmū'*, an-Nawawi (may Allah bestow mercu upon him) said, "Know that being acquainted with the views of the *salaf*, along with their evidences, is of paramount importance. This is because their differing on the detailed rulings is a mercy[1] and because mentioning their views with their evidences enables the qualified researcher to differentiate between the stronger and weaker positions, and it clarifies for him and others where the problem lies, and it shows him priceless points of benefit. Additionally, it trains the reader to answer questions, and it broadens his scope of thinking and makes him intellectually distinguished, and it teaches him to discern between authentic and weak hadith(s), and between stronger and weaker arguments. It also teaches him to reconcile between [apparently] contradictory hadith(s) and those which are literally applied versus those which are figurative. Nothing [after all that] will perplex him except a handful of rare cases."[2]

رابعاً: المتلقي لأحكام دينه من فقه أي مذهب من المذاهب المدونة يخرج باطلاعه على أدلتها في هذه الكتب من ربقة الجمود على التقليد المحض المذموم في القرآن إلى الاتباع المقرون بالبصيرة الذي اشترطه الأئمة فيمن يتلقى العلم عنهم.

يقول النووي- رحمه الله تعالى- في مقدمة كتابه المجموع: «واعلم أن معرفة مذاهب السلف بأدلتها من أهم ما يحتاج إليه؛ لأن اختلافهم في الفروع رحمة [١]، وبذكر مذاهبهم بأدلتها يَعرف المتمكن المذاهب على وجهها والراجح من المرجوح، ويتضح له ولغيره المشكلات، وتظهر له الفوائد النفيسات، ويتدرب الناظر فيها بالسؤال والجواب، ويتفتح ذهنه ويتميز عند ذوي البصائر والألباب، ويعرف الأحاديث الصحيحة من الضعيفة، والدلائل الراجحة من المرجوحة، ويقوم بالجمع بين الأحاديث المتعارضات، والمعمول بظاهرها من المؤولات، ولا يشكل عليه إلا أفراد من النادر»[٢].

---

1 This statement, in the absolute sense, is not correct. Rather, mercy is in agreement. As for disagreements caused by various understandings of the revealed texts, this is a necessity that simply cannot be avoided.
2 *Al-Majmū'* 1/5

١ هذا القول على إطلاقه ليس صحيحاً، بل الرحمة الاتفاق، أما الاختلاف الذي سببه الاختلاف في فقه النصوص فإنه ضرورة لا مناص منها.
٢ المجموع: ١/ ٥.

Compiling Books on the Principles of *Fiqh*

The Muslims realized from the very beginning that many of the Qur'anic verses were general, bearing loads of meanings in a few words. For instance, when the Messenger (ﷺ) was asked about the donkeys, he replied, **"Nothing has been revealed to me except this unique, comprehensive verse: 'So whoever does good equal to the weight of an atom (or a smallest ant) shall see it; and whoever does evil equal to the weight of an atom (or a smallest ant) shall see it.'[1]"[2]**

The Prophet was gifted with comprehensive speech. Of what falls under this are the hadith(s) on fundamental rulings and broad principles. For instance, the hadith, "Verily, actions are but by intentions,"[3] applies to most branches of *Fiqh*. Imam as-Shāfi'i used to say, "This hadith applies to 70 chapters of *Fiqh*. It leaves no excuse for a falsifier, aggressor or conartist, until the meeting with Allah, the Most High."[4]

The scholars differed on which hadith(s) the principles of Islam revolve around,[5] and an-Nawawi (may Allah bestow mercy upon him) collected forty hadith(s) of this kind.

At times, the jurists took some of these hadith(s) and turned them – using their exact wording – into a principle of *Fiqh*, such as the hadith, "No harm [should ensue], nor any reciprocating harm." Other times, they may reword these hadith(s) to produce the juristic principle. For example, the great principle in *Fiqh* which states, "Matters are [judged] by their aims," is taken directly from the hadith which states, "Verily, actions are but by intentions."

تدوين علم القواعد الفقهية

تنبه المسلمون منذ بداية الأمر إلى أن كثيراً من آيات القرآن آيات جامعة، تحمل المعاني الكثيرة في الألفاظ القليلة، وقد سئل الرسول ﷺ عن الحُمُر، فقال: «لم ينزل عليَّ فيها إلا هذه الآية الجامعة الفاذة: ﴿فَمَن يَعْمَلْ مِثْقَالَ ذَرَّةٍ خَيْراً يَرَهُ﴾[١] »[٢].

وأوتي الرسول ﷺ جوامع الكلم، ومن هذه الأحاديث أحاديث في الأحكام تعد أصولاً وقواعد جامعة، فمثلاً حديث: «**إنما الأعمال بالنيات**» يدخل في غالب مسائل الفقه وأبوابه، ويرى الشافعي أنه «يدخل في سبعين باباً من الفقه، وأنه لم يترك لمبطل، ولا مضار، ولا محتال حجة إلى لقاء الله تعالى»[٣].

وقد اختلف العلماء في الأحاديث التي هي قواعد الإسلام[٤]، وقد جمع النووي- رحمه الله- هذه الأحاديث فبلغت أربعين حديثاً.

وقد أخذ الفقهاء بعض هذه الأحاديث بلفظها وجعلوها قواعد فقهية، كحديث: «**لا ضرر ولا ضرار**»، وأحيانا يصوغون هذه الأحاديث صياغة قريبة أو بعيدة، وتصبح بذلك قاعدة فقهية، كالقاعدة العظيمة الشأن «الأمور بمقاصدها»، فإنها مأخوذة من قوله ﷺ: «**إنما الأعمال بالنيات**».

---

1 Sūrat az-Zalzalah – Verse 7
2 Reported by al-Bukhāri.
3 Reported by al-Bukhāri.
4 *Fayd al-Qadīr* 1/32, *al-'Ayni 'alā al-Bukhāri* 1/22 and *Jāmi' al-'Ulūm wal-Ḥikam* 1/61 by Ibn Rajab
5 See our book *Maqāṣid al-Mukallafīn* 90.

١ الزلزلة: ٧.
٢ أخرجه البخاري: ٢٣٧١، ومسلم ٩٨٧، وانظر تفسير ابن كثير: ٨/ ٤٦١-٤٦٢، سورة الزلزلة، الآية: ٧.
٣ فيض القدير: ١/ ٣٢، العيني على البخاري: ١/ ٢٢، وجامع العلوم والحكم لابن رجب: ١/ ٦١ الحديث الأول.
٤ انظر كتابنا: مقاصد المكلفين:٩١.

In his book *al-Ashbāh wan-Naẓā'ir*, as-Suyūṭi has mentioned many of these principles, and he would first introduce each principle with its basis in the hadith(s) and Companions' statements.

At times, we may not find an explicit text from which the *Fiqh* principle was taken. Instead, when the great scholars and *Imām*(s) scanned the rulings of the Islamic Sharia, they notice certain constants in its resembling rulings, and from that they extracted the principle.

Examples

Some of these principles are: "certainty cannot be removed by doubt," "the default rule is acquittance," "the default in matters is permissibility, unless a proof indicates its prohibition," "hardship necessitates leniency," "necessities permit the forbidden," "the default in speech is the literal meaning," "There is no *ijtihād* when a text is present," "preventing harm takes precedence over attaining benefit" and "profiting entails risk."

The Benefit of Knowing These Principles

These rules are considered the foundation upon which the laws of Sharia were built. The one who is well-versed in these rules begins to discover many of the secrets behind the Sharia rulings and learns the objectives behind these rules. Knowing them also trains one on how to extract the proper rulings, especially those that are not explicitly addressed by the texts, for they usually fall under one of these broad principles instead. Regarding this, al-Qarāfi said, "The second category is that of general, holistic principles which are many in number, widely applicable and encapsulate the secrets and wisdoms of the Sharia. Every one of these principles has countless applications that fall beneath it. Thus, these principles are of great importance in *Fiqh*, and a jurist's skill and prestige grow to the degree that one encompasses and masters these principles."[1]

1 *Al-Furūq* 2-3 by al-Qarāfi

وقد ذكر السيوطي في كتابه الأشباه والنظائر قواعد كثيرة، وصدَّر كل قاعدة بأصلها من الحديث والأثر.

وقد لا نجد نصّاً معيناً أخذت منه القاعدة الفقهية، ولكن الأئمة الكرام، والعلماء الأوائل استقروا أحكام الشريعة الإسلامية، واستخلصوا من أحكامها المتشابهة قاعدة جامعة.

أمثلة:

ومن هذه القواعد الفقهية: اليقين لا يزال بالشك، الأصل براءة الذمة، الأصل في الأشياء الإباحة حتى يدل دليل على التحريم، المشقة تجلب التيسير، الضرورات تبيح المحظورات، الأصل في الكلام الحقيقة، لا اجتهاد مع النص، درء المفاسد أولى من جلب المصالح، الغنم بالغرم.

فائدة العلم بهذه القواعد:

تعد هذه القواعد هي الأصول التي بنيت عليها الأحكام الشرعية، والذي يتمرس في هذه القواعد يطلع على كثير من أسرار الأحكام الشرعية، ويتعرف على مآخذ الأحكام، ويتدرب على كيفية استخراج الأحكام، وخاصة تلك الأحكام التي لم ينص على حكمها فإنها تكون في كثير من الأحيان مندرجة تحت قاعدة كلية من هذه القواعد، يقول القرافي: «والقسم الثاني قواعد كلية فقهية جليلة كثيرة العدد، عظيمة المدد، مشتملة على أسرار الشرع وحكمه، لكل قاعدة من الفروع في الشريعة ما لا يحصى، وهذه القواعد مهمة في الفقه، عظيمة النفع وبقدر الإحاطة بها يعظم قدر الفقيه ويشرف»[1]، ويقول السيوطي: «اعلم أن فن الأشباه والنظائر فن عظيم، به يطلع على حقائق الفقه ومداركه، ومآخذه وأسراره،

١ الفروق للقرافي: ٢، ٣.

As-Suyūṭi said, "Know that the science of *al-Ashbāh wan-Naẓā'ir* (comparable cases) is a great science. Using it, one realizes the facts, sources and secrets of *Fiqh*. It enables one to understand and remember, and makes one capable of correctly attributing one ruling to its resembling cases, and directs one to the rulings on matters for which nothing is expressly stated, or those new cases which never come to an end. For this reason, our companions said, 'The essence of *Fiqh* is knowing *al-Ashbāh wan-Naẓā'ir*.'"[1]

The Books Compiled on These Principles

The Ḥanafi scholars were those most concerned with authoring works on the principles of *Fiqh*. One of those who wrote on this topic was Abū Zayd ad-Dabūsi, who died in 430 A.H. He wrote a book called *Ta'sīs an-Naẓar*, which mentioned 86 principles. Ibn Nujaym, who died in 970 A.H., was another of these authors who compiled a book called *al-Ashbāh wan-Naẓā*'ir.

Among the Shāfi'is, as-Suyūti, who died in 911 A.H., wrote about this topic. He also wrote the book *al-Ashbāh wan-Naẓā*'ir.

Among the Mālikis, al-'Izz ibn 'Abdis-Salām, who died in 660 A.H., compiled the book *Qawā'id al-Aḥkām fī Maṣaliḥ al-Anām*. The Māliki jurist al-Qarāfi, who died in 684 A.H., compiled the book *al-Furūq*.

Among the Ḥanbalis, Sulaymān ibn 'Abdil-Qawi aṭ-Ṭūfi al-Ḥanbali compiled two books in this regard: the first was *al-Qawā'id al-Kubrā* and the second was *al-Qawā'id aṣ-Ṣughrā*. He died in 710 A.H.

Ibn Rajab al-Ḥanbali, who died in 795 A.H., also compiled a book on the principles of *Fiqh* which vividly illustrated his knowledge and strength.

Dr. Muhammad Salām Madkur considered the book by al-'Izz ibn 'Abdis-Salām, the book by al-Qarāfi and the book by Ibn Rajab to be more of general parameters and classifications on *Fiqh*, and that their content differed greatly from the principles of *Fiqh* we have come to know and studied.[2]

1 *Al-Ashbāh wan-Naẓā*'ir 6
2 *Al-Madkhal lil-Fiqh* 186 by Muhammad Sallām Madkūr

ويتمهـر في فهمـه واسـتحضاره، ويقتـدر عـلى الإلحـاق والتخريـج، ومعرفـة أحـكام المسـائل التـي ليسـت بمسـطورة، والحـوادث والوقائـع التـي لا تنقـضي عـلى ممـر الزمـان، ولهـذا قـال أصحابنـا: الفقـه معرفـة الأشـباه والنظائـر»(١).

الكتب المدونة في القواعد:

الأحنـاف هـم أكـثر مـن عنـوا بالتأليـف في قواعـد الفقـه، ومن الذيـن ألفـوا فيهـا أبـو زيـد الدبـوسي المتـوفى سـنة ٤٣٠هـ ألـف كتابـاً سـماه تأسيس النظـر، وقـد اشـتمل عـلى سـت وثمانـين قاعـدة، ومنهـم ابـن نجيـم، المتـوفى سـنة ٩٧٠هـ وله كتـاب الأشـباه والنظائـر.

وممـن ألـف في هـذا الفـن مـن الشـافعية السـيوطي المتـوفى سـنة ٩١١هـ لـه كتـاب الأشـباه والنظائـر.

ومـن المالكيـة العـز بـن عبـد السـلام المتـوفى سـنة ٦٦٠هـ- ، لـه كتـاب «قواعـد الأحـكام في مصالـح الأنـام»، وللقـرافي المالـكي المتـوفى سـنة ٦٨٤هـ كتـاب «الفـروق».

ومـن الحنابلـة سـليمان بـن عبـد القـوي الطـوفي الحنبـلي المتـوفى سـنة ٧١٠هـ لـه كتابـان: أحدهـما: القواعـد الكـبرى، والثـاني: القواعـد الصغـرى.

ولابـن رجـب الحنبـلي المتوفى سـنة ٧٩٥هـ كتـاب في القواعـد يـدل عـلى علـم ومعرفـة.

ويـرى الدكتـور محمـد سـلام مدكـور أن كتـاب العـز بـن عبـد السـلام وكتـاب القـرافي وكتـاب ابـن رجـب كلهـا تتضمـن مجـرد تقسـيمات وضوابـط أساسـية في موضوعـات فقهيـة، وهـي تختلـف كثـيراً عـن القواعـد التـي عرفناهـا وعنيناهـا(٢).

١ الأشباه والنظائر: ٦.
٢ المدخل للفقه لمحمد سلام مدكور: ١٨٦.

Summary of Unit 10

1) In this era, the jurists of the four *madhhab*(s) continued compiling juristic works in general and abridged texts and explanations in particular.

2) Some jurists in this era compiled *Fiqh* books that followed the methods of the *salaf* (predecessors). They were keen to mention the evidences, the views of the earlier generations and the views of the great scholars from various lands. Of these books was *al-Muḥallā*, *al-Mughni* and *al-Majmū'*.

3) This era also witnessed the documentation of the juristic principles, wherein many scholars composed books in this regard.

خلاصة الوحدة

نخلص من دراسة هذه الوحدة إلى ما يلي:

١- استمر فقهاء المذاهب الأربعة - في هذا العصر- في تدوين المؤلفات الفقهية عامة والمتون والشروح خاصة.

٢- دون بعض الفقهاء في هذا العصر مجموعة من الكتب الفقهية ساروا فيها على منهاج الأوائل حيث اهتموا فيها بذكر الأدلة، وأقوال السلف، وعلماء الأمصار، مثل كتاب: المحلى، والمغني، والمجموع.

٣- تم في هذا العصر تدوين على القواعد الفقهية، وصنف العلماء فيها التصانيف.

Notes

NOTES

Unit 11

The Causes of Intellectual Stagnation and its Effects

Contents of Unit 11

1) The causes of intellectual stagnation and its effects.
2) The causes of intellectual stagnation and *madhhab* fanaticism.
3) The effects resulting from intellectual stagnation and *madhhab* fanaticism.

Importance of this Unit

This great transformation from the era of the *Mujtahid Imām*(s) wherein *Fiqh* flourished to the era of *taqlīd* and stagnation did not appear from thin air. Rather, there were several reasons for it. Of them was the excessive praise of their *Imām*(s), which was a door to much evil that opened upon the Muslims and one that afflicted their *Fiqh* with stagnation and backwardness. Another major cause was the weakness that plagued the Muslim *Ummah*, as this played a direct role in burying the sciences, *Fiqh* included. Another major cause was the rulers endorsing the scholars belonging to the *madhhab* they themselves followed. In this era, when the rulers and sultans would adopt a *madhhab*, they would spread it and even limit the judiciary and mufti positions to it. These practices drove the people to follow that one *madhhab* blindly (*taqlīd*) and to avert their attention from the Qur'an and Sunnah.

Our aim in this unit is to familiarize ourselves with these causes and others in further detail.

Learning objectives

By the end of this unit, readers should be able to:

1) Mention the causes that lead to the intellectual stagnation and *madhhab* fanaticism.
2) Refute the claim made by some scholars that "every *mujtahid* is correct."
3) Point out the effects resulting from intellectual stagnation and *madhhab* fanaticism.
4) Refute those who claim that the door of *ijtihād* has been closed.

الوحدة الحادية عشر

أسباب الجمود الفكري وآثاره

محتويات الوحدة الحادية عشرة

١- أسباب الجمود الفكري وآثاره.
٢- أسباب الجمود الفكري والتعصب المذهبي.
٣- الآثار المترتبة على الجمود الفكري والتقليد المذهبي.

أهمية دراسة الوحدة:

لم يأت هذا التحول الكبير من عصر ازدهار الفقه في عهود الأئمة المجتهدين إلى عصر الجمود والتقليد من فراغ، بل كانت له أسباب عدة منها: الغلو في تعظيم الأئمة، فلقد كان هذا باب شر كبير انفتح على المسلمين، وكان سبباً فيما أصاب الفقه من جمود وتراجع، وأيضاً من أسباب حالة الوهن والضعف التي دبت في جسد الأمة الإسلامية فلقد كان هذا له أثره المباشر في تراجع الناحية العلمية ومنها الفقه، وكان من الأسباب أيضاً تمكين السلاطين لأتباع المذهب الذي يعتنقونه، وذلك أن الحكام والسلاطين في ذلك العصر، تبنوا مذهباً ومكنوا له ونشروه، وقصروا مناصب القضاء والإفتاء عليه دون غيره، وقد صرف هذا هم الناس إلى إتباع المذاهب، وتقليدها، وترك الاشتغال بعلوم الكتاب والسنة.

هذه الأسباب وغيرها نتعرف على تفصيلاتها من خلال دراستنا لهذه الوحدة.

الأهداف التعليمية:

يتوقع منك أيها الدارس الكريم بعد دراستك لهذه الوحدة أن تكون قادراً على أن:

١- تذكر الأسباب التي أدت إلى الجمود الفكري، والتعصب المذهبي.
٢- تُفند دعوى بعض العلماء «أن كل مجتهد مصيب».
٣- تُبين الآثار المترتبة على الجمود الفكري، والتقليد المذهبي.
٤- ترد على القائلين بإغلاق باب الاجتهاد.

The Causes of Intellectual Stagnation and *Madhhab* Fanaticism

There were many causes that lead to intellectual stagnation and *madhhab* fanaticism in this era. We will try to point out these causes in this section.

I. Excessively Praising the Imām(s)

Excessively praising the righteous is of the great tribulations that inflicted the nations throughout history, including this one. The polytheism of the people of Noah, for instance, resulted from excessively praising the righteous people. The idols of the people of Noah were righteous people living in the period between Adam and Noah. They continued being exalted by their people until they were eventually worshipped along with Allah. In *Ṣaḥīḥ al-Bukhāri*, it was narrated by Ibn Jurayj, through 'Aṭā', that regarding the explanation of Allah's words **"And [they] said, 'Never leave your gods, and never leave Wadd or Suwā' or Yaghûth and Ya'ûq and Nasr,'"**[1] Ibn 'Abbās said, "These are the names of righteous men from the people of Noah. When they died, Satan inspired their clansmen to erect statues in their places of gathering and to call these idols by the names of these men. They did so, but they were not [immediately] worshipped. When these [erecters] died off and knowledge [of the idols' origin and purpose] had faded, they were worshipped [by the following generations]."[2]

The Children of Israel had loved 'Uzayr (Ezra) to the degree that they eventually raised him to the status of Godhood, and the Christians over-exalted Jesus until they said he was God, the son of God or part of a trinity. Thus, Allah prohibited them from such extremism in His words, **"O People of the Book, do not commit excess in your religion or say about Allah except the truth. The Messiah, 'Īsā, the son of Maryam, was but a Messenger of Allah and His word which He directed to Maryam and a soul [created at a command] from Him."**[3]

1 Sūrah Nūh – Verse 23
2 Reported by al-Bukhāri: 4920.
3 Sūrat an-Nisā' – Verse 171

أسباب الجمود الفكري والتعصب المذهبي

هناك عدة أسباب أدت إلى الجمود الفكري والتعصب المذهبي في هذا العصر، وسنحاول أن نوضح هذه الأسباب في هذا المبحث.

أولاً: الغلو في تعظيم الأئمة:

الغلو في تعظيم الصالحين من أعظم البلاء الذي أصيبت به الأمم كما أصيبت به هذه الأمة، فشرك قوم نوح كان أصله الغلو في الصالحين، فآلهة قوم نوح كانوا رجالاً صالحين بين آدم ونوح، عظَّمَهم قومهم ثم عبدوهم من دون الله، ففي صحيح البخاري، من حديث ابن جريج عن عطاء عن ابن عباس عند تفسير قوله تعالى: **﴿وَقَالُوا لَا تَذَرُنَّ آلِهَتَكُمْ وَلَا تَذَرُنَّ وَدًّا وَلَا سُوَاعًا وَلَا يَغُوثَ وَيَعُوقَ وَنَسْرًا﴾**(١)، قال: هذه أسماء رجال صالحين من قوم نوح، فلما هلكوا أوحى الشيطان إلى قومهم أن انصبوا إلى مجالسهم التي كانوا يجلسون فيها أنصاباً وسموها بأسمائهم، ففعلوا فلم تعبد، حتى إذا هلك أولئك، ونسخ العلم (نسي ودرس) عبدت(٢).

وبنو إسرائيل أحبوا العزير حتى رفعوه إلى مرتبة الألوهية، والنصارى غلو في عيسى حتى قالوا: هو الله أو ابن الله أو ثالث ثلاثة، وقد نهاهم الله عن هذا الغلو في قوله: **﴿يَا أَهْلَ الْكِتَابِ لَا تَغْلُوا فِي دِينِكُمْ وَلَا تَقُولُوا عَلَى اللهِ إِلَّا الْحَقَّ إِنَّمَا الْمَسِيحُ عِيسَى ابْنُ مَرْيَمَ رَسُولُ اللهِ وَكَلِمَتُهُ أَلْقَاهَا إِلَى مَرْيَمَ وَرُوحٌ مِّنْهُ﴾**(٣).

١ نوح: ٢٣.
٢ أخرجه البخاري: ٤٩٢٠.
٣ النساء: ١٧١.

One manifestation of this dispraised excessiveness is to glorify the views of the *Imām*(s) to the extent that they are given precedence over the revealed texts which are clear and straightforward. Another manifestation is to obligate every legal accountable person, who has reached the age of puberty, with abiding by a *Fiqh madhhab* or forbidding a Muslim to violate their *madhhab* and adopt a ruling from another.

Allah has dispraised the People of the Book for their rejection of what has been revealed of Allah's words and the words of His messengers and for the sake of blindly following their scholars and monks. Allah, the Most High, deemed this to be a form of worshipping those scholars and monks. The Most High says, **"They have taken their scholars and monks as lords besides Allah..."**[1]

The Prophet (ﷺ) pointed out the meaning of taking them as lords, by saying, "They did not [ritually] worship them, but when they used to deem something [that was forbidden] as lawful for them, they [too] would consider it lawful, and when they used to deem something [that was permissible] as unlawful for them, they [too] would consider it unlawful."[2]

II. The Way Books Were Compiled

a) The Multitude of Compilations on Fiqh

There was a surplus of compilation in this era. Books were written, abridged, explained, commented on and footnoted. The people's preoccupation with these books, at the expense of the Qur'an and Sunnah, resulted in much harm. Ibn Khaldūn allotted a section in his book *al-Muqaddimah* to this matter, under the title "Excessive Compilation on a Science Impedes its Acquisition." In that section, he said, "Know that of what harms people in the pursuit of knowledge and its mastery is excessive compiling, using different terms when teaching, various teaching methods, and then requiring the teacher and student to retain [all] that in order to be considered knowledgeable. In other words, the student must memorize all this or most of it, and take its methods into consideration. However, his entire lifetime would not be enough to read everything composed on a single science, and hence he would inevitably fail at becoming a person of knowledge."[3]

1 Sūrat at-Tawbah – Verse 31
2 Reported by at-Tirmidhi: 3095, and he deemed it *ḥasan*. See: *Jāmi' al-Uṣūl* 2/161, and the referencing for it by Shaykh Nāsir in his work on al-Mawdūdī's *al-Musṭalaḥāt al-Arba'ah* 18.
3 *Muqaddimat Ibn Khaldūn* 531

ومن الغلو المذموم تعظيم أقوال الأئمة بحيث تقدم على النصوص الواضحة الصريحة، وإيجابهم على كل مكلف بلغ سن الرشد أن يلتزم أحد المذاهب الفقهية، وتحريمهم خروج المسلم على مذهبه، كما يحرمون عليه الأخذ من المذاهب الأخرى.

وقد ذم الله أهل الكتاب لأنهم يردون ما جاءهم من كلام الله وكلام رسله تقليداً لأحبارهم ورهبانهم، وعد سبحانه وتعالى فعلتهم هذه عبادة منهم لهم، فقال سبحانه: **﴿اتَّخَذُوا أَحْبَارَهُمْ وَرُهْبَانَهُمْ أَرْبَاباً مِّن دُونِ اللهِ﴾**(١).

وقد بين الرسول ﷺ المراد باتخاذهم أرباباً فقال: «**أما إنهم لم يعبدوهم، ولكنهم كانوا إذا أحلوا لهم شيئاً استحلوه، وإذا حرموا عليهم شيئاً حرموه**»(٢).

ثانياً: طريقة التدوين والتأليف:

أ- كثرة التأليف في الفقه.

كثر التدوين في هذا العصر واتسع وتفرع فوضعت الكتب، واختصرت وشرحت، ووضعت الحواشي، واشتغل الناس بها، وكان ذلك على حساب الاشتغال بالكتاب والسنة، وقد أضر ذلك كثيراً، وقد عقد ابن خلدون فصلاً في مقدمته عنون له بقوله: «فصل في أن كثرة التأليف في العلوم عائقة عن التحصيل» وقال في هذا الفصل: «اعلم أنه مما أضر بالناس في تحصيل العلم والوقوف على غاياته: كثرة التأليف، واختلاف الاصطلاحات في التعاليم، وتعدد طرقها، ثم مطالبة المتعلم والتلميذ باستحضار ذلك، وحينئذ يسلم له منصب التحصيل، فيحتاج المتعلم إلى حفظها كلها أو أكثرها، ومراعاة طرقها، ولا يفي عمره بما كتب في صناعة واحدة إذا تجرد لها، فيقع القصور ولابد دون رتبة التحصيل»(٣).

١ التوبة: ٣١.
٢ رواه الترمذي (٣٠٩٥) وحسنه، وانظر جامع الأصول: ٢/ ١٦١، وتخريج الشيخ ناصر له في تخريج المصطلحات الأربعة للمودودي: ١٨.
٣ مقدمة ابن خلدون: ٥٣١.

b) The Abridged *Fiqh* Books

Another aspect that led to the intellectual stagnation that dimmed the minds and pushed the scholars and students of knowledge in directions most distant from the blessed path of Fiqh were the books that focused on summarizing the books of *Fiqh*. This resulted in the student and teacher busying themselves with decoding these juristic phrases that resembled riddles. Ibn Khaldūn mentioned this in *al-Muqaddimah*, "Section: Excessively Abridging the Books of a Science Impedes its from being Taught."

We can summarize the harmful consequences of these abridged works, as mentioned by Ibn Khaldūn, in the following points:[1]

• The writers being obsessed with abridging led them to become less eloquent and harder to understand. For that reason, their works needed explanations, and their explanations needed footnotes.

• This spoiled the learning process, because it compelled beginner students to undertake the study of these advanced encyclopedias. A beginner is supposed to climb the ladder of knowledge gradually and from the ground up. Thus, Ibn 'Abbās used to interpret the word "*rabbāni*" (pious to God) in Allah's words, **"Be pious [scholars] of the Lord because of what you have taught of the Scripture and because of what you have studied,"**[2] as those who raise people upon the primaries of knowledge before its advanced levels.

• Busying the student of knowledge with deciphering the abbreviations and shortened expressions, as well as trying to understand them, wasted much of their time without benefit. This drove them to return to the clearer books that are self-explanatory, and only then would the riddles be solved and the meanings clarified.

1 *Muqaddimat Ibn Khaldūn* 532
2 Sūrah Āl-'Imrān – Verse 79

ب - المختصرات الفقهية:

مما ساعد على الجمود الفكري الذي بلد الأذهان، وأدخل طلبة العلم والعلماء في متاهة بعيدة عن المسيرة الفقهية المباركة تلك المؤلفات التي عنيت باختصار الفقه، بحيث أصبح هم المعلم والطالب حل تلك العبارات الفقهية التي تشبه الألغاز، يقول ابن خلدون في مقدمته «فصل في أن كثرة الاختصارات المؤلفة في العلوم مخلة بالتعليم».

ويمكننا أن نوجز المفاسد الناتجة عن هذه المختصرات التي ذكرها ابن خلدون في النقاط التالية (١).

• إغراق المؤلفين في الاختصار أدى إلى الإخلال بالبلاغة، وصعوبة الفهم، ولذلك احتاجوا إلى الشروح، والشروح احتاجت إلى الحواشي.

• إفساد التعليم؛ لأنهم يقصدون إلى المدونات التي هي غايات في العلم ويلزمون الطلبة المبتدئين بدراستها، والطالب المبتدئ ينبغي أن توضع له أوائل العلوم، وقد فسر ابن عباس «ربانين» في قوله تعالى: **﴿وَلَكِن كُونُوا رَبَّانِيِّينَ بِمَا كُنتُمْ تُعَلِّمُونَ الْكِتَابَ وَبِمَا كُنتُمْ تَدْرُسُونَ﴾** (٢)، أي: يربون الناس بصغار العلم قبل كباره.

• إشغال طالب العلم والعالم بحل رموز العبارة وبيان معانيها لشدة اختصارها وفي هذا ضياع للوقت في أمر ليس له فائدة، وكان الواجب الرجوع إلى الكتب الواضحة العبارة التي تبين عن نفسها بنفسها، وبذلك يزول الإلغاز، وتتضح المعاني.

١ مقدمة ابن خلدون: ٥٣٢.
٢ آل عمران: ٧٩.

• This method destroys the ability to think critically, and thus the skill of critical thinking died off and/or would not fully develop. Were the students of knowledge trained upon studying the rulings in light of the Qur'an, Sunnah and the scholars' understandings of these texts, then the talents would have been nourished, the skills would have developed and scholars would have surfaced that resembled the scholars of the first generations.

• Moreover, their objective behind abridging was never attained. For example, *al-Mudawwanah* in the Māliki *madhhab* was composed of three volumes; Ibn Abi Zayd abridged it in al-Qayrawān, then al-Barādhi'i came and authored *at-Tahdhīb* wherein he abridged the abridgement of Ibn Abi Zayd. Then, Abū 'Amr ibn al-Ḥājib came midway through the seventh century and abridged *at-Tahdhīb* by al-Barādhi'i. Then, Khalīl came in the eighth century and abridged the abridgement of Ibn al-Ḥājib, making it a radically abridged work. In other words, *Mukhtaṣar Khalīl* is an abridgement of an abridgment of an abridgment of the original abridgment!

Mukhtaṣar Khalīl was more of a riddle than an academic book. For that reason, it required elaborate explanations; al-Kharshi explained it in six volumes, az-Zarqāni explained it in eight volumes, as did ar-Rahūni as well. A Māliki jurists was incapable of simply trusting his understanding of *Mukhtaṣar Khalīl* without first reading these 22 volumes. By abridging, they sought to lessen the words in order to facilitate its memorization and save time, but the outcome was the exact opposite. Were they to rely on the original work *al-Mudawwanah*, it would have been easier and more beneficial, for it was understandable by itself and most of it did not require explanation.[1]

• هذه الطريقة فيها إفساد للملكة العلمية، ولذلك فإن الملكة العلمية تنعدم أو تنشأ قاصرة، ولو درب طلبة العلم على دراسة الأحكام من خلال النصوص من الكتاب والسنة ومن خلال فهم العلماء لهذه النصوص لصقلت المواهب، ونمت الملكات، وبرز العلماء الذين يحاكون علماء العصور الأولى.

• ثم إن الفائدة التي رجوها من وراء الاختصار لم تتحقق، فالمدونة في فقه المالكية مكونة من ثلاثة أسفار، اختصرها ابن أبي زيد في القيروان، ثم جاء البراذعي وألف «التهذيب» اختصر فيه مختصر ابن أبي زيد، ثم جاء أبو عمرو بن الحاجب واختصر تهذيب البراذعي في أواسط القرن السابع، ثم جاء خليل في القرن الثامن واختصر مختصر ابن الحاجب، فبلغ غاية الاختصار، فمختصر خليل مختصر مختصر مختصر المختصر.

لقد كان مختصر خليل أقرب إلى الألغاز منه إلى الكتب العلمية، ولذلك احتاج إلى شروح مطولة، وقد شرحه الخرشي في ستة أسفار، والزرقاني في ثمانية أسفار، والرهوني في ثمانية أيضاً، والفقيه المالكي لا يثق بفهمه لمختصر خليل إلا إذا طالع هذه الأسفار التي بلغت اثنين وعشرين سفراً، كان مرادهم من الاختصار تقليل الألفاظ تيسيراً على الحفظ، واختصار الزمن، فانعكست الآية، ولو اعتمدت المدونة لكان أسهل وأنفع؛ لأنها مفهومة بنفسها لا تحتاج إلى شرح في غالب مواضعها (١).

---

1 See *al-Fikr as-Sāmi* 2/401.

١ انظر الفكر السامي: ٢/ ٤٠١.

c) The Absence of Academic Reliability in Verification

Many of the verifying scholars complained about the reliability of the books compiled in this era. Of them was Abū Shāmah (may Allah bestow mercy upon him) who said, "The compilers among our companions who were described with the aforementioned qualities... their works were very flawed from two major aspects."[1] These were:

1) They differed greatly in what they reported from ash-Shāfi'i and/or confirmed about him. There arose various routes of transmission, such as a Khurasāni route and an Iraqi route, each reporting about their *Imām* differently, although it was all supposed to be the views of one *Imām* whose books are compiled and available. They could have returned to the books of ash-Shāfi'i, for example, and verified what has been reported about him elsewhere. Unfortunately, they did not do that and simply relied on what every group had of narrations that were ascribed to ash-Shāfi'i (may Allah bestow mercy upon him). This made knowing the actual authorized position in the *madhhab* a most challenging endeavor and subsequently gave rise to much discrepancy. Imām an-Nawawi (may Allah bestow mercy upon him) said, "Know that the books on the [Shāfi'i] *madhhab* are a matter of much disagreement between its followers. Thus, a reader cannot be confident that what an author wrote is actually the position of the *madhhab* until he reads most of the famous books on the *madhhab*."[2]

1 *Mukhtaṣar Kitāb al-Mu'ammil* 3/28, taken from Jāmi' ar-Rasā'il al-Munīriyyah

2 *Al-Majmū'* 1/4

ج - عدم اتباع المنهج العلمي في التوثيق:

وقد اشتكى كثير من محققي العلماء من المؤلفات التي ألفت في هذا العصر، ومن هؤلاء أبو شامة- رحمه الله-، يقول: «ثم إن المصنفين من أصحابنا المتصفين بالصفات المتقدمة... قد وقع في مصنفاتهم خلل كثير من وجهين عظيمين»(١).

١- ١- اختلافهم كثيراً فيما ينقلونه من نصوص الشافعي، وفيما يصححونه منها، وصارت لهم طرق مختلفة خراسانية وعراقية، وكل أصحاب طريقة ينقلون عن إمامهم خلاف ما ينقله هؤلاء، مع أن المرجع في هذا كله إمام واحد، وكتبه مدونة مروية موجودة، وكان بإمكانهم الرجوع إلى كتب الشافعي، والتحقق من النقول التي نقلت عنه، ولكنهم لم يفعلوا، واعتمد كل فريق على ما عنده مما نسب إلى الشافعي- رحمه الله تعالى-، ومن هنا أصبح معرفة المعتمد في المذهب في غاية الصعوبة، وحصل فيه اضطراب شديد، يقول النووي- رحمه الله تعالى-: «اعلم أن كتب المذهب «يعني مذهب الشافعي» فيها خلاف شديد بين الأصحاب، بحيث لا يحصل للمطالع وثوق بكون ما قاله المصنف منهم هو المذهب، حتى يطالع معظم كتب المذهب المشهورة»(٢).

١ مختصر كتاب المؤمل- جامع الرسائل المنيرية: ٣/ ٢٨.

٢ المجموع: ١/ ٤.

2) The frequent citation of weak and fabricated hadith(s) as proofs to support their views. On top of that, they would not even quote these texts accurately. Instead, they would add and subtract from the wording of the hadith(s) because they did not return to the reliable books of hadith for verification. Thus, you find the author reporting from another book of *Fiqh*, and subsequently reports the mistake that others fell into. Abū Shāmah mentions that some of the major jurists of the Shāfi'i *madhhab* were of this category, such as al-Ghazāli and Abū al-Ma'āli al-Juwayni.[1] It was mentionied by ash-Shawkāni that when al-Ghazāli and al-Juwayni spoke on hadith, they would say things that were comical to hear, and this was due to their frequent citation of weak and fabricated hadith(s). Similarly, despite az-Zamakhshari and ar-Rāzi being of those who authored books on hadith, they had no knowledge of this science and would quote weak hadith(s) a great deal.[2]

The scholars of Hadith tried to fill this gap in the *Fiqh* books, and this was by producing works that verified the hadith(s) found in the most famous *Fiqh* books in circulation.

III. The Weakness of the Islamic State

There is no doubt that the establishment of an Islamic state, wherein people find security and stability, was of great help to the scientific life that was prevalent in the Islamic world. Likewise, the weakness and eventual collapse of the Islamic state harmed the sciences greatly, *Fiqh* included. Ibn Khaldūn set a special section in *al-Muqaddimah* to point out how the sciences flourish proportionately with the advancement of civilizations. According to Ibn Khaldūn, "the reason for this is that disseminating knowledge was one of the crafts, and crafts are more commonly found in the developed cities. To the degree that these cities grow, become developed and enjoy luxuries, thus will be the degree of quality and abundance of their crafts. This is because these crafts are not essential for everyday life, so whenever the residents of a city have enough of their bare necessities, their attention becomes geared towards that which is beyond their livelihood and survival, namely the sciences and crafts which only the human beings are capable of."[3]

1 *Mukhtaṣar Kitāb al-Mu'ammil* 3/28, taken from Jāmi' ar-Rasā'il al-Munīriyyah
2 *Adab aṭ-Ṭalab* 53
3 *Muqadimmat Ibn Khaldūn* 434

٢- ٢- كثرة الاستدلال بالأحاديث الضعيفة والموضوعة على ما يذهبون إليه نصراً لقولهم، وهم مع ذلك لا يأتون بالنصوص كما وردت، بل يزيدون وينقصون من ألفاظ الأحاديث، بسبب عدم رجوعهم إلى كتب الحديث والأخذ منها، فتجد المؤلف ينقل عن كتب الفقه، فينقل الخطأ الذي وقع فيه غيره، ويذكر أبو شامة أن بعض كبار فقهاء الشافعية من هذا الصنف أمثال الغزالي وأبي المعالي الجويني(١)، ويذكر الشوكاني أن الغزالي والجويني إذا تكلموا في الحديث جاؤوا بما يضحك منه سامعه، وذلك لكثرة استشهادهم بالضعيف والموضوع، والزمخشري والرازي مع كونهم يؤلفون في الحديث فإنه لا علم لهم به، واستشهادهم بالضعيف كثير(٢).

وقد حاول المحدِّثون سدَّ هذه الثغرة في المؤلفات الفقهية، فاتجهوا إلى تخريج المؤلفات الفقهية المشهورة المتداولة.

ثالثاً: ضعف الدولة الإسلامية:

لا شك أن قيام دولة إسلامية يجد الناس فيها الأمن والاستقرار قد ساعد كثيراً في تلك الحياة العلمية التي كان يموج بها العالم الإسلامي، وقد أثر ضعف الدولة ثم تمزقها وانهيارها بعد ذلك في الحياة العلمية، ومنها الفقه، وقد عقد ابن خلدون في مقدمته فصلاً لبيان: «أن العلوم إنما تكثر حيث يكثر العمران، وتعظم الحضارة»، «والسبب في ذلك- كما يقول ابن خلدون- أن تعليم العلم من جملة الصنائع، والصنائع إنما تكثر في الأمصار، وعلى نسبة عمرانها في الكثرة والقلة والحضارة والترف تكون نسبة الصنائع في الجودة والكثرة لأنه أمر زائد على المعاش، فمتى فضلت أعمال أهل العمران عن معاشهم انصرفت إلى ما وراء المعاش من التصرف في خاصية الإنسان وهي العلوم والصنائع»(٣).

١ مختصر كتاب المؤمل- مجموعة الرسائل المنيرية: ٣/ ٢٨.
٢ أدب الطلب: ٥٣.
٣ مقدمة ابن خلدون: ٤٣٤.

IV. Sultans Supporting the Followers of the Madhhab They Adopted

The rightly-guided caliphs, the rulers of the Umayyad state and some of the rulers in the Abbasid dynasty did not adopt a particular *madhhab*. They used to glorify the scholars at large, and especially the *Mujtahid Imām*(s) among them. When someone would excel in the sciences of the Qur'an and Sunnah and was well-versed in the views of the righteous predecessors, they would grant them judiciary positions and other reputable posts. As a result, people aspired to acquire knowledge of the Qur'an and Sunnah and to become distinguished in that.

As for the era of *taqlīd*, the rulers in every period and land used to adopt one *madhhab* or another and then endorse it, spread it and restrict the judiciary and mufti positions to it. Also, some of the wealthy used to build schools and allocate endowments for its teachers and scholars, but would stipulate that none is hired for such positions except their *madhhab* of choice.

This averted the people's aspirations away from the sciences of the Qur'an and Sunnah and toward blindly following a *madhhab* instead.

As-Sayyid Sābiq said, "Of what helped spread this backward spirit was the rulers and affluent establishing schools but restricting its teaching to a certain *madhhab* or *madhhab*(s). This led people to favor this *madhhab* and abandon the exercise of *ijtihād*, in order to safeguard their salaries. Abū Zur'ah once asked his Shaykh, al-Balqini, 'Why didn't Shaykh Taqi ad-Din as-Subki perform *ijtihād* despite being qualified to do so?' Al-Balqini remained silent, so Abū Zur'ah said, 'In my opinion, he only refrained because job opportunities were only available for the jurists of the four *madhhab*(s), and whoever ventures beyond them receives nothing, is disqualified from any judiciary post, cannot assume a mufti position and is accused of heresy.' In response, al-Balqini smiled and expressed his agreement."[1]

1 *Fiqh as-Sunnah* 1/13

رابعاً: تمكين السلاطين لأتباع المذهب الذي اعتنقوه:

كان الخلفاء الراشدين وحكام الدولة الأموية، وبعض حكام الدولة العباسية- لا يتبنون مذهب إمام بعينه، وكانوا يعظمون أهل العلم خاصة أهل الاجتهاد منهم، ويسندون القضاء والمناصب لمن برع في علم الكتاب والسنة وأقوال السلف الصالح، فانصرفت الهمم إلى تحصيل علم الكتاب والسنة، والنبوغ فيهما.

أما في عصر التقليد فإن الحكام في كل مصر وزمان تبنوا مذهباً من المذاهب ومكنوا له ونشروه، وقصروا مناصب القضاء والإفتاء عليه، وبعض أهل الثراء كانوا يبنون المدارس ويوقفون الأوقاف على مدرسيها ومشايخها، ويشترطون أن لا يتولى ذلك إلا أصحاب مذهب من المذاهب يسمونه.

وقد صرف هذا همم الناس إلى اتباع المذاهب وتقليدها وترك الاشتغال بعلوم الكتاب والسنة.

يقول السيد سابق في هذا: «وكان مما ساعد على انتشار هذه الروح الرجعية- ما قام به الحكام والأغنياء من إنشاء المدارس، وقصر التدريس فيها على مذهب أو مذاهب معينة، فكان ذلك من أسباب الإقبال على تلك المذاهب، والانصراف عن الاجتهاد، محافظة على الأرزاق التي رتبت لهم، سأل أبو زرعة شيخه البلقيني قائلاً: ما تقصير الشيخ تقي الدين السبكي عن الاجتهاد وقد استكمل آلته، فسكت البلقيني، فقال أبو زرعة: فما عندي أن الامتناع عن ذلك إلا للوظائف التي قدرت للفقهاء على المذاهب الأربعة، وأن من خرج عن ذلك لم ينله شيء من ذلك، وحرم ولاية القضاء، وامتنع الناس عن إفتائه، ونسبت إليه البدعة، فابتسم البلقيني، ووافقه على ذلك»[1].

١ فقه السنة: ١/ ١٣.

Look at the condition reached by the scholars of this era; ash-Sha'rāni said in *al-Mizān*, "Muhammad ad-Dahhān, the grammarian, was a Ḥanbali jurist that later adoped the Shāfi'i *madhhab*. Then, he became a Ḥanafi when the caliph requested a grammarian to teach his child grammar. Then, he became a Shāfi'i when a job opportunity arose to teach grammar in an-Niẓāmiyyah school, but its owner stipulated that only Shāfi'i instructors be hired. There was no one more knowledgeable in Fiqh and grammar than him."[1]

Due to each ruler supporting one *madhhab* in particular, many *madhhab*(s) became extinct, like those of Sufyān ath-Thawri, Sufyān ibn 'Uyaynah, 'Abdullāh ibn al-Mubārak, Abū 'Amr al-Awzā'i, 'Abdur-Raḥmān ibn Abi Laylā, al-Layth ibn Sa'd, Dāwūd ibn 'Ali, Abū Thawr, Ibn Jarīr aṭ-Ṭabari and others.

V. The Claim of Some Scholars that Every Mujtahid is Correct

Of the factors that deepened the rifts of disagreement was the claim of some scholars that every *mujtahid* is correct. Based on that, they permitted that Allah be worshipped according to the *madhhab* of any *Mujtahid Imām*. Subsequently, some of the contemporary scholars considered the views of the *Imām*(s) and their respective *madhhab*(s) equivelant to the Sharia itself, whereby it is permissible to accept any of their views, deem them an undisputed part of the religion, bind their followers to them and base rulings on them.

1 *Al-Mizān* 1/37

وانظر إلى الحال التي وصل إليها العلماء في هذا العصر، قال الشعراني في الميزان: «محمد الدهان النحوي كان حنبليًا انتقل إلى مذهب الشافعي، ثم تحول حنيفاً حين طلب الخليفة نحويًا يعلم ولده النحو، ثم إنه تحول شافعيًا حين شغرت وظيفة النحو بالنظامية لما شرط صاحبها ألا ينزل فيها إلا شافعي المذهب، ولم يكن هناك أحد أعلم بالفقه والنحو منه»[1].

وبسبب انتصار كل حاكم من الحكام لمذهب معين من المذاهب انقرض كثير من المذاهب كمذهب سفيان الثوري، وسفيان بن عيينة، وعبد الله بن المبارك، وأبو عمرو الأوزاعي، وعبد الرحمن بن أبي ليلى، والليث بن سعد، وداود بن علي، وأبو ثور، وابن جرير الطبري، وغيرهم.

خامساً: دعوى بعض العلماء أن كل مجتهد مصيب:

ومن الأسباب التي أدت إلى تعميق الخلاف وتأصيله ما ذهب إليه بعض العلماء من أن كل مجتهد مصيب، وتجويزهم أن يعبد الله على أي مذهب من مذاهب العلماء المجتهدين، وقد جعل بعض المعاصرين أقوال الأئمة ومذاهبهم بمثابة الشرع، وجوزوا الأخذ بأي رأي من آرائهم، وجعله ديناً يلزمون به أتباعهم، ويبنون عليه الأحكام.

١ الميزان: ١/ ٣٧.

This claim that "every *mujtahid* is correct" is an old fallacy which the scholars disproved. Ibn 'Abdil-Barr dedicated a chapter regarding this in his book *Jāmi Bayān al-'Ilm* titled "Proof from the Statements of the *Salaf* that Disagreements Entail Correctness and Incorrectness, and that Pursuing the Evidences is Mandatory in Such Cases."[1] Therein, he mentioned examples of when the Companions and those after them accused one another of being mistaken in matters of *Fiqh* disagreements. Of these instances was when Abū Bakr as-Siddiq rejected the view of some Companions who believed it was not permissible to fight the apostates. Another instance was when 'Umar ibn al-Khaṭṭāb ended the disagreement between the Prophet's Companions regarding the number of *takbīr*(s) in a *janāzah* (funeral) prayer and returned it to being four.

Ibn 'Abdil-Barr mentioned the likes of these examples regarding the Successors and the *Mujtahid Imām*(s) after them. Then, he commented, "These incidents are abundant in the books of the scholars. In fact, the differences between the Companions, Successors and those after them, wherein one would accuse the other of being mistaken, can hardly ever be encompassed in a book, nevertheless in this chapter. However, what we mentioned is sufficiently indicative of what we left out. Additionally, the Companions of the Messenger (ﷺ) referring back to one another is a clear proof that their respective views were either correct or incorrect."[2]

Ibn 'Abdil-Barr also mentioned the statement of Imām Mālik, "The truth is but one. Two contradictory views cannot both be correct. Correctness and the truth are but one thing."[3]

1 *Jāmi' Bayān al-'Ilm* 2/104
2 Ibid
3 Ibid: 2/109

وقد ظهر هذا القول «كل مجتهد مصيب» قديماً، فأنكره العلماء وبينوا خطأه، وقد عقد ابن عبد البر في كتابه «جامع بيان العلم» باباً عنون له بقوله: «باب ذكر الدليل في أقاويل السلف على أن الاختلاف فيه خطأ وصواب يلزم طلب الحجة عنده»(١)، وقد ذكر فيه بعض ما خطأ الصحابة ومن بعدهم فيه بعضهم بعضاً، وأنكره بعضهم على بعض عند الاختلاف، فمن ذلك أن أبا بكر الصديق رد قول الصحابة الذين ذهبوا إلى عدم جواز محاربة المرتدين، وقطع عمر بن الخطاب اختلاف أصحاب رسول الله ﷺ- في التكبير على الجنائز، وردهم إلى أربع.

وذكر مثل ذلك عن التابعين ومن بعدهم من العلماء المجتهدين، وعقب على ذلك قائلاً: «هذا كثير في كتب العلماء، وكذلك اختلاف أصحاب النبي ﷺ، والتابعين ومن بعدهم من المخالفين، وما ورد فيه إنكار بعضهم على بعض لا يكاد يحيط به كتاب، فضلاً عن أن يجمع في الباب وفيما ذكرناه منه دليل على ما عنه سكتنا، وفي رجوع أصحاب رسول الله ﷺ بعضهم إلى بعض لدليل واضح على أن اختلافهم خطأ وصواب»(٢).

وذكر قول مالك: «ما الحق إلا واحد، قولان مختلفان لا يكونان صواباً جميعاً، ما الحق والصواب إلا واحداً»(٣).

١ جامع بيان العلم: ٢/ ١٠٤.
٢ المصدر السابق.
٣ المصدر السابق: ٢/ ١٠٩.

Mujtahid(s) are Excused and Rewarded, Even if They are Mistaken

One must never assume that a *mujtahid,* who exerted his utmost effort to discern a ruling, is sinful for being mistaken. This is incorrect; a *mujtahid* is reward in all cases. He receives two rewards for being correct, a reward for exerting his effort (*ijithād*) and a reward for being correct. If he was mistaken, he still receives the reward for the effort he exerted.

Ibn ʻAbdil-Barr mentioned in his book *Jāmiʻ Bayān al-ʻIlm* "that the position of Mālik (may Allah bestow mercy upon him) with regard to *mujtahid*(s) who exercise *ijtihād* and *qiyās,* and then differ in speculative matters wherein different interpretations are possible, is that the truth of their disparate views is only one in the sight of Allah. However, if each *mujtahid* excercised *ijtihād* properly, as he was commanded [by Allah], and exhausted his efforts, was of those skilled in this craft and was qualified to perform *ijtihād,* then he has fulfilled his duty, is not obligated with anything else and is rewarded for seeking correctness, even though the truth is one in the sight of Allah."

He then said, "This is the view followed by most of ash-Shāfiʻi's companions and is the more famous view of Abū Ḥanīfah, as reported by Muhammad ibn al-Ḥasan and Abū Yūsuf, and their most accurate companions, such as ʻĪsā ibn Abān, Muhammad ibn Shujāʻ, al-Balkhi and those who came after them."[1]

Mujtahid(s) are rewarded regardless of whether their exercised *ijtihād* in the fundamental matters or the detailed rulings. According to Ibn Taymiyah, none but the Muʻtazilah considered a *mujtahid* sinful for being mistaken in the fundamental matters of the religion but not the detailed rulings. Ibn Taymiyah (may Allah bestow mercy upon him) said, "None of the *salaf,* Companions or Successors viewed that a *mujtahid,* who exerted his utmost effort to discern the truth, is sinful in either the fundamental matters or the detailed rulings. This differentiation was first made by the Muʻtazilah, and some of those who narrated this about them later applied it to *Uṣūl al-Fiqh* [as well]." It was reported that ʻUbaydullāh ibn al-Hāsan al-ʻAnbari said, "Every *mujtahid* has exacted," and he meant that he is not sinful.

This is the view held by all the great *Imām*(s), like Abū Ḥanīfah, ash-Shāfiʻi and others."[2]

---

1 Ibid: 1/90

2 *Majmūʻ Fatāwā Shaykh al-Islām* 13/125

المجتهدون معذورون مأجورون وإن أخطأوا:

لا يذهبن بك الظن إلى أن المجتهد الذي بذل وسعه في التعرف على الأحكام مأزور في خطئه، فذلك غلط، فالمجتهد مأجور له في صوابه أجران: أجر على اجتهاده، وأجر على صوابه، والمخطئ مأجور على اجتهاده.

وقد ذكر ابن عبد البر في كتابه جامع بيان العلم «أن مذهب مالك- رحمه الله- في اجتهاد المجتهدين والقائسين إذا اختلفوا فيما يجوز فيه التأويل من نوازل الأحكام أن الحق من ذلك عند الله واحد من أقوالهم واختلافهم، إلا أن كل مجتهد إذا اجتهد كما أمر، وبالغ، ولم يأل، وكان من أهل الصناعة، ومعه آلة الاجتهاد، فقد أدى ما عليه، وليس عليه غير ذلك، وهو مأجور على قصده الصواب، وإن كان الحق عند الله من ذلك واحداً.

قال: وهذا القول هو الذي عليه عمل أكثر أصحاب الشافعي، قال: وهو المشهور من قول أبي حنيفة فيما حكاه محمد بن الحسن وأبو يوسف، وفيما حكاه الحذاق من أصحابهم، مثل عيسى بن أبان ومحمد بن شجاع البلخي ومن تأخر عنهم...»(١).

والمجتهدون مأجورون سواء أكان اجتهادهم في الأصول أو الفروع، والذين قالوا بإثم المجتهدين في الأصول إذا أخطؤوا دون الفروع هم المعتزلة كما يقول ابن تيمية، يقول- رحمه الله- في هذا: «ولم يقل أحد من السلف والصحابة والتابعين: إن المجتهد الذي استفرغ وسعه في طلب الحق يأثم لا في الأصول، ولا في الفروع، ولكن هذا التفريق ظهر من جهة المعتزلة، وأدخله في أصول الفقه من نقل ذلك عنهم، وحكوا عن عبيد الله بن الحسن العنبري أنه قال: كل مجتهد مصيب، ومراده أنه لا يأثم.

وهذا قول عامة الأئمة كأبي حنيفة والشافعي وغيرهما»(٢).

---

١ المصدر السابق: ١/ ٩٠.

٢ مجموع فتاوى شيخ الإسلام: ١٣/ ١٢٥.

The Effects Resulting from Intellectual Stagnation and *Madhhab* Fanaticism

Whoever reflects on the era of *taqlīd* and closely examines the effects left behind by such intellectual stagnation and *madhhab* imitation will find awfully painful effects that sadden the heart, wrench the soul and consume the mind. We will mention just some of these effects here.

I. Forsaking the Sciences of Ijtihād

Previously, the *mujtahid* scholars used to busy themselves with the sciences of *ijtihād*. They would study the Arabic language, learn the Qur'an, study the Sunnah, collect the knowledge of their righteous predecessors and exert great efforts to correctly diagnose the newly emerging circumstances of their times. By doing that, they broadened their horizons, strengthened their skills and became beacons of light by which others were guided. However, when the students of knowledge neglected the sciences of *ijtihād* and limited themselves to the statements and books of human beings, they consequently severed themselves from the gushing rivers that gave life to the minds and illuminated the hearts. Then, when knowledge diminished and *taqlīd* became prevalent, many of its people called for the door of *ijtihād* to be closed. This was done under the pretext that many of the ignorant were claiming to be *mujtahid* when in reality they did not qualify, and thus they went astray and led others astray with them.

There is no doubt that some of the ignorant claiming to be qualified for *ijtihād* had dangerous effects, but one wrong is not fixed by committing another. The correct treatment of this phenomena is embodied in reviving the sciences of *ijtihād* and facilitating the means to make that possible. Moreover, the call to close the door of *ijtihād* and pressure the *mujtahid*(s) from exercising it failed at preventing what they claimed to fear. Claimants to knowledge still remained in every age that appointed to themselves the post of giving *fatwa*. In fact, their numbers increased and their harms grew.

الآثار المترتبة على الجمود الفكري والتقليد المذهبي

الذي ينظر في عصر التقليد والاجتهاد، ويتمعن في الآثار التي خلفها ذلك الجمود الفكري والتقليد المذهبي- يجد أموراً سيئة، وآثاراً مؤلمة، يحزن لها القلب، وتأسى لها النفس، وينشغل لها الفكر، وسنذكر بعض هذه الآثار.

أولاً: ترك الاشتغال بعلوم الاجتهاد:

كان العلماء المجتهدون يشتغلون بعلوم الاجتهاد، فيدرسون اللغة العربية، ويتعلمون القرآن ويدرسون السنة، ويأخذون علم السلف الصالح، ويجتهدون في معرفة وقائع عصرهم ونوازله؛ وبذلك تتسع آفاقهم، وتقوى ملكاتهم، ويصبحون منارات يهتدي بها، فلما ترك طلبة العلم علوم الاجتهاد، وحصروا أنفسهم في كلام الرجال، وكتب الرجال، انقطعوا عن النهر الفياض الذي يحيي العقول، وينير القلوب، وعندما قلَّ العلم، وكثر التقليد نادى كثير من المقلدين بإغلاق باب الاجتهاد، ودعواهم في ذلك أن كثيراً من الجهلة ادعوا الاجتهاد وهم ليسوا بأهل لذلك، فضلوا وأضلوا.

ولا شك أن ادعاء بعض الجهلة الاجتهاد له آثار سيئة وخطيرة، ولكن لا يعالج الخطأ بخطأ آخر، وكان العلاج الحق يتمثل في إحياء علوم الاجتهاد، وتهيئة الأسباب التي تحقق ذلك، زد على هذا أن الدعوة إلى قفل باب الاجتهاد، والحظر على المجتهدين، والتضييق عليهم- لم يحقق الغرض الذي قصدوه من دعواهم، فقد بقي أدعياء العلم في كل عصر ينصبون أنفسهم للفتوى، بل زاد أمرهم، وكثر شرهم.

The door of *ijtihād* remains open, and it is not permissible for anyone to call for its closure for many reasons:

1) *Ijtihād* is a matter legislated by Allah, the Most High, which He directed us to and chose that it be the fourth source of the Sharia. No one possesses the right to close a door that Allah has opened or to call for its closure, as that entails defying Allah and His Messenger.

2) Closing the door of *ijtihād* under the pretext that no one exists who qualifies for practicing it after the fourth century is but a presumption, a claim to know the unseen and a restriction of Allah's mercy. How do they know that Allah will not bring forth a *mujtahid* or send this *Ummah* someone to revive its religion for it? In fact, this call implies belying the Messenger (ﷺ) who informed that Allah will send for this *Ummah* at the head of every century those who will revive its religion.

Furthermore, reality itself belied this claim, for we have seen a number of *mujtahid*(s) in the eras of *taqlīd* that played major roles in *Fiqh*, such as Ibn Taymiyah, Ibn al-Qayyim, al-'Izz ibn 'Abdis-Salām, ash-Shawkāni, aṣ-Ṣan'āni and many others.

3) *Ijtihād* is an absolute necessity for the survival, preservation and continuinity of the Islamic Sharia. That is because the newly emerging events are endless. Hence, it was from the wisdom of Allah that he legislate the process of *ijtihād* through which the Muslims could extract the proper rulings from the texts of the Sharia, its general principles and via comparing the similar and resembling cases. Practicing *ijtihād* was exercised by the Messenger (ﷺ), his Companions, the Successors and those who followed them. Therefore, *ijtihād* is a matter that has forever been practiced by our righteous predecessors and the best of this *Ummah*, and we were obligated to follow in their footsteps.

باب الاجتهاد مفتوح لا يغلق، ولا يجوز لأحد أن ينادي بإغلاقه لأمور:

١- الاجتهاد أمر شرعه الله تعالى، وأرشد إليه وجعله رابع مصادر الشريعة، ولا يجوز لأحد أن يغلق باباً فتحه الله، أو ينادي بإغلاقه ففي ذلك محادة لله ورسوله.

٢- الدعوة إلى إغلاق باب الاجتهاد بحجة أنه لا يوجد من يصلح لهذا المنصب بعد القرن الرابع- رجم بالغيب، وقول بالظن، وحجر لرحمة الله، فمن أدراهم بأن الله لن يوجد مجتهداً، ولن يبعث لهذه الأمة من يجدد لها أمر دينها، بل هذا تكذيب للرسول ﷺ الذي أخبر بأن الله سيبعث لهذه الأمة- على رأس كل قرن- من يجدد لها أمر دينها.

والواقع المشاهد أكذب هذه الدعوى، فإننا نرى مجموعة من المجتهدين في عصور التقليد كان لهم دور عظيم في الفقه، أمثال ابن تيمية وابن القيم، والعز بن عبد السلام والشوكاني والصنعاني وغيرهم كثير.

٣- الاجتهاد ضروري جداً لبقاء الشريعة الإسلامية وحياتها واستمرارها؛ ذلك لأن الحوادث متجددة غير محصورة، فكان من حكمة الله أن شرع للمسلمين الاجتهاد يستنبطون بواسطته الأحكام من نصوص الشريعة وقواعدها العامة، ويقيسون الأشباه على الأشباه والنظير على النظير، وقد اجتهد الرسول ﷺ، واجتهد الصحابة، والتابعون وتابعوهم، فالاجتهاد أمر قد مضى عليه السلف الصالح وخيار الأمة، وعلينا اتباع سنتهم واقتفاء هديهم.

II. Combating Those who Insisted on the Sciences of Ijtihād

The supporters of *taqlīd* waged a fierce war against those who tried to break free from its shackles and busy themselves with the sciences of *ijtihād*. The people of *taqlīd* bombarded those who tried to rescue the *Ummah* from its diseases with an array of accusations. For instance, they alleged that these people wanted to establish new *madhhab*(s), that these people were heretic innovators and that these people opposed the consensus of Muslim scholars. All this was said to keep the Muslims chained by *taqlīd* and to dissuade those who rode the path of the righteous predecessors and great *Imām*(s) from continuing.

Many of the great scholars received the brunt of this, such as Shaykh al-Islām Ibn Taymiyah, who the people of *taqlīd* harmed greatly. He was imprisoned because of this matter and died in prison.

Likewise his student, the great verifier and scholar, Ibn al-Qayyim al-Jawziyyah was imprisoned with his teacher Ibn Taymiyah for a period of time.

Another of their targets was ash-Shawkāni. He was afflicted greatly by the people of *taqlīd*, who evoked hatred for him among the rulers of his lands. They persuaded these rulers to imprison and kill him, and they incited a great tribulation in Ṣan'ā' during his time, but Allah safeguarded him, elevated his status among the people and benefitted His slaves using him.

Around the beginning of the thirteenth *hijri* century, the esteemed scholar of ash-Shām, Shaykh Jamāl ad-Dīn al-Qāsimi (may Allah bestow mercy upon him) was accused of a dangerous charge: *ijtihād*. A special court was convened for him, and he was summoned to appear before it. There, his books were investigated and confiscated for a period of time.[1]

1 See *Qawā'id at-Taḥdīth* 1/25 by Muhammad Jamāl ad-Dīn al-Qāsimi

ثانياً: محاربة الذين يشتغلون بعلوم الاجتهاد:

أعلن المقلدون حرباً حامية الوطيس على الذين يحاولون الخروج من ربقة التقليد والاشتغال بعلوم الاجتهاد، وقد اتهم المقلدون هؤلاء الذين أرادوا تخليص الأمة من أدوائها بتهم كثيرة، كادعائهم بأنهم يريدون إنشاء مذاهب جديدة، وأنهم أصحاب بدعة جديدة، وأنهم خالفوا الإجماع، كل ذلك يقال لإبقاء المسلمين تحت ربقة التقليد، وثني الذين ساروا على درب الأئمة والسلف الصالح عن مواصلة الطريق.

وقد نال العلماء الأعلام من هذا شيء كثير فمن هؤلاء شيخ الإسلام ابن تيمية، فقد ناله من المقلدين أذى كبير، وسجن بسبب ذلك، وتوفي سجيناً.

وكذلك تلميذه العلامة المحقق ابن قيم الجوزية، وقد سجن مع شيخه مدة من الزمان.

ومنهم الشوكاني، فقد أصابه من المقلدين بلاء، فقد وشوا به عند أمراء بلده، وحسنوا لهم سجنه وسفك دمه، وأقاموا فتنة في صنعاء في عهده، ولكن الله حفظه منهم، ومكن له، ونفع به عباده.

وفي أوائل القرن الثالث عشر الهجري اتهم علامة الشام الشيخ جمال الدين القاسمي- رحمه الله تعالى- بتهمة خطيرة هي «الاجتهاد»، وألفت له محكمة خاصة، دعي للمثول أمامها، وفتشت كتبه وصودرت فترة من الزمان[١].

١ انظر قواعد التحديث لمحمد جمال الدين القاسمي: ١/ ٢٥.

III. The Phenomena of Debate and Argumentation

One of the dangerous effects of differing in this era was the spread of debates and arguments. They did not take place for the sake of identifying the truth and learning the intended meanings of Allah's words. Instead, they were for the sake of defending the *madhhab* and refuting the views of the opposition who belonged to other *madhhab*(s). Imām al-Ghazāli talked about the evils of such debates and the destructive morals they produce. He said, "Know that the type of debate which is held for the sake of defeating others, stumping them, showing one's superiority and seeking to impress the people and gain their attention is the core of every evil trait in the sight of Allah and every praiseworthy quality in the sight of Allah's enemy Satan. Its relationship to the internal evils – such as arrogance, conceit, envy and self-praise – is like the relationship of wine to the external evils of fornication, slander, murder, and theft."[1]

IV. Disunity, Enmity and Hatred

Unity, fraternity, and love are of the favors that Allah has preferred this *Ummah* with. Allah says, **"And hold firmly to the rope of Allah all together and do not become divided. And remember the favor of Allah upon you - when you were enemies and He brought your hearts together and you became, by His favor, brothers."**[2]

Of the greatest afflictions that plagued the Muslims was their division into sects and parties, through which enmity and hatred replaced the love and affection that existed among the followers of this religion. Subsequently, they began to forsake one another and then shed the blood of one another. All this resulted from their neglecting the Books of the Allah and the Sunnah of His Messenger (ﷺ). Allah, the Glorified, informed that this disease had plagued the previous nations as well, **"And they did not differ except after knowledge had come to them - out of jealous animosity between themselves.**

1 *Iḥyā' 'Ulūm ad-Dīn* 1/45
2 Sūrah Āl-'Imrān – Verse 103

ثالثاً: شيوع المناظرات والجدل:

ومن الآثار الخطيرة للخلاف والانقسام شيوع المناظرات والجدل، وكانت تعقد لا لبيان الحق، والتوصل إلى مراد الله من كلامه- وإنما انتصاراً للمذهب، ورداً لأقوال الخصوم من أصحاب المذاهب الأخرى، وقد ذكر الغزالي آفات هذه المناظرات، وما يتولد منها من مهلكات الأخلاق فقال: «واعلم أن المناظرة الموضوعة لقصد الغلبة والإفحام وإظهار الفضل والشرف والتشدق عند الناس والمماراة واستمالة وجوه الناس- هي منبع جميع الأخلاق المذمومة عند الله، المحمودة عند عدو الله إبليس، ونسبتها إلى الفواحش الباطنة من الكبر والعجب والحسد والمنافسة وتزكية النفس كنسبة شرب الخمر إلى الفواحش الظاهرة من الزنا والقذف والقتل والسرقة...»[(١)].

رابعاً: الاختلاف والعداوة والبغضاء:

الوحدة والألفة والمحبة من نعم الله التي أنعم بها على هذه الأمة: ﴿وَاعْتَصِمُوا بِحَبْلِ اللهِ جميعاً وَلاَ تَفَرَّقُوا وَاذْكُرُوا نِعْمَتَ اللهِ عَلَيْكُمْ إِذْ كُنْتُمْ أَعْدَاءً فَأَلَّفَ بَيْنَ قُلُوبِكُمْ فَأَصْبَحْتُمْ بِنِعْمَتِهِ إِخْوَاناً﴾[(٢)]، وكان من أعظم مصاب المسلمين تفرقهم إلى شيع وأحزاب ومذاهب، وحلول العداوة والبغضاء محل المحبة والمودة بين أتباع هذا الدين، ثم هجران بعضهم بعضاً، وسفك بعضهم دم بعض، وكل هذا نتيجة إعراضهم عن كتاب الله وسنة رسول الله ﷺ، وهذا الداء أصاب الأمم الماضية: ﴿فَمَا اخْتَلَفُوا إِلاَّ مِن بَعْدِ مَا جَاءَهُمُ الْعِلْمُ بَغْياً بَيْنَهُمْ إِنَّ رَبَّكَ يَقْضِي بَيْنَهُمْ﴾[(٣)]، ﴿وَلَوْ شَاءَ اللهُ مَا اقْتَتَلَ الَّذِينَ مِن بَعْدِهِم مِّن بَعْدِ مَا جَاءَتْهُمُ الْبَيِّنَاتُ وَلَكِنِ اخْتَلَفُوا

١ إحياء علوم الدين: ١/ ٤٥.
٢ آل عمران: ١٠٣.
٣ الجاثية: ١٧.

Indeed, your Lord will judge between them on the Day of Resurrection concerning that over which they used to differ."[1] In another verse, Allah, the Almighty, says, **"If Allah had willed, those [generations] succeeding them would not have fought each other after the clear proofs had come to them. But they differed, and some of them believed and some of them disbelieved. And if Allah had willed, they would not have fought each other, but Allah does what He intends."**[2]

Allah had ordered the Muslims to return to the Book of Allah and the Sunnah of His Messenger (ﷺ) in cases of dispute, but they referred these matters to the sayings of men instead. Allah, the Majestic, states, **"And if you disagree over anything, refer it to Allah and the Messenger,"**[3] meaning to the Book of Allah and the Sunnah of His Messenger (ﷺ).

The Disparity between the Disagreements of the Mujtahid Imām(s) and Those of the People of Taqlīd

The Companions, as well as those *Mujtahid Imām*(s) who followed them, disagreed on many issues. However, their disagreement was necesarry due to each's different understanding of the texts. It was not voluntary and for the sake of argument. Therefore, this type of disagreement could not have been avoided. As for the people of *taqlīd*, they would discover the evidence from the Qur'an or Sunnah and still not dismiss their own view. Instead, they would cast the implications of Allah's Book behind themselves.

Also, the differences among the Companions and *Mujtahid Imām*(s) did not lead to them hating one another and becoming divided. They used to supplicate to Allah for one another and would pray behind one another. As for the people of *taqlīd*, they showed enmity for one another, hated one another, refused praying behind those who oppose their *madhhab* and some of them even prohibited marrying a woman who followed another *madhhab*.

1 Sūrat al-Jāthiyah – Verse 17
2 Sūrat al-Baqarah – Verse 253
3 Sūrat an-Nisā' – Verse 59

فَمِنْهُم مَّنْ آمَنَ وَمِنْهُم مَّن كَفَرَ وَلَوْ شَاءَ اللَّهُ مَا اقْتَتَلُوا وَلَكِنَّ اللَّهَ يَفْعَلُ مَا يُرِيدُ﴾[1]، وقد أمر الله المسلمين برد المختلف فيه إلى كتاب الله وسنة رسوله، فردوه إلى آراء الرجال: **﴿فَإِن تَنَازَعْتُمْ فِي شَيْءٍ فَرُدُّوهُ إِلَى اللَّهِ وَالرَّسُولِ﴾**[2]، أي إلى كتاب الله، وسنة رسوله ﷺ.

الفرق بين اختلاف المجتهدين والمقلدين:

اختلف الصحابة ومن بعدهم من العلماء المجتهدين، وكان اختلافهم عن ضرورة واختلاف طبيعي في الفهم، لا اختياراً للخلاف، ومثل هذا لا يمكن التخلص منه، أما المقلدون فإن الواحد منهم يظهر له الدليل من الكتاب والسنة فلا يدع مذهبه، وينبذ كتاب الله وراء ظهره.

ولم يؤد اختلاف الصحابة والأئمة المجتهدين إلى التباغض والتفرق، فكان يدعو بعضهم لبعض، ويصلي بعضهم وراء بعض، أما هؤلاء المقلدون فقد تعادوا وتباغضوا، وتركوا الصلاة خلف من يخالفهم في المذهب، وأفتى بعضهم بعدم جواز الزواج من المرأة التي تخالفهم في مذهبهم.

١ البقرة: ٢٥٣.
٢ النساء: ٥٩.

V. The Followers of the Madhhab(s) Restricting Themselves

Before this era, the Muslims lived under the wide umbrella of the Qur'an and Sunnah. Therein, they would find a solution for every newly emerging problem in life. However, when the Muslims fell into *taqlīd*, the followers of every *madhhab* became trapped in their own *madhhab*, since no one *madhhab* embodies Islam in its entirety. We find the Imām ash-Shāfi'i (may Allah bestow mercy upon him) himself said, "Every person is oblivious to one Sunnah [or another] belonging to the Messenger of Allah (ﷺ)."[1]

Similarly, when Abū Ja'far al-Manṣūr asked Imām Mālik for permission to spread his book *al-Muwaṭṭa'* everywhere and impose it upon the people, Mālik said to him, "Do not do it, for the Companions dispersed in every direction and narrated the hadith(s) of Ḥijāz which I approve of. People then took them [and based their views on them], so leave them upon what they received."

Regarding this same point, Ibn Taymiyah said, "Encompassing [every] hadith of the Messenger of Allah (ﷺ) has never been done by anyone of the *Ummah*."[2]

About this point, Muhammad Sallām Madkūr said, "The jurists of this era restricted their research to one small circle: the *Fiqh madhhab* of a previous *Imām* which they refuse to look beyond. They consider every opinion held by the other *madhhab*(s) to be mistaken, and that everything the *Imām* they imitate has stated can never be wrong. Such *madhhab* fanaticism reached the extent that the famous Ḥanafi jurist, al-Karkhi, would actually say, 'Every verse or hadith that opposes the sayings of our *Imām*(s) is either abrogated or must be interpreted differently.'" Therefore, the statements of their *Imām*(s) had become sources from which rulings should be derived.

1 *Mukhtaṣar Kitāb al-Mu'ammil lir-Radd lil-Amr al-Awwal* 3/23, taken from Majmū'at ar-Rasā'il al-Munīriyyah
2 *Raf' al-Malām* 12

خامساً: تضييق أتباع المذاهب على أنفسهم:

كان المسلمون قبل هذا العصر يحيون في دائرة واسعة إطارها الكتاب والسنة، وكانوا يجدون حلاً لكل مشكلات الحياة المتجددة، فلما وقع المسلمون في التقليد انحصر أتباع كل مذهب في إطار مذهبهم، وليس هناك مذهب يحيط بالإسلام كله، هذا الشافعي- رحمه الله تعالى- يقول: «ما من أحد إلا وتذهب عليه سنة لرسول الله ﷺ، وتعزب عنه»[١].

وهذا أبو جعفر المنصور يطلب من مالك بن أنس أن يأذن له بتفريق كتاب الموطأ في الآفاق ليحمل الناس عليه، فقال له مالك: لا تفعل، فإن الصحابة تفرقوا في الآفاق، ورووا أحاديث أهل الحجاز التي اعتمدتها، وأخذ الناس بذلك، فاتركهم على ما هم عليه.

ويقول ابن تيمية في هذا: «الإحاطة بحديث رسول الله ﷺ لم تكن لأحد من الأمة»[٢].

ويقول الدكتور محمد سلام مدكور في هذا: «فقهاء هذا العصر حصروا أبحاثهم في دائرة ضيقة محدودة في حدود مذهب فقيه سابق لا يحيد عنه، وأصبح في نظرهم أن الآراء في المذاهب الأخرى خاطئة، وأن كل ما قاله الإمام الذي يقلده صحيح لا يحتمل الشك، وقد وصل التعصب المذهبي إلى أن يقول الكرخي الفقيه الحنفي: «كل آية أو حديث يخالف ما عليه أصحابنا فهو مؤول أو منسوخ»، فأصبحت عبارة أئمتهم مصدراً يتخذون منها أحكامهم...»[٣].

١ مختصر كتاب المؤمل للرد للأمر الأول- مجموعة الرسائل المنيرية: ٣/ ٢٣.
٢ رفع الملام: ١٢.
٣ المدخل للفقه الإسلامي: ٩٥.

The followers of every *madhhab* restricting themselves in this manner resulted in many harmful effects. Among them were:

1) They deprived themselves of the efforts made by the scholars and jurists of other *madhhab*(s), especially when every *madhhab* excelled at a subject that could be non-existent in the *madhhab* of another. For that reason, they sometimes found themselves stuck regarding newly emerging situations they encountered. At times, their pressing needs forced them to adopt the views of other *madhhab*(s). Other times, such limitations caused the ignorant to assume that the Sharia of Islam does not suffice the needs of the society it governs, and that led to the call for taking from man-made laws. In reality though, the matter is not likes this; the flaw comes from binding ourselves to a particular *madhhab*. Had they considered all the *Fiqh madhhab*(s) and made the evidence the only determining factor for what is and is not acceptable, they would have found the Islamic Sharia to be a spacious arena that is comprehensive enough to govern life and not restrict it.

2) Trapping oneself inside a single *madhhab* causes narrow mindedness. The followers of every *madhhab* assume themselves to be on the truth, and that everyone else is upon falsehood. They may even be daring enough to shed blood on the basis of such narrow thinking. Ibn al-'Arabi said, "Our Shaykh, Abū Bakr al-Fihri, used to raise his hands upon *rukū'* (bowing), and upon rising again from it, as this is the opinion of Mālik and ash-Shāfi'i. One day, he visited me in Mahras ash-Shu'arā' at the time of ẓuhr prayer. He entered the masjid and proceeded to the first line, and I was in the rear sitting by the windows that overlooked the sea and taking in the breeze due to the scorching heat. The commander of the sea brigade, Abū Thumnah, was sitting in the same line as me with his companions, awaiting the prayer and looking at the boats. When Shaykh al-Fihri raised his hands upon *rukū'* and upon raising his head from it, Abū Thumnah said to his companions, 'Did you see this Easterner?! How dare he enter our masjid! Get up and kill him, and throw him into the sea so that no one will see you.' My heart jumped inside of me, and I said, 'Glorified is Allah! This is at-Tartushi, the jurist of our time!' They said to me, 'Then why did he raise his hands?' I said, 'This is the practice of the Prophet (ﷺ), and this is the opinion of Mālik according to the narration of the people of Madinah about him…' and I continued quieting and calming them until he finished his prayer."[1]

1 *Al-'Itiṣām* 1/113 by ash-Shāṭibi

وقد سبب هذا التضييق الذي أخذ به أهل كل مذهب أنفسهم مفاسد عدة، منها:

١- عدم استفادتهم من جهود العلماء الآخرين: أئمة وفقهاء المذاهب الأخرى، خاصة وأن عند كل مذهب علما قد لا يوجد عند الآخرين؛ ولذلك يجدون أنفسهم في ضيق في بعض الأحيان أمام الوقائع والنوازل التي تلم بهم، وقد يضطرون إلى الأخذ بالمذاهب الأخرى تحت ضغط الحاجة، وقد يظن بعض الذين لا يعلمون أن الشريعة الإسلامية لا تفي بحاجات المجتمعات التي تحكمها، فينادون بالاقتباس من الشرائع الوضعية، والأمر ليس كذلك، وإنما الخطأ هو في الالتزام بفقه مذهب بعينه، أما لو نظرنا في جميع المذاهب الفقهية، جاعلين الدليل هو الفيصل بين ما يجوز قبوله، وما لا يجوز، فيسجدون الشريعة الإسلامية ميداناً فسيحاً رحباً، تحكم الحياة وتسعها، ولا تضيق عنها.

٢- الانحباس في إطار المذهب الواحد يسبب ضيقاً في الأفق؛ إذ يظن أتباع كل مذهب أن الحق عندهم، وأن ما عند غيرهم باطل، وقد يقدمون على سفك الدماء بسبب ضيق الأفق، «قال ابن العربي: كان شيخنا أبو بكر الفهري يرفع يديه عند الركوع، وعند رفع الرأس منه، وهو مذهب مالك والشافعي، قال: فحضر عندي يوماً في محرس أبي الشعراء بالثغر موضع تدريس عند صلاة الظهر، ودخل المسجد من المحرس المذكور، فتقدم إلى المصنف الأول وأنا في مؤخرة قاعداً على طاقات البحر، أتنسم الريح من شدة الحر، ومعي في صف واحد أبو ثمنة رئيس البحر وقائده في نفر من أصحابه ينتظر الصلاة، ويتطلع على مراكب المنار، فلما رفع الشيخ الفهري يديه في الركوع وفي رفع الرأس منه، قال أبو ثمنة لأصحابه: ألا ترى إلى هذا المشرقي كيف دخل مسجدنا! قوموا إليه فاقتلوه وارموا به في البحر فلا يراكم أحد.

فطار قلبي من بين جوانحي، وقلت: سبحان الله! هذا الطرطوشي فقيه الوقت، فقالوا لي: ولم يرفع يديه؟ فقلت: كذلك كان النبي ﷺ، وهو مذهب مالك في رواية أهل المدينة عنه، وجعلت أسكتهم وأسكنهم حتى فرغ من صلاته»[١].

١ الاعتصام للشاطبي: ١/ ١١٣.

Abū Isḥāq ash-Shāṭibi also spoke about the danger of confining a student in the science of *Fiqh* to just one *madhhab*. He said, "Habituating the student upon not looking into any but one *madhhab* causes one to become averse to and intolerant of every other *madhhab* whose proofs one has not come across. In turn, this will prevent one from recognizing the virtue of *Imām*(s) whose virtue is agreed upon by the people, in addition to their religiosity and their experience in the objectives of the Sharia and the understanding of its aims."[1]

Among what proves the correctness of this statement by ash-Shāṭibi is the claim made by some fanatics among the Mālikis that "Whoever swears that every hadith in *al-Muwaṭṭa'* is authentic has not broken his oath, while anyone who swears that every hadith in *Ṣaḥīḥ al-Bukhāri* and *Ṣaḥīḥ Muslim* is authentic has broken his oath."[2]

VI. Busying Themselves with Hypothetical and Impossible Scenarios

We have previously seen how the Companions and Succesors denounced busying oneself with these types of scenarios. We have also seen that some *imām*(s) busied themselves with hypothetical *Fiqh*. In the era of *taqlīd*, the jurists drowned themselves in these matters. As stated by Professor az-Zarqā, this made *Fiqh* distant from addressing the practical needs of the people and their time-sensitive interests. Some of the issues they addressed were nearly impossible to take place and studying them was a waste of time.[3]

وقد نبه أبو إسحاق الشاطبي على خطورة قصر طالبي علم الفقه على مذهب واحد، فقال: «إن تعويد الطالب على أن لا يطلع إلا على مذهب واحد، ربما يكسبه ذلك نفوراً وإنكاراً لكل مذهب غير مذهبه، ما دام لم يطلع على أدلته، فيورثه ذلك حزازة في الاعتقاد في فضل أئمة أجمع الناس على فضلهم، وتقدمهم في الدين، وخبرتهم بمقاصد الشرع وفهم أغراضه»(١).

ويؤكد كلام الشاطبي هذا قول بعض متعصبي المالكية: إن من حلف على أن جميع ما في كتاب موطأ مالك من الأحاديث صحيح لا يحنث، أما من حلف أن جميع ما في البخاري ومسلم من الأحاديث صحيح فإنه يحنث في يمينه(٢).

سادساً: الاشتغال بالفرضيات والمسائل المستحيلة الوقوع:

رأينا كيف كان الصحابة والتابعون ينهون عن الاشتغال بهذا النوع من المسائل، ورأينا كيف اشتغل بعض أئمة المذاهب بالفقه التقديري، وقد أغرق الفقهاء في عصر التقليد بالاشتغال بهذه المسائل، وبذلك ابتعد الفقه- كما يقول الأستاذ الزرقا- في كثير من أحكامه عن الحاجة العملية والمصالح الزمنية، ووجدت فيه طائفة من المسائل يكاد يكون وقوعها مستحيلاً، ودراستها إضاعة للوقت(٣).

1 *Mā Lā Yajūz fīhi al-Khilāf* 93
2 Ibid
3 *Al-Madkhal* 1/186 by az-Zarqā

١ ما لا يجوز فيه الخلاف: ٩٣.
٢ ما لا يجوز فيه الخلاف: ٩٣.
٣ المدخل للزرقا: ١/ ١٨٦.

Summary of Unit 11

We can summarize our study of this unit in the following points:

1) There were several factors that lead to intellectual stagnation and *madhhab* fanaticism in this era. Of them was:

- The excessive praise of the *Imām*(s)
- The faulty style of book compilation
- The weakness of the Islamic state
- The sultans only supporting the followers of their *madhhab*
- The claim of some jurists that every *mujtahid* is correct

2) The intellectual stagnation and *madhhab* fanaticism of this era left behind many painful effects. Of them was:

- Forsaking the sciences of *ijtihād*
- Combating those who insisted on the sciences of *ijtihād*
- The phenomena of debate and argumentation
- Differences that caused enmity and hatred
- The *madhhab* followers restricting themselves
- Being busied with hypothetical and impossible scenarios

خلاصة الوحدة

نخلص من دراسة هذه الوحدة إلى ما يلي:

١- هناك عدة أسباب أدت إلى الجمود الفكري، والتعصب المذهبي في هذا العصر ومنها:

- الغلو في تعظيم الأئمة.
- الأسلوب المختل في التدوين والتأليف.
- ضَعْف الدولة الإسلامية.
- تمكين السلاطين لأتباع المذهب الذي اعتنقوه دون غيرهم.
- دعوى بعض العلماء أن كل مجتهد مصيب.

٢- خلّف الجمود الفكري، والتقليد المذهبي في هذا العصر، آثاراً مؤلمة، وأموراً سيئة منها:

- ترك الاشتغال بعلوم الاجتهاد.
- محاربة الذين يشتغلون بالاجتهاد.
- شيوع المناظرات والجدل.
- الاختلاف المسبب للعداوة والبغضاء.
- تضييق أتباع المذاهب على أنفسهم.
- الاشتغال بالفرضيات والمسائل المستحيلة الوقوع.

Notes

Notes

Unit 12
Fiqh in Contemporary Times

Contents of Unit 12

1) Removing the Sharia from Governance
2) The Printing of *Fiqh* Books
3) Using *Fiqh* Views in State Law
4) *Fiqh* Encyclopedias
5) *Fiqh* Assemblies
6) The Renaissance of *Fiqh*
7) The Righteousness of the Jurist

Importance of this Unit

In our contemporary times, there were many admirable efforts made by the scholars which were instrumental in reviving *Fiqh*. Of these efforts was the printing of *Fiqh* books which present the views of the jurists, compare them and determine the preponderant view based on the evidences. Another major effort was printing the books which collected the Sunnah and their explanations. Additionally, the unrelenting attempts of a group of Hadith scholars, jurists and researchers to revive the *Fiqh* of Sharia were of paramount importance. This effort was represented in their authorings, their juristic encyclopedias and their juristic conferences. It was also evident in their establishment of colleges, institutes and assemblies that focused on the *Fiqh* of Sharia, in addition to holding seminars and conventions that investigated the rulings of *Fiqh* and particularly those pertaining to newly emerging issues in their times.

Come, let us now study this unit in order to understand – by Allah's grace – all of these details.

Learning Objectives

By the end of this unit, readers should be able to:

1) Know what is meant by turning the Islamic *Fiqh* into laws, its history, its benefits and its flaws.
2) Distinguish between *Fiqh* encyclopedias and the original compilations of comprehensive *Fiqh* books.

الوحدة الثانية عشرة
الفقه في العصر الحاضر

محتويات الوحدة الثانية عشرة

١- إقصاء الشريعة عن الحكم.
٢- طباعة الكتب الفقهية.
٣- تقنين الفقه الإسلامي.
٤- الموسوعات الفقهية.
٥- المجامع العلمية.
٦- كيف ننهض بالفقه.
٧- صلاح الفقيه.

أهمية دراسة الوحدة:

هناك جهود مشكورة قام بها أهل العلم في عصرنا هذا، كان لها أثر كبير في النهوض بالفقه، فمن ذلك طباعة أمهات الكتب الفقهية التي تعرض أقوال الفقهاء وتوزان بينها، ثم ترجح القول الأقوى دليلاً، وأيضاً طباعة كتب السنة وشروحها، وكذلك المحاولات الدائبة التي يقوم بها مجموعة من المحدثين والفقهاء والباحثين لإحياء فقه الشريعة، والتي تمثلت في المؤلفات والموسوعات الفقهية والمؤتمرات الفقهية وإنشاء المعاهد والكليات والمجامع التي تعنى بفقه الشريعة، وانعقاد الندوات والمؤتمرات التي تبحث في القضايا الفقهية وخاصة النوازل.

هيا بنا لدراسة هذه الوحدة لنتعرف - بفضل الله سبحانه- على كل هذه التفاصيل.

الأهداف التعليمية:

يتوقع منك أيها الدارس الكريم بعد دراستك لهذه الوحدة أن تكون قادراً على أن:

١- تُعرف معنى تقنين الفقه الإسلامي، وتاريخه، وفوائده، وعيوبه.
٢- تُفرق بين الموسوعات الفقهية، والمدونات من أمهات كتب الفقه.

3) Mention the most important *Fiqh* assembles and centers in the Muslim world.
4) Compare between the classical jurists and those of later generations.
5) Identify the conditions that must be fulfilled in a *mujtahid*.

Fiqh in Contemporary Times

Prelude: The Condition of *Fiqh* in This Era

This last phase began in the second half of the 13th *hijri* century and continues until our present day. We specifically chose the second half of the 13th century because it marked a pivotal event in this age, namely the removal of Sharia from the sphere of governance in the lands of Islam. Even though this dangerous shift was enacted after some time, it was first initiated during the second half of the 13th century.

Anyone who reflects on this era will feel much grief over the condition to which Islamic *Fiqh* had plummeted. At the same time, one may be pleased upon noticing a number of promising factors that suggest a renaissance in *Fiqh*, new life being breathed into it and its emancipation of some of the flaws that plagued it during the era of *taqlīd*.

Grief and sorrow sprout from the Sharia being removed from governance and replaced with man-made laws over the course of the past 150 years. Therein, the Sharia courts were limited to judging on civil matters only, and even in this limited sphere, the man-made laws still crowded the Islamic Sharia and overrode it at times.[1]

٣- تذكر أهم المجامع والمراكز الفقهية في العالم الإسلامي.

٤- تُقارن بين فقهاء السلف، وفقهاء الأعصار المتأخرة.

٥- تُحدد الشروط التي يجب توافرها في المجتهد.

الفقه في العصر الحاضر

تمهيد: حال الفقه في هذا العصر:

الدور الأخير يبدأ من النصف الثاني للقرن الثالث عشر الهجري، ويمتد إلى أيامنا هذه، وإنما حددنا النصف الثاني من القرن الثالث عشر لوجود معلم مهم من معالم هذا العصر، وهو إقصاء الشريعة الإسلامية عن الحكم في الديار الإسلامية، وهذا المنحنى الخطير وإن لم يتم إلا بعد فترة، إلا أن بدايته كانت في النصف الأخير من القرن الثالث عشر.

والمتأمل في هذا العصر يحزن أيضاً للحال التي وصل إليها الفقه الإسلامي، ويسر أحياناً لوجود مبشرات تؤذن بنهضة الفقه، وعودة الحياة إليه، وتخلصه من بعض السلبيات التي أصابته في عصر التقليد.

فالأسى والحزن لأن الشريعة الإسلامية أقصيت عن الحكم واستبدلت بها القوانين الوضعية على مدار المائة والخمسين سنة الماضية، وانزوت المحاكم الشرعية لتحكم في الأحوال الشخصية فقط، وحتى هذا القسم الضيق، فإن القوانين الوضعية ما فتئت تزاحم الشريعة الإسلامية فيه(١).

---

1 Review our book *ash-Sharīʿah al-Ilāhiyyah*.

١ راجع كتابنا: الشريعة الإلهية.

Glee and optimism sprout from the printing of *Fiqh* books, which present the views of the jurists, compare them and determine the preponderant view based on the stronger evidence. Another promising occurrence was printing the books which collected the Sunnah and their explanations, which would serve to spread the guiding light that gave life to *Fiqh* in the first eras. Also, the unrelenting attempts of a group of Hadith scholars, jurists and researchers to revive the *Fiqh* of Sharia were of paramount importance. This effort was represented in their authorings, their juristic encyclopedias and their juristic conferences. It was also evident in their establishment of colleges, institutes and assemblies that focused on the *Fiqh* of Sharia, in addition to holding seminars and conventions that investigated the rulings of *Fiqh*, particularly those pertaining to newly emerging issues in their times.

We will try to shed light on all these aspects, both the positive and the negative, and Allah is the source of strength.

Removing the Islamic Sharia from Governance

Islamic *Fiqh* has never been as severely hurt as this modern age, when the enemies of Islam succeeded at removing the Islamic Sharia from governance. The Sharia courts were dissolved, replaced with civil courts, and what remained of Sharia courts in most Muslim countries were confined to ruling on very limited cases.

When Napoleon occupied Egypt in 1798, he had tried to interfere with the Islamic Sharia, but his dreams crumbled upon being driven out of Egypt after a short period of time.

In 1840, man-made laws began creeping into the Islamic Caliphate in Turkey. These laws were gradually mixed with the Islamic Sharia until they ultimately led to the abolishment of the Sharia rulings altogether. In fact, the caliphate itself collapsed in 1924. Its new constitution declared that Turkey was a secular state, and its previous article – that stated that the country's official religion was Islam – was removed.

والسرور والاستبشار لطباعة أمهات الكتب الفقهية التي تعرض أقوال الفقهاء وتوازن بينها، ثم ترجح القول الأقوى دليلاً، وطباعة كتب السنة وشروحها مما ينشر النور الذي أحيا الفقه في أدواره الأولى، وكذلك المحاولات الدائبة التي يقوم بها مجموعة من المحدثين والفقهاء والباحثين لإحياء فقه الشريعة، والتي تمثلت في المؤلفات والموسوعات الفقهية، والمؤتمرات الفقهية، وإنشاء المعاهد والكليات والمجامع التي تعنى بفقه الشريعة، وانعقاد الندوات والمؤتمرات التي تبحث في القضايا الفقهية، وخاصة النوازل.

وسنحاول أن نلقي الضوء على كل جانب من هذه الجوانب سيئها وخيرها، والله المستعان.

إقصاء الشريعة الإسلامية عن الحكم

لم يصب الفقه الإسلامي بمصاب كما أصيب به في العصر الحديث حيث نجحت جهود أعداء الإسلام في إقصاء الشريعة الإسلامية عن الحكم، وقد ألغيت المحاكم الشرعية، واستبدل بها المحاكم النظامية والمحاكم المدنية، وبقيت المحاكم الشرعية تحكم في نطاق ضيق محدود في أكثر الديار الإسلامية.

وقد حاول نابليون التلاعب بالشريعة الإسلامية عندما احتل مصر في عام ١٧٩٨ م، ولكنه لم يبلغ مناه لاضطراره للخروج من مصر بعد فترة وجيزة.

وقد تسللت القوانين الوضعية إلى دولة الخلافة في تركيا ابتداء من عام ١٨٤٠ م، ولم تزل القوانين تخالط أحكام الشريعة الإسلامية شيئاً فشيئاً حتى انتهى الأمر إلى إلغاء الأحكام الشرعية، بل إلغاء الخلافة الإسلامية في سنة ١٩٢٤ م، بل نص الدستور أن تركيا دولة علمانية، وألغى النص السابق القاضي بأن دين الدولة الإسلام.

In India, the laws of the Islamic Sharia were removed since 1856. In the year 1875, the French laws were translated to Arabic in Egypt, and they became the official governing laws in the mixed courts. In the year 1883, these laws become the sole legislation in the lands of Egypt. In 1955, the little that remained of the Sharia court in Egypt were abolished and turned over to the oridinary judiciary.

By the middle of the 14th *hijri* century, the man-made laws were the only governing law in the Muslim world, except for the Kingdom of Saudi Arabia.

The Printing of *Fiqh* Books

One of the milestones of this era is the appearance of the printing press. The science of *Fiqh* benefitted a great deal from this, as some vital *Fiqh* books were on the verge of being lost. Thus, when some finally became motivated to print these books, all they could find for some of them were one or two manuscripts remaining in existence. That is because they were majorly unappreciated in the era of *taqlīd*, and consequently these books were left for the worms or dwindled over the years due to warfare, storms, rainfall and aging. For this reason, the phenemona of printing, alongside the efforts of a few exceptional Muslims throughout history, preserved these priceless works. Presently, thousands of copies of these valuable books are made available, after nothing but a single manuscript could be found of them in the past.

Using *Fiqh* Views in State Law

The History of Lawmaking

When law practitioners use the term legislation or lawmaking, they are referring to the act of documenting the legal code under the auspices of the legislative authority. At times, the term legislation is also used in reference to the legal code itself which has been generated by that authority.[1]

1 *Uṣūl al-Qānūn* 83 by Dr ʻAbdul-Munʻim aṣ-Ṣudah

وفي الهند ألغيت أحكام الشريعة الإسلامية منذ سنة ١٨٥٦ م، وفي سنة ١٨٧٥ م، ترجمت القوانين الفرنسية إلى العربية في مصر، وأصبحت هي القوانين التي تحكم في المحاكم المختلطة، وفي سنة ١٨٨٣ م جعلت هذه القوانين هي القوانين التي تحكم الديار المصرية، وفي سنة ١٩٥٥ م ألغيت البقية الباقية من المحاكم الشرعية في مصر وحول اختصاصها إلى القضاء العادي.

ولم يأت منتصف القرن الرابع عشر الهجري حتى أصبحت القوانين الوضعية هي المهيمنة في كل الديار الإسلامية باستثناء المملكة العربية السعودية[١].

طباعة الكتب الفقهية

من معالم هذا العصر ظهور الطباعة، وقد استفاد الفقه من الطباعة استفادة عظيمة، فقد أوشكت بعض الكتب الفقهية المهمة على الضياع، وعندما انبعثت الهمم لطباعة هذه الكتب، لم يوجد من بعضها إلا نسخة واحدة أو نسختان، ذلك أن العناية بها في عصر التقليد قلت، فعاثت بهذه الكتب الديدان، واجتاحتها الحروب والأعاصير والأمطار ومرور الأيام، فكان ظهور الطباعة وعناية بعض الأفذاذ في هذه الأمة بنشرها سبيلاً لحفظها، فكثير من الكتب الفقهية القيمة يوجد منها اليوم ألوف من النسخ وعشرات الألوف بعد أن لم يكن موجوداً منها إلا بعض النسخ.

تقنين الفقه الإسلامي

تاريخ التقنين:

يريد القانونيون بالتشريع وضع القواعد القانونية في صورة مكتوبة بواسطة السلطة المختصة بذلك، ويطلق اصطلاح التشريع كذلك على القواعد القانونية ذاتها التي تضعها هذه السلطة[٢].

١ فصلنا القول في هذه المسألة في مبحث مستقل بعنوان «الشريعة الإلهية لا لقوانين الجاهلية».

٢ أصول القانون للدكتور عبد المنعم الصدة: ٨٣.

As for codifying legislation, this refers to collecting the legal codes pertaining to any particular branch of law in the form of a book, compilation or treatise. This takes place after reviewing these laws, organizing them, sifting out the contradictions and grouping them based on subject. Each group is comprised of articles, and these articles address the rulings related to the various legal aspects that full under the subject matter of this group. Civil law, for example, is a culmination of the legal codes which organize the interpersonal relationships within a society. Commercial law, as another example, is what systematically regulates trade practices and the relationships between merchants.[1]

The idea of codifying law is ancient. Of the oldest known codifications is that of the Hamurabi Law in 2000 B.C. Then, there was the appearance of the twelve tables of Rome in 450 B.C. Following that was the Justinian records in 534 C.E. Additionally, some of the most famous codes which appeared in the past were the Manu Law of India, the Pharoanic Law of Bokharis and the Greek Law of Solon.

France was the first to codify laws in the modern age. Napoleon assigned four law experts with the task of codifying a bill on civil law. This law was entered into force in the year 1804 C.E. and was named the Napoleonic Code.

European countries soon followed the footsteps of France; a legal code surfaced in Austria in 1811 C.E., Italy in 1869 C.E., Switzerland in 1881 C.E., and Germany in 1900 C.E.[2]

أما تقنين التشريع فيريدون به تجميع القواعد القانونية المتعلقة بفرع معين من فروع القانون في شكل كتاب أو مدونة أو مجموعة واحدة، وذلك بعد مراجعة هذه القواعد وتنسيقها، ورفع التناقض منها، وتبويبها بحسب الموضوعات التي تنظمها، والمجموعة تظهر في شكل مواد، وتشمل مختلف النصوص الخاصة بالأحكام القانونية المتصلة بفرع من فروع القانون، فالمجموعة المدنية مثلاً تتضمن القواعد القانونية التي تنظم روابط الأفراد فيما بينهم، والمجموعة التجارية تعرض لتنظيم الأعمال التجارية والعلاقات بين التجار...[(١)].

وفكرة التقنين قديمة، ومن أقدم ما عرف من التقنينات قانون حمورابي عام ٢٠٠٠ قبل الميلاد، ثم ظهرت الألواح الاثنا عشر عند الرومان عام ٤٥٠ قبل الميلاد، ثم ظهرت مدونة جوستينيان عام ٥٣٤ ميلادية، ومن أشهر التقنينات التي ظهرت قديماً أيضاً قانون مانو الهندي ومجموعة بوخوريس الفرعونية ومجموعة صولون الإغريقية.

وأول من اتجه إلى التقنين في العصر الحديث فرنسا، فقد عهد نابليون إلى أربعة من رجال القانون بمهمة وضع مجموعة للقانون المدني، وقد كان التقنين المدني الذي صدر عام ١٨٠٤ هو نتيجة عمل تلك اللجنة، وقد صدرت باسم مجموعة نابليون.

وقد حذت الدول الأوروبية حذو فرنسا، فظهر التقنين النمساوي في سنة ١٨١١م، والتقنين الإيطالي في سنة ١٨٦٩م، والتقنين السويسري في سنة ١٨٨١م والتقنين الألماني في سنة ١٩٠٠ م[(٢)].

---

1 *Muḥāḍarāt fī Naẓariyyat al-Qānūn* 234 by Dr Muhammad ʿAli al-Imām

2 *Muḥāḍarāt fī Naẓariyyat al-Qānūn* 243, 246

١ محاضرات في نظرية القانون للدكتور محمد علي إمام: ٢٣٤.

٢ محاضرات في نظرية القانون: ٢٤٣، ٢٤٦.

The History of Codifying Fiqh as Law

1) The laws of the Islamic Sharia existed in the Qur'anic verses and Prophetic hadith(s), and the Qur'an was compiled in writing during the era of the Companions, and the Sunnah was also compiled a hundred years later.

It was easy for the judges, rulers and mufti(s) to refer back to the Qur'an for judgment because most of them had memorized the Book of Allah. Likewise, when the Sunnah was compiled shortly thereafter, resorting back to it for the rulings it contained was an easy task as well.

2) Differences appeared in *Fiqh* rulings at the time of the Companions but on a very small scale. The scope of differences later widened, and the Muslims suffered a great deal from these differences. Its effects became evident between the *fatwa* and judicial spheres, since the decision given by a judge would sometimes contradict the *fatwa* given by a mufti. In the earlier generations, their abidance by the evidences, in addition to the presence of great jurists, protected them from such disputes. There is no doubt that there were rulers, jurists, judges and mufti(s) that deliberated a great deal on putting an end to this problem or at least minimizing it. For example, the fundamental principles laid down by Imām ash-Shāfi'i, and then later refined by him, was but one of the many approaches which sought to unify the method by which rulings were extracted.

3) The Abbasid caliph Abū Ja'far al-Manṣūr had once tried to turn *al-Muwaṭṭa'* of Imām Mālik into the official *madhhab* of the nation. He wanted to oblige the people to strictly abide by it, but Imām Mālik refused because the hadith(s) of the Messenger (ﷺ) were scattered throughout the lands and not entirely collected in *al-Muwaṭṭa'*.

تاريخ تقنين الفقه الإسلامي:

١- تناولت الشريعة الإسلامية الأحكام الشرعية القانونية في الآيات القرآنية والأحاديث النبوية، وقد جمع القرآن ودُوِّن في عهد الصحابة، ودونت السنة بعد ذلك بمائة سنة.

وقد كان من السهل أن يرجع القضاة والحكام والمفتون إلى الأحكام التي تضمنها القرآن، فقد كان أكثر هؤلاء يحفظون كتاب الله، ثم دونت السنة، وصار الرجوع إلى الأحكام التي تضمنتها سهلاً ميسوراً.

٢- ظهر الاختلاف في الأحكام الفقهية في عهد الصحابة، وابتدأ ضيقاً، ثم اتسع، وقد عانى المسلمون من هذا الخلاف، وظهرت آثاره في الفتوى والقضاء؛ إذ تتعارض الأحكام الصادرة من المفتين والقضاة في بعض الأحيان، وقد كان التقيد بالدليل، ووجود الفقهاء العظام في الرعيل الأول عاصماً من الفتنة، ولا شك أن الحكام والفقهاء والقضاة والمفتين قلَّبوا وجوه النظر للقضاء على هذه المشكلة أو تقليصها، وما القواعد الأصولية التي وضعها الشافعي، ونماها مَنْ بعده- إلا نمط من الأنماط لتوحيد طريقة استخلاص الأحكام، وقد وجدت أنماط أخرى من التفكير.

٣- فكر الخليفة العباسي أبو جعفر المنصور بأن يجعل موطأ الإمام مالك المذهب الرسمي للدولة، وذلك بحمل الناس على التزامه والأخذ به، ولكن الإمام مالك رفض ذلك؛ لأن أحاديث الرسول ﷺ كانت مفرقة في الأمصار، فالموطأ لم يجمع السنة كلها.

4) Ibn al-Muqaffa' had suggested to the caliph, al-Manṣūr, that he unify the protocol of all the courts. This suggestion was raised to the sultan, but no records have reached us indicating that this suggestion was accepted. The suggestion was preserved in *Risālat aṣ-Ṣaḥābah*[1] by Ibn al-Muqaffa'. In this letter, he spoke about the judges differing on rulings that could lead to unwarranted bloodshed, without any evidence, and cited the practices of some Umayyad rulers to support his argument. Then, he suggested that the caliph adopt a single position in the controversial matters of *Fiqh*, and then have everyone abide by that position in order to eliminate the differences among the judges and rulers.

5) The Abbasids advocated the *madhhab* of Abū Ḥanīfah, which granted his followers great standing in the state, and earned them the mufti and judicial positions.

6) When the Ottomans took rule, they also advocated the *madhhab* of Abū Ḥanīfah, as this was the *madhhab* they followed. They used to allot the Grand Mufti position, and most of his assistants, only to the Ḥanafi scholars.

Majallat al-Aḥkām al-'Adliyyah (The Justice Department's Rulings Magazine)

Toward the end of the 13th *hijri* century, civil courts were established in Turkey, and some of the cases originally handled by the Sharia courts were transferred over to them. The judges of these new courts were not well-versed in *Fiqh*. Therefore, they were incapable of extracting the rulings from the *Fiqh* books due to their various styles and diverse views. Also, differentiating between these views requires a special training and talent, and none of that was found in these non-Sharia judges.[2]

---

1 Note: the term *Ṣahābah* here refers to the companions of the sultan, not the Companions of the Messenger (ﷺ).

2 The establishment of civil courts, and instating laws in this regard, resulted from the Ottoman state gradually assimilating to the European nations.

٤- عرض ابن المقفع على الخليفة المنصور توحيد العمل في المحاكم ورفع فكرته هذه إلى السلطان، ولكننا لم نجد لها صدى فيما وصلنا من مراجع، وقد حفظ هذا الاقتراح في رسالة الصحابة(١) التي وضعها ابن المقفع، وقد تحدث ابن المقفع فيها عن اختلاف القضاة في الأحكام، مما يؤدي إلى الأمر بسفك الدماء من غير بينة ولا برهان احتجاجاً بفعل بعض من سبق من حكام الدول الأموية، ثم عرض على الخليفة أن يتبنى في المسائل المختلف فيها رأياً ينهي اختلاف القضاة والحكام، ويجعل الرأي والحكم واحداً فيما اختلفوا فيه.

٥- ناصر العباسيون مذهب أبي حنيفة فأصبح لأتباعه مكانة كبيرة في دولتهم، وتولوا القضاء والإفتاء.

٦- لما تولى العثمانيون الحكم ناصروا مذهب أبي حنيفة؛ لأنهم كانوا من أتباع مذهبه، وكانوا يختارون شيخ الإسلام ومعظم معاونيه من الأحناف.

مجلة الأحكام العدلية:

في أواخر القرن الثالث عشر الهجري أنشئت في تركيا المحاكم النظامية، ونقل إليها بعض اختصاصات المحاكم الشرعية، ولم يكن قضاة هذه المحاكم من الفقهاء المتمرسين بالفقه؛ ولذا لم يكن في استطاعتهم أخذ الأحكام من الكتب الفقهية، لاختلاف أساليبها، وكثرة الآراء فيها، ولأن التمييز بين تلك الآراء يحتاج إلى ملكة فقهية خاصة، وتدريب خاص، ولم يتوافر لهؤلاء القضاة غير الشرعيين شيء من ذلك(٢).

---

١ يقصد صحابة السلطان، لا صحابة الرسول ﷺ.

٢ المحاكم النظامية ووضع القوانين على هذا النحو كان بسبب تأثر الدول العثمانية بالدول الأوروبية.

To traverse this hurdle, the *Fiqh* rulings had to be collected and codified like laws in order to facilitate finding and using them. A command was issued from the sultanate to form a committee of the eminent jurists and that it be lead by the minister of justice. It took seven years for this committee to complete its task – between the years 1285 and 1293 A.H. (1869-1876 C.E.).[1] The committee produced a group of rulings which were chosen from the *Fiqh* of the Ḥanafi *madhhab* and arranged its sections in accordance with the typical chaptering found in *Fiqh* books. However, it separated the rulings into articles and assigned to each a serial number, just like the other laws. This was sought to facilitate reviewing it and making reference to it. Its total number of articles was 1,851.[2]

Some weaker opinions within the *madhhab* were adopted into this magazine because they suited the interests of that age. In the year 1293 A.H., the sultanate decreed that this set of laws be acted upon in all the courts throughout the nation. By doing that, it became a public civil law that was selectively chosen from among the wide spectrum of *Fiqh* rulings. Since these rulings were now backed by the sultan's authority, nothing contrary to them in any *Fiqh* book was seen to have legitimacy any longer. Judges would only resort back to the statements of the Muslim jurists in matters that were not addressed by the magazine.[3]

This was applied in Turkey and in the other nations which were subordinate to the Turks' rule.

The Codification of Personal Laws

After the magazine was no longer applied in Turkey and the nations under its rule, no remnants of Islamic Sharia could be found in the court systems except for personal law. The first personal law issued in Turkey, which was enacted in 1917 C.E. (1336 A.H.), was named "the family rights law." In Lebanon, this law remains in effect until today.[4]

1 *Al-Madkhal lit-Ta'rīf bil-Fiqh* 116 by Professor Muhammad Muṣṭafā Shalabi
2 *Al-Madkhal* 1/210 by Professor az-Zarqā
3 Ibid: 1/211
4 *'Aqd az-Zawāj wa* Āthāruh 20 by Abū Zahrah

واقتضى الأمر علاج المشكلة السابقة بجمع أحكام المسائل وصياغتها على هيئة قانون ليسهل الرجوع إليها، وأخذ الأحكام منها، فصدرت إرادة سلطانية بتأليف لجنة من مشاهير الفقهاء برياسة وزير العدلية، وأتمت اللجنة عملها في سنوات (١٢٨٥- ١٢٩٣هـ/ ١٨٦٩- ١٨٧٦م)(١)، وقد وضعت اللجنة مجموعة من الأحكام منتقاة من فقه المذهب الحنفي، ورتبت مباحثها على الكتب والأبواب الفقهية المعهودة، ولكنها فصلت الأحكام بمواد ذات أرقام متسلسلة كالقوانين، ليسهل الرجوع إليها والإحالة عليها، وقد جاءت في (١٨٥١) مادة(٢).

وقد أخذت بعض الأقوال المرجوحة في المذهب للمصلحة الزمنية التي اقتضتها، وقد صدرت الإرادة السلطانية في سنة ١٢٩٣هـ بلزوم العمل بها، وتطبيق أحكامها في محاكم الدولة، وبذلك أصبحت قانوناً مدنيّاً عامّاً منتخباً من الأحكام الفقهية فما وجد فيه لا يعول على ما يخالفه في كتب الفقه لاقترانه بالأمر السلطاني، وإنما يرجع القضاة إلى نصوص الفقهاء فيما لا نص عليه في المجلة(٣).

وقد طبقت في تركيا وفي الدول التي كانت تهيمن عليها الدولة التركية.

تقنين الأحوال الشخصية:

بعد أن توقف العمل بالمجلة في تركيا والديار التي كانت تابعة لها لم يبق من الشريعة الإسلامي ما يطبق في المحاكم في الديار الإسلامية إلا الأحوال الشخصية، وقد كان أول قانون صدر للأحوال الشخصية في تركيا باسم «قانون حقوق العائلة» صدر في سنة (١٣٣٦هـ- ١٩١٧م)، وما زال هذا القانون معمولاً به في لبنان، إلى اليوم(٤).

١ المدخل للتعريف بالفقه للأستاذ محمد مصطفى شلبي: ١١٦.
٢ المدخل للأستاذ الزرقا: ١/ ٢١٠.
٣ المصدر السابق: ١/ ٢١١.
٤ عقد الزواج وآثاره لأبي زهرة: ٢٠.

Unofficial Codifications

1) The Works of Muhammad Qadri

There were some scholars who codified the rulings of the Islamic Sharia into law form, but the government did not instruct that these laws be adopted, nor that the judges be bound to them, as they did with the previously mentioned rulings magazine. For that reason, these laws never took effect, and thus we named them unofficial laws.

The first of these works was prepared by Muhammad Qadri Bāshā in Egypt. It appears that he was initially authorized by the Egyptian government, in order to absorb some of the public rage that was triggered by the adoption of the Napoleonic Laws in Muslim lands. In response, the government commissioned Muhammad Qadri Bāsha with compiling a book of Sharia rulings in order to sedate the people's fury for a while.

Muhammad Qadri relied on the Ḥanafi *madhhab* in his collection of Sharia rulings and used the justice department's rulings magazine as a guide. What he gathered in this regard was divided into three books:

The **first** was specific to interpersonal relations, and he named it *Murshid al-Ḥayrān fī Ma'rifat Aḥwāl al-Insān*. It consisted of 941 articles and was printed by the government in 1890 C.E.

The **second** was specific to endowments, and he named it *al-'Adl wal-Inṣāf fī Mushkilāt al-Awqāf*. It consisted of 646 articles and was printed in 1893 C.E.

The **third** was specific to the rulings on personal law, in which he talked about bequests, interdiction, wills, and inheritance. This book became the only recognized book on personal law in many Islamic countries.

التدوين غير الرسمي:

١- أعمال محمد قدري:

قام بعض العلماء بتقنين أحكام الشريعة الإسلامية، ولكن لم يصدر أمر من الدولة بتبني هذه القوانين وإلزام القضاة بها، كما حدث في مجلة الأحكام؛ ولذلك لم تعتبر هذه الأعمال قوانين نافذة، ولذلك سميناها قوانين غير رسمية.

وأول عمل من هذا القبيل قام به «محمد قدري باشا» في مصر، ويبدو أن عمله هذا كان في بدايته بتفويض من الحكومة المصرية لامتصاص النقمة التي أثارها تحكيم قانون نابليون في رقاب المسلمين، فعهدت الحكومة إلى محمد قدري بتدوين كتاب الأحكام الشرعية لتهدئ من روع الناس إلى حين.

وقد جمع محمد قدري الأحكام الشرعية معتمداً على مذهب أبي حنيفة، مسترشداً بمجلة الأحكام العدلية، وجعل ما جمعه في هذا في ثلاثة كتب:

الأول: خاص بالمعاملات وسماه: «مرشد الحيران في معرفة أحوال الإنسان»، ويحتوي على (٩٤١) مادة، وقد طبعته الدولة في سنة ١٨٩٠م.

الثاني: خاص بالوقف وسماه: «العدل والإنصاف في مشكلات الأوقاف»، ويحتوي على (٦٤٦) مادة، وطبع أيضاً سنة (١٨٩٣م).

الثالث: خاص بأحكام الأحوال الشخصية، وقد تكلم فيه عن «الهبة والحجر والإيصاء والميراث»، وقد أصبح المعول على هذا الكتاب في الأحوال الشخصية في كثير من الديار الإسلامية»[1].

١ راجع فلسفة التشريع: ١١٧؛ المدخل لمدكور: ١١١؛ محاضرات في فقه القانون: ٢٣٦؛ المدخل لمحمد محمود الطنطاوي: ٢٢٤، طبعة دار النهضة العربية، القاهرة (١٣٩٨

2) A Summary of Sharia Rulings Based on the Authorized Positions of the Māliki Madhhab

The late M. Muhammad 'Āmir gathered many of the Māliki *Fiqh* principles in the form of legal articles, and he entitled this work *Mulakhaṣ al-Aḥkām ash-Shar'iyyah 'alā al-Mu'tamad min Madhhab Mālik.*[1]

3) The Sharia Rulings Magazine Based on the Ḥanbali *Madhhab*[2]

This magazine was prepared by the judge Shaykh Aḥmad ibn 'Abdillāh al-Qāri al-Makki (d. 1359 A.H.). It is comprised of 21 books; each book had a number of chapters, and every chapter had a number of sections.

Throughout this magazine's 675 pages, its books discussed an array of subjects. Of them were sales, rentals, loans, endowments, gifts, ransoms and others.

These [21] books included, within their chapters and sections, 2,382 *Fiqh* based articles in total. The magazine relied on the primary sources of Ḥanbali *Fiqh*, the most important of them being *al-Mughni* and *ash-Sharḥ al-Kabīr*.

The Benefits and Harms of Codifying Fiqh as Laws

Codification serves to collect all the rulings pertaining to a specific branch of law in one record. Then, it classifies these rulings into chapters, arranges them in a academically coherent fashion and reconciles between whichever of these laws contradict one another. This process makes finding and studying these laws much easier. Consequently, people are able to know their rights and duties in transactions, the authorities are able to apply them easily and the judges are able to judge based on them with regard to the cases and disputes that are presented to them. These are the benefits of codifying man-made laws which are taken from the customs of the people and the intellections of the wise among them.

1 *Buḥūth fī ash-Sharī'ah al-Islāmiyyah wal-Qānūn* 2/38 – Published by Cairo University (1977 C.E. / 1397 A.H.)

2 Verified by the two professors Dr 'Abdul-Wahhāb Ibrāhīm Abū Sulaymān and Dr. Muhammad Ibrāhīm Aḥmad 'Ali. It was published by ar-Risālah Foundation in Jeddah.

٢- ملخص الأحكام الشرعية على المعتمد من مذهب مالك:

قام المرحوم محمد محمد عامر بوضع الكثير من قواعد فقه المذهب المالكي في صورة مواد قانونية تحت عنوان «ملخص الأحكام الشرعية على المعتمد من مذهب مالك»(١).

٣- مجلة الأحكام الشرعية على مذهب أحمد(٢):

مجلة الأحكام الشرعية على مذهب الإمام أحمد بن حنبل من عمل الشيخ القاضي أحمد بن عبد الله القاري المكي المتوفى سنة (١٣٥٩هـ)، وتعرض المجلة لواحد وعشرين كتاباً، كل كتاب يندرج تحته عدد من الأبواب، وتحت كل باب عدد من الفصول.

والكتب التي تناولتها المجلة عبر صفحاتها التي تبلغ ستمائة وخمس وسبعين صفحة من القطع المتوسط هي واحد وعشرون كتاباً، منها: كتاب في البيوع، كتاب الإيجارات، وكتاب القرض، وكتاب الوقف، وكتاب الهبة والرهن، وغيرها.

وتضم هذه الكتب بما تحتويه من أبواب وفصول (٢٣٨٢) مادة فقهية وقد اعتمدت المجلة على المصادر الأساسية للفقه الحنبلي، ومن أهمها المغني والشرح الكبير.

فوائد التقنين وعيوبه:

التقنين يجمع القواعد المتعلقة بفرع من فروع القانون في مدونة واحد، ثم يبوب هذه القواعد، ويرتبها على أساس علمي منطقي، ويرفع ما بين القواعد من تناقض، وهذا يؤدي إلى سهولة التعرف على هذه القواعد، وبذلك يعرف الناس حقوقهم، وواجباتهم في أمور المعاملات، ويسهل على أولي الأمر تطبيقها، وعلى القضاة الحكم بمقتضاها في القضايا والمنازعات التي تعرض عليهم، هذه هي فوائد تقنين الشرائع الأرضية البشرية التي تؤخذ من عادات الناس وما يسنه لهم عقلاؤهم.

١ بحوث في الشريعة الإسلامية والقانون، المجموعة الثانية: ٣٨، مطبعة جامعة القاهرة (١٣٩٧هـ- ١٩٧٧م).

٢ قام على تحقيقها الأستاذان: الدكتور عبد الوهاب إبراهيم أبو سليمان، والدكتور محمد إبراهيم أحمد علي، ونشرتها مؤسسة الرسالة بجدة.

As for the Islamic Sharia, its rulings are preserved and well-known. Ordinary individuals from this *Ummah* memorize its primary source of legislation, the Qur'an, not just the scholars. Its two primary sources, the Qur'an and Sunnah, have been transcribed and compiled into books. In addition, there are compilations which have specifically gathered the verses and hadith(s) pertaining to rulings and clearly explained them.

There are substantial harms in codifying the Islamic Sharia into law. It freezes the rulings that were turned into law and halts the exercise of *ijtihād* since the people and judges are forced to abide by one *madhhab*, one law or one set of laws. In essence, this is a form of monopolizing *Fiqh*, since it does not allow for the consideration of anything except what has been codified as law.

Such codification diverts the scholars from considering the rulings, in light of the Qur'an and Sunnah, to the confined sphere of the state's legal code, and it turns the revealed texts of the Sharia into mere historical records of the current "Islamic legal code." This is what made the pious jurists refrain from taking part in the codification since the codifier's actions imply claiming that these rules are undoubtedly the rulings of Allah, and that may not always be the case.

It is not necessary for us to exaggerate regarding the harms of codifying the Sharia rulings into laws, for the Islamic Sharia is documented and preserved and referring back to its rulings remains an easy task. We are unlike the non-Muslim countries which mainly depend on a wide array of sources for legislation, and thus require codifying their laws in order to eliminate the disagreements and disputes between the judges.

أما الشريعة الإسلامية، فإن أحكامها محفوظة معروفة، فالأشخاص العاديون من الأمة يحفظون مصدرها الرئيس وهو القرآن، فضلاً عن علمائها وأهل الرأي فيها، والمصدران الرئيسان فيها مدونان، وهما الكتاب والسنة، وهناك مدونات جمع فيها مدونوها آيات التشريع وأحاديث التشريع وشرحوها وبينوها.

وتقنين أحكام الشريعة له سيئات فهو يجمد الأحكام القانونية، ويوقف الاجتهاد؛ لأنه يلزم الناس والقضاة جميعاً باتباع مذهب واحد، أو مادة واحدة أو فصل واحد، وهو أيضاً من نوع الحجر على الأحكام؛ لأنه يمنع من النظر في غير ما قنن.

إن التقنين ينقل العلماء من النظر في الأحكام من خلال النصوص في الكتاب والسنة إلى دائرة ضيقة هي القواعد القانونية المقننة، ويجعل النصوص الشرعية مجرد مصدر تاريخي للقانون الإسلامي المقنن، وهذا يجعل الفقهاء الأتقياء يتحرجون من التقنين، خاصة وأن المقنن يجزم بنسبة الأحكام إلى الله، وقد لا يكون الأمر كذلك.

ولا يجب أن نبالغ في إعطاء تقنين الأحكام الشرعية على النحو المعروف في القانون أهمية عظيمة؛ ذلك أن الشريعة الإسلامية مدونة، والرجوع إلى أحكامها سهل ميسور، أما الدول الكافرة التي تعتمد في تشريعها على مصادر متفرقة فإنها تحتاج إلى التقنين لإزالة الخلاف والفرقة التي تحدث بين القضاة.

Take the nations of England and America, for example. They had not compiled their laws, and hence the court decisions in Britain are based primarily on custom and previous judicial cases. Judges in these two nations present what are called "precedents," and in light of the verdicts previously delivered by the higher courts do the lower courts function. As for the higher courts themselves, they are bound by their previous verdicts, making these "precedents" the basis for their judgments. Such "precedents" cannot be easily changed, and thus brings some consistency into their judicial process.

Researchers and law practictioners in the Muslim world 150 years ago assumed that codifying the rulings – as Europe had done – would rid these lands of backwardness and subjugation and that it would make them one of the developed mentions. After these long years, we discovered that codification was but a façade. Had the rulings of the Islamic Sharia actually been upheld, the condition of the Muslims would have been improved, and we would have become one of the most advanced nations.

Fiqh Encyclopedias

In the past, the jurists exhausted themselves to author books. It is known that "the ultimate objective in every academic science is facilitating its acquisition for the learner and making it more easily understood. Such an aim is only possible by arranging it in a wise manner that is most suitable for that respective craft.[1] This drove the scholars to "categorize the rulings, arrange them accordingly, and publish them under their appropriate principles. This made them more quickly understood, more likely to be mastered and easier to memorize – which in turn increased their scope of benefit."[2]

1 *Badā'i' aṣ-Ṣanā'i'* 1/2 by al-Kāsāni
2 Ibid: 1/2

وها هي الأمة الإنجليزية والأمة الأمريكية لم تدونا قانونيهما، والأحكام التي يصدرها القضاة في بريطانيا تقوم أساساً على مبادئ العرف والسوابق القضائية، فالقضاة في هاتين الدولتين يتقيدون بما يسمونه «السابقات»، فالمحاكم البدائية ملزمة باتباع اجتهاد المحاكم العليا، والمحاكم العليا تتقيد باجتهادها السابق بصورة تجعل من «السابقات» أساساً ثابتاً لأحكامهم، لا يمكنهم تغييره بسهولة، وتجعل الاجتهاد موحداً معلوماً.

لقد ظن الباحثون ورجال الحكم في الدول الإسلامية منذ أكثر من مائة وخمسين عاماً أن تقنين الأحكام- كما فعلت أوربا- سيخلص هذه البلاد من التخلف والاستعباد، وسيجعلنا نلحق بركب التقدم، وها نحن نكتشف بعد هذا الزمن الطويل أن التقنين أمر شكلي، فلو كانت أحكام الشريعة الإسلامية نافذة قائمة لصلح حال المسلمين، ولأصبحوا في طليعة الأمم.

الموسوعات الفقهية

لقد أجهد الفقهاء في العصور السابقة أنفسهم في التصنيف، ومن المعلوم أن «المقصود الكلي من التصنيف في كل فن من فنون العلم هو تيسير سبيل الوصول إلى المطلوب على الطالبين، وتقريبه إلى أفهام المقتبسين، ولا يلتئم هذا المراد إلا بترتيب تقتضيه الصناعة، وتوجبه الحكمة»[١]، وهذا أحوجهم إلى «تصفح أقسام المسائل وفصولها، وتخريجها على قواعدها وأصولها، ليكون أسرع فهماً وأسهل ضبطاً، وأيسر حفظاً، فتكثر الفائدة، وتتوفر العائدة»[٢].

١ بدائع الصنائع للكساني: ١/ ٢.
٢ المصدر السابق: ١/ ٢.

In order to achieve this aim which al-Kāsāni just explained, some of the contemporary scholars believed *Fiqh* should be compiled into encyclopedia.

Encyclopedias are inclusive compilations that contain a comprehensive record of information on one or more sciences. This information is presented under customary headings, ordered in a systematic fashion that does not require any experience or training to navigate through. Its facts are written in simple terms which don't need explanation or an instructor to comprehend. Rather, anyone with an average degree of general education, and a bit of background on the topic at hand is sufficient. Alongside all this, the referencing of its facts to reliable sources provides its readers with confidences regarding its contents, especially when its compilers are those credible and qualified to speak on such topics.

Therefore, an encyclopedia must gather a number of unique qualities to deserve its name; it must be comprehensive, easily arranged, simply worded and reliable.

Hence, *Fiqh* encyclopedias are different from what we call compilations, elaborate, abridged and comprehensive books of *Fiqh* because none of these have all the above mentioned qualities. At times, these older books may coincidentally share in one of these qualities, like being comprehensive, and that explains why they are sometimes called encyclopedias. However, this is meant in the figurative sense, not the literal, because they still lack some of the most important qualities, like being arranged specifically to be easily researchable, explaining in coherent terms and being harmonious in nature.[1]

1 *Al-Mawsū'ah al-Fiqhiyyah al-Kuwāytiyyah* 1/53

وتحقيقاً لهذا الهدف الذي قرره الكاساني رأى بعض المعاصرين أن يدونوا الفقه في موسوعات.

والموسوعة أو دائرة المعارف أو المَعْلمة تطلق على المؤلف الشامل لجميع معلومات علم أو أكثر، معروضة من خلال عناوين متعارف عليها، بترتيب معين، لا يحتاج معه إلى خبرة وممارسة، مكتوبة بأسلوب مبسط لا يتطلب فهمه توسط المدرس أو الشروح، بل يكفي للاستفادة منه الحد الأوسط من الثقافة العامة مع الإلمام بالعلم الموضوعة له، ولابد مع هذا كله من توافر دواعي الثقة بمعلوماتها بعزوها للمراجع المعتمدة، أو نسبتها إلى المختصين الذين عهد إليهم بتدوينها ممن يطمأن بصدورها عنهم.

فخصائص الموسوعة التي توجب لها استحقاق هذه التسمية هي: الشمول، والترتيب السهل، والأسلوب المبسط، وموجبات الثقة.

فالموسوعة الفقهية تخالف ما نطلق عليه اسم المدونات أو المطولات أو المبسوطات، أو الأمهات من كتب الفقه؛ لأنها لم تراع جميع الخصائص المشار إليها، وإن وجد خصيصة منها أو أكثر بالقصد أو التوافق، ولا سيما شمول قدر كبير من المادة الفقهية الموثقة هو الذي يسيغ إطلاق اسم الموسوعات عليها، من باب التجوز لا الحقيقة؛ لأنها تفتقر إلى أهم الخصائص: اتخاذ المصطلحات المرتبة أساساً للبحث فيها، فضلاً عن سهولة الأسلوب وإطلاق الحدود للبيان المتناسق(١).

١ الموسوعة الفقهية الكويتية: ١/ ٥٣.

The Need for Fiqh Encyclopedias

The difficulties encountered by the students of *Fiqh* is what led to the compilations of *Fiqh* encyclopedia. These difficulties can be summarized with the following points:

1) The *Fiqh* books of every *madhhab* are not uniform in their arrangement, wherein they follow a single pattern. Instead, what one *madhhab* discusses first can be discussed last by another *madhhab*, and what one *madhhab* includes in a particular chapter could not be included by another *madhhab* under that same chapter.

2) There is no detailed indexing in such books which directs the researcher to the issue one investigates. For instance, we find the topic of "abortion and coitus interruptus" in *Hāshiyat Ibn* ʿĀbidīn under "the ruling on practicing coitus interruptus with a slave-girl" which is found in the book on slavery. Similarly, the ruling on a sick person dealing with his wealth is found under "emancipating during sickness." Similarly, dealing with the non-Muslims and polytheists living under the protection of the Muslim state is found under "the rulings on guardianship." Putting rulings in improper places makes finding them extremely difficult.

3) Many of the *Fiqh* terms are difficult to understand and the way the *Fiqh* books were written contains much complexity.

History of Fiqh Encyclopedias

The first explicit call to undertake this project came from the Islamic *Fiqh* Conference held in Paris (1370 A.H. / 1950 C.E.). Of its concluding recommendations was the call to compile a *Fiqh* encyclopedia which presents the Islamically sanctioned "rights" written in a modern style and arranged in alphabetical order.

The first attempt to advocate this project was initiated by the Sharia College in the University of Damascus. This took place in 1375 A.H. / 1956 C.E., and it became the vanguard in setting the framework upon which the encyclopedia would be built. On the path to producing the encyclopedia, some preliminary works were produced, like *Muʿjam Fiqh Ibn Ḥazm* and *Dalīl Mawāṭin al-Baḥth ʿan al-Musṭalaḥāt al-Fiqhiyyah.*

الحاجة إلى الموسوعة الفقهية:

والذي دعا إلى إنشاء الموسوعة الفقهية تلك الصعوبات التي تقف في وجه الدارسين للفقه، ويمكن أن تلخص هذه الصعوبات فيما يأتي:

أولاً: كتب الفقه غير مرتبة في كل المذاهب الفقهية ترتيباً واحداً، يمضي على نسق واحد، فما يقدمه مذهب قد يؤخره مذهب آخر، وما يدخل في باب معين في مذهب قد لا يدخله المذهب الآخر في نفس الباب.

ثانياً: لا توجد فهرسة دقيقة ترشد الباحث إلى المسألة التي يريدها، فمثلاً تجد موضوع «الإجهاض والعزل» في حاشية ابن عابدين مندرجين في موضوع «حكم العزل عن الأمة» في كتاب «الرق»، وإقرار المريض وتصرفاته بماله تجدهما في مبحث «العتق في المرض»، ومعاملة أهل الذمة والمشركين تجدها في «أحكام الوصي».

ووضع الأحكام في غير مظانها يجعل الوصول إلى المسألة في غاية الصعوبة.

ثالثاً: صعوبة المصطلحات الفقهية، فالأساليب التي كتبت بها بعض كتب الفقه فيها شيء كثير من التعقيد والجفاف.

تاريخ الموسوعة الفقهية:

أول نداء صريح ارتفع مطالباً بإنجاز هذا المشروع هو ذلك النداء الذي صدر عن مؤتمر الفقه الإسلامي في باريس (١٣٧٠هـ- ١٩٥١م)، فقد كان من بين توصياته الدعوة إلى تأليف موسوعة فقهية تعرض فيها المعلومات الحقوقية الإسلامية وفقاً للأساليب الحديثة والترتيب المعجمي.

وكانت أول محاولة لإبراز هذا الموضوع هو العمل الذي ابتدأته كلية الشريعة في جامعة دمشق في عام (١٣٧٥هـ- ١٩٥٦م)، وكان لها فضل السبق في وضع خطة تقوم الموسوعة على أساسها، وقد صدر عن الموسوعة بعض الأعمال التمهيدية كمعجم فقه ابن حزم، ودليل مواطن البحث عن المصطلحات الفقهية.

In 1381 A.H. / 1961 C.E., the Egyptian Ministry of Endowments began a project to produce a *Fiqh* encyclopedia and issued 17 volumes of it before stopping abruptly.

In Kuwait, its Ministry of Endowments began producing a *Fiqh* encyclopedia in 1386 A.H. / 1967 C.E and stopped in 1971. During that period, three subjects - out of 50 - were issued, in addition to publishing *al-Mughni* on Ḥanbali *Fiqh*. The Ministry resumed its work in 1975, and the first volume of the encyclopedia was finally issued in 1981. By the year 2003, the entire encyclopedia was nearly complete.

Academic Assemblies

Contemporary scholars strove in modern times to establish institutes, colleges, assemblies for *Fiqh* research and *Fiqh* conferences. Collegiate institutions that teach Sharia are widespread all over the Muslim world, and they are well-known. There are also Islamic universities that each the various branches of Sharia, the oldest of which being Al-Azhar University in Egypt and Zaytuna University in Tunisia. Other similar universities are Imām Muhammad ibn Saud University in Riyadh of Saudi Arabia, Umm Durman Islamic University in Sudan and the Islamic University in Madinah, Saudi Arabia.

The most important academic and *Fiqh* assemblies, centers, and institutions are:

1) *Majma' al-Buhūth al-Islāmiyyah* (The Islamic Research Assembly)

This assembly was established in Al-Azhar University, Cairo, in the year 1961 C.E. This assembly is comprised of esteemed scholars, from all over the Muslim world, that are known for their qualifications in both the Islamic sciences and in Islamic law.

Annually, the assembly holds a session wherein its members present their new research, which they have prepared regarding the newly emerging transactions in Islamic *Fiqh*. Furthermore, it serves to disseminate Islamic scholarship as well as codify the Islamic *Fiqh*.

وفي عام (١٣٨١هـ- ١٩٦١م) ابتدأت وزارة الأوقاف المصرية مشروعاً لموسوعة فقهية، وقد صدر عن الموسوعة سبعة عشر جزءاً ثم توقفت.

وفي دولة الكويت قامت وزارة الأوقاف بإنشاء موسوعة فقهية عام (١٣٨٦هـ- ١٩٦٧م)، وقد توقف العمل فيها في عام (١٩٧١م) بعد أن أصدرت ثلاثة موضوعات من بين خمسين موضوعاً أنجزتها في تلك الفترة، كما أنجزت ونشرت معجم المغني في فقه الحنابلة.

ثم عاودت العمل في هذا المشروع في عام ١٩٧٥م، وصدر أول جزء عن الموسوعة في عام ١٩٨١م، وقد قاربت الموسوعة على الاكتمال في عام ٢٠٠٣م.

المجامع العلمية

نشط العلماء في إقامة المعاهد والكليات والمجامع العلمية والفقهية، والمؤتمرات الفقهية، في هذا العصر، والمعاهد الكلية التي تقوم بتدريس الشريعة منتشرة في شرق العالم الإسلامي وغربه، وهي مشهورة معروفة، وهناك جامعات إسلامية تدرس مختلف فروع الشريعة، وأقدمها جامعة الأزهر في مصر، وجامعة الزيتونة في تونس، ومن هذه الجامعات: جامعة الإمام محمد بن سعود في الرياض بالمملكة العربية السعودية، وجامعة أم درمان الإسلامية بأم درمان بالسودان، والجامعة الإسلامية بالمدينة المنورة.

ومن أهم المجامع أو المراكز أو الهيئات الفقهية أو العلمية ما يأتي:

١- مجمع البحوث الإسلامية:

أقيم «مجمع البحوث الإسلامية» بالأزهر الشريف بالقاهرة في سنة ١٩٦١ م، ويتكون هذا المجمع من كبار العلماء المشهود لهم بالكفاءة العلمية في العلوم الإسلامية والقانون الإسلامي، وقد تكون من العلماء في جميع البلاد الإسلامية.

والمجمع يعقد جلسة كل عام يقدم فيها الأعضاء أبحاثهم الجديدة التي أعدوها فيما جد في أبواب المعاملات، ويقوم بنشر التراث الإسلامي، ويعمل على تقنين الفقه الإسلامي.

2) *Al-Majlis al-'Ilmi* (The Academic Council) in India

Other academic assemblies and councils were established, some of which were civic and others governmental. Of the civic kind was *al-Majlis al-'Ilmi* which exists in Surat, India and disseminates the primary books on the Islamic sciences It has published many invaluable Islamic books, such as *Musnad al-Humaydi, as-Sunan* by Sa'īd ibn Manṣūr and *Naṣb ar-Rāyah.*

3) *Al-Majlis al-A'lā lish-Shu'ūn al-Islāmiyyah* (The Supreme Council for Islamic Affairs) in Egypt

This council was established under the auspices of the Endowments Ministry. Its assembly was comprised of scholars that were distinguished in various sciences. It published many of the classical Islamic works, in addition to printing the researches of contemporary experts and specialists. Notably, they were the overseers of the Islamic *Fiqh* Encyclopedia that was eventually produced.

4) *Al-Markaz al-'Ālami li-Abḥāth al-Iqtiṣād* (The International Center for Economic Research) in Mecca

This was founded in King 'Abdul-'Azīz University in 1397 A.H. / 1977 C.E. to carry out, endorse and synchronize the research pertaining to Islamic economics on a higher level. This center held several conferences on the topic of Islamic economics, in addition to publishing a bi-annual academic magazine specialized in Islamic economics, in both Arabic and English.

5) *Majma' al-Fiqh al-Islāmi* (The Islamic Fiqh Assemly) in Jeddah

During the 12th Islamic Conference held by the foreign ministers, which took place in Baghdad (Iraq) in 1401 A.H. / 1981 C.E., it was decided to establish *Majma' al-Fiqh al-Islāmi*. This new assembly holds a yearly seminar to discuss a wide array of *Fiqh*-related matters, in addition to publishing a yearly magazine that discusses the subjects that were researched in the conference.

٢- المجلس العلمي بالهند:

وقامت مجامع ومجالس علمية أخرى، بعضها شعبية وبعضها حكومية، فمن المجالس العلمية الشعبية: المجلس العلمي الكائن في سملك سورث بالهند، وهو يقوم على نشر أمهات الكتب الإسلامية، وقد صدر عنه عدة كتب مهمة، مثل: مسند الحميدي، والسنن لسعيد منصور، ونصب الراية.

٣- المجلس الأعلى للشؤون الإسلامية في مصر:

وقام في مصر المجلس الأعلى للشؤون الإسلامية، وهو تابع لوزارة الأوقاف، وقد تكونت لجانه من العلماء البارزين في العلوم المختلفة، ونشر كتباً كثيرة من كتب التراث، كما نشر الأبحاث والمؤلفات للخبراء والمتخصصين، وعنه صدرت موسوعة الفقه الإسلامي.

٤- المركز العالمي لأبحاث الاقتصاد بمكة:

وقد أسس في جامعة الملك عبد العزيز في سنة (١٣٩٧هـ- ١٩٧٧م) «المركز العالمي لأبحاث الاقتصاد الإسلامي» لإجراء ودعم وتنسيق الأبحاث العلمية في الاقتصاد الإسلامي على أرفع مستوى. وقد عقد المركز عدة مؤتمرات في مجال الاقتصاد الإسلامي، كما أصدر مجلة علمية متخصصة في الاقتصاد الإسلامي بالعربية والإنجليزية تصدر مرتين في العام.

٥- مجمع الفقه الإسلامي بجدة:

قرر المؤتمر الإسلامي الثاني عشر لوزراء الخارجية المنعقد في بغداد بالجمهورية العراقية (١٤٠١هـ- ١٩٨١م) إنشاء مجمع الفقه الإسلامي، وهو يعقد دورة سنوية لبحث القضايا الفقهية في مختلف الموضوعات، كما يصدر مجلة سنوية تحتوي الموضوعات التي تم بحثها في كل دورة.

The Mudhakirat al-Amānah al-'Āmmah chose the city of Jeddah (KSA) to be the central Islamic location of the assembly, while reserving for the assembly its right to establish branches and offices in any Muslim land.

It was decided by al-Mudhakkirah that the assembly had two aims:

a) To achieve Islamic unity, in theory and practice, via humane morals, on the individual, societal and international levels – in light of the rulings enjoined by the Islamic Sharia.

b) To pull the Muslim Ummah toward its creed, to study the contemporary problems of everyday life and overcome them via sound *ijtihād* that retrieves the proper solutions from the Islamic Sharia.

6) *Al-Munaẓamah al-Islāmiyyah aṭ-Ṭibbiyyah* (The Islamic Medical Organization)

This organization is located in Kuwait and was established in 1405 A.H. / 1984 C.E. It focuses on holding conferences and forums that discuss the *Fiqh* rulings related to contemporary medical issues. Of the matters it researched was:

- Reproduction in light of Islamic law
- The beginning/end of human life from an Islamic perspective
- An Islamic outlook on certain medical practices
- Human organ transplant from an Islamic perspective
- The medical definition of death

It has also hosted several international conferences.

7) *Al-Hay'ah ash-Shar'iyyah al-'Ālamiyyah liz-Zakāh* (The Islamic International Organization for Zakāh)

This organization is also located in Kuwait and was founded in 1408 A.H. / 1987 C.E. with the aim of holding conferences to discuss issues pertaining to *zakāh*.

وقـد اختـارت الأمانـة العامـة مدينـة جـدة لتكـون المقـر الإسـلامي للمجمـع، وللمجمـع أن ينشـئ فروعـاً ومكاتـب في أي بلـد إسـلامي.

وحددت المذكرة أهداف المجمع بهدفين:

الأول: تحقيـق الوحـدة الإسـلامية نظريّـاً وعلميّـاً عـن طريـق السـلوك الإنسـاني ذاتيّـاً واجتماعيّـاً ودوليّـاً وفقـاً لأحـكام الشريعـة الإسـلامية.

الثاني: شـد الأمـة الإسـلامية لعقيدتهـا ودراسـة مشـكلات الحيـاة المعـاصرة والاجتهـاد فيهـا اجتهـاداً أصيـلاً بغـرض تقديـم الحلـول النابعـة مـن الشريعـة الإسـلامية.

٦- المنظمة الإسلامية الطبية:

ومقـر هـذه المنظمـة دولـة الكويـت، وأنشـئت في عـام (١٤٠٥هـ- ١٩٨٤م)، وقـد عنيـت بإقامـة المؤتمـرات والنـدوات التـي تبحـث في المسـائل الطبيـة الفقهيـة المعـاصرة.

ومن المشكلات التي تم بحثها:

- الإنجاب في ضوء الإسلام.
- الحياة الإنسانية بدايتها ونهايتها في المفهوم الإسلامي.
- الرؤية الإسلامية لبعض الممارسات الطبية.
- رؤية إسلامية لزراعة بعض الأعضاء البشرية.
- التعريف الطبي للموت.
- كما عقدت عدة مؤتمرات عالمية.

٧- الهيئة الشرعية العالمية للزكاة:

ومقـر هـذه الهيئـة الكويـت، وقـد تـم تأسيسـها في سـنة (١٤٠٨هـ- ١٩٨٧م)، وقـد عنيـت بإقامـة المؤتمـرات والندوات المتخصصـة بقضايـا الـزكاة.

This organization is not subordinate to any country or *zakāh* institution in particular. It is strictly a research organization whose members are notable Sharia jurists and other experts specialized in sciences related to *zakāh*.

Of the issues discussed in its conferences and seminars are the following:

- Guidelines for calculating *zakāh* in modern times
- *Zakāh* on unlawful money
- *Zakāh* on retirement pension or end of service award
- *Zakāh* and satisfying one's essential needs
- The concept of ownership and its implications on the due *zakāh*
- A contemporary *Fiqh* perspective on investing *zakāh* money
- Attracting the hearts toward Islam through *zakāh*
- Managing *zakāh* collection and distribution

The Renaissance of *Fiqh*

These efforts that are making waves all over the Muslim world and serve to re-erect *Fiqh* from its stumble and reintroduce its distinct heavenly glory are great efforts that will surely yield their fruits by the permission of Allah, the Most High.

In the following section, I will try to correct a mistake that I believe many jurists and reasearchers fall into, in order to further improve our strategies, and eliminate a bit of their imperfection. I would like to point out that – from my perspective – the potential fruits of these marvelous efforts will not be harvested without a specific class of jurists carrying them out. I will briefly identify this special class of scholars upon which our hopes can be fastened.

The path to producing these types of jurists is simple. I will point out the three branches of knowledge that a *mujtahid* needs and the necessary amount of each that one is required to possess. I will also point out how the earlier generations paved the way for these three sciences. Then, I will conclude by discussing two vital matters for every *mujtahid* jurist: the inherent talent for *Fiqh* and the concern for the jurist's righteousness.

وهـذه الهيئـة لا تختـص بدولـة أو مؤسسـة مـن مؤسسـات الـزكاة، وتجمـع في عضويتهـا فقهـاء شرعيـين معنيـين، وعلـماء الاختصاصـات ذات الصلـة بهـا.

ومن القضايا التي بحثتها في مؤتمراتها وندواتها ما يأتي:

- الأصول المحاسبية للتقويم في الأموال الزكوية.
- زكاة المال الحرام.
- زكاة مكافأة نهاية الخدمة والراتب التقاعدي.
- الزكاة ورعاية الحاجات الأساسية الخاصة.
- مبدأ التمليك ومدى اعتباره في صرف الزكاة.
- استثمار أموال الزكاة رؤية فقهية معاصرة.
- تأليف القلوب على الإسلام بأموال الصدقات.
- إدارة والي مال الزكاة «أو مصرف العاملين».

كيف ننهـض بالفقـــــه؟

هـذه الجهـود التـي يمـوج بهـا العـالم الإسـلامي الهادفـة إلى إقامـة الفقـه مـن عثرتـه وإبـرازه في حلـة قشـيبة واضحـة المعـالم، جهـود مشـكورة، وسـتؤتي ثمارهـا إن شـاء اللـه تعـالى.

وسـأحاول في هـذا المبحـث أن أُقـوّم خطـأ أظـن أن كثـيراً مـن الباحثـين مـن الفقهـاء يقعـون فيـه حتـى يتحـدد المسـار، ويُقـوَّم شيء مـن الاعوجـاج، وأحـب أن أبـين في هـذه النظـرة أن الثمار المرجوة مـن خـلال الجهـد الدائـب لـن تظهـر مـا لم يقـم بهـا نـوع خـاص مـن الفقهـاء، وسـأحدد في هـذه العجالـة نوعيـة هـذا الصنـف الـذي يمكـن أن تُعقَـد عليـه الآمـال.

والطريـق لتخريـج هـذا الـضرب مـن الفقهـاء ميسرة، وسـأبين المقـدار الـلازم مـن ثلاثـة علـوم يحتـاج إليهـا المجتهـد، كـما سـأبين كيـف مهـد السـابقون الطريق في هـذه العلـوم الثلاثة، وفي الختـام سـأتحدث عـن أمريـن ضروريـين للفقيـه المجتهـد، وهـما: إيجـاد الملكـة الفقهيـة، والعنايـة بصـلاح الفقهـاء.

Correcting Our Approach to ***Fiqh***

In this era, many jurists tried to escape the epidemic of *madhhab* fanaticism and attempted to consider all the various *Fiqh* approaches with fairness and objectivity. They accepted the notion that any of these *ijtihād*-based views in *Fiqh* can be a possible understanding of the Islamic Sharia and began searching the *madhhab*(s) to choose the most suitable opinions for the spheres of codification, compilation, education and giving *fatwa*.

This phenomena is both useful and necessary, for it resets the *Fiqh* procedure to its correct functioning and rids the people of their awful *madhhab* fanaticism. It opens the eyes of the jurists and researchers to a broader spectrum of interpretations and broadens the horizons of their thinking. However, this approach brought along a shade of deviance that must be corrected, lest it drown the jurists and researchers in its depths.

We can summarize the mistakes that this approach was subjected to in a number of points:

1) Those who adopted this approach consider the various views of the different *madhhab*(s) to all be legitimate Sharia rulings which represent the Islamic Sharia. Based on that perception, they select from between these different views whatever appears more beneficial to them. This is problematic because there are major differences between the Sharia and the jurists' understanding of the Sharia. The opinions of the jurists are subject to error, while the Sharia is not. The opinions of the jurists many times contradict one another, while the Sharia is void of a single contradiction.

2) The type of comparative studies prominent among many researchers in this era fall short of intellectually preparing jurists to exercise *ijtihād*. This is because these researchers are merely weighing between the different views and opinions. As a result, the researcher usually remains incapable of understanding how rulings are extracted and deduced to begin with, for his preferred choice is not made based on an impartial inference. Rather, it is usually based on the fact that he assumes this view to be most appropriate for the demands of his situation and the needs of his age.

تقويم المسار الفقهي:

حاول كثير من الفقهاء في هذا العصر التخلص من العصبية المذهبية، والنظر إلى التراث الفقهي نظرة فيها إنصاف واعتدال، فعدوا جميع الآراء والاجتهادات الفقهية فهماً للشريعة الإسلامية، وأخذوا يبحثون في هذه المذاهب لاختيار الأصلح والأفضل في مجال التقنين والتدوين والتعليم والإفتاء.

وهذا اتجاه جيد وضروري، وهو يعيد الأمر إلى نصابه، ويخلص الناس من العصبية المقيتة، وهو يفتح أعين الفقهاء والباحثين على الفقه الإسلامي كله، وبذلك يجدون المجال واسعاً، والأفق أكثر رحابة، إلا أن هذا الاتجاه يحمل في طياته شيئاً من الانحراف ينبغي تقويمه قبل أن يغرق الباحثون والفقهاء في المضي فيه.

ويمكن أن نوجز الأخطاء التي تلبس بها هذا الاتجاه في عدة أمور:

الأول: أن أصحاب هذا الاتجاه يرون أن كل الآراء التي في المذاهب الإسلامية أحكام شرعية، تمثل الشريعة الإسلامية، ومن ثم فإنهم يقومون بالانتقاء من الآراء المختلفة بحسب ما يبدو لهم أنه الأنسب والأصلح، وهذا غير سديد، فإن فقه الفقهاء للشريعة غير الشريعة، وآراء الفقهاء فيها الصواب وفيها الخطأ، ثم إن الاجتهادات والآراء الفقهية تتضارب وتتعارض، والشريعة الإسلامية صواب كلها، وليس فيها تعارض ولا تضارب.

الثاني: الدراسة المقارنة التي اعتمدها كثير من الباحثين في هذا العصر قاصرة عن تهيئة الذهنية الاجتهادية، فالذي يقوم به الدارسون والباحثون إنما هو الموازنة بين الآراء والأقوال، ويبقى الباحث في الأغلب عاجزاً عن التعرف على طريقة استنباط الأحكام؛ لأن اختياره للآراء لم يكن قائماً على قوة المدرك، بل على ما يظهر له غالباً من موافقة هذا الحكم لمتطلبات الواقع وحاجات الزمان.

3) Many researchers considered the views of the sects within Islam to be equivelant to the views of the Companions, the four *madhhab*(s) and the major scholars of mainstream Islam. In reality, when the views of the deviant sects of Islam contradict the views of *Ahl as-Sunnah wal-Jamā'ah,* they are to be rejected. Some of the incorrect rulings wherein some deviant sects violated the consensus of *Ahl as-Sunnah* are: the permissibility of *mut'ah* (temporary) marriage, the impermissibility of a Muslim marrying a Jewish or Christian woman and women only inheriting wealth and not qualifying for land or estates. Similarly, of the rulings wherein the *Khawārij* sect opposed the consensus of *Ahl as-Sunnah* are: their belief that the previously married fornicator is flogged and not stoned, their belief that only the mother and sister via nursing are impermissible for marriage and their belief that marrying a woman and her aunts – paternal and maternal – is permissible.
It is mandatory that the jurists and researchers only consider the opinions that are based on evidence and only choose the opinion or view with the strongest evidence. By doing that, we can accurately consider the vast resources of *Fiqh* works through the lenses of the revealed texts, and this will illuminate for us the path, reveal for us the mistakes, advocate the truth and expose us to those best skilled at juristic deduction based on sound principles.

The Ideal Jurist

We do not wish to produce jurists like those who existed in the era of *taqlīd*. Rather, we need those who deserved such a title in the age of the Companions, Successors and great *Imām*(s). The jurist in their times is what we now call a *mujtahid*; until one is qualified to exercised *ijtihād*, one would not be called a jurist among them. At-Tahānawi said, "*Fiqh* is the science of the practical Islamic rulings and their detailed evidences. A *faqīh* (jurist) is the one who mastered this science, also known as a *mujtahid*. At-Taftazāni, the verifying scholar, said in his footnotes on [al-'Aḍudi], 'It appears from their words that a jurist who is not a *mujtahid* is something unimaginable, and there can never be a *mujtahid* that is not a jurist.'"[1]

1 *Kashf Iṣṭilāḥāt al-Funūn* 5/1157 by at-Tahānawi

الثالث: عد كثير من الباحثين جميع فقه الفرق الإسلامية مساوياً لفقه الصحابة، وفقه مذاهب علماء الأمصار والمذاهب الإسلامية، مع أن فقه الفرق الإسلامية المخالف لفقه أهل السنة والجماعة مرفوض، لا يجوز الأخذ به، فمن ذلك الأحكام التي خالف فيها بعض الفرق إجماع أهل السنة؛ كتجويز نكاح المتعة، وحرمة تزوج المسلم من الكتابية، وعدم توريث النساء من الأرض والعقار، ووقف توريثهن على المال المنقول فقط، ومن ذلك الأحكام التي خالف فيها الخوارج إجماع أهل السنة، فقد ذهبوا إلى أن الزاني المحصن لا يرجم، بل يجلد، ولم يحرموا من الرضاع إلا الأم والأخت، وأجازوا الجمع بين المرأة وعمتها، والمرأة وخالتها.

ويجب أن يتجه الباحثون والفقهاء إلى الفقه القائم على الدليل، ويختارون الرأي أو القول الأقوى دليلاً، وبذلك ننظر إلى هذه الثروة الفقهية العظيمة من خلال النصوص، فتتضح لنا السبل، وتكشف لنا الأخطاء، وينصر الحق، وتظهر الملكات الفقهية التي تحسن الانتقاء على أسس قويمة.

الفقيه الذي نريد:

لا نريد إيجاد الفقيه بالمعنى المعروف في عصر التقليد، وإنما نريد الفقيه الذي كان يستحق هذا الاسم في عصر الصحابة والتابعين والأئمة، فقد كان الفقيه عندهم هو المجتهد عندنا، وإذا لم يبلغ درجة الاجتهاد لا يطلق عليه اسم الفقيه، يقول التهانوي: «الفقه: العلم بالأحكام الشرعية العملية من أدلتها التفصيلية، والفقيه من اتصف بهذا العلم، وهو المجتهد، قال المحقق التفتازاني في حاشيته على العضدي: ظاهر كلام القوم أنه لا يتصور فقيه غير مجتهد، ولا مجتهد غير فقيه على الإطلاق»(١).

١ كشاف اصطلاحات الفنون للتهانوي: ٥/ ١١٥٧.

Aḥmad ibn Ḥamdān al-Ḥanbali said, “A real jurist is someone fully qualified to identify the rulings on a multitude of matters at will. This skill is based on his knowing the major Sharia rulings, then applying *ijtihād* and due consideration, and having them readily available in his memory. Therefore, every jurist is in fact a *mujtahid* and judge.”[1] In those ages, they would not permit anyone to give legal opinions or assume judgeship until one reached this degree of qualification.[2]

Presently, the road to becoming a *mujtahid* jurist has been paved smooth, and it is easier today than it was during the time of the righteous predecessors. The sciences needed have already been compiled, printed, organized and chaptered. The Qur’an is available, as are its sciences. The Sunnah and its collections are easily accessible, as well as the books that explain both the Qur’an and Sunnah. These are all fruits of the gargantuan efforts contributed by the scholars. They spent their lives collecting and documenting, many of which would journey for years to acquire and record this information.

As-Subki reports that Abū Shāmah said, “Indeed, Allah has facilitated – praise be to Him – the documentation of the hadith(s) that have been confirmed authentic and the avoidance of those which are weak via the collections of the *ḥuffāẓ* of Hadith, such as *Ṣaḥīḥ al-Bukhāri*, *Ṣaḥīḥ Muslim*, *al-Mustadrak*, the collections Ibn Khuzaymah, at-Tirmidhi, Abū Dāwūd, an-Nasā’i, Ibn Mājah, Ibn Ḥibbān, ad-Dāraquṭni and al-Bayhaqi. Therefore, there is no excuse for anyone to not rely on these books. The same applies for the *Fiqh* rulings that are based on linguistic implications; this was all made available by the scholars of the Arabic language. Hence, reaching the degree of *ijtihād* has been eased greatly and is definitely easier today than it was before – if it was not for the lowly ambitions and absence of those who would realize [that].”[3]

1 *Ṣifat al-Fatwā* 14
2 Ibid: 5
3 *Ma‘ni Qawl al-Muṭṭalibi: Idhā Saḥ al-Ḥadīth fa Huwa Madhhaby* by as-Subki. It has been printed within *Majmū‘at ar-Rasā’il al-Muniriyyah* 3/107.

وقال أحمد بن حمدان الحنبلي: «الفقيه على الحقيقة من له أهلية تامة يمكنه أن يعرف الحكم بها إذا شاء معرفته جملة كثيرة، عرفها من أمهات مسائل الأحكام الشرعية الفروعية العملية بالاجتهاد والتأمل، وحضورها عنده، فكل فقيه حقيقة مجتهد قاض»[١]، ولم يكونوا يجيزون في تلك العصور لمن لم يبلغ هذه المرتبة الفتيا ولا القضاء[٢].

والطريق التي تؤدي إلى بلوغ مرتبة الفقيه المجتهد اليوم ميسرة مذللة، وهي اليوم أسهل منها في عهد السلف الصالح، فالعلوم التي يحتاجها مدونة مطبوعة، مرتبة مهذبة مبوبة، هذا القرآن وهذه علومه، وتلك السنة ودواوينها، والكتب التي شرحت الكتاب والسنة، وهي ثمرة جهود هائلة من العلماء، أفنوا أعمارهم في تدوينها وتحصيلها، وكان الرجل منهم يقضي السنوات الطوال في الرحلة والتنقل لتحصيلها وتدوينها، يقول السبكي: «ومما قاله أبو شامة إن الله يسر- وله الحمد- الوقوف على ما ثبت من الأحاديث، وتجنب ما ضعف منها، مما جمعه الحفاظ؛ كالصحيحين والمستدرك عليهما وابن خزيمة والترمذي وأبي داود والنسائي وابن ماجه وابن حبان والدارقطني والبيهقي، فلا عذر في ترك الاشتغال بها، وكذلك المسائل المثبتة الفقهية المبنية على اللغة، كل ذلك إلى علماء اللسان، فالتوصل إلى الاجتهاد سهل ميسور، وأسهل منه قبل اليوم لولا قلة همم المتأخرين وعدم المعتبرين»[٣].

١ صفة الفتوى: ١٤.
٢ المصدر السابق: ٥.
٣ معنى قول المطلبي: «إذا صح الحديث فهو مذهبي» للسبكي، وهو مطبوع ضمن مجموعة الرسائل المنيرية: ٣/ ١٠٧.

The Required Amount of Knowledge in Arabic, Qur'an and Hadith

1) The Arabic Language

The jurist must have a thorough understanding of the Arabic language because the Qur'an which encapsulated the Sharia is Arabic, and the Sunnah which explains it is Arabic as well. The Arabic sciences are grammar, morphology, linguistics, semantics and rhetoric. The amount of Arabic required for the jurists, as al-Ghazāli said, is "that which enables one to understand the language of the Arabs and what they customarily intend by their terms, so that one can discern from their statements that which is definitive, vague, explicit, general, specific, literal, figurative, decisive, speculative, absolute, definitive, explicit, implicit, etc."[1] Al-Ghazāli did not stipulate "that a person reach the degree of al-Khalīl or al-Mubarrid, whereby one masters the entire language and becomes an expert in grammar. Rather, the amount which clarifies the Qur'an and Sunnah, allows one to grasp their words and illustrates their intended meanings [is sufficient]."[2]

2) The Noble Qur'an

Imām as-Shāfi'i (may Allah bestow mercy upon him) stipulated that a jurist memorize the entire Qur'an. This is only befitting for someone who partakes in this noble field, especially since the jurists must have a pious heart and a sound creed, and the earliest class of jurists all fulfilled this condition. However, this is not mandatory for producing jurists that are scholarly in the practical detailed rulings. Rather, it suffices them to memorize the Qur'anic verses pertaining to legal rulings.[3]

المقدار اللازم من العربية والقرآن والحديث

١- العلم بالعربية:

لابد للفقيه من أن يكون عالماً باللغة العربية؛ لأن القرآن الذي نزل بهذه الشريعة عربي، ولأن السنة التي هي بيانه جاءت بلسان عربي، وعلوم العربية هي النحو والصرف واللغة والمعاني والبيان، والقدر المحتاج إليه منها كما يقول الغزالي: «الذي يفهم به خطاب العرب وعاداتهم في الاستعمال إلى حد يميز بين صريح الكلام وظاهره ومجمله، وحقيقته ومجازه، وعامه وخاصة، ومحكمه ومتشابهه، ومطلقه ومقيده، ونصه وفحواه، ولحنه ومفهومه»(١)، ولا يشترط الغزالي: «أن يبلغ درجة الخليل والمبرد وأن يعرف جميع اللغة ويتعمق في النحو، بل القدر الذي يتعلق بالكتاب والسنة، ويستولي على مواقع الخطاب، ودرك حقائق المقاصد منه»(٢).

٢- القرآن الكريم:

وقد اشترط الشافعي- رحمه الله- أن يحفظ القرآن كله، وهذا هو الذي يليق بمن يتصدر لهذه المهمة الجليلة، خاصة وأن الفقيه ينبغي أن يكون فقيه النفس، سليم الاعتقاد، وهكذا كان النمط الأول من الفقهاء، إلا أن ذلك غير واجب لتخريج الفقهاء العلماء بالفروع؛ لأن القسم الذي يحتاج إليه الفقيه من القرآن هو آيات الأحكام(٣).

---

1 *Al-Mustaṣfā* 1/352

2 Ibid

3 We previously mentioned the compilations that collected the verses and hadith(s) pertaining to rulings.

١ المستصفى: ١/ ٣٥٢.

٢ المصدر السابق.

٣ سبق ذكر المؤلفات في آيات الأحكام وأحاديث الأحكام.

3) The Prophetic Sunnah

It is necessary that those who study *Fiqh* be well-grounded in the Prophetic Sunnah. Early scholars such as Sufyān ath-Thawri, Yaḥyā ibn Maʿīn, Aḥmad ibn Ḥanbal, ash-Shāfiʿi, al-Bukhāri, Muslim, Abū Dāwūd and others exerted their utmost efforts in collecting and compiling the Sunnah. One of them would journey for months, traveling from country to country, in pursuit of the hadith(s). Then, they arranged for us the Prophetic hadith(s) and chapters, so as to aid the student of knowledge in locating them and benefittng from them.

Some of the exceptional scholars like al-Bukhāri, Muslim and Ibn Khuzaymah put together compilations of only authentic hadith(s) so the students of knowlege could take from them while reassured of the source. Other scholars verified the books that contained a mix of authentic and weak hadith(s), like what Shaykh Aḥmad Shākir did with *al-Musnad* of Imām Aḥmad, and what Shaykh Nāṣir ad-Dīn al-Albāni did with *as-Sunan* of Abū Dāwūd.

Some scholars gathered many of the Sunnah collections into one compilation, as was the case in *Mishkāt al-Maṣābīḥ* and *Jāmiʿ al-Uṣūl*.

Whoever wishes to become advanced in *Fiqh* must dwell on rehearsing the books of the Sunnah, especially their strictly authentic collections if they are not yet capable of discerning the authentic from unauthentic chains of transmission.

Recognizing the Authentic and Weak Hadith(s)

As we discussed, the jurist must understand the principles of Hadith terminology. This is what enables one to recognize the authentic and weak hadith(s), as well as the books that were composed regarding the narrators of these hadith(s). We have already explained these matters in a previous unit.

٣- السنة النبوية:

ومما ينبغي أن يشتغل به السائرون في طريق الفقه السنة النبوية، وقد أتعب العلماء الأوائل أمثال سفيان الثوري، ويحيى بن معين، وأحمد بن حنبل، والشافعي والبخاري ومسلم وأبو داود وغيرهم أنفسهم في طلب السنة وجمعها وتدوينها، فكان الواحد منهم يرحل في طلب الحديث من قطر إلى قطر، ويقضي في سبيل ذلك شهوراً، وقد رتبوا لنا الأحاديث النبوية وبوبوها؛ كي يسهل على طلبة العلم الاستفادة منها والرجوع إليها.

وقد أفرد بعض العلماء الأفذاذ كتباً خاصة بالأحاديث الصحيحة بحيث يستقي منها طلبة العلم وهم آمنون من صفاء المورد؛ أمثال البخاري ومسلم وابن خزيمة، وقام آخرون بتخريج أحاديث الكتاب التي اختلط فيها الصحيح بالضعيف كما فعل الشيخ أحمد شاكر بمسند الإمام أحمد، والشيخ ناصر الدين الألباني بسنن الإمام أبي داود.

وقد قام بعض العلماء بجمع كثير من كتب السنة في كتاب واحد كما هو الحال في مشكاة المصابيح وجامع الأصول.

وعلى من يريد أن يبلغ في الفقه مرتبة متقدمة أن يديم النظر في كتب السنة، وليحرص على النظر في الكتب التي التزمت بإيراد الصحيح إن لم يكن بصيراً بمعرفة الإسناد والتمييز بين الصحيح والضعيف.

معرفة الصحيح من الضعيف:

لابد للفقيه- كما أشرت- من معرفة قواعد مصطلح الحديث التي يتم بها معرفة الصحيح والضعيف، ومعرفة الكتب التي وضعت في رجال الحديث، وقد سبق بيان ذلك والحديث عنه.

Becoming Skilled at *Fiqh*

Not everyone that memorizes the verses and hadith(s) pertaining to rulings, nor those who read up on the views of the jurists, will automatically become jurists themselves. The proof to that is the statement of the Messenger (ﷺ), "Perhaps, a bearer of *Fiqh* [may convey] to one who is more comprehending than him, and perhaps a bearer of *Fiqh* may not himself be a *faqīh*."[1]

Of the statements reported about Imām Mālik in this regard was, "*Fiqh* is not a matter of memorizing many rulings. Rather, *Fiqh* is a light that Allah grants to whoever of His creation He wills."[2] An example of this is what Ibn 'Abdil-Barr reported about Abū Yūsuf, Abū Ḥanīfah's companion, who said, "When al-A'mash and I were once alone, he asked me about a specific matter, and I answered him. He said, 'Where did you get this answer, O Ya'qūb?' I said, 'From the hadith you narrated to me,' and I narrated it back to him. He said, 'O Ya'qūb, I had memorized this hadith before your parents ever met, but I just now understood its meaning.'"[3]

For this reason, they likened the one who memorizes the hadith(s) but does not comprehend their meanings to the pharmacist that memorizes the names of all the drugs but does not know who to prescribe them to.

Becoming skilled at *Fiqh* is achieved through two matters:

The **first** is divinely-gifted talent, which people have no control over. Imām ash-Shāfi'i (may Allah bestow mercy upon him) was one of those who were granted this. It was noticed in him by Imām Mālik (may Allah bestow mercy upon him) when ash-Shāfi'i first came as a youngster to learn under him. Upon discovering it, Mālik said to him, "Indeed, Allah has cast a light upon your heart, so do not extinguish it with sins."[4]

1 Narrated by Abū Dāwud (3660) and others. Its chain is authentic, and its referencing was previously mentioned.
2 *Jāmi' Bayān al-'Ilm* 2/21
3 Ibid: 2/31
4 *Al-Ikmāl fī Asmā' ar-Rijāl* by al-Khatīb al-Baghdādi. It was attached to the back end of *Mishkāt al-Maṣābīḥ* 3/793.

تكوين الملكة الفقهية

ليس كل من حفظ نصوص آيات الأحكام وأحاديث الأحكام ونظر في مسائل الفقه أصبح فقيهاً، والدليل على ذلك قول الرسول ﷺ: «**رب حامل فقه إلى من هو أفقه منه، ورب حامل فقه ليس بفقيه**»(١).

ومن الأقوال التي أثرت عن الإمام مالك: «ليس الفقه بكثرة المسائل، ولكن الفقه نور يؤتيه الله من يشاء من خلقه»(٢)، ومن الأمثلة التي تروى في هذا الموضع ما ذكره ابن عبد البر بإسناده إلى أبي يوسف صاحب أبي حنيفة قال: سألني الأعمش عن مسألة، وأنا وهو لا غير، فأجبته، فقال لي: من أين قلت هذا يا يعقوب؟ فقلت: بالحديث الذي حدثتني أنت، ثم حدثته، فقال لي: يا يعقوب، إني لأحفظ هذا الحديث من قبل أن يجتمع أبواك، ما عرفت تأويله إلا الآن(٣).

ولذا شبهوا من يحمل الأحاديث ثم لا يفقه معانيها بالصيدلاني الذي يحفظ الأدوية ولا يدري كيف يستعملها، وفي هذا يقول الشاعر(٤):

إن من يحمل الأحاديث ولا // يعرف فيه التأويل كالصيدلاني
حين يلقي لديه كل دواء // وهو بالطب جاهل غير وان

والملكة الفقهية تتأتى بأمرين: **الأول**: هبة إلهية، وهذه لا حيلة للعبد بها، وممن رزقها الإمام الشافعي- رحمه الله تعالى- وقد تبينها فيه الإمام مالك- رحمه الله تعالى- عندما قدم عليه الشافعي وهو غلام يطلب العلم عليه، وقال له: «إن الله ألقى على قلبك نوراً، فلا تطفئه بالمعصية»(٥).

١ رواه أبو داود (٣٦٦٠)، وغيره، وإسناده صحيح، وقد سبق تخريجه.
٢ جامع بيان العلم: ٢/ ٢١.
٣ المصدر السابق: ٢/ ٣١.
٤ المصدر السابق: ٢/ ٨٤، والشاعر هو أبو محمد اليزيدي.
٥ الإكمال في أسماء الرجال للخطيب التبريزي، ملحق في آخر مشكاة

Aṣ-Ṣanʿāni said, "It's no secret that *ijtihād* is a gift from Allah which He bestows upon whoever of His slaves He wishes. Not everyone who learns the sciences applies them accordingly, and not everyone who learns the principles remembers to employ them when a case arises that has no specific evidence addressing it."[1]

This skill we speak of, which aṣ-Ṣanʿāni calls "a gift from Allah," was described as an "inherent talent" by Imām ash-Shāfiʿi (may Allah bestow mercy upon him). When Imām ash-Shāfiʿi was discussing the conditions that must be met for someone to qualify for giving *fatwa*, he said, "It is not permissible for anyone to give *fatwa* in the religion of Allah except for one with thorough knowledge of the Qur'an, its abrogating verses as well as its abrogated… and must also be well-versed on the hadith(s) of the Messenger of Allah (ﷺ)… and must also be skilled in the Arabic language and its poetry… and must also be familiar with the differences between the scholars of the Muslim world… and after all that, must be inherently talented."[2]

The **second** is training and practice, preferably at the hands of a sharp, insightful jurist that can gradually advance his students along the stairway of *Fiqh*. Other factors that develop one's skill in *Fiqh* are:

- Frequent rehearsal of the Noble Qur'an and the Prophetic Sunnah
- Studying the books that interpret the Qur'an and Hadith
- Becoming familiar with the positions of the scholars
- Sitting in the circles of knowledge
- Being keen to act upon one's knowledge, for this evokes of the blessings of knowledge.

1 *Irshād an-Nuqqād ilā Taysīr al-Ijtihād*, taken from *Majmūʿat ar-Rasāʾil al-Munīriyyah* 1/21
2 *Iʿlām al-Muwaqqiʿīn* 1/48

يقول الصنعاني: «لا يخفى أن الاجتهاد موهبة من الله، يهبه لمن يشاء من العباد، فما كل من أحرز الفنون أجرى من قواعدها العيون، ولا كل من عرف القواعد استحضرها عند ورود الحادثة التي يفتقر إلى تطبيقها على الأدلة والشواهد.

وما كل من قاد الجياد يسوسها

ولا كل من أجرى يقال له مجري»(١)

وهذا الذي سميناه ملكة، وقال عنه الصنعاني هو «موهبة من الله» سماه الإمام الشافعي- رحمه الله-: قريحة، فقد تحدث الشافعي- رحمه الله- عن الشروط التي ينبغي أن تتوافر فيمن يتصدر للفتوى، فقال: «لا يحل لأحد أن يفتي في دين الله إلا رجلاً عارفاً بكتاب الله بناسخه ومنسوخه... ويكون بعد ذلك بصيراً بحديث رسول الله ﷺ... ويكون بصيراً باللغة بصيراً بالشعر... ويكون بعد هذا مشرفاً على اختلاف الأمصار، وتكون له قريحة بعد هذا»(٢).

والثاني: بالدربة والمران، ويحسن أن يكون ذلك على يد فقيه عليم بصير، يحسن الترقي بتلاميذه في مدارج الفقه، ومما يكون الملكة الفقهية النظر في كتاب الله وسنة رسوله ﷺ، وفي كتب التفسير، وشروح كتب الحديث، والتعرف إلى أقوال العلماء، والجلوس في مجالس العلم، والحرص على العمل بما يعمل؛ فذلك من بركة العلم.

المصابيح: ٣/ ٧٩٣.

١ إرشاد النقاد إلى تيسير الاجتهاد- مجموعة الرسائل المنيرية: ١/ ٢١.
٢ إعلام الموقعين: ١/ ٤٨.

Were a person to follow these steps, that person would become a jurist. If that person were asked about a matter or gives a lesson on a subject, its evidences and the scholar's statements about it are readily in mind. If this person wishes, it is also easy for this person to return to its references in the books of Quranic interpretation, Hadith, *Fiqh* or *Uṣūl*. Ibn Ḥazm said, "The term *Fiqh* applies to a quality that resides within a person, namely one's understanding of what one knows. It also denotes knowing the actual meanings of the Qur'an and Hadith, after having studied them, and that being present in one's mind to call upon it whenever one pleases."[1]

A Jurist's Ignorance of Some Rulings Does Not Exclude One from Being a Jurist

If the jurist is skilled in *Fiqh* and well-grounded in understanding the rulings, then it is not harmful to be ignorant of some rulings or undecided about them. This was the case with the greatest scholars among the Companions and those after them. On countless occassions, the pious caution of the early jurists drove them to say "I do not know" when asked about a matter that was unclear to them. Jalāl al-Maḥalli said, "Covering all branches of knowledge [to qualify as a jurist] does not contradict Imām Mālik's saying 'I don't know' about 36 out of 40 questions presented to him – for without doubt, Imām Mālik was of the greatest jurists. This was by virtue of him being equipped to understand the rulings, and deliberate regarding them. Using the term 'knowledgeable' about those equipped for a science is a known practice. For instance, saying that a person is knowledgeable in grammar does not mean that every detailed grammatical fact is present in that person's mind. Rather, it means that this person is equipped to call upon it when needed."[2]

1 *Iḥkām al-Aḥkām* 5/697

2 *Sharḥ al-Jalāl al-Maḥalli 'alā Matn Jam' al-Jawāmi'* 1/45

فإذا كان كذلك أصبح فقيهاً، إذا سئل عن مسألة أو حاضر في موضوع استحضر الأدلة وكلام العلماء، وسهل عليه أن يعود إلى الموضوع في مظانه من كتب التفسير والحديث والفقه والأصول، يقول ابن حزم: «اسم الفقه واقع على صفة في المرء، وهي فهمه لما عنده، وتنبهه على حقيقة معاني ألفاظ القرآن والحديث ووقوفه عليها، وحضور كل ذلك في ذكره متى أراده»(١).

جهل الفقيه ببعض المسائل لا يخرجه من دائرة الفقهاء:

إذا كانت للفقيه ملكة فقهية، وكان متهيئاً للعلم بالأحكام- لا يضيره أن لا يعلم بعض الأحكام الشرعية أو يتوقف فيها، فقد كان هذا حال أكابر العلماء من الصحابة ومن بعدهم، وكم كان الفقيه الورع يسأل عن المسألة فلا يتبين له فيها وجه الصواب، فيقول: لا أدري، يقول الجلال المحلي: «وكون المراد بالأحكام جميعها لا ينافيه قول مالك وهو من أكابر الفقهاء في ست وثلاثين مسألة من أربعين سئل عنها: لا أدري؛ لأنه متهيئ للعلم بأحكامها بمعاودة النظر، وإطلاق العلم على مثل هذا التهيؤ شائع عرفاً، يقال: فلان يعلم النحو، ولا يراد أن جميع مسائله حاضره عنده على التفصيل، بل إنه متهيئ لذلك»(٢).

١ إحكام الأحكام: ٥/ ٦٩٧.

٢ شرح الجلال المحلي على متن جمع الجوامع: ١/ ٤٥.

The Righteousness of the Jurist

The type of jurist we need is the righteous, pious jurist that fears Allah and obeys Him. Among the first generations, it was only these types of scholars that were seen as deserving of being called a jurist.

This is the jurist whose *fatwa* should be accepted. As for the jurists who acquire knowledge of the Sharia sciences but do not couple that with piety, they are a tribulation to this *Ummah*. Instead of treating its illnesses, they became one of the factors that led to its misery and the loss of its religion. This is because their misguidance entails the misguidance of the creation, for the people act upon their *fatwa*(s), and the enemies of Islam could manipulate them for their interests.

One of the conditions stipulated by al-Ghazāli for a *mujtahid* jurist's *fatwa* to be accepted was that jurist's uprightness. He said, "The second condition is that he be an upright person who avoids the sins that tarnish his credibility. This is a condition for the permissibility of relying on his *fatwa*; whoever is not upright should not have their *fatwa* accepted."[1]

In later times, many jurists drifted away from the qualities of the first jurists. To them, *Fiqh* was nothing but a craft by which they earned a living. Listen to how Ibn Khaldūn described the jurists of his time by saying, "Know that to most of the jurists of this age, and its surrounding ages, the Sharia was a bundle of statements they carried, regarding how to perform rituals and how to carry out transactions, which they orate to those interested in acting upon them. Even with the greatest of them, that is their utmost commitment [to knowledge], except in a few cases. On the other hand, the *salaf* (may Allah be pleased with them) and the pious Muslims throughout history carried the Sharia by infusing it with their lives."[2]

1 *Al-Mustaṣfā* 2/350 by al-Ghazāli
2 *Muqaddimat Ibn Khaldūn* 224

صلاح الفقيه

الفقيه الذي نريده هو الفقيه الورع التقي الذي يخشى الله ويتقيه، وهذا هو الذي كان يدعى فقيهاً في الصدر الأول.

وهو الفقيه الذي تقبل فتواه، أما الفقهاء الذين يحصلون العلم الشرعي ولا يجمعون معه التقوى فهؤلاء بلاء على هذه الأمة، وبدلاً من أن يعالجوا أدواءها يصبحون من الأسباب التي تؤدي إلى شقائها وضياع دينها؛ لأن ضلالهم يسبب ضلال الخلق، فالناس يصدرون عن فتاويهم، ولأن أعداء الإسلام قد يُسَخِّرون هؤلاء في مصالحهم.

وقد عد الغزالي من الشروط التي تشترط في قبول فتوى الفقيه المجتهد: العدالة، قال «الشرط الثاني: أن يكون عدلاً مجتنباً للمعاصي القادحة في العدالة، وهذا يشترط لجواز الاعتماد على فتواه، فمن ليس عدلاً فلا تقبل فتواه»[١].

وقد ابتعد كثير من الفقهاء في العصور المتأخرة عما كان يتصف به الفقهاء الأول وأصبح الفقه بضاعة عندهم، انظر إلى ما يصف به ابن خلدون فقهاء عصره: «اعلم أن الفقهاء في الأغلب لهذا العهد وما احتف به إنما حملوا الشريعة أقوالاً في كيفية الأعمال في العبادات، وكيفية القضاء في المعاملات، ينصونها على من يحتاج إلى العمل بها، هذه غاية أكابرهم، ولا يتصفون إلا بالأقل منها وفي بعض الأحوال، والسلف- رضوان الله عليهم- وأهل الدين والورع من المسلمين حملوا الشريعة اتصافاً بها»[٢]، ثم يقسم الفقهاء ثلاثة أقسام فيقول: «فمن حملها اتصافاً بها وتحقيقاً دون نقل فهو من الوارثين.

١ المستصفى للغزالي: ٢/ ٣٥٠.
٢ مقدمة ابن خلدون: ٢٢٤.

Then, Ibn Khaldūn continued to categorize the jurists into three types and said, "Those who carry it (i.e., knowledge of the Sharia) by infusing it with their lives [via practice], but not transmitting it [to others], then they are of its inheritors. As for those who combine between both matters, then these are the scholars, and they are its real inheritors – like the jurists among the Successors, predecessors, and four *Imām*(s). The third category of jurists, who do not [even] practice these acts of worship, then this type has not inherited anything whatsoever. They merely have memorized phrases which they orate to us regarding how to perform certain practices, and these are the majority of the jurists in our age."[1]

In the eyes of the first generations, a person of *Fiqh* was the one who knows the right path to the Hereafter, refines one's own soul, abstains from the sins that corrupt one's deeds, sees this world as insignificant, earnestly aspires for the Hereafter and has a heart captivated by the fear of Allah. The Most High said, **"For there should separate from every division of them a group [remaining] to obtain understanding in the religion and warn their people when they return to them..."**[2]

This kind of *Fiqh* is what effectively warns the people, not the complex details that are found in the *Fiqh* rulings of divorce, emancipation, accusations of adultery, sales and renting. These matters do not warn the people – as mentioned in the verse – or develop within them the fear of Allah. In fact, focusing on only these sciences hardens the heart and makes it barren of any god-fearing qualities. For that, Allah described those who fear the slaves more than the Lord of the slaves as not having any *Fiqh*, **"You [believers] evoke more fear within their breasts than Allah. That is because they are a people who do not *yafqahūn* (understand)."**[3] Here, Allah attributed their lesser fear of Allah, and their greater fear of being harmed by the people, to their lack of *Fiqh*.

1 Ibid – slightly modified
2 Sūrat at-Tawbah – Verse 122
3 Sūrat al-Ḥashr – Verse 13

ومن اجتمع له الأمران فهو العالم، وهو الوارث على الحقيقة مثل فقهاء التابعين والسلف والأئمة الأربعة، ومن اقتفى طريقهم وجاء على أثرهم.

والفريق الثالث الفقيه الذي ليس بعابد، فهذا لم يرث شيئاً، إنما هو صاحب أقوال ينصها علينا في كيفيات العمل، وهؤلاء أكثر الفقهاء في عصرنا»[١].

وقد كان أهل الصدر الأول يَصِفون بالفقه من عَلِم طريق الآخرة، وأصلح نفسه، وترك الذنوب والمعاصي المفسدة للأعمال، وهانت في عينه الدنيا، واشتدت رغبته في الآخرة، واستولى على قلبه الخوف من الله، قال تعالى: **﴿فَلَوْلَا نَفَرَ مِن كُلِّ فِرْقَةٍ مِّنْهُمْ طَائِفَةٌ لِّيَتَفَقَّهُوا فِي الدِّينِ وَلِيُنذِرُوا قَوْمَهُمْ إِذَا رَجَعُوا إِلَيْهِمْ﴾**[٢].

وما يحصل به الإنذار والتخويف هو هذا الفقه دون تفريعات الطلاق والعتاق واللعان والسلم والإجارة، فذلك لا يحصل به الإنذار ولا التخويف، بل التجرد له على الدوام يقسي القلب، وينزع الخشية منه كما نشاهد الآن المتجردين له؛ ولذلك وصف الله الذين يخافون العباد أكثر من رب العباد بأنهم لا يفقهون: **﴿لَأَنتُمْ أَشَدُّ رَهْبَةً فِي صُدُورِهِم مِّنَ اللَّهِ ذَٰلِكَ بِأَنَّهُمْ قَوْمٌ لَّا يَفْقَهُونَ﴾**[٣]، فأحال قلة خوفهم من الله واستعظامهم سطوة الخلق على قلة الفقه، وسئل سعد بن إبراهيم الزهري: أي أهل المدينة أفقه؟ فقال: «أتقاهم لله تعالى»[٤]، وقال الحسن البصري: «إنما الفقيه الزاهد في الدنيا، الراغب في الآخرة، البصير بدينه، المداوم على عبادة ربه، الورع، الكاف نفسه عن أعراض المسلمين، العفيف عن أموالهم،

١ المصدر السابق بتصرف يسير.
٢ التوبة: ١٢٢.
٣ الحشر: ١٣.
٤ إحياء علوم الدين: ١/ ٣٢.

Sa'd ibn Ibrāhīm az-Zuhri was once asked, "Who has the most *Fiqh* in Madinah?" He answered, "The most fearful of Allah, the Most High."[1] Similarly, al-Ḥasan al-Baṣri said, "A *faqīh* is one who shuns this worldly life, aspires for the Hereafter. He is the one who has a deep understanding of his religion, consistently worships his Lord, employs *wara'* (pious caution), abstains from [violating] the honor of the Muslims, refrains from [indulging in] their wealth and remains a sincere advisor to the masses of them."[2] Notice how he did not include someone who memorizes the *fatwa*(s). It is true that the term *faqīh* includes the detailed juristic branches, but we do not want to differentiate between the well-versed jurist and the pious, ascetic scholar. The expected norm is that jurist is someone that is ascetic, pious and god-fearing.[3] Thus, Imām Abū Ḥanīfah used to define *Fiqh* as the science of spirituality – knowing what will benefit the soul and what will harm it.[4]

Drowning in the study of *Fiqh* without giving due attention to the righteousness of the *Fiqh* students – meaning the refinement of their hearts and actions – has grave consequences. In my opinion, some of those responsible for the religious education delivered in some universities contributed to this perversion that afflicted the current carriers of *Fiqh*. For example, Al-Azhar University used to consider the subject of *Fiqh* their prime objective. From the first moments after admission, the students are programmed to believe that this subject is the most important reason they are seeking knowledge there and that all the other branches of knowledge serve this goal. For this reason, their earliest classes in the past were always reserved for this subject. *Fiqh* was constantly given the first hours of the day, as well as the longest, most conducive hours for learning.[5]

الناصح لجماعتهم»[١]، ولم يقل الحافظ للفتاوى، صحيح أن اسم الفقيه يشمل الفروع الفقهية، ولكننا لا نريد هذا الفصل بين العالم بالفروع والتقي الورع الزاهد، فالأصل أن يكون الفقيه زاهداً تقيّاً ورعاً[٢]، وقد عرَّف الإمام أبو حنيفة الفقه بأنه معرفة النفس ما لها وما عليها[٣].

فالإغراق في دراسة الفقه دون العناية بصلاح طلبة الفقه: صلاح قلوبهم وأعمالهم، ينتج عواقب وخيمة، وفي ظني أن بعض القائمين على أمر التعليم الديني في بعض الجامعات ساهموا في هذا الانحراف الذي أصاب كثيراً من الذين يحملون الفقه، فقد كان الأزهر يعتبر مادة الفقه هي الأساس الأول، ويلقن طلابه منذ انتسابهم إليه أن تلك المادة هي الغرض الأساس من طلب العلم فيه، وأن جميع العلوم خدم لها، ولهذا كان قديماً يجعل دراستها في باكورة النهار، ويرصد لها أطول الأوقات وأغرها»[٤].

1 *Iḥyā' 'Ulūm ad-Dīn* 1/32
2 *Iḥyā' 'Ulūm ad-Dīn* 1/32
3 The definition of *faqīh*, according to the first generations, was summarized from *Ihyā' 'Ulūm ad-Dīn* 1/32.
4 *Kash Iṣṭilāḥāt al-Funūn* 1/30
5 *Muqaddimat Takhrīj al-Furū' 'alā al-Uṣūl* 27 by Dr Muhammad Sallām Madkūr

١ إحياء علوم الدين: ١/ ٣٢.
٢ تعريف الفقيه عند أهل الصدر الأول، لخصناه من إحياء علوم الدين: ١/ ٣٢.
٣ كشاف اصطلاحات الفنون: ١/ ٣٠.
٤ مقدمة تخريج الفروع على الأصول للدكتور محمد سلام مدكور: ٢٧.

Dr Muhammad Sallām Madkūr reports from his Shaykh, Mahmūd an-Nawawi, the religious studies inspection manager in Al-Azhar, that he said, "At one point in time, Al-Azhar used to consider studying subjects other than *Fiqh* to be a strictly ritualist matter by which blessings are evoked. Some of the instructors used to consider it enough, in their study of Hadith, to merely recite its words upon their students."[1]

In this same regard, Shaykh al-Islām Ibn Taymiyah[2] talked about how distant those specialized in *Fiqh* had become from spirituality and the acts of worship performed by the heart – namely being sincere for Allah, relying upon Him, loving Him, fearing Him and similar. He explained why they were satisfied with performing certain acts, and staying away from others, but only on the external level, without any true devotion, reliance, love, fear and hope in their hearts.

Summary of Unit 12

We can summarize our study of this unit in the following points:

1) Man-made laws made their way into the Islamic Caliphate in Turkey, in 1840 C.E. and continued to gradually mix with the Islamic Sharia until the rulings based on Sharia were annulled altogether. In fact, the Islamic Caliphate itself came to an end in 1924 C.E.

2) *Fiqh* benefitted greatly from the widespread appearance of the printing press in this era. Some of the important classical books were on the brink of being lost, due to them not receiving much attention during the era of *taqlīd*. Thus, printing was a means by which they were preserved and disseminated.

1 Ibid

2 See *Majmū' al-Fatāwā* 20/72 by Shaykh al-Islām.

وينقل الدكتور محمد سلام مدكور عن بعض مشايخه: وهو الشيخ محمود النواوي مدير تفتيش العلوم الدينية بالأزهر قوله: إنه أتى على الأزهر حين من الدهر كان يعتبر فيه دراسة ما عدا الفقه من علوم الدين دراسة على سبيل التبرك، وأن بعض الشيوخ كان يكتفي في دراسة الحديث بتلاوته على الطلاب»(١).

وقد تحدث شيخ الإسلام(٢) عن كثرة انحراف المتفقهين عن طاعات القلب وعباداته: من الإخلاص لله، والتوكل عليه، والمحبة له، والخشية له، ونحو ذلك، وبيّن أن سبب وقوفهم عند المشروع من الأفعال الظاهرة فعلاً وتركاً، من غير أن يحصل لقلوبهم إنابة وتوكل ومحبة، وخوف ورجاء.

خلاصة الوحدة

نخلص من دراسة هذه الوحدة إلى ما يلي:

١- تسللت القوانين الوضعية إلى دولة الخلافة في تركيا ابتداء من عام ١٨٤٠م، ولم تزل القوانين تخالط أحكام الشريعة الإسلامية شيئاً فشيئاً حتى انتهى الأمر إلى إلغاء الأحكام الشرعية، بل إلغاء الخلافة الإسلامية في عام ١٩٢٤م.

٢- استفاد الفقه من ظهور الطباعة في هذا العصر استفادة عظيمة، فبعض الكتب القديمة المهمة كانت قد أوشكت على الضياع، بسبب قلة العناية بها في عصر التقليد، فكان ظهور الطباعة سبباً في حفظها ونشرها.

١ المصدر السابق.

٢ راجع مجموع فتاوى شيخ الإسلام: ٢٠/ ٧٢.

3) The phrase "codifying legislation" refers to collecting the legal codes pertaining to any particular branch of law in the form of a book, compilation or treatise. This takes place after reviewing these laws, organizing them, sifting out the contradictions and grouping them based on subject. Of the most noteworthy attempts to codify the Islamic *Fiqh* in this era was *Majallat al-Ahkām al-'Adliyyah* (The Justice Department's Rulings Magazine).

4) During this era, there appeared what is called *Fiqh* encyclopedias. These were elicited by the difficulties faced by the student of *Fiqh*, such as the absence of a precise index for the books of *Fiqh*. These encyclopedias direct the researcher to the exact issue one is investigating. Likewise, another factor that called for these new compilations was the lack of uniformity between the various *madhhab*(s) when it came to the subject order in their books.

5) In these contemporary times, the scholars became motivated toward establishing institutes, colleges, academic and *Fiqh* assemblies.

6) For a person to reach the station of qualifying to exercise *ijitihād*, a number of conditions must first be met. Of them is knowledge of the Arabic language, knowledge of the Noble Qur'an, and knowledge of the Prophetic Sunnah – both its chains and texts. Also, of the conditions for a *mujtahid* is that this person develops one's skills in *Fiqh* and that this person is upright and acts upon one's knowledge.

٣- يراد بـ «تقنين التشريع» تجميع القواعد القانونية المتعلقة بفرع معين من فروع القانون في شكل كتاب أو مدونة أو مجموعة واحدة، وذلك بعد مراجعة هذه القواعد وتنسيقها، ورفع التناقض منها، وتبويبها بحسب الموضوعات التي تنظمها، ومن أبرز محاولات تقنين الفقه الإسلامي في هذا العصر «مجلة الأحكام العدلية».

٤- ظهر في هذا العصر ما يسمى بـ «الموسوعة الفقهية»، والذي دعا إلى إنشائها تلك الصعوبات التي تقف في وجه الدارسين للفقه، مثل عدم وجود فهرسة دقيقة لكتب الفقه، ترشد الباحث إلى المسألة التي يريدها، وكذلك عدم ترتيب الموضوعات الفقهية في كل المذاهب ترتيباً واحداً.

٥- نشط العلماء في هذا العصر في إقامة المعاهد والكليات والمجامع العلمية والفقهية

٦- يشترط لبلوغ الإنسان مرتبة الاجتهاد عدة شروط منها: العلم باللغة العربية، والعلم بالقرآن الكريم، والسنة النبوية، رواية ودراية، وكذلك من شروط المجتهد أن تتوافر لديه الملكة الفقهية، وأن يكون عَدْلاً عاملاً بما يعلم.

Notes

Conclusion

Fiqh is one of the noblest branches of the Islamic sciences, and thus the Sharia highlighted its importance and stressed learning and mastering it. It means the knowledge of the practical Islamic rulings which are derived from their detailed evidences. The circumstances of Islamic *Fiqh* varied greatly throughout the ages, beginning from the lifetime of the Prophet (ﷺ), then the Companions, the Successors, the *Mujtahid Imām*(s) and continuing until our present age. Some of the exceptional scholars contributed by tracing out for us the methods by which one can extract the Sharia rulings, and these methods became known as the *Fiqh madhhab*(s). The *madhhab*(s) which still exist and have a following until today are those of Imām Abū Ḥanīfah, Imām Mālik, Imām ash-Shāfi'i and Imām Aḥmad ibn Ḥanbal.

In this book, we have tried to shed some light on the development of *Fiqh*, its history, its primary sources and the phases it went through. While doing that, we tried our best to be brief so it could be easily understood by the readers, and from Allah comes all success, and only He guides to the straight path.

خاتمة

الفقه من أعظم وأشرف علوم الشريعة الإسلامية، والتي حث الشرع على تعلمها وإتقانها، ومعناه العلم بالأحكام الشرعية العملية المكتسب من أدلتها التفصيلية، وقد اختلفت أحوال الفقه الإسلامي باختلاف الأعصار ابتداءً من عصر النبوة، ومروراً بعصر الصحابة والتابعين والأئمة المجتهدين، وانتهاءً بمسيرة الفقه في العصر الحاضر، وقد اختط بعض العلماء الأفذاذ طريقة سلكوها في التعرف على الأحكام الشرعية، وقد عُرِفَت هذه الطرق باسم المذاهب الفقهية، والمذاهب الفقهية المتبوعة الباقية إلى اليوم هي:

مذهب الإمام أبي حنيفة، والإمام مالك، والإمام الشافعي، والإمام أحمد بن حنبل.

وقد حاولنا في هذا الكتاب أن نُلقي الضوء على نشأة الفقه وتاريخه ومصادره الأساسية ثم أطواره التي مر بها، وقد توخينا في ذلك الإيجاز حتى يسهل على الطالب استيعابه والإلمام به.

والله الموفق والهادي إلى سواء السبيل ،،،

Notes

www.ingramcontent.com/pod-product-compliance
Lightning Source LLC
Chambersburg PA
CBHW081507220526
45467CB00010B/2820
9798688801156